FRANCES M. YOUNG
with Andrew Teal

From Nicaea to Chalcedon

A Guide to the Literature and its Background

Second Edition

Baker Academic

a division of Baker Publishing Group
Grand Rapids, Michigan

© 1983, 2010 by Frances M. Young

Second edition published in North America by Baker Academic
a division of Baker Publishing Group
P.O. Box 6287, Grand Rapids, MI 49516-6287
www.bakeracademic.com

ISBN 978-0-8010-3915-7

Published by an arrangement with SCM Press
13–17 Long Lane
London EC1A 9PN

First edition published 1983 by SCM Press

Printed in the United States of America

Library of Congress Cataloging-in-Publication Data is on file
at the Library of Congress, Washington, DC

Typeset in London by Regent Typesetting

Contents

Preface to the Second Edition

A generation has passed since the first edition of *From Nicaea to Chalcedon*, and a flood of scholarship has passed under the bridge in that time. The history and politics of the Arian controversy between 325 and 381 has been radically reconceived, and Christological sympathies have tended to shift from Antioch to Alexandria. There has been a number of full-scale biographical studies of particular individuals, a significant growth of attention paid to the Cappadocians and a burgeoning of interest in asceticism and the monastic movement, as well as early Byzantine society and politics, and Syriac studies. This new edition endeavours to take account of all this.

As the Preface to the original edition indicated, the period from Nicaea to Chalcedon is one of the most significant in the formation of the doctrine of the Church. Yet the average student of Christian doctrine rarely gets to grips with the background or the literature of the period, let alone the theological argumentation to be found in the texts. The book set out to be a companion to standard textbooks, providing background material, an introduction to the characters involved in the disputes, to the literary sources and the critical questions which they pose. Thus the subject-matter of the traditional Patrology was given more discursive presentation, and the critical issues and questions of interpretation discussed by patristic scholars were communicated to a wider audience. That purpose remains the same. This guidebook presents a series of essays on a number of significant literary figures, laymen, bishops and heretics of the fourth and fifth centuries, essays which offer biographical, literary-critical and theological information. Some were chosen for their importance in the history of doctrine, some because new material has thrown light upon their work, some because they broaden the reader's understanding of the culture and history of the period or of live issues in the Church at the time; in this edition some additional figures appear, reflecting their increasing importance in current scholarship: Marcellus of Ancyra, Evagrius Ponticus, Pseudo-Macarius and Ephrem the Syrian.

So this book bridges several different approaches: the historian tends to see but a collection of warring prelates and hard-headed politicians, the biographer often borders on the hagiographical, the churchman is only interested in whether they were orthodox or not, the patristic scholar is immersed in critical questions, tracing fragments, establishing texts, and the historian of doctrine tends to flatten the characters into ciphers for particular doctrinal standpoints. Of course I exaggerate – but here is offered an attempt to bring together the fruits of these many different approaches and so put them all in a different perspective.

The original guide was also intended to help the student with bibliography by identifying what was available in English for the beginner, and for the graduate student updating the lists in a standard Patrology, that of Quasten (published in 1960). There are now many more bibliographical aids available, such as *Bibliographia Patristica (Internationale Patristische Bibliographie)* (Berlin: Walter de Gruyter, 1959–), *Clavis Patrum Graecorum* (Turnhout: Brepols, 1974–), as well as resources on the Internet. So there is here no attempt to provide anything like comprehensive lists, but a similar dual purpose has informed the referencing. For the beginner there are regular suggestions for further reading in English provided within the body of the chapters, and the references at the back are arranged as introductory bibliographies of the most important material for graduate students.

The original edition owed much to Judith Lieu, then my research student, and to Professor Maurice Wiles, my Doktorvater; my debt to them remains. Now I am also grateful for the assistance of the Revd Dr Andrew Teal, who provided the first draft of the new Chapter 2, traced more complete publication details of old material cited, helped with identifying and gaining access to new material of which we needed to take account, assisted with the final editing of the typescript for submission to the publisher and prepared the index. Errors which remain are mine. Experts on each subject treated will no doubt easily detect shortcomings. All I can do is offer the excuse that only the finest scholars can encompass more than a very small area in depth. I have endeavoured to learn from the experts as far as possible.

The encouragement of James Ernest of Baker Publishing Group generated this edition, which we have undertaken in the hope that the new edition will prove as useful as the first. We have been grateful for the patience of Natalie Watson at SCM Press – the scanning and editing took substantially longer than we had promised!

Frances M. Young
September 2009

Abbreviations

General and Primary sources

Ad M.	Ad Monachos
Apol.	Apology
Bibl.	Bibliotheca
C. Arianios	Contra Arianos
CG	Contra Gentes
Comm.	Commentary
De fide et inc.	De Fide et Incarnatione
De O.	De Oratione
De Trin.	On the Trinity
Dem. Evang.	Demonstratio Evangelica
DI	De Incarnatione
Ep(p).	Epistle(s)
ET	English translation
Fr(s).	Fragment(s)
Haer.	Panarion against all Heresies
HE	Ecclesiastical History
Heb.	Hebrews
Hom.	Homily
Hom. Cat.	Catechetical Homilies
Jn.	John
KG	Kephalaia gnōstika
KMP	Kata Meros Pistis
L	Lietzmann (1904)
Laus	Laus Constantini
LXX	Septuagint
Matt.	Matthew
MS(S)	manuscript(s)
Myst. Cat.	Mystagogical Catecheses
n.	note
NS	New Series
NT	New Testament
OT	Old Testament
Orat.	Oration
Poem.	Poemata
Praep. Evang.	Praeparatio Evangelica
proph.	Prophet

Rom.	Romans
VA	Vita Antonii
Vir.	De Viris Illustribus
Vita	Vita Constantini

Journal and Series Titles, Secondary Sources

References conform to Schäferdiek (1997), apart from the following:

ACO	Acta Conciliorum Œcumenorum, Berlin: de Gruyter.
CCG	Corpus Christianorum, Series Graeca, Turnhout: Brepols.
CCL	Corpus Christianorum, Series Latina, Turnhout: Brepols.
CSCO	Corpus Scriptorum Christianorum Orientalum, Louvain/ Leuven: Peeters.
FC	Fathers of the Church, Washington, DC: Catholic University of America Press.
JECS	Journal of Early Christian Studies (Journal of the North American Patristic Society – formerly The Second Century), Baltimore: John Hopkins University Press.
JEH	Journal of Ecclesiastical History, Cambridge: Cambridge University Press.
JTS	Journal of Theological Studies, Oxford: Oxford University Press.
NPNF	A Select Library of the Christian Church: Nicene and Post-Nicene Fathers.
PG	Patrologia Graeca
PL	Patrologia Latina
SC	Sources Chrétiennes, Paris.
SJT	Scottish Journal of Theology, Edinburgh: T. & T. Clark.
SP	Studia Patristica. Papers presented at the Oxford Patristics Conferences. Formerly Berlin, Akademie-Verlag; Oxford, Pergamon; Kalamazoo, MI: Cistercian Publications; Leuven: Peeters.
TZF	Texte zur Forschung: Darmstadt: Wissenschaftliche Buchgesellschaft.
WS	Woodbrooke Studies
ZNW	Zeitschrift für die neutestamentlische Wissenschaft und die Kunde der älteren Kirche, Berlin: Topelmann.

1

The Birth of Church History
and its Sequel

I Eusebius of Caesarea

Eusebius sums up an age of transition. His works reflect the Church's movement from being a persecuted minority to being the dominant faith of the Roman Empire, in terms of influence if not yet numbers. It was perhaps the perfect moment for 'the father of Church history' to take up his pen. It was the end of one era, the start of another.

It is natural to think of Eusebius as belonging to the fourth century, for his extant literary output belongs to its early decades. Besides he was involved in the deliberations of Nicaea and subsequent events. But Eusebius was nearing forty by the turn of the century, and in many ways his outlook reflects the presuppositions of the third century. In most of his work an apologetic element can be discerned, and in spite of moving eagerly with political developments, he has seemed unequal in his theological thinking to the new demands and difficulties of the Arian controversy.

However, this in itself makes him a more interesting figure. We can be pretty sure that he spoke for a solid mass of conservative churchmen, facing with dread and uncertainty apparent innovations to their faith, yet welcoming with sincere idealism the conversion of the emperor and the triumph of the Church. In the pages of his works we meet what 'Origenism' had become, the faith of the ordinary educated church leader, surprisingly literal-minded in its approach to scripture and doctrine. In his actions we may see compromise, but if so it was probably born out of a genuine desire for the preservation of the traditional faith and the unity of the Church.

1 Life

Surprisingly little is known of Eusebius' life.[1] He seems to have been born in the early 260s, probably in Palestinian Caesarea, which remained his home throughout his life. Caesarea had been Origen's base for the last twenty years of his life, and it was probably on this account that the city attracted Euse-

---

1 Barnes (1981) provides a summary chronological table on pp. 277–9; his somewhat quixotic dates have been contested, however, and an alternative chronological scheme may be found tabulated in Carriker (2003), pp. 37–41, following Burgess (1997).

bius' teacher, Pamphilus, an eager collector of Origen's works. The early career of Eusebius is particularly obscure, apart from his acknowledged devotion to Pamphilus, whose name he took, Εὐσέβιος ὁ Παμφίλου.[2] The house of Pamphilus became a school, based around a remarkable library, probably originating from the collections made by Origen to which Pamphilus tirelessly added material;[3] here he and Eusebius worked in collaboration with one another. Eventually they produced a joint defence of the great scholar to whom they both owed so much.[4] If the collection of quotations to be found in Eusebius' work are anything to go by, the library must have been quite a comprehensive collection,[5] not only of Christian literature, but of a wide range of literature in the Greek language, especially philosophical works. Under Pamphilus, Caesarea also became a centre for the correction of manuscripts, and it was from Eusebius that Constantine later ordered fifty copies of the scriptures for his new churches in Constantinople.[6]

Eusebius grew up in a time of peace. The Decian persecution had faded into the past. The Church was expanding throughout the Empire. He was forty or more when renewed persecution hit the Church with the edict of Diocletian in AD 303. For ten years he lived through Rome's final bitter onslaught on Christianity, and it is from his pen that we have detailed eyewitness accounts of the effects of persecution in Egypt and Palestine. Eusebius apparently toured these areas, and could report many incidents first hand; he and other Christians openly visited those suffering for their faith in prison or in the mines, apparently unmolested. In 307 Pamphilus was imprisoned, and eventually died as a martyr in 310; while in prison he composed his *Defence of Origen* with Eusebius' help. Exactly how Eusebius survived we do not know; he was apparently imprisoned in Egypt (sometime in 311–13), and was later accused of compromising in order to secure his release. In spite of the fact that the library housed many copies and versions of the scriptures – the first target of the authorities – it was apparently not destroyed. We can only conclude that the persecution was carried out somewhat sporadically and unsystematically.

In 313, the persecution ceased and Eusebius became bishop of Caesarea. This position he held for the rest of his life. He must have been nearly seventy when he was elected bishop of Antioch after the deposition of Eustathius. Wisely he

---

2 Controversy has raged over the implications of this. Since Photius, some have understood it to mean 'slave of' or 'freedman of' Pamphilus, but the form is probably to be understood as a patronymic, with the implication that Pamphilus adopted Eusebius as his son and heir, and maybe he inherited the library. See Gifford (1903), III.1, pp. vi–xi, for discussion. It remains possible that Eusebius simply took Pamphilus' name after his death as a token of respect.

3 See Carriker (2003); he dismisses the idea that Origen's library was destroyed in the Decian persecution, and suggests that it had probably come under episcopal control prior to Pamphilus' arrival in Caesarea.

4 Their joint *Apologia pro Origene* exists only in Rufinus' Latin version; text: Amacker and Junod (2002).

5 Carriker (2003), p. 311 documents all that we know of its contents from Eusebius' voluminous works. He comments on 'its wealth of religious literature, its dearth of classical history, poetry and oratory, and its strength in Middle Platonic works'.

6 Eusebius, *Vita* iv.36.

refused the honour, ostensibly on grounds of careful adherence to canon law as established at Nicaea,[7] but perhaps also on account of devotion to his library.

But if he remained bishop of Caesarea, this did not mean that he lived peacefully in an ecclesiastical backwater. His later years as bishop are better known to us, as he became involved in the politics of the newly established official Church, and stormy years they were. At Antioch (Spring 325) his orthodoxy was impugned, and his acquiescence at Nicaea (Summer 325) apparently caused him some embarrassment. However, in spite of the doctrinal conclusions of Nicaea, Eusebius' admiration for Constantine was augmented rather than diminished, and Constantine seems to have recognized the distinction and usefulness of so accomplished a Christian scholar. Immediately after the council, Constantine celebrated the twentieth anniversary of his succession with the bishops present; at the thirtieth anniversary Eusebius would deliver a panegyric in his honour. Immediately before the latter, he took a prominent part in the councils of Antioch and Tyre, proceedings which dealt with the 'ultra-Nicene' bishops, Eustathius and Athanasius; and he wrote at length against Marcellus,[8] deposed around the same time. As a result of this confrontation with the young upstart of Alexandria, not to mention other manoeuvres during his episcopacy, Eusebius has continually faced charges of 'semi-Arianism', or of trimming his sails to fit the political wind. The justice of these charges will be considered later, but in fairness to Eusebius, we should remember that already at the time of Nicaea, he had probably reached sixty, and the Council of Tyre was ten years later. He was an old man, profoundly thankful for the triumph of the Church and perhaps a little out of his depth in the rapidly moving controversies and developments of the new era. It is hardly surprising that an aged and respected bishop with an essentially conservative outlook should find the intense single-mindedness of the young Athanasius distinctly uncongenial, even offensive. All Eusebius wanted was peace in the Church for the triumphant celebration of Constantine's Tricennalia. He lived on to see out Constantine's reign, and died about AD 340, having spanned a significant turning-point in Christian history.

2 The *Ecclesiastical History* and earlier historical writings

One consequence of our meagre knowledge of Eusebius' life is difficulty in the matter of dating his writings, a question to which much scholarly work has been devoted. The matter is complicated by the successive editions and redactions through which his work seems to have passed. The general order of composition can to some extent be established by cross-references, and the dating of certain sections is fixed fairly generally by allusions to the contemporary situation. But his works are massive, and must have been assembled over considerable periods of time.

The *Ecclesiastical History*[9] clearly went through several editions. At one time there was general acceptance of the theory of E. Schwartz that the first edition

---

7 Eusebius, *Vita* iii.61.

8 Text: Klostermann (1972). See Chapter 2, pp. 56–61.

9 Text: Schwartz (1903–9); Bardy (1952–60). ET Lawlor and Oulton (1932); Williamson (1965/89).

consisting of eight books appeared in approximately 312; that Book IX was added in 315, Book X in 317; and that a final edition appeared about the time of Nicaea, when the character of the references to the Emperor Licinius was changed to conform with his downfall. It is generally agreed that the final complete edition dates from 325–6, and that the final books underwent substantial modification over a period; but a number of investigators have tended to put the date of the first edition, consisting of only seven books, much earlier, even prior to 303,[10] and to posit considerable revision of these earlier sections in later editions – indeed, Grant characterized the work as a 'process'.[11] The early dating has subsequently been challenged, and substantial reasons advanced for regarding it as unlikely that there was an edition prior to 313, the first version consisting of eight books.[12] The considerable differences between Books I—VII and the subsequent material[13] may be accounted for by suggesting that Eusebius was inspired to write the history when he realized that the Great Persecution was the Final Persecution; so Books I—VII trace the history up to its brink, while VIII (and eventually VIII—X) tells of the course of persecution and deliverance from it.

Prior to the *Ecclesiastical History*, Eusebius composed the *Chronicle*,[14] and arguments about the dating of both revolve around the various editions of this earlier compilation.[15] The Greek original is no longer extant, though part of the work survives in translations: an Armenian version perhaps renders a somewhat abbreviated Greek edition,[16] while Jerome's Latin explicitly brought it up to date and incorporated more Western material. The missing first part apparently consisted of a continuous prose narrative of the histories of various nations, made up largely of excerpts from accounts accessible to Eusebius with some attempt at cross-reference; the second part, known as the *Chronological Tables*, is a note-form summary in parallel columns, a tabulated conspectus which brings into line the different systems of dating and displays the parallel development of the major peoples of the ancient Near Eastern and Mediterranean areas. The idea of such a table was probably Eusebius' own, and may have been inspired by the parallel columns of Origen's *Hexapla*.[17]

Chronological schemes had been attempted before, but Christian versions, such as that by Julius Africanus, had been constructed in the interests of apol-

---

10 For example Wallace-Hadrill (1960); Grant (1980); Barnes (1981) even puts it before 300.

11 Grant (1980), p. 10.

12 Louth (1990); Burgess (1997).

13 Well summarized in Louth (1990), who also accounts for it along the line here suggested. See further discussion in Tabbernee (1997).

14 Text: Karst (1911); Helm (1913).

15 Some have argued that the *Tables* originally ended in 303, or even earlier (Barnes 1981), and like the *History* went through successive editions – hence the interconnections over the issue of dating. See Wallace-Hadrill (1955) and Burgess' critique (1997). Grant (1980) exploits differences between the two works to discern changes made to the early books of the *Ecclesiastical History*.

16 See Mosshammer (1979) for discussion of the textual issues and Eusebius' sources; Burgess (1997) contends that the same version underlies both the Armenian and Jerome's translation.

17 Noted first by Barnes (1981); developed by Grafton and Williams (2006).

ogetic and eschatology – to show that Moses and the prophets lived before Plato by whom they were plagiarized, and to fit everything from creation to incarnation into 5,500 years on the assumption that after 6,000 years would come the Millennium, the Great Sabbath. Moses' priority continued to matter to Eusebius; indeed his chronographical investigation may have been stimulated by Porphyry's challenge to the consensus that synchronized Moses and Inachus (500 years before the Trojan War)[18] – Porphyry had brought Moses' date back even earlier, to 800 years prior to the fall of Troy. Eusebius himself reduced the priority to 350 years, making Moses contemporary with Cecrops, the first king of Attica. He also calculated on the basis of Septuagintal information 5,199 years between Adam and the incarnation, noting that the Hebrew was different. These two moves undercut the millenarian scheme. Eusebius was necessarily dependent on predecessors for material – in fact it has been noted that in general he tends to be more reliable when dependent on documentary evidence for the past than when recounting events of his own day – but he did his own comparative research; and he tolerated a degree of doubt, given the differences between versions of the Bible and the difficulties in using historical documents – he simply could not reconcile the long time spans in Egyptian and Chaldean sources with biblical material. He quoted Acts 1.7, about not knowing the times or seasons, to allow for investigation and uncertainty.[19]

Yet, for all this scholarly attention to detail, Eusebius cannot be entirely absolved of the charge of distortion for the sake of propaganda.[20] His principal interest can be discerned in the fact that by the time of Augustus the parallel columns were reduced to two: only imperial and Christian chronology now mattered. Yet living in Palestine, Eusebius must have been all too aware of the neighbouring Persian Empire, and other works show that he knew of Christian missions outside Roman boundaries. It is hard not to conclude that Eusebius' *Chronological Tables* were deliberately framed to fit one of his favourite apologetic themes – namely the providential coincidence of the incarnation and the establishment of world peace under Augustus.

In his prologue to the *Ecclesiastical History*, Eusebius states that it is an amplification of the information collected in the latter part of the *Chronological Tables*.[21] It seems then that the *Ecclesiastical History* arose naturally out of the *Chronicle* as Eusebius' next major project. This background helps us to understand the somewhat strange divisions of material in the *Ecclesiastical History*: the work evolved out of chronography, and so chronological rather than logical sequence is followed. The imperial succession provides one framework of the narrative, and information about Christian leaders like Justin Martyr and Origen is divided up and put in different sections under the reigns of different emperors. Eusebius states in his preface, probably added at the end as a review of what he has done

---

18 Burgess (1997), p. 489; the Appendix prints Eusebius' Preface – Burgess notes that the first word is 'Moses', and Eusebius immediately sets out the problem of Moses' date.

19 William Adler, 'Eusebius' *Chronicle* and its legacy' in Attridge and Hata (1992).

20 *Pace* Barnes (1981), who dates the *Chronicle* to the third century and regards the early Eusebius as primarily a scholar, admittedly limited by his resources, who only took up apologetic as the peace of the Church was shattered after 303.

21 *HE* I.i.2.

rather than an anticipation of what he intended to do,[22] that his purpose is to trace the lines of succession from the holy apostles, the names and dates of the heretics, the calamities which have overtaken the Jews since their conspiracy against the Saviour, and the persecutions and heroic martyrdoms suffered for the faith. These other subjects tend to impose their own schemes, and the various episcopates interlock with the imperial reigns. The result is an apparent confusion of order and subject, which is somewhat bewildering to the reader.

Eusebius was first and foremost a scholar, not of the clear thinking philosophical type,[23] nor with an overriding commitment to objectivity given his apologetic interests, but still an antiquarian who loved to sort evidence and amass information. His attention to detail can amount to pedantry.[24] As a historian, he was not very imaginative; but from posterity's point of view, his chief asset is his love of documents, of quoting the actual texts to demonstrate what he was recording. Attention is drawn to the nature of his work by the fact that a modern selection of texts illustrating Church history is entitled *A New Eusebius*.[25] Without Eusebius, our knowledge of the early Church would be considerably impoverished.[26] Apart from some oral resources, his repertoire was almost certainly limited to the literary works and dossiers of letters contained in the libraries of Caesarea and Jerusalem, but that was a substantial resource.[27] He had problems dating and evaluating his material, and his perspective is anachronistic, projecting back the Church he knew in his own time.[28] To some extent, we can correct and amplify his information from other works available to us, though this is not always the case and then his inadequacies become tantalizing: what exactly did Paul of Samosata teach and why was he condemned? Eusebius preserves details of his immoral life and anti-ecclesiastical conduct, but never fully explains his heretical doctrines, simply implying a link with Ebionites and Artemon.[29] Maybe he doubted the 'usefulness'[30] of recording false teachings, since he is equally vague about most heresies; but he also thought that heresies were short-lived, and so needed little discussion.[31] For all his inadequacies, however, Eusebius is indispensable: he provides us with our only fragments of Papias' writings, in spite of his somewhat derogatory opinion of his intelligence; and to him we owe the survival of very early martyrologies, and extracts from such important figures as Melito of Sardis and Dionysius of Alexandria. Besides this, he lists the works of the more important ecclesiastical

22 Grant (1980).

23 Barnes (1981, p. 100) calls him 'philosophically confused'; but Lienhard (1999) and Robertson (2007) challenge the common estimate of Eusebius' theology as unsophisticated – see further below.

24 Kofsky (2000), p. 251.

25 Stevenson (1957).

26 Lawlor reckoned that half the quotations in the HE would be otherwise unknown to us; see Lawlor and Oulton (1927), II, p. 19.

27 Nautin (1961); Carriker (2003).

28 Barnes (1981).

29 For discussion see Grant (1980), pp. 92–3.

30 Eusebius insists on the utility of the material he quotes and his overall project: Grant (1980), p. 23.

31 Grant (1980), p. 85.

authors, and provides a chronological scheme, which, though needing some modification, remains a basic guide for reconstructing the general sequence of events in Church history from New Testament times to his own day.

Eusebius is chiefly known for his work on Church history. Yet here, as well as in his theology, modern scholarship has made him the butt of criticism. He has been accused of deliberate distortion of facts and mutilation of documents;[32] the tendentious character of his work, his lack of judgment and insight, his disregard for social and political factors, have all been remarked. In particular, the value of his accounts of the events of his own time has been the subject of much dispute. Books VIII—X of the *Ecclesiastical History*, and the associated pamphlet, the *Martyrs of Palestine*, are concerned with the progress of the persecution years. The *Martyrs of Palestine* exists in two recensions, a longer version only extant in Syriac, and a shorter Greek version, appended in four manuscripts to Book VIII of the *Ecclesiastical History*. Eusebius claims to have been an eyewitness of many of the events described, and for the effect of persecution on the Christian population they are invaluable contemporary documents. But when it comes to detail, reconstruction of the chronology of the persecution from Eusebius' account is extremely difficult,[33] and inscriptions cast doubt on the reliability of Eusebius' transmission of contemporary rescripts.[34] The whole account is influenced by Eusebius' point of view: Licinius, for example, is blackened after being hailed as a hero, and the actions of Maximin are distorted to comply with Eusebius' vicious judgment on his character as persecutor. Eusebius' honesty has been impugned; he deliberately rewrote imperial history to suit his own purposes, it has been claimed.

Perhaps, however, his qualities as a historian should be judged in the light of contemporary norms rather than by modern standards. The thing that makes Eusebius dull and difficult to follow is the very methodology which distinguishes his work from pagan historical writing. History was a literary form, 'a rhetorical work with a maximum of invented speeches and a minimum of authentic documents'.[35] But Eusebius, although an educated man, did not attempt to follow the traditional path of Thucydides and Livy. Of course Eusebius was not working entirely in a vacuum. In various ways the works of pagan historians and philosophers anticipated his interests. Disciples of Aristotle wrote histories based on 'successions', showing how one master followed another in a particular subject (for example Aristoxenus' *History of Music*); and Diogenes Laertius in his *Life and Opinions of the Philosophers* mixes biography with explanations of doctrines, lists schools and heads of schools, and discusses *haireseis* (divergent opinions). So Eusebius' lists of bishops had pagan precedents, as did his discussion of heretical sects.[36] Furthermore Eusebius' overall understanding of history was framed as a reaction to what his pagan predecessors had made of

---

32 Lawlor estimated that over fifty non-biblical quotations are mutilated, though this he attributed to incompetent copyists employed by Eusebius to transcribe passages. See Lawlor and Oulton (1927), pp. 20–5. For numerous examples of exclusions, distortions and falsifications, see Grant (1972, 1975, 1980).

33 Lawlor (1912); and the debate between Baynes, Lawlor and Richardson (1924–5).

34 See Grant (1972, 1975, 1980) for this and the following points.

35 Momigliano (1963); amplified by Markus (1975).

36 Bardy (1952–60), Introduction, vol. IV, p. 79.

it all: fate and fortune had been their preoccupation, free will and providence is Eusebius' answer.[37] However, in his reliance on documentary evidence, in his refusal to produce creative writing, he was inventing a new kind of historical presentation. He himself claims to have been 'the first to venture on such a project and to set out on what is indeed a lonely and untrodden way',[38] and for this reason he begs the pardon of his readers for his deficiencies. He had no precedent to follow, because this history was not a study of human politics or military strategy; it was not written to please or exhort. It was intended to convince of the truth of Christian claims, and thus introduced the methods of a controversialist into historical composition. Its purpose was apologetic;[39] and so evidence is piled up to prove points, and an erudition is displayed which is not found in pagan historical writing. Perhaps, as Momigliano suggested,[40] Eusebius anticipated the development of modern historiographical methodology, based on careful documentation.

Eusebius relied on evidence because he was an advocate seeking to establish truth and convince his readers of it; he had no intention of being impartial. His work was that of a Christian theologian presenting events as a history of salvation; in this respect, he followed in the tradition of Jewish historical writing, as found in scripture, and to some extent in Josephus. It is not surprising that, having developed his theory of the historical process, he should see events in the light of his conclusions. He was presenting the triumph of orthodoxy against heresy, of Christianity over idolatry; he was bearing witness to the judgment of God and the providential activity of the divine Logos, as discerned in the events of history. Inevitably, distasteful facts were suppressed, like the pervasiveness of millenarian beliefs in the second century;[41] inevitably awkward facts were distorted – he would not attribute persecution to the 'good emperor', Marcus Aurelius. Judgments were passed and revised in the light of his Christian prejudices, as in the case of Licinius. Eusebius was certainly not an objective historian in the modern sense; he was a propagandist. Yet his search for facts and his desire to present evidence was in itself ahead of his time. Eusebius set a precedent and evolved a pattern that was to become standard for writing ecclesiastical history. Most of his successors made no attempt to replace his work, but rather continued it and brought it up to date – surely a testimony to their estimate of his achievement.

3 Apologetic works

The *Church History*, whatever its date, was just one of Eusebius' many projects. His first truly apologetic work was *Against Hierocles*,[42] a hasty answer to an

---

37 Chesnut (1977), chapters 1 and 2.

38 *HE* i.1.2.

39 *Pace* Barnes (1981); see Arthur J. Droge, 'The Apologetic Dimensions of the *Ecclesiastical History*' in Attridge and Hata (1992).

40 Momigliano (1963).

41 Grant (1980), pp. 131–6, argues that Eusebius changed his mind about the canonicity of the Johannine Apocalypse, and so also his estimate of Papias' intelligence.

42 Text: Forrat with des Places (1986); ET Conybeare (1921).

imperial official who launched an attack on Christianity just prior to the out-break of persecution. At some point (303 or 313?), in reply to Hierocles' attempt to convince people that Jesus was outclassed by Apollonius of Tyana, Eusebius subjected Philostratus' *Life of Apollonius* to detailed criticism.[43] The *General Elementary Instruction* in ten books (mostly lost) seems to have been directed at interested outsiders, but may have been a substitute for catechetical instruction after the congregating of Christians was banned.[44] The period of persecution also saw the production of the *Defence of Origen*,[45] the *Life of Pamphilus*, and the massive answer to Porphyry's great work *Against the Christians*, mostly lost but all referred to in other works. Eusebius' large extant works of apology, the *Praeparatio Evangelica*[46] and its accompanying *Demonstratio Evangelica*,[47] probably date from post-persecution days, though some passages suggest that persecution was still in progress, or at least might be expected again in the near future.[48]

Whatever the exact date of these huge compilations, many of the governing ideas had probably been worked out already. Much of the *Demonstratio*, we can see, is based on the extant *Prophetic Eclogues*,[49] a collection of Old Testament texts fulfilled in Christ, which constituted Books VI–IX of the *General Elementary Instruction*. With revised dating the question of priority may be less clear than it once seemed, but theories sketched in the *Ecclesiastical History* are certainly developed and proved in greater detail in these volumes. In fact, the more one reads Eusebius, the more one is struck by his ability constantly to restate the same arguments and reuse the same material in a new context. The culmination of the process is seen in the *Theophania*,[50] probably written late in life and declaring in final form the proofs of the superiority of Christianity which had concerned Eusebius throughout his life. We even find the familiar Eusebian arguments in his panegyric delivered at Constantine's Tricennalia.

The historian was at heart an apologist,[51] and his apologetic interests are given their full scope in the *Praeparatio* and *Demonstratio*.[52] The character of these works is similar to that of his historical writings, relying heavily on extracts from the wealth of material in his library. One could imagine him reproducing his card index with connecting sentences; without such convenient aids, his labours, or those of his scribes, must have been considerable – checking references in a roll

---

43 See Forrat with des Places (1986) for a full discussion and introduction to this text and its date.

44 Barnes (1981), p. 168.

45 Amacker and Junod (2002).

46 Text: Mras (1982–3); des Places (1974–91); ET Gifford (1903).

47 Text: Heikel (1913); ET Ferrar (1920).

48 *Dem. Evang.* iv.16; viii.1.

49 Text: Migne, *PG* 22.

50 *Theophania*: Greek fragments – Gressmann (1904); full text only in Syriac; ET Lee (1843).

51 Frede (1999) warns against treating everything Eusebius wrote as apologetic – so diffuse a notion becomes meaningless; on the other hand, Eusebius himself can use the term both in a narrow sense for a definite literary genre, and also for anything that defends Christianity.

52 For a detailed study, see Kofsky (2000).

cannot have been easy, and the non-scriptural writings were unlikely to be in codex form. The *Praeparatio evangelica* and its companion volume are massive works reflecting massive research, not just in Christian archives, but in much of Greek prose literature. The central themes of traditional apology are given support from the very words of the opposition, the anti-Christian Porphyry being cited with remarkable frequency and at great length. Eusebius' method, though invaluable to posterity, is not conducive to readability. He is more of an editor or compiler than an author; to a greater extent even than in the *Ecclesiastical History*, he seems dominated by his vast resources of material. Yet scholars interested in tracing the lost works of pagan philosophers and historians cannot be too grateful to Eusebius.[53]

The impression given by these works, then, is that Eusebius was setting out to confirm the Church's position, rather than discover new ideas and insights. He prefers to reproduce the thoughts and statements of others. Yet it has been argued that Eusebius has given apologetic a new and original historical perspective. This is based on the frequency with which Eusebius presents the primitive religion of the Hebrews (by which he means the biblical patriarchs) as the perfect ideal restored in Christianity.[54] In the light of this, it is claimed, we can stand back and see beneath the mass of detail an overall vision of the religious history of humanity,[55] inspired partly by Porphyry's theory that a purer and simpler worship of the heavenly bodies preceded the development of bloody sacrifices and the deification of heroes and natural forces, partly by the traditional Christian explanation of idolatry and polytheism as the seductive activity of evil demons. This overall picture may be summarized as follows: at the time of the Fall, humanity had turned from the true God to worship the material. At first, they had worshipped the stars, which were at least heavenly bodies, but then they had gone on lowering their sights, worshipping the elements, natural forces and finally their own famous ancestors, as gods. The evil demons had made the most of human free will and encouraged their downfall with their seductive temptations. Thus polytheism had evolved. Meanwhile, the Logos had undertaken the salvation of humankind, and revealed the true religion to Abraham and his successors; but their descendants had lost the vision, and Moses was chosen to establish a legal set-up which would preserve the essential features of the true religion in symbols, in a materialist form which weak and sinful human beings could grasp. So we find polytheism and Judaism, both materialistic, both the result of human folly and ignorance, but one deriving from a divine attempt to save humanity from the worst excesses. Then, at a carefully prepared moment in history, and in fulfilment of the prophecies given to the Jews, the Logos came himself in the flesh to reveal again the true religion and re-establish purity and faith among all nations. Thus Christianity came into

---

53 Gifford (1903) lists the fragments for which we are indebted to Eusebius; it is a very remarkable collection, including virtually all we know of Numenius the Pythagorean, and the Platonist Atticus, not to mention the extracts from Philo Judaeus and Porphyry; see also Carriker (2003).

54 *Praep. Evang.* vii; *Dem. Evang.* i.

55 For discussion of Eusebius' historical ideas, I am much indebted to Sirinelli (1961). See also the similar account in Chesnut (1977), chapter 4. Kofsky (2000) draws attention to some of the inconsistencies and difficulties inherent in this overall account.

being, not as an innovation, but as a return to the primitive religion which was alone pure and true. Basically Christianity for Eusebius is a revelation of the right way to worship the one true God, and in this respect is distinguishable from all other religions.

It is hardly Eusebius' main purpose to present this history, and he never quite succeeds in bringing it out with perfect consistency; the status of the primitive astral religion varies, as well as his estimate of Moses' role. Ideas of this kind, however, certainly seem to underlie his material; and to spell them out helps to make sense of his apologetic works. Into the scheme Eusebius incorporated the classic apologetic weapons,[56] in particular the old accusation that all Greek knowledge, religion and philosophy had been plagiarized from the barbarians. He acknowledges, like so many Christians before him, that Plato had discovered the truth, though he got it from Moses. He repeats traditional arguments against astrology and belief in fate; he uses standard attacks to expose the error of each school of philosophy. He explains the source of oracles, and their cessation at the time of Christ, in terms of the battle between the Logos and the evil demons. He incorporates the long-standing Christian argumentation from the evidence of prophecy and its fulfilment. No available stone is left unturned in the endeavour, on the one hand to discredit paganism in both crude and more sophisticated forms, and on the other hand to answer the standard charges against Christianity, that Christians abandoned their ancestral religion for a new superstition, and that they fell between two stools in being neither Jew nor Greek.[57] It is arguable that having already answered Porphyry's *Against the Christians* blow by blow, he was here presenting a more general case for Christianity against the background of Porphyry's attack, and utilizing Porphyry to bolster his own argument.[58]

Yet through all the mass of documentation and argumentation, it is possible to discern an understanding of providence in human history which has convinced Eusebius of the truth of Christianity. What impresses him most, and has contributed to the scheme already outlined, is (i) the fulfilment of prophecy, (ii) the miraculous success of Christianity and (iii) the evidence of providential coincidence. To each of these arguments Eusebius constantly returns, and it is worthwhile to look briefly at each theme.

(i) In the *Eclogae propheticae* and the *Demonstratio*, the argument from prophecy is used with force. Jesus Christ was the only one who fulfilled the prediction of another prophet like Moses, the only one to establish a new covenant and set up a new law. He alone was the fulfilment of the prophecies.[59] Eusebius draws on traditional Christian proof-texts, and for him the Old Testament scriptures are divinely inspired oracles which, being fulfilled in Christ, constitute proof of

---

56 Plagiarism: *Praep. Evang.* x; Moses' priority: *Praep. Evang.* xi—xiii (cf. *Theophania* ii, 44f.); fate and astrology: *Praep. Evang.* vi; anti-philosophers: *Praep. Evang.* xv; oracles: *Praep. Evang.* iv—v; prophecy: *Dem. Evang.*, passim.

57 This is stated as the purpose of the two works in the opening prefaces to the *Praeparatio* and the *Demonstratio*.

58 Kofsky (2000), pp. 250–75, has a useful account of the relationship between Porphyry's *Against the Christians* and Eusebius' purpose in the *Praeparatio* and *Demonstratio*.

59 *Dem. Evang.* i.7; iii.2.

the Christian claims. 'The new scriptures shall prove the old, and the gospels set their seal on the prophetic evidence.'[60]

However, in Eusebius' estimate of Moses, we find all the ambiguity of the relationship between Christianity and Judaism. Without Moses, there would have been no record of the ideal religion of the patriarchs; without Moses, there would have been no prophecies. Moses was indispensable – and yet he was the originator of Judaism. The Jews to whom the scriptures belonged were the implacable enemies of Christianity; their charges had to be met. Besides, Christians, while accepting the scriptures, refused in certain crucial respects to obey their directives. Eusebius appreciated the force of these facts, and in the *Demonstratio* he set out to account for them.

By way of explanation, he utilizes the estimate of the Jewish law traditional since Paul. The legal system, the polity, established by Moses had a pedagogical purpose; it was not the whole truth about God and his worship – it was a prophetic symbol, and when the truth came, the symbol had to be done away with. Besides this, Eusebius produced a number of very practical objections to the suggestion that Gentiles as well as Jews were to obey the law; all nations, for example, could not travel to Jerusalem to perform sacrifice.[61] Moses was a lawgiver for the Jews; Jesus Christ was like Moses, in that he too was a lawgiver, but his law was superior; it was universal and replaced the Mosaic code which was now obsolete.

The replacement of the law, however, was not to detract from the scriptures as a book of prophecy. The Mosaic writings were divinely inspired and had the truth enshrined in them; they were to be carefully distinguished from other oracles and prophetic writings, whose source was the demons.[62] The Jews had failed to see the truth when it had been unveiled in Christ; therefore their nation and polity was destroyed by the Romans under the providence of God. In fact this had been predicted in veiled terms in their own prophecies. Clinging to the materialist symbol, they failed to discern spiritual reality and made permanent what was intended to be an interim measure. Christianity was the revelation of the reality behind the symbol.

Thus the argument from prophecy, also used to good effect in the *Ecclesiastical History* as well as the *Eclogae propheticae*, was presented in his apologetic works as still standing; clearly Eusebius found it a forceful one.

(ii) The miraculous success of Christianity was another compelling fact in Eusebius' eyes. The argument becomes more and more forceful with the progress of political developments; but already before the final triumph of Constantine it was being utilized. The rapid spread of the gospel to all lands and nations, the conversion of humanity from 'devilish polytheism in all its forms', were described with enthusiasm in the *Ecclesiastical History*.[63] Still more would Eusebius wax eloquent in his more political works, when his readers could be encouraged to step on the band-wagon of the triumphant Church with its magnificent imperially supported new buildings and multitudinous congregations. Yet it was the miraculous success of the gospel in its early days which

60 *Dem. Evang.* iv.15.
61 *Dem. Evang.* i.3.
62 *Dem. Evang.*, introduction to Book v.
63 *HE* ii.3.

remained one of Eusebius' chief weapons against pagan scoffers. If Christianity was a massive hoax perpetrated by the disciples of a false magician, how could it have survived as a pure philosophy of life requiring abstemious and sacrificial behaviour from its adherents? How could illiterate, Syriac-speaking rustics have pulled off such a hoax on the sophisticated Graeco-Roman world? Why should people be prepared to die for something they knew to be false? Eusebius is perhaps at his most forceful in developing these particular arguments,[64] and he recognizes this by reproducing them in the *Laus Constantini* and again in the *Theophania*.

(iii) The evidence of providential coincidence was for Eusebius the most powerful argument of all. One of the features of Eusebius' concept of historical development is his identification of Christianity with civilization and peace. Idolatrous humanity is depicted as savage and barbarous; and the establishment of civilized peace under Augustus is not merely coincidental with the incarnation, but almost consequent upon it. Two great powers sprang up together to give peace to all,[65] the Roman Empire and the Christian Church; this miracle is attributed to the work of providence providing conditions for the rapid spread of Christian missions, and the overthrow of polytheism.

But what then of the persecutions? If the peace of Rome and the peace of the Church are to be almost identified, how is the conflict between the Church and the Empire to be explained? Eusebius seems to have tried various methods of accounting for this. In the *Ecclesiastical History* the earlier persecutions are attributed to 'bad emperors', or to the misleading of 'good emperors' by wicked advisers. God allowed occasional confrontations in order to prove that the Church did not owe its success to the connivance of the secular power. God permitted persecution so that the glorious deeds of the martyrs might shine forth as yet another proof of the power of Christianity, overcoming even death. But how was Eusebius to face and justify the final bitter onslaught?

Eusebius begins his account of the great persecution[66] by a description of the peace and success of the Church in the years immediately preceding it. These were the early years of his life. He had not experienced the days of suppression; he saw the authorities tolerating large congregations and great church buildings. On looking back, however, he decided that outward success must have sapped the spiritual strength of the Church; abuse and disagreement, hypocrisy and worldliness had taken over. So God fulfilled the warnings of the prophets, and in his own time Eusebius saw churches in ruins, scriptures in flames, bishops in hiding and the faithful in prison. This was God's judgment on the Church, purifying and chastening it. Later he reverts to old theories of 'bad emperors', as the persecution inexplicably drags on; and eventually he sees confirmation of this in the terrible misfortunes which overtook the persecuting princes, and the success of the Christian sympathizer, Constantine.[67] Finally he comes to see the sequence of events as a demonstration of divine judgment in history, preparing the way for the glorious climax in Constantine's

---

64 *Dem. Evang.* iii.
65 *Theophania* iii.2, and frequently.
66 *HE* viii.1.
67 *HE* viii.13–16.

victory and the establishment of peace on earth.[68] His long-standing views on providence had been vindicated by the political events of his own lifetime. The unity of Church and Empire was fully realized. What greater proof could there be of the truth of Christianity?

4 Political writings

Constantine was the most convincing proof in Eusebius' eyes; it was that fact which clinched his apologetic argument. Now perhaps we can understand Eusebius' attitude to the emperor. We can hardly wonder that in panegyrics like the *Laus Constantini* he comes close to blind adulation and Constantine's personal faults are ignored. Not only is this consistent with the conventional form of panegyric, but it was inevitable in view of the significance of Constantine as confirmation of Eusebius' religious convictions. Eusebius may be criticized for short-sightedness in his unqualified surrender to imperial glory, but nevertheless it is utterly comprehensible in the light of his understanding of divine activity in history.

It is also comprehensible in the light of contemporary culture. Eusebius foreshadowed the imperial theology of the Byzantine Empire in his descriptions of Constantine's role. In his panegyrics, the empire on earth is seen as an imitation of God's sovereign rule in heaven. Imperial epithets are used of God and divine epithets of the emperor. Monarchy alone ensures peace; democracy means anarchy. So there is one God and one emperor under God.[69] Close parallels have been traced between such views and the theory of kingship developed by Hellenistic philosophy, as found in Plutarch and Diotogenes;[70] and similar vocabulary is found in pagan panegyrics.[71] Eusebius has taken up and Christianized the theory of kingship found in the popular philosophy of his day. Constantine has become the ideal 'philosopher-king',[72] who has the right to rule others because he has learned to govern his own unruly passions; he is depicted as ascribing all his success to God, refusing excess flattery, caring nothing for his gorgeous apparel, for the paraphernalia of his office, for the sheer power of his position. His humility, generosity and piety are stressed, and direct communication with the Logos is attributed to him. Thus he becomes the example and teacher of his subjects, as well as their ruler; like a radiant sun, he illuminates the most distant subjects of his empire. When Constantine feasts the bishops, it is like feasting in the kingdom of God. Eusebius comes near to seeing in Constantine a new manifestation of the Logos on earth. In adopting the language of the imperial cult, Eusebius oscillates between exaggerating the specifically Christian aims of the emperor, and suppressing distinctively Christian themes in the interest of achieving religious unity and consensus in the Empire – in other words, he readily became a spokesman for what seems to

---

68 *HE* ix.8.
69 *Laus* i—iii.
70 Baynes (1933/55).
71 Setton (1941); see also Chesnut (1977), chapter VI.
72 Philosopher-king, etc.: *Laus* v; *Vita* iv. 48. Teacher: *Vita* iv. 29. Sun: *Laus* iii. Feast of the Kingdom: *Vita* iii.15.

have been Constantine's general religious policy.[73] Eusebius' attitudes were not unrealistic at the time, and as yet the dangers of the subservience of the Church to its political masters was not apparent.

This discussion assumes that the dossier of works concerned with Constantine is genuine, but in fact it has been the subject of much controversy. The four books of the *Vita Constantini*[74] constitute a seemingly unfinished work of ambiguous genre – an encomium, written after the death of Constantine to celebrate his achievements, which then transmutes into something like the *Ecclesiastical History* with inserted documents. The work is tendentious, suppressing uncomfortable facts and exaggerating the emperor's Christian virtue. However, the author states that he is only concerned to present 'those royal and noble actions which are pleasing to God, the Sovereign of all',[75] because it would be disgraceful if the evil deeds of a Nero should be given fine rhetorical treatment, while Constantine's goodness were passed over in silence. In other words, he is writing in the traditions of imperial panegyric, and there is no pretence at exhaustive biographical treatment. He is to give an account only of circumstances which have reference to Constantine's religious character.[76] So maybe the author should not be dismissed as a dishonest historian on the basis of the omissions and distortions of this particular work. To this work are appended a speech by Constantine (*Ad Coetum sanctorum*), the panegyric which Eusebius offered to the emperor on the occasion of the Tricennalia, and a treatise dedicated to the emperor describing the great new church he built over the Lord's sepulchre in Jerusalem. The latter two works are together known as the *Laus Constantini*.[77]

But was Eusebius the author of the *Vita Constantini*? Are authentic documents preserved within the encomium and appended to it? A long history of doubt has largely been laid to rest.[78] It is noticeable that some passages of the *Vita* are closely paralleled in the *Ecclesiastical History* and the *Laus*; and we have already remarked on Eusebius' propensity for reusing material. A. H. M. Jones noted that a papyrus (*PLond.* 878) is a contemporary copy of the edict quoted in *Vita Constantini* ii.27–28;[79] there being no doubt about the authenticity of this document, the implication is that the rest are genuine. Jones further remarks that he finds it 'difficult to believe that a later forger would have troubled to search out the original of old documents and copy them *in extenso*', so adding weight to the accumulation of arguments against posthumous forgery. But the work is

---

73 Drake (1976). Barnes (1981) contests the widespread notion that Eusebius became an adviser to Constantine – he only met him four times, it would seem, and few of the letters were specifically personal. But that Eusebius endorsed Constantine's policies and articulated them seems incontestable.

74 Texts of the *Vita Constantini* and the *Laus Constantini*; Winkelmann (1975); ET of *Vita* – Cameron and Hall (1999); of *Laus* – Drake (1976).

75 *Vita* i.10.

76 *Vita* i.11.

77 Drake (1976) and Cameron and Hall (1999) have useful discussions of both the critical and historical problems of these texts.

78 Baynes (1929) discusses all the objections and argues for their authenticity in the very full footnotes.

79 Jones (1954).

certainly not a documentary history of what actually happened; Eusebius was creating a portrait to set the record straight, embracing the techniques of apologetic and hagiography as well as panegyric.[80]

The emphasis and style of Eusebius' writings on the emperor is very much in line with his previous work and his most important ideas. Constantine, like Moses, had direct experience of God before becoming priest, legislator and teacher.[81] Called by God, he has come to fulfil his destiny, as the final proof of God's activity in history, judging the wicked and overcoming evil and idolatry in all its forms and ensuring peace in the world and in the Church. The consonance of this with Eusebius' views on providence may explain the exaggerated view of Constantine's measures against idolatry and his glossing over the nature and seriousness of the doctrinal disputes in the Church. It is interesting that concerns similar to those of Eusebius are reflected in Constantine's speech and can be found in many of his rescripts: the desire for peace in the Church, the assertion of the superiority and truth of Christianity, the arguments against polytheism and philosophy, the justification of the incarnation. Eusebius was prepared to make himself the mouthpiece of the imperial policy,[82] to respond to Constantine's attempts at rapprochement between pagan and Christian, to give Constantine a special place in relation to the Supreme God even at the expense of playing down distinctively Christian ideas, not simply because he was an abject time-server, but because Constantine's advent confirmed his theology and his philosophy of history.

All this serves as a reminder that during the years of the Arian struggle, there were other issues at stake which seemed far more important. For Constantine and Eusebius, the primary issue was Christianity's claim to be the truth in the face of the pagan majority. It was this which made the unity of the Church so vitally important to both. Internal squabbles undermined their overall purposes. The actions and compromises of both are explained by this background. It is far from surprising that Eusebius' accommodating attitudes commended themselves more to the emperor than Athanasius' intransigence. The bishop of Caesarea stood for inclusiveness; the bishop of Alexandria for exclusiveness.

5 Eusebius' Christology

The part played by Eusebius in the Arian controversy and the proceedings at Nicaea has been the subject of much discussion by historians and theologians alike.[83] Eusebius' Christological position cannot be exactly identified with that of either side in the dispute. He thought in terms of one transcendent Supreme God, incomprehensible and inexpressible, who mediated the divine self to the world through the Logos. This Being he regarded as divine, but not God in the

---

80 Averil Cameron, 'Eusebius' *Vita Constantini* and the construction of Constantine', in Edwards and Swain (1997).

81 Cameron in Edwards and Swain (1997).

82 See Drake (1976) and Storch (1971).

83 On Eusebius' Christology, see Luibheid (1978); Hanson (1985), pp. 253–6, (1988), pp. 46–59; Lienhard (1999); Delcogliano (2006), pp. 471–6; Parvis (2006); Robertson (2007).

same ultimate sense as the God from whom he genuinely derived his being; the ultimate source of all things was not divided or reduced by the generation of the Logos, which was beyond human comprehension – he was the 'perfect creation of a perfect Creator'.[84] To this extent, Eusebius was Arian in tendency, though he certainly did not subscribe to the Arian conclusion that the Logos was mutable or made out of nothing.[85] This 'second God' was produced from the First Cause, and fashioned after his image,[86] 'the living image of the living God'.[87] Eusebius was convinced of the Son's perfection and changelessness, even in the context of the incarnation, and this belief had the same quasi-docetic results in some of Eusebius' statements as appear in anti-Arian exegesis;[88] the Logos himself did not suffer on the cross, but only his body. However, Eusebius could see nothing wrong, it seems, in believing in a hierarchy of divine beings; a radical distinction between divine and non-divine did not appear on his map of the universe.

Nevertheless, he did believe in a *de facto* distinction between the one Supreme God to whom worship should be offered, and all other inferior spiritual beings, whether angels or demons, who should not receive worship.[89] Where was the Logos to fit into the monotheism versus polytheism debate? Eusebius apparently follows traditional 'Origenist' patterns and fails to see the problems involved. There is a fundamental tension between his monotheism and his Christology. 'Even the only-begotten of God and the first-born of the whole world, the beginning of all, commands us to believe his Father alone true God, and to worship only him.'[90] Yet the Logos is also to receive worship, for he is God's vice-gerent, his image and his instrument, a second Lord.[91] Eusebius goes to a great deal of trouble to prove that there is only one God, and so there can only be one Logos; but one God plus one divine Word, on the face of it, makes two divine beings, both of whom are to receive worship. One feels that Eusebius can easily be charged with ditheism, especially in the rhetorical and loose expressions of the *Theophania*.

Eusebius may thus appear a little confused and self-contradictory in his assertion of the uniqueness of God, while defending the divinity of the Word and his right to receive worship. His position may be comprehensible in terms of the Platonic/Origenist heritage on which he drew. Already the second-century Neo-Pythagorean Numenius had spoken of a second God, and Eusebius is

---

84 *Dem. Evang.* iv.2.

85 *Dem. Evang.* v.1. Robertson (2007) notes that Eusebius did not like the idea that anything was created out of nothing, for nothing comes from nothing (a Greek commonplace) – rather everything was '*ek Theou*', or made from God's will, in the sense that God was the ultimate First Cause. This puts a different perspective on the ways in which Eusebius shared and did not share ideas with Arius and other associates.

86 *Praep. Evang.* vii.12, 13, 15. Eusebius quotes Philo as well as proof-texts from the scriptures.

87 *Dem. Evang.* v.1.

88 *Dem. Evang.* iv.3, 13. See below, pp. 63–4.

89 *Praep. Evang.* iv.10, 17, 21.

90 *Praep. Evang.* vii.15.

91 *HE* i.2.

responsible for preserving the vast majority of Numenius' fragments.[92] In both cases the need for a secondary divine being arose from the classic problem of the Platonic–Pythagorean tradition, the need for some ontological connection between the One and the Many. Like Origen, Eusebius cast the Logos in this mediatorial role: God is the One who utterly transcends the Many; the Logos is both One and Many, being the image of God and at the same time pervading all things. He is the Neoplatonic World-Soul;[93] the instrument through which God created and sustains the world, and the mediator who reveals and displays providential love in his direction of the world and its history. This account of the Logos' mediation in Eusebius has been challenged, but also refined, by the insistence that Numenius was not necessarily the source, but rather provided 'corroboration for what Eusebius believed to be correct Christian doctrine', ultimately deriving from scripture; as mediator the Logos had to be both similar to and different from both God and creatures.[94]

The Logos then could in no sense be identified with God; to admit that he was 'of one substance with the Father' in the sense of having a common identity was to undermine both God's uniqueness and the mediatory position of the Logos. The Logos 'was necessary because the uncreated and immutable substance of Almighty God could not be changed into the form of a man'.[95] So close did Eusebius come to denying his own belief in the changelessness of the Logos. No wonder he found the language of the Arians more in line with his conservative thinking. As far as he was concerned, the Logos must remain an intermediary link between God himself and the beings he had created.

One reason for Eusebius' failure to appreciate the position of the anti-Arians was his soteriological outlook. Eusebius was an intellectual Christian. 'We have been delivered by the grace and beneficence of Almighty God, by the ineffable power of our Saviour's *teaching* in the gospel, and by *sound reasoning*'; 'we have received these proofs after subjecting them to the tests and enquiries of a critical judgment.'[96] Such sentences have at times been regarded as witnessing to Eusebius' conversion, though he may well have been born and brought up a Christian. Nevertheless, they do make the point that his faith was the reasoned faith of an intellectual who found the Christian account of things more convincing than that of its rival religious philosophies. He seems not to have been driven by deep religious passions. As von Campenhausen suggested, monotheism and morality was the heart of the gospel for Eusebius.[97] The work of Christ was that of teacher and revealer pointing the way to the true religion and overcoming ignorance and idolatry. It is true that Eusebius uses and interprets the imagery of sacrifice to explain Christ's death, which he sees as a triumph over the opposing powers of evil. He even describes salvation as deification,

---

92 des Places (1975).

93 Ricken (1967); Lyman (1993). Luibheid (1978) probably fails to take Eusebius' Platonist and Origenist background seriously enough; though Kannengiesser probably overdoes the tracing of Origenist elements in every aspect of Eusebius' work in 'Eusebius of Caesarea, Origenist' in Attridge and Hata (1992).

94 Robertson (2007), p. 41.

95 *HE* i.2.

96 *Praep. Evang.* ii.4; *Dem. Evang.* iii.4.

97 von Campenhausen (1963), chapter V.

using a word similar to Athanasius' θεοποίησις (*theopoiēsis*).[98] But always the conventional images are expounded in such a way as to account for the death of Christ within Eusebius' understanding of his revelatory function; the providential oversight and progressive education of wandering humanity involved conquering the powers of evil, destroying false religion, and cleansing human beings of their sins and weaknesses.[99] For Eusebius the important result of the coming of the Lord remained fundamentally the establishment of the true religion, the revelation of the true God over against the error and vice of idolatry. This is particularly apparent if we contrast the main emphasis of the argument of the *Theophania* with that of Athanasius in the *Contra gentes* and *De incarnatione*, even though the similarities are striking.[100] Unlike Athanasius, Eusebius did not argue from Christ's revelatory and redeeming work to his essential, undiluted divinity; in fact this would undercut the ability of the Logos to act as an intermediary. A second Lord might become incarnate, whereas this was inconceivable for the transcendent First Cause. An image can reveal without being identical with the original; a deputy can act with the delegated powers of his superior. Eusebius' position was far from unreasonable within the terms of his own understanding of Christian salvation, just as it was acceptable within the terms of contemporary thought. But it belonged to the third-century world, to a hierarchical understanding of the spiritual world which many would go on assuming for some decades.[101] Now, however, Arius had raised new questions and forced on the Church a more sophisticated and critical statement of its claims. Was Christ really divine? How is divinity to be defined? In what sense if any at all, is the Logos to be regarded as God? Eusebius' prime concern was to envisage how the Logos mediated God. Arius spoke a language he understood; his opponents seemed to confuse his carefully conceived scheme. So he championed Arius and found himself excommunicated at a synod in Antioch in 324.

The hints and silences in the accounts of the proceedings at Nicaea are particularly tantalizing. Eusebius describes the occasion in the *Vita Constantini*, and in a letter to his church at Caesarea he tells how agreement was reached on the creed.[102] From these accounts it might be concluded that Eusebius himself gave the opening address; then later he produced the traditional baptismal creed of his church as a possible compromise document, and accepted the addition of certain terms, with which he found it hard to agree, only when they had been carefully expounded to his satisfaction by the emperor. But the course of events seems to have been somewhat compressed and distorted in the accounts he

---

98 *Dem. Evang.* iv.14. For Athanasius' use of the concept, see below, pp. 55, 62, 64.

99 *Dem. Evang.* iv.12.

100 See below, pp. 51–2.

101 Weber (1965) suggests that Eusebius' position is pre-Nicene and entirely in line with tradition; Athanasius and Marcellus were the innovators. Ricken (1967), Luibheid (1978) and Lienhard (1999) agree that he was not a creative genius, but is one of the best documented examples of a theological school that dominated the Greek East for much of the fourth century, with variant forms in Arius, the Eastern councils and the homoiousians. See further pp. 21, 24–5, 41.

102 Preserved by Athanasius in his *De decretis Nicaenae Synodi*; see below, Chapter 2 references, p. 65 n. 120, 121.

gives. To many it has seemed a fair stretch of the critical imagination to take the Nicene creed as a revised version of the Caesarean creed quoted by Eusebius,[103] and it is far more likely, especially in view of his recent condemnation at Antioch, that Eusebius produced his creed to rehabilitate himself. It undoubtedly represented the traditional faith of the Church and cleared his name, but it had no relevance to the theological matter in dispute.

Eusebius eventually signed the new creed, with its *homoousion*, presumably in deference to the emperor's wishes and for the sake of peace in the Church; but in his letter to his church, his embarrassment is evident. Does this mean that Eusebius sacrificed principle to political expediency?

Such a judgment is probably unfair. The Christological section of the *Demonstratio evangelica* suggests that Eusebius disliked 'substance' terminology, because of the danger of its being understood in a materialist sense.[104] His analogies concentrate on the fragrance emanating from an object, or a ray of light issuing from its source; and even these he describes as earthly images, illustrations far transcended by theology which is not connected with anything physical. The Son was begotten unspeakably and unthinkably.[105] He certainly accepted that the Logos was derived from the Father in a unique sense – the father–son relationship is not, after all, the same kind of thing as the craftsman–artefact relation; but in God's case the manner of the Son's generation surpassed human understanding. So, in spite of his distrust of the terminology produced, Eusebius was prepared to be accommodating, if only others would make concessions too. If we compare the *Demonstratio* with his later dogmatic treatises, it is clear that the signing of the Nicene Creed made no basic change to his Christology.

In the old days of controversy, it is hardly surprising that some condemned Eusebius, others tried to defend the 'father of Church history' from the charge of heresy. Clearly Eusebius' position was neither on one side nor the other, and like Constantine himself, in some bewilderment, he acted primarily in the interests of Church unity. He wanted to steer a middle course. What then of the sequel to Nicaea? Was Eusebius similarly motivated in his subsequent actions?

Nicaea produced a formula; the problem now was its interpretation[106] – that was how it seemed by hindsight. But at the time, Eusebius was involved in proceedings against Eustathius, Marcellus and Athanasius on grounds, it seems, not directly associated with the Nicene Creed as such. The rights and wrongs of the case brought up at Tyre are far from clear. If Athanasius' works seem to prove that all the charges were trumped up, nevertheless his own followers were equally unscrupulous, and we cannot doubt that there was suppression and distortion of the evidence on both sides. No compromise was possible, and the only way of ensuring peaceful and successful celebrations for the thirtieth year of Constantine's reign was to remove the most intransigent customer. If it were not for Athanasius, the dream of Church unity might be realized, and this

---

103 Kelly (1950), pp. 217ff.; though Eusebius' account has been reinstated by Parvis (2006), acknowledging a debt to Vinzent.

104 For the following discussion I am indebted to Stead (1973).

105 *Dem. Evang.* iv.3; v.1.

106 Athanasius, *De Decretis Nic. Syn.* 3. Socrates, *HE* i.23.

was fundamental to Eusebius' political theory and historical philosophy. So Athanasius was condemned at Tyre. In the case of Marcellus, Eusebius took up his pen, replying to Marcellus' attack on his own theology in *Against Asterius*.[107] In the hasty work, *Contra Marcellum*, long quotations from Marcellus are left to speak for themselves with little real attempt at refutation;[108] but *De ecclesiastica theologia* spells out the sort of theology prevalent in the Greek East at the beginning of the fourth century, steering a course between Arius and Marcellus.[109] Eusebius' insistence on the mediatory position of the Logos is reinforced.[110] It was all too obvious to Eusebius that Marcellus' theology was wrong and dangerous, and that his own position represented the traditional theology of the Church. This only goes to prove Eusebius' essential conservatism. The other work of his old age, the *Theophania*, shows that throughout his life Eusebius was more concerned with upholding the true religion against polytheism than in refining his somewhat confused and anachronistic understanding of the relationship between God and the Logos. His heart lay in the defence of a united Church, and the promulgation of the truth of Christianity, whose success he regarded as the goal of the historical process.

6 Eusebius as a biblical scholar

One surprising consequence of the later dating of Eusebius' major works is that it suggests that he produced virtually no composition of his own until after the death of Pamphilus, when he was around fifty years old and bishop of Caesarea. The nature of the community around Pamphilus perhaps provides some explanation.[111] Pamphilus was not just a collector of books, but one who engaged in collation, correcting and copying, who prepared and gave away copies of the scriptures, and engaged his disciples in this oral and collaborative process. Over years Eusebius doubtless worked alongside him, built up experience and studied the *Hexapla*. Perhaps it was not until after persecution, with Pamphilus gone, that he realized the need to justify Christianity, and embarked on a different kind of 'collation', namely, the composition of the great 'mosaics' of quotations already described, and his constant revisions, projects to which the army of scribes would have had a crucial contribution to make. As bishop he probably ceased to be physically involved in hands-on book production, employing many assistants – hence his ability to undertake the mammoth task of supplying fifty copies of the scriptures for Constantine's new churches in Constantinople.

Like Origen, Eusebius allowed for multiple possibilities, and set things side by side for investigation: here the *Hexapla* was probably an important influence, a work to be used as a 'treasury of exegetical materials, some of them perplex-

---

107 Text of *Contra Marcellum* and other doctrinal works: Klostermann (1972). For Marcellus, see Chapter 2, pp. 56–61.

108 Parvis (2006) follows Vinzent (1997) in suggesting that this was the dossier used to condemn Marcellus at the Synod of Constantinople.

109 Lienhard (1999), though see the critique in Parvis (2006).

110 Robertson (2007), pp. 99ff.

111 On Pamphilus and book production, see Grafton and Williams (2006).

ing, rather than an effort to provide a stable, perfect text of the Bible'.[112] So one of Eusebius' great contributions was to conceive of systems for the organization of information for easy reference and retrieval. His first endeavour of this kind is likely to have been the Gospel Canons, tables which enabled those studying the Gospels to identify parallel passages.[113] Yet for Eusebius the New Testament was the authentic record of the historical Jesus, and he faced seriously the discrepancies between the Gospels, seeking to explain them in *Gospel Questions and Solutions*,[114] assuming that a historical explanation could be found. Another example of his predilection for sorting things is the *Onomasticon*,[115] alphabetically arranged lists of biblical places intended to help with site identification. The lists group references in the Pentateuch, book by book, and then the history books of the Old Testament, sometimes adding Gospel sites but by no means comprehensively, which has given rise to the notion that Eusebius took over a Jewish compilation. It seems that Eusebius meant it to be an exegetical aid, not yet foreseeing the need for a pilgrims' handbook.[116]

We possess little of Eusebius' exegetical work, though he was renowned in his day as a student of the Bible. Considerable fragments of a *Commentary on the Psalms* and a *Commentary on Isaiah* had been found in the Catenae, but there was little else of significance before the discovery of an almost complete copy of the latter in a manuscript in Florence.[117] On the whole it confirms previous conclusions regarding Eusebius' Old Testament exegesis, which were based on his treatment of Old Testament texts in the *Prophetic Eclogues* and the *Demonstratio evangelica*. Several features are striking: first, his frequent discussion of Greek versions other than the LXX, and occasional reference to Hebrew – he must have worked with the *Hexapla* beside him;[118] second, his understanding of the literal meaning of a prophecy as its fulfilment in a later historical event. Occasionally in the *Demonstratio* he offers two interpretations, literal and figurative – an example is provided by the prophecies of peace at the coming of Emmanuel: literally they refer to the peace of the Empire at the time of the incarnation, figuratively to the peace of the individual soul who receives 'God with us'.[119] In the *Commentary on Isaiah* it is clear that Eusebius' prime interest is in discerning God's activity in the world rather than seeking an individualist or intellectualist spirituality – here is his main difference from Origen. Eusebius

---

112 Grafton and Williams (2006), p. 170.

113 See Nestle-Aland's *Novum Testamentum Graece*, 26th edn, pp. 73–8, along with the marginal annotations.

114 Epitome and fragments of the *Quaestiones Evangelicae* in Migne, PG 22.

115 Text of the *Onomasticon*: Klostermann (1904). ET and commentaries will be found in Freeman-Grenville, Taylor and Chapman (2003), which places an ET of Jerome's Latin version alongside that of Eusebius, enabling a comparison of differences between the 320s and 380s; and Notley and Safrai (2005), which sets out the Greek and the Latin with English in three columns.

116 Wilken (1992); Walker (1990) underlines the difference between Eusebius and Cyril of Jerusalem in attitude to the Holy Places; see further below, p. 191.

117 Möhle (1934) reported the find of the *Commentary on Isaiah*. Text: Ziegler (1975). See also van Cangh (1971, 1972).

118 Though Hollerich (1999), pp. 80–1, notes that his access to Hebrew was through the literal translation of Aquila, so he may have used the *Tetrapla*.

119 *Dem. Evang.* vii.1.

distinguished between direct and veiled predictions, the latter notion permitting not only the treatment of the text as prefigurative but also, at times, a rather arbitrary application of texts to future events through the use of allegory to unpack metaphors and the symbols found, for example, in numbers, animals and natural phenomena. For Eusebius, Old Testament history was a living reality, fulfilled in the present. It has been suggested[120] that the *Commentary on Isaiah*, written soon after the Nicene Council in 325, gives a better insight into Eusebius' overriding interests than the panegyrical works on Constantine – for it focuses more on the ecclesiastical than the imperial, depicting the Church as embodying the 'godly polity' prefigured in scripture, and bishops as leaders of the visible and concrete ecclesiastical community foreseen by the prophets.

Eusebius inherited Origen's critical spirit rather than his bent for allegorical exegesis. But he was also heir to Origen's intellectualist approach, which, though open-minded towards the culture and learning of the pagan world, still saw Christianity as the truth to be defended. From Origen came his concept of the universe as the home of a hierarchy of spiritual beings, and his understanding of the Logos as the intermediary between the transcendent God and his multifarious creation. From Origen came his avoidance of crude millenarian beliefs and his concentration on the moral education of humanity by the Logos. The chief difference was that, whereas Origen emphasized the progress of the individual soul, Eusebius saw this education as a long-term evolutionary process worked out in the course of history.[121]

Thus the concrete historical reality of the Christian Church was of far greater significance to Eusebius than to his theological master; and he it was who became the first ecclesiastical historian. He also became the first theoretician of Byzantine 'Caesaro-papism'. He had his faults – his tendency to suppress awkward information, his over-enthusiastic response to Constantine, his conservative mentality in theology; but at least he pioneered the writing of Church history, and others were able to follow where he had led.

For Further Reading

English translations

Cameron, A. and Stuart G. Hall, 1999. *Eusebius. The Life of Constantine* (introd., trans. and commentary), Oxford: Clarendon Press.

Drake, H. A., 1976. *In Praise of Constantine: a Historical Study and New Translation of Eusebius' Tricennial Orations*, Berkeley: University of California Press.

Ferrar, W. J., 1920. *The Proof of the Gospel (Demonstratio Evangelica)*, 2 vols, London: SPCK.

Gifford, E. H., 1903. *Eusebii Pamphili Evangelicae Praeparationis Libri XV* (text and ET), Oxford: Oxford University Press.

Lawlor, H. J. and J. E. L. Oulton (ET and notes), 1927. *Eusebius, Bishop of Caesarea, The Ecclesiastical History and the Martyrs of Palestine*, 2 vols, London: SPCK.

Lee, S., 1843. *Eusebius. On the Theophaneia*, Cambridge: Cambridge University Press.

---

120 For a full discussion of Eusebius' *Commentary on Isaiah*, see Hollerich (1999).
121 Kannengiesser in Attridge and Hata (1992).

Notley, R. S. and Z. Safrai, 2005. *Eusebius*, Onomasticon. *The Place-Names of Divine Scripture. A Triglott edition with Notes and Commentary*, Leiden: Brill.

Williamson, G. A., 1965/89. *Eusebius. The History of the Church from Christ to Constantine*, rev. edn A. Louth, Harmondsworth and Baltimore: Penguin books.

Studies

Attridge, H. W. and G. Hata (eds), 1992. *Eusebius, Christianity and Judaism*, Leiden: Brill.

Barnes, T. D., 1981. *Constantine and Eusebius*, Cambridge, MA: Harvard University Press.

Chesnut, Glenn F., 1977. *The First Christian Histories: Eusebius, Socrates, Sozomen, Theodoret and Evagrius*, Paris: Éditions Beauchesne.

Grafton, Anthony and Megan Williams, 2006. *Christianity and the Transformation of the Book. Origen, Eusebius, and the Library of Caesarea*, Cambridge, MA: Harvard University Press.

Grant, R. M., 1980. *Eusebius as Church Historian*, Oxford and New York: Clarendon.

Kofsky, Aryeh, 2000. *Eusebius of Caesarea Against Paganism*, Leiden: Brill.

Lienhard, J. T., 1999. Contra Marcellum: *Marcellus of Ancyra and Fourth Century Theology*, Washington, DC: Catholic University of America Press.

Luibheid, C., 1978. *Eusebius of Caesarea and the Arian Crisis*, Dublin: Irish Academic Press.

Robertson, Jon M., 2007. *Christ as Mediator. A Study of the Theologies of Eusebius of Caesarea, Marcellus of Ancyra, and Athanasius of Alexandria*, Oxford: Oxford University Press.

Wallace-Hadrill, D. S., 1960. *Eusebius of Caesarea*, London: Mowbray.

II Eusebius' Successors

Subsequent attempts to write Church history all indicate the dominating influence of Eusebius' work. When Rufinus of Aquileia introduced Church history to the Latin world, he basically translated the *Ecclesiastical History* of Eusebius together with the now lost continuation added by Gelasius, a later bishop of Caesarea. For the next century and a half, Greek historians of the Church did not attempt to replace the work of Eusebius,[122] but rather chose to take up the story where he left off. Four of those who assumed his mantle deserve attention: Socrates, Sozomen, Philostorgius and Theodoret.

Hindsight meant that the historians of the early fifth century constructed the story of the fourth century in terms of a struggle between 'Nicenes' and 'Arians'. From the encomium on Athanasius delivered by Gregory of Nazian-

---

122 The *Christian History* of Philip of Side, published in the 430s, is perhaps an exception, but it was apparently more like an encyclopaedia than a history. Socrates (*HE* vii.27) describes it as a collection of 'very heterogeneous materials', containing a 'medley of geometrical theorems, astronomical speculations, arithmetical calculations and musical principles' with geographical details and other irrelevant material. It was an attempt to cover the whole of history from the creation, according to Photius (*Bibl.* 35). All is lost apart from a few fragments.

zus at Constantinople in 379 and the subsequent triumph of orthodoxy in 381, that binary perspective shaped all accounts for some 1,600 years, and Socrates' revision of his first two books in the light of a dossier of documents from Athanasius doubtless reinforced the process. Only in the late twentieth century with the deconstruction of that narrative, largely created by Athanasius himself, did the complexities and shifting alliances of the period between Nicaea and Chalcedon begin to be exposed.[123]

While the possibility remains that the 'losing party' of Eusebians at Nicaea systematically plotted a 'reversal of fortunes',[124] it is now widely regarded as doubtful whether any of the leading protagonists in the period immediately after the Nicene Council saw the creed agreed there as authoritative over local traditions, or themselves as defending or opposing the *homoousion* as such. Conflicts were generated by ethical issues, and political and personal antagonisms, as much as doctrinal differences, and the last did not necessarily arise from 'Arianism' or reaction against it: the cases of Eustathius, Marcellus and Athanasius provide examples.[125] Bishops gathering in 341 refused to be labelled 'Arians' on the grounds that they were not followers of a mere presbyter but bishops of the Church defending the true tradition of the faith. It is not impossible that this was a response to the fact that Athanasius had begun to dub all his enemies, whatever their actual position, 'Ariomaniacs', thus endeavouring to 'elevate his struggle to the ideological plane'.[126] The career of Cyril of Jerusalem[127] suggests that his theological position, like that of Eusebius of Caesarea at an earlier date, was simply ambiguous in relation to the particular binary divide produced by hindsight, and that it was not commonly held doctrine which determined the 'party' with which he had contacts at any given time; while the early associations of Basil of Caesarea[128] demonstrate that there was no clear conception of a 'pro-Nicene' party until well into the 360s. Accommodations and realignments then began to prepare for a coalescing of groups around Nicaea as a unifying focus, and once Theodosius I arrived in Constantinople, conditions were ripe for 'orthodox' leadership to supplant 'Arian' bishops across the Empire. Read back, however, the labels impose a clarity which 'blurs the differences between those who had much in common',[129] while obscuring the shifts that would eventually produce 'Nicene' theology. Nor is it helpful simply to characterize Constantius and Valens as 'Arian' emperors, despite their influence on the

---

123 For this shift in perspective see for example Barnes (1993); Barnes and Williams (1993); and Ayres (2004a), building on Hanson (1988) and other previous work on Arianism, Neo-Arianism, Nicene and Neo-Nicene alliances, etc. Work on Marcellus (see Chapter 2 below), on Aetius and Eunomius (see Vaggione (2000) and Chapter 4 below), has played a considerable role, as well as the reassessment of Athanasius' presentation of the conflict (see Kannengiesser (1974), Chapter 2 below).

124 For the twenty years after Nicaea traced in detail, see Parvis (2006). Though emphasizing a power struggle between parties, she still identifies the construction of 'Arianism' as a heresy as the work of Athanasius and Marcellus in Rome in 340.

125 See further, Chapter 2 below.

126 Barnes (1993), p. 53.

127 See below, Chapter 5, Section II.

128 See below, Chapter 4.

129 Ayres (2004a), p. 13.

course of events; in both cases they prove to be pragmatic rulers seeking the most unifying outcome of their patronage of ecclesiastical dignitaries.

Despite this revisionism, however, the Church historians reviewed here provide documents and evidence of undeniable value, if critically examined, in tracing what happened between Nicaea and the reign of Theodosius II.[130] Socrates' instinct that contentiousness lay at the root of disputes in the Church is perhaps truer to his subject-matter than the framework of classic struggle into which the material tends to be fitted.

1 Socrates Scholasticus

Little is known of Socrates apart from what we can glean from his work. He was apparently a citizen of Constantinople by birth, and may never have left the city, although descriptions of local customs elsewhere suggest that he perhaps travelled a bit. His exact dates cannot be determined. His *Ecclesiastical History*[131] ends in 439, and allusions to at least one revision of the work suggest that he lived for a time after that date. He was probably old enough to have some memory of about the last forty years he describes. He was a layman, perhaps a lawyer by profession;[132] the final year of his history corresponds to the date of the publication of the Theodosian Code, and the work is dedicated to a man named Theodore – was this the Theodore who was one of the nine law commissioners who supervised the Code's compilation? Perhaps Socrates was commissioned to produce a historical survey to aid the commissioners in their selection of ecclesiastical legislation;[133] the controversies of the previous century clearly complicated the task in relation to the legislation of 'Arian' emperors. Socrates begins with the reign of Constantine and the Arian controversy, a fact which might lend support to this hypothesis. But in fact Socrates shows no interest in the Code and cites no laws.[134] His treatment in the final book of both Proclus, the archbishop, and of the emperor, Theodosius II, might suggest that his history was intended to show how, after all the intervening tribulations, Theodosius II was successful in uniting Church and Empire, so paralleling the achievements of Constantine.[135]

Socrates consciously and deliberately began where Eusebius left off, feeling it necessary to explain the overlap at the beginning. He regarded Eusebius' treatment of Constantine's reign and the rise of Arianism as inadequate, pointing out that in the *Life of Constantine*, Eusebius was 'more intent on the rhetorical finish of his composition and the praises of the emperor than on an accurate statement

---

130 See Barnes (1993), Appendices 5, 6 and 7, for tabulations of (i) Socrates' chronology and its mistakes, (ii) the material and sources Sozomen used independently of Socrates, and (iii) additional information found in Theodoret.

131 Text: Hansen (1995); Hansen, Périchon and Maraval (2004, 2005, 2006, 2007); ET in *NPNF*.

132 This is based on the attachment of Scholasticus to his name; Urbainczyk (1997), pp. 13–14, shows that this is late and probably has no basis.

133 Chesnut (1977), pp. 168f.

134 Urbainczyk (1997), p. 37.

135 Urbainczyk (1997).

of facts'.[136] So his first book deals with the reign of Constantine, and imperial reigns mark off the limits of each subsequent book. Whatever the occasion or purpose of Socrates' history, its model was Eusebius, though Socrates mentions some aspects where he differs. Perhaps the most notable is that Eusebius differentiated his work from classical historiography by contrasting narratives of war with the peace of the Church, while Socrates sees disputes in the Church and the Empire's wars as integrally linked – indeed the subject-matter of his history.[137]

It has been suggested that, like Eusebius, Socrates was an Origenist,[138] though there is little to go on except a few approving comments. He defends Eusebius against charges of Arianism by appeal to Origen,[139] opponents of Origen, like Theophilus of Alexandria, come in for sharp criticism, and he defends Origen against his detractors.[140] But Socrates generally avoids discussing theological niceties, so his own position is not easy to discern. Like Eusebius, he espouses a Christian humanism of a scholarly and critical kind, which could stem from a respect for Origen, but equally could have come from adopting the Academy's position of 'methodical doubt' whereby various opinions were marshalled alongside each other and the inadequacy of human knowledge demonstrated. In Socrates' case, this approach was coupled with a remarkably tolerant spirit; he shows respect for Novatians, and even Arian presbyters with whom he had contact. Socrates hated most the heretics who arrogantly claimed to know the whole truth, accusing them of 'sophistry' and love of dispute. He was not given to reverence for contentious bishops either. He approved the search for unity rather than contentiousness.

But Socrates' attitudes were very different from those of Eusebius at a number of points:

(i) Where Eusebius was anxious to camouflage disputes in the Church, Socrates regards these as the material for history-writing. He concludes his work by praying that the Church everywhere may live in peace, and adds the comment: 'as long as peace continues, those who desire to write histories will find no materials for their purpose.' Elsewhere he claims that he would have been silent if the Church had remained undisturbed by divisions.[141]

(ii) Eusebius was intolerant of heresy and schism, but Socrates praises imperial tolerance towards heretics,[142] and openly expresses admiration for the Novatian sect, whose strict standards certainly appeared attractive compared with the worldly ecclesiastics of orthodoxy. He can even be charitable towards contemporary Arians, especially those who held Origen and Plato in esteem. However, for all his tolerance and lack of enmity, he writes from the standpoint of post-Arian orthodoxy, and subscribes to the theory that heresies, once

---

136 Socrates, HE i.1.
137 Eusebius, preface to Book v of his HE; Socrates, preface to Book v of his HE; discussion in Urbainczyk (1997), pp. 69–70.
138 Chesnut (1977).
139 HE ii.21.
140 HE vi.13.
141 Socrates, HE i.18.
142 Imperial tolerance: v.20; vii.41–2. Novatians: frequently, but cf. vii.46. Arians: vii.6.

divorced from the orthodox Church, inevitably subdivide into multifarious sects.[143] Generally he disclaims any attempt to analyse or understand the philosophical and theological issues at stake in doctrinal disputes. He simply adopts the view that disorder is bad, heresy is bad and lack of charity is bad.

(iii) Eusebius wrote with enthusiasm and respect of the heroes, scholars and leaders of the Church. Socrates is almost cynical about ecclesiastics and ecclesiastical politics. The subject of his work is the 'contentious disputes of bishops and their insidious designs against one another'; for 'the bishops are accustomed to do this in all cases, accusing and pronouncing impious those they depose, but not explaining their warrant for so doing'.[144] He deliberately refrains from using honorific titles for the bishops, like 'most dear to God' or 'most holy'.[145] Socrates is not afraid to criticize: in telling the story of John Chrysostom, he does not attempt to hide the faults of the recently reinstated saint. He is prepared to examine and assess Nestorius' views for himself rather than join automatically in the witch-hunt. On the whole he makes realistic assessments of the characters involved, and is not disposed to hagiography. He recognizes that ambition and jealousy now affect ecclesiastical politics.[146]

(iv) Eusebius welcomed with enthusiasm the new link between Church and state, regarding it as providential. Socrates, just over a century later, is less enthusiastic, recognizing its ambiguous character. When Socrates reflected on how the affairs of state were closely interwoven with ecclesiastical history, he produced the theory that Church and state were somehow linked in a kind of cosmic sympathy (an idea with Neoplatonic roots).[147] The result was that dissensions in the Church produced dissensions in the state, and vice versa. Likewise peace and prosperity in either Church or state would mean peace and prosperity for the other. The emperors had a key role in Church history 'because from the time they began to profess the Christian religion, the affairs of the Church depended on them, so that even the greatest synods have been and still are convened by their appointment'.[148] Socrates believed that it was the emperor's task to foster harmony in both political and ecclesiastical spheres. This he did through his piety (εὐσέβεια), through the power of his prayers, through his virtue and orthodoxy. In the past, state patronage had not always enhanced the unity of the Church; Socrates explained the problems in terms of 'bad emperors', rather as Eusebius had explained the persecutions. But 'although nonhomoousian emperors are detrimental for the state, Socrates excuses them as being mistaken or ill advised by heretical clerics'.[149] By contrast, the current emperor, Theodosius II, deserved a eulogy[150] – for peace and prosperity were now established. So for all his scepticism, Socrates could be as unrealistic as

---

143 Attitude to heresy: v.20ff. Refusal to examine disputes: i.22. Disorder, etc.: ii.1.

144 *HE* v. introd.; i.24.

145 *HE* vi. introd.; the rest of Book vi deals with the Chrysostom affair. Chrysostom's relics were reburied in Constantinople in 438 by Theodosius II, i.e. shortly before Socrates wrote the history. That incident is described in vii.45.

146 *HE* vi.20; on Nestorius, see vii.32.

147 Chesnut (1975); and (1977), pp. 186ff.

148 Socrates, *HE* v. introd. On the emperor's role, see Downey (1965).

149 Urbainczyk (1997), p. 152.

150 Socrates, *HE* vii.20.

Eusebius: his work ends with a premature and over-enthusiastic assessment of the situation, written a few years before the Council of Chalcedon and the subsequent schism with anti-Chalcedonians.

(v) Where Eusebius was anxious to show the workings of providence in history, Socrates disclaims any attempt to analyse the mysterious reasons for the providences and judgments of God, virtually claiming that an objective account of the disputes in the Church is his sole purpose.[151] About the cause of a hailstorm, popularly ascribed to divine vengeance for the deposition of John Chrysostom, he professes agnosticism. Yet he has not entirely abandoned the idea of providence; he seems to understand it as channelled through the emperor, as long as he has the necessary piety. Thus Socrates did recognize as an act of God the subjugation of the enemies of Theodosius II; and thunderbolts and plagues, fulfilling a prophecy in Ezekiel, deterred recent barbarian ravages – for God rewarded the meekness of Theodosius. (Modern historians would call it weakness!)

Socrates' aims and interests in writing his history were therefore not always very close to those of Eusebius. The apologetic interest is less obvious (though Downey traced several apologetic motifs),[152] and within the limits imposed by his culture, Socrates seems to have attempted to give a tolerant and unbiased account of the events of that stormy century. The methods of Eusebius he did adopt, examining and quoting original documents to support and amplify his account, thus preserving many invaluable texts. He speaks of the laborious task of sifting documents, testing evidence, and of enquiring of a variety of witnesses whose accounts inevitably conflicted.[153] He recognizes that facts can be suppressed or distorted by partiality and prejudice. He tries to distinguish between hearsay and genuine information. But at times, Socrates falls uncritically into reproducing popular estimates of people and events which are not always consistent with his efforts at considered judgment. It is Philostorgius and the pagan historians who tell us how Constantine murdered his son Crispus, a fact suppressed by all orthodox Christian writers, including Socrates. Furthermore, he was certainly limited in the achievement of his ideals by the source material available to him.

What source material did Socrates use? He began with the works of Eusebius and Rufinus; on a number of occasions he acknowledges his debt to the latter, or deliberately corrects his errors.[154] He accepted these histories not uncritically, and used alongside them records of conciliar decisions, letters and other documents he had available. Some light is thrown on his methods by the Introduction to Book II, which explains why he revised his first two books. He first wrote them following Rufinus, then he came across the writings of Athanasius and other contemporaries of the events he was describing, and these he assumed to be more accurate than later conjectures. For this reason he made his revision in the light of this new material. But the problem is that Athanasius' apologetic writings and dossiers of documents are themselves tendentious, putting only his side of the case. Socrates did not confine himself to 'orthodox' sources, as

---

151 *HE* vii.32.
152 Downey (1965).
153 *HE* vi. introd.; for suppression and distortion, see i.10.
154 E.g. *HE* i.12, 15; ii.1.

is shown by his use of Sabinus, a Macedonian heretic who made a collection of conciliar acts.[155] Yet he was bound to view the events of the last century from the current 'official' view, and he is critical of Sabinus for his tendentious remarks and selection of material. He could not entirely divorce himself from contemporary prejudices. Furthermore, he was unable or unwilling to appreciate the real issues involved and was thus blind to the sort of considerations which gave each group its theological and political impetus. His descriptions of the battle between Eusebius of Caesarea and Athanasius is concerned not with the issues, nor even with the personalities, but rather with retrieving Eusebius' reputation as orthodox; so he generalizes the situation, affirming that they and others at this time were engaged in a 'contest in the dark', neither party understanding distinctly the reasons for the dispute, each writing 'as if' they were adversaries![156] Socrates' failure to clarify the issues reduces his overall value to those now trying to appreciate what was involved in the disputes. Besides, in detail he sometimes failed to make accurate reconstructions and telescoped events or characters; he confuses Maximin and Maximian, for example, and conflates the council which deposed Athanasius in 338/9 with the 'Dedication' Council of 341, both of which met in Antioch.

Compared with other historians of his day, however, Socrates' achievement was considerable. Sozomen, Philostorgius and Theodoret more consciously and deliberately represented a point of view than Socrates. They, like Socrates, wrote histories which began where Eusebius left off, and covered approximately the same period. Inevitably their chief matter was what was perceived as the long Arian conflict, and this was bound to give their work a different character from that of Eusebius. It was no longer possible to present a picture of a single successful institution, ironing out or suppressing differences in belief and practice. Now the historian could not help belonging to a party. For Sozomen, far more than for Socrates, the subject and purpose of his history was to tell the story of the gradual but triumphant progress of orthodoxy against political and ecclesiastical odds. Eusebius' apologetic search for the providential hand of God in events is again at the centre. The same is true for Philostorgius, but he was an ardent follower of Eunomius, and therefore his interpretation of the course of events is exactly opposite that of Sozomen. For him, history is now progressing to its dreadful climax, as truth is suppressed and God's true prophets and servants persecuted. It is surprising that his 'heretical' history survived long enough to be epitomized by the ninth century Patriarch, Photius, though we can only regret its loss in our attempts to understand the disputes of the fourth century.[157] We have enough in Photius' précis and other surviving fragments to see how recrimination and distortion of fact were the weapons used on every side. Personal slanders were the natural accompaniment of doctrinal disputes, and to advance a plausible charge of adultery sufficient to condemn the beliefs of the opposition. For Philostorgius, if not for the orthodox historians, the scandalous charges advanced against Athanasius were true.[158] On both

---

155 *HE* i.8; ii.15, 17.

156 *HE* i.23. Cf. ii.21, where Socrates devotes a whole chapter to defending the orthodoxy of Eusebius with long quotations to prove his point from the *Contra Marcellum*.

157 Text: Bidez (1972/81).

158 Philostorgius, *HE* ii.11.

sides, the heroes of the faith were regarded as spotless in virtue and inspired with miraculous powers. Their enemies were the enemies of God, dogged by a hostile providence. Such is the picture presented by Philostorgius and Sozomen, though from opposite sides of the fence. By contrast, it is refreshing to meet the amused anticlericalism and tolerance of Socrates. The mere fact that he was prepared to read Nestorius for himself rather than regurgitate malicious gossip says a great deal for his insight and critical ability in such a period.

2 Philostorgius

Unlike Socrates, Philostorgius consciously and deliberately set out to disclose the providential designs of God in the course of history. Miracles and portents figure largely in his presentation. Those who are sympathetic to the 'true faith' prosper; disaster attends those rulers who persecute the Eunomians. Illness is a sign of divine punishment; earthquake a scourge of divine wrath. This pattern is truly in the tradition of Eusebius' work, though it is worked out somewhat more crudely, and with an apocalyptic and astrological flavour that Eusebius would certainly have repudiated. The sack of Rome is no brief incident of the past for Philostorgius, but a sign of the approaching end of the world, fore-shadowed by the appearance of the comet in 389.[159] Recent events are described in vivid apocalyptic imagery: famine, pestilence, ravages of wild beasts and barbarians, water and fire pouring from heaven, hailstorms and snow, gales and earthquakes, all reveal the anger of God. The disastrous reign of Theodo-sius II is heralded by an eclipse of the sun and the appearance of a meteor. The scourges of divine wrath descended upon the earth. It seems that Philostorgius intended to create the impression that the Empire was entering its last days, and Photius' summary does not entirely obscure this.

What kind of man was Philostorgius? He was a Cappadocian, who went to Constantinople at the age of twenty. He is said to have come from an Arian family, and in the capital soon attached himself to Eunomius, who clearly made a deep impression on him. Unlike Socrates, Philostorgius is inclined to hagio-graphy, and most of the honours go to Eunomius, who is acclaimed for his intelligence and virtue, his grace and dignity – even his lisp and his skin disease adding to his elegance and majesty![160]

Philostorgius had great powers of description and was remarkably sensitive to natural beauty as well as uncommon wonders.[161] The capital city made a powerful impression on him and he revels in the account of its foundation and splendid buildings. He appears to have enjoyed travel and describes the won-ders of the Holy Land at first hand. He had a geographical curiosity which allows us some insight into current conceptions of the world, like the speculation that the great rivers of the world (including the Nile!) all flowed from Para-dise, which was located somewhere in the East. Philostorgius was fascinated

---

159 Illness, *HE* vii.10; earthquakes, xii.9; signs in heaven, x.9; for the other examples in this paragraph see xi.7, xii.8, 9.
160 *HE* x.6.
161 *HE* iii. 11; for Constantinople, see ii.9; for the rivers, see iii.7–10.

by strange phenomena of all kinds,[162] comets and visions and portents, prodigies from heaven, abnormalities like giants and dwarfs and weird grotesque creatures. He was a cultured layman according to the educational standards of the time, and it is instructive to see the importance granted to astrology and the miraculous in the sophisticated society of this period. Credulity was more common than scepticism. Philostorgius explicitly rejects a rationalist explanation of madness in favour of demon possession.[163]

Philostorgius, like Eusebius, was concerned in the debate with pagans. He tells us that he wrote a work against Porphyry on behalf of the Christians, and he is concerned to show that Christians do not worship martyrs nor the image of Constantine.[164] Contemporary pagans attributed the disasters of Theodosius' reign to the abandonment of the old gods. Philostorgius, as we have seen, produces a somewhat different interpretation. Indeed, he directs a good deal of his history to polemic against the heathen. He tells with enthusiasm of Christian missions outside the Roman Empire in the reign of Constantius, and groans at the indignities inflicted on Christians under Julian, taking the same attitude towards him and his policies as any of the so-called orthodox writers.

Philostorgius' *Church History* was probably written in the early 430s, that is, a little earlier than the work of Socrates. It was ostensibly a continuation of Eusebius, a history and apology for the 'true Church' as it confronted paganism and false orthodoxy. The great events for Philostorgius were those which affected the Eunomian Church.[165] Photius was not completely wide of the mark when he described the work as not so much a history as a panegyric of the heretics. Philostorgius does not mention a single bishop of the great centres of the Church, Antioch, Constantinople, Rome or Alexandria (apart from his *bête noire*, Athanasius). All who oppose Eunomius tend to be bracketed together, whether homoousian or homoiousian, even Arians![166] Every other party did at least agree that the reality of the Godhead is ultimately shrouded in mystery, whereas Eunomius insisted that theology can be exactly exposed to the full light of knowledge. Philostorgius therefore praises Eusebius as historian while accusing him of erroneous opinions in matters relating to religion, because he considered the deity as unintelligible and incomprehensible.[167] Arius himself is castigated for the absurd error of affirming that God cannot be known or comprehended or conceived by the human mind. Eunomius alone purified the doctrines of the faith obscured by the passage of time, and then held to them consistently. He would not approve of the title 'Neo-Arian' used by modern scholars.[168]

Yet Philostorgius was not merely a narrow sectarian. He shows admiration for the wisdom and literary style of Eunomius' chief opponents, Basil of

---

162 *HE* iii.26, x.9, xii. 8; vii.14; x.11, iii.11 provide examples of the phenomena mentioned.

163 *HE* viii.10.

164 *HE* ii.17; for missions, see ii.5, iii.4–6; for Julian vii.4.

165 Note esp. viii.2–4, where describing the Eunomians' period of prosperity.

166 *HE* x.3.

167 *HE* i.2; for Arius, see ii.3, x.2.

168 Barnes (1993), p. 137, suggests that the issues raised by Aetius and Eunomius were new, and not a reprise of Arius' views.

Caesarea and Gregory Nyssen. He had some competence in literary criticism and a breadth of interest in secular events and the natural world which is hardly paralleled among the orthodox historians. Furthermore it is clear that he used sources, particularly non-Nicene sources, which are no longer available to us. We can only regret that more 'unorthodox' literature has not survived.

One surprising feature of Philostorgius' work is his indifference to the monastic movement. His heroes are renowned for sanctity and miraculous powers, but there appears to be no mention of the ascetic ideals which gripped Christian leaders in this period.[169] Some have seen ascetic features in the glowing description of Theophilus, his ideal missionary traveller, but Philostorgius is in fact more interested in his doctrines and miracles. Socrates, in his more comprehensive and balanced survey of the history of the Eastern Church, gives some attention to the origins, ideals and literature of monasticism,[170] and notices the influence of the monks in the events he is describing. It is Sozomen, however, who gives great emphasis to ascetic characters.

3 Sozomen

Sozomen's work[171] sometimes gives the impression of being a gossip column rather than serious history. It is full of anecdotes and biographical details. He clearly delights in describing the ascetic feats and consequent miracles of his heroes. One of his purposes is to present monasticism as the true philosophy, and in each period he devotes chapters to the lives of contemporary ascetics, martyrs and saints. He uses a great deal of biographical and hagiographical sources and surveys the celebrated monks of Egypt, Palestine, Syria and Persia, as well as those who introduced monasticism to Asia Minor and Europe. Furthermore, the testimony of a monk like Antony is sufficient in his mind to allay all doubts about the legitimacy of Athanasius' succession to the Alexandrian see, and the destruction of heresy is ultimately attributed to popular admiration for the ascetics, as they were always faithful to the Nicene faith.[172]

In his Preface, Sozomen tells us some of the things which influenced his decision to write a history. He is impressed by the miraculous change made by the advent of Christianity, by the destruction of the ancient cults of the nations and the impressive witness of Christian martyrs. He felt drawn to give an account of these events from the beginning, but was deterred by the work of his predecessors, particularly Eusebius, and chose instead simply to summarize events up to the deposition of Licinius and begin a full narration at that point. His summary is no longer extant.

Sozomen goes on to list his aims and methods. He claims to follow in the tradition of seeking not only oral testimony but records of earlier events, laws, proceedings of synods, epistles. The bulk of the material he found so great that

---

169 See Vaggione, 'Of monks and lounge lizards: "Arians", polemics and asceticism in the Roman East', in Barnes and Williams (1993), for a discussion of the difference in views of asceticism between Eunomians and others.

170 Socrates, HE i.21; iv.23.

171 Text: Bidez and Hansen (1960); Bidez et al. (1983, 1996); ET in NPNF.

172 Sozomen, HE vi.27; for Athanasius, see ii.17.

he decided to summarize the contents of documents rather than quote verbatim. Compared with Socrates, he reproduces very few actual texts. He mentions the existence of collections of documents made by the partisans of each sect to support their own viewpoint, and claims to have sought historical accuracy and truth in spite of all obstacles. Nevertheless, truth for him is the demonstrable fact, proved by history, that the doctrine of the catholic Church is the most genuine, having survived all attacks through the providential guidance of God. He proposes to survey not merely events connected with the Church in the Roman Empire, but also the Church among the Persians and barbarians; nor will he confine his account to Church politics, since, as we have seen, the character and deeds of the monks are both relevant to ecclesiastical history and important to record. In fact, he begins his history with Constantine's triumph, the prosperity of the Church and the virtue of the monks, denying the Arian controversy priority of place in his opening book.

In certain respects Sozomen is the true successor of Eusebius, since the tracing of God's providence in history is his primary purpose. He writes from the point of view of a largely intolerant orthodoxy seeing its triumph as the triumph of God. Fulfilled prophecy and miracle attest the truth of God's activity in events. Christianity is the true and universal religion. The enforcement of doctrinal conformity (though not uniformity in practice[173]) is proper for orthodox rulers, if not for those who supported the Arians: thus Valens is treated as a cruel oppressor while Constantine and Theodosius the Great are glorified for efforts to suppress paganism and heresy. Theodosius' weak but orthodox successors are given excessive flattery. Sozomen thus reflects the same attitude as his predecessors, idealizing the emperor because his pious orthodoxy was thought to ensure the safety of Church and state. His dedicatory preface shows that he wrote his history to attract the emperor's literary patronage and submitted it to the palace for revision.

As a historian, Sozomen leaves much to be desired. He is far less successful than Socrates in carrying out his aims, and really makes no attempt at objective judgment. He lacks critical ability and accepts statements in his sources at their face value. He sometimes presents several different views, as when he gives five different accounts of the death of Arius! He thus gives the appearance of being fair, while attempting no analysis or sifting of the evidence available. Besides, he does not follow his predecessors in acknowledging his most important sources. Much of his work runs closely parallel to that of Socrates, and it is clear that he used Socrates' history at least as a guidebook and directory to sources, without acknowledging his debt. He has added a good deal of supplementary material, some of it based on additional sources and documents, though much of it is anecdotal material and fuller narratives. He is more prepared to make use of rumour and popular speculations, without critical assessment of their value, especially reporting current views as to the divine mercy or wrath to be seen in a particular event. He is utterly uncritical as far as the miraculous is concerned. He falls easily into flattery and seeks to defend heroes like John Chrysostom from criticisms such as those adduced by Socrates. He is quick to blacken or whitewash, giving even Constantius the benefit of the doubt, sure

---

173 *HE* vii.19.

34

that he really upheld the Nicene faith under a different slogan.[174] Did Sozomen really fail to see any difference between *homoousios* and *homoiousios*? He does, after all, protest his lack of dialectical ability. Or does this lift the curtain a little, acknowledging the fact that Constantius largely followed the policies of his father and during his reign was regarded as a pious Christian emperor?

It seems that Sozomen left his work unfinished. In the dedication to the emperor, he mentions his intention to continue to Theodosius' seventeenth consulship (that is 439, the year in which Socrates concluded his work), but the ninth book breaks off abruptly in 425. Probably the most satisfactory explanation is that he died before completion of the work.[175] Perhaps he undertook the project late in life after an active career as a lawyer. His exact dates are difficult to determine, but he was clearly a contemporary of Socrates. He originated from Palestine and seems to have travelled widely before settling in Constantinople. He gives us more information about the Syrian and Western Church than Socrates. His style is superior to that of Socrates, who specifically aims at simplicity and tends to be dull. Sozomen certainly had descriptive powers, and was not afraid to write in a style to please an educated public. Quite why he wrote a history so obviously overlapping with Socrates is unclear, but he may have wanted to provide something more delightful to read, which also corrected Socrates' assessments, demonstrating more vigorously the role of providence and celebrating more fulsomely the saints and heroes of the faith.

4 Theodoret

Far from being merely a historian, Theodoret was bishop of Cyrus near Antioch and one of the leaders of the so-called Antiochene school during the Christological controversies of the fifth century. He wrote dogmatic and exegetical treatises, as well as apologetic and history; a good deal of his correspondence is extant, and he also compiled a collection of lives of Syrian ascetics, known as the *Historia Religiosa*.[176]

The *Ecclesiastical History* of Theodoret[177] differs from that of the others we have been considering precisely because it was written by a bishop who was deeply involved in the controversies of his own time – he stops short before getting involved in these. The book is extremely partisan, the heretics being consistently blackened and dubbed 'Ariomaniacs', afflicted with the 'Arian plague'. At times one feels that he is deliberately correcting the assessments of Socrates, and camouflaging the faults of 'good' bishops and emperors. Typical is his embarrassment at the story of Chrysostom's conflict with the empress:[178] neither side could be criticized, so the imperial names are concealed to avoid the difficulty. Thus the story is skated over and the causes of Chrysostom's exile and disfavour suppressed. Luckily Theodoret is not our only source, or we should be left guessing about the course of events. Throughout, Theodoret's

---

174 *HE* iii.18.
175 The various suggestions are discussed by Chesnut (1977), p. 195 n. 20.
176 See Chapters 3 and 6 below; here is discussion only of history and apologetic.
177 Text: Parmentier (1954/98); Parmentier et al. (2006, 2009); ET in *NPNF*.
178 Theodoret, *HE* v.34.

narrative is more compressed than that of the other historians, and he does not waste words explaining his purpose and method. He sometimes simply strings documents together with brief comments.

The work of Theodoret draws particular attention to the problem of the interrelationship between the various historians of the period. There seems to be little doubt that he knew Socrates and Sozomen, and possibly Rufinus and Philostorgius. It used to be thought that he was largely a plagiarist, producing a clerical account of matters inadequately treated by uncomprehending laymen. More recently, however, attention has been drawn to the fact that Theodoret produces different documents from Socrates on a number of occasions, and that his wording suggests independent use of the same sources. Theodoret's one comment on his purpose is to the effect that he is attempting 'to record in writing events in ecclesiastical history hitherto omitted'. Omitted by whom? It is true that he only specifically refers to Eusebius, but he adds, 'I shall begin my history from the period at which his terminates.' Is this what he means by the events hitherto omitted? One suspects rather that he is alluding to the work of his contemporaries and indicating that he intends to fill in details they overlooked and correct their presentation where it was at fault. A comparison between his first book and that of Socrates confirms this impression. Where Socrates referred to collections of letters written by Alexander and Arius, quoting selected examples, Theodoret makes brief reference to a letter reproduced by Socrates and then himself quotes another.[179] Although elsewhere he makes the same selection as Socrates,[180] Theodoret does seem to have refrained from slavish copying and done his own research.

Theodoret's chief importance lies in the additional documentary sources that he reproduces. His assessment of the course of the Arian controversy has no independent value; for him, the Arian heresy was simply explicable as a work of the devil, inspired by jealousy at the sight of the Church prosperous, peaceful and successful under Constantine: Satan was 'unable to bear the sight of the Church sailing on with favourable winds' and 'eager to sink the vessel steered by the Creator and Lord of the universe'.[181] As Christians, the Greeks had given up worshipping the creature instead of the Creator, so, not daring to declare open war on God, the evil one insidiously set about reducing the Creator to a creature, by playing on the ambition of Arius and instigating his heresy. Like Eusebius, Theodoret saw history as the triumph of the true Church against enemies, external or internal, in league with the evil powers.

Also like Eusebius, Theodoret refrained from offering any account of the controversies in which he himself was involved. Both had reason for feeling some embarrassment about the situation. Eusebius favoured Arius, who had been condemned; Theodoret had favoured Nestorius and continued to oppose the victorious party after Nestorius' condemnation. In the events of their own time, each came under fire for upholding truth as they saw it; each felt the unity of the Church threatened. Each avoided raising the issues in their historical works. Theodoret's history concludes at the death of Theodore of Mopsuestia, whose

---

179 Socrates, *HE* i.6; compare Theodoret, *HE* i.2–3.
180 Compare Theodoret, *HE* i.14–16 with Socrates, *HE* i.9.
181 Theodoret, *HE* i.1.

teaching had profoundly influenced the author himself, and also stimulated the Nestorian view. The consequent disruption of the Church is concealed, and the work ends with a list of bishops of the great cities during the period covered, thus drawing together the lists of contemporary bishops which punctuated the narrative throughout. Such a finale reminds us that his interest in presenting the Church as a successful, God-directed institution was greater than that of the lay historians. On the other hand, the work seems to date from the 440s when there was a lull in the conflict, and Theodoret may have been trying to encourage unity by reminding all sides of their common war against the Arians.

Like Eusebius, Theodoret was an apologist as well as an historian.[182] His *Graecarum affectionum curatio* (*Cure for Pagan Maladies*) was the last attempt at a comprehensive work of apology. In an age when Christianity was dominant, the need for apologies in the old tradition gradually died out. The question is whether Theodoret's work was purely a literary activity or whether it really spoke to the conditions of the time.

As suggested by its subtitle: *The Truth of the Gospel proved from Greek Philosophy*, the work has much in common with Eusebius' *Praeparatio evangelica*. It cannot be denied that Theodoret owed a great deal to the apologetic tradition and the contributions of his predecessors; he used not only their arguments and themes, but also their citations from pagan literature. Clement's *Stromateis* and Eusebius' *Praeparatio* are particularly important in this regard. The extent of his dependence has led to low estimates of his originality and of the relevance of the work when the Empire had been Christian for a century.

There is no doubt that this is to underestimate Theodoret's achievement. For all its dependence on Eusebius' *Praeparatio*, in many ways it is a superior work. Often more careful and exact references to the sources are given, which suggests independent checking and erudition of his own. Furthermore, where Eusebius had simply provided a framework of topics and strung together long quotations with brief introductory comments in a diffuse and repetitive sort of way, Theodoret constructed a careful argument into which the much briefer quotations are fully integrated. Besides this, it has been shown that Theodoret adapted the traditional material and arguments for his own purposes, and moulded it to fit contemporary issues. His intended audience was cultivated and educated, steeped in the literature and traditions of the Graeco-Roman heritage, scornful of the barbarous origins of Christianity and the crudity of its holy books, suspicious of its novel and irrational tendencies and scandalized by the veneration of the dead in the martyr-cult and the excesses of the extreme ascetics. They were the sort who had comparatively recently supported the pagan revival under Julian the Apostate, and attributed imperial disasters to the rejection of the ancient traditional gods. We should not forget that Augustine's *City of God* was approximately contemporary with this work. Paganism still had its attractions and its adherents, especially among the upper classes with a literary education. Antioch still remembered the prowess of the pagan sophist, Libanius, the tolerant but unconverted teacher of so many Christian leaders, including John Chrysostom. To such people, faith was inadequate as a

---

182 For the following paragraphs I am indebted to Canivet (1957); and his edition of the text, Canivet (1958/2000). Pásztori-Kupán (2006) translates selections of this work.

source of knowledge, creation out of nothing was philosophically absurd, and Christian, especially monastic, ideals were a mockery compared with a life of culture and virtue. Theodoret set out to undermine their false preconceptions about Christianity and to show it consistent with, and indeed superior to, the best traditions of Greek philosophy. He diagnosed and prescribed for the illnesses of the soul which was unable to overcome its inherent distaste for the truth of the gospel.

Theodoret's most original contribution was his organization of the material to meet contemporary criticisms. Each book is devoted to a particular topic and skilfully compares and contrasts Christian and pagan views. Books II—XI cover traditional topics: the First Principle and origins of the universe, angels and spiritual beings, matter and cosmogony, concepts of human nature, providence, sacrifices and cults, veneration of the martyrs, laws and customs, true and false prophecies, and the prospect of final judgment. In each case, however much he is indebted to earlier apologists, Theodoret gives his own carefully worked out and coherent exposition of the issue, maybe not making any brilliant contribution, but with clarity and relative brevity. The prominence of his discussion of the martyr-cult, which is given a whole book, reflects his awareness of the particular issues which were causing scandal in his own time. Besides this, the traditional material and arguments are given a particular bent and emphasis by being put within a certain framework: Book I meets the philosopher's dislike of being asked to rely on faith rather than reason, and the last book, XII, deals with the practical outworkings of faith in Christian virtue. It is in these two areas that Theodoret comes closest to originality and proves that he was not merely writing an anachronistic work based only on traditional material. He updated the traditional arguments and faced current issues in the confrontation between Christian and pagan values. It is not for nothing that his work has been regarded as the last and most beautiful apology for Christianity.

Apart from this major treatise, Theodoret produced other works of an apologetic nature, in particular the *Ten Discourses on Providence*.[183] They were most probably delivered to the cultured Greek congregation of Antioch, sometime between 431 and 435. Unlike most sermons, they are reasoned arguments, lectures rather than homilies on scriptural texts. They indicate the need to confirm fashionable Christians in their faith, but also to convince fringe members of congregations in an age of official Christianity. They reflect the same qualities as the *Curatio* in that they are heavily dependent on the many previous discussions of the theme, both pagan and Christian, while being a brilliantly clear restatement of the arguments. Theodoret also claims to have written an apologetic work against the Jews,[184] another concern he shared with Eusebius. A possible fragment of this lost work has been the subject of much dispute; it has even been suggested that no such treatise ever existed, the references to anti-Jewish as well as anti-pagan writing being in fact allusions to the *Curatio*.[185]

So, among other interests, Theodoret shared the chief preoccupations of Eusebius, namely apologetic and history. In both activities he drew on the work

---

183 Text: Azéma (1954); ET Halton (1988).
184 Theodoret, *Epp.* 113, 116, 145.
185 Canivet (1957).

of others, but made his own modifications to fit the temper of the times or the truth as he saw it. His history may reveal a lack of sympathy for freethinkers, but his apologetic work shows him a man of culture, an impression confirmed by his correspondence.[186] Like others in this period, he had a somewhat schizophrenic mentality, open to the richness of the Graeco-Roman literary heritage, but closed to speculation and deviation in matters of belief.

For Further Reading

English translations

ET of Socrates, Sozomen and Theodoret in *NPNF*.

Studies

Ayres, Lewis, 2004. *Nicaea and its Legacy*, Oxford: Oxford University Press.
Chesnut, Glenn F., 1977. *The First Christian Histories: Eusebius, Socrates, Sozomen, Theodoret and Evagrius*, Paris: Éditions Beauchesne.
Hanson, R. P. C., 1988. *The Search for the Christian Understanding of God*, Edinburgh: T. & T. Clark.
Lienhard, J. T., 1999. Contra Marcellum: *Marcellus of Ancyra and Fourth Century Theology*, Washington, DC: Catholic University of America Press.
Parvis, Sara, 2006. *Marcellus of Ancyra and the Lost Years of the Arian Controversy 325–345*, Oxford: Oxford University Press.
Urbainczyk, Theresa, 1997. *Socrates of Constantinople, Historian of Church and State*, Ann Arbor: University of Michigan Press.
Vaggione, R. P. C., 2000. *Eunomius of Cyzicus and the Nicene Revolution*, Oxford: Oxford University Press.

Conclusion

In this chapter we have moved from Nicaea to Chalcedon, and also from the atmosphere of the third century, when the Church was a persecuted minority still seeking intellectual and social acceptability, to the very different ethos of the early Byzantine period with its cultured Christian élite and its popular devotion to martyrs, saints and holy men. Yet there is a continuous religious and literary tradition which spans the centuries. Theodoret shares the interests and the culture of Eusebius in more than one respect; for if in the realm of philosophical theology Eusebius had hardly moved with the times, in other ways he anticipated the attitudes and outlook of the Christian Empire and the imperial Church of the Byzantine world. The Church was now in a position to review its past; and while popular Christianity developed the cult of its dead heroes, the cultured produced literary works most of which were concerned to glorify the triumph of the one true catholic and orthodox Church. In this atmosphere both hagiography and Church history flowered.

---

186 See further Chapter 6, Section VII.

2

Athanasius and the Shaping of
Nicene Theology

Introduction

The history and theology of the fourth century is dominated by the 'pivotal' figure of Athanasius.[1] As patriarch of Alexandria, he was to forge a remark-able link with Rome and the West, publicize Egypt's monastic movement and win over the monks themselves to catholic orthodoxy, and against all odds courageously uphold the faith of Nicaea through skilful politics and theological acumen. Athanasius became a legendary figure, to some extent even in his own lifetime, but especially in subsequent conflicts, throughout the fourth and fifth centuries and beyond, where he is claimed by warring factions as guarantor of each party's own orthodoxy.[2] The aim in this chapter is critically to exam-ine and evaluate that legend, while providing an interpretation of his overall theological position.

Athanasius designated his opponents 'Ariomaniacs' – the crazed followers of a certain Arius, one-time priest of Baucalis in Alexandria. Thus Arius gave his name to one of the bitterest disputes in the history of the early Church, and a complex and shifting web of alliances and theological positions was reduced to a binary opposition between 'Nicenes' and 'Arians',[3] a single controversy said to rumble on from Nicaea (325) to Constantinople (381). For the Church at large this struggle, polemically oversimplified or not, had wide political and theological implications. On the one hand it stimulated the discussions which led to the formulation of the Trinitarian dogma and ultimately the Chalcedon-ian definition; on the other, much to the chagrin of Constantine and Eusebius of Caesarea, it also shattered the unity of the Church just as it acquired peace, power and influence in the Empire, and it even exacerbated the unhappy state

---

1 Anatolios (1998), p. 1.

2 While the use of Athanasius in Cyril of Alexandria is scarcely surprising, it is also true that the Antiochenes appealed to him: e.g. the florilegia in the *Eranistes* of Theodoret of Cyrus and citations of Athanasius in the Nestorian *Book of Heracleides*. See further, Chapter 6 below.

3 The deconstruction of the received picture of faithful 'Nicenes' versus 'Arian' heretics, with 'semi-Arians' wavering according to political winds, emerges from much recent scholarship; see, for example, Barnes and Williams (1993), Barnes (1993), Williams (1987), Hanson (1988), Ayres (2004a), Parvis (2006), Gwynn (2007). Weinandy (2007) rebuts this challenge to the received picture. See also above, pp. 24–6.

of the Catholic West when it fell a century later before the barbarian invaders – for the barbarians were converts to the Arian version of Christianity.[4]

So 'Arianism' certainly caused havoc, and Arius came to be regarded as the 'archetypal heretic'.[5] His opponents believed that his ideas were deliberately framed to deceive the unwary and corrupt the gospel. But how far was their estimate of Arius just? It is by no means clear that what he actually taught deserved the vilification it has received from his own day into modern times, and he was after all merely the trigger which set off the conflagration. The main protagonists were the leading bishops of the East, now frequently redesignated the 'Eusebians', and the issues became both more subtle and, at the same time, more clouded with political concerns as the controversy developed. Arius' views need to be distinguished from the sophisticated philosophies of the later Arian sophists, Aetius and Eunomius, whose teachings the Cappadocians challenged.[6] To many of his own contemporaries he certainly did not appear in the same light as he did in retrospect; for it is quite clear that at first many found his position more in line with traditional Christianity than that of his opponents. The ambivalent reaction of Eusebius of Caesarea we have already noted;[7] the ambiguous position of Cyril of Jerusalem will be observed later.[8]

So in late twentieth-century scholarship, Arius himself has to some extent been rehabilitated,[9] while the received account of the polemics and parties of the period has increasingly been challenged through examining the sources more acutely.[10] The purpose of this chapter is not to provide yet another account of fourth-century struggles, but rather to focus on a re-evaluation of Athanasius and his work, this being enhanced by incorporating a critical introduction to the figure of Arius (as distinct from other Arians), and an outline of the now shadowy theology of one of Athanasius' foremost allies, Marcellus of Ancyra. Neither side was, after all, homogeneous.

For Further Reading

Ayres, L., 2004a. *Nicaea and its Legacy: An Approach to Fourth-Century Trinitarian Theology*, Oxford: Oxford University Press.
Hanson, R. P. C., 1988. *The Search for the Christian Understanding of God*, Edinburgh: T. & T. Clark.

---

4 The depth of the Arian religion of the Goths is difficult to assess: Ulfila apparently subscribed to the Homoian creed of 359. His consecration as bishop in charge of the Goths by Eusebius of Constantinople (formerly of Nicomedia) was read by Sozomon and Theodoret as the reason for the lack of carnage at the fall of Rome to the Goths in 410: they had acquired something of the gentleness of Christ even through deficient faith.

5 Wiles (1996), pp. 1–26.

6 Hanson (1988), Barnes and Williams (1993). See further, Chapter 4 below on the Cappadocians.

7 See above, Chapter 1.

8 See below, Chapter 5.

9 Wiles (1962); Gregg and Groh (1981); Lyman (1993).

10 See note 3, above.

I Arius

Arius was a native of Libya, but Alexandria had become his place of residence. At the time when his views became controversial, probably but not certainly around 318,[11] he was serving as a relatively senior priest in the city, and apparently his preaching attracted a large following. Sozomen suggests that before this he had connections with the Melitians, a group of schismatics who had split with Bishop Peter at the time of the Great Persecution, but there are good reasons to question this.[12] He was probably ordained deacon by Peter, made priest by his successor, Achillas, and at first held in high esteem by Bishop Alexander.[13] Socrates claims that Arius spoke out because of a sermon preached by Alexander which seemed to him to be dangerously Sabellian.[14] However, the evidence suggests that it is unlikely that Alexander was instrumental in initiating the controversy, even if he unconsciously stimulated it – rather he was reluctantly drawn in when it became apparent that Arius' views were causing considerable disruption in the Church. According to Rufinus, Alexander was a 'gentle and quiet' man,[15] and there is evidence that he went out of way to secure a fair hearing for Arius; this is reflected in Sozomen's account of his wavering between the opposing views expressed by his clergy,[16] and contemporary charges of irresolution and excessive forbearance.

At this point, then, we can reconstruct a picture of a gentle and tolerant bishop gradually forced to move against a popular preacher whose controversial views were finding increasing support among sections of the community. Perennial difficulties in holding the Alexandrian Church together is a likely broader context.[17] The spread of Arius' ideas among the populace was stimulated by the composition of songs 'for the sea, for the mill, and for the road'.[18] A synod of Egyptian bishops eventually excommunicated Arius, who then toured the major Eastern sees building up support for himself.[19] Eusebius of Nicomedia became his most persistent and influential advocate, and Eusebius of Caesarea allowed him to preach.

It is from this period that our earliest evidence of Arius' views comes. Epiphanius preserves several letters written by Arius, and reports that in his day seventy letters from Alexander to episcopal colleagues in the East were extant.[20]

---

11 Schwartz suggested 323; for discussion of the date, see articles by Telfer (1946, 1949) and Baynes (1948); Boularand (1972) adopts the date 322.

12 Williams (1986, 1987); Hanson (1988).

13 Sozomen, *HE* i.15.

14 Socrates, *HE* i.5.

15 Rufinus, *HE* i.1.

16 Sozomen, *HE* i.15.

17 Williams (1987).

18 Philostorgius, *HE* ii.2.

19 Telfer (1936), pp. 60–3, threw doubt on the story of Arius' visits to bishops in Palestine and Asia Minor. Gwynn (2007) notes the political value of this depiction of Arius to his opponents, and judges it a deliberately polemical orthodox construct; Parvis (2006), however, is reluctant to imagine Arius and his companions not forming a network in the controversy.

20 Epiphanius, *Panarion* 69.4.

The first of Arius' letters[21] that we know is an appeal to Eusebius of Nicomedia, written before he left Egypt, complaining that he has been excommunicated because he says that the Son had a beginning, whereas God is without begin-ning. Arius contrasts his position with that of Alexander who persecutes him for refusing to preach the eternal generation of the Son. The second letter of Arius is addressed to Alexander,[22] and is usually attributed to his time at Nicomedia.[23] It is an ἔκθεσις πίστεως, a public letter outlining his position. He claims that he is setting out the faith of their forefathers, carefully stressing his credentials and arguing from propositions of a strictly monotheistic character: God alone is ingenerate (ἀγέν[ν]ητος – *agen(n)ētos*),[24] alone eternal, alone with-out beginning, alone true, alone has immortality, alone is wise, alone good, alone sovereign. The Son is not co-eternal with the Father, but God is before all things, being Monad and Beginning of all. Arius appeals to Alexander by sug-gesting that this is no different from the faith he learned from him, his bishop, and claims that his condemnation of Sabellian and Adoptionist errors is equal to Alexander's. The representation of Alexander's views is rather different from that given in his earlier appeal to Eusebius, but this is surely no more than should be expected in the circumstances. The first was written in the heat of anger at his excommunication, the second is an appeal to sink their differences and recognize their common ground.

On the other side, two of Alexander's letters to episcopal colleagues, pre-served by Socrates and Theodoret, show that once convinced of Arius' error and intransigence, the bishop remained firm in his condemnation. The first[25] contains Alexander's own summary of Arius' teaching, which largely confirms the impression gained from Arius' own extant writings; the second[26] warns a number of bishops outside Egypt about Arius and his followers, accusing them of hiding their corrupting doctrine with all too persuasive and tricky discourses, and attacking some of the standard Arian assertions.

The subsequent history is well known. Constantine was moved to intervene and, at the first Ecumenical Council at Nicaea, the majority condemned Arius and accepted the Nicene Creed. However, the embarrassment of Eusebius of Caesarea, an embarrassment quite evident in his explanatory letter to his home church,[27] indicates that even at the time misgivings were felt. Conflict was bound

---

21 Epiphanius, *Panarion* 69.6; also in Theodoret, *HE* i.5. = Opitz (1934) no. 1.

22 Epiphanius, *Panarion* 69.7; also in Athanasius, *De Synodis* 16 = Opitz (1934) no. 6.

23 But see Telfer (1936), who argues that Arius wrote this letter in Egypt since, in his view, Arius never toured the East at all (as noted above, note 19).

24 The additional ν (n) is placed in brackets to indicate the ambiguity inherent in the word which made Arius' argument possible. It was Athanasius who clearly distinguished between ἀγένητος, (*agenētos*) from γίνομαι (*ginomai* = I come into being) meaning 'unoriginate' or 'uncreated', and ἀγέννητος (*agennētos*) from γεννάω (*gennaō* = I beget) meaning 'unbegotten'. See further Prestige (1933, 1936, chapters II and VII).

25 Socrates, *HE* i.6 = Opitz (1934) no. 4b. This appears also in some MSS of Athanasius' works, headed *Deposition of Arius and his associates*, with a covering letter requesting the clergy of Egypt to sign it.

26 Theodoret, *HE* i.4 = Opitz (1934) no. 14.

27 Appended to some MSS of Athanasius' *De Decretis* (33); quoted in Socrates, *HE* i.8 and Theodoret, *HE* i.12 = Opitz (1934) no. 22. ET in *NPNF* II.IV.

to break out again. Few refused to accept Arius when Constantine recalled him from exile and sought his reinstatement as priest. During these negotiations, Constantine obtained from Arius a confession of faith, a letter which simply produced a creed, written in straightforward biblical phrases and avoiding all controversial language. Socrates and Sozomen,[28] who preserve this letter, differ as to whether it was required before Arius' recall or before the Council of Tyre in 335. Only a year after that council, Arius died.[29]

Arius has been dismissed as of small literary importance.[30] It is true that little survives beside the letters referred to above, but his use of verse forms may not be unimportant in the history of hymnography.[31] Some of the popular songs referred to already may have been incorporated in his one literary work, the *Thalia* (Banquet). This survives only in quotations made by opponents for the purpose of refuting the views expressed; the text must have disappeared very early since no one quotes more than the standard Arian formulae after Athanasius and Marcellus of Ancyra. Reconstruction of the work has proved virtually impossible, since Athanasius, our main source in two key passages,[32] makes some direct quotations but frequently seems to paraphrase, collects random examples out of context, and some citations are vague enough to cast doubt on whether his source is always the *Thalia*. Moreover, Athanasius explicitly scorns it as an imitation of the dissolute drinking-songs of the Egyptian Sotades and accuses Arius of 'dancing and joking in his blasphemies against the Saviour',[33] but it may not be fair to trust this, hardly balanced, judgment. Some quotations seem to indicate that the work was indeed written in verse – the opening seven lines suggest the presence of an acrostic poem – but the metrical form has been difficult to establish. Some have resorted to the suggestion that the work was not wholly in metrical form, but possibly contained some formal argument and exegesis.[34] It was apparently during his stay with Eusebius of Nicomedia that Arius put his heresy on paper in this rather unusual fashion, though this interpretation of the evidence has been challenged.[35]

In spite of vast extant literature from Arius' opponents, our knowledge of Arius' original teaching, its sources and inspiration, is limited. Fifth-century Church historians give the impression that he was a superb dialectician and

---

28 Socrates, *HE* i.26 and Sozomen, *HE* i.27 = Opitz (1934) no. 30.

29 Barnes (2009) defends Schwartz's datings (reflected here) against the editors of *Athanasius Werke* 3.1.3 (Brennecke et al. 2007), who argue for considerably earlier dates, locating Arius' death in or before 328 on the assumption that the emperor's urging of Athanasius to readmit 'those around Arius' in a letter of 328 implied that Arius himself was already dead. Barnes defends the integrity of attestations to Arius' readmittance to communion: 'it seems probable, therefore, that Arius went to Libya in 328 after his first readmission to communion and stayed there until he travelled to Constantinople shortly before his death in the summer of 336' (pp. 126–7).

30 Altaner (1960), p. 310.

31 Böhm (1992).

32 *C. Arianios* i.5–6; *De Synodis* 15.

33 *C. Arianos* i.2, 4; *PG* 26.16, 20.

34 For a detailed discussion, see Bardy (1927); Bardy publishes here the text of the fragments. See, however, the article by Stead (1978). Also discussion in Williams (1987).

35 *De Synodis* 15. Opitz (1935a), p. 242. But see the discussion by Kannengiesser (1970a).

was misled by his own logical powers.[36] From this, the conclusion has usually been drawn that Arius was simply trying to work out the logical consequences of his philosophical presuppositions.

The general view was that Arius began with the proposition that the essential attribute of God is that the divine being is underived (ἀγέν[ν]ητος – *agen(n)ētos*); the Son was begotten (γεννητός– *gennētos*), and this derivative state means that he differs essentially from true God. Therefore, he must be a creature, though, as traditional phrases indicated, he was the first and greatest of God's creatures, a creature not as the creatures in creation, but the agent through whom the rest of creation was formed. Since he was a creature, he was fallible and pass-ible; furthermore, being other than the Father, he could not know him perfectly and accurately. It was these corollaries which showed up the extreme to which Arius' logic had taken him. Alexander reports that Arians were even willing to admit that, though in fact sinless, the Word of God could have fallen like the devil. Arius' opponents, then, would assert that Arius' theories struck at the heart of the Christian gospel of redemption and revelation through the very Word of God himself, and reduced the Lord they worshipped to the level of a demigod or demon. Thus a widespread estimate of Arius has been that he was moved more by logic than by faith, that his monotheism was more philo-sophical than scriptural and that, as his contemporaries said, it was no better than paganism. Pollard put it thus: Arius transformed the 'living God of the Bible' into the 'Absolute of the philosophical schools'.[37] Some have continued to emphasize the logical grounding of Arius' position: that Arius forged vari-ous fluid ideas in a system with 'remorseless logic' was Barnard's conclusion;[38] and Williams, after careful examination of Arius' philosophy, suggests that his argumentation has a logic which can be expressed in three syllogisms:

1 The Logos of God is the rational ground of the world; that rational ground has no existence independent of the world; therefore the Logos does not pre-exist creation.
2 God the Father is absolute unity while God the Son is multiplicity; absolute unity cannot be conceptualized without implying multiplicity (something over against the conceiving subject); therefore the Son can have no concept of the Father's essence. It is noteworthy, by the way, that Arius' apophat-icism sharply differentiates him from the Neo-Arians who believed God the Father entirely simple and comprehensible.
3 The Logos exists as a subject distinct from the Father; the defining qualities of one subject cannot be shared with another; therefore the divine attributes traditionally applied to the Son must be true of him in a different sense from that in which they are true of the Father.

However, the notion that Arius was moved more by cosmological or logi-cal considerations than any sense of salvation in Christ is open to question; for a Saviour who realistically faced and conquered genuine temptations to which, being τρεπτός (changeable), he might have succumbed but over which

---

36 Socrates, *HE* i.5; Sozomen, *HE* i.15.
37 Pollard (1958), p. 104.
38 Barnard (1970, 1972); Williams (1987), pp. 231–2.

he nevertheless triumphed κατὰ χαρίν (by grace), has some soteriological advantages over a divine being who triumphs willy-nilly.[39] Following up this possibility has produced some startling results; for it has been suggested that examination of the thrust of the arguments used by Arius' opponents confirms the hints found in the extant fragments that, whatever the form in which they are expressed, Arius' views basically *arose* out of such soteriological considerations.[40] The nub of the argument between Arius and his opponents concerned the nature of sonship, the Arians insisting that the Son was Son by grace and obedience on the grounds that our salvation depended upon his identity with us. 'Christ's limitations are exactly ours (willing, choosing, striving, suffering, advancing) and likewise Christ's benefits and glories are exactly ours ... What the Arians are proclaiming is not a demotion of the Son, but a promotion of believers to full and equal status as Sons.'[41] The issues were less Trinitarian, as older textbooks suggested, than soteriological, ethical and Christological.

Such revisions of Arius' theology and motivation may yet prove to have gone too far in rejecting standard estimates of Arius, but there are other reasons for questioning the traditional characterization of Arianism as a pagan or philosophical distortion of Christian truth. After all being led astray by philosophy was an all-too present motif in Christian polemic – if it could be established that novel ideas were the result of improper blending with the Schools, the protagonists were rhetorically outed as innovators. So the accusation is to be expected, and a number of evident facts do not accord well with that as a judgment of Arius' real intent:

(i) His position could be presented as thoroughly scriptural – at Nicaea his opponents were forced to adopt the non-scriptural, philosophical term *homoousios* (of the same substance) in order to exclude his views.[42] He proved during his career that he had no difficulty in accepting creeds couched in traditional scriptural language.

(ii) The argument with Arius revolved around certain key texts of scripture, and often his opponents had to produce very forced exegesis to counter his position. Some studies have therefore taken very seriously the possibility that Arius' views had their starting-point in scripture, rather than philosophy. Boularand[43] noted Theodoret's observation that Arius had been put in charge of scriptural exposition, as well as Hilary's statement that Arius' principal doctrine, that there is only one God, is Mosaic in origin. The character of Arius' teaching presupposes not any current philosophical monotheism, some have argued, but an exegetical debate within Christian circles about the status of the Logos. Arius adopted a literalist interpretation of those texts which attributed progress and human weakness to the Son of God, and found this confirmed by John 14.28: 'My Father is greater than I'. He accepted the traditional view that Wisdom in Proverbs 8 is identical with the Logos, and, on the basis of verse 22, concluded that the Logos was God's creature.

---

39 Wiles (1962); Gregg and Groh (1981) emphasize soteriological motivations in Arian exegesis and thought.

40 Gregg and Groh (1977). See further Gregg and Groh (1981).

41 Gregg and Groh (1977), p. 272.

42 Kelly (1950), for example pp. 213, 235, 253; cf. Athanasius, *De Decretis 18−21*.

43 Boularand (1972), chapter IV *passim*.

Of course Arius used certain philosophical terms, like Monad and ἀγέν[ν]ητος. But then so did everyone else. Some studies of the philosophy of Arius converged to show that Arius himself, unlike the later Arian Sophists Aetius and Eunomius, is unlikely to have imported philosophical considerations into his theology; rather he inherited them through the Christian tradition itself. Barnard[44] demonstrated important connections between the thought of Arius and that of the earlier apologist, Athenagoras, and Stead[45] suggested that 'Arius draws upon a Platonic tradition evolving within the Church rather than representing a violent incursion of alien philosophy'. Yet Williams finds in Arius a post-Plotinian break with earlier Christian Platonism, discerning a radical streak in Arius' fundamentally conservative intentions.[46] The complex question of his antecedents becomes more and more crucial in estimating his contribution.

There has been considerable controversy over what those antecedents were. A less than respectable background was suggested by Arius' ancient opponents, and some investigators have accepted that their accusations had some basis in fact. Alexander's encyclical accuses Arius of resurrecting the heresies of Ebion, Artemas, Paul of Samosata and Lucian, his successor; if this can be accepted as evidence, it suggests that Arius' ideas were ultimately derived from the notorious Paul of Samosata, heretical bishop of Antioch, through a continuing adoptionist tradition there. The evidence is good that Arius received theological education in the school of Lucian of Antioch; he appeals to Eusebius of Nicomedia as a 'fellow-Lucianist', and Lucian's pupils, who included a number of bishops around the Eastern Mediterranean, apparently united in Arius' defence when opposition became evident. The connection between Lucian and Paul of Samosata, however, is hard to establish on the meagre evidence we have; we know little of Paul's actual position and virtually nothing of Lucian's teaching.[47] That Lucian was a revered martyr, and a textual critic who probably made an important contribution to establishing the Byzantine text of the New Testament, is the sum total of our knowledge. Arius' literalism in scriptural interpretation may well be one of the features inherited from this Antiochene connection: but whether Arianism had its doctrinal roots in Antioch is less certain.

It is the case, however, that links can be traced between Arius' views and those of earlier Alexandrians, even if a continuous or coherent tradition cannot be established. Arius' doctrine of God has affinities with Athenagoras and Clement, his subordinationism has elements consistent with aspects of the Origenist tradition, his theological method is anticipated in Dionysius of Alexandria, and his biblical literalism may be connected with Bishop Peter.[48] Arius was guilty perhaps not so much of demoting the Son as exalting the Father;

---

44 Barnard (1970, 1972).

45 Stead (1964), p. 30.

46 Williams (1987); cf. Williams (1983).

47 Bardy (1936) is an exhaustive study of the evidence we possess concerning Lucian and his pupils. Pollard (1958) argues in support of Alexander's evidence, against the views of Bardy et al. For a comprehensive survey of the suggested possibilities, see Boularand (1972), chapter V; and Williams (1987).

48 Barnard (1970). The following remarks are based upon the work of Barnard and Stead, especially Stead (1978), but also Stead (1976).

for, as Stead has shown, he taught (or at the very least assumed) a hierarchical Trinity of the Origenist type – this was obscured by Athanasius for his own polemical purposes, but is confirmed by the reaction of Eusebius of Caesarea. Athanasius emphasized the fact that Arius ranked the Logos among the creatures; whereas Arius' main concern was probably to avoid attributing physical processes like emanation or generation to God, a traditional point developed earlier against the Gnostics. Arius therefore expressed coherently what many Christians had long since assumed.

Sozomen tells us that Arius originated these disputations 'under a pretext of piety and of seeking a complete discovery of God'. These phrases suggest that Arius was a Christian teacher with honest intentions, though the hint is masked by the charge of pretext. Alexander's reference to Arius' persuasive and tricky discourses no doubt reflects the fact that Arius' account of Christian belief was attractive. Indeed, the popularity of his biblical solution to the tension between monotheism and faith in Christ is beyond dispute; and there is no reason to doubt Arius' sincerity. His opponents attributed his popularity to deception, but it is more likely that it was a response to one who was enthusiastic in his pursuit of what he thought to be the true meaning of the Christian confession. There was a long tradition in Alexandria of somewhat independent teachers, exploring ways of interpreting the Bible so as to make sense of it within the current philosophical context. Maybe Arius' misfortune was his assumption that he could still operate as an inspired Christian teacher, even questioning the views of his bishop, when that 'school-based' Christianity was giving way to episcopal authority and the political demand for ecclesial unity.[49]

Yet perhaps this estimate is attributing too much initiative to Arius. It is not impossible that he was simply a die-hard conservative who dared to challenge what he considered the innovations of his bishop, and who attracted a following merely on the grounds that he voiced what so many others felt about dangerous theological developments. If the way in which Arius formulated his views raised questions in a new way, those who were opposed to Arianism found it difficult to find a formula which would effectively exclude his line of interpretation, simply because he had a serious claim to be voicing tradition; he genuinely believed that he was setting forth 'our faith from our forefathers'. Maybe, just like Eusebius, he was principally concerned about 'monotheism and morality'.[50] If that estimate is right, then Arius was not in himself the 'archetypal heretic', nor even much of an enquirer; rather, he was a reactionary, a rather literal-minded conservative who appealed to scripture and tradition as the basis of his faith.

For Further Reading

Gregg, Robert and Dennis Groh, 1981. *Early Arianism: a View of Salvation*, Philadelphia: Fortress Press.

Williams, R. D., 1987. *Arius: Heresy and Tradition*, London: Darton, Longman & Todd.

---

49 Williams (1987); but surely the figures of Hieracas and Didymus show that school-based Christianity survived into much later in the century; see further pp. 93–4 below.

50 See above, p. 8.

II Athanasius: The Legend and its Critique

It was Alexander's successor, Athanasius, who would bear the brunt of the controversy into which his predecessor had been drawn. In his early years he served Alexander as deacon and personal secretary, and was in this capacity present at Nicaea. Of the two, Athanasius undoubtedly had the stronger personality, and posterity has given him credit for inspiring Alexander's determined opposition to Arius. Gregory of Nazianzus represents him as taking a stand against the Arian 'plague' at the actual council, even though he was not yet a bishop.[51] In fact it is not likely that a young deacon would have had any opportunity of contributing to the discussions of such a venerable collection of episcopal dignitaries, and even if he influenced his own bishop, Alexander's part in the proceedings does not appear to have been crucial. Athanasius was hardly responsible for introducing the key Nicene formulation, and it is now clear that he only gradually came to see the value of the *homoousion* as an expression of Nicene theology.[52]

The enhanced role of Athanasius at Nicaea is one feature of the 'legend of Athanasius' which rapidly developed. This 'good tradition' has affected all the main sources, for Athanasius' own apologetic works were a primary source for the historians. Thus the classic picture is of a steadfast saint and theologian who almost single-handedly defended the Nicene formula through the reigns of Arian emperors, and finally engineered a reconciliation among anti-Arian parties in the East. Until critical examination in the late twentieth century, a typical reconstruction of the troubled but triumphant life depicted in the sources would have run something like this:

Athanasius was still only in his thirties when he succeeded Alexander as bishop in 328. The seat he inherited proved to be a somewhat uncomfortable one. Constantine's aim at Nicaea had been to establish unity in the Church, but the *homoousion* formula was received with considerable misgivings by the majority of Eastern bishops, and when it became politically expedient, few refused to accept Arius and his associates into communion with the Church. Athanasius was the only really influential figure who remained entrenched *contra mundum*. Charges of murder and black magic secured his deposition at the scarcely impartial Synod of Tyre (335), and appeal to Constantine merely induced the conspirators to produce the simpler but more disturbing charge that Athanasius had interfered with the sailing of corn-ships from Alexandria to the capital. This accusation aggravated any suspicions the emperor already harboured that the bishop was becoming too powerful in Egypt, and gave him an opportunity of removing the one obstacle to the restoration of peace in the Church. Athanasius was sent into exile at Trier.

This was merely the beginning of Athanasius' troubles. After Constantine's death in 337, Athanasius returned home, but the Eastern empire was now

---

51 Gregory Nazianzen, *Oration* 21.14, PG 35.1096.

52 *De Decretis*, written in the early 350s is where Athanasius first defends the term. Cf. Ayres (2004b), p. 339: 'A term originally chosen for polemical purposes and without any dense, well-established theological meaning, was gradually identified as a key marker of pro-Nicene theology.'

under Constantius, an Arian sympathizer, and the Eastern bishops were, on the whole, prepared to toe the imperial line. In 339, Athanasius fled again to the West, where the Pope and Constans were in sympathy with him. It is said that Athanasius introduced the new monasticism to the Western Church during his exiles, as well as building up formidable support for his own position. From 340, the Western and Eastern halves of empire and Church were divided by the Arian doctrines, a tragic situation exemplified in the irreconcilable split in 343 at the Council of Sardica.

After the death of Gregory, the usurper of Athanasius' see, Constantius gave way to pressure from Constans and Athanasius was reinstated (346); but once his imperial advocate had been murdered, his position was far from secure. Athanasius' career shows how it was becoming increasingly difficult for a far-flung and diverse community like the Church to maintain independence from the political power of its most illustrious lay member. The presence of Constantius, now sole emperor, coerced even a Western Council (Milan 355) to depose Athanasius, and in 356 imperial soldiers arrived at his Church door. George the Cappadocian, who superseded Athanasius amid scenes of plunder and violence, was intensely unpopular with the people of Alexandria, who stood by their deposed bishop throughout his third exile. This time Athanasius did not flee abroad, but stayed concealed among the loyal monks of Egypt, sometimes even within the city of Alexandria itself. Many were the legends told of how Athanasius eluded the imperial detectives during this period, sometimes escaping very narrowly; as the 'invisible patriarch', he successfully administered the Church of the faithful who protected him, kept him informed of the situation, and distributed the apologetic pamphlets which he wrote in hiding. Twice more under Julian the Apostate and Valens the Arian, Athanasius spent short periods of exile concealed in this fashion by his local supporters. It was during Athanasius' episcopacy that a close alliance was forged between the archbishop of the city and the monks of the countryside, an alliance which proved a powerful political force in the following century. In the wider sphere, Athanasius attained such respect that he was appealed to as an authority by Basil of Caesarea, and he made a genuine ecumenical attempt to bring together the various anti-Arian parties in the later years of his life, notably in his *Tomus ad Antiochenos*, a conciliar letter addressed to the split Church in Antioch.

Athanasius died in 373, an aged but triumphant upholder of his convictions. During his forty-five years as bishop, he had only two extended periods of relatively peaceful residence in his seat, from 346 to 356, and the last seven years of his life. He had lived as a martyr for the sake of truth.

Alongside this 'good tradition', however, there are traces of a less favourable estimate of Athanasius current among his contemporaries.[53] Certainly, he must have been a politician capable of subtle manoeuvres; the first seems to

---

[53] For the following points I am indebted to several essays in Kannengiesser (1974): chiefly, W. G. Rusch, 'À la recherche de l'Athanase historique', pp. 161–80, but also Annik Martin, 'Athanase et les Mélitiens (325–335)', pp. 31–62, and L. W. Barnard, 'Athanase et les empereurs Constantin et Constance', pp. 127–44. On the Melitians, see also Barnard (1975), pp. 183–9, and Martin (1996). That these criticisms have become standard is

have been in his own election, which was definitely contested, may have been illegal and looks as though it was enforced. There seems to have been a pitiless streak in his character – that he resorted to violence to achieve his own ends is implied by a good deal of evidence. When he succeeded Alexander, he inherited a volatile local situation. The surprising strength of the Melitian party in Egypt has often been overlooked through preoccupation with the Arian problem, but there is evidence to suggest that thirty-five out of sixty-five Egyptian bishops were Melitians. Athanasius managed to antagonize this group rather than facilitate their reconciliation according to the provisions of Nicaea, and it was evidence supplied by the Melitians which made Athanasius vulnerable to attack at the Council of Tyre. That he did not scruple to use force in his dealings with this group can hardly be doubted, and his deposition at Tyre was based, not on doctrinal considerations, but upon his misconduct in Egypt. Rusch is certainly right in suggesting that the hostile reports of Philostorgius, the evidence of the papyri, and the criticisms that Gregory Nazianzen felt that he had to answer in his panegyric, must be admitted as evidence in the search for the 'historical Athanasius'.

Besides this, the idea that Athanasius' influence dominated the Eastern Church from 345 to 373 has been subjected to searching criticism by Leroux.[54] According to his interpretation of the evidence, Athanasius was out of touch: he went on fighting the old battle against Arius when everyone else was struggling with the much subtler issues raised by Aetius and Eunomius; he had no idea of the real situation in Antioch; Basil only appealed to him because he had influence in the West; and the *Tomus ad Antiochenos* was addressed only to the quarrelsome ultra-Nicenes. Thus, in Egypt alone did Athanasius have the ascendency attributed to him, and even here he had had to defend himself; his apologetic works were a means of justifying his dubious career to his own flock and were not widely disseminated elsewhere. Ecclesiastical politics in the East mostly passed him by.

This 'deflation' of Athanasius may go too far; some elements in the good tradition are certainly right. By the end of his life, Athanasius had forged a remarkable alliance with the Coptic monks and had won complete ascendency over Egypt. It was on the power base he had established that successors like Theophilus and Cyril were to challenge the authority of Constantinople and of the emperor himself. If his local position was so shaky to start with, his political skills must have been the more considerable.[55] Furthermore, he did obstinately hold out for a particular theological position, and with the backing of the West, upheld it whatever the cost. What was the driving force behind his single-mindedness? And how was it that his Nicene theology eventually became sufficiently acceptable in the East that it could triumph in 381 after the accession of Theodosius I?

The second question raises more complex issues, but we are in the fortunate position of having plenty of material in which to try and find the answer to the

---

proved by the estimate of Athanasius in Barnes (1993) and the reaction in Weinandy (2007).

54 J. M. Leroux, 'Athanase et la seconde phase de la crise arienne (345–373)' in Kannengiesser (1974), pp. 145–56.

55 Frend (1976).

first. In spite of his turbulent career, Athanasius' literary output was enormous, and most of it is concerned with the controversies in which he was involved. His own writings allow us to see the force of his argumentation, the adaptability of his terminology, the underlying consistency of his theological thinking and the sincerity of his belief that he was safeguarding the truth of scripture, the tradition of the Church and the faith for which the martyrs had died during his early years. We can here detect the presuppositions of his faith, and so appreciate why it was that the refutation of 'Arianism' became for him a matter of life and death, for which he would face all difficulties and every form of persecution.

For Further Reading

Barnes, T. D., 1993. *Athanasius and Constantius: Theology and Politics in the Constantinian Empire*, Cambridge, MA and London: Harvard University Press.

III The Fundamentals of Athanasius' Theology: *Contra Gentes – De Incarnatione*

Some development can be traced in Athanasius' thought as far as details and means of expression are concerned, but the central core of his position was never touched. His earliest writings are in fact the key to his life and his dogmatic argumentation. The view that the *Contra Gentes* and the *De Incarnatione*, two volumes of a single apologetic work, were written before the outbreak of the Arian controversy is no longer the scholarly consensus. The grounds on which this dating rested lie in the absence of any reference to Arius in these works, but this argument is not necessarily conclusive, since there is no reference to Arius in the *Festal Letters* of 329–35;[56] surely a warning would be more appropriate in a pastoral letter than in a work intended to interest nonbelievers? Supporters of an early date suggested that Athanasius, as yet barely in his twenties, wrote the work as a theological essay not intended for publication. The shorter and longer versions of the work evidenced in the textual traditions are explained as two different drafts, both found among Athanasius' papers at the end of his life.[57] If this were correct, Athanasius would have laid the foundations of his mature faith at a remarkably early age. A later date seems on the face of it much more likely. Furthermore, the relationship between these volumes and Eusebius' *Theophania* is less puzzling if they are assigned to Atha-

---

56 Kannengiesser (1964a).

57 Cross (1945); Meijering (1968) also regards the work as the theological essay of a young man, as does Parvis (2006). For detailed discussions of the textual problem, namely the relationship between the Short and Long Recensions, see the survey and further research of Kannengiesser (1964b, 1965, 1966). The existence of the Short Recension was first noticed by J. Lebon, and was studied in detail by R. Casey: see Ryan and Casey (1945/6). The commonly accepted view that the Short Recension was Athanasius' own revision has been challenged by Kannengiesser, but he agrees (against Opitz 1935b) that no doctrinal motivations can be detected in the redactional process; Casey described the shorter version as a secondary literary revision.

nasius' first exile at Trier, or perhaps just before it.[58] The *Theophania* undoubtedly appeared no earlier than the mid-320s. It is hardly likely that the aged and respected scholar and historian, Eusebius, would have drawn from the apologetic work of a young deacon scarcely out of his teens. Either the similarities must be attributed, somewhat implausibly, to a common apologetic tradition and a common cultural and religious milieu,[59] or else we must accept a much later date for Athanasius' work. That Athanasius made use of Eusebius' work is made all the more probable by the parallel connections between their exegesis of the Psalms; Rondeau[60] showed that here Athanasius uses the historical and philological erudition of Eusebius, but has a quite different theological perspective. So Athanasius is likely to have used Eusebius' apologetic work similarly, plundering it for material but correcting it theologically so as to present overall a somewhat different outlook.[61] There are indications that this was Athanasius' intention. Eusebius attributes evidential value to Christ's death and resurrection, while Athanasius emphasizes the soteriological aspects, stressing Christ's identification with humanity in his death and resurrection. Furthermore, some expressions seem to contain veiled criticism of the inadequate understanding of the Arians, with whom Eusebius was sympathetic, as in the reference to 'the true Son of God who is the Power and the Wisdom and the Word of the Father'.[62] Where Eusebius, and probably Arius, had a fundamentally cosmological approach, Athanasius began with the saving act of the incarnation.

As his first literary endeavour, then, Athanasius not merely assembled well-worn arguments against paganism, but presented systematically what the Christian gospel really meant.[63] Here we find set out the basic presuppositions

---

58 Recent reconsideration of the date was initiated by Nordberg (1961a, b). He dated the work(s) as late as the reign of Julian the Apostate on the grounds that this provided an occasion for such an apologetic undertaking. But see the discussion by Kannengiesser (1970b). The date he suggests, namely the exile at Trier, was accepted by Roldanus (1968), following Kannengiesser's earlier article (1964). A number of scholars expressed the fact that they are not convinced; see for example van Winden (1975). The relationship between the work of Athanasius and that of Eusebius seems to be almost decisive, however. Pettersen (1982) and Slusser (1986) slightly revised Kannegiesser's view, suggesting composition just prior to the first exile. Barnes (1993) compromises on the late 320s (after Eusebius' *Theophania* c.325), but later dating is now widely acknowledged; for example Hanson (1988), Anatolios (1998), Weinandy (2007), Steenberg (2009).

59 Van Haarlem (1961). Cross (1945) suggested that Athanasius was influenced as a theological student by Eusebius' visit to Alexandria in 311, but that is pure speculation. Anatolios (2004) maintains that this work represents Athanasius' reworking of Irenaeus in a manner deliberately counter to Eusebius' *Theophania*.

60 Rondeau (1968).

61 Cf. Anatolios (2004).

62 *CG* 46; the case is presented by Roldanus (1968), Appendix; see p. 375 n. 5 for further examples. See also E. Mühlenberg, 'Verité et Bonté de Dieu' in Kannengiesser (1974), pp. 215–30.

63 Pettersen (1982) suggested the work was not so much apology as catechesis. The work is often used to detect Athanasius' fundamental approach to theology: for example, Pettersen (1995), Anatolios (2004), Weinandy (2007).

that lay behind his long life of conflict and controversy. The *Contra Gentes*,[64] the first volume, follows many of the classic Jewish and Christian arguments against polytheism and idol-worship. The traditional religio-philosophical problems of the origin of evil and the existence of the soul appear. Theism is proved by the argument from design. The possibility of natural theology is admitted, though regarded as remote. Yet, even here, we can detect the characteristics of Athanasius' thought, which appear more obviously in the *De Incarnatione*. There we see that the truth of salvation in Christ is the only thing that really matters, as far as Athanasius is concerned.[65] What then is his understanding of salvation in Christ?

Each of these volumes begins with an account of the original state of the human race and the fall from grace. The two differing accounts highlight the two primary concerns of Athanasius' soteriology, human irrationality and human mortality, both alike caused by the same disaster. For humanity, along with the rest of creation, was called into existence out of τὰ οὐκ ὄντα (*ta ouk onta* – the non-existent). But God chose to endow this creature with his own image, with a share in the rational being of the Logos himself, so that he might enjoy, at least in a partial way, the eternal life of God himself. However, humanity forfeited its share in the Logos by disobedience. The incarnation, Athanasius argues, was the only solution to the consequences:

(i) *Human irrationality*. In the *Contra Gentes* (2—5) the human creature who originally had θεωρία (*theōria* – vision) of God and all that was good, turned to 'things nearer to itself', the material rather than the spiritual; humankind became corrupted by selfish desires and worshipped the creature instead of the Creator. This theme is taken up in the *De Incarnatione* (11—16); human beings could not be λογικοί (*logikoi*) once they had lost the Logos of God; they were reduced to the level of beasts, and worshipped idols in bestial form; indeed, idolatry is the proof of human irrationality. Humanity might have learned of God by contemplating the harmony and order of the universe he created, or by listening to the prophets and wise men God sent, or by living according to the law which God gave to the Jews but intended for all nations. But even so, human beings could not have regained full knowledge of God without their share in the Logos. Ultimately, the only solution was to renew God's image in humankind, and this was accomplished by the Logos himself dwelling in a human being; he came and taught them at their own level and revealed God through direct contact with them. True revelation of God was a prime necessity for salvation.

(ii) *Human mortality* (*De Incarnatione* 6—10). God had given humanity a share in the Logos, and had also given human beings free will. So God tried to safeguard this gift by making it conditional upon obedience to a particular law. If that law were broken, humankind would be turned out of paradise and left to inevitable submergence under the forces of death and corruption; returning to

---

64 Text and ET of the *CG* and *DI*: Thomson (1971). Also Kannengiesser (1973/2000), Camelot (1977), Meijering (1984), Meijering and van Winden (1989).

65 Weinandy (2007) follows many others in emphasizing the soteriological basis of Athanasius' theological thought.

the nothingness from which it came. Humanity disobeyed, and forfeited the principle of life, the Logos.

For Athanasius, this left God in an intolerable position. It was unthinkable that God should go back on his word; humanity having transgressed must die; God could not falsify the divine self. But it was not worthy of God's goodness that the divine work should perish, especially in the case of beings which had been endowed with the nature of the Logos himself; it would have been better never to have created them. This has been described as the 'divine dilemma';[66] somehow God's integrity had to be salvaged while the demands of divine love were met.

The answer was the incarnation. The Logos took a human body capable of dying; when the Logos died the death owed by all humanity, the debt to God's honour was paid and death itself was overcome. The corrupt nature of humanity was re-created when the body of the Logos was raised and clothed in incorrupt-ibility. The indwelling Logos restored the lost image of God to humanity, and God was reconciled to himself.

Athanasius has frequently been accused of being so concerned with death that he neglects the seriousness of sin and the need of salvation from guilt.[67] Certainly his emphasis in the De Incarnatione is on death, but it must be remem-bered that death is the direct outcome of human disobedience to God's express command. Athanasius shows a predominant interest in death because it was the curse of sin, the mark of the loss of that nature which humanity had possessed. If it had been a case of a mere trespass, he says,[68] repentance could have solved the problem; but the human situation was worse than that, for the result of sin had been a corruption of nature and a loss of grace which only the re-creating power of the Logos could restore. Creation and re-creation were both performed by the same Logos of God.

Re-creation is Athanasius' main understanding of salvation in Christ. Humanity would have lived ὡς θεός (as God), if it had not been for the Fall. Scripture says, 'Ye are all gods and sons of the Most High.'[69] Here are the seeds of Athanasius' doctrine of θεοποίησις (theopoiēsis – deification), first hinted at towards the end of the De Incarnatione, where he sums up his position in a much quoted sentence: αὐτὸς γὰρ ἐνηνθρώπησεν, ἵνα ἡμεῖς θεοποιηθῶμεν (He became man/human, that we might become god/divine).[70]

Salvation in Christ, understood in terms of revelation and re-creation, is the faith that Athanasius was prepared to defend to the uttermost. Everything else he came to stand for is merely a corollary of this central fact of his religious consciousness. His fight against the 'Arians' would be motivated by soteriolo-gical concerns. Never again did he give a full account of his position, but behind

---

66 It appeared as a chapter heading in an English translation by a religious of CSMV (published in 1953), and has been taken up since in a number of expositions of the CG–DI.

67 For example, van Haarlem (1961).

68 DI 7.

69 DI 4.

70 DI 54. Note the difficulty of conveying Athanasius' thought in English. He did not mean that we become God in the sense that God is God; but he did mean something more than 'divine'. See discussion below p. 62.

all his theological arguments against his opponents this twin understanding of salvation can be detected. In the course of the long and diffuse polemic of the *Orationes contra Arianos*, his two major concerns constantly recur as the basis of argument. Revelation and re-creation involved the restoration to humanity of the true Logos of God; so right from the start Athanasius' soteriology implied that God alone could be the source of salvation, that God alone could take the initiative and deal with humanity's sorry plight. This conviction spurred him in defence of the essential Godhead of the Logos; the Logos is not a creature but is of 'out of the substance of the Father' (ἐκ τῆς οὐσίας τοῦ πατρός) because only so is our salvation fully realized and guaranteed: that was Athanasius' central argument.

For Further Reading

English translation

Thomson, Robert W., 1971. *Athanasius. Contra Gentes-De Incarnatione*, text and ET, Oxford: Clarendon Press.

Studies

Studies of Athanasius' thought will be grouped at the end of the chapter.

IV Marcellus: Ally or Embarrassment?

In the year 339, sent into exile again, Athanasius arrived in Rome. A few months later so did Marcellus of Ancyra, an experienced bishop, some fifteen years senior to Athanasius. The year 340 they spent together, and it is after that year that 'a new animal emerges in the writings of both: the full-blown Arian heresy, modelled on the constructs of the old heresiologies'.[71] It is likely that during that time they together drew up a series of propositions: those on which they agreed and those they both denied and ascribed to Arius and his associates – these can be identified through the parallels between Marcellus' *Letter to Julius* and *Contra Arianos* I. Given the likely influence of Marcellus on Athanasius at this point, it is necessary to know a little more about him, his literary activity and his career.

Indeed, there has been a very significant resurgence in interest in this shadowy figure at the outset of the new millennium. He was identified by the great nineteenth-century historian Adolf von Harnack as a 'most interesting phenomenon in the history of dogma',[72] a judgment which signified that Marcellus was perhaps doing something more sophisticated than simply attempting to

---

71 Parvis (2006), 181. Cf. pp. 181–5 for their common set of propositions.

72 von Harnack (1931), p. 242. Loofs (1902) together with Vinzent (1997) and Parvis (2006) share an excitement about the creativity of Marcellus' Christological accomplishment.

construct Christology in the mould of a more ancient Logos-theology.[73] It is, however, far from clear how Marcellus may be evaluated, his assured texts being limited to the fragments selected in a polemic against him by Eusebius, together with other fragments and a letter to Pope Julius I preserved in Epiphanius.[74] These texts are not set in Marcellus' own context or connecting narratives or arguments:[75] it is notoriously difficult to make sense of so much silence.

In his lifetime Marcellus was clearly a significant figure. As bishop of Ancyra in Galatia he was a participant in the Arian controversies until the council of Serdica in 343, after which he seems to have kept a low profile until his death around 374–5,[76] aged over ninety years; yet his name remained notorious and his purported views the measure against which the next generation defined themselves. Already a bishop, he was present at the Synod of Ancyra in 314 – probably the president, as it took place in his see; this faced issues concerning the rehabilitation of the lapsed (and other offenders excluded from Christian fellowship), and he may well have had a hand in the drawing up of its canons.[77] Marcellus was at Nicaea in 325, an entrenched opponent of Arius and champion of the *homoousios*, so it was hardly surprising that when 'those around Eusebius' deposed Eustathius and Athanasius, Marcellus, too, found himself cast out at Constantinople in 336. At issue was his refutation of Asterius' defence of the Nicomedian Eusebius, about a sixth of which survives in quotations in the *Contra Marcellum* of Eusebius of Caesarea together with further reportage in Epiphanius.

Asterius of Cappadocia, a co-Lucianist with Arius, had supported Arius from the beginning of the conflict before Nicaea. Though his apostasy in the final persecutions at the outset of the fourth century was a fact that his opponents did not allow to be forgotten, he would be recognized as a strong theological opponent by Athanasius, and clearly Marcellus had felt the need to respond to his defence of Eusebius of Nicomedia. Asterius' work seems to have divergent emphases – fragments of his *Syntagmation*, a response to Nicaea's unexpected inclusion of *homoousios*, are preserved by Athanasius. This work would seem to be outspokenly supportive of Arius, and radically subordinationist. Marcellus, however, preserves a much more subtle style in Asterius' defence of Eusebius – the Son is the image, no different from the Father in divinity, substance and

---

73 That Marcellus, like the early apologists, restated the Stoic distinction between the *logos endiathetos* and the *logos prophorikos*, thus resurrecting an 'economic trinitarianism', has been frequently stated; for example, Kelly (1958).

74 Eusebius, *Contra Marcellum* and *De ecclesiastica theologia*; Epiphanius *Adv. Haer.* 72.2.3. A critical Greek text is established in Vinzent (1997); there is not a complete English translation, though fragments are translated in Robertson (2007) and Parvis (2006), who has indicated her intention to provide a critical edition with English translation and commentary. Other works have been speculatively attributed to Marcellus, of which the *De Sancta Ecclesia* is the most widely accepted; see Lienhard (1999). Parvis (2006), p. 190, accepting this work as Marcellus' and dating it to 340, describes it as the 'first expression of the perfecting of the myth of Arianism by Athanasius and Marcellus during their year together in Rome'.

75 Ayres (2004a), p. 2.

76 Epiphanius *Panarion* 72.1.2.

77 See Parvis (2006), pp. 11–30.

power. He remains, though, but the image: 'the Father is *allos* (distinct), who begot from himself the only-begotten Logos and first born of all creation . . . the exact image of his substance and will and glory and power'.[78] Asterius' moderation prompts Marcellus to stress further the ontologically identical nature of Father and Logos in his response. He agrees that 'image' implies two entities, one of which images the other, but refuses to allow 'two' or 'three' to be applied to the Godhead.

As a result, a conventional interpretation of Marcellus is that he was consumed by a desire for strict monotheism;[79] this is set by Chadwick in the context of Neo-Pythagorean mathematics: 'the Monad contains the potential to engender the dyad and the triad, but is primary'.[80] However, Lienhard observes that '[t]o make the expansion of the Monad into a Triad the keystone of Marcellus' thought is to distort his theology.'[81] It would seem that scripture and the accomplishment of Nicaea, which anathematized any teaching that denied the unity of God and posited more than one *hypostasis*, was a more powerful prompt for Marcellus than late antique philosophy proper – though clearly this was the milieu in which much debate took place. For Marcellus, the Logos and the Father are one *hypostasis*, indistinguishable in nature, but that leaves the issue of the nature of Jesus very exposed: 'was Jesus more than a mere man? To critics [Marcellus] . . . seemed to combine Sabellius with Paul of Samosata. They thought that to affirm the incarnate Lord to be God entailed his distinctness from the transcendent Father, and Marcellus seemed to prejudice both propositions.'[82]

The eternal Word was indeed the dynamic power of the Godhead, eternally silent within the divine, but spoken at creation.[83] Lienhard depicts Marcellus as construing three economies – (i) in creation the Word proceeds from the Father but has no distinct *hypostasis*; (ii) in the incarnation the Word becomes flesh and becomes 'Son' – it is here that other 'names' applicable to the Word are possible; (iii) the dyad expands into a triad on Easter night with the Holy Spirit, the Word being distinct from the Spirit. However, at the end of time (after 1 Corinthians 15.24–8) God will again be 'all in all' – the absolute Monad.[84] By his restriction to the incarnate economy of other Christological names, including image and even Son, Marcellus preserved his 'mia-hypostatic' position – only the Logos is 'God of God, Light of Light . . . of one being with the Father'.

However, it was this perceived radical disconnection – at once elevating the Logos and diminishing the 'one Lord Jesus Christ' – that provoked a concerted

---

78 Fr. 21.

79 Robertson (2007), p. 97, notes that as this is something common to all parties it hardly differentiates Marcellus from anyone else: the point is that the two clusters of 'parties' in the Nicene conflict had different strategies to ensure this – those who wanted to include Christ in the unity of God, and those who sought to exclude him from essential divinity in order to protect that unity.

80 Chadwick (2003), p. 234.

81 Lienhard (1999), p. 57.

82 Chadwick (2003), p. 234.

83 Parvis (2006), p. 31, following Zahn, emphasizes the continuity with the theology of Irenaeus of Lyons as an important foundational component of Marcellus' own.

84 Lienhard (1982), p. 489.

effort to repudiate Marcellus further: letters warning of his errors were sent to Rome in 339, inviting Julius to condemn him. Marcellus' response, his own *Letter to Julius*, outlined his faith and convinced Julius of his orthodoxy. The earliest written text of the Roman Baptismal Creed, despite its presumed antiquity, appears here – presumably Marcellus is using it for diplomatic reasons; but there are interesting variants. Marcellus omits 'Father' in the opening article, 'I believe in one God the Almighty', and adds 'eternal life' in the conclusion.[85] The omission of 'Father' may be significant, implying perhaps his exclusion of the generation in eternity of the Son, and intimating that, at the end, as in the beginning, God will be one. This suggests that the Trinity is itself a response to the fallen condition of humankind, a temporal solution, necessary as human beings, and their sin, both exist and need to be redeemed in time. It also offers a way of protecting the divine nature from ontological change at an absolute level: the strategic 'expansion' of the Monad into Dyad and ultimately Triad offers a protection to the Ultimate God from diminution: the power and priority of the Monad is maintained.

Robertson's study of the notion of mediation in Marcellus makes it clear that a major concern of Marcellus, one that Athanasius shared, was a deep opposition to the idea of the mediating Christ as somehow more approachable – and therefore less sublimely transcendent and powerful than the Father.[86] Paulinus of Tyre (Antioch) urged the importance of a depiction of Christ which showed '"a more human God" (ἀνθρωπικώτερος θεός), that is, a God with whom humans could reasonably have discourse, as opposed to the Father'.[87] The Eusebian party identified Marcellus' theology as endangering the notion of mediation in the sense of 'standing between' two different parties: the divine *becoming* the mediator cannot meet this obligation. Marcellus absolutely rejects any notion of mediation which posits ditheism, dividing God's own Word from God.[88] To divide the divine into three *hypostases* would make it impossible to conceive of as a single divine being; the single divine being had to be prior to any kind of differentiation, which, as we have observed, was his solution.[89] Marcellus was perhaps more able than his opponents to accept the unmediated engagement of the Creator God with the creation, as Athanasius was and Irenaeus had been.

In the winter of 340–1 both Athanasius and Marcellus were acquitted of heresy in Rome, and Pope Julius communicated this to the Eastern bishops. Julius' findings, however, were rejected at the Dedication Council in Antioch in 341. Later, at Sardica, the Eastern bishops refused to allow Athanasius and Marcellus to sit in synod; East and West were divided over their (significantly divergent) insistence on the eternity and divinity of the Logos. The West, however, continued to be impressed by Marcellus. When, in the mid-340s, the Third Antiochene Synod condemned both Marcellus and his disciple Photinus in the lengthy doctrinal text, the *Ekthesis Makrostichos*, the Council of Milan in 345, though upholding the condemnation of Photinus, rejected the call for Marcellus' anathematization. It seems likely, however, that at this time Athanasius

---

85 Vinzent (1997), p. 126. See discussion in Parvis (2006), pp. 181–5.
86 Robertson (2007), pp. 97–126.
87 Robertson (2007), p. 98.
88 Fr. 117.
89 Fr. 47.

– perhaps seeing more clearly the dangers of refusing the eternal generation of the Son – broke with Marcellus; it is not impossible that *Contra Arianos III* is directed against Marcellus' pupil Photinus. Marcellus now becomes silent until around 370, when his companions ask for his readmission.[90]

Had Marcellus by then modified his position? Lienhard suggests that he and his followers had gradually 'abandoned most of the teachings he had put forth – perhaps as speculation – in the *Contra Asterium*, in order to hold on to two points he considered essential: the eternal existence of the Son and the propriety of calling God one *hypostasis*'.[91] Despite being replaced by Basil of Ancyra in 340, Marcellus seems to have quietly led a continuing group in Ancyra which confessed an eternal Triad ἐν ὑποστάσει (*en hypostasei*); Athanasius accepted them as orthodox, as did Basil of Caesarea in 375 after Marcellus' death. But the creed of Constantinople in 381 would continue to fend off Marcellus' threat with the clause 'whose kingdom shall have no end'.

Newman, somewhat romantically, saw Athanasius' breach with Marcellus 'as a tragic tale of two comrades-in-arms, the one eventually forced to break with the other on account of his tainted theology, the second divinely preserved so that they might be silently reconciled in extreme old age'.[92] Contemporaries found the relationship more enigmatic; Epiphanius wrote:

> I myself once asked the blessed pope Athanasius about this Marcellus, what his opinion of him was. He neither defended him nor expressed hostility towards him. He only smiled, and indicated that he was not far from error, but he considered him excused.[93]

Marcellus has been described as 'a dark burnt-out star, itself invisible but deflecting the orbit of anything that comes near it'.[94] Silence seems something of a *leitmotif* when it comes to Marcellus. Before anything was made there was ἡσυχία (silence)[95] – the Word was not spoken yet; and might it be that Athanasius' silence – his abstention from using *homoousios* – was because it was a word 'tainted' by Marcellus and thereby connected with a quasi-Sabellian depiction of the Trinity evolving in time to meet the human condition?[96] Parvis, citing Epiphanius, suggests that 'Marcellus allowed himself to vanish from fourth century history, slowly becoming more and more insubstantial until all that was left was Athanasius' smile'.[97]

90 Tetz (1973), pp. 78–84.

91 Lienhard (1999), pp. 242–3.

92 Parvis (2006), p. 249, referring to J. H. Newman (1881), *Select treatises of St Athanasius in Controversy with the Arians, Freely Translated*, 2nd edn, London: Pickering, vol. 2, pp. 197–8.

93 Epiphanius, *Panarion* 72.4; ET as quoted by Lienhard (1993), p. 78.

94 Lienhard (1993), p. 65.

95 Fr. 76.

96 Ayres (2004a), p. 96.

97 Parvis (2006), p. 252; Epiphanius, *Panarion* 72.4.4.

For Further Reading

Lienhard, J. T., 1999. Contra Marcellum: *Marcellus of Ancyra and Fourth-Century Theology*, Washington, DC: Catholic University of America Press.
——, 1993. 'Did Athanasius Reject Marcellus?' in Barnes and Williams (1993), pp. 65–80.
Parvis, S., 2006. *Marcellus of Ancyra and the Lost Years of the Arian Controversy, 325–345*, Oxford Early Christian Studies, Oxford: Oxford University Press.

V Orations against the Arians

Marcellus faded into silence as Athanasius' increasing output gradually began to set the decision at Nicaea at the centre of his own defence. Though as yet reticent about the *homoousion*, the three *Orations against the Arians*,[98] which together constitute Athanasius' most important dogmatic work, became the anti-Arian classic, and the argumentation developed here was later followed very closely by others, for example, by Cyril in his *Thesaurus de sancta et consubstantiali Trinitate*.[99] The first offers a defence of the true Sonship of the Logos against the Arian position, and the rest deals with the favourite Arian proof-texts. At first sight it appears as though the urgency of Athanasius' argumentation leads him to disregard literary form; for his presentation seems ill-arranged and repetitious to the point of boredom. Kannengiesser argued that the work consists of an original nucleus to which further material was added later, in particular suggesting that Book III stands apart and may not be by Athanasius.[100] For the moment, however, we will assume that the *Orations I–III* can be used together and that they do provide material for understanding Athanasius' impressively consistent theological position.[101]

Arius maintained that the Logos, while different from all other creatures, including angels and heavenly beings, was even so a creature and not essentially God himself. That at least was what Athanasius understood him to mean and obviously this doctrine compromised his whole understanding of salvation. True revelation of God was not possible if the Logos was not God. So in the *Contra Arianos* he constantly returns to this theme. Johannine texts like 'No one knows the Father except the Son', 'I and the Father are one', and many others are quoted over and over again. Hebrews 1.3 where Christ is described as the radiance of God's glory and the very stamp of the divine nature is a

---

98 *Orationes contra Arianos*: text, PG 26, and Bright (1884); Tetz (1998, 2000); Kannengiesser is preparing a new edition for *Sources Chrétiennes: Athanasius: Orations Against the Arians*, ed., trans., and commentary: SC, Paris: Cerf: 2009, forthcoming. Translation in NPNF II.4. ET selections in Anatolios (2004).

99 Liébaert (1951). See below, pp. 308–9.

100 Kannengiesser (1973, 1982). His attribution of *C. Arianos III* to Apollinarius has not generally proved convincing; see also Meijering (1996). *Contra Arianos IV* is generally held to be pseudonymous, and has been identified, with convincing evidence, to be a text against Asterius of Cappadocia, Eusebius of Caesarea and Marcellus of Ancyra (Vinzent 1996).

101 As do many others, for example, Barnes (1993), Anatolios (2004), Weinandy (2007).

favourite text, expounded in such a way as to highlight the unity of Father and Son in their revelatory activity. Likewise, the re-creation of human nature could only be accomplished by God himself. Only if the Lord of life himself submitted to death, could death be overcome for all humanity; he became the first-born of the dead by his resurrection. At this point, however, Athanasius' emphases have changed a little since the *De Incarnatione*. He concentrates more on redemption from sin and the curse, on Christ's bearing our sins and weaknesses. He seems to have become more aware of the depths of evil and suffering from which Christ freed humankind. But this does not weaken the argument: a mere creature could no more cleanse humanity from the depths of sin than raise it to new life; the Logos must be God.[102] Besides this, Athanasius' characteristic idea of θεοποίησις or υἱοποίησις (*theopoiēsis* – deification or *huiopoiēsis* – filiation)[103] is far more prominent than in the *De Incarnatione*. The Logos took a body, so that in it we might be renewed and deified;[104] by being σύσσωμοι with him (*syssōmoi*, i.e. sharing in a common body), we are transformed into perfect humanity, we ascend to heaven, and this is to be made divine.[105] Only if the Logos is himself God could he accomplish this for us.

This raises some of the difficulties of Athanasius' position.

(i) In what sense do we become divine? In fact, Athanasius himself is concerned to elucidate this. We never become θεοί (gods) or sons of God in the same sense as the Logos is θεός and son of God: he is Son in nature and truth, we are sons by appointment and grace.[106] Insistence on this difference was important since Arius appeared to teach that the Logos was son in the same limited sense as we are. Athanasius instinctively felt that this jeopardized our sonship – there could be no adoption without the true Son in whom we participate by the Spirit; if there is divinization through the Logos, it must be because he is by nature and substance true God of true God.[107] The involvement of the Spirit in the ontological aspect of salvation will lead Athanasius later to extend the description ὁμοούσιος (*homoousios*) to the Spirit – 'the Holy Spirit shares the same unity with the Son, as the Son does with the Father'.[108]

(ii) Did the Logos dwell in an individual man, or in collective humanity, a sort of Platonic idea of Man?[109] Athanasius certainly did not have the sort of interest in the concrete and historical situation of Christ's earthly life which a modern investigator has. Details of Christ's life appear in his writings only because of their soteriological significance: he wept and was afraid in Gethsemane in order to prove that he had really taken a human body and really bore

102 C. *Arianos* ii.67.

103 For the history of this idea before and after Athanasius, see Russell (2004).

104 C. *Arianos* ii.47.

105 Detailed references for Athanasius' recurrent ideas are too numerous to record here. This applies to most of the material in the present paragraph.

106 C. *Arianos* iii.19–21; Christensen and Wittung (2007), Meyer (1998).

107 C. *Arianos* i.9ff. and frequently.

108 *Ad Serapionem* 1.2. Cf. Hanson (1988), pp. 748–60; Weinandy (2007), pp. 103–19. ET selections in Anatolios (2004).

109 van Haarlem (1961), English summary chapter 5. Bouyer (1943), chapter 3. Kelly (1958), p. 378.

our weaknesses.[110] Besides, there are many passages which seem to suggest that the incarnation automatically sanctified human nature as a whole. On the other hand, in some passages, he certainly does not describe an automatic transformation; it depends on the individual's participation in the Logos through the Spirit, on being 'created in him'. This may not seem far from the Pauline conception that Christians are 'in Christ' and die and rise with him, crucifying the old self and accepting new life; but even the language of participation has Platonic overtones, and the most satisfactory understanding of Athanasius' viewpoint is in terms of such philosophical presuppositions – by this time they were common currency in intellectual circles, so that their use implies no great philosophical sophistication. The humanity of Christ in Athanasius' thought is certainly not quite ordinary humanity, if only because its relation to our humanity is different from that of any other human being.

(iii) Does not Athanasius' account of the incarnation seem docetic? On many occasions, Athanasius' exegesis seems forced and unnatural. The texts implying weakness or ignorance he explains as merely referring to the incarnation-situation. All is subordinated to the purpose of showing that the Logos in himself had all the attributes of divinity, such as impassibility, omniscience, etc. Arius' explanation of such texts – that the Logos was fallible and a mere creature – had to be refuted at all costs. At one point, Athanasius even goes so far as to say τὰ ἡμῶν ἐμιμήσατο – he imitated our circumstances.[111] However, the context in which Athanasius made that remark suggests that for him it certainly did not carry docetic implications – the saints and heroes of the faith can share in Christ's incorruptibility through receiving and imitating him precisely because he 'imitated' our circumstances.[112] The soteriological motivation remains paramount, and implies real incarnation.

Nevertheless, the weight of the evidence supports those who argue that Athanasius did not think that Christ had a human soul; his was a Word–flesh Christology, and he was Apollinarian before Apollinarius.[113] But this does not necessarily mean that Athanasius was crypto-docetic in his outlook. Again an explanation can be found in current philosophy. To Platonists, human existence was the soul's experience of being trapped in the flesh and succumbing to its temptations. If Athanasius understood human life in this way, then in general terms his view of the incarnation was perfectly legitimate. The Logos had the experience of being human because he, like us, was trapped in flesh and, like us, was tempted by it; but the subject of the experience being the Logos, he did not in the process succumb to sin, because of his very nature. This was no docetic charade, but a real experience of the conditions of human life, the only difference being that he could have no guilt or sinfulness. In fact, docetism would have entirely undermined Athanasius' soteriology; only if the Logos assumed real human flesh could he have any relationship with us.[114] Nevertheless, changeless involvement in the human condition was not easy to

---

110 C. *Arianos* iii.54–7.

111 C. *Arianos* iii. 57. See the classic article by Richard (1947).

112 Brakke (1995).

113 See below, pp. 245–53.

114 See further below, pp. 67–8, and Young (1971); also Pettersen (1980). Many others have now challenged the 'Word–Flesh' category, and the excessive weight put on the

conceive, and Athanasius' position led him into the sort of forced exegesis we have referred to.

Athanasius himself does not seem to have reflected on these problems at all. They simply fell outside his perspective. Current assumptions about humanity's dual nature (soul and body) may appear in his work, but he had no great interest in anthropological analysis for its own sake, and still less an interest in developing a philosophical theology. If we think through what he has to say in his own terms, then the problems of his theology become less pressing. Athanasius' fundamental ideas all derive from his radical distinction between the Creator and everything created out of nothing. Human intelligence and permanence depended upon relationship with the Creator, and the incarnation was the means of establishing that relationship at a more secure level. Christ had to share humanity's creatureliness, just as he had to share the divinity of the Creator, so that Creator and creature could be united in him. Θεοποίησις (deification) could never obliterate the ontological distinction between God and creatures, but the humanity of the Logos made participation in God possible through incorporation in him. The question of the human soul of Christ did not appear within Athanasius' horizon; yet docetism would have destroyed his soteriology.[115] The conjunction of Creator and creature in the incarnation, a conjunction which overcame the inherent passibility and destructibility of the creature – this it was that dominated Athanasius' thought. In attributing a *theological* significance to the humanity, Athanasius leaves clear Christological water between himself and Apollinarius (and later Alexandrian Christological expression): ἃ γὰρ τὸ ἀνθρώπινον ἔπασχε τοῦ λόγου, ἵνα ἡμεῖς τῆς τοῦ λόγου θεότητος μετασχεῖν δυνηθῶμεν (For the humanity of the Logos suffered, so that we may be empowered to participate in the divinity of the Logos).[116]

The date of the *Orations against the Arians* is contested. It was usual to assign them to Athanasius' third exile among the monks in Egypt, but the question of date was reopened by Kannegiesser's literary analysis – he would put the original nucleus as early as 340.[117] It has also been observed that the *homoousion* is mentioned only once, and Nicaea does not yet seem to lie at the heart of the theological polemic in these works. Rather, the argumentation in these *Orations* is grounded in the soteriology expounded in the *De Incarnatione*, though its presentation implies some development in outlook and considerable reflection on its application to Arianism. How long the interval was between those early apologetic treatises and this extended work of polemic depends on detailed critical examination of the relationship between this work and Athanasius' other

<hr>

notion of a human soul in the discussion: for example Anatolios (2004), Weinandy (2007).

115 See further Roldanus (1968); also Louth (1985). Kannengiesser (1973) makes some interesting comments on Athanasius' interest in the νοῦς (mind) rather than the soul; the νοῦς of man should be fixed on God, the νοῦς is κατ' εἰκόνα θεοῦ (according to God's image). The true image of God is the Logos; the incarnation made possible direct encounter with the image of God become Man, the 'Logos-in-body'. Cf. Kannengiesser (1972).

116 *Ep. Ad Epictetum* 6, MPG 26.1060C, cited in Theodoret of Cyrus *Eranistes*, MPG 292, Ettlinger (1975), p. 235.

117 Roldanus (1968) also dates the work as early as 339.

writings. His *Encyclical Letter to the Bishops* was written, probably in Rome, in 339. Protesting at the persecution of the true faith, he here describes the events accompanying the violent installation of Gregory at Alexandria and his own expulsion. The *Orations against the Arians* probably followed to substantiate the claim that his opponents were heretical. The fact that Asterius is attacked alongside Arius had suggested some input from Marcellus, also in exile in Rome; and Sara Parvis has been able to document detailed parallels.[118] So it would appear that Athanasius produced these *Orations* between 339 and 345, well before the spate of other, more personal, apologetic writings.

VI Self-justification, Retrospective History and Shifting Theological Alliances

After Constans forced Constantius to allow him back to Alexandria in 346, Athanasius began to assemble a number of pamphlets in defence of his own position. Many of these apologetic works take the form of dossiers of relevant documents, like letters and quotations from conciliar proceedings; this makes them most valuable for reconstructing the history of events during these troubled years, and indeed Athanasius' own biography. Yet their objective appearance is deceptive to the extent that the documents were carefully selected to support Athanasius' case, and their tendentious nature needs to be assessed in the light of other sources.[119]

A rough consensus about the dating of Athanasius' self-defensive writings has emerged. The first pamphlet would seem to be the *Apologia contra Arianos*,[120] possibly compiled in its original version to send to the bishops in council at Antioch in 349. It surveys the various charges brought against him since 328. The council's condemnation of Athanasius was overtaken by events, and for the moment he survived in Alexandria.

Next came the *De Decretis Nicaenae Synodi* in about 353;[121] this defends the Nicene formula, and gives some account of the proceedings which produced it – in fact, this is the point at which Athanasius first explicitly nailed his colours to this mast. Here is quoted Eusebius' letter to his Church in Caesarea, Athanasius' adapting those arguments for his own ends, and, as Ayres has argued, using the *homoousion* as a 'cipher' for doctrinal statements he regarded as more fundamental: his primary concern was to affirm that the Son is the Father's own, indeed from the Father's proper substance and not from 'outside'

---

118 The observation of a potential connection was made, for example, by Kannengiesser, Barnes, Vinzent et al.; Parvis (2008) provides the evidence.

119 The most detailed reconstruction of Athanasius' career has been produced by Barnes (1993). His introduction and appendices critically assess the sources. It is generally recognized now that the *Historia acephala* and the *Festal Index* prefacing the collection of *Festal Letters* are vital; texts in Martin with Albert (1985).

120 Texts of the works discussed in the following paragraphs are to be found in Opitz (1935a). See also Szymusiak (1958/87); Heil (1999). Translations will be found in *NPNF* II.4.

121 ET selections in Anatolios (2004).

(ἔξωθεν).[122] This was quickly followed by the *De Sententia Dionysii* defending the orthodoxy of a predecessor in the episcopal seat at Alexandria who had criticized the *homoousion*. In both of these works he insists on the necessity of removing material implications in the generation of the Son: the language of 'true offspring' is to be understood in ways appropriate to the divine.

In the mid-350s came the *Apologia ad Constantium imperatorem*, which seems to imply that despite everything Athanasius still hoped to come to terms with the one who was now sole emperor. This did not transpire, however, and the *Encyclical to the Bishops of Egypt and Libya* warns them of the heretics as he goes into exile in 356. This exile he spent in hiding among the monks and ascetics of Alexandria and the desert. The year 357 saw him produce the *Apologia de fuga* and the *Historia Arianorum ad monachos*; this 'fiercely polemical'[123] work is an appeal to the Egyptian monks which was intended to be privately circulated, for the reader is instructed to return the document when read.

The epistle *De Synodis Arimini et Seleuciae* he probably penned soon after the meeting in 359 of that double council, at which Constantius hoped to engineer Church unity among the 'centre' parties of both East and West, excluding the extremes represented by Eunomius and Athanasius. By now Acacius of Caesarea, the successor of Eusebius, had long stepped into his predecessor's shoes, preserving the library,[124] attacking Marcellus, and leading the core of Eastern bishops who resisted Athanasius' return and supported Constantius' search for unity. To avoid the language of *ousia* seemed to express the common faith of the people. So he proposed that the Son was like the Father according to the scriptures. In the *De Decretis* Athanasius had already implied that Acacius' position was Arian; now the *De Synodis* places Acacius and associates firmly among the 'Ariomaniacs', while recognizing that those opposed to the Homoian creed were close to the emerging pro-Nicene position. Retrospectively the years 325–60 are now seen in terms of this single struggle; yet this oversimplified picture enabled Athanasius to recognize that, despite hesitations about the actual word *homoousios*, those ready to use *ousia* language and accept everything else agreed at Nicaea were effectively his allies. Rapprochement with the homoiousians would seal his triumph and secure his legendary reputation.

Meanwhile other issues had begun to emerge. Four *Letters to Bishop Serapion*,[125] dating around 359–61, use the arguments already traced in relation to the Logos in order to establish the essential divinity of the Holy Spirit. Since our salvation depends on a relationship with God which is grounded in participation in the Spirit, the Spirit must be *homoousios* with God; he cannot be a creature. He is of the Holy Triad; he is the vital activity and gift whereby the Logos sanctifies and enlightens. It is hardly surprising that Athanasius was quick to see that the same principles applied. Explicitly these letters were occasioned by Serapion writing to Athanasius about certain persons who had given up the Arian account of the Logos, but understood the Holy Spirit in Arian terms as one of the minister-

---

122 Ayres (2004b).

123 Hanson (1988).

124 Jerome, *Vir. Ill.* 98.

125 Four *Letters to Serapion*: text, PG 26.525ff.; emended version by Lebon (1947). ET Shapland (1951), ET of selections in Anatolios (2004). See the comprehensive article by Campbell (1974).

ing spirits who differed from the angels only in degree. However, it may be significant that in the 360s we find Acacius, true to the hierarchical view of the Origenist tradition, denying the Holy Spirit's divinity, as being lower than the Logos if higher (in status though not ontology) than the angels.[126]

The Christological problem of the relation between divinity and humanity in Jesus Christ also became more explicit towards the end of Athanasius' life. The *Letters to Epictetus, Adelphius and Maximus*[127] attempt to deal with this problem. Athanasius yet more emphatically insists that the Logos must have become truly human, because it was human nature that needed saving; but his basic position remained unchanged. The Logos, being divine, could not suffer or be weak; but his body wept and suffered and died, and since it was the body of the Logos, the Logos, who was not 'outside it', could be said to be involved in the suffering of his own flesh. He admits it is a paradox that the impassible, divine Logos shared in the passion; but had he not been impassible and unchangeable his victory over the weaknesses of the flesh would not have been achieved. It is noticeable that, as ever, soteriological considerations direct Athanasius' argumentation.

As already noted, debate over Athanasius' Christology has centred on the issue of the human soul of Jesus. It seems highly unlikely that Athanasius thought of the incarnate Logos as having assumed a human soul.[128] The anti-Apollinarian literature attributed to him is certainly not genuine, and his authentic writings do not make any use of the idea. It has been argued, however, that at the end of his life Athanasius came to recognize the need to assert the presence of a human soul in the Saviour; appeal is made in particular to a phrase in the *Tomus ad Antiochenos* which Athanasius wrote on behalf of the Council of Alexandria in 362. It was apparently at this council that Athanasius first met the question, and he accepted the force of the soteriological argument that 'the salvation effected in the Word himself was a salvation not of body only, but also of soul'; therefore 'it was not possible, when the Lord became man for us, that his body should be without intelligence'.[129] If there was any way of winning Athanasius' support, appeal to soteriological principles was it. But Athanasius may not have interpreted the words οὐ σῶμα ἄψυχον οὐδ' ἀναίσθητον εἶχεν (the Saviour had 'not a body without a soul nor without sense or intelligence') as an assertion that the Saviour had a human soul; he probably envisaged a body animated and made intelligent by the presence of the Logos.[130] This would have been all his soteriology required. In fact, Athanasius never made any constructive use of the idea of Christ's human consciousness, even subsequent to this council. The Logos took a body, human flesh; the Logos remained the subject of all the incarnate experiences, triumphing over the sins and weaknesses of his humanity. The body was his temple; it was impersonal – τὸ ἀνθρώπινον; it was the instrument by which he effected the sanctification of human nature. Only because the Logos is by nature unchangeable, is the triumph over temptation and sin ensured. A fallible

---

126 Leroux (1966), pp. 82–5.
127 *Letters to Epictetus, Adelphius and Maximus*: text, PG 26.1049ff. ET in *NPNF*.
128 Richard (1947); for the opposing view, see Galtier (1955).
129 *Tomus ad Antiochenos* 7; text in PG 26.796ff.; translation in *NPNF*.
130 Kelly (1958), pp. 288f. That Apollinarius himself interpreted the *Tome* in this way is clear; see below, pp. 248–9, and Galtier (1955).

human soul, which could have explained the fears and ignorance of the human Jesus, had no place in Athanasius' view of the matter. His thought remained within the soteriological framework with which he began. Salvation, understood as revelation and re-creation, depended on the unchangeable, invincible power of the Logos assuming human nature and triumphing over its weakness and sin.

In other ways too the *Tomus ad Antiochenos* presents us with interpretative problems. To what extent did it achieve the reconciliation of anti-Arian factions, or indeed address the schism between 'Nicenes' in Antioch? Many have presented this as an ecumenical achievement: summoned on Athanasius' initiative, the Council of Alexandria in 362 produced the *Tome*, a document which took its stand simply on the Nicene Creed, refusing to get into endless controversy over vocabulary when the intention of the disputants was the same. Athanasius' success in effecting a reconciliation in the Church at this council was rewarded by his fourth exile; for the occupant of the imperial throne was Julian the Apostate, and the last thing this pagan revivalist wanted was a peaceful Church attracting new converts. So here at the end of his life, it is said, Athanasius appears as not uncompromising, except where the heart of his convictions were attacked. He was prepared to be flexible. This flexibility and moderation is then read back into the fact that Athanasius hardly uses the word *homoousios* in his *Orations against the Arians* or even his works of defence; he hesitated to over-employ this word because he knew how controversial it was and how readily it lent itself to a number of different interpretations. The *Orations* are full of intended periphrases expressing the same idea, and his reticence was probably the result of his 'fine theological tact'.[131]

But there are difficulties with this view. Athanasius' avoidance of the word *homoousios* need not reflect 'tact' towards other parties; as we have seen, he himself only gradually recognized its usefulness. Furthermore, the Antiochene schism was not healed by the *Tome*, and it is possible that the document never intended to address itself to the fundamental split in the Antiochene Church – nothing is said about Bishop Meletius, who though no Arian, led the majority Church. The Synod at Alexandria in 362 is likely to have been a local reunion of exiled bishops, without the universal character ascribed to it.[132] In any case, Julian was already trying to get rid of Athanasius before the Synod met.[133] Athanasius' flexibility may well have been overestimated, along with the extent of his authority and influence outside Egypt. To the chagrin of Basil of Caesarea, Athanasius and the West continued to support Paulinus against Meletius in Antioch, and the schism was still not healed at the Council of Constantinople in 381.

Some of the criticisms need to be taken seriously, yet in the reaction against the accepted view, the pendulum may have swung too far. There are some indications that Athanasius did have the followers of Meletius in mind when he urged reunion and tolerance;[134] and the *Tome* itself clearly indicates both that he did adopt a noncommittal attitude towards use of the word *hypostasis*, and

---

131 Kelly (1950), pp. 257ff.
132 Leroux in Kannengiesser (1974); Hanson (1988).
133 Armstrong (1921).
134 Tetz (1975).

that he did appeal to those united in spirit to sink verbal differences for the sake of peace. Athanasius' intransigence can be exaggerated as much as his saintliness; and Julian's repeated, and increasingly wrathful, letters ordering his departure from Alexandria indicate that the emperor thought he was a force to be reckoned with in the wider sphere of ecclesiastical politics.

For Further Reading

English translation

Russell, Norman, 2004. *The Doctrine of Deification in the Greek Patristic Tradition*, Oxford: Oxford University Press.
Shapland, C. R. B., 1951. *The Letters of St. Athanasius concerning the Holy Spirit*, London: Epworth.

VII Other Works

Whatever the actual situation in his lifetime, Athanasius very rapidly acquired legendary status as the one who defended Nicene orthodoxy pretty well single-handed through the years of Arian ascendency. Many dogmatic works of the period came to be attributed to him, like the twelve books *De Trinitate* and the *Athanasian Creed*, both of which originated in the West. Some anti-Apollinarian treatises bear his name, but it is now generally agreed that they are not the work of Athanasius; they differ from his authentic work in language and style, and were probably written after his death.[135] The genuine work of Athanasius, as we have indicated, had a tendency towards Apollinarianism – in fact, Apollinarian tracts were circulated in the fifth century under Athanasius' name, and some of the characteristic terminology of Cyril of Alexandria seems to have originated from these pseudonymous pamphlets, which for Cyril had the authority of his great predecessor.[136] In Athanasius' lifetime, the issues had not yet been so explicitly raised as to demand a response.

The legend of Athanasius presents him as a fine leader motivated by honesty, faith and charity. It might be nearer the truth to say that he was vehement to the point of violence, and that his 'charity' was the face of an astute politician out to achieve his own ends. There is little doubt that Athanasius had a tendency to see things in black and white; you were either for him or against him. Yet clearly Athanasius was a leader capable of inspiring deep loyalty – otherwise his legend could never have developed. As pastor and ascetic he came to enjoy the love and respect of Egypt, including the extreme ascetics of the desert. Some extant material is not primarily concerned with the controversial issues of the day, but reflects these other aspects of his activities. We may suspect underlying political motives; but taken at face value, they throw interesting light on the fundamentally Christian aims of Athanasius' life. The works on virginity and

---

135 For details of the spurious works, consult the Patrologies and the *Clavis Patrum Graecorum*.
136 See below, p. 316.

the *Life of Antony* are dealt with elsewhere.[137] Here it remains only to mention the *Festal Letters*.

As a pastor, Athanasius never neglected his episcopal duties, in so far as he was able to carry them out. Almost every year, often in the most difficult of circumstances, he followed the custom of writing to the Egyptian churches announcing the date of Easter.[138] Apart from a few fragments, all these epistles were lost until a Syriac version of thirteen Festal Letters dating from 329 to 348 turned up in a desert monastery early in the nineteenth century.[139] In these letters, Athanasius deals with pastoral problems, like the influence of evildoers or heretics, or which books are to be regarded as Holy Scripture (incidentally, the thirty-ninth letter, which deals with this question is particularly interesting, since it contains the first list of New Testament books which *exactly* corresponds with the twenty-seven later canonized); but his principal aim is to inspire his flock to keep the Christian Passover by fasting and then feasting in a spirit of true worship and purity. His letters are full of scriptural quotations,[140] traditional typology and simple piety, consistent with the lack of philosophical subtlety and the forceful argument which are the hallmarks of his writing.

Conclusion

This chapter began with the description of Athanasius as 'pivotal' in the struggle for theologically consistent articulations in the fourth century. But how was he 'pivotal'? In one sense, while never losing his commitment to what he saw to be the fundamental theological issues, he also exhibited – alongside this tenacity – a capacity to recover the balance point in confused times when key phrases, in particular *homoousios*, acquired meanings rather counter to what Athanasius would later explicate. He showed himself as loyal to Marcellus and Apollinarius as he could, but also careful to reach out to homoiousian concerns and see beyond the differences of expression in the desire to reach theological settlement. It is this capacity that makes him core to both Alexandrian and Antiochene theological traditions, and a key player in the Christological controversies of the fifth century.[141] His genius and significance can be described as pivotal not least because 'he emphasizes the generosity of Christ's work without defining its boundaries'.[142]

---

137 See below, pp. 74–8.

138 This practice no doubt derived from the victory of the Alexandrian church in the Synodal Letter appended to the Canons of Nicaea concerning the correct celebration of the date of Easter.

139 Syriac text: Cureton (1848); Lefort (1955). ET in *NPNF*. Cureton discovered a catalogue of all the letters, which has proved invaluable for reconstructing the chronology of Athanasius' life; in addition to the Syriac find, others have turned up in Coptic.

140 On Athanasius' use of scripture, see Young (1997a) and Ernest (2004): especially important is his use of scripture's overall 'scope' or 'mind' to counter piecemeal use of texts in argument, or pleas that *homoousios* is not a scriptural word, for example, in *De Decretis*.

141 Wessell (2004).

142 Stead (1992), p. 95.

But this is not to deny that he was also a controversial figure – described as 'wily, brutal and unscrupulous'.[143] If he was loyal and inspired loyalty in others, he also provoked conflict and opposition. He may well have been a highly politicized figure, could be tyrannical, and certainly if he was not personally responsible for violence, acts of cruelty were committed in his name. Yet this troublemaker was to become a saint within a generation. Less than ten years after his death, Gregory Nazianzen delivered a glowing panegyric at Constantinople.[144] He was a pillar of the Church, he cleansed the temple in imitation of Christ, with powerful actions and persuasive argument. He was to become known as the 'Father of Orthodoxy', and deserved this title not merely because of his stubborn resistance to every attack upon his person and the principles for which he stood, but also because of his careful closeness to the nuances of theological development so that the orthodox tradition owes an enormous debt to his theological writings. In the later theological controversies, he will be the one all sides seek to own; and he alone of the Eastern Fathers had an immediate, direct, and lasting influence on the West.

So Athanasius remains honoured as the victorious captain of the fight against Arius and his archetypal heresy: his pivotal significance was also because he managed to connect with the *lex orandi* – appealing to the Christian experience of salvation in Christ, to monks, bishops and lay people alike. After Athanasius, any diminution of the divinity of the Son even in technical theology would be connected with impiety and error: 'He became human that we might be deified; he revealed himself in a body so that we might perceive the Mind of the unseen Father; and he endured shame from men that we might inherit immortality.'[145]

This pivotal and core Christian insight was Athanasius' starting point, and from here he was to argue throughout his eventful life that revelation and θεοποίησις depended upon the Son sharing the essential nature of the Godhead perfectly. Arian thought and argument simply did not take account of the power of this in the Church – and so, despite 'Arianism' appearing to be near to victory in the battles by night of the first half of the fourth century, Athanasius was to win the war conclusively. The consequences of his achievement are indeed pivotal for the development of Christian theology.

For Further Reading

English translation

Anatolios, K., 2004. *Athanasius*, London: Routledge.

Studies

Anatolios, K., 1998. *Athanasius: The Coherence of his Thought*, Routledge Early Christian Monographs, London: Routledge.
Ayres, L., 2004b. 'Athanasius' Initial Defense of the term ὁμοούσιος; re-reading the *De Decretis*', *JECS* 12, pp. 337–59.

---

143 Frend (1965), p. 157.
144 Gregory Nazianzen, *Orat.* 21.
145 *DI* 54.

Gwynn, D. M., 2007. *The Eusebians: The Polemic of Athanasius of Alexandria and the Construction of the 'Arian Controversy'*, Oxford Theological Monographs, Oxford: Oxford University Press.

Pettersen, Alvyn, 1980. *Athanasius and the Human Body*, Bristol: Bristol Press.

——, 1995. *Athanasius*, London: Geoffrey Chapman.

Weinandy, T. G., 2007. *Athanasius: A Theological Introduction*, Aldershot: Ashgate.

3

Heroes of the Faith: the Literature of the Desert

Introduction

When Eusebius wrote his *Martyrs of Palestine* he entered a long-standing tradition – that of collecting *Acts* of the martyrs, transcripts of trials and biographical accounts of the heroes of the faith.[1] During Eusebius' lifetime, however, persecution ceased and martyrdom became a thing of the past. Others came to be presented as the 'athletes' of Christ, carrying on the war against the powers of evil; the monks in the deserts replaced the martyrs as the heroes and saints.[2] Most of the works to be considered in this chapter can be regarded as belonging to an established literary genre.

Yet the so-called monastic movement stimulated its own literary tradition, which itself contributed to stimulating the movement. Indeed, it has been suggested that it constituted propaganda for an emerging style of asceticism and was accompanied by the suppression of earlier forms. The first major contribution was the *Life of Antony* attributed to Athanasius. This publicized the ideals of withdrawal to the desert throughout the Christian world and, by using a literary and philosophical dress, ensured that often illiterate Copts became models of life even for the educated and sophisticated. The deserts of Egypt became the goal of pilgrims and the subject of a flourishing literature: in Greek, the *History of the Monks in Egypt* and the *Lausiac History* of Palladius; in Latin, the works of Jerome, Rufinus and John Cassian. Later the various collections of *Apophthegmata patrum* were assembled and took literary form. Meanwhile, Theodoret produced his account of the rather different asceticism of Syria, with which the *Homilies of (Pseudo-)Macarius* are probably to be associated, despite their attribution to a great hero of Egyptian monasticism.

This chapter is far from comprehensive. It does not cover the huge range of historical sources, nor does it discuss recent developments in reconstructing the history of asceticism. While there is some discussion of the extent to which the literature discussed is literary fiction, there is no attempt to unpick its distortions to establish what the real history might be,[3] and notable by its absence is any treatment of Pachomius.[4] Then there is plenty of other literature concerned

---

1 See, for example, Musurillo (1972).

2 Malone (1950).

3 See further Goehring (1999).

4 An introduction may be found in Harmless (2004); see Rousseau (1999) for fuller treatment.

with virginity, or with regularizing monastic life, or celebrating saints' lives: some of this will be noticed elsewhere – for example, Basil's *Rules* in the chapter on the Cappadocians. The Greek material discussed here is but the tip of a large iceberg of other sources, some extant in other ancient languages, much lost. This chapter will introduce the most influential Greek accounts of the fourth-century movement in Egypt and Syria, and explore the writings of three characters associated with the ascetic movement: Didymus the Blind, Evagrius Ponticus and 'Macarius'.

For Further Reading

Brown, Peter, 1988. *The Body and Society: Men, Women and Sexual Renunciation in Early Christianity*, London/Boston: Faber & Faber.

Elm, Susanna, 1994. *'Virgins of God': The Making of Asceticism in Late Antiquity*, Oxford: Clarendon Press.

Goehring, James E., 1999. *Ascetics, Society and the Desert: Studies in Egyptian Monasticism*, Harrisburg, PA: Trinity Press International.

Harmless, William, SJ, 2004. *Desert Christians: An Introduction to the Literature of Early Monasticism*, New York: Oxford University Press.

Rousseau, Philip, 1978. *Ascetics, Authority and the Church in the age of Jerome and Cassian*, Oxford: Oxford University Press.

I Athanasius and the Life of Antony

Virginity and asceticism had deep roots in the Christian tradition.[5] Christian sexual abstinence was already remarked on by Galen,[6] and long before the time of Athanasius dedicated virgin women were a feature of Church life. Preserved in Coptic is his first *Letter to Virgins*, in Syriac his second *Letter to Virgins*, while his *De Virginitate* is preserved in Syriac and Armenian. The authenticity of these texts is disputed, but it has been defended by Brakke,[7] who has not only offered an English translation, but has also built up a picture of how Athanasius sought to regulate the practice and integrate dedicated virgins within the life of the Church. It is clear that men too could follow 'a more rigorous regime of fasting, prayer and vigils than other Christians',[8] while continuing to live near villages or in the city and worshipping at the local church; one practice Athanasius was concerned about was men and women setting up house together as ascetics, a

---

5 See Brown (1988).

6 Brown (1988), p. 3.

7 Brakke (1995). See also Elm (1994). Elm places the works on virginity after 350; Brakke, however, places them in the early part of Athanasius' life, and suggests a change of focus around 350 to the desert monks. Either way, it seems clear that Athanasius both sought to regulate and forged an alliance with ascetics of all types so as to minimize the influence of Melitians and Arians.

8 Brakke (1995), p. 9.

practice which appears as widespread and suppressed in many different locations during the fourth century.[9]

Asceticism was not therefore a new phenomenon, but in the time of Athanasius new types of ascetic life began to emerge in Egypt. The focus on Antony as the first monk might be specified more accurately in terms of being the first to withdraw into the great desert – for he himself began by learning from a local 'solitary'; but even this may exaggerate his innovatory character, for others were doing similar things around the same time if not earlier.[10] It is noticeable that of the five periods of exile Athanasius suffered, the last three (in the 350s and 360s) were all spent in Egypt, hidden among the monks. His alliance with the ascetics was politically astute, and cemented by the publication of the *Life of Antony* in c.357, assuming that he wrote it.

The spread of the monastic ideal owed much to this work. Two Latin translations appeared almost immediately, and we also know of Syriac, Armenian and Arabic versions. Its widespread influence is attested by many – Gregory of Nazianzus, for example, Jerome and John Chrysostom; it was a factor in Augustine's conversion.[11] In the immediate future, it would seem, Athanasius' reputation rested on his contribution to monastic literature, as much as his defence of Nicene orthodoxy. Yet his authorship of this work is contested.[12] There are intriguing differences between the Syriac and the Greek,[13] which suggest there may have been a Coptic original; and there are some grounds for thinking that the one who reworked the Coptic *Life* in Greek, as 'an Alexandrian refurbishment more attuned to the spiritual yearnings of an urban Mediterranean culture', was not Athanasius.[14] The discussion following this challenge[15] has clarified the profound ways in which the *Life of Antony*, for all its difference from other words of Athanasius, nevertheless can be seen as presenting a figure who is the embodiment of Athanasius' theology, an 'icon' of deification.[16] The desert life re-creates a miniature Eden, and in Antony divine passionlessness (ἀπάθεια – *apatheia*) is made visible.[17]

The *Life of Antony*[18] has been plausibly attributed to the period in Athanasius' life when he was in exile soon after Antony's death in 356.[19] It has been suggested that one of its purposes was to foster Athanasius' good relations with the monks of Egypt, and, like the *Historia Arianorum ad monachos*, it was intended

9 Elm (1994).
10 Harmless (2004), pp. 418–23.
11 Gregory Nazianzen, *Orat.* 21.5; Jerome, *Vir.* 87; Chrysostom, *Hom. in Matt.* 8.5; Augustine, *Confessions* 8.16.
12 For a summary discussion, see Harmless (2004), pp. 111–13.
13 Draguet (1980).
14 Barnes (1986).
15 Tetz (1983); Louth (1988); Lorenz (1989); Brakke (1994).
16 Harmless (2004), p. 90.
17 Harmless (2004), pp. 92–3.
18 *Vita Antonii*: text in Bartelink (1994); ET Meyer (1950); Gregg (1980).
19 The date is discussed in Barnard (1974); see the reply by Blennan (1976). The following remarks are derived from this exchange. For the question of historicity, see Dörries (1966); Rubenson (1990) and note 22 below.

for private circulation. Internal evidence,[20] however, together with a remark by Evagrius that the work was written for 'foreign brothers', may indicate that it was destined for a readership overseas, possibly monks who wished to vie with the Egyptians; so perhaps the recipients were to be the contacts Athanasius had made during his exiles in the West. According to the Prologue, Athanasius had been personally acquainted with Antony, had seen him many times and even acted as his attendant; but these personal contacts are almost certainly exaggerated.[21] The *Life* is an idealized picture intended as a pattern of discipline, a curious blend of traditional and legendary material with philosophical and ecclesiastical ideals.[22] Miraculous cures, exorcisms, supernatural visions and graphically depicted battles with the devil give a predominantly mythological flavour; but the author is at pains to state that Antony never had dealings with Melitians, Manichaeans or Arians, that he observed the rule of the Church and submitted to the clergy,[23] that he strove for virtue and *apatheia* (freedom from passion) – for likeness to the divine.[24] The work seems to have been modelled on some literary 'Life', like that of Plotinus or Apollonius, and according to literary convention long discourses, to monks, to pagans, punctuate the work; yet Antony's lack of culture and illiteracy is also stressed, so as to highlight his remarkable wisdom; he was θεοδίδακτος (taught by God).[25] The work was to have an appeal to educated and non-educated alike, to the extremes of those attracted to monasticism, the illiterate Copts and the philosophically inclined.

It has been claimed that the *Vita Antonii* reflects a different theology and a different asceticism from Athanasius' other works. Up to a point this is undoubtedly true; the work has a very different tone. The predominance of the devil and the demons is the most obvious example; they hardly appear elsewhere in Athanasius' writings. But this contrast can be exaggerated. The *De incarnatione* celebrates Christ's victory over the powers of death and sin rather than the devil; but the devil appears in the Long Recension, and the theme is

---

20 The Preface suggests that the addressees are vying with the monks in Egypt; *VA* 93 refers to Antony's fame reaching Spain, Gaul, Rome and Africa. See Brakke (1995), p. 262, footnote.

21 Brakke (1995), pp. 205ff.

22 How much of this picture of Antony is historical has been addressed by Rubenson (1990). He argues for the authenticity of some letters attributed to Antony, and then uses the evidence to assess both Athanasius' *Life* and the sayings attributed to Antony in the *Apophthegmata*. The conclusion would seem to support the characterization of the *Life* as an idealized picture, with some misleading and inconsistent features (such as Antony's illiteracy and lack of knowledge of Greek), but nevertheless 'much of the philosophical and theological background that is presupposed in the presentation of the hero of the *Vita* is shared by the author of the letters', even though 'there are important differences, which reveal a tendency in the *Vita* that is alien to the letters' (p. 140). See also Frazier (1998) for an analysis of the literary structure of parts of the text.

23 *VA* 67–9, 82, 91.

24 *VA* 14, 20f., 67, 74.

25 *VA* 72. The survival of the letters (note 22 above), assuming their authenticity (which is disputed), may bring into doubt his illiteracy; see Harmless (2004), pp. 78–81 for discussion and bibliography.

one of victory.[26] For the Antony of the *Life*, too, the theme is victory over the powers of evil. Christ has cut the sinews of the devils; their power is destroyed since Christ overcame death, dispelled ignorance and freed humankind from idolatry, magic and astrology. To display one's belief in this by brandishing the weapon of prayer and uplifting the sign of the cross disarms them completely. With these weapons, the devils' own territory, the tombs and the desert, can be invaded with success. In the accounts of visions, miracles and temptations, we are given a lively picture of the victorious Christ working through Antony to overcome evil and confuse the worldly wise. Victory is attributed to God; Antony, the ideal ascetic, is the instrument of God's saving activity: 'This was Antony's first triumph over the devil – or rather the first triumph of the Saviour in Antony.'[27] The power of the divine Logos is displayed as effecting salvation through victory over human sin and mortality. Antony becomes the instrument of the Logos, as the humanity of Christ had been the Logos' instrument in the incarnation. The ascetic is represented, not as retiring into solitariness simply for the salvation of his own soul, but as marching into the desert to engage the devils in battle, and so make a positive contribution to the salvation of the world by participating in the Logos' saving work. Philosophical ideals of striving for mastery over the passions, the subjection of the physical to the spiritual, the achievement of likeness to the divine – these ideals, along with the psychological struggles of the ascetics which will become familiar in the later compendia of desert experiences, are assimilated to the Christian ideal of θεοποίησις (*theopoiēsis*)[28] which was so important to Athanasius' soteriology.

The issue of authenticity, then, may not easily be put to rest; but that takes nothing away from the significance of this work for the early monastic movement. Here we find themes that keep recurring in the later material: the restoration of the Garden of Eden in the desert; the focus on moral reformation rather than intellectual contemplation; on mastery of the body and its desires so as to receive that incorruption of the body made possible by the incarnation of the Logos; on taking up the triumphant cross daily in the on-going struggle with the powers of evil.

For Further Reading

English translations

Gregg, R. C. (trans.), 1980. *The Life of Antony and the Letter to Marcellinus*, CWS, New York: Paulist Press.
Meyer, R. T., 1950. *The Life of Antony*, ACW 10, Westminster, MD: Newman Press.

Studies

Brakke, David, 1995. *Athanasius and Asceticism*, Baltimore/London: Johns Hopkins University Press.

---

26 For further discussion of the links between the *VA* and *CG–DI*, see Brakke (1995), pp. 218–26; and, for parallels with Athanasius' theology in general, Harmless (2004), pp. 85ff.
27 *VA* 7; cf. 22–8, 38, 78, 84.
28 *VA* 14, 74.

Louth, Andrew, 1988. 'St Athanasius and the Greek *Life of Antony*', *JTS* NS 39, pp. 504–9.

Rubenson, S., 1990. *The Letters of St. Antony: Origenist Theology, Monastic Tradition and the Making of a Saint*, Bibliotheca Historico-Ecclesiastica Lundensis 24, Lund: Lund University Press.

II The Histories: the *Lausiac History* and *Historia monachorum*

Two rather similar accounts of the early monks in Egypt achieved great popularity in the Middle Ages, that of Rufinus and the *Lausiac History* of Palladius. Modern researches have revealed that both of these works have a very complicated textual history. A Greek text which corresponds to the bulk of Rufinus' Latin work is now recognized as original and known as the *Historia monachorum in Aegypto*.[29] The authorship of this work is a matter of much speculation; the only known fact is that it was by a monk connected with Rufinus' community on the Mount of Olives. This could explain Rufinus' use of the material in his Latin account. The Greek original, which was probably written about the year 400, describes a visit to the great monastic centres of Egypt made by a party of seven pilgrims in 394–5. The work is very similar in content to that of Palladius – indeed at points they report the same anecdotes – but this work is arranged in the form of a travelogue, describing one after another the ascetic centres passed on a journey northwards along the Nile, thus giving a striking picture of the surge of monastic life in Egypt at this time.[30]

The *Lausiac History* purports to be autobiographical, and to describe what Palladius learned of the ascetic movement from his own visit to the great centres of Egypt. What he describes belongs almost exactly to the same period, that is the 390s, though his work was written some years later, round about 420. In the case of this work too, critical problems have beset the investigator. The textual confusion is the first difficulty. The work was so popular that it exists in many different versions: Latin, Syriac, Armenian, Coptic, Ethiopic, Arabic and Old Sogdian. Besides this, the Greek manuscripts contain a number of different redactions: material was inserted, rearranged and rewritten at will. Credit for sorting all this out went to Dom Cuthbert Butler,[31] who showed that of the two basic text-types, the longer recension was a combination of Palladius' *Lausiac History* with the *Historia monachorum*, whereas the shorter version represents the original. Controversy has pursued his work, however, particularly since R. Draguet insisted that he gave too little attention to an important manuscript in Oxford.[32] However, for practical purposes, Butler's text has provided

29 *Historia Monachorum*: text Festugière (1961/71); earlier edition in Preuschen (1897). Preuschen argued for Rufinus' priority; but see Festugière (1955). A French translation of the *Historia Monachorum* will be found in Festugière (1965). An English translation is by Russell (1981). For complex questions about the manuscript tradition, see Bammel (1996).

30 For the phenomenon of pilgrimage to visit 'living saints', see Frank (2000).

31 Butler (1904); for an English translation, see Meyer (1965).

32 Draguet (1949, 1950). Chitty (1955) defended Butler; Draguet (1955) replied.

a reasonably reliable working base. A further development, however, has been the acceptance of the authenticity of material in the longer Coptic version; it seems likely that, for the *Lausiac History*, Palladius abbreviated *Lives*, of Pambo, Evagrius, Macarius the Egyptian and Macarius the Alexandrian, which he had written earlier in a fuller form.[33]

The second difficulty is the relationship between this material and other parallel texts. Did Palladius make use of the *Historia monachorum*? Did Sozomen use these two works as sources for the monastic chapters of his history, or did all three use a common source? It looks as though the *Historia monachorum* and Palladius are independent witnesses which largely confirm each other; and that Sozomen did use both these texts as sources (Socrates after all knew and referred to Palladius' work).[34]

However, the continuing discussion of these questions is related to the third difficulty, namely the question of historical reliability. The nineteenth-century rationalist tendency to dismiss all material containing miraculous elements gave way to attacks of a literary-critical kind. Discussion has focused on three areas: the question of the autobiographical framework, the picture of Pachomius' foundations at Tabennesi and the account of John of Lycopolis. The basic charge made is that Palladius' material was drawn from earlier written sources and then artificially strung together by the provision of a fictitious autobiographical framework. Bousset argued this thesis,[35] finding confirmation of his view in Nau's *Histoire de S. Pachome*, which made available some hitherto unpublished Greek material together with a translation of a Syriac version: the chapters in the *Lausiac History* were clearly dependent on this material. Then Peeters[36] discovered that a Coptic *Life of John of Lycopolis* had used both the *Historia monachorum* and the *Lausiac History* as sources and, when they contradicted each other, preferred the former; this preference, Peeters argued, was based on local knowledge, and he proceeded to show that most of Palladius' narrative is exactly what one would expect if he were 'writing up' an imaginary visit to the famous hermit. Furthermore, the supposed date of Palladius' visit cannot be integrated with the autobiographical material offered in Palladius' book. In fact, the difficulty of reconstructing a chronologically coherent account of Palladius' movements gives plausibility to the charges advanced, quite apart from the fact that considerable evidence has been produced which seems to indicate that some parts of the work are based on literary sources rather than being the reminiscences of an eyewitness.[37]

However, the case for Palladius' trustworthiness has not gone by default. Halkin,[38] who collected together and edited all the Greek lives of Pachomius, argued that the dependence claimed by Bousset went the other way: Palladius was the original. Others have shown important weaknesses in Peeters'

---

33 For an introduction and bibliography, see Harmless (2004), pp. 303, 305–8.

34 Socrates, *HE* iv.23.

35 It was suggested first by Reitzenstein, and pursued by Bousset (1917, 1922); Nau's material had appeared in 1908.

36 Peeters (1936). His arguments are summarized in English by Telfer (1937).

37 Draguet (1944, 1945, 1947b).

38 Halkin (1930). For his work on the Greek lives, see Halkin (1929); and his edition of the text (1932).

arguments.[39] Derwas Chitty, the author of the classic book on Egyptian and Palestinian monasticism, *The Desert a City*, is not alone in regarding Palladius as a more sober and reliable source than the *Historia monachorum*, whose author appears extremely gullible.[40] Harmless[41] contrasts these works in the following terms:

> Both authors are portrait painters, similar in frame but different in accent. Palladius is a miniaturist with a taste for morality plays, while the anonymous author of the *History of the Monks* is an iconographer with a taste for magical realism.

Partial use of sources should certainly not undermine all Palladius' claims, nor should overall estimates of the work be based on problematic details. A case in point is the tale of Potamiaena. Her martyrdom is described by Eusebius,[42] who dates it to the persecution in 202–03; Palladius puts it in the time of Diocletian's co-emperor, Maximian, that is, about a hundred years later. But granted the discrepancy, the fact that Palladius tells the story at all is a point of some interest. Potamiaena was not one of his edifying ascetics, and so does not really fit into his work; yet Palladius devoted a section to recounting the tale. He told the story because he had heard it from Isidore, who had heard it from Antony – in other words, he passed it on as one of the good stories circulating orally in the desert community. This is perhaps a clue to the character of the book. What Palladius provides is a somewhat haphazard collection of tales, based partly on hearsay, partly on sources, partly on his own experience. It reflects the traditions and legends floating around the monastic communities to which he himself belonged for a dozen or so years. Prophecy, miracles and extraordinary ascetic feats were the stuff of the tradition, part of the atmosphere built into that particular outlook and style of life. The prevalence of marvellous stories is no reason for doubting Palladius' good faith, since it faithfully reflects the attitude of mind which he shared with his readers: 'armchair pilgrims' looked for the evocation of an exotic world.[43] And the structure of the book may not be so haphazard after all; for Buck[44] has shown that it is best understood as autobiographical, each item being placed according to the context in which Palladius received the information. To treat the book thus can help to resolve some of the chronological puzzles. So, making some allowance for a tendency to exaggeration and idealization, there seems little reason to dispute eyewitness statements and descriptions given by Palladius himself; and even the chronological haziness may be best attributed to the inconsistencies of an old man's memory, retracing events of thirty or forty years earlier.

---

39 For example, Buck (1976).
40 Chitty (1966), pp. 51f.
41 Harmless (2004), p. 299.
42 Eusebius, *HE* vi.5.
43 Frank (2000) brings out features of both the *Historia Monachorum* and Palladius' *Historia* that indicate that they are meant to evoke another world which is distant and exotic: these include the travelogue motif and the miraculous.
44 Buck (1976).

So it seems most likely that Palladius was a contemporary observer of much that he describes, and that his work must be regarded as an important source for the study of the early monastic movement, its ideals and its mentality. It is not a work of ascetic theory, nor a defence of monasticism against its critics, but a collection of anecdotes, 'memorable, even entertaining', intended to edify the reader: 'Discipline of the body is really a way to discipline the spirit'.[45] The failures and weaknesses of some are not concealed behind the achievements of the greatest; for it all provides useful material for example or warning. As a manual of spiritual edification, the work drew its authority from the fact that its author spoke of his own encounters with the holy men[46] – but not just men: he promises to write of the 'deeds of the Fathers, male and female', and devotes a whole chapter to 'manly women . . . to whom God granted the capacity to fight struggles equal to those of men'.[47]

What was it that Palladius admired in these ascetics? Theoretically he was primarily interested in the suppression of passion; but he was also quick to criticize spiritual pride: 'Drinking wine within reason is better by far than drinking water in arrogance.' Questions of diet are a constant preoccupation; but his heroes are also remarkably well versed in the scriptures, and live a life of quiet industry and prayer. There are tales of tempting demons and ministering angels, of miraculous cures and prophecies fulfilled. But the dominating note is the conquest of bodily weakness. His heroes try to deny the need for sleep and undergo in the open the fierce midday sun and the cold air of midnight. They are preoccupied with suppressing sexual passions: near the time of his death, Evagrius said: 'This is the third year that I have not been tormented by carnal desires'; reporting this, Palladius offers the comment, 'this, after a life of such toil and labours and continual prayer'. Yet some of the strangest stories betray a genuine awareness of the spiritual aim of physical mortification:

Early one morning when [Macarius] was sitting in his cell, a gnat stung him on the foot. Feeling the pain, he killed it with his hands and it was gorged with his blood. *He accused himself of acting out of revenge*, and he condemned himself to sit naked in the marsh of Scete out in the great desert for a period of six months. Here the mosquitoes lacerate even the hides of the wild swine just as wasps do. Soon he was bitten all over his body, and he became so swollen that some thought he had elephantiasis. When he returned to his cell after six months he was recognized as Macarius only by his voice.[48]

Palladius' aim was to convince the imperial chamberlain, Lausus, to whom the work is dedicated (hence *Lausiac History*), that it is possible to rise above physical needs and self-regard. That is why he responded to his request that he should record the stories of the Fathers, those he had seen and others he had heard about, through his own life and travels in the great monastic centres.[49]

---

45 Harmless (2004), p. 287.
46 Hunt (1973).
47 Elm (1994), especially chapter 10 – 'All experiments included women'.
48 The translations in this paragraph mostly follow Meyer (1965); quotations are from the prologue and chapters 38 and 18.
49 On the *Lausiac History*, see further Molinier (1995).

What information can we glean about the author of this work? Some details of his life remain in dispute. When did he spend three years in Jerusalem? Did he make a journey to the borders of India? How did he visit John of Lycopolis and return to Asia Minor in time to be consecrated bishop of Helenopolis within a space of six to twelve months? However, for all the difficulties, it is possible to reconstruct a fairly clear picture from his writings.

Palladius was a Galatian, born in the early 360s. He went to Egypt, after some time in Jerusalem, in order to see the saints for himself, beginning in 388 in Alexandria, where he met Didymus the Blind four times over ten years. He approached Isidore, an old man of seventy who had accompanied Athanasius to Rome fifty years before. Isidore refused to take on the training of Palladius, and passed him on to Dorotheus, a solitary who had lived for sixty years in a cave five miles from the city. After three years, Palladius had to abandon his apprenticeship there owing to a breakdown in health; he describes Dorotheus' life as squalid and harsh – perhaps as an excuse for his failure, but one suspects that he did not feel a great respect for extreme asceticism. When he enquired why Dorotheus subjected his body to such extreme tests, he received the reply, 'It kills me, I will kill it.' Undeterred, however, Palladius went on to visit the mountain of Nitria, close to 'the great desert which stretches as far as Ethiopia and the Mazicae and Mauretania'. Here there were some 5,000 anchorites. After a year with the most notorious of these, he passed on to the innermost desert and to Cellia, where he attached himself to Evagrius Ponticus for nine years. Evagrius, as we shall see, was the writer of many ascetical treatises which had a profound influence on Eastern devotion and spirituality; Palladius' work is permeated with Evagrius' teaching, though it is expressed in his assumptions and vocabulary, in his descriptions of the monks' lifestyle, rather than in theoretical exposition.[50]

The rest of Palladius' career arose from his involvement with the Origenist party.[51] After further travels in Egypt (he claims that he visited the Pachomian monasteries and that John of Lycopolis prophesied his future involvement in ecclesiastical politics – but these are sections where his dependence on sources has been canvassed), he left for Palestine – on medical advice, he states, but it was just about the time when Egypt became too hot for known Origenists. In Palestine, he was in close contact with the Origenists based on the Mount of Olives – Rufinus and Melania. He went to Constantinople and was consecrated bishop of Helenopolis by John Chrysostom. Thus he became embroiled in the controversy over John's behaviour, was himself charged with Origenism at the Synod of the Oak in 403, and even travelled to Rome in his efforts to plead the cause of 'the blessed John'. In exile, he composed a Platonic dialogue, the *Dialogus de vita sancti Joannis Chrysostomi*, a work to which further reference will be made in Chapter 5. He spent his exile in Egypt, so again had ample chance to glean information from the famous monastic centres. The *Lausiac History* was written around 420 after he had returned to Asia Minor, a move made possible by the rehabilitation of John's memory. According to Socrates,[52] Palladius

---

50 Draguet (1946, 1947a). Also Meyer (1970).

51 Hunt (1973) studies this relationship in detail. For further material on the Origenist controversy, see Chapter 5 below.

52 Socrates, *HE* vii.36.

became bishop of Aspouna, and he tells us himself that when he composed the *Lausiac History* he had been a monk for thirty-three years, a bishop for twenty, and he was fifty-six years old. The date of his death is unknown.

There is another work attributed to Palladius, the *De gentibus Indiae et Brag-manibus*. Its authenticity was defended by Coleman-Norton,[53] and in the 1960s the appearance of new editions of the text indicated resurgent interest in the work.[54] The author claims to have travelled to the borders of India, a journey which does not fit into any other information we have about our Palladius, but it cannot be decisively ruled out, especially as there are stylistic connections. The actual information about India is in fact all second-hand; the author got it from another traveller, a Theban called Scholasticus, and rounds off with a commentary on Arrian's *Anabasis*. An interest in the ascetic practices of the Brahmins is not out of character with what we know of Palladius from the *Lausiac History*.

For Further Reading

English translations

Meyer, R. T., 1965. *Palladius: The Lausiac History* (ACW 34), New York: Newman Press.

Russell, Norman, 1981. *The Lives of the Desert Fathers: The 'Historia monachorum in Aegypto'*, CS 34, Kalamazoo, MI: Cistercian Publications.

Studies

Frank, Georgia, 2000. *The Memory of the Eyes: Pilgrims to the Living Saints in Christian Late Antiquity*, Berkeley: University of California Press.

Hunt, E. D., 1973. 'Palladius of Helenopolis: A Party and its Supporters in the Church of the late Fourth Century', *JTS* NS 24, pp. 456–80.

Meyer, R. T., 1970. 'Palladius and Early Christian Spirituality', *SP* 10, pp. 379–90.

III The *Apophthegmata Patrum*

The *Lausiac History* and the *Historia monachorum* are literary works, similar to Athanasius' *Life of Antony* in that they were written by cultured Greek visitors; less overlaid with philosophical goals perhaps, they nevertheless reflect the interests and style of their authors – not to mention their propensity for gossip and idealization. The same sort of thing could be said of the Latin literature of Rufinus, Jerome and Cassian: all had visited the desert and experienced it at first hand, yet all were to some extent outside admirers. Some of the famous ascetics were themselves Greek-speaking immigrants and scholars, like Evagrius Ponticus and Arsenius, but many were uneducated Copts who knew no Greek and were often illiterate. The stylized material of the *Apophthegmata patrum* enables us to some extent to lift the curtain of polish and culture and take a

---

53 Coleman-Norton (1926).
54 Editions: Derrett (1960); Berghoff (1967).

peep at the oral traditions. The collections are admittedly later in date, and the critical questions surrounding them are desperately complex; yet here can be traced something like the sources that must have provided Palladius and others with a good deal of their material. Although some of Palladius' heroes were figures of obscurity, many were the leaders of early monasticism, like Amoun and Pachomius, or characters so famous that their sayings were handed down and can be found in the *Apophthegmata*, people like Pambo, Macarius the Great and Macarius the Alexandrian, Moses the Ethiopian and Paul the Simple. For the most part, the *Apophthegmata* complement Palladius' information, rather than overlapping it; and the larger collections of anecdotes and sayings tend to come from the great figures of the next generation.

1 Origins, critical questions, historicity

One-seventh of the Alphabetic collection is attributed to Poemen, one such second-generation figure; even though it is possible that more than one Poemen has been confused, it is plausible that Poemen's associates, the generation which retreated from the old centre at Scetis after barbarian devastation (407–8), were responsible for the nucleus of the collections.[55] On the other hand, parts of the Alphabetic collection seem dependent on a small collection made by Abba Isaias at Gaza in the mid-fifth century; this survives in Syriac and begins: 'My brethren, what I saw and heard with the Old Men, these things I relate to you, taking away nothing and adding nothing.' The anecdotes are then related as told to Isaias. Isaias also originated from Scetis, and this may be a more reliable clue to the origins of the written collections.[56] It is now generally accepted that the written collections originated in Palestine, though the material is almost entirely concerned with the monastic communities of Lower Egypt from the early fourth to the mid-fifth century.[57]

However, the immensity of the problems confronting the investigator must not be minimized. The variety of texts, collections and versions makes the field a highly complicated one in which conclusions are inevitably tentative. The nature of the literature is such that precise dating is impossible. Edifying sayings and anecdotes were added or rearranged, attributed to different Fathers, expanded or given a new context. Each monastery may have had its own *Gerontikon* or *Paterikon*, with which collections from elsewhere might be integrated. Oral and written material seems to have coexisted, and each affected the other. Much of the material exists still only in manuscripts in a range of languages, and critical texts are lacking even for much of the published material. Most of the material is now accessible through the French translations published by the monks of Solesmes; but in some cases the original text which they translated remains unpublished.[58]

55 Bousset (1923), §19.

56 Chitty (1971, 1974). He had already dropped hints in his book (1966), pp. 74 and 80 n. 117, and found confirmation when the Syriac was published by Draguet (1968). Translation: Draguet (1970).

57 Regnault (1987); accepted by Gould (1993a) and Harmless (2004).

58 Regnault et al. (1966, 1970, 1976, 1981, 1985, 1992).

Generally speaking, the collections can be classified into two main types – the Alphabetic and the Systematic – according to the pattern adopted for arranging the individual pericopae. The Latin version, a translation made in the mid-sixth century by Pelagius the deacon and John the subdeacon, is the best known example of the topical or systematic arrangement, whereby the material is classified under headings of the twenty or so monastic virtues: 'of quiet', 'of patience', 'that a monk might not possess anything', 'that nothing ought to be done for show', 'of humility' and so on.[59] A number of Greek manuscripts have the same arrangement, and the publication of the Greek version has been started.[60] The best known Greek text, however, belongs to the other main type in which the arrangement is made alphabetically, according to the name of the particular ascetic of which the anecdote is told, or the saying reported.[61] Anonymous logia do not appear at the end of the text as promised in the Preface, but the deficiency was partially made up by the publication of some material from the Codex Coislinianus 126.[62] Subsequently Guy has published the remainder, and examined other material of the Alphabetic-Anonymous type found in manuscripts which are probably to be regarded as superior and more complete.[63] Within the two basic types of collection, there are considerable variations in content and order; and the situation is further complicated by the existence of other Latin collections as well as Syriac, Coptic, Armenian and Ethiopic collections.

The first survey of this material was that of Bousset.[64] He concluded that the Alphabetic collection dated from around AD 530, though it is clearly based on an earlier less systematic collection dating probably from the second half of the fifth century. The topically arranged collection was in turn dependent on the *Alphabeticon*. However, these conclusions were based on the published texts alone, and they have been questioned by the studies of J.-C. Guy, who suggested on the basis of the evidence of the Greek manuscripts, that the relationship is more complex, the two types deriving independently from earlier less systematic collections. Within each type, a history of development, of scribal additions and rearrangements can be traced. Guy based this study on the Greek evidence only, and Derwas Chitty doubted his conclusions:[65] the Latin version is based on an earlier stage in the development than any of the Greek manuscripts, and this, he believes, is demonstrably dependent on the *Alphabeticon*. The critical questions remain far from being resolved. Rubenson argued that the two types of collection evolved independently, and subsequently influenced each other, but his conclusions have not been entirely convincing.[66] Whether or not

59 The work is known as the *Verba Seniorum*; text in PL 73.851–988, translation in Waddell (1936) (selections only). (Quotations from the *Verba Seniorum* are normally from this translation, though I have made occasional modifications.)
60 Guy (1993) publishes the text of books 1—9 with French translation; 10—21 remains unpublished. Regnault (1992) translates the complete text.
61 *Alphabeticon*: text in Guy (1968). Guy (1962) provides some supplementary material. Translation: Ward (1975a). (Quotations from the *Alphabeticon* are from this translation.)
62 Codex Coislinianus ed. Nau (1907-9 and 1912-13). Translation: Ward (1975b).
63 Guy (1962); complete translation Regnault (1985).
64 Bousset (1923).
65 Chitty (1974).
66 Rubenson (1990); cf. Gould (1993b).

further investigation will call in question the other generally accepted conclusion, namely that the written collections in Greek antedate the various versions extant in Coptic, remains to be seen.

In spite of the problems, can anything be said about the authenticity of the material? Basically what we have are anthologies of wise sayings or 'oracles' from the most famous Egyptian solitaries, and anecdotes concerning their amazing feats. As in the case of Palladius, the rationalist dismissal of this material as totally legendary met with a reaction in the twentieth century, and many have stressed the value of the material as a source for understanding the spirit and history of the monastic communities, even if some scepticism remained about the specific historicity of individual pericopae given their occasional attribution to different figures in different versions. Methods of comparative assessment or 'form criticism' developed, J.-C. Guy[67] proposing an analysis into (i) primary material consisting of charismatic or prophetic words of the spirit-filled 'abba' for a specific occasion; (ii) secondary, literary apophthegms of more general application; and (iii) edifying episodes, miracle-stories and biographical anecdotes which became associated with the sayings-collections. Guy regarded it as highly likely that the processes of oral transmission and written collection coexisted over a long period of time, each developing and being adapted to the needs of the communities, and each affecting the other. Something of this process can still be seen at work in the textual transmission of the material as available to us, modifications and additions being clearly in evidence.

Guy tended to literary analysis, and to scepticism about origins. Latterly, Regnault, followed by Gould,[68] stressed the oral nature of the material, and the probability that recollections were accurately passed on. The material itself points to the continuities in the tradition and, appealing to the fact that most of it comes from a geographic space and a time period which are fairly narrowly defined, Gould argued for a greater confidence in the historical reliability of such an oral tradition. The coherence of the collections, he suggests, is found in their focus on the origins and development of a community 'conscious of its own identity'.[69] He shows how the founders, the subsequent generation and the *diaspora* are interconnected in the traditions and recorded stories, while there is little interest in the Church outside the monastic community, or indeed in other monastic communities such as that of Pachomius. The fundamental relationships in the community are of teacher and disciple, and some sayings actually speak of one 'Father' saying that he heard another 'Father' say the word he is now passing on to the next generation. Some sayings suggest falling standards in the third generation compared with the 'Fathers'. Such examples show a consciousness 'of the links which bound their monastic community to its past history'.

---

67 Guy (1955).
68 Regnault (1987); Gould (1993a).
69 Gould (1993a), p. 14.

2 The world of the *Apophthegmata*

The *Apophthegmata* originated in an unliterary, indeed occasionally anti-literary, milieu, a milieu in which books, writing and dogma took second place to attitudes and way of life. Whatever the authenticity of the individual pericopae, the contents give a graphic, impressionist picture of life in the Egyptian deserts, the excesses and graces of the heroes of the faith. It is instructive to remember how influential was this literature in shaping the ideals of Christian piety for many centuries. Inevitably some anecdotes strike the modern reader as bizarre, and the obsession with sexual temptations now seems psychologically inevitable in the situation to which they subjected themselves; yet there are also pearls of perennial wisdom and scenes with a delightfully natural and human touch. A brother goes away from the community hoping to overcome his anger if there is no one around to arouse him; his jug of water falls over three times, and in a great rage he breaks it. Back he goes to the community having learned the need for struggle, patience and, above all, help from God, in *all* places.[70]

Most of the vivid pictures lose their effect when reduced to bald summaries. To read the texts themselves is to come away with a moving impression of the patience and gentleness, the wisdom and humility, the hospitality and sincerity of the characters depicted. By and large the stories show people expressing their faith in humility, chastity and the struggle against demonic temptations, a struggle which they knew they experienced directly, even if now we might attribute it to over-heated imaginations. On the whole, extremes of asceticism gave way to moderation and common sense: 'we have not been taught to kill our bodies, but to kill our passions', said Abba Poemen to Abba Isaac.[71] And some of the demand for patience arose from very human situations:

> Another day when a council was being held in Scetis, the fathers treated Moses (the Ethiopian) with contempt in order to test him, saying, 'Why does this black man come among us?' When he heard this he kept silence. When the council was dismissed, they said to him, 'Abba, did that not grieve you at all?' He said to them, 'I was grieved, but I kept silence.'[72]

Such incidents of racism may not always have been contrived as a test.

A superficial estimate of the anchorite's ideal might suggest that his outlook was self-centred – a search for personal salvation ignoring the welfare of society. Typical is the saying of Antony:

> Who sits in solitude and is quiet has escaped three wars: hearing, speaking, seeing; yet against one thing shall he continually battle: that is, his own heart.[73]

But there is also the anonymous logion:

---

70 *Verba Seniorum* vii.33 // Codex Coislinianus 126.201.
71 *Alphabeticon: Poemen* 184.
72 *Alphabeticon: Moses* 3 // *Verba Seniorum* xvi.7.
73 *Verba Seniorum* ii.2 // *Alphabeticon: Antony* 11.

If you see a young man ascending to heaven by his own will, catch him by his feet and throw him down to the earth, for it is not expedient for him.[74]

The *Apophthegmata* reveal a genuine desire to eradicate the self and in humility put first the good of others. Particularly attractive is the story of Abba John: he and others were travelling by night and the guide lost the way. Rather than upset and shame the guide, John pretended to be unwell and unable to proceed before morning.[75]

Indeed, the world we enter through these texts is one of mutual learning and teaching. In Guy's view, the basis of the spiritual education in the desert was the charismatic word;[76] the saying of the experienced ascetic was full of the Spirit, and able to effect action in the disciple. So a dialogue between master and pupil is a form which frequently appears. The *Apophthegmata* instil obedience, but it is not obedience to a set of rules; it is obedience in the context of a relationship between the 'elder' who is the model, and the disciple who imitates.

A brother asked Abba Poemen, 'Some brothers live with me; do you want me to be in charge of them?' The old man said to him, 'No just work first and foremost, and if they want to live like you, they will see to it themselves.' The brother said to him, 'But it is they themselves, Father, who want me to be in charge of them.' The old man said to him, 'No, be their example, not their legislator.'[77]

Such a story throws light on the character of *Apophthegmata* themselves; the repetition of precept and example took the place of learning rules, and occasionally quite contradictory advice can be found if individual pericopae are compared. Building on Guy's observations, others[78] have developed a picture of the community in which master and apprentice grew together towards spiritual maturity.

Represented in these texts is, paradoxically, a society of solitaries, a 'school' where teaching and learning were to a fair extent conducted in silence. The request for a 'word' is often met with a surprising twist meant to redirect attention away from word to example, or away from the master's supposed competence to the enquirer's inappropriate expectations. The 'word' is not usually some universally applicable piece of advice, but specific to the situation, arising from inspired discernment of what the enquirer needs to hear. Sometimes there is no word, sometimes an acted parable instead. Often there is a task to be carried out obediently and precisely, from which the disciple learns renunciation of his own will – for the majority of the material revolves around the intimate relationship of abba and disciple: it is in the process of living together that endurance and obedience is developed.

---

74 *Verba Seniorum* x.lll // Codex Coislinianus 126.244.

75 *Alphabeticon: John the Dwarf* 17 // *Verba Seniorum* xvii.7.

76 Guy (1974); cf. Burton-Christie (1993) and Gould (1993a).

77 *Alphabeticon: Poemen* 174.

78 Gould (1993a), to whom I am indebted for the substantive points made in the following paragraph; but also Rousseau (1978) and Regnault (1987, 1990).

Abba Poemen said, 'Do not assess yourself but adhere to someone who lives well.'[79]

The beginner submits to a monk with more experience, and in that relationship tempting 'thoughts' are disclosed and progress is made in their healing, sometimes facilitated by the master's self-disclosure of his own continuing battles with temptation, or by his penitential solidarity with his disciple. Above all teaching is by example not precept. Poemen spoke of the teacher who did not do what he taught as being 'like a spring which gives drink to all and cleanses all, but cannot purify itself'.[80] Abba Isaac tells how he was frustrated that Abba Cronius never told him what to do, but the old man refused to give orders, and suggested that the brother should do 'what he sees me doing'.

From then on if the old man was about to do anything, I used to anticipate him and do it. If he did anything he did it silently, and this taught me to act silently.[81]

The humility of the old experienced teacher is presented time and again as an element in the relationship with the younger monk in which the teacher's endurance and integrity is also tested.

The mutual testing of brothers in the desert is most tellingly revealed by stories about the relationship between simple, unlettered monks and sophisticated outsiders. One of the most famous ascetics was Arsenius, who had been tutor to the princes, Arcadius and Honorius:

One day Abba Arsenius consulted an old Egyptian monk about his own thoughts. Someone noticed this and said to him, 'Abba Arsenius, how is it that you, with such good Latin and Greek education, ask this peasant about your thoughts?' He replied, 'I have indeed been taught Latin and Greek, but I do not even know the alphabet of this peasant.'[82]

Perhaps there is a little evidence of tension between Greek and Copt, educated and illiterate, in the *Apophthegmata*. There are differing estimates of the value of books, and anecdotes like the story told of Evagrius:

One day at the Cells [Cellia], there was an assembly about some matter or other and Abba Evagrius held forth. Then the priest said to him, 'Abba, we know that if you were living in your own country you would probably be a bishop and a great leader; but at present you are here as a stranger.' He was filled with compunction, but was not at all upset and bending his head he replied, 'I have spoken once and will not answer, twice but I will proceed no further' (Job 40.5).[83]

---

79 *Poemen* 73, as quoted by Gould (1993a), p. 28.
80 *Alphabeticon: Poemen* 25, as quoted by Gould (1993a), p. 58.
81 *Alphabeticon: Isaac of Kellia* 2, as quoted by Gould (1993a), p. 61.
82 *Alphabeticon: Arsenius* 6 // *Verba Seniorum* xv.7.
83 *Alphabeticon: Evagrius* 7 // *Verba Seniorum* xvi.2.

Another anecdote shows the embarrassment on the other side. An old man was shocked to find Arsenius lying on a bed with a pillow; he was ill and was tended by a priest. The priest questioned the man, who agreed that as a shepherd he had lived a hard life and he was actually more comfortable in his cell. The priest said:

> You see this Abba Arsenius. When he was in the world he was the father of the emperor, surrounded by thousands of slaves. . . . Beneath him were spread rich coverings. While you were in the world as a shepherd you did not enjoy even the comforts you now have, but he no longer enjoys the delicate life he led in the world. So you are comforted while he is afflicted. The old man saw the point and begged for forgiveness.[84]

The emphasis on practical discipline rather than spiritual speculation or book learning is evident in a number of stories, and there are some which seem to discourage even engagement with scripture. Arsenius, we are told, never wanted to reply to questions concerning scripture.[85] Poemen would not respond to someone who spoke 'of the scriptures, concerning heavenly and spiritual things'; when asked why, he replied,

> He is great and speaks of heavenly things, and I am lowly and speak of earthly things. If he had spoken of the passions of the soul, I should have replied, but he speaks to me of spiritual things and I know nothing of that.[86]

A story is told of Antony asking some brothers what they made of a certain text in scripture. To each reply he said, 'You have not understood it'. So asked how he explained it, he said, 'I do not know'. However, the old assumption that the desert monks were predominantly illiterate and that the Bible was not at the heart of their way of life has now been vigorously contested.[87] The scriptures were memorized; verses from scripture were cited to challenge demonic temptations; meditation on scripture, which meant its oral recitation, accompanied manual labour. Psalms were chanted and scriptures read at gatherings for liturgy. In fact scripture permeated the lives of the monks, but theirs was not the careful, enquiring exegesis of the scholar, but the practical and insightful adaptation of the scriptural word or image to their situation, often through allegory.

Conclusion

All this material, together with the more literary works mentioned earlier and such material as the *Lives* and *Rule* of Pachomius, is a vast and interconnected area of study with many fascinations. We find pictures drawn at two different levels. In the more literary works, a philosophic ideal overlays the

---

84 *Alphabeticon: Arsenius* 36.
85 *Alphabeticon: Arsenius* 42.
86 *Alphabeticon: Poemen* 8.
87 Rubenson (1990) for Antony; Burton-Christie (1993) for the *Apophthegmata*.

material, an ideal which could and did attract the sophisticated and educated, the Cappadocians and Augustines of the time. Yet even here, lying behind the literary presentation, it is possible to discern the picture given in the collections of *Apophthegmata*. Greek-speaking, educated ascetics measure themselves by the harsh simplicity of Copts retreating from the social, economic and political dominance of Graeco-Roman civilization. The problem of the manuscript traditions, the relationship between the various sources, the question of the reliability of each pericope, the effects of turning oral material into literary material and of translation from one language to another – all these problems make the study of this literature, in general terms at least, somewhat analogous to study of the gospels. Whatever the detailed solutions to the critical problems, these documents provide us with important source material for the origins and character of Egyptian and Palestinian monasticism, a movement which had an enormous influence on the wider Church scene in the period with which we are dealing. In general terms we cannot doubt that the impression they create is a reliable reflection of the ethos that developed in the desert communities.

For Further Reading

English translations

Waddell, Helen, 1936. *The Desert Fathers*, London and New York: Burns, Oates & Washbourne.
Ward, Benedicta, 1975(a). *The Sayings of the Desert Fathers*, London: Mowbrays.
Ward, Benedicta, 1975(b). *The Wisdom of the Desert Fathers*, Oxford: SLG Press.

Studies

Burton-Christie, Douglas, 1993. *The Word in the Desert: Scripture and the Quest for Holiness in Early Christian Monasticism*, New York/Oxford: Oxford University Press.
Chitty, D., 1966. *The Desert a City*, Oxford: Oxford University Press.
Gould, Graham, 1993(a). *The Desert Fathers on Monastic Community*, Oxford: Clarendon Press.

IV Didymus the Blind

Didymus spent his life in Alexandria rather than the desert, but there are reasons for placing him in this chapter: Palladius[88] includes him among the famous monks he visited in Egypt, and he was known to Rufinus and Melania. Antony is said to have visited him; and Evagrius praises him as a 'great and gnostic teacher', citing his advice in his *Gnōstikos*.[89] That he was an ascetic is universally attested, and presumably he may be regarded as in the older tradition of practising asceticism by domestic withdrawal within the urban environment.

---

88 Palladius, *Lausiac History* 4.
89 *Gnōstikos* 48.

There he was, like the leading desert ascetics, a master with his disciples, but unlike them he was clearly at the centre of a more 'academic' circle. Like Evagrius, Didymus represents the Origenist traditions which were to split the Egyptian desert in the last decade of the fourth century, after both had died. However, the consequence for both was the loss of much of their work after the condemnation of Origen in 553. In the case of Didymus this has been dramatically reversed, at least partially, by the chance discovery of a considerable number of papyri in a munitions dump at Tura during the Second World War. Interestingly, some of this new material takes the form of questions and answers – in other words, they are transcripts of discussions between Didymus and his students. His teaching was clearly conducted in the more formal setting of regular instruction in a school,[90] rather than by responding to the request for 'a word' in the manner of the 'Desert Fathers'. Yet it is also made clear that Didymus' primary concern was the process of learning whereby spiritual maturity is attained – an interest held in common with the heroes of the desert.

1 Didymus the teacher

Didymus lived until 398, by which time he was eighty-five. The predominant impression found in contemporary sources, is of an aged and revered teacher, highly respected in ecclesiastical circles around the Mediterranean for his outstanding erudition and prodigious memory. His reputation was enhanced by his simple asceticism and by the fact that his remarkable learning had been acquired in spite of his being afflicted with blindness from childhood. This picture of Didymus' life and character comes from the years at the end of the fourth century, and is drawn from a number of his disciples. Origen's translator and apologist, Rufinus, spent a total of eight years at Didymus' feet,[91] obtained a treatise on the death of infants from his master,[92] and drew on Didymus' commentary on Origen's De principiis when he made his Latin translation of the work.[93] Jerome, the great biblical scholar from the West, acknowledges his debt to Didymus in the preface to many of his commentaries,[94] and apparently made a point of going to Alexandria in order to meet him and get him to clarify certain of his perplexities.[95] It was at Jerome's request that Didymus wrote his Commentary on Zechariah,[96] and it was Jerome who ensured an abiding reputation for Didymus in the West by translating his treatise on the Holy Spirit. After so many expressions of respect, Jerome's later condemnation of Origen, and with him, his late disciple, Didymus, was particularly abhorrent to the loyal Rufinus.[97]

---

90 Layton (2004); see further below.
91 Rufinus, *Apologia in Hieronymum* (Defence against Jerome) ii.12.
92 Jerome, *Adversus Rufinum* iii.28.
93 Jerome, *Adversus Rufinum*, ii.11; Bardy (1910), p. 33.
94 Jerome, *In Ep. ad Gal.; In Matt.; In Osee proph.; In Isaiam; In Danielem*, etc.
95 Jerome, *In Ep. ad Ephes.*, prolog.; *Ep.* 84.
96 Jerome, *In Zech.*, prolog.; *De viris illistribus* 109.
97 Rufinus, *Apol. in Hier.* ii.8, 12, 23, 25, etc.

Despite this widespread reputation, Didymus was an Alexandrian by birth and never ventured far from the city. At the age of four, before he had started school or learned to read, he lost his sight. He was obviously a scholar from birth, for despite this handicap, he succeeded in attaining competence in all the subjects that constituted higher education in his day: our sources list dialectic, geometry, arithmetic, astronomy, music, poetry, rhetoric and philosophy, including Aristotle's syllogisms and Plato's eloquence.[98] Sozomen tells us that he taught himself by feeling letters that had been carved on a tablet,[99] but his greatest asset seems to have been a memory which retained everything that was read to him. Rufinus gives the impression that he deliberately cultivated this ability by quietly recalling and ruminating on what he had heard during the long hours when sighted people needed to sleep.[100] The wide range of accomplishments attributed to Didymus is not obviously reflected in his extant writings,[101] though the vast quantity of quotations (in particular from biblical and Christian sources, though if the De Trinitate is authentic then also pagan literature) bears witness to his remarkable powers of memory and the breadth of his literary knowledge. Anecdotes concentrate on the contrast, so impressive to his contemporaries, between his physical blindness and his mental perspicacity. For example, Antony, the founder of monasticism, is said to have visited him and told him not to grieve over the loss of his sight, which even ants and flies possess, but to rejoice in having the vision of angels, the ability to discern God.[102] Jerome regularly calls him Didymus the Seeing, rather than Didymus the Blind.

Rufinus[103] tells us that 'taught by God', Didymus had such learning and knowledge that he became 'a teacher in the Church school', having been 'approved by Bishop Athanasius' and other learned churchmen. It used to be assumed that this meant he was head of the famous Catechetical School which had flourished in the past under Clement and Origen;[104] but the continuous existence of such an institution has long since been questioned.[105] The history of Christianity in Alexandria seems to suggest a number of 'schools' gathered around various Christian teachers, not all of whom were acceptable to the bishop – one thinks of Valentinus and others, of Demetrius' ups and downs with Origen,

---

98 Rufinus, HE ii.7; Socrates, HE iv.25f.; Theodoret, HE iv.26.

99 Sozomen, HE iii.15.

100 Rufinus, HE ii.7.

101 For detailed discussion, see Bardy (1910), pp. 218ff.; in the De Trinitate, references can be found to the Iliad and Odyssey, Orpheus, Pindar, Diagoras of Melos, Sophocles, Euripides, Plato the Comedian, Aratos, Hermes Trismegistus and the Sybillines. Plato, Aristotle and Porphyry are mentioned, though Didymus' philosophical views are mainly eclectic and second-hand. Studies of the newly discovered material confirm this general impression, though suggest that his knowledge of pagan literature was largely through second-hand Christian scholarship; see Layton (2004).

102 Rufinus, HE ii.7; Socrates, HE iv.25; cf. Sozomen, HE iii.15.

103 Rufinus, HE ii.7.

104 Philip Sidetes lists Didymus among the heads of the Catechetical School. Gauche (1934) claims to reconstruct the syllabus of the university and treats Didymus as Origen's successor in a formal sense.

105 Bardy (1937, 1942).

and of the school of biblical exegesis around Arius.[106] Athanasius himself was against a certain Hieracas of Leontopolis,[107] who seems remarkably like Didymus, an ascetic teacher with groups of pupils or disciples. Maybe in contrast to others the bishop approved Didymus, who certainly seems to have been pro-Athanasian. He remained faithful to the Nicene position all his life – indeed Socrates ranks him as the Alexandrian counterpart to Basil of Caesarea and Gregory of Nazianzus – a bulwark against Arianism raised up by God's providence.[108]

One of the great gains of the Tura discovery is the evidence they provide for 'early Christian educational aims, practices, and institutions'.[109] Layton's study focuses on this aspect, the way in which the rediscovered commentaries reveal a 'scholasticism' which promotes 'moral progress toward ideals of virtue', pressing 'an assertive Christian identity in the wider conflicts of Alexandria'. Didymus is shown as one who 'listened, taught, learned, and argued with pagans, Jews, Manichees, and an array of rival Christian teachers, many of whom he regarded as heretics'. But the commentaries also demonstrate how the language of Hellenistic schools was 'shaped into novel patterns by its filtering through biblical narratives', and these narratives then establish the 'pattern and language of virtue to which the students aspired'. It is a 'mimetic' tradition: like most educational and exegetical activity in the ancient world, it provided 'types' to be enacted in the life of the learner. But it is also a 'scholastic' process in that it is 'occupied with securing the rational foundations of a received authoritative tradition and applies a method of inquiry to identify and resolve potential inconsistencies and contradictions within that tradition'.

The method was clearly not just exposition in lectures, but also debate, and the aim was 'to live according to philosophy and virtue'.[110] As already noted, some of the debate is transcribed in the rediscovered material, revealing a community 'dedicated to the collaborative investigation of the biblical texts'. They apparently 'met twice daily to hear the master's expositions on scripture'. The lectures presuppose a continuity of listeners in the class, since reference back is given no explanation; and the questions suggest 'more than an elementary level of educational attainment' on their part – textual variants, theological controversies and the use of philosophical categories for interpretation are raised. This systematic engagement, together with the location in the city, differentiates Didymus' school from the apparently occasional teaching of the desert ascetics, though what they have in common is the attraction of disciples who see in their teacher one to emulate. It is assumed that the 'proper teacher' is a model, while Rufinus and others regard Didymus as a 'lamp shining with divine light'. Didymus 'sought ways to inculcate the desert within the city', and was recognized for what he did by Antony and Evagrius, as well as Athanasius.

---

106 Pearson, 'Egypt' and Young, 'Towards a Christian *Paideia*', in Mitchell and Young (2006); Williams (1987), pp. 84ff.

107 Brakke (1995), pp. 44ff.

108 Socrates, *HE* iv.26.

109 Layton (2004); quotations in this paragraph come from the Introduction.

110 Layton (2004); quotations in this paragraph are from Chapter 1.

2 Literary works

Rufinus puts great store on having heard Didymus teach in person by word of mouth.[111] But Didymus also produced a vast collection of written works for which he was well known outside Egypt, perhaps especially in the West.[112] As noted, little of Didymus' work survived his condemnation as an Origenist in 553. In the sixteenth century, all that was known was the *De Spiritu Sancto* in Jerome's Latin version and a Latin text of the *Commentary on the Catholic Epistles*. Since then, the Greek texts of several dogmatic works have been traced among the works of other more respectable Fathers of the Church. The most important of these is the treatise *De Trinitate* which Mingarelli recognized as Didymus' work in the eighteenth century.[113] There are cross-references to the authentic treatise *On the Holy Spirit*[114] which seemed to establish the attribution. Twentieth-century scholarship reopened the question;[115] but even though Didymus' authorship of this treatise can no longer be regarded as absolutely assured it will be assumed here that it was Didymus' work. Also plausibly attributed to Didymus is a work *Against the Manichees*. More contentious is the view that Didymus was the author of Books IV and V of Basil's *Contra Eunomium*,[116] and of the important little treatise *Adversus Arium et Sabellium* attributed to Gregory of Nyssa.[117] The latter is the earliest work in which the formula 'one *ousia* and three *hypostases*' appears: was Didymus the architect of this brilliant solution to the contentions of the East?

Didymus was best known in his own day as a biblical commentator, and extensive quotations from his commentaries, particularly the *Commentary on the Psalms*, have been identified in the Catenae.[118] But our knowledge of Didymus'

---

111 Rufinus, *Apol. in Hier.* ii.12.

112 Jerome acknowledges his debt to many commentaries; even before he made his translation of Didymus' *De Spiritu Sancto*, Ambrose drew heavily from it for his own treatise on the subject, and his *De mysteriis* was probably influenced by Didymus' *De Trinitate*. Augustine came under his influence. See Bardy (1910), pp. 241–9.

113 Text edited by Hönscheid (1975) and Seiler (1975).

114 Now in a critical edition, Doutreleau (1992).

115 Doutreleau (1957) questioned the attribution; Béranger (1963) showed that none of Mingarelli's arguments are conclusive, and that the attribution has to be demonstrated, if it can be, on other grounds.

116 There is general agreement that *Contra Eunomium* IV and V do not belong to Basil's treatise and were not written by Basil; but discussion about whether they should be restored to Didymus continues. Two papers were delivered at the Oxford Patristic Conference 1979, one arguing that they were the work of Didymus (Hayes 1982), the other reviving the suggestion that the author might have been Apollinarius (Hübner 1989 presents the full case in monograph form). The latter case is accepted by the editor of the text, Risch (1992). Details of the earlier discussion will be found in the Patrologies; see for example Lebon (1937); and Pruche (1970).

117 Holl (1928), pp. 298–309, reprints the article in which he argued that Didymus was the author, but he did not convince Bardy.

118 See, for example, Mühlenberg (1975–8); Petit (1986, 1992–5); Hadegorn and Hadegorn (1994–2000).

exegetical work is dramatically increased by the Tura discovery.[119] The first text to be published was the *Commentary on Zechariah*, which appeared in the *Sources Chrétiennes* series in 1962,[120] to be followed a good many years later by the *Commentary on Genesis*.[121] Meanwhile, the *Commentary on Job*,[122] the *Commentary on the Psalms*[123] and the *Commentary on Ecclesiastes*[124] have gradually appeared in a somewhat cumbersome typescript form in the series *Papyrologische Texte und Abhandlungen*.

With the publication of the material, scholarly discussion of its significance has begun to get under way. First impressions suggested that it did not make a great deal of difference to what we already knew.[125] It had long been clear that scripture was Didymus' chief inspiration – we already knew that he had written commentaries on Genesis, Exodus, Leviticus, Job, the Psalms, Proverbs, Ecclesiastes, Song of Songs, Isaiah, Jeremiah, Daniel, Hosea, Zechariah, and the whole of the New Testament except Mark and some of the shorter Pauline Epistles. His dogmatic treatises are saturated with unnecessarily long quotations from scripture, by which he is led into rambling digressions – the *De Trinitate*, for example, is mainly a vast collection of scripture proofs, arranged by topics. Didymus, we knew, regarded speculation as sophistry and searching the scriptures as the way of wisdom.[126]

We knew too that Didymus was an Origenist who used the allegorical method in his commentaries, and this also is generally confirmed by the new discoveries. Origen in expounding his method distinguished three senses of scripture, but in practice his exegetical work is based on a distinction between the literal meaning and one or more allegorical meanings. First impressions of Didymus' techniques, based on the new information provided by the *Commentary on Zechariah*, suggested that he was content with distinguishing two senses, though he had a range of descriptions of the 'higher meaning', like ἀναγωγή (*anagōgē*), ἀλληγορία (*allēgoria*), θεωρία (*theōria*), τροπολογία (*tropologia*), διαλογία (*dialogia*); this meaning was reached by interpreting symbolically, mystically or spiritually.[127] As for Origen, so for Didymus, everything was potentially a symbol, especially numbers and descriptive passages. Thus, in the Zechariah commentary, elaborate sums are supposed to elucidate the mystical significance of the date on which Zechariah had his vision;[128] the man on the horse is the Saviour made man; the mountains are the two Testaments, which are described as cloud-covered because they are fertile and rich in thoughts of God

---

119 Doutreleau surveyed the find in two articles, Doutreleau and Aucagne (1955); and Doutreleau and Koenen (1967).

120 Doutreleau (1962).

121 Nautin and Doutreleau (1976, 1978).

122 Henrichs, Hadegorn and Koenen (1968–85).

123 Doutreleau, Gesché and Gronewald (1968–70).

124 Binder, Liesenborghs, Kramer, Krebber and Gronewald (1969–83).

125 Doutreleau (1961).

126 *De Trinitate* i.18, PG 39.341.

127 For fuller discussion, see Doutreleau's (1962) Introduction to the *Commentary on Zechariah*. A similar account of Didymus' exegetical methods will be found in Gesché (1962).

128 *In Zech.* i.17–19, SC I, 198ff.

and the incarnation; the vision occurs at night, since there is plenty of obscurity in the enigmatic and profound prophecies of the two Testaments.[129] As in Origen, so in Didymus, references to God's anger or other anthropomorphic traits are allegorized away: God is immutable, beyond change and emotion, but he seeks the repentance and education of sinful men by means of chastisement.[130] Allegorical interpretation is popularly regarded as a way of importing into the scriptural text a philosophy alien to it; at points, Didymus seemed to extract such speculative meanings, and to differ in no very significant ways from his great master, Origen.

Closer study of Didymus' commentaries, however, suggested that more precise definition of his methodology might advance our entire understanding of the Alexandrian allegorical tradition. Debate centred on definition of his technical terms; is it really true that he made no attempt to distinguish *allēgoria* and *anagōgē*? Bienart suggested that it might be possible to restrict *anagōgē* to Christological, as distinct from general philosophical or mystical, meanings.[131] Then Tigcheler, on the basis of a study of the *Commentary on Zechariah*,[132] grounded the distinction in a sophisticated hermeneutical procedure whereby Didymus carefully distinguished between the 'wording' and the 'reference' of the text at both literal and spiritual levels, so that *allēgoria* led to the recognition of a figurative sense in the language, *anagōgē* to the reality to which the figurative language refers. Hill's[133] impression, however, after translating the whole of the *Commentary on Zechariah*, was that Didymus' hermeneutic lacks a consistent set of principles, has no clear methodological approach, and does not always distinguish *allēgoria* and *anagōgē*. He simply moves quickly from literal or historical comment to the spiritual level, flicking through his mental concordance and suggesting that none of the parallels are inappropriate, all are possible.

Didymus' allegory, however, does seem modified, more perhaps than Origen's, by a sense of scriptural unity, of the primacy of Christological understanding, and the importance of ecclesiastical rather than heretical interpretations. Over and over again interpretation is offered simply in the form of collections of texts from elsewhere in scripture, often, it is true, texts with only allusive or verbal connections with the passage under discussion; yet one guiding principle is that scripture points to God in Christ. So, for example, in Zechariah 3, the high priest, Joshua, stands accused by Satan, but vindicated by God; and to Didymus, the passage is a description of Jesus, the great high priest after the order of Melchizedek, who freed mankind by bearing their sins on the cross and overcoming the power of the devil.

However, the overriding thrust of Didymus' exegesis, as Layton[134] has shown, relates to his pedagogy. 'Two interpretive issues' preoccupy him: 'first, the clarification of difficulties that a reader might encounter and, second, the disclosure of the interior meaning of the text'. Layton suggests that it is the first which Didymus regards as 'literal' interpretation, the second as 'spiritual', accepting

---

129 *In Zech.* i.21f., SC 1, 200ff.
130 *In Zech.* i.9, 15, 56–8, etc.
131 Bienart (1972).
132 Tigcheler (1977).
133 Introduction to Hill (2006), pp. 12, 15, 17, 19–20.
134 Layton (2004); quotations from pp. 26–7, 39, 87, 94, 112.

that there is no real distinction between allegory and anagogy. Focusing on three of the newly found commentaries, on the Psalms, on Job and on Genesis, Layton demonstrates how the theme of the soul's movement towards virtue runs through the digressive debates, lengthy expositions and accumulations of parallel biblical texts. In Didymus' verse by verse treatment, the narrative of the soul as it matures and acquires the ability 'to undertake the contemplative life' is what gives unity to the biblical material, rather than the immediate context of the text literally understood. Mutability is the condition which permits the journey towards perfection, the Psalms expressing the longing and the struggle of the pilgrim, while Job is the hero whose courage is to be emulated. The Genesis commentary develops 'a narrative of human moral formation', Christ becoming 'the pattern according to which humanity is created and the agent that impresses this image upon the virtuous'. These 'narratives concerning the life of virtue' are not 'contained within the discourse of the biblical text itself, but emerge from the interaction of reader and text' in Didymus' circle, where reading is a communal activity.

3 Contribution to doctrine

Didymus was a man of the Bible. He was broadly Origenist in his method of exposition. The extent of Didymus' dependence on Origen was discussed as early as Jerome. The work that could have told us most, his commentary on Origen's *De Principiis*, is unfortunately lost. We gather from Jerome[135] that it was a defence of Origen against current attacks, in which Didymus gave an interpretation of Origen's Trinitarian doctrine which conformed with later orthodoxy, but accepted uncritically what became his most controversial doctrines, like the pre-existence of souls and the ἀποκατάστασις (*apokatastasis* – the universal restoration of all things to the original state of perfection). In his extant works, there are hints that he accepted the latter doctrine,[136] while he clearly believed the former,[137] along with 'the denial of the possession of flesh in the resurrection'.[138] Didymus found inspiration in Origen and defended him on points where current debate had not yet fixed the rules, but he was far from unaware of the contemporary theological climate. Jerome had to admit, even in his anti-Origen phase, that Didymus was certainly orthodox in the matter of the Trinity. In fact, Didymus was an intelligent contributor to contemporary debate.

Intelligent, but not brilliantly original, Didymus seems to have absorbed ideas from many sources and presented them with ample documentation in formulae that would be easily assimilated. He may or may not have invented

---

135 Jerome, *Adv. Ruf.* i.6; ii.16.

136 There is a summary of the situation in Quasten's *Patrology* III.99; but this is superseded by the evidence from the newly discovered commentaries. In the *Commentary on Job* Didymus speculates that Satan might have the capacity for repentance, Layton (2004), p. 152.

137 Didymus, *De Trin.* iii.1 (PG 39.773–6); and 'widely represented in the Tura commentaries', Layton (2004), p. 152.

138 Layton (2004), p. 152.

the formula 'one *ousia* in three *hypostases*',[139] but, assuming the *De Trinitate* is his work, he hammered it home with pages and pages of scriptural proofs. His argumentation against the Arians and the Macedonians, who applied Arian arguments to the Holy Spirit rather than the Logos, follows the pattern developed by his predecessors and contemporaries, but it was Didymus, perhaps, who amassed the material and produced scholarly monographs on the divinity of the Holy Spirit and the nature of the Trinity. His dogmatic works reveal a mind averse to philosophical speculation, desiring only to press home relevant biblical passages and express the traditional faith of the Church in the formulae which now appeared to be the only adequate expression of that faith. To open the pages of the *De Trinitate* is to find an essentially pious man, concentrating on the ἰσοτιμία (equality of honour), the fact that the three *hypostases* are worshipped as one saving God.[140]

Didymus' most interesting contribution to contemporary debate was in the field of Christology. The bitter controversies of the fifth century were still in the future, but already the question of whether the Logos assumed a soul as well as flesh in the incarnation had come into the open. In Didymus' works, there are no explicit references to Apollinarius, but he constantly uses anti-Apollinarian formulae, stressing that the Saviour did not assume a body without a soul and a mind.[141] The debates which interested him more directly were with the Arians and Manichaeans, and the interesting thing is that he has realized the relevance of this assertion to these other problems. Both of these opponents were docetic, the latter explicitly so, regarding the body of Christ as a fantasy, the former effectively so, by denying that the body had a human soul.[142] He reproaches the Arians on the same grounds as Athanasius had, accusing them of attributing human characteristics to the Divine Logos instead of his flesh; but, unlike Athanasius, he recognizes that their exegesis is possible because it rests on the presupposition that the indwelling Logos replaced the soul in the Saviour's body.[143] Neither soulless flesh, nor divinity needs food or sleep, he says; therefore the ineffable incarnation was not without soul.[144] The weaknesses and passions of Jesus Christ which are described in scripture, should be attributed to his fallible human soul. He maintained all the consequences of being made man; he was entirely like us; he assumed not merely bodily pains and weaknesses, but also psychological tensions and mental suffering.[145] The difference between the soul of Jesus and that of other human beings was a difference in quality, not nature: he remained sinless in spite of temptation and the possibility of succumbing to it. Layton's[146] exploration of Didymus' use of προπάθεια (*propatheia*) in discussing Christ's agony in Gethsemane refines this general outline: Christ's

---

139 See above, p. 95 and note 117.

140 For a detailed discussion of Didymus' Trinitarianism, see Bardy (1910), chapter 3. This is, of course, largely based on the *De Trinitate*.

141 Bardy (1910), chapter 3; Doutreleau (1962), Introd., I, 88. See also Gesché (1962).

142 De Trin. iii.21 (*PG* 39.904).

143 De Trin. iii.21 (*PG* 39.900); cf. iii.30.

144 De Trin. iii.2 (*PG* 39.797).

145 De Trin. iii.21 (*PG* 39.900–16).

146 Layton (2000) and (2004), pp. 121–7; Didymus' discussion is in the *Psalms Commentary* 221.34—222.6.

soul is never separated from the divine Word by thought (λογισμός) or idea or disturbance, but it experiences that agitation called προπάθεια, which is not itself sin, but tempts the rational soul to give in: 'it would have no glory or dignity or praise or crowns if it were not agitated'.

Didymus, then, assigns to the soul of Jesus a genuinely positive role in the incarnation. The Saviour's human soul was fallible, but in fact by remaining sinless, it conformed perfectly with the intention of its Creator. So, not needing salvation itself, it became the instrument of our salvation. It seems likely that at this point Didymus was indebted to Origen, according to whom the Logos united himself with humanity through the medium of the one soul that had remained sinless.[147] But another factor in his thinking could well have been his interest as a teacher in inculcating virtue; for in a sense Christ is the virtue to which Didymus aspires. 'Virtue exists essentially in God and humans have virtue through participation in the Trinity', a participation which takes place through Christ as mediator.[148] For Christ is the image according to which human beings were created and the likeness to which the soul aspires; progress is through deeper participation in the pattern of virtue provided by Christ.[149] Following this line of thought, Didymus saw its relevance to contemporary discussions and made a constructive contribution by assimilating this idea to the soteriological tradition so well represented by Athanasius.[150] It was because the Logos had assumed human nature in its totality, that the whole being, body, soul and mind, was saved in him.

Conclusion

Didymus was first and foremost a learned ascetic. His reputation rested on scholarship and his ability as a teacher. The *De Trinitate* and other dogmatic works confirm this characterization. Socrates remarked that anyone wanting to get an idea of Didymus' vast erudition would discover it by consulting the enormous volumes he produced.[151] Being blind, he relied on secretaries to produce his manuscripts, and often it is clear that the written text is largely based on teaching material. This is true of the rediscovered Commentaries, and already Mingarelli, who discovered the *De Trinitate* in the eighteenth century, thought that large parts of this treatise were originally prepared as lectures.[152]

---

147 Note especially Gesché (1959); also Wiles (1965) and Bouteneff (2001).

148 Placid Solari, 'Christ as Virtue in Didymus the Blind' in Luchman and Kulzer (1999), pp. 67–88, quoting from the *Commentary on the Psalms*.

149 Layton (2004).

150 See Young (1971).

151 Socrates, *HE* iv.25.

152 Mingarelli's introduction and notes to the *De Trinitate* are reproduced in *PG* 39 with the text. Gauche (1934), pp. 96ff., discusses Didymus' teaching methods on the basis of this theory and mentions the work of de Regnon (1892–8), III.118–20, who referred to *De Trin.* iii.4 'as an orderly and well-planned lecture of a capable teacher'. Gesché (1962), p. 38, speaks of the Psalms commentary as 'un cours professoral'. This is now supplemented by work on the newly discovered commentaries noted above.

Didymus repudiates the attempt to produce polished literary work,[153] and his style is diffuse and repetitious as if he were pressing home his points to a class.[154] He documents his arguments with detailed quotations. He digresses onto interesting side-issues, clarifying minor points *en passant*. He concentrates on easily memorable formulae. He summarizes his arguments, outlines his chain of reasoning, lists all his points.[155] He had the ability of a good teacher to absorb ideas from others and present them in a form that others would find easy to assimilate.

Didymus was a scholar and a teacher; but for all his academic attainments, he was essentially a pious monk and a conservative churchman. His scholarship was entirely devoted to the elucidation of scripture and the doctrines of the Church. In these areas of speciality, he displayed little originality, though he undoubtedly contributed to the consolidation of the orthodox position. His main source-book, his real inspiration, was the Bible, and in the long term, it was as an exegete that he had some abiding influence. The discovery of the *Commentary on Zechariah* revealed the extent to which mediaeval allegory unconsciously followed Didymus through the medium of Jerome, who did not hesitate to draw from Didymus' work when composing his own influential commentary.[156] It is good to see new discoveries and research rehabilitating the memory of a simple, scholarly churchman, who based his faith on study of scripture and the search for ascetic virtue.

For Further Reading

English translations

Hill, R. C. (trans.), 2006. *Didymus. Commentary on Zechariah, FC*, Washington, DC: Catholic University of America Press.

Studies

Bouteneff, P. C., 2001. 'Placing the Christology of Didymus the Blind', *SP* 37, pp. 389–95.
Layton, Richard A., 2004. *Didymus the Blind and His Circle in Late-Antique Alexandria*, Urbana and Chicago: University of Illinois Press.

V Evagrius Ponticus

Like Didymus, Evagrius has been emerging from the shadows through twentieth-century scholarship.[157] The substantial loss of his work, as in the case of Didymus, is directly attributable to his later condemnation as an Origenist

---

153 *De Spiritu Sancto* 63 (PG 39.1086).

154 Note especially his own justification of his style in *De Trin.* iii.1 (PG 39.781–4).

155 See *De Trin.* iii.2 – a summary of all the arguments used in the earlier books, giving a total of fifty-five brief points.

156 Doutreleau (1962), Introduction, 136.

157 Konstantinovsky (2009) provides bibliography and a critical survey.

in 553. Some of his writings, like some of Didymus', survived through attribution to others; many more survived through translation, particularly into Syriac or Armenian. Just before the earlier outbreak of controversy in 399, Evagrius died, as did Didymus, but it was Evagrius' associates and disciples who found themselves fleeing Egypt as their theology attracted the opposition of the so-called Anthropomorphites. So, even though he was not directly implicated at the time, Evagrius' thought may well have played a part in generating that first Origenist controversy.[158]

Nevertheless, Evagrius made a major contribution to providing a theoretical basis for ascetic practice, the significance of which has become the more apparent through the rediscovery of many of his writings and a resurgence of interest in this scholarly monk. He gave the wisdom of the desert a systematic and written form, and, directly or indirectly, did much to shape the monastic spirituality of the Eastern churches.

1 Life and influences

What we know of Evagrius' life essentially comes from Palladius,[159] the apparent source for others, like Socrates and Sozomen. He was born around AD 345 in Ibora, a city of Helenopontus, the area just north of Cappadocia in Asia Minor. As a young man he came under the influence of Basil of Caesarea, and was ordained lector. His earliest writing, *On the faith*, has now been identified among Basil's letters (no. 8). He followed Gregory of Nazianzus to Constantinople, and served as his archdeacon. That it was through these two that Evagrius met Origen's theology is more than likely; they had, after all, collaborated in producing the *Philocalia*, a collection of extracts from Origen.[160]

Evagrius was present at the Council of Constantinople in 381. After Gregory's resignation, he stayed on serving Gregory's successor, but within a year or so got involved in an affair with a married woman, and had a vision in a dream which precipitated his departure to Jerusalem. There he had a protracted illness, but was rescued by Melania's prayers and adopted the monastic life. Melania sent him to join her contacts in the Egyptian deserts, but his association with 'Origenists' like Rufinus clearly dates from this period. Evagrius was in Nitria for a couple of years, then around 385 moved on to Cellia. There he remained till the end of his life. He learned from the great names of the desert, Macarius the Great and Macarius the Alexandrian; he apparently met Antony and visited John of Lycopolis. He had his own disciples, including Palladius and John Cassian; it is through the writings of John Cassian that Evagrius' ideas, though never directly acknowledged, were transmitted to the West. Rather than weaving rope or baskets, he apparently worked as a calligrapher, as well as writing his own works, but like other educated outsiders, he sought to learn the alphabet of the illiterate saints among whom he lived.[161] He was one of the

---

158 Clark (1992), chapter 2; though see the critique in Konstantinovsky (2009).
159 *Lausiac History* 38.
160 For the Cappadocians, see Chapter 4.
161 See above, p. 89.

monks Theophilus would have made a bishop[162] if he had not escaped, it is said, to Jerusalem – he clearly kept in touch with his friends there. Anecdotes concerning Evagrius are preserved in the literature of the desert, the histories and the *Apophthegmata*.

Evagrius more than once mentions both Gregory of Nazianzus and Macarius the Great as his teachers, and his theological work would appear to be the outcome of a kind of meeting between the two – a mind shaped by Cappadocian theology and committed to Nicene Orthodoxy,[163] finding expression in the manners of speech and ascetic ideals of the Egyptian desert. Many of Evagrius' writings take the form of collections of short 'chapters' – brief, memorable, often proverb-like sayings, not unlike the *apophthegmata* remembered in the later collections.[164] This, together with the fact that a major concern is to help the monk deal with 'thoughts', or inner demons, roots Evagrius' work in the desert communities. Yet his description of the ultimate goal of the inner journey through the desert struggle with temptation, while owing something to a conception of the origin and destiny of creation derived from the work of Origen, was also conceived with reference to the apophatic and Trinitarian theology developed by the Cappadocians in response to the Neo-Arians.[165]

2 Writings

Like Didymus, Evagrius was, in general terms, well known all along: reference to his literary activity is found in Jerome, Gennadius, Rufinus and Socrates, as well as Palladius. Some of his ascetic writings, especially those which bore no marks of 'Origenist' teaching, survived in Greek collections of monastic treatises, sometimes attributed to Evagrius himself, sometimes to Nilus of Ancyra. Much else, it turns out, survived in fragmentary form in anthologies and catenae. Lost works have been identified in Syriac or Armenian, while the identification of Greek material as his, and some reconstruction of writings that had disappeared, has been made possible by comparison with such early versions where material was correctly attributed to Evagrius. Sorting it all out has been a somewhat delicate job, not yet complete, but it is increasingly possible to study Evagrius' work with greater access to critical texts than was once the case, and more confidence that we know what he actually wrote.

According to an epistolary prologue (the letter to Anatolius), the *Praktikos* (100 chapters) was the first treatise of a trilogy, followed by the *Gnōstikos* (50 chapters) and the *Kephalaia gnōstica* (600 chapters); this trilogy was surely Evagrius' major work. The *Praktikos* is known from five Greek manuscripts, three Syriac versions and versions in Armenian, Arabic and Georgian. Most, but not all, of the Greek manuscripts attribute this work to Evagrius, and there are many other witnesses to parts of the treatise. All this material has been sorted out by Antoine and Claire Guillaumont, and a critical text published in

---

162 Socrates, *HE* 4.23.
163 *Pace* Konstantinovsky (2009), who minimizes Cappadocian influence.
164 See above, pp. 83–91.
165 See below, Chapter 4.

the *Sources Chrétiennes*.[166] There are some grounds for thinking that there were two redactions of this work; the final chapters, a collection of anecdotal sayings of the 'sages' and desert 'Fathers', together with the prologue and epilogue which are addressed to Anatolios, were probably added later to allay suspicions of 'Origenism'.

The subsequent members of the trilogy are not so well documented. The *Gnōstikos* is only found in its entirety in Syriac and Armenian, though some of the Greek text is found in fragments; what is traceable in Greek has been reconstructed by the Guillaumonts in the *Sources Chrétiennes*, and filled out from the ancient versions to provide a French translation of the whole.[167] The complete, unexpurgated *Kephalaia gnōstica* was discovered by Antoine Guillaumont in 1952 in a Syriac manuscript in the British Museum;[168] this led to his argument that it was the Origenism of Evagrius which was condemned in 553.[169]

The opening words of the *Praktikos* are: 'Christianity is the doctrine of our Saviour Christ, composed of the πρακτική (*praktikē*), the φυσική (*physikē*), and the θεολογική (*theologikē*)' (doubtless a variation on Origen's ἠθική (*ēthikē*), ψυχική (*psychikē*) and ἐνοπτική (*enoptikē*)). The trilogy covers these three stages of the spiritual life, though the three volumes do not correspond to this threefold division, and Evagrius often seems to focus on a twofold scheme, the πρακτική and the γνωστική (*gnōstikē*). Only with the first of these stages would Evagrius appear retrospectively to have been on safe ground, and it is this that is preserved in Greek, along with other treatises which develop similar material, such as *On the Eight Spirits of Evil* (or *Thoughts*) and *On Thoughts*; all these are often found in Greek manuscripts containing monastic anthologies, as are the *Foundations of Monastic Life*, the *Ad Monachos* and *To the monk Eulogios*. Indeed, the *Praktikos*, together with *On Prayer*, would become the two most important works to survive in Greek. *On Prayer* is among the classics gathered in the eighteenth-century anthology, the *Philocalia*, but there it is attributed to Nilus of Ancyra; its attribution to Evagrius was effectively argued by Irénée Hausherr in the 1930s,[170] and it is so attributed in the Syriac and Arabic traditions. The Greek Ascetic Corpus is more conveniently accessible in English than in critical editions, as it is collected together and translated with introduction and commentary by Robert E. Sinkewicz.[171]

Besides the trilogy and works already mentioned, other writings too have been identified. The *Antirrhetikos* survives in Syriac and Armenian, and consists of 487 temptations, listed under the eight 'thoughts' characteristic of Evagrius' analysis, with scripture texts provided as an antidote to each. There are also some letters preserved in Syriac, including the early work *On the Faith* (= Basil, *Ep.* 8) and one addressed either to Melania or Rufinus. Extracts from biblical commentaries have been traced in the Catenae, including *scholia* on the Psalms and wisdom literature; as scholia, brief comments on the text, they bear compar-

---

166 Guillaumont and Guillaumont (1971, 1972).
167 Guillaumont and Guillaumont (1989).
168 Guillaumont (1958).
169 Guillaumont (1962).
170 Hausherr (1959, 1960) provides a discussion of authenticity as well as introduction, French translation and commentary. His earlier articles are listed in Sinkewicz (2003).
171 Sinkewicz (2003); see bibliographies in this work to trace Greek texts.

ison with the brief 'chapters' of Evagrius' other work and illustrate his 'spiritual' exegesis – the *Scholia on Proverbs* provides a good example.[172] The grounding of Evagrius' thought in scripture is a subject that would repay further exploration. A sample of the range of material now attributed to Evagrius is provided by the translation of excerpts in the volume by A. M. Casiday.[173]

3 Interpreting Evagrius

Evagrius' short 'chapters' seem intended for pondering. Interpreting the aphorisms is often a challenge, and the method generally adopted by Evagrian scholarship[174] is to interpret Evagrius by Evagrius – in other words correlate things he says in one place with what he says elsewhere. *To the Monks* (*Ad Monachos*) is of particular interest because Driscoll[175] has shown that underlying the collection of proverbs, despite its apparently haphazard character, there is in fact a very precise shape, designed to reflect the progress of the spiritual life as Evagrius understood it. Thus one can see that the works preserved in Greek in fact presuppose teachings which only become explicit in once lost material. We will shape the discussion around the trilogy, drawing in other texts along the way, and then return to the *Ad Monachos*.

Praktikos

For Evagrius this term involves the cultivation of detachment, the practical outworking of asceticism in challenging the desires of body and soul: 'the practical life is the spiritual method for purifying the passionate part of the soul'.[176] Evagrius accepted the Platonic tripartite division of the soul: the rational (νοῦς – *nous*), the desirous (or concupisciple: ἐπιθυμία – *epithymia*) and the irascible (θυμός – *thumos*). The passions he located in the latter two parts,[177] and the object of πρακτική was to achieve ἀπάθεια (passionlessness). To this end Evagrius identified eight 'thoughts' (λογίσμοι), often treated as the precursors of the seven deadly sins; he also discussed the ways in which dreams indicate the ascetic's inner state. The focus, then, is on interiority, the inner temptations of the desert monk: gluttony, for example, is 'the temptation to mitigate one's ascetic discipline'[178] rather than acts of genuine gluttony. Evagrius indicated that 'thoughts' or temptations were inevitable – the crucial question was whether you gave in

---

172 Géhin (1987); cf. also Géhin (1993) for the *Scholia on Ecclesiastes*.

173 Casiday (2006); see for comment on Evagrius' interest in scripture and for further detail on tracing original texts.

174 Driscoll (2003), p. x note 1, with reference to Guillaumonts et al.

175 Driscoll (2003).

176 *Praktikos* 78. For the difference between this understanding and the usual contrast between the active and contemplative life, rooted in Aristotle's distinction between the *bios praktikos* and *bios theorētikos*, see Louth (1981), p. 102.

177 Though here he is not entirely consistent; vainglory and pride arise out of apparent success in suppressing the passions, and he sometimes hesitates to assign these to the concupiscible or irascible parts of the soul. See Sinkewicz (2003), p. 138, especially note 6.

178 Louth (1981), p. 105.

to them.[179] 'He never claims that human beings are sinless or passionless ...
Instead he is describing the integration of attractions and repulsions in a tran-
quil personality shaped by grace.'[180]

In the *Praktikos* Evagrius first sets out briefly the eight 'thoughts': gluttony,
fornication, avarice; anger, sadness, ἀκηδία (*akēdia* – which means a combination of boredom, loss of commitment and despondency); vainglory (the
expectation of being highly thought of) and pride; and then he offer remedies.
His treatment of the 'thoughts' in the *Praktikos* lies between his brief treatise,
Eight Thoughts (or the *Eight Spirits of Evil*) and the longer work *On Thoughts*:[181]
the former is in the form of wisdom sayings, and is quite introductory, while
the latter seems to be for the more advanced and consists of more discursive
paragraphs. Despite the alternative title of the former, the sayings there focus
on the eight thoughts without turning them into a demonology. A few examples highlight the imagery and the biblical allusions:

'Fog conceals the sun's rays; and heavy consumption of food darkens the
mind' (1.16).

'A tent-peg, passing unnoticed, destroyed an enemy's jaw-bone (Judges 4.21);
and the principle of abstinence has put passion to death' (1.9).

'A wandering monk is like a dry twig in the desert; he is still for a little while
and then is carried off unwillingly' (6.10).

On Thoughts, on the other hand, uses reference to the demons to explore the
relationship between the various 'thoughts', how one exploits another, how
mental representations, memories and dreams can stir up passions, how the
demons exploit inner motivations and twist them, how easy is self-deception,
the need for constant watchfulness and discernment, and pitfalls, such as the
danger of excessive asceticism. Knowing the enemy is all important for success
in the battle; so Evagrius provides analysis of the forces ranged against the
ascetic.

Here, too, he associates the thoughts with different parts of the soul: gluttony, fornication and avarice arise from the desirous part of the soul (linked
with the bodily appetites); anger, depression and ἀκηδία arise from the irascible
(the site of the emotions – the reactions or repulsions stimulated by things);
vainglory and pride arise from a consciousness of making progress in overcoming the passions. Where abstinence cuts away the passions of the body, those
of the soul yield to spiritual love.[182] However, in the *Praktikos* Evagrius is quite
clear that attaining full passionlessness is not possible in this life.

Evagrius seeks not to suppress the emotional and driving force of the soul,
but rather to harness it: the desirous is meant to long for virtue, and the irascible to struggle for that goal.[183] There are these 'two major energy sources in the

---

179 *Praktikos* 74—5.
180 Stewart in Luchman and Kulzer (1999), p. 8.
181 Sinkewicz (2003).
182 *Praktikos* 35—6.
183 *Praktikos* 86.

human personality': the 'source of desire and attraction' has as its pathology lust, but its health is in love of God and others and attraction to virtue; while the 'source of resistance and repulsion' has anger as its pathology, and its health is resistance to sin and the struggle against temptation.[184] The ultimate aim of πρακτική is not ἀπάθεια in the sense of 'insensibility, like that of a stone' (as Jerome mockingly suggested[185]), but rather 'emotional integration',[186] or that detachment which is essential to love, for love that is possessive is self-oriented rather than true love for the other. 'Love is the offspring of impassibility, and impassibility is the blossom of the practical life';[187] 'the end of the practical life is love'.[188]

Since the rational soul is tripartite according to our wise teacher [possibly Gregory of Nazianzus], when virtue arises in the rational part it is called prudence, understanding, and wisdom; when it arises in the concupiscible part it is called chastity, love and abstinence; and when it arises in the irascible part it is called courage and perseverance; but when it penetrates the entire soul it is called justice . . .

Evagrius comments on each of these virtues, for example:

The work of chastity is to look without passion upon objects that set in motion within us irrational fantasies. The work of love is to conduct itself towards every image of God in much the same way as it would towards the archetype . . . The role of justice is to cultivate concord and harmony between the parts of the soul.[189]

Gnōstikos

The middle work of the trilogy is the briefest, and is clearly transitional: Socrates[190] provides evidence that it was treated as a separate work, though one Syriac version presents it as continuous with the *Praktikos*; in other respects it is an introduction to the much larger *Kephalaia gnōstika*.[191] Evagrius explains that the πρακτικός is one who has reached the point where the 'pathetic' part of the soul has become ἀπαθής; the γνωστικός is the one who plays the part of salt to purify the impure, and light for those purified.[192] In other words, the role of the γνωστικός ('knower') is to teach others, and that in effect is his way of almsgiving, since he has no money.[193]

The focus of this treatise is not on the knowledge the knower has, but on

---

184 Stewart in Luchman and Kulzer (1999), p. 13.
185 Jerome, *Ep.* 133; quoted Guillaumont and Guillaumont (1971), I.98–100.
186 Stewart (2001).
187 *Praktikos* 81.
188 *Praktikos* 84.
189 *Praktikos* 89.
190 *HE* 4.23.
191 Guillaumont and Guillaumont (1989), Introduction.
192 *Gnōstikos* 2, 3.
193 *Gnōstikos* 7.

the demeanour of the teacher; what can be taught to whom; the interpretation of scripture, its allegorical and literal passages and how they relate to the
πρακτική, the φυσική and the θεολογική; and the ongoing temptations and virtues of the teacher. 'The conscience of the γνωστικός is for him a severe critic,
and he cannot hide anything from it, for it knows the secrets of his heart.'[194]
The work ends with quotations from Gregory of Nazianzus, Basil of Caesarea,
Athanasius, Serapion of Thmuis and Didymus the Blind,[195] all pointing to the
work's conclusion that πρακτική means purifying the intellect and ensuring it is
impassible, while φυσική means discerning the truth hidden in created things,
and the gift of θεολογική is to turn the intellect from material things towards the
First Cause.

Kephalaia Gnōstica

The 'chapters' of this work are arranged in six 'centuries' and at the end we are
told that these represent the six days of creation; in fact, and despite the letter to
Anatolios, there are ninety in each 'century' rather than a hundred. The *Skemmata* (*Reflections*) are sometimes considered to supply missing chapters – indeed
'this opinion goes back to Mar Babai ... (569–628), who wrote a massive commentary on the *Kephalaia Gnōstika*'.[196]

In this work we come closer to the knowledge of the knower, but it is far from
a linear composition. Its enigmatic material has been called 'polyphonic',[197]
with many points progressing at the same time, as themes are interwoven,
broken off and returned to; one suspects that this work might repay the careful attention Driscoll gave to the *Ad Monachos*. Guillaumont, though admitting
the elusiveness of any outline, suggested that the work begins with cosmology
and the present condition of created beings, moves on to those contemplations
by which the intellect can progressively elevate itself to its original state, then
considers Christ and his soteriological role, with the final 'century' introducing
eschatology and the final restoration. But all these themes spiral back and forth,
and an overall scheme for the work is hard to trace.

The opening lines[198] assert that there is no opposition in the primary Good,
simply because it is Good in its Being, and nothing might be opposite to its
Being. By contrast, opposition is found in attributes, and these belong to bodies,
so opposition is a feature of creatures. With such a Platonic-sounding opening
it is perhaps not surprising that one major supposition in the first 'century'
concerns the 'movement' away from Unity, involving oppositions and separation, coming about through negligence, and being the cause of ignorance and

---

194 *Gnōstikos* 39.
195 See Young (2001), p. 71 for an evaluation of these key figures as 'proximate images
of Christ – men who were part of the living memory at the end of the fourth century ...
a plurality of icons image Christ "the archetype"'.
196 Sinkewicz (2003), p. 210; cf. Muyldermans (1931) for the Greek text and Harmless
and Fitzgerald (2001) for discussion and another English translation.
197 Guillaumont (1962).
198 *Kephalaia gnōstika* (hereafter cited as *KG*) I.1–2.

evil, which is a sickness of the soul.[199] Evagrius affirms that while there was a time when evil did not exist, there never was a time when virtue did not;[200] and most chapters focus on what is needed for recovery, namely, the πρακτική and contemplation. The need for a spiritual sense to discern spiritual things, and the identification of that with impassibility produced by God's grace,[201] together with occasional references to the struggle with demons, link the reflections back to the *Praktikos*, the indispensable starting-point. But meanwhile[202] Evagrius has set out the five principal 'contemplations': contemplation of the Holy and adorable Trinity, contemplation of incorporeals and of bodies, contemplation of judgment and providence – later he explains that the judgment of God is the genesis of the world by which God gave to each of the λογικοί the appropriate body; and states that while the first trumpet means this genesis of bodies, the last trump indicates their destruction.[203]

The second 'century' opens by stating that things that have come into existence from nothing are a mirror of God's goodness; so we are led into exploring the φυσική, the 'natural contemplation' that points to providential causes and the wisdom of the Creator.[204] Soon we meet the idea of four transformations: the passage from evil to virtue; then from impassibility to contemplation of the 'second creation' (corporeal things); then to contemplation of the incorporeals; and finally to knowledge of the Holy Trinity.[205] The integration of the progressive stages of return is fundamental and recurring in Evagrius' ascetical and mystical thought: knowledge heals the νοῦς (mind), love the θυμός (emotion) and chastity the ἐπιθυμία (desire).[206]

Already in the first 'century', God is treated as the one by whose wisdom everything is produced, but the divine self is not itself a 'part' to be counted among beings.[207] The Holy Trinity simply cannot be put in the same category as contemplation of sensible or intelligible beings, and cannot be counted with objects: it is 'essential knowledge'.[208] 'Natural contemplation' is distinguished from such 'essential knowledge' as only possible after the genesis of bodies; yet the whole creation carries 'signs' because 'God made everything with wisdom' (Ps. 103.24).[209] It is notable that Evagrius has such a high sacramental view of the material creation.[210] But his estimate of bodies is deeply ambiguous – in

---

199 *KG* I.2, 4, 40, 41, 49, 50, 51; cf. III.22 ('the first movement of the *logikoi* is separation of the *nous* from the Unity which is in it') and 28.

200 *KG* I.40–1.

201 *KG* I.33–7; cf. II.35 which speaks of the five senses of the *nous*.

202 *KG* I.27.

203 *KG* III.38, 66; cf. VI.79.

204 *Physikē* is 'not the observation of or enjoyment of the wonders of nature – though it does not exclude that . . . – but rather a discovery of the reasons (*logoi*) with which the Logos made the world'; Driscoll (2003), p. 14.

205 *KG* II.4.

206 *KG* III.35.

207 *KG* I.43.

208 *KG* II.47.

209 *KG* II.66–7, 70.

210 See further Konstantinovsky (2009), for example pp. 47, 56ff.

some sense a punishment and a liability, the body is also holy, and any who denigrate it 'blaspheme against the Creator'.[211]

Yet the one who sees the Creator from the harmony of beings does not know God's nature but the wisdom with which God made everything, and even then not 'essential wisdom' but rather what appears in beings – how foolish, then, are those who claim to know God's nature![212] Here Evagrius reflects the Cappadocian arguments against Eunomius.[213] It is simply not possible to know the nature of the Holy Trinity.[214] Like God, however, νοῦς (mind) is also 'incomprehensible' – if only because it is susceptible of the Holy Trinity.[215] Just as a fire overpowers its 'body', so the *nous* can overpower the soul if it is entirely 'mixed' with the Holy Trinity;[216] and just as Adam became a 'living soul' after the 'breathing in' (Gen. 3.7), so the νοῦς becomes a 'living mind' when it has received the Holy Trinity.[217] There is a real tension here between Evagrius' sense of God's otherness and his expectation of attaining 'knowledge in which the knower and the known are one';[218] yet that possibility rests in the incomprehensibility that νοῦς shares with God – it is not possible for us to comprehend what is a nature susceptible of the Holy Trinity, nor to comprehend the Unity, nor 'essential knowledge', Evagrius states.[219]

What we inherit as heirs with Christ is knowledge of the Unity.[220] The opening of the fourth 'century' develops this a little further: the co-heir of Christ is the one who arrives in Unity and delights itself in contemplation with Christ.[221] Evagrius' understanding of Christ is particularly elusive. Some of the 'chapters' seem to distinguish between Christ and the Word – indeed, to state that he is not connatural with the Trinity, though he alone has in him all 'essential knowledge' inseparably, and the Word of God is in him.[222] Many commentators assume that Christ is conceived here as the one λογικός or νοῦς which did not fall, as in Origen's thought. There are also sayings which seem to suggest that Evagrius sees Christ as the 'One-Many' that holds together the variety of created beings with the ultimate One: repeatedly Evagrius uses of Christ the phrase from Ephesians (3.10), 'the wisdom of God in its rich variety'.[223] Yet Christ alone belongs within the Unity and has the Unity within himself – for 'the Father alone knows the Son, and the Son the Father' (Matt. 11.27).[224] Ulti-

---

211 *KG* IV.62; see discussion in Konstantinovsky (2009), especially pp. 122ff.

212 *KG* V.50–1.

213 See Chapter 4, pp. 156–9.

214 *KG* V.62; cf. V.55–6 against the possibility of applying analysis to God.

215 *KG* II.11.

216 *KG* II.29.

217 *KG* III.71.

218 Louth (1981), p. 109, following Hausherr, puts Evagrius with Origen in opposition to the 'radical unknowability' of Gregory of Nyssa; cf. 'in all contemplation the object of contemplation is over against the mind, except in contemplation of the Holy Trinity' (*KG* IV.87).

219 *KG* II.11.

220 *KG* III.72.

221 *KG* IV.8.

222 *KG* IV.18, 21; V.48. For discussion, see Konstantinovsky (2009), chapter 5.

223 *KG* I.43; II.2, 21; III.11, 13, 81; IV.7; V.84.

224 *KG* III.1–3.

mately Christ will deliver up his kingdom to the Father, so that God will be all in all.[225] The *Skemmata*[226] provide a couple of sayings which perhaps confirm this mediating position:

> Christ, in that he is Christ, possesses [essential] knowledge; in that he is creator, he possesses the reasons of the ages [i.e. the created order]; in that he is incorporeal, he possesses the reasons of incorporeal beings.

> Christ is a rational nature, possessing within himself that which is signified by the dove that alighted upon him (cf. Matt. 3.16).

Sinkewicz[227] cites a text which explains this in terms of the wings of the dove being contemplation of bodies and the incorporeals, through which the mind is raised on high and comes to rest in the knowledge of the Holy Trinity. Evagrius picks up biblical themes in his understanding of Christ as the one through whom we are created and in whom we are redeemed – yet they are transmuted into his own terms.

Enigmatic sayings often allude to scripture, and usually imply an intellectualizing interpretation. The high priest's dress is symbolic, the 'intelligible breastplate', for example, being the hidden knowledge of God's mysteries.[228] Intelligible 'unleavened bread' is the state of the rational soul constituted of pure virtues and true doctrines.[229] The resurrection of the body is the passage to a higher character, the resurrection of the soul is the return to an impassible state, while the resurrection of the *nous* is the passage from ignorance to true knowledge.[230] The kingdom of God is contemplation of beings.[231] The 'intelligible temple' is the pure *nous* which now has in itself the wisdom full of God's rich variety (Eph. 3.10); the temple of God is one who sees holy Unity, and the altar of God is contemplation of the Holy Trinity.[232] The crucifixion of Christ is mortification of our 'old man', the annulling of the sentence against us and remission which makes us return to life; the death of Christ is the mysterious operation which restores to eternal life those who hoped in him in this life.[233] But traditional statements like these last occur in a context in which Egypt signifies evil, the desert the πρακτική, the land of Judah the contemplation of bodies, Jerusalem that of the incorporeals and Sion is a symbol of the Trinity;[234] so they clearly carry a distinctly Evagrian meaning.

---

225 Konstantinovsky (2009), p. 164, quoting *Scholion* 118 to Prov. 10.3, which quotes 1 Cor. 15.28.

226 *Skemmata* 1 and 5; ET Sinkewicz (2003), p. 211; I have substituted 'essential' for 'substantial' for consistency.

227 Sinkewicz (2003), note on p. 285.

228 *KG* IV.66.

229 *KG* IV.28.

230 *KG* V.19, 22, 25.

231 *KG* V.35.

232 *KG* V.84; cf. *Skemmata* 34: 'the mind is the temple of the Holy Trinity' (Sinkewicz 2003, p. 214).

233 *KG* VI.40, 42.

234 *KG* VI.49.

The above paragraphs are inevitably based on a rather arbitrary selection from the *Kephalaia gnōstika*; yet they should provide a little insight into the allusive nature of this work. One should probably avoid too easily reading it in the light of the anti-Origenist strictures of 553, or indeed of a preconceived metaphysical scheme;[235] yet it would seem appropriate to discern its overall viewpoint by reference to the so-called *Letter to Melania*. This opens with the ancient commonplace that a letter brings together those who are separate, and treats this as a 'type' of the 'rift' between God and fallen beings, which God bridges through the creation. Someone who contemplates creation becomes aware of the Creator's loving intention, as the reader of a letter senses the letter-writer. The Son and the Spirit are signs of the Father, rational creation is a sign by which the Son and Spirit are known (Gen. 1.26), and the visible, material creation is a sign of the intelligible, immaterial creation. But all this differentiation will be superseded when everything is raised to the order of the mind. When the mind fell through free will, it was called soul, and descended again into body; but at some point it will rise to its former creation. The unification of rational beings with God the Father will be like many streams entering the 'intelligible, infinite and immutable sea'. Before sin made a separation between the minds and God, they were one with him; when the sin between the minds and God is expunged, they will be one and not many.[236] Constantly Evagrius glosses this scheme with assurance that the Trinity remains eternally Trinity, before and after the minds mingle with it. Here again is the integral place of πρακτική, φυσική and θεολογική in the journey back to unity with God: the first purges body and soul of its passions, the second discerns God's providential intentions in creating the material world (the second creation), the third is the attainment of 'essential knowledge' of the Trinity. The *Kephalaia gnōstika* would seem to invite meditation on aspects of this over-arching picture of the spiritual journey.

Ad Monachos

The short collection *Ad Monachos* appears to be a focused presentation in condensed form of this whole schema. It is surely meant to be pondered line by line, not hastily surveyed; yet Driscoll's overview reveals that its arrangement is a skilful representation of the πρακτική and the γνωστική, with the central section roughly corresponding to the *Gnōstikos* in the trilogy, and having a similar transitional role.

What emerges very clearly is that the bridge between πρακτική and γνωστική is love:

In front of love, passionless marches;
in front of knowledge, love.[237]

---

235 Casiday (2006), pp. 25–35; Konstantinovsky (2009). Casiday provides ET of the *Letter to Melania*.

236 For the return to Unity (ἀποκατάστασις), see discussion in Konstantinovsky (2009), chapter 6; Evagrius' thought led logically to universalism through the destruction of all that is evil.

237 *Ad Monarchos* (hereafter cited as *Ad M.*) 67.

Driscoll notes how the importance of the other virtues lies in the way they lead to the supreme virtue of love:[238] Evagrius 'moves the reader' on 'through a sustained meditation' at 'the center of the text' on 'the inextricable relation between πρακτική and knowledge'; this is 'the key to the whole, virtue leading to love and love leading to knowledge'. The opening of the whole collection makes the same point:

> Faith: the beginning of love.
> The end of love: knowledge of God. [239]

Knowledge appears off and on from the beginning, but when we reach the last thirty chapters, we clearly turn to the wisdom of investigating 'the reasons of God' (physikē) and soon focus on the supreme knowledge of the Trinity.[240]

> Contemplations of worlds enlarge the heart;
> Reasons of providence and judgement lift it up;[241]

> While knowledge of incorporeals raises the mind
> And presents it before the Holy Trinity.[242]

We have reached θεολογική, but Evagrius' reserve is noticeable. Elsewhere in his writings it is clear that before God there is only silence. It is to this aspect of Evagrius' thinking that we now turn.

4 Imageless prayer

The other treatise which survived to influence Eastern spirituality was On Prayer. Evagrius defines prayer as 'the communion of the mind with God' and makes it clear that a prerequisite is the 'four primary virtues' – prudence, continence, courage and justice.[243] He also states that 'prayer is the offshoot of gentleness and freedom from anger' and a defence against sadness and discouragement (ἀκηδία).[244] In other words, the πρακτική is the essential starting-point; 'the state of prayer is an impassible habit, which by means of a supreme love carries off to the intelligible height the spiritual mind beloved of wisdom'.[245] 'Undistracted prayer is the mind's highest form of intellection', for 'prayer is the ascent of the mind towards God'.[246] Furthermore, 'one who prays "in spirit and in truth" (John 4.23–4) honours the Creator no longer on the basis of creatures, but praises him for himself'.[247] 'If you are a theologian, you will pray

---

238 Driscoll (2003), p. 151.
239 Ad M. 3.
240 Ad M. 110.
241 Ad M. 135.
242 Ad M. 136.
243 De Oratione (hereafter De O.) 3 and 1.
244 De O. 14, 16.
245 De O. 52.
246 De O. 34a, 35.
247 De O. 59.

truly; and if you pray truly, you will be a theologian.'[248] Prayer, though presupposing the πρακτική and the φυσική, is profoundly linked with the ultimate stage of the spiritual ascent, the θεολογική.

But this pure prayer is only realized if you 'do not form images of the divine within yourself, nor allow your mind to be impressed with any form, but approach the Immaterial immaterially and you will come to understanding': 'The Divinity is without quantity and without form'.[249] So it is particularly in prayer that the demons attack by forming 'some strange fantasy' in the mind, which is 'easily brought into submission' because 'it is habituated to associating with mental representations'.[250] Prayer is 'the laying aside of mental representations'; so 'make no attempt at all to receive a figure or colour during the time of prayer'.[251]

This aspect of Evagrius' thought has generated considerable discussion. It is clear that the 'image of God' was a major issue in the Egypt of the fourth century. Theophilus zealously attacked idolatry, and in his festal letter of 399 (it would seem) promulgated the view that God was incorporeal – according to the historians this provoked rioting among the monks. Most of our reports suggest that these 'Anthropomorphites' had a naïve understanding as recent converts from paganism. It seems likely, however, that there were deeper theological issues reflecting debate that had been going on for some time, issues arising from scripture and tradition about humanity being created in God's image, about the incarnation and about the Eucharist, all of which could put a different complexion on the conflict. Despite Socrates' scepticism about Theophilus' motives, maybe the fact that he responded to such arguments is reflected in the anecdote that, confronted by angry monks, he replied, 'In seeing you I behold the face of God'. Certainly a Coptic source would support such an interpretation. It was after this volte-face that Theophilus drove the so-called Origenist monks out of Egypt. Evagrius' teaching about the purgation of all images from the mind in prayer, and its possible rooting in an Origenist view of protology and eschatology, would seem to have had some responsibility for this, especially as he was closely associated with Ammonius, one of the Tall Brothers, with Palladius, and with Rufinus and Melania, all part of the Origenist network.[252]

However, even more than the theology of Origen, which posited a kinship between the λογικοί (rational beings) and God, the anti-Arian theology, which insisted on a distinction between God and created intelligences, would seem to have been a crucial factor for Evagrius. He had learned from the Cappadocians that God cannot be defined or conceived by the creaturely mind: 'anyone who introduces number or creature when confessing the Son of God or the Holy Spirit, introduces a material and circumscribed nature unawares'.[253] Nicene Orthodoxy demanded the removal of all mental representations or images. But even more significant, the notion of imageless prayer is profoundly integrated with

248 *De O.* 60.
249 *De O.* 66–7.
250 *De O.* 68.
251 *De O.* 70, 114.
252 For fuller exposition of this view, see Clark (1992), who builds on the work of Guillaumont and others.
253 *Epistula Fidei* (= Basil's *Ep.* 8) 2 (8).

Evagrius' overall thought, a point well demonstrated by Columba Stewart;[254] it coheres with his suspicion of mental representations as a source of temptation, and his determination to resist spiritual self-deception. Characteristic of Evagrius are 'cautions against mistaking sensory phenomena for experiences of God'. But Stewart also explores the fact that ἀναισθησία (*anaisthēsia*) allows for συναίσθησις (*sunaisthēsis*) in 'spiritual prayer'. For Evagrius often draws upon biblical imagery, especially references to the divine light, and allows it to function as a stepping stone to the 'place of God', the 'chamber in which we behold the holy and hidden Father'.[255] Indeed, exegesis and the pondering of scripture is more significant for Evagrius' thought than most accounts suggest; the weaving together of biblical and philosophical terminology is characteristic, and in Evagrius, Driscoll suggests, 'the philosophical language does not contaminate the Christian content but makes it possible to think about it more profoundly'.[256] In the *Skemmata*, the person at prayer sees himself 'resembling sapphire or the colour of heaven' (cf. Exod. 24.9–11) – this is the state of the mind 'to which the Holy Trinity comes in the time of prayer'; for 'the mind is the temple of the Holy Trinity', and 'prayer is a state of the mind that arises under the influence of the Trinity's unique light'.[257] Imageless prayer is perhaps a foretaste of that 'essential knowledge' which is a transcendent mystical union in which knower and known become incomprehensibly one.

We might add that alongside the statements which resist images are some that urge monks to treat colleagues as they would the One whose image they bear – Evagrius constantly holds different perspectives in balance. Thus, seven beatitudes provide a climax, though not the ending, of the chapters *On Prayer*. The first four reinforce the imageless character of pure prayer – a couple of examples:

Blessed is the mind which has acquired perfect freedom from the impressions of forms during the time of prayer.[258]

Blessed is the mind which during the time of prayer has acquired perfect detachment from the senses.[259]

The others, however, put this into a different perspective – such as:

Blessed is the monk who considers all people as God after God.[260]

As for Origen, so for Evagrius, the spiritual life was a journey of the mind. As

---

254 Stewart (2001); note his discussion of how this relates to Evagrius' understanding of how the mind works. See also Konstantinovsky (2009), pp. 33ff. on Evagrius' epistemology – images, which are 'the building blocks of knowledge', may be edifying or demonic; yet 'finally the mind becomes completely disengaged from the multiplicity of the universe's forms and colours', p. 81.

255 Cf. Harmless and Fitzgerald (2001).

256 Driscoll in Luchman and Kulzer (1999).

257 *Skemmata* 2, 4, 34, 27; for further discussion see Konstantinovsky (2009), chapter 4.

258 *De O.* 117.

259 *De O.* 120.

260 *De O.* 123; cf. *Praktikos* 89, quoted earlier.

for Didymus, so for Evagrius, the narrative of that spiritual journey could be discerned in scripture. As for the Cappadocians, so for Evagrius, the infinite otherness of the Trinity put the mind of the theologian in its place. As for the desert ascetics, so for Evagrius, patient daily struggle with internal temptations, whether arising from the appetites of body or soul, was the arena which enabled the growth of true love and pure prayer.

For Further Reading

English translations

Casiday, A. M., 2006. *Evagrius Ponticus*, The Early Christian Fathers, London and New York: Routledge.
Driscoll, Jeremy, OSB, 2003. *Evagrius Ponticus: Ad Monachos*, Translation and Commentary, ACW 59, New York: Newman Press.
Sinkewicz, Robert E., 2003. *Evagrius of Pontus. The Greek Ascetic Corpus*, Oxford Early Christian Studies, Oxford: Oxford University Press.

Studies

Konstantinovsky, Julia, 2009. *Evagrius Ponticus: The Making of a Gnostic*, Farnham: Ashgate.
Stewart, Columba, 2001. 'Imageless Prayer and the Theological Vision of Evagrius Ponticus', *JECS* 9, pp. 173–204.

VI The 'Macarian' Homilies

The 'Macarian' material may provide a bridge from Egypt to other streams of the fourth-century ascetic movement. Attributed in the majority manuscript tradition to Macarius of Egypt, one of Evagrius' teachers, whom we have already met also in Palladius and the *Apophthegmata*, these texts had widespread and considerable influence on Eastern monasticism and Protestant pietism. Twentieth-century scholarship, however, confirmed earlier hunches that their provenance is more likely to be Syria, or its borderlands with Asia Minor, and that their teaching is somewhat uncomfortably close to Messalianism, an ascetic heresy repeatedly condemned. As a result, there has been a tendency to contrast the 'Macarian' spirituality of the heart with Evagrius' focus on the mind,[261] despite the interest of both in ἀπάθεια as a prerequisite for receiving the Holy Spirit in the soul; and to contrast 'Macarian' affirmations about seeing God with Evagrius' imageless prayer, despite the fact that they share a mysticism of light and the *Spiritual Homilies* point to deeper ways of seeing.[262] The work of Golitzin and Plested,[263] however, has bucked these trends:

---

261 Louth (1981), p. 116.
262 Konstantinovsky (2009), p. 104.
263 Golitzin (2002); also 'Temple and Throne of the Divine Glory: "Pseudo-Macarius" and Purity of Heart, together with some remarks on the limitations and usefulness of scholarship' in Luckman and Kulzer (1999); Plested (2004).

while accepting the Syrian connections, they demonstrate that different influences intertwine in the 'Macarian' writings and parallels with Evagrius can be drawn, so that it is not after all so surprising that the two combined to shape the monastic spirituality of the Eastern Church. These homilies, then, may indeed provide a bridge between ascetic worlds.

1 Critical questions

The critical questions surrounding these texts are complex. Researches into the manuscript tradition have revealed the existence of several different collections.[264] The best-known Greek collection, printed in Migne[265] and available in English translations,[266] is now designated Collection II. It contains the traditional fifty 'spiritual homilies', some including questions from disciples and answers from their teacher. Collection I[267] has sixty-four *logoi*, consisting of a similar range of 'homilies' and some letters; the first of these *logoi* is the so-called *Great Letter*, a text with a clear literary relationship to the *De Instituto Christiano* of Gregory of Nyssa, and so the subject of considerable debate about priority, the general consensus now being that priority lies with 'Macarius'.[268] Collection III[269] has forty-three homilies, twenty-one of them not paralleled elsewhere, while Collection IV contains twenty-six homilies, all of which are included in the Collection I – the largest. In addition to Greek manuscripts there are versions in Syriac, Arabic, Georgian, Latin and Slavonic.

The work of Dörries established the Messalian connection. An article by Villecourt in 1920 had put the issue of the provenance of this material on the agenda. Some features of these texts mirror the reported reasons given for the repeated condemnations of Messalianism as a heresy; and Dörries[270] discovered that Pseudo-Macarian material was sometimes attributed to a Symeon of Mesopotamia, and a Symeon is listed among those condemned as Messalian by Flavian of Antioch in 380s or 390s. Some scholars have simply accepted that these texts are Messalian; others have suggested that they represent a 'reforming tendency' in the direction of a more orthodox position. This raises issues about the nature and history of Messalianism, as well as the origins of these texts.

It is generally recognized that the Messalians took their name from the Syriac for 'those who pray'. They are first mentioned in the 370s by Ephrem the Syrian[271] and Epiphanius,[272] and Jerome refers to 'heretics who are all over

---

264 Dörries (1941).

265 For a critical edition, see Dörries, Klostermann and Kroeger (1964).

266 Maloney (1992) – quotations are usually made from this English version; cf. Mason (1921).

267 For the text, and discussion of the collections and their relationship, see Berthold (1973).

268 Jaeger (1954) argued for 'Macarius' being dependent on Gregory; this judgment has been reversed since Staats (1968, 1984).

269 Klostermann and Berthold (1961); Desprez (1980).

270 Dörries (1941, 1978).

271 In *Against the Heresies* 22.4; cf. Chapter 5 for Ephrem.

272 *Ancoratus* 13 and *Panarion* 80; cf. Chapter 5 for Epiphanius.

Syria, whom they perversely call by a native word, *Massalianos*, *Euchites* in Greek'.[273] The charges against Messalianism include the notions (1) that evil, sin or 'the demon' dwells in each person from birth and cannot be cut out by baptism; (2) that continuous prayer alone can expel the indwelling demon; (3) that after the body and soul come into *apatheia*, the presence of the Holy Spirit can be felt entering a person, who then feels in communion with the heavenly bridegroom; (4) that then fasting and other disciplines are no longer necessary; and (5) that the Holy Trinity can be seen with the eyes of the body by those perfected. Furthermore, they are accused of being possessed, and calling their dreams and fantasies prophecies. They are said to reject the sacraments and the efficacy of ecclesiastical liturgies and authorities; but also to deny that such charges apply to them.

One of the important contributions made by Columba Stewart[274] was to sort out the sources for Messalianism, the stages of the controversy and the charges against it, and then detail the parallels in the Macarian material. Tracing a coherent heretical movement behind the condemnations is problematical, he suggests, and it is even more problematical to try and construct Messalianism from the 'Macarian' material. Stewart's other contribution was to track distinctive aspects of these Greek texts which reveal their background in Syrian traditions, something assumed rather than documented before. Thus he both affirms the Syrian contribution to Greek monastic spirituality through these texts, and assesses Messalianism as an 'irruption into the Hellenistic world of ascetical practices and imagistic language far more characteristic of Syriac Christianity than of the imperial Church centred on Constantinople', and hence misunderstood.

Later work, as already hinted, has stressed the range of different influences on the 'Macarian' material, creating a 'rich synthesis' of Syrian themes, Hellenistic philosophy, Origen's theology, Egyptian monasticism and Alexandrian Christology,[275] and taking seriously also the links with the Cappadocians which this author, whoever he was, shared with Evagrius.

2 Ascetic teaching

Sin and struggle

'Macarius' is certainly convinced that sin is pervasive in human life, and only God can effectively deal with it. Sin is 'mixed' with the soul, and inhabits 'the members of our soul and body'. 'It is impossible to separate the soul from sin, unless God should calm and turn back this evil wind', this 'stiff blowing wind of sin' by which a person is 'buffeted and shaken'. Liberation is found only when 'the divine wind of the Holy Spirit' comes, 'breathing through and refreshing souls who live in the divine light'.[276] Stewart notes that sin is not a 'substance' in the Pseudo-Macarian homilies, but it is 'an evil reality working with all power

---

273 *Dialogue against the Pelagians.*
274 Stewart (1991).
275 Stewart reviewing Plested (2004) in *JEH* 59 (2008), p. 528.
276 Collection II.ii.4; quotations from Maloney (1992).

and sensation', 'the robber in the house of the soul'; sin and grace are 'two presences or players in the heart' (πρόσωπα). Though not dualistic in the same sense as Gnostics or Manichaeans, the language used 'veers in the direction of dualism': 'he can even apply to the work of evil spirits language he ordinarily reserves for the energizing effect of the Holy Spirit'.[277]

Satan 'agitates and entices the whole human race, infected by the sin of Adam'. Human beings are like 'wheat in a sieve', 'sifted by restless thoughts of this world', 'tossed to and fro by earthly cares, desire and absorption in a variety of material concerns'.[278] There is constant struggle, but it is an inner struggle: the soul engages in 'war' in one's 'inner thoughts' against 'arrogance, presumption, unbelief, hatred, envy, deceit, hypocrisy', and all sorts of other sins.[279] The opposition is hidden passions, invisible bonds; and in fact, the person enmeshed in material affairs or seduced by passions, does not even recognize there is a struggle. It is the person who has set out on the path of withdrawal who 'discovers the opposition, the hidden passions, the invisible bonds, the unseen warfare, the battle and the interior struggle'.[280] To 'begin to seek God' is 'to enter into a battle with your nature in its old habits and custom', 'putting thoughts against thoughts, mind against mind, soul against soul, spirit against spirit'. This is because 'a certain hidden and subtle power of darkness is revealed that has been entrenched in the heart'.[281]

But the person who discovers this receives the heavenly armour of the Spirit, described by the Apostle, 'the breastplate of justice, the helmet of salvation, the shield of faith and the sword of the Spirit' (Eph. 6.14).[282] The good thing is that 'the Lord is near to your soul and body, seeing your battle. And he puts in you secret, heavenly thoughts and he begins interiorly to give you rest.' Discipline and grace come from the Lord, who is like a tutor.[283] Even when a person is 'deep and rich in grace, there still remains inside of him a remnant of evil', since 'it lives in our heart and there operates by suggesting wicked and obscene thoughts and by not allowing us to pour out pure prayers'. But 'if one constantly puts his hope in God, evil to a certain degree diminishes and dries up'.[284]

'Macarius' is clear that baptism by itself does not effect the transformation necessary, arguing from the reality of post-baptismal sin.[285] Sin can always get an entry, without constant watchfulness and prayer. There would certainly seem to be some kind of connection between the charges against the Messalians and this aspect of 'Macarian' teaching; but the ongoing struggle with sin is certainly not unique to these homilies, as sufficiently demonstrated by the other ascetic writings already explored in this chapter.

---

277 Stewart (1991), pp. 75–6.
278 Collection II.v.1–6.
279 Collection II.iii.4.
280 Collection II.xxi.4–5.
281 Collection II.xxxii.9–10.
282 Collection II.xxi.5.
283 Collection II.xxxii.9–10.
284 Collection II.xvi.4, 6.
285 Collection II.xv.14.

Grace, perfection and the Holy Spirit

This war can only be brought to a conclusion through grace and the power of God; none can save themselves.[286] 'Only those escape who have been reborn from above and have been transported in mind and heart to another world, as it was said: "Our citizenship is in heaven" (Phil 3.20).' The 'difference between true Christians and the rest of human beings is that the mind and intellect of Christians are always centred on heavenly thoughts', because 'they participate in the Holy Spirit', 'have been born above from God and are children of God in truth and power' and 'have arrived, through many labours and sweat' at a 'state of equilibrium, tranquillity and peace, freed from further sifting'. The language of grace, of renewal and of new creation is used; 'they have received in the inner person another Spirit'. Nevertheless few successfully complete the race; it takes complete self-denial.[287]

'Macarius' is a theologian of the Holy Spirit, and of transformation or trans- figuration. 'If anyone is in Christ, he is a new creature', he says, quoting 2 Corinthians 5.17; 'for our Lord Jesus Christ came for this reason, to change and transform and renew human nature, and to recreate this soul that had been over- turned by passions through the transgression'. Christ came to 'mingle human nature with his own Spirit of the Godhead', to effect in those who believe 'a new mind and a new soul and new eyes, a new spiritual tongue, and, in a word, new humans', to 'pour into them new wine which is his Spirit'.[288] The Spirit is 'the Lord himself shining in their hearts', and the one who possesses the Spirit fulfils 'all the commands justly and practices all the virtues without blame, purely without forcing and with a certain ease'.[289] To reach this state hearers are encouraged to force themselves to observe the commandments, begging God to grant the gift of 'the heavenly grace of the Spirit'.[290] There is a practical recogni- tion of synergism: the co-operation of divine grace and human will.

Striving for perfection in Christ lies at the heart of Macarius' teaching. There are frequent references to 'a "mixing" of the Holy Spirit with the human soul', 'to becoming "one spirit" with the Lord, to being changed into a "divine nature"', and 'to other ways of describing full communion with God'. God comes to dwell in the soul, and then obedience to the commandments becomes 'natural and easy'. 'The "mature" Christian is the one who has grown up through the ascetical struggle, and been "completed" by the gift of the Spirit.' Hence 'the emphasis on growth and progress'.[291] Many passages develop Ephesians 4.13, which speaks of advancing 'to maturity, to the measure of the full stature of Christ' (cf. Col. 1.28), or the Hebrews' reference to progressing from children's milk to the solid food of the mature (Heb. 5.12–14). There is a profound oscil- lation between the need for constant struggle, and the promise of reaching the goal, which is a return to Paradise and restoration of the image of God; 'sin is uprooted' and 'the first creation of the pure Adam' received. However, renewal

---

286 Collection II.xxi.4.
287 Collection II.v.1–6.
288 Collection II.xliv.1.
289 Collection II.xviii.1–2.
290 Collection II.xix.7.
291 Quotations in the last few sentences from Stewart (1991), pp. 78–82.

goes further than that: 'by the power of the Spirit and the spiritual regeneration', one 'not only comes to the measure of the first Adam, but also reaches a greater state than he possessed. For man is divinised.'[292]

Again there are apparent connections with the charges against the Messalians; but there are also distinct similarities to the thinking of the Cappadocians. Basil had associated the process of sanctification with the work of the Holy Spirit, and the ascetic teaching of Gregory of Nyssa points to constant growth to maturity and perfection, through effort and struggle, but also by becoming a receptacle of the Spirit and of God's grace.[293] The textual overlap of Gregory's *De Instituto Christiano* and the *Great Letter*, which is a summary distillation of 'Macarian' ascetic teaching, reflects a profound similarity in outlook.[294] Needless to say the notion of 'divinization' is common in fourth-century theology, from Athanasius to the Cappadocians and Ephrem the Syrian.

The scriptural element

The account given above implicitly draws attention to the biblical basis of the 'Macarian' spirituality.[295] The text is riddled with biblical quotations and allusion – sometimes great collages are created:

> We have not yet been immersed in the leaven of sincerity (I Cor. 5.8), but we are still in the leaven of evil . . . 'We have not yet put on the new man who has been created after God in holiness' (Eph. 4.24), because we have not yet put off 'the old man that is corrupt according to the sinful lusts' (Eph. 4.22). We have not yet 'given birth to the image of the heavenly' (I Cor. 15.49) nor have we been made 'conformed to his glory' (Phil. 3.21). We have not yet adored 'God in spirit and in truth' (Jn. 4.24), since 'sin reigns in our mortal body' (Rom. 6.12) . . . We have not yet been 'transformed by a renewal of the mind', since we are still 'conformed to this world' (Rom. 12.2) 'in the vanity of the mind' (Eph. 4.17). We are not yet 'glorified with Christ' because we have not yet 'suffered with him' (Rom. 8.17) . . .[296]

And so it goes on, citing mainly but not exclusively Pauline texts.

Another habit is reference to biblical stories and models. Perseverance in the face of temptation is graphically illustrated by reference to one biblical hero after another: Joseph, David, Moses, Abraham, Noah. 'We have offered these examples from Holy Scripture to show that the power of divine grace is in man

---

292 Collection II.xxvi.2.

293 See further Chapter 4.

294 Despite the fact that the consensus now is that the 'Macarian' Great Letter has priority, the discussion in Jaeger (1954) of Gregory's ascetic teaching and of the similarities is still valuable.

295 It is striking that 'Macarius' uses many of the same texts as John Wesley, who was certainly influenced in his reading of the New Testament by Greek patristic material, especially 'Macarius'. Wesley's diary entry for 30 July 1736 records that he read Macarius and sang. Later, he published excerpts from the Macarian Homilies in the first volume of his *Christian Library*. See further Young (2002).

296 Collection II.xxv.3–5.

and the gift of the Holy Spirit which is given to the faithful soul comes forth with much contention, with much endurance, patience, trials and testings.'[297] Accounts of Elijah withholding and then commanding rain, Moses turning the rod into a serpent and back, David overcoming Goliath, Joshua impotently besieging Jericho till God commanded the walls to tumble down – all these and more are taken to be a 'figure and shadow' of true realities, to be applied to the spiritual journey. Like Jericho's walls, for example, the walls of evil 'that obstruct your mind' will fall by God's power.[298] Traditional 'types' interiorize the Law,[299] circumcision becoming circumcision of the heart, baptism of the flesh becoming baptism with Holy Spirit and fire, the sacrifices under the old covenant signifying Christ's sacrifice, while spiritual laws are written on the 'fleshy tablets of the heart' rather than tablets of stone. The Passover and Exodus are all about human slavery to the Egyptians (that is the demons) and the deliverance accomplished in Christ; he leads the soul out of Egypt, away from darkness, and God patiently

> tests it to see whether it remains faithful, whether it has love for him. For God has planned such a road, leading to life (Mt 7.14), to be fraught with affliction and narrow escapes, in much testing and extremely bitter trials so that from there the soul may afterward reach the true land of the glory of the children of God.[300]

Many of the images and metaphors 'Macarius' uses are developments from biblical usage: themes like light and fire, water and oil, wind and trees, seed and fruit, bread and wine, mirrors and garments, pearls and treasure. He refers to biblical parables, and invents his own: Take the example of a rich woman with no protection, he says[301] – she searches for a powerful husband, and after much struggle finds a 'strong wall'; in the same way the soul searches for its bridegroom.[302] This is not the only time he uses this kind of parable, and the idea of the heavenly bridegroom of the soul recurs time and again.[303] The scriptural basis of the 'Macarian' teaching is clear on page after page, but it is scripture read in order to discern what is true for the heart on its spiritual journey to union with God, picking up typological traditions and open to the charge of allegory.

This constant recourse to scripture, and the allusive and imaginative way it is developed, can be paralleled in the poetic writing of Ephrem the Syrian, but it also bears comparison with Gregory of Nyssa; one thinks of the *Life of Moses* and the *Commentary on the Song of Songs*. The motif of the bridegroom of the soul will reappear repeatedly in Theodoret's account of Syrian asceticism, the *Historia Religiosa*. 'Macarius' provides a striking example of a widespread hermeneutic.

---

297 Collection II.ix.2–7.
298 Collection II.l.1–3.
299 Collection II.xlvii.1ff.
300 Collection II.xlvii.13.
301 Collection II.xlv.5.
302 Collection II.xlv.5.
303 For example, Collection II.iv.6–7; x.1, 4; xv.2; xxv.8; xxvii.1; xxviii.5; etc.

Interiority and prayer

The account of the scriptural element in 'Macarian' teaching has already alerted us to its pervasive interiority. The focus is on experience, assurance, sensation, communion,[304] and this is found in prayer:

> One kneels down in prayer and at once his heart is filled with the power of God. And his soul exults in the Lord as a bride with the bridegroom ... It happens that he is the whole day occupied by his work and can give himself to prayer for only an hour. The interior man is caught up in prayer and plunged into the infinite depths of that other world with great sweetness ...
> At times the fire flares out and burns with more vehement flames. At other times it burns more gently and slowly ... It is always burning and giving off light, but when it is especially trimmed, it burns more brilliantly, as though intoxicated by the love of God.[305]

But 'Macarius' admits that this intensity is not permanent: 'there are times when grace burns more brightly, consoles and refurbishes more completely. Then at other time the grace subsides and is clouded over.' One reason for this is that if a person stays on the top step of grace, the highest level of perfection, he could not bear to take any interest in anything else, preaching or work, but would simply 'sit in a corner lifted up and intoxicated'. He affirms that he has 'not yet seen any perfect Christian'. No matter how much a person is 'at rest in grace', 'experiencing mysteries, revelations, and the immense consolation of grace', 'sin still abides in him'. Those who claim to be perfect are deceived by lack of experience.

Yet he affirms that there are 'spiritual senses' – five rational senses of the soul.[306] 'Everyone should realize there are eyes deeper within than these physical eyes and there is hearing deeper within than this hearing'. Just as a friend or loved one is recognized by physical senses, so 'the true friend, the sweetest and greatly desired bridegroom' is seen and recognized by one spiritually enlightened. 'Seeing with the mind the desirable and only ineffable beauty, such a person is pierced with divine passionate love and is directed in the way of all virtues by the Spirit.'[307]

All the ascetic endeavour possible makes a person 'salt without savour', unless he 'feel in his soul ... the pleasure of the Spirit', unless he be 'clothed ... with the clothing of the light of the Godhead', unless he 'know with assurance the satisfaction of the communion of the heavenly bridegroom in his soul' and 'the joy of the Spirit interiorly', unless he 'receive the heavenly consolation of grace and a divine filling in the soul in the appearance to him of the glory of the Lord'.[308] Reading scripture profits nothing if a person does not receive the gift of life. This perspective is surely that in which to read what little is said about

---

304 Stewart (1991) explores the distinctive Greek vocabulary used for this range of responses.
305 Collection II.viii.1, 2.
306 Collection II. iv.7.
307 Collection II.xxviii.5.
308 Collection II.xlix.1.

sacraments: baptism and Eucharist and everything else are nothing worth if they do not effect inner transformation. 'Macarius' speaks of 'a baptism of fire and of the Holy Spirit', and of 'bread and wine' offered up in the Church as 'the antitype of his flesh and blood', and of those 'who received of the visible bread' eating 'spiritually of the flesh of the Lord', and receiving the Holy Spirit.[309] Since visible things are the type and shadow of hidden ones, so the exterior performance of the 'mystery' of the Eucharist is received as 'an illustration [of what is] worked in a soul by grace'. In other words these texts suggest 'a sacramental conception of the indwelling presence of the Lord in the human person, analogous to the sacramental economy of the institutional Church'.[310] Church and soul are type and antitype.[311] The human body is a temple of God, and the human heart is an altar of the Holy Spirit.

Again this stress on interiority illustrates the overlap of 'Macarian' teaching on asceticism with the charges against Messalianism: baptism is not enough to get rid of the sin or 'demon' which dwells in everyone; continuous prayer is the way to expel it; and the Holy Spirit can be felt when a person enters into communion with the heavenly bridegroom. But again there are many other connections to be made, with Syriac material, with Origen and the Cappadocians, with Evagrius. Interiority constantly parallels ecclesiology when the focus is on anticipation of the eschaton.

Christ and salvation

'Macarius' always has a practical homiletic outlook rather than a theoretical interest; so Christology is not something that figures abstracted from ascetic teaching. Christ gives 'true prayer, genuine love,' he says, 'which is himself made all things in you: paradise, tree of life, pearl, crown, builder, cultivator, sufferer, one capable of suffering, man, God, wine, living water, lamb, bridegroom, warrior, armor, Christ, all in all'.[312] Again, in the *Great Letter* we find names of Christ catalogued, names 'received analogically' 'due to the economy of salvation for mankind'. He is a rock because of his unshakable and impenetrable strength, a door because he is the entrance to eternal life, an axe because he cuts out the roots of evil, a way because he leads the worthy to a knowledge of the truth, a vine from which wine is produced that exhilarates the human heart, and bread that strengthens the heart of the rational animal. Such cataloguing of scriptural 'names' for Christ connects these homilies with Origen, Athanasius and many others.[313]

We also find repeated use of biblical titles, such as Redeemer, Saviour, King, Prophet.[314] Christ is High Priest, Lamb of God[315] and Shepherd:

309 Collection II.xxvii.17.
310 Stewart (1991), pp. 219–20, quoting Collection I.7.18 and I.52. Cf. Golitzin (2002).
311 See Collection II.xxxvii.8.
312 Collection II.xxi.4.
313 Young (1987).
314 Collection II.iv.20; cf. for King v.6; x.4; xv.30, 33, 37; xvii.1; xxiii.2; xxv.23, 25; xxvii.4; xxviii.3; xxxix.1, xlvii.17; etc.; for Redeemer xi.6; xxxi.2; for Saviour xxv.23.
315 High Priest: collection II.i.6,8; xxxii.5; xliv.4. Lamb: collection II.xi.10; xxviii.5,6; xlvii.8, 11.

As a shepherd is able to heal the scabby sheep and to protect it from wolves, so the real Shepherd, Christ, came and alone was able to heal and convert the lost and scabby sheep, namely humanity, for the scab and leprosy of sin.[316]

As the true physician, Christ is able to heal all sickness and disease of the soul.[317] He is also the liberator who sets free those bound to sin.[318]

The cross is crucial to this healing. Moses fixed a bronze serpent on a pole as an antidote to bites from serpents in the desert. 'The dead serpent conquered over the living serpents as a type of the body of the Lord.' He raised the body he took from Mary on the cross; so the dead body slew 'the serpent, living and creeping into the hearts of men'. But there is more to it than that. For 'just as Moses made a new thing when he fashioned the likeness of a serpent, so the Lord created a new thing from Mary' – 'a new and sinless body'. 'The heavenly Spirit touched humanity and brought it to divinity.' So 'a dead body overcame the live serpent'. Triumph over the sin that inhabits human nature is the focus of homilies which enjoin ascetics to interior struggle, and it is this triumph that Christ accomplished.[319] The cross is something in which to glory, to which to be attached.[320]

Christ is also an example: suffering mockery, wearing a crown of thorns, he 'bore the spittings, the buffets, and the cross. If God so lived on earth, then it will become you to imitate him.' The hearers are to be crucified with the crucified, suffer with the one who suffered – 'the bride must suffer with the Bridegroom and so become partner and co-heir with Christ'.[321]

The most important designations of Christ, however, are 'light' and 'image', since transformation or transfiguration is the ultimate goal of the ascetic's life. At one point 'Macarius' describes Christ as a portrait painter, endeavouring to reproduce his own image in the believer. The soul needs to have Christ stamped on it if it is to be coin in the treasuries of the kingdom.[322] The bodies of the saints are like lamps lit from the fire of Christ:

> For as the body of the Lord was glorified when he climbed the mount and was transfigured into the divine glory and into infinite light, so also the bodies of the saints are glorified and shine like lightning.[323]

Their transfiguration takes place by 'putting on Christ', the 'garment of salvation', the 'ineffable light'. Once clothed in Christ, the garment

> will never be put off for all eternity. But in the resurrection of their bodies also will be glorified by the glory of the Light with which the faithful and noble persons are even now clothed.[324]

---

316 Collection II.xliv.3; cf. xii.13.
317 Collection II.xliv.3; cf. xv.30; xx.4; xxv.23; xxx.9; xlvi.2; xlviii.4.
318 For example, Collection II.xxv.23.
319 Collection II.xi.10.
320 Collection II.viii.6; xxxviii.5, etc.
321 Collection II.xii.4–5; cf. xxvii.1–2.
322 Collection II.xxx.4–5.
323 Collection II.xv.38.
324 Collection II.xx.1–3.

So Christ lies at the core of the 'Macarian' transformative reading of the Bible; Christians become his friends, his brothers, his fellow-heirs, participators of the divine nature, conformed to his glory.[325]

The most fascinating passage exemplifying the re-creative role of Christ is found in what appears as Homily i of Collection II. Here is a reflection on Ezekiel's vision of the chariot-throne of God – the Merkabah, a passage which figured large in Jewish mystical speculations and so was treated with great caution by the Rabbis. 'Macarius' starts off by saying that the prophet 'described it in human terms but in a way full of mysteries that completely surpass the powers of the human mind'. He insists that what the prophet saw, whether in ecstasy or in a trance, was true and certain. He thinks, however, that the 'mystery hidden for generations' (Col. 1.26) has been revealed 'in our time, at the end of the ages' (1 Peter 1.20) when Christ appeared. What Ezekiel's vision is about is the 'mystery of the human soul that would receive its Lord and would become his throne of glory'. The soul 'is covered with the beauty of ineffable glory of the Spirit', 'with the beauty of the ineffable glory of the light of Christ, who mounts and rides upon the soul'. It is 'Christ who drives, guides, carries and supports the soul about and adorns and decorates the soul with his spiritual beauty'. The animals that bore the chariot represent the will, the conscience, the mind and the power of loving. The Rider – the authentic Charioteer – is mounted on the soul and guides it with the reins of the Spirit. What we seem to have here is an astonishing adaptation of the Platonic notion of reason controlling the soul's passions. Christ takes control and he knows the way – elsewhere 'Macarius' speaks of Christ as a Pilot of the soul. With Christ in the driving seat, the whole soul becomes eye, totally light – 'all light, all face, all eye', 'all glory, all spirit'. This happens while in the body, and anticipates the resurrection. So, as Golitzin suggests,[326] 'Macarius' is affirming that it is no longer necessary to go up to heaven, as in apocalyptic visions, to see God on the glorious throne. The ascetic teaching is an interiorization of the cosmic struggle of apocalyptic, and the soul becomes the locus of theophany – the pure in heart shall see God.

The Christology of 'Macarius' is not without a sense of the great gulf between God, with whom Christ is one in substance,[327] and the created soul: God is without limits and is incomprehensible; God is in heaven and also here; God cannot undergo change and contains all things, being infinite.[328] But it is this transcendence which makes God's humility so astonishing: 'just as his greatness is incomprehensible, so also is his littleness', and this is a model for renunciation. 'He took flesh from the earth and joined it with his divine Spirit, so that you also, of the earth, might receive the heavenly soul.'[329] Macarius found the soul itself incomprehensible: 'if you cannot understand the thoughts of your own soul, how can you scrutinize the thoughts of God and his very mind?' 'The more you wish through knowledge to search and penetrate God, the more deeply you descend away from him and you comprehend nothing. Those visits

325 For example xxv.4–5, quoting NT texts; and many other examples, such as xxvii.1; xlviii.2.

326 Golitzin (2002); and in Luckman and Kulzer (1999).

327 The *Great Letter*.

328 Collection II.xvi.5.

329 Collection II.xxxii.6–7.

of God to you that happen each day, they are so mysterious and incomprehensible. You can receive them only with gratitude and belief.'[330]

Conclusion

The Macarian material offers a spirituality of experience and of the heart. But this should not be misunderstood. The heart is not the seat of emotion, but the 'inner self',[331] the place where the mind and thoughts reside, but also the depths within we scarcely understand ourselves, where dwell dragons, lions and poisonous beasts, rough roads and precipices, but also God, angels, life and light.[332] And when grace enters the heart, it penetrates the body also – for this is perhaps the most striking difference from Evagrius: the body is not transcended but transfigured.[333]

Whether belonging to Asia Minor or Syria, 'Macarius', despite the traditional attribution of his works, has come to represent ascetic teaching beyond the Egyptian tradition, and so provides a bridge to what purports to be an account of the famous monks of Syria.

For Further Reading

English translations

Maloney, G. A., SJ (trans.), 1992. *Pseudo-Macarius. The Fifty Spiritual Homilies and the Great Letter*, CWS, New York: Paulist Press.
Mason, A. J. (trans.), 1921. *Fifty Spiritual Homilies of St. Macarius the Egyptian*, London: SPCK.

Studies

Golitzin, A., 2002. 'A Testimony to Christianity as Transfiguration: The Macarian Homilies and Orthodox Spirituality' in S. T. Kimbrough, Jr (ed.), *Orthodox and Wesleyan Spirituality*, Crestwood, NY: St Vladimir's Seminary Press.
Golitzin, A., 'Temple and Throne of the divine Glory: "Pseudo-Macarius" and Purity of Heart, together with some remarks on the limitations and usefulness of scholarship', in Harriet A. Luchman and Linda Kulzer (eds), 1999. *Purity of Heart in Early Ascetic and Monastic Literature*, Collegeville, MN: Liturgical Press.
Plested, Marcus, 2004. *The Macarian Legacy: The Place of Macarius-Symeon in the Eastern Christian Tradition*, Oxford Theological Monographs, Oxford: Oxford University Press.
Stewart Columba, 1991. *'Working the Earth of the Heart': The Messalian Controversy in History, Texts, and Language to AD 431*, Oxford: Clarendon Press.

---

330 Collection II.xii.11.
331 See further the Preface to Maloney (1992) by Kallistos Ware.
332 Collection II.xliii.7.
333 Golitzin (2002).

VII Theodoret's *Historia Religiosa*

With Theodoret's *Historia religiosa*[334] we definitely move to Syria. Syrian asceticism had a character and history of its own, and almost certainly had independent roots.[335] Radical discipleship, taking literally the demand to forsake all and follow Christ, seems to have been characteristic of primitive Syrian Christianity, including the universal requirement of chastity after baptism; and the early Christian monks seem to have assimilated to their Christian discipleship a local ascetic tradition whereby individuals abandoned civilized life and reverted to the natural life of wild beasts, eating uncooked the natural produce of the earth, and wandering through the wilderness. In its developed form, Syrian asceticism went to strange extremes, so that ancient and modern critics alike have written deprecatingly of the way in which the holy men of Syria and Mesopotamia vied with each other in ascetic exercises. To pray and sing hymns continually while deliberately subjecting the body to unheard-of discomforts seems to have been the main object in view. The ascetics lived in permanent darkness in caves or tombs, or on high mountain-tops unprotected from the extremes of the climate. Not content with simple food and clothing, they fasted completely for ever-increasing periods, and clad themselves in iron so that they were bent continually to the ground, or their skin was chafed till the blood ran. The culmination was Symeon Stylites' thirty-odd years on a sixty-foot pillar, an example which subsequently produced a 'pillar-saint' tradition in the early Byzantine period. We seem a long way from the saying of the *Apophthegmata* against doing things for show, though a few of Theodoret's heroes take the same view as the wise reply of Abba Poemen to the question how one should fast:

> I would have it so that every day one should deny oneself a little in eating, so as not to be satisfied . . . (for) all these things did the great old men try out and they found that it is good to eat a little every day, and on certain days a little less.[336]

Theodoret had close personal connections with the monks of the Syrian provinces and the Euphrates region;[337] and whatever our reaction may be, it is clear that he regarded the Syrian ascetics with a mixture of veneration and criticism. The critique is subtle: of a solitary he comments that 'living like recluses he looked after his own soul',[338] and reports a rebuke by one ascetic to another that he cannot escape the charge of self-love when 'the divine law prescribes loving one's neighbour'.[339] The veneration is explicit: every life ends with a plea for the holy man to bless or intercede for the author; and the rhetorical prologue com-

---

334 Text edited Canivet and Leroy-Molinghen (1977, 1979); ET Price (1985).

335 For further details see Vööbus (1958, 1960). There are excellent summary articles by Murray (1975) and Brock (1973). Cf. Chapter 5, Section I on Ephrem Syrus.

336 *Vitae Patrum* x.44 // Alphabeticon: *Poemen* 31.

337 See further Chapter 6, Section VII.

338 *Historia religiosa* XX.2.

339 *Historia religiosa* IV.4.

pares these characters with the heroes of the theatre and the games, describing them as athletes or gladiators who take on the whole armour of God to struggle against unseen enemies. Yet he will not write 'encomia' exalting their spiritual prowess as individuals; for their exploits are charismata, mysterious workings of the Holy Spirit, demonstrating 'philosophy' – ἀπάθεια (passionlessness) in a body subject to passion (παθητός), zeal for incorporeal nature and heavenly citizenship. The monks live the lives of angels, for they imitate while in the body the life of non-bodily beings. Theodoret's work is clearly intended to edify, and he claims to write a record for posterity; but was there some other purpose?

Theodoret refers to his *Historia religiosa* in his *Ecclesiastical History*, and by relating it in various ways to his other writings, as well as considering internal evidence, it is possible to date the work fairly definitely to around 440. At this time Theodoret had been bishop of Cyrus for nearly twenty years, and during the extended, though not unruffled, lull in the Christological battle with Alexandria, had devoted himself to composing scriptural commentaries. Theodoret's literary activity was very wide-ranging – he seems to have tried out more or less every ecclesiastical genre from apologetics to history, to exegesis, to anti-heretical tracts. It is possible that he had no greater motive than to contribute to the growing literature of spiritual edification through telling the deeds of the saints. Indeed, this may even be linked to his concentration on biblical commentaries during the lull in the Christological controversy. Scripture is constantly quoted or alluded to, the 'types' of Moses, David, Elijah, Peter and others recur, and the devotion of his heroes to the Bridegroom reminds us that Theodoret wrote a commentary on the Song of Songs. Krueger has shown how pervasive is explicit reference to biblical precedents, how typology is used as 'a mode of reading the saints', and 'if the saints . . . are like the biblical heroes, then the text that tells of them is like the biblical texts, a true account of the work of God among his holy people'.[340]

However, the possibility of political motivations has been repeatedly canvassed. Peeters, in a study of the *Lives* of Saint Symeon,[341] advanced the view that Theodoret wrote under immediate pressures, his purpose being to rehabilitate his reputation among the monks of Syria; he was tarred with the Nestorian brush, was at loggerheads with John of Antioch over the Formulary of Reunion and was getting a cold reception among the ascetics. So he wrote the *Historia religiosa* to prove his championship of the Syrian ascetics against the Egyptian monks who flocked to Cyril's support. This view met with some trenchant criticisms. Richard[342] showed that relations with John of Antioch had long since been restored, and that there are no signs of the conflict Peeters imagined in the period when the *Historia religiosa* was written. It is true that some of his letters show him trying to ensure the monks' support when renewed conflict broke out; but, Canivet argued,[343] these letters are not so much concerned with his personal position as the need to involve the monks in ecclesiastical affairs and to guarantee their orthodoxy. It is significant that impeccable orthodoxy

---

340 Krueger (1997).
341 Peeters (1943).
342 Richard (1946).
343 Canivet (1977), pp. 77ff. My discussion owes much to Canivet's work, here and the edition of the text, Canivet and Leroy-Molinghen (1977, 1979).

is the mark of every one of the characters portrayed in the *Historia religiosa*; but Theodoret's aim was to keep the potentially autonomous monastic communities under episcopal authority and in line with the episcopate on doctrinal issues – self-defence, it was said, was not among his intentions.

However, building on such earlier studies, Urbainczyk[344] has shown that Theodoret's presentation of these characters does suggest personal as well as ecclesiastical motivations. We are reminded that much of his life was passed in active engagement in the long power struggle between Egypt and Syria, in which both John Chrysostom and Nestorius had been deposed as bishops of Constantinople; we are also reminded that episcopal concern about the independence of the monks is evident in this period, not least in the canons of Chalcedon. Against this background, the *Historia religiosa* becomes a 'political tract' with 'three functions': (i) 'it argues for a prominent position for Syria in ecclesiastical affairs by demonstrating that it, as well as Egypt, has produced individuals remarkable for their piety'; (ii) 'it portrays these as deferring to the Church, thus providing a model for how ascetics should behave'; (iii) 'it demonstrates the unique authority Theodoret enjoys in the region'.[345] Careful attention to the text shows that Theodoret himself is a persistent character in the story, a witness in seventeen out of the twenty-eight lives he recounts; and his mother appears in four. Converted from living a high life by one, Peter, who also cured her eye complaint, she becomes pregnant with Theodoret after thirteen years of marriage when Macedonius tells her to dedicate her child to God. She takes him to visit holy men as a child, and the stories hint at them giving him respect. Theodoret is thus subtly invested with a biblical 'typology'. When Theodoret moves on to the living holy men around his diocese, they all indicate 'their extraordinary esteem for Theodoret'.[346] This implicit personal theme is interwoven with explicit motifs about their recognition of episcopal authority: bishops 'receive honor, and Theodoret receives more than others'.[347]

Theodoret probably had a number of somewhat mixed motives, and apologetic for the ascetic movement may also have been an important purpose. Theodoret was clearly addressing a cultured audience, and as Canivet observes, we have considerable evidence that in this period cultivated and civilized people, especially pagans, despised the monks as ignorant rustics or hypocrites undermining society. There are also traces of criticism directed particularly against the ascetic practices of the Syrians, which were unfavourably compared with those of the heroes of Palestine and Egypt. Although Theodoret generally does not make this apologetic purpose explicit, answering criticisms only in the Epilogue, which seems to be a later addition to the original work,[348] his choice of irreproachable examples and his presentation of the anchorites as the prototypes of the Christian life, as the heroes of a new kind of epic, as the champions in a new kind of conflict, as the incarnation of a new type of humanity – all this suggests that he is offering a reply to detractors. He says he means to avoid panegyric and write a *historia*: but history in the ancient world meant present-

---

344 Urbainczyk (2002).
345 Urbainczyk (2002), p. 68.
346 Urbainczyk (2002), p. 141.
347 Urbainczyk (2002), p. 129.
348 Urbainczyk (2002), p. 62, on the epilogue, *On Divine Love*.

ing moral examples, and his collection of 'lives' is in the fashionable tradition of 'Lives of the Sages'. The true philosophy is presented by means of a series of biographical portraits. Theodoret's title was *Philotheos historia*, perhaps an echo of Galen's *Philosophos historia*.

This background accounts for the somewhat different form of Theodoret's work compared with those considered earlier. Theodoret does not offer a rather diffuse collection of sayings and anecdotes, nor an autobiographical account of his travels, but a series of 'Lives of the Saints'. The work is usually divided into thirty chapters (originally twenty-eight – XXII and XXIII belong together and were separated at some point, as also XXIV and XXV),[349] with a prologue and a concluding essay, *On Divine Love*, which was probably written a few years later. For the most part each chapter deals with one individual: each was either the founder of a monastery (usually referred to by Theodoret as a 'wrestling-school' or a 'choir'), in which case disciples may be invoked in the same chapter, or a great individual exponent of the anchorite life, and all are presented as faultless models of the monastic ideal in one way or another. Generally we learn a little about the background of each, the style of their asceticism, a few anecdotes, something about their relationship with people, bishops, and others, their miracles and their pupils.

Theodoret gives some hints about the intended arrangement – it more or less follows a chronological and geographical scheme. Thus, Theodoret introduces first heroes of the past who have died, starting with James of Nisibis, then turns to people still alive, again beginning with a James, the local holy man of his diocese of Cyrus, to whom he devotes the longest chapter in the collection. The other long 'Life', that of Symeon Stylites, appears among these later saints, and the paragraph referring to his death is almost certainly an interpolation.[350] Again, many of the earliest accounts concern people associated with Antioch, some of whom Theodoret had known in his youth – Aphrahat, Peter, Zeno, Macedonius; while the later chapters largely deal with monks around Cyrus. Men are in the majority, but the final three are holy women. A few of the 'Lives' are brief notices, but in many cases the chapter gives some account of the origin of the subject, his methods of asceticism, and a number of anecdotes, each one being a literary piece potentially independent of the entire work. This is particularly true of the 'Life of Symeon', the relationship of Theodoret's account with other early Lives being in this case a critical question of some complexity.[351]

This brings us to the question of sources. Theodoret, anxious to provide guarantees of the extraordinary things he relates, affirms that he has seen some facts with his own eyes, and what he has not seen himself, he has heard from those who had been witnesses. This seems to exclude written sources, and Canivet[352] argues that that is the case. Theodoret reports the popular legends which had grown up around such early figures as Jacob of Nisibis.[353] He frequently tells us

---

349 Devos (1979).

350 This is generally acknowledged in all discussions of this material. A full critical account of the manuscript tradition will be found in Leroy-Molinghen (1964). The signs are that a new edition was produced by a later hand.

351 See Doran (1992).

352 Canivet (1977), chapter V.

353 Cf. Chapter 5, Section II; Jacob was Ephrem's bishop.

where he got his information from, where possible naming a reliable witness like his pious mother or Acacius of Beroea. Even the 'Life of Symeon' distinguishes between what Theodoret had himself seen and what he had heard from others. Canivet is disposed to take Theodoret's word for it. Yet the 'Life of Symeon' is far more of a 'Saint's Day Sermon' or exhortation to pilgrims than the other chapters; it is more like a panegyric, tends towards the rhetorical in style, comparing its hero with Old Testament prophets. Furthermore, it presents an apology for 'Stylitism' which closely resembles that of the Syriac Life written in 474; so far from the Syriac being dependent on Theodoret, as Delahaye suggested,[354] the most likely explanation is that of Festugière, namely that both drew on the 'official' apologetic legend composed by the attendant monks.[355] Theodoret himself speaks of other accounts already existing in the saint's lifetime. That Theodoret's account is a patchwork, partially drawing on source-material and partially on his personal experience, seems most likely; but clearly the critical questions surrounding this aspect of Theodoret's work remain complex.

Without Theodoret's *Historia religiosa*, our knowledge of Syrian monasticism would be seriously depleted; Canivet counted references to seventy-five ascetics, many not mentioned in other material.[356] Yet Theodoret confesses in a number of places to being selective, and some have commented on his 'patchy knowledge of the past history of Syrian monasticism'.[357] There is also a sense in which he has attempted to 'domesticate' the wilder elements of the movement he describes.[358] Extreme ascetic practices are reported, but Theodoret tends to avoid dwelling on them, approves of ecclesiastics, including himself, who tried to moderate them and hastens to characterize the 'angelic life' of his characters. In what respects did they live the life of angels? Most obviously in their virginity – for immortal beings do not need to propagate the species; then also in their remarkable transcendence of normal human needs and limitations – through excessive fasting and extreme physical endurance; and most importantly in their perpetual worship – the work of angels is to dance in heaven and sing to the glory of the Creator. Chanting psalms and singing hymns, contemplating the divine beauty through reading the scriptures – these were the principal activities for the sake of which the monk abandoned the world and sought to eliminate all distractions. Physical needs were neglected for the sake of continual prayer and prostration. True, there is an element of deliberate mortification of the flesh which might imply a rejection of the body as an alien element – dualism was never far away in the Orient; but disciplining the body can also signify an attempt to make it a worthy temple of the Holy Spirit. Theodoret himself appears sympathetic to marriage in his other writings, and like most of the Fathers, definitely opposed the extreme dualism of Manichaeans and others. Even the ideal of ἀπάθεια (passionlessness) which figures so prominently in

---

354 Delahaye (1923), p. ix.

355 Festugière (1959), pp. 346–87; see further the discussion of the few overlapping sections in Doran (1992).

356 Canivet (1977), p. 83.

357 Price (1985), introduction, xviii.

358 The following discussion owes much to Canivet (1977), chapter X.

the *Historia religiosa*, he elsewhere recognizes to be an attribute of God alone, unattainable for created beings. On the whole, even in this work, Theodoret favours moderation, serenity, gentleness and meekness, so much so that there is sometimes a certain incongruity between his factual reports of the ascetics and his generalizing descriptions. Part of this taming process he achieved by 'Hellenizing' his characters, depicting them according to the philosophical and heroic models of the genre he had chosen; thus Theodoret attributes to his new-style philosophers the cardinal Greek virtues: σωφροσύνη, δικαιοσύνη, ἀνδρεία and σοφία (temperance, justice, courage and wisdom) – though in the epilogue, he sees their highest motivation in terms of Christian virtue, ἀγάπη (love), and there are hints of this in the portraits he offers, particularly those occasional references to devotion to the Bridegroom. What really impresses Theodoret about the ascetics is that they surpass the normal capabilities of human nature – they represent the new humanity constituted in Christ.

While there is little emphasis here, when compared with the literature from Egypt, on interior psychological battle with demons, Theodoret's heroes have undertaken a campaign against evil and paganism, a combat with the devil who is overcome by their exorcisms, evangelization and miraculous cures, a race in which they will win an imperishable crown; for they are the imitators of God's prophets, indeed the imitators of Christ himself. This gives them παρρησία (freedom to speak familiarly) before God and authority among human beings. For another role performed by the angels is the protection of nations and individuals. So the ascetics were angels on earth with power and authority in the world of affairs. Although their ideal was to avoid human contact and converse with God (Symeon's column got higher and higher to avoid the crowds), it is clear that the holy men, so far from merely providing an edifying example, actually played a positive role in the half-Christian society of the late Roman Empire.[359] They were sought out by the populace for cures to diseases of the flesh as well as social and political ills, for judicial decisions and advice of all sorts. In these pages we not only read of Symeon Stylites on his pillar dispensing justice, comfort and spiritual assistance to all comers regularly at the ninth hour, and then returning to prayer at sunset until the ninth hour of the following day – but we also see how natural Theodoret regards it that his pleasure-loving young mother should have sought a cure from Peter the Galatian when suffering from an eye-complaint, and that his childless parents should have turned for help to Macedonius the 'barley-eater'. Furthermore, we find anecdotes in which holy men stood up to heretic emperors, and acted as *'patroni'* for citizens subject to imperial displeasure. Their extraordinary feats set them apart as holy, and their holiness gave them a freedom of speech in the courts of earth and heaven which was denied to others. So their intercessory powers were highly valued, and non-Greek-speaking provincials acquired a prestige which made them a new social élite. The outstanding ascetic, of whatever social class, surpassed human limitations and belonged to the angelic world. This was Theodoret's justification of what was already a social fact: the extraordinary impact of 'wild vagrants in skins . . . [who] disquieted the Graeco-Roman world by their his-

---

359 Brown (1971a).

trionic gestures',[360] and the consequent shift in power and influence that took place in the society and culture of the late Roman Empire.

Theodoret's picture of the monks living an 'angelic life' picks up a motif already found in the *Historia monachorum*. In the prologue to that work, we also find the monks depicted as new prophets, true servants of God, not preoccupied with food and clothing but with continuous prayer and hymn-singing, awaiting the return of Christ in the desert. Syrian asceticism may have had its own characteristics and its own roots, yet the similarities run deep. In Egypt and Syria alike, the anchorites were sought out for cures, and consulted like the oracles of the classical world. And in all the monastic literature the monks have taken the offensive against false gods and the powers of evil;[361] they have marched into the desert or up mountains to meet the demons on their own territory; they have tackled them through healing and exorcism; they have captured their citadels, the tombs; and they continue the struggle to the end. Thus the monks followed Christ with a faith capable of moving mountains. Is it any wonder that miracles and prodigies flourished, that the wild beasts were tamed, and heaven anticipated on earth? They belong to a different world. As far as the literature of monasticism is concerned that is their point.

For Further Reading

English translations

Doran, Robert, 1992. *The Lives of Simeon Stylites*, trans. with introd., Kalamazoo, MI: Cistercian Publications.

Price, R. M., 1985. *Theodoret of Cyrrhus. A History of the Monks of Syria*, trans., Kalamazoo, MI: Cistercian Publications.

Studies

Brock, S. P., 1973. 'Early Syrian Asceticism', *Numen* 20, pp. 1–19.

Brown, Peter, 1971a. 'The Rise and Function of the Holy Man in Late Antiquity', *JRS* 61, pp. 80–101.

Krueger, D., 1997. 'Typological Figuration in Theodoret of Cyrrhus's *Religious History* and the Art of Postbiblical narrative', *JECS* 5, pp. 393–419.

Urbainczyk, Theresa, 1997. *Theodoret of Cyrrhus: The Bishop and the Holy Man*, Ann Arbor: The University of Michigan Press.

---

360 Brown (1971b).
361 A. J. Festugière (1965) I, chapter 1, explores this theme fully.

4

The Cappadocians

The political eclipse of Arianism in its various forms came with the appointment of Theodosius to the Eastern throne. By this time, AD 379, the defenders of orthodoxy would be recognized in three bishops from the province of Cappadocia. It is true that Basil, the great bishop of Caesarea, had not survived to see this triumphant day, but his friend, Gregory Nazianzen, and his brother, Gregory Nyssen, were consciously carrying on his work and perpetuating his influence. Hindsight saw these three as having stood by Nicene orthodoxy in days of persecution, though their place among the shifting alliances of the 360s and 370s was surely less clear cut; but now in days of peace, their work was to provide the theological basis for the lasting definition of Eastern Trinitarianism.

This important contribution, however, by no means exhausts their interest and significance. One striking feature of their writings is the wealth of their religious language and imagery, their comprehensive acceptance of biblical, devotional and doctrinal traditions. But these traditions were not fossilized, and each of the three had a very personal contribution to make, not only to the articulation of Trinitarian doctrine, but also to various aspects of the Christian life. Perhaps the most fascinating aspect of their work is the evidence it provides concerning two areas of tension in the contemporary Church: first the tension and accommodation between faith and culture, that is, the pagan culture embedded in the educational system of the Graeco-Roman world with which the new official religion had to come to terms; and then the tension and accommodation occasioned by the rise and dominance of the monastic ideal. In both cases, it was only because leaders like the Cappadocian Fathers found a balance between extremes, that the Church did not sell itself to the world, or withdraw from the world into the desert. Yet this balance was hardly intentional; it arose out of circumstances, out of the inconsistencies of ingrained attitudes, as the consequences of each individual's character.

I Biographical

The lives of the three Cappadocians were closely interlinked,[1] and so was their work. However, the tendency to treat the three together has been increasingly

---

1 The most important sources are the writings of the Cappadocians themselves, particularly Gregory Nazianzen, *Orat.* 43 on Basil and *Carmen de vita sua*; Gregory Nyssen, *Vita Macrinae*, and the collections of their correspondence. Modern biographies have tried to discount the hagiographical and apologetic aspects of these texts; for example, Rousseau (1994).

contested, and the received account of their lives and personalities has been subject to revision by 'reading between the lines' of their rhetoric – for we know a great deal about them from their own writings, but each would seem to have suppressed some things and reshaped their past for apologetic reasons.[2]

All three came from well-established Christian families. Of a family of nine, Basil, Gregory and Peter became bishops; their grandparents had been martyrs, their mother and sister would be recognized as saints. Their friend, Gregory, was the son of the bishop of Nazianzus, a convert, won by his Christian wife. So all three grew up under the influence of committed parents; they speak with the conviction of a faith into which they had been born, a faith whose images, expressions, vocabulary and attitudes were second nature to them. Yet each apparently experienced the stimulus of a more radical call to faith.

Nor was their experience narrow and sectarian. Their families were Christian, but they also belonged to the higher classes of Cappadocia;[3] they were rich enough and proud enough to provide their sons with a first-class classical education, the father of Basil and Gregory Nyssen being himself a rhetor. Basil studied in Caesarea, the capital of Cappadocia, in Constantinople[4] and finally Athens, the leading university of the world. In Caesarea he had already been acquainted with Gregory from Nazianzus, and now, in Athens, the friendship blossomed into intimacy. Gregory's educational career had in fact been very similar, though while Basil was at Constantinople, he and his brother Caesarius had visited the famous centres of Christian learning, Palestinian Caesarea and Alexandria, both, of course, known for their connection with Origen. Athens, however, was Gregory's enthusiasm. He spent most of his twenties there, unable to tear himself from the pursuit of learning. Reluctantly, he followed Basil back to Cappadocia in about 357.

The friendship seems to have meant more to Gregory than to Basil; Gregory was deeply hurt when Basil appeared to let him down. The story of their love and their quarrels is woven into the course of Gregory's vacillating career. In their correspondence, Gregory refers to an agreement they had made while at Athens to share a 'life of philosophy' together.[5] But for Basil, this may have been mere student idealism. On his return to Caesarea, he found himself the centre of admiring attention, and quickly proved a success as a rhetorician. He probably enjoyed his reputation and riches. But if Basil was to dominate others, he himself is said to have found a dominating influence in his sister, Macrina, who had already dedicated herself to an ascetic life[6] – though it is

2 For Basil, see Rousseau (1994); for Gregory Nazianzen, see McGuckin (2001).

3 For general background see Mitchell (1993), especially vol. 2; also the trilogy by Van Dam (2002, 2003a, 2003b), which explores further social and familial contexts.

4 Some (for example Meredith (1995)) have assumed that Basil had studied in Antioch because of his links with Libanius; but it is likely that Libanius was in Constantinople at the time Basil was acquainted with him.

5 Gregory Nazianzen, *Ep.* 1; though see the caveats in Rousseau (1994).

6 Gregory Nyssen, *Vita Macrinae*; Silvas (2008) translates all texts relevant to understanding Macrina. See Rousseau (1994) for the suggestion that there was more ambivalence in Basil's relationship with Macrina and his family than Gregory suggests. For a discussion of Macrina as a *type* of holy woman, see Warren Smith (2004), pp. 57f., and for a discussion of her domestic role, see Rousseau (2005), pp. 165f.

likely that the more important influence was Eustathius of Sebaste.[7] Basil soon gave up his career, received baptism and set out on a long journey through Egypt, Palestine, Syria and Mesopotamia to visit the monks and solitaries of the deserts. He returned to found a monastery, become the major influence in the organization of monastic communities in Asia Minor and eventually carve out the role of monk-bishop,[8] which was to become the norm in Eastern Orthodoxy.

In monastic retreat, Basil looked for the support of his friend. He wrote and urged Gregory to join him in Pontus. Gregory had already received baptism, possibly in Athens after a storm at sea en route from Alexandria. In this period to be baptized implied a resolution to give up worldly ambitions but now Gregory was reluctant to commit himself to the ascetic life, at least as Basil practised it. His ageing parents, in need of help and support, provided an excuse. He visited Basil for a short time, but returned. His letters reveal ambivalence between idealism and joking parodies of Basil's over-enthusiasm.[9] Several times he returned to Pontus, but never for long. He and Basil compiled the *Philocalia*, a collection of extracts from Origen, and Basil probably discussed early versions of his Rules for monastic organization with his friend.[10] But Gregory's position with regard to monasticism remained equivocal; he was sufficiently held by the ideal of philosophic retreat to resent it when others forced him to renounce it – the future will show that the less he was free to retire from the world, the more he felt the urge to do so; but his understanding of retreat was perhaps different from that of Basil. Basil, meanwhile, appeared to throw himself into ecclesiastical politics with a certain unscrupulousness, as if conscious that the monastery was too small a stage for his abilities. Gregory became more and more sensitive to his friend's apparent disloyalty to their ideals.

The first blow to Gregory's ever-frustrated intentions was his ordination. His dominating father compelled him to accept the priesthood and help with the running of his diocese. Gregory fled to Pontus, but soon realized he had no alternative but to accept his new status.[11] Already Basil had been active outside the walls of his monastery and moved in episcopal circles – he was with Eustathius of Sebaste and Basil of Ancyra at a synod in Constantinople in 360. In 360, both Dianius, the bishop of Caesarea, and Gregory's father signed the Creed of Constantinople, Constantius' final attempt to engineer unity. Each had renounced his error under the influence of Basil and Gregory, respectively. Now, the new bishop of Caesarea, Eusebius, who was a theological novice, persuaded Basil to become his assistant; so he, too, was ordained priest. For a spell

---

7 The importance of Eustathius has been recognized since Loofs (1878); Rousseau (1994) shows how Basil and his brother, Gregory, wrote this influence out of Basil's past after the rupture in relationship in the 370s.

8 Sterk (2004).

9 Basil, *Ep.* 14; Gregory, *Epp.* 4, 5, 6. See Ruether (1969); Bernardi (1995); McGuckin (2001).

10 In *Ep.* 2, Basil outlines the essentials of his monastic ideals to Gregory. On Basil's ascetic works, see further below, pp. 152–6. The conventional view is that the *Philocalia* was compiled at this stage, but this is purely conjectural. For an alternative, see Junod (1972).

11 Gregory Nazianzen, *Orat.* 1 and 2.

he returned to his monastery when relations with Eusebius became strained; but his friend, Gregory, was instrumental in effecting a reconciliation between the two and Basil returned to his duties. He was needed to defend the Church in the last period of Arian ascendency, under Valens.[12]

We know very little of the early career of Gregory, Basil's younger brother.[13] He himself affirms that he owed his education to Basil,[14] and certainly he never benefited, as Basil had, from travel to the educational centres of the time. Yet wherever he received his education, he is scarcely inferior to the other two in the rhetorical skills admired in that period, and his debts to philosophy are, if anything, more evident than those of his brother and his friend.[15] He seems to have been destined for the priesthood, and was ordained early as a lector. It is possible that he was for a time living the ascetic life with Basil in Pontus,[16] but a letter from Gregory Nazianzen reveals that he had suddenly thrown over his ecclesiastical career.[17] He turned rhetor, like his father before him, and it is likely that during his 'worldly' period he married.[18] Neither his marriage nor his rhetorical career lasted long, however – it may be that his wife died in child-birth.[19] Whether through grief, disillusionment, the effect of Gregory's letter or the influence of his family (quite apart from anything else, Macrina seems to have been a formidable sister, and Gregory was susceptible to dreams induced by his repressed guilt[20]), he soon abandoned worldly pursuits.

In 370, Eusebius died. Basil seemed his obvious successor. The stuff of politics, however, is ambition, competing groups and frantic lobbying. Basil realized that the Church was not immune from such pressures and his election was by no means secure. He was not above entering the arena on its own terms. Unfortunately he misjudged the sensibilities of his friend and nearly sacrificed his support by feigning ill-health in order to secure Gregory's immediate presence. The disillusioned Gregory could see nothing but self-seeking ambition in

---

12 See Sozomen, HE vi.15, and Gregory Nazianzen, Orat. 43. Basil's subsequent confrontation with Valens is a curious episode which poses some problems for the historian.

13 The lack of a full biographical study is partially made up by Silvas (2007).

14 Gregory Nyssen, Ep. 13 (if genuine) addressed to Libanius; he also calls Basil his teacher in his Hexaemeron and the De Opificio Hominis.

15 Rist argues, in 'Basil's "Neoplatonism": its Background and Nature' in Fedwick (1981), pp. 137–220, that neither Basil nor his friend, Gregory, show much awareness of contemporary philosophy and are mostly hostile to philosophy; however, it is possible that Basil's brother, Gregory, stimulated some interest in Plotinus on Basil's part, since Basil's De Spiritu Sancto and Gregory's De Virginitate, both written around the same time, reveal definite allusions to treatises now known from the Enneads: 5.1 and 6.9 in the De spiritu Sancto; 1.6 and 6.9 in the De Virginitate. See also Peroli (1997).

16 Basil, Ep. 223.

17 Gregory Nazianzen, Ep. 11.

18 Gregory Nyssen, De Virginitate 3. Gregory Nazianzen, Ep. 95 has led some to think his wife was called Theosebeia, but it seems more plausible to suggest that his sister of this name, a dedicated virgin, acted as his housekeeper when he was a bishop. See Silvas (2007).

19 Silvas (2007).

20 The account of Gregory's dream is found in his homily In 40 martyris. See Cherniss (1930); Silvas (2007).

Basil's activities. Nevertheless, his father realized the value of securing Basil's election as metropolitan of Cappadocia and the quarrel was patched up. Basil was indebted to the aged bishop of Nazianzus for his influential support.[21]

But trouble did not end with his election. Politics makes enemies. Basil was envied his abilities and suspected of pride. To add to his difficulties, the emperor, Valens, divided the province of Cappadocia into two, ostensibly for administrative reasons. Since ecclesiastical provinces conventionally followed those of the empire, a potential rival to Basil was created in the new capital of Tyana, whose bishop, Anthimus, did not hesitate to take the opportunity of declaring himself metropolitan of Cappadocia Secunda. Basil entered a power struggle and tried to consolidate his own position by appointing people he could trust to newly created sees. Gregory of Nazianzus found himself consecrated bishop of a strategically important crossroads, Sasima, with customs inspectors and innkeepers as virtually his only parishioners. He felt insulted and a mere pawn in the hands of Basil's ambition. The fourth century was a time of reluctant bishops, but none more so than Gregory.[22] Meanwhile another new bishop appeared in the country town of Nyssa, namely Gregory, Basil's younger brother.

Basil was not altogether fortunate in his choice of support. His friend never took up his episcopacy at Sasima, and his brother proved tactless and incompetent in ecclesiastical affairs,[23] succumbing eventually to 'Arian' plots and being deposed for misappropriating church funds. Both looked back with respect after Basil's premature death and their own rise to influential positions; but severe strain was put on Basil's relationship with both Gregories by the politics of his episcopacy. On the one side, Basil's patience was much tried by their weaknesses; on the other, his friend resented Basil's betrayal of their youthful ideals, and his brother, one suspects, had an inferiority complex. Basil himself seems to have suffered from considerable insecurity, and many of his friendships were jeopardized during his episcopacy.[24]

Nevertheless, Basil's achievements as bishop were enormous.[25] At a purely practical level, he established charitable institutions, hospitals and schools; he organized monasteries and brought administrative skill to the running of the diocese. He reformed the liturgy of his cathedral and was formidable in preaching and exegesis. He provided strong moral leadership in a time of laxity, basing his ideas on a return to the simple life of the primitive Church. In the troubled days of an 'Arian' emperor, he came to be seen a fortress of Nicene orthodoxy which the imperial power dared not directly touch – his personal confrontation with Valens became legendary. His vast correspondence with the leading Nicene theologians has been regarded as a testimony to his indefatigable energy in the service of truth as he understood it. It was not without reason that he became known as Basil the Great. A more nuanced and complex

---

21 Gregory Nazianzen, *Epp.* 40–6.

22 Gregory Nazianzen, *Epp.* 47–9; *Carmen de vita sua*. For a fuller exploration of the complexities of these events, see McGuckin (2001).

23 Basil, *Epp.* 58–60, 100. See Daniélou (1965).

24 For discussion, see Rousseau (1994).

25 The panegyric by Gregory Nazianzen, *Orat.* 43, provides a glowing summary, though still revealing his own hurt feelings.

reconstruction of Basil's personal commitments may reveal the anachronistic character of that judgment;[26] yet he had already challenged the Anomoian, Eunomius, before becoming bishop, and his treatise on the Holy Spirit offered a 'careful and limited gloss on the simple teaching of Nicaea'.[27]

Basil died in 379, just before the triumph of Nicene orthodoxy was assured. He was only forty-nine, but his health had been ruined by over-enthusiastic asceticism. For Gregory of Nazianzus, this was the last of a number of deeply felt bereavements. In the early 370s, he had found himself delivering funeral orations for his brother, his sister and his father,[28] whose death was soon followed by that of his mother. Gregory refused to succeed his father, and after administering the diocese for a while, retired to a monastery in Seleucia, as he had so long desired. It was here, himself confined to a sickbed, that he heard of Basil's death.

But Gregory was not to lie in Seleucia for long. Representations arrived on behalf of the tiny community of faithful Nicene Christians in Constantinople. The capital city was a hotbed of religious differences, and the home town of vacillating courtiers who followed the creed of the current emperor. Consequently the churches had been in the hands of the 'Arians' for most of the previous fifty years. With the accession of Theodosius, the hour had come for the Nicenes to establish their position, and in Gregory Nazianzen they thought they had found the required leader. In vain, Gregory pleaded his devotion to ascetic retirement. He gave way to what appeared to be a call to duty, protesting that he had no ambition for high places in the Church or in the world.[29] Perhaps he protests too much; the compliment to his abilities must have been sweet after the insult of Sasima.

And in fact Gregory was a resounding success. His brilliant oratory attracted crowds to the tiny chapel of the Anastasis (Resurrection). His *Five Theological Orations*[30] brought disarray in the enemy camp. He suffered from Arian violence and hostile plots, but the Nicene forces steadily grew. His reputation was somewhat diminished by his unfortunate support for a scheming adventurer, the philosopher Maximus, who ingratiated himself with Gregory and then had himself secretly consecrated archbishop. Doubts about Gregory's judgment, however, were soon dissipated; the Emperor Theodosius arrived, routed the Arians and installed him in the cathedral as potential archbishop.

Meanwhile Gregory of Nyssa, now restored to his see, was sorting out the episcopal succession in Sebaste and contending with Pneumatomachians. Basil's death had been rapidly followed by that of his sister Macrina, events which led him consciously to adopt the mantle of his lost brother, and he entered a period of vast literary activity. It would seem that the one work written before Basil's death, and perhaps indeed at his brother's request, was his *De Virginitate*, but now he undertook to defend his brother's works in specially written apologies; he carried on the debate with Eunomius, he pursued the defence of the Holy Spirit. Gregory did not follow Basil slavishly; he was prepared to cor-

26 Rousseau (1994).
27 Rousseau (1994), p. 276.
28 *Orat.* 7, 8 and 18.
29 *Orat.* 33; *Carmen de vita sua* 592ff.
30 *Orat.* 27–31; see further below, pp. 162–4.

rect and develop.[31] Yet Basil's Rules lie behind the *De Instituto Christiano*,[32] and his *Hexaemeron* inspired the *De Opificio Hominis*.[33] In 381, Basil's shadow lay over the Council of Constantinople; as his brother, defender and representative, Gregory achieved prominence, and his theology seems to have had more than a little influence on the council's deliberations.[34] So the one who had once given the impression of being a bad administrator and a tactless negotiator suddenly came to wield considerable influence.

At this council, called by Theodosius to seal the triumph of the Nicene position, the two Gregories came together as defenders of orthodoxy; but while one was to continue to enjoy the favour of the imperial court and the esteem of the orthodox world, the other was to retire into obscurity. The council began by confirming Gregory Nazianzen's election to Constantinople, and after the death of Meletius of Antioch, he became president. But he soon withdrew in disgust at the political wrangling of the assembled bishops, and in his absence, the delayed Egyptian delegation arrived and began to sow doubts about the legality of his election. According to the Nicene canons, bishops could not be transferred from one see to another, and Gregory had been consecrated to Sasima. The one thing Gregory feared was accusations of ambition and self-seeking; so he let his case go by default. He offered his resignation and returned home, intending once more to live an ascetic life, and continue the fight for orthodoxy with his pen – the council after all resisted his strong affirmation of the Godhead of the Spirit and produced a vague credal statement, lacking the *homoousion* he had long before urged upon Basil.[35] In Nazianzus he actually found himself forced to sort out the affairs of the diocese, since no successor to his father had yet been appointed. Finally a successor was installed, and Gregory retired to his estate to nurse his ill-health and his hurt feelings, finding solace in the composition of poetry, and in overseeing the publication of his contribution to Christian literature in the form of *Letters*, *Orations* and *Poems*.[36] He died about 390.

The other Gregory, however, had had the distinction at Constantinople of delivering the Funeral Oration on Meletius of Antioch; later he also pronounced the funeral Orations on the Emperor's daughter and wife. Furthermore, the bishop of humble little Nyssa was one of three appointed to regulate ecclesi-

---

31 Balas (1976) discusses an interesting example of this; cf. also Meredith in Mateo-Seco and Bastero (1988). For the chronology of Gregory's works, see Daniélou (1966a).

32 But see above, p. 117 note 268, p. 121 for its dependence on Macarius. Gregory seems to have had links with Syriac traditions; see, for example, Drobner in Spira and Klock (1981).

33 So closely did the two become associated in their discussion of human origins that in the various manuscript traditions, each has assigned to him some homilies on the creation of man, which are clearly intended to supplement the nine homilies on the *Hexaemeron*; the authorship of these homilies remains disputed: *Sources Chrétiennes* published them as Basil's (Smets and van Esbroek 1970), and Jaeger's edition of Gregory's works includes them in a supplement. See also Lim (1990).

34 Jaeger (1966). See further Daniélou (1966a) and May (1966).

35 Bernardi (1995), and NB McGuckin (2001) on the view that the Creed of Constantinople only seems to support the position of Gregory Nazianzen because his work has been treated as the exegesis of the credal statement for so many centuries.

36 McGuckin (2001); McGuckin in Børtnes and Hägg (2006).

astical affairs, and in succeeding years he found himself travelling around the East arranging elections and fulfilling imperial missions; it was probably after Constantinople that he visited Jerusalem.[37] The 380s also seem to have been intense in terms of literary activity. Declining influence and personal differences with Basil's successor marred Gregory's final years, but the quality of his literary productions did not suffer as he turned to producing his 'mystical' works of exegesis. The last mention we have of him is his attendance at a synod in Constantinople in 394.

All three Cappadocians left voluminous writings,[38] including valuable collections of correspondence.[39] This means that very precise and detailed reconstructions can be produced of certain episodes in their careers. Only thirty letters have reached us from the pen of Gregory Nyssen, but the others were extremely prolific. Basil's correspondence runs to a collection of 365 epistles, though some are addressed to him rather than being his own composition. Some of the letters cannot be dated, but those that can cover the course of his career, 1–46 coming from the early period and 47–291 from his episcopal years. These letters provide a rich supply of information about the Church in this period, as well as Basil's own life and interests. Doctrinal and administrative problems are discussed as well as personal matters. The letters are written with the elegance of style customary in the period, though they were not in the first place intended for publication.

Gregory Nazianzen was apparently the first Greek author to publish a collection of his own epistles,[40] at the request of a young admirer, who also asked for advice on epistolary composition. Gregory suggested that letters should be short, clear, simple and charming, citing Basil's letters as models of the art of letter writing.[41] Of Gregory's letters 244 survive, some of them being early correspondence, including several to his friend Basil, but many being the conscious literary creations of his last years. A few letters deal with doctrinal issues, the letters to Cledonius being important statements of the case against Apollinarius (the first of these was in fact officially adopted by the Council of Chalcedon). But the vast majority are personal and autobiographical – often apologetic, and they reveal most clearly the tensions of conflicting ideals in the course of his life.

---

37 *Ep.* 2; Silvas (2007), p. 48, contests the suggestion that it was after the Council of Antioch in 379.

38 The only complete edition in each case is to be found in the volumes of Migne, *PG*. However, *Sources Chrétiennes*, Budé and others have produced editions of major works of Basil and Gregory Nazianzen; those available are listed in the Bibliography. Jaeger began an edition of Gregory of Nyssa, which others have continued – referenced here as Jaeger et al. (1960–), generally cited as *GNO*. English translations of selections are to be found in *NPNF*, with some more recent translated selections provided in Daley (2006) and Meredith (1999). For specific works discussed later in this chapter, editions and translations will be referenced.

39 Texts of the letters: Basil, Courtonne (1957, 1961, 1966); Hauschild (1973, 1990, 1992). ET: Deferrari (1926, 1928, 1930, 1934); also in *NPNF* and Way (1951, 1955). Gregory Nazianzen: three editions, all by Gallay (1964, 1967); (1969); Gallay and Jourjon (1974); ET selection in *NPNF*. Gregory Nyssen: Jaeger et al. (1960–) = *GNO* vol.VIII; ET of selection in *NPNF*; Silvas (2007).

40 Quasten (1960), p. 247; see Bernardi (1995) chapter xi on Gregory as a letter-writer.

41 Gregory Nazianzen, *Epp.* 51–4.

For Further Reading

English translations

Daley, Brian E., 2006. *Gregory of Nazianzus*, London and New York: Routledge.
Silvas, Anna M., 2007. *Gregory of Nyssa: The Letters. Introduction, Translation and Commentary*, Leiden: Brill.
Silvas, Anna M., 2008. *Macrina the Younger, Philosopher of God*, Turnhout: Brepols.
Way, Sister Agnes Clare, 1951, 1955. *Saint Basil. Letters*, 2 vols, FC, Washington, DC: Catholic University of America Press.

Studies

McGuckin, J., 2001. *Gregory of Nazianzus*, Crestwood, NY: St Vladimir's Seminary Press.
Meredith, A., 1995. *The Cappadocians*, London: Geoffrey Chapman.
Mitchell, Stephen, 1993. *Anatolia: Land, Men and Gods in Asia Minor*, 2 vols, Oxford: Clarendon Press.
Rousseau, Philip, 1994. *Basil of Caesarea*, Berkeley/Los Angeles/London: University of California Press.
Van Dam, Raymond, 2002. *Kingdom of Snow. Roman Rule and Greek Culture in Cappadocia*, Philadelphia: University of Pennsylvania Press.
——, 2003a. *Families and Friends in Late Roman Cappadocia*, Philadelphia: University of Pennsylvania Press.
——, 2003b. *Becoming Christian: The Conversion of Roman Cappadocia*, Philadelphia: University of Pennsylvania Press.

II Withdrawal and Involvement

Already, in tracing the lives of the three Cappadocian Fathers, we have seen illustration of the areas of tension and accommodation mentioned earlier. The personal tensions produced by the monastic ideal are most clearly illustrated by the indecisiveness of Gregory Nazianzen. Gregory, it seems, was sensitive, introspective, over-enthusiastic, unsure of himself, easily slighted and easily depressed; yet his problems were not simply of his own making. They reflect tension in contemporary attitudes. In his career has been traced the personal outworking of the conflict between philosophy and rhetoric, a conflict inherent in the classical tradition since Socrates and the Sophists.[42] Be that as it may, the impact of the monastic movement among Christians aggravated the conflict of ideals – the conflict between withdrawal for contemplation and duty to the community, leadership, success. It was in this century that potential Christian leaders first had to weigh the rival claims of the active and contemplative life, to balance the demands of duty to the Church against the desire for personal salvation reached only, according to the ideals of the time, by withdrawal from the world. Gregory's ideal would seem to have been a Christianized version of the 'classical' model, of a leisured and educated élite pursuing philosophy and

42 Ruether (1969).

eschewing worldly ambitions. By contrast, Basil's family apparently adopted an egalitarian model, involving hard, physical labour, alongside emancipated slaves, to support a simple lifestyle – far too harsh for Gregory.[43] Though it has been suggested that he deliberately chose a middle way,[44] Gregory probably never resolved the tensions satisfactorily; his career illustrates the pull of duty on the one hand and, on the other, retreat as soon as he was frustrated by conflict. He has been described on the basis of his letters and orations as an 'active energetic pastor', engaged in 'theological controversy, ecclesiastical politics, liturgical leadership, and the care of the poor', who nevertheless 'frequently portrays himself as a hermit out of his proper place, an ailing contemplative forced into action . . .'[45] Nevertheless, his experience did produce an influential discussion of the qualities and dedication requisite for ordination to the priesthood, a discussion that presented responsible service as not only a perfectly valid way of obedience to God, but indeed a more arduous one.[46] However much he saw practical virtue as a possible path towards the preliminary purification required, for Gregory the goal remained θεωρία (contemplation); but the priest, 'deified and deifying',[47] is charged with the responsibility of bringing others to God. Gregory's view influenced others, such as John Chrysostom, who within decades would try to be an ascetic while patriarch of Constantinople, only to find the seat too hot for a hair shirt.

Basil was one of those who pioneered this route, and he appears not to have been so deeply troubled in spirit by the apparent conflict of ideals. As priests, both Basil and Gregory of Nazianzus had occasion to deal with opposition to the local bishop from monastic groups; the fact that there had long been tensions between monks and bishops in Asia Minor is evident from the canons of the Council of Gangra. Unfortunately the precise date of this council is unclear, but the practices of Basil's hero, Eustathius,[48] were then the object of criticism, and the canons suggest that in Asia Minor ascetics were a 'kind of counter-cultural community within the urban milieu'.[49] By now, however, Eustathius was himself a bishop, and he embodied for Basil the ideal of the philosopher who put his talents to the service of the community – in this case, the Church. Already Athanasius had chosen and ordained bishops from the monastic groups in Egypt, and the Cappadocians were instrumental in providing models and biblical justifications for this kind of integration. Moses was Basil's ideal 'type': forty years of training, forty years of contemplation, forty years of care for humanity and community leadership.[50] On the face of it, we have in Basil a consistent character, a man who renounced the world and devoted himself to the service of the Church.

---

43 McGuckin (2001).

44 Beeley (2008).

45 Daley (2006).

46 Gregory Nazianzen, *Orat.* 2.

47 Russell (2004), p. 219.

48 Rousseau (1994) shows how Basil 're-wrote' his past once he had fallen out with Eustathius; that Basil's asceticism was influenced by Eustathius has been recognized since Loofs (1878).

49 Sterk (2004), p. 30.

50 Sterk (2004), p. 62.

Yet Basil's ideals and achievements were perhaps not entirely reconcilable, and maybe he was more insecure than has been recognized.[51] The rule of obedience was possibly his most original contribution to the development of coenobitic monasticism;[52] yet Basil was obedient to none. He was domineering as a bishop, and insensitive to the scruples of his friend and his brother. Humility and self-denial were required of the brethren in his communities; yet Basil was ambitious for his see and jealous of his authority. That he was accused of pride and haughtiness is clear from Gregory's defence of his character in his panegyric: 'What they term pride', says Gregory, 'is, I fancy, the firmness and steadfastness and stability of his character'.[53] Yet Gregory himself never ceased to regard his consecration as bishop of Sasima as an act of tyranny on Basil's part.[54] It was no doubt for the good of the Church that a character like Basil failed to put his own theory into practice. However, in his life and his writings, Basil provides a revealing illustration of the difficulty of living in accordance with the conscious ideology of the period when responsibilities made their own inescapable demands, demands seemingly well suited to the character and temperament with which he had been endowed.

Basil's brother, Gregory of Nyssa, was perhaps the most successful in integrating the tensions. From his earliest writing, *De Virginitate*,[55] we learn about his marriage, but the apparent contradiction between this fact and his immediate topic was perhaps what enabled him to realize that the real issues were not properly understood in terms of marriage and celibacy – rather the soul's non-attachment (ἀπάθεια) was the key element in union with God, and this implied the re-education of desire.[56] An account of Gregory Nyssen's political manoeuvrings may make strange reading alongside his 'mystical' writings. Scripture, however, provided models for living with this tension. To both Gregories, the great figures of the Bible, like Moses and Paul, appeared as mediators, whose mystical experience of God was transmitted to the people[57] – indeed, it could be that Nyssen's *Life of Moses* was intended for a priest.[58] So their ideal was to aim at balance, and in the long term, the development of this ideal was of more significance than any personal tensions from which it evolved.

For Further Reading

Studies

Coakley, Sarah (ed.), 2003. *Re-Thinking Gregory of Nyssa*, Oxford: Blackwell.

---

51 Rousseau (1994).

52 Amand de Mendietta (1949).

53 *Orat.* 43.

54 *Carmen de vita sua* 530ff.; *Epp.* 17, 50.

55 Text in Jaeger et al. (1960–) = VIII.1; ET Callahan (1967).

56 See Laird, 'Under Solomon's Tutelage: The Education of Desire in the Homilies on the Song of Songs' in Coakley (2003), referring to earlier articles by Hart.

57 Gregory Nazianzen, *Orat.* 2; Gregory Nyssen, *In Ps.* 7, *De Vita Moysis*. Spidlik (1971).

58 Heine (1975). Text in Jaeger et al. (1960–) = *GNO* VII.1; ET Ferguson and Malherbe (1978).

Ruether, Rosemary, 1969. *Gregory Nazianzen, Rhetor and Philosopher*, Oxford: Claren-
don Press.
Sterk, Andrea, 2004. *Renouncing the World Yet Leading the Church: The Monk-Bishop in
Late Antiquity*, Cambridge, MA: Harvard University Press.

III Christianity and Contemporary Culture

When pagan culture and Christian tradition are put in the scales, we find a
similar unstable but significant balance. The balance is hardly surprising when
one remembers that the theological lineage of the Cappadocians goes directly
back to Origen,[59] whose devotion to the text of scripture was counterbalanced
by engagement with the Greek philosophical tradition. Nevertheless, it is interesting to witness the conscious and unconscious interplay of two traditions in
the minds of these three, an interplay that was the inevitable result of their
family background and education, and yet could only be achieved by a certain
inconsistency in their attitudes.

When Basil was baptized and renounced the world, he at the same time
renounced pagan culture – later he would write that he had wasted his youth
on 'the wisdom made foolish by God'.[60] In accordance with Christian traditions,
he denounced the philosophers. The same conventional polemic appears in the
works of both Gregories. Dabbling in philosophy was the source of heresy.
Grudging recognition might be given to Plato, but only if his dependence on
Moses was stressed. In theory only the Bible pointed the way to truth.[61] In fact,
the extant works of all three Cappadocians reveal how much they had assimilated the literary and philosophical heritage of antiquity. The roots of their
education remain alive, even where they are unwilling to admit it. Rhetoric
and philosophy may be renounced for their own sake, but become the hand-
maid of theology. Modern studies have revealed the very considerable range
of literature known to them all – at least from school textbooks and probably
often first-hand. Quotations and allusions are there, even though they are not
acknowledged.[62] But more than this, the spirit and methods of contemporary
intellectual pursuits remain alive in their ecclesiastical works.

Basil's shift towards rejection of the culture in which he was educated was

---

59 Cappadocia was evangelized by Gregory Thaumaturgus, Origen's pupil, who
converted Basil's grandmother, Macrina the Elder. However, see Gribomont (1963),
who explores Basil's ambivalence towards his Origenist heritage, and the discussion
in Rousseau (1994). None of them refer to Origen directly, for the most part, but the
influence has been repeatedly documented.

60 *Ep.* 223.

61 All three made strong statements of this kind, particularly in anti-heretical works.
For discussion of Gregory Nazianzen, see Fleury (1930); and for Gregory Nyssen,
Cherniss (1930) and Meredith (1976) which ascribes some of Gregory's statements to
traditional anti-heretical motifs.

62 For example allusions to passages in Homer, Hesiod, Theognis, Solon, Simonides,
Pindar, the tragedians, Aristophanes, Callimachus, Herodotus, Thucydides, Plutarch,
Demosthenes, Lysias, Isocrates, Plato, Aristotle, Plotinus and many others have been
traced. See Amand de Mendietta (1945); Fleury (1930), Courtonne (1934), Cherniss
(1930), etc.

slow and never quite complete.[63] Basil claims to have given up cultural pursuits,[64] but at some unknown date he wrote *An Address to Young Men on How They Might Derive Benefit from Greek Literature*.[65] He accepts that training in pagan literature is a useful preparation for the difficulty of scriptural exegesis. Where there is an affinity with Christian values the two traditions should be set side by side; the fruit of the soul is truth, but 'external wisdom' (that is, non-Christian wisdom) may adorn it. His main concern, however, is the moral content of the literature. He warns that the soul must be watched in case pleasure in the poet's words leads the reader to accept the more evil sort of influence like those who take poisons with honey: the reader is to take what is appropriate and useful, and guard against what is harmful, a commonplace since Plutarch and others had found themselves defending literature against Plato's criticisms.[66] So Basil collects examples of virtue and good philosophy from Hesiod, Homer, Plato and many others. He recognizes that the classical tradition provided the only method of education, and recommends its acceptance at least as a *praeparatio evangelica*. The 'startling thing' is the 'apparent ease with which he supposed he could marry . . . the biblical message and the classical voice'.[67]

In his Homilies on the *Hexaemeron*[68] Basil draws on his learning to inspire his audience to praise of the Creator. He considers the solutions of various philosophical traditions to intellectual problems concerning the nature and origin of the universe; he argues the validity of the Christian doctrine of creation as a viable solution to these problems. The methods and questions of the philosophers are his presuppositions, and their examples, illustrations and suggestions provide much of his material. His principal interest is moral and spiritual, but still he presents his hearers with a complete Christian philosophy, not just ethics but cosmogony and physics. Yet here more than anywhere the tensions and contradictions are apparent. Basil is preaching to a congregation; he is the official representative of the Church and he reflects the traditional attitudes.[69] So he expresses contempt for the philosophers and scientists who busy themselves in vain with unanswerable questions and produce solutions which are the arrogant demonstrations of human reason. Their mutual contradictions prove their folly. Their elaborately clever systems distract them from the one truth worth knowing. Christians do not need any information which is not provided by scripture, and they should avoid 'busy-bodying' curiosity about the

63 Rousseau (1994).

64 Basil, *Ep.* 223; also the correspondence with Libanius (if genuine, which is disputed).

65 Basil, *An Address to Young Men on How They Might Derive Benefit from Greek Literature*: text: Boulenger (1935); text with ET in Deferrari (1926ff.). More recent ET: Wilson (1975). For a discussion of the occasion of this address, see Moffatt (1972).

66 Plutarch, *On the Education of Children* and *How the Young Man should study Poetry* in *Moralia* I.

67 Rousseau (1994), p. 59.

68 Basil, *Homilies on the Hexaemeron*: text: Giet (1968); Smets and van Esbroeck (1970); Amand de Mendietta and Rudberg (1997). ET in *NPNF* and Way (1963). Courtonne (1934) is a detailed study of the *Hexaemeron* and its sources.

69 See further Amand de Mendietta (1976); Rousseau (1994) suggests that his 'confident rejection of ancient culture came only slowly and ambiguities persist'.

universe, the shape of the earth, the number of the heavens. Scripture alone suffices. Yet even as he mocks the philosophers, he displays his own knowledge of astronomy. There is a real sense in which the bishop tied to orthodox tradition breathes the Greek spirit of enquiry; the monk renouncing the world appreciates the natural order. By careful assimilation, Basil has in fact achieved a remarkable synthesis between biblical teaching and selected elements of the profane systems.[70]

But what exactly was Basil's own point of view? It is likely that he modified his own views over the years: classical allusions are far more frequent in his early letters than in those of the episcopate. Be that as it may, quite clearly Basil was capable of adapting his style and his approach to his audience, quoting only the Bible in his ascetical works, but being freer in his use of quotations and allusions in other literary genres.[71] Even so, many of his compositions show a remarkably unselfconscious marriage of cultures, which is perhaps especially well evidenced in the collocation of biblical and Hellenic motifs in his letters of consolation.[72]

Basil's rather grudging recognition provides a contrast to the enthusiasm of his friend, Gregory. It was Julian's attempt to deny education to Christians which roused Gregory more than anything. He asserts that he has given up all other worldly things, riches, nobility, fame, etc., but 'words' – that is, literature, culture, argument – these he cannot renounce. We should remember that he had spent ten years of his life in Athens where his studies had overlapped those of Julian, that he was reluctant to leave and may even have refused the offer of a chair of rhetoric there when he followed Basil back to Cappadocia – indeed it is possible that he was almost directly affected by Julian's law against teachers in so far as he had pupils or disciples in Nazianzus between arriving home and being ordained in 361.[73]

Gregory's *Orations against Julian* were probably never delivered at anything more than a private reading, and were completed after Julian's death.[74] They are somewhat unattractive pieces of invective, but of interest here because we can see how Gregory attacks the claim that the Greek language, mathematics, poetry, etc. belong to paganism. No race or religion has an exclusive claim to culture, for culture has been derived from many sources. Julian's edict and Gregory's intense reaction to it bear witness to the contemporary tension in the Church. Julian had taken the Christians at their word: if nothing is required beyond orthodox faith, if the wisdom of the world is vanquished by God's foolishness, if literature and philosophy are superfluous beside the scriptures, then it is inconsistent for Christians to be professional teachers of rhetoric. Therefore they were to be excluded from this profession. By this edict, Julian aimed to turn the schools into centres of pagan propaganda. If the pagan reaction had been stronger and more lasting than it proved to be, the Church could have found itself deprived of educated leaders within a generation. Gregory knew that the Church could not afford to lose the only intellectual tools available

---

70 Orphanos (1975), p. 42.
71 Gribomont (1975); Rousseau (1994).
72 Gregg (1975); McGuckin (2001).
73 See McLynn's careful reading between the lines in Børtnes and Hägg (2006).
74 Gregory Nazianzen, *Orat. 4–5*; edition – Bernardi (1983).

for the education of theologians and the development of apologetic argument. Gregory's eventual publication of his collected *Orations*, *Epistles* and *Poems* may well have been intended to show that Christians were not uneducated, but also to provide a body of Christian literature to be used in enhancing the training of Church leaders.[75]

But Gregory's anger was not merely academic; his emotions and personality were involved. In spite of some conventional polemic against literature and philosophy, he of all people could not disclaim the classical heritage. In his epistles and poems, we see his real feelings, his genuine devotion to literature, philosophy and rhetoric. These he regarded as the auxiliaries of Christian doctrine. In him, more than in any other of the Fathers, accord between Hellenism and Christianity was realized, concludes Fleury.[76] In his panegyrics on Caesarius, Athanasius and Basil,[77] Gregory particularly stresses the fact that they were men of culture, men who had enjoyed a comprehensive education. Gregory was prepared to admit that Christianity owed much to 'external wisdom', since, for him, classical culture was an ancient and treasured heritage, a legacy for all; indeed, culture was the foundation of human, as distinct from bestial, life. Pagan philosophy was only false because it tended to be distracted by beautiful discourse and inessential vanities; philosophy Christianized, however, related human *logos* to the divine Logos, producing practical virtue and contemplation, and so leading to the truth.[78]

Gregory Nazianzen, then, set out to be a man of literature.[79] His *Orations*,[80] speeches on themes rather than homilies on texts, are fine examples of contemporary rhetoric, used not slavishly but intelligently, to express Christian ideas and sentiments. His *Letters*[81] were collected as specimens for emulation. In his *Poems*,[82] he consciously imitated the classics of the past, inspired by a desire to create a parallel Christian literature. The extent of his *Poems* is extraordinary – 19,000 lines are extant, Jerome attested 30,000; while his styles range through dactylic hexameters, elegiac couplets, epic dialect and iambic trimeters, with archaisms and rare Homeric forms on the one hand, and neologisms on the

---

75 McGuckin (2001), p. 118.

76 Fleury (1930), p. 99.

77 *Orat.* 7, 21, 43.

78 *Orat.* 25; on this see Coman (1976).

79 On his use of literary and biblical exempla, see Demoen (1996).

80 The text of all Gregory's *Orations* will be found in *PG* 35–6; but now for *Orat.* 1–3 see Bernardi (1978), for 6–12 Calvet-Sebasti (1995), for 20–3 Mossay and Lafontaine (1980), for 24–6 Mossay and Lafontaine (1981), for 27–31 (the *Theological Orations*) Mason (1899) and Gallay and Jourjon (1978), for 32–7 Moreschini (1985), for 38–41 Moreschini (1990), for 42–3 Bernardi (1992). ET of select orations in *NPNF*; also McCauley et al. (1953), Vinson (2003) and Daley (2006); ET of the *Theological Orations* Norris, Williams and Wickham (1991).

81 *Epp.* 51–3.

82 The text of Gregory's *Poems* is to be found in Migne, *PG* 37–8, though some are spurious or doubtful; some modern editions are available – Werhahn (1953), Jungck (1974), Palle (1985), Meier (1989), Moreschini and Sykes (1996), Tuilier et al. (2004), Simelidis (2006). ETs of select poems: McGuckin (1986/9), Meehan (1987), White (1996), Moreschini and Sykes (1996), Gilbert (2001).

other.[83] It seems likely that composing poetry was a lifelong interest, not simply a retirement activity; and a number of different motivations can be discerned. For example, thirty-eight of the poems were occasioned by the necessity of opposing heretics in their own terms – for Apollinarians, like Arians, had resorted to poetic propaganda; while his personal poems clearly contain apologetic elements. But his own account of why he wrote poetry lists the need to restrain himself by struggling with metre, the desire to offer something enjoyable to the young to induce them to progress to the good, the wish to demonstrate that pagans do not have greater literary talent than 'we' Christians, and for his own comfort.[84] Reading between the lines one can also detect an interest in meeting Plato's rejection of poetry with a body of inspired poetic material which genuinely provides a παιδεία (training) that leads to divine contemplation.[85] That most of his verses lack the quality of originality and inspiration is a judgment often made, but they belong to their time; they reflect the contemporary 'classicism', the exclusive interest in a golden age long past, an attitude which shaped the educational tradition of many centuries and would continue to do so for many more to come.[86]

The bulk of Gregory Nyssen's work consists of anti-heretical, dogmatic, exegetical and ascetical treatises – in other words, he did not on the face of it utilize contemporary literary forms as much as the other Gregory. Yet he had once embarked on a career as rhetor, and rhetorical norms pervade his work, especially his homilies. His panegyrics on saints and martyrs, and the three funeral orations delivered at Constantinople, are notable examples of his adaptation of pagan oratorical techniques to Christian use, and his work *On Infants' Early Deaths* is an elaborate rhetorical exercise which conforms to the rules of Isocrates.[87] However much Gregory sneers at Eunomius for being a mere rhetor who enjoys playing with words for effect, he is himself tarred with the same brush. As for his charges that Eunomius makes too much use of pagan philosophy and Aristotelian logic, there is in fact 'not a little of these elements to be found in him'.[88] He uses the *Categories* to refute his opponent, and is often treated as one of the greatest philosophical minds of the early Church. His *Dialogue on the Soul and the Resurrection*[89] is a Christian *Phaedo*, a literary account of a conversation with his sister Macrina on the eve of her death, Macrina becoming Gregory's mouthpiece as Socrates had been Plato's. Both this and many of his other works reveal that Gregory knew the Platonic dialogues and was able to make a constructive adaptation of Plato's reasoning. Gregory seems to have known the works of the Neoplatonists, Plotinus, Porphyry and Iambli-

---

83 McGuckin in Børtnes and Hägg (2006).

84 *Poem.* II.1.39; ET 'To his own verses' in White (1996).

85 McGuckin in Børtnes and Hägg (2006).

86 For discussion, see Sykes (1970); McGuckin (1986/9, 2001); Moreschini and Sykes (1997); McGuckin in Børtnes and Hägg (2006).

87 Mann (1977). Cf. Daniélou (1966b). Text in Jaeger et al. (1960–) = GNO III.2. See also Ramelli (2007).

88 Meredith (1976); for Gregory's debt to philosophy in respect of particular theological themes, see Zachhuber (1999); Turcescu (2005); etc.

89 Text in Migne, *PG* 46; ET in *NPNF*.

chus, as well as the traditions of the contemporary Platonic school at Athens.[90] It is not at all clear where and how he acquired his philosophical education, but he certainly had it. In fact, so wholeheartedly did he accept the approach and attitude of ancient philosophy that one critic suggested that he was really a born philosopher reluctantly forced into the straitjacket of orthodoxy by his domineering family.[91] This estimate hardly does justice to the complexities of Gregory's character and thought, but it does highlight the extent of his unacknowledged debt to the pagan philosophical tradition.

Over the centuries the Church had adapted itself and its message to the contemporary situation, partly consciously, partly unconsciously. It is not surprising that people see the Christian tradition with the cultural spectacles of their own time. Yet at the same time, the Church had always distinguished itself not merely from other religions, but from the world, its ideals and purposes, its wealth and its wisdom. This double-edged tradition affected the stance of the Cappadocians. The Church was now beginning to take over the world, not merely in political terms, but in the sphere of philosophy and culture. The ambivalent attitude expressed in the writings of the Cappadocians reflects the emergence of a Christianized culture. This new culture is dependent on the pagan culture of the past, but it has to be distinguished from it. It must disown its inheritance, while embracing its newly acquired riches. It must renounce the world and its wisdom, but to win the world, it had to talk its language. For all its superficial inconsistency, this attitude served the needs of the day.

For Further Reading

English translations

Gilbert, Peter, 2001. *On God and Man: The Theological Poetry of St. Gregory of Nazianzus*, Crestwood, NY: St Vladimir's Seminary Press.
McGuckin, J. A., 1986/9. *St Gregory Nazianzen: Selected Poems*, Oxford: SLG Press.
Meehan, D., 1987. *St Gregory of Nazianzus. Three Poems*, FC, Washington, DC: Catholic University of America Press.
Moreschini, C. (ed.) and D. A. Sykes (ET and Commentary), 1997. *Gregory of Nazianzus: Poemata Arcana*, Oxford: Clarendon Press.
Roth, Catherine, 1993. *On the Soul and the Resurrection*, Crestwood, NY: St Vladimir's Seminary Press.
Silvas, Anna M., 2008. *Macrina the Younger, Philosopher of God*, Turnhout: Brepols.
Way, Sister Agnes Clare, 1963. *Saint Basil. Exegetic Homilies*, FC, Washington DC: Catholic University of America Press.
White, C., 1996. *Gregory of Nazianzus: Autobiographical Poems*, Cambridge Medieval Classics, Cambridge: Cambridge University Press.

---

90 Daniélou (1967). For the more general points, see Daniélou in Harl (1971), a useful review article which indicates the more specialized studies on which these statements are based. Latterly there has been greater reserve about the extent of Gregory's knowledge of contemporary philosophy, for example Rist in Fedwick (1981); but see Heine (1995) for evidence that he followed the hermeneutical approach of Iamblichus; and Turcescu (2005) for a survey of discussion of Gregory's acquaintance with philosophy.

91 Cherniss (1930).

Wilson, N. G., 1975. *Saint Basil on the Value of Greek Literature*, London: Duckworth.

Studies

Cherniss, H. F., 1930. *The Platonism of Gregory of Nyssa*, New York: Burt Franklin.
Demoen, K., 1996. *Pagan and Biblical Exempla in Gregory Nazianzen: A Study in Rhetoric and Hermeneutics*, Corpus Christianorum, Turnhout: Brepols.
Gregg, Robert C., 1975. *Consolation Philosophy: Greek and Christian 'Paideia' in Basil and the Two Gregories*, Philadelphia: Philadelphia Patristic Foundation.

IV Basil and the Ascetic Movement

Basil's involvement in the organization and regulation of ascetic communities was the genesis of a body of works that ultimately influenced the development of monasticism in East and West. Research has increasingly suggested that he was not quite the innovator once presumed;[92] that there was a variety of ascetic modes of life already around in Asia Minor, from extreme rejection of social norms to urban communities, domestic asceticism and 'spiritual marriages'; that much of the developed pattern represented in Basil's works was anticipated by Eustathius, who had had a long-standing relationship with Basil's family; and that it is quite possible that the type of community Basil encouraged had already been gradually worked out by his sister, Macrina, whose ascetic life was initiated under Eustathius' influence. Nevertheless, it is clear that Basil himself had influence among ascetics, and likely that the various stages in the development of the *Great Asketikon*,[93] stages evident from its complex textual history, reflect development not only in the family monastery at Annesi but also in his own thinking about the ascetic life, its proper regularization and its relationship with Church and society.

A desire to return to the simplicity of the primitive church in Jerusalem determines the flavour and tone of Basil's ascetic teaching. It is true that his ideals are affected by contemporary presuppositions about the soul and the body; it is also true that the ethical teaching of Hellenistic philosophers has influenced his maxims; nevertheless, scripture provides his means of expression. For him, scripture was the only rule; his own *Rules* are merely systematic aids for those seeking spiritual perfection.[94]

The *Ascetica* attributed to Basil constitute a considerable collection of writings, some undoubtedly inauthentic.[95] The collection has a long history of use in the Eastern Church, and so has been preserved in a number of textual traditions and versions; inevitably then, study of these documents has been fraught with prior critical questions, a sense of which can be gleaned from Silvas's introduction to her translation of the *Asketikon*; but no serious student of the material

---

92 For the following points, see Elm (1994); Rousseau (1994); Silvas (2005).
93 Rousseau (2005), Appendix; Silvas (2005).
94 Cf. Basil, *Ep.* 22. The discussion of Basil's ascetic teaching in this section is much indebted to Amand de Mendietta (1949). See also Rousseau (1994).
95 Texts in *PG* 31. ET: Clarke (1925); Wagner (1950); Silvas (2005).

can get far without consulting the major works of Gribomont, Rudberg and Fedwick.[96]

It appears probable that Basil's first ascetic treatise was the work known as the *Moralia*; Gribomont is not alone in suggesting that it was composed about 360 while Basil was at his monastery in Pontus. The character of this work suggests that it might be a pastoral work belonging to the years of his episcopate, but the case has not proved entirely convincing.[97] It consists basically of lists of scriptural citations, the author merely providing links and headings. Who was the collection made for? What was its purpose? Since sections 70–9 are concerned with the proper duties of ministers of the word, married people, parents, slaves, soldiers and magistrates, it was hardly intended only for monks. Gribomont[98] suggested that the ascetic movement in Basil's eyes was a movement of reform in the Church. Basil was here setting out the evangelical basis of the movement, emphasizing continence rather than condemnation of marriage and riches, overcoming the fears of extremism aroused by such groups as the Messalians. He was looking for New Testament norms in a situation where ascetic propaganda was causing dissension. Whatever its original intention, the treatise certainly appears to be authentic, and the theoretical basis not only of much of Basil's ascetic teaching, but his ecclesiology.[99] What is notable is its entirely scriptural content. It seems we should not distinguish monastic from moral teaching in Basil's case; he was primarily concerned with the inner life of the serious Christian – radical renunciation could be practised without becoming a monk. Interior intensity is what delivers appropriate outward and visible behaviour.[100]

If we assume that the *Moralia* was the first work, the second seems to have been the work known as the *Small Asketikon*. This does not survive in its original form in Greek, but Rufinus' translation and a Syriac version appear to be good witnesses. It consisted of answers to practical questions, the questions presupposing a somewhat Messalian atmosphere, the answers deliberately counselling restraint. At this stage Basil seems to have been much under the influence of Eustathius of Sebaste, which perhaps explains Sozomen's comment that some attributed the ascetic treatises to Eustathius rather than Basil. Basil's own ideas were more fully developed as later versions appeared.

The *Small Asketikon* was expanded into the *Great Asketikon* during Basil's episcopacy, possibly in several stages, but was developed further by a redactor in the sixth century.[101] The work consists of the *Longer Responses* and the *Shorter Rules*, the former discussing the fundamental principles of monasticism in fifty-five sections, while the latter take the form of question and answer, providing brief applications (313 of them) to the details of daily life. In this work, which became known as the *Rules*, Basil seems to be trying to regulate and reform ascetic communities under his episcopal jurisdiction, or at least to be providing a compendium of his teaching for the use of monks. Yet they do not really

---

96 Silvas (2005); Gribomont (1953); Rudberg (1953); Fedwick (1993–2004).

97 Lèbe (1965); Rousseau (1994), p. 228.

98 Gribomont (1957).

99 Amand de Mendietta (1949); Fedwick (1979); Rousseau (1994).

100 Rousseau (1994).

101 Silvas (2005) provides a helpful account.

establish a monastic rule in the sense of a code of practice. Rather they trace out an ascetical way of life on the basis of the New Testament,[102] very much as his earlier treatises did. Basil had been evolving monastic 'regulations' ever since his letter to Gregory on the monastic life, and these documents appear to be the culmination of the process, a synthesis of his teachings for the use of monks.

The most refreshing aspect of Basil's ascetic teaching, apart from its profoundly scriptural basis, is his recognition of the need for community, for a society in which alone true Christian virtue can be expressed. Having explored the various ascetic traditions of Syria and Palestine, he recognized the dangers and eccentricities involved in an individualistic search for personal purity in isolation from others; he perhaps adopted the communal ideas of Pachomius, though Gregory of Nazianzus suggests that his vision was a unification of the solitary and communal life, and it is likely that he was drawing together various ascetic strands already prevalent in Asia Minor, seeking the best of each to excise the excesses of each.[103] But this was not merely a response to practical problems. The strong escapist currents of contemporary soteriology were tempered in Basil's thought by an unusually profound insight into the nature of New Testament ethics. He saw that it was impossible to practise the law of love in solitude. The solitary neglected to feed the hungry and clothe the naked. He therefore failed to obey the commands of God, and total obedience is the radical demand of Christ. The Christian virtues of humility, obedience and love can only be worked out in the context of a community serving the needs of society.

This ideology was probably forged in Pontus with the composition of the *Moralia*, but it was certainly reinforced by Basil's experience in the famine of 369, when he was priest in Caesarea. It is likely that this event created the germ of the Basileiados – the 'new city'[104] on the outskirts of Caesarea, which eventually made up a whole collection of buildings for the relief of the poor and destitute, the care of the sick, a refuge for lepers and a monastery. It is intriguing that Valens offered patronage to Basil's foundation after his visit in 372.

The most important source of Basil's teaching was the Acts' account of the primitive Christian community. Undoubtedly his family background, the writings of Origen, the examples of Antony, Pachomius and other famous ascetics, the outlook of contemporary philosophy, Christian tradition and the ascetic leadership of Eustathius, all made large contributions to the total picture. Basil's asceticism bears the characteristic marks of the period: celibacy and withdrawal from worldly pursuits, the search for union with God through meditation and prayer, refusal of all but the barest necessities of life – these are inevitably the basic features of his teaching. Yet certain characteristics undoubtedly drew inspiration from the teaching of Jesus and the example of his first disciples. All things were to be held in common and to be used for the benefit of the

---

102 A useful summary in English will be found in Murphy (1976).

103 Gregory Nazianzen, *Orat.* 43. Cf. Elm (1994); Crislip (2005).

104 The phrase comes from Gregory Nazianzen, *Orat.* 43; see Crislip (2005) for discussion of the character and potential antecedents of this foundation. See Holman (2001) for Basil's famine relief and charitable activities, along with (possibly) supporting sermons of the two Gregories; and Finn (2006) for Basil's combination of motifs from classical euergetism and Christian traditions of almsgiving.

sick and the needy. The monastery was to be situated within reach of suffering humanity, and provide a hospital and schools. The monk was to engage in manual work for the maintenance of the community and its welfare services. Thus Basil sought to resuscitate and perpetuate the fervour of the early Church in his monastic communities, but also to bring ascetics under the discipline of the local church and the bishop.

In fact, Basil's organization would inevitably tend to breed subservience. Obedience and humility were notably lacking among the individualistic ascetics of the desert, who accepted the authority of none but the Lord; for Basil, the community was necessary not only to nurture love, but also to provide a specific context in which obedience and humility could be fostered. For this reason, the monk had to discipline himself to unquestioning obedience to his superior, and to calm acceptance of the judgment and criticism of his fellow-monks. No doubt this required a greater self-sacrifice than merely giving up worldly goods and ambitions, but it meant that institutionalization was inevitable, and the primitive fervour Basil sought to re-create would be dampened by the discipline of routine, by the deliberate destruction of emotion, by authoritarianism. The counter-cultural threat of undisciplined ascetics was certainly tamed in the process.

Nevertheless, for Basil, the monk was the authentic Christian who set out to live Christianity in its fullness. In theory, Basil could not tolerate a dual morality: every Christian is called to utter obedience to every precept in the gospels. But in practice, he saw monasteries as providing the conditions in which this ideal could flourish and be perfected. The spirit of self-sacrificial love for others is at least the mainspring of Basil's teaching, whether or not it could be realized most effectively in the monastic conditions which he envisaged.

For Further Reading

English translations

Callahan, V. Woods, 1967. *Gregory of Nyssa. Ascetical Works*, FC, Washington, DC: Catholic University of America Press.

Silvas, Anna M., 2005. *The Asketicon of St. Basil the Great*, Oxford: Oxford University Press.

Wagner, M. M., 1950. *Saint Basil. Ascetical Works*, FC, Washington, DC: Catholic University of America Press.

Studies

Crislip, Andrew T., 2005. *From Monastery to Hospital: Christian Monasticism and the Transformation of Health Care in Late Antiquity*, Ann Arbor: University of Michigan Press.

Elm, Susanna, 1994. *'Virgins of God': The Making of Asceticism in Late Antiquity*, Oxford: Clarendon Press.

Fedwick, Paul J., 1979. *The Church and the Charisma of Leadership in Basil of Caesarea*, Toronto: Pontifical Institute of Mediaeval Studies.

Finn, Richard, 2006. *Almsgiving in the Later Roman Empire: Christian Promotion and Practice (313–450)*, Oxford: Oxford University Press.

Holman Susan R., 2001. *The Hungry are Dying: Beggars and Bishops in Roman Cappadocia*, Oxford: Oxford University Press.

V The Dogmatic Debates

All three Cappadocians were involved in the dogmatic controversies of their time, and a considerable amount of their published work was directly concerned with these issues. In the confused state of the 360s and 370s Basil moved to cement alliances with Athanasius and the West, and consolidate a 'Neo-Nicene' position which was then defended by his friend and his brother, especially at and after the Council of Constantinople in 381. The tendency to treat the three as holding a single position is increasingly challenged as the nuances of the thought of each is observed,[105] but still their theology was shaped similarly by key debates.

1 Eunomius

All three were provoked by the theology of a fellow-Cappadocian, Eunomius,[106] who, following Aetius, insisted on the unlikeness of the essence of the Father and the Son (the Anomoian position, sometimes called 'Neo-Arian'). Basil was engaged in refuting his position in the early 360s, possibly first when attending the council in Constantinople in 360 with Basil of Ancyra and Eustathius of Sebaste, both leading homoiousians, but principally in writing a treatise[107] against the recently published *Apologia* of Eunomius. The first three books of the *Contra Eunomium* are genuine, the other two being erroneously added on to the end.[108] Book I argues that ἀγεννησία (*agennēsia* – ingenerateness) is *not* the essential characteristic of the deity; the other two, while rarely using the *homoousion*, in fact argue for the essential equality with the Father of the Son (Book II) and of the Spirit (Book III). After Basil's death, Gregory Nazianzen tackled the Eunomian position in orations in Constantinople, while Gregory his brother was inspired to answer Eunomius' reply to Basil. All three treat Eunomius with considerable disdain – he did not come from the same 'aristocratic' level of Cappadocian society.

Gregory of Nyssa composed at least four treatises against this opponent. The order of these books became confused in the manuscript tradition, but has now been restored in the new critical edition.[109] Gregory also defended the divinity

---

105 For example, Beeley (2008).

106 See Vaggione (1987, 2000) for extant texts and biographical study.

107 For a critical account of this work, see Anastos in Fedwick (1981), pp. 67–136; for Basil's Trinitarianism, see Hildebrand (2007).

108 Text of the *Contra Eunomium*, PG 29, Sesboüé, de Durand and Doutreleau (1982, 1983). On books IV—V, see Hayes (1972) and Risch (1992). See Chapter 3, Section IV, note 116 for discussion of the attribution to Didymus.

109 The enumeration of Jaeger et al. (1960–) = *GNO* I & II is followed here. ET in *NPNF* is based on earlier editions and therefore differently ordered and entitled; for more recent

of the Holy Spirit in several small treatises, one of which appears among Basil's correspondence, an indication of the confused state in which Gregory's works have survived. Another treatise, the *Ad Ablabium*, or *On not Three Gods*, which has been at the centre of debate about the 'social' understanding of the Trinity in the East,[110] probably dates from the end of his career.

In these controversial writings, we find many of the standard polemical ploys. The heretic is accused of being unbiblical and impious; of using sophistry and syllogisms to trample on the being of God. The debate with Eunomius became a personal feud, pamphlet following counter-pamphlet, slanders and misrepresentations being the tricks of the trade. Yet in the midst of what may seem uncharitable and offensive argument, the fundamentals of Trinitarian orthodoxy were finally fashioned.[111]

The heart of Eunomius' position lay in his insistence that God is knowable – indeed, completely comprehensible because God is simple unity. With respect to the Being (οὐσία – *ousia*) by which the divine is one, he affirms, God is not separated or divided into more, nor is 'becoming sometimes one and sometimes another, nor changing from being what God is, or split from one οὐσία into a threefold ὑπόστασις (*hypostasis*): for God is always and absolutely one, remaining uniformly and unchangeably God'.[112] Gregory of Nyssa undoubtedly shares Eunomius' definition of divinity,[113] in spite of the scorn with which he quotes his words. The whole basis of Gregory's Trinitarian doctrine is the idea that God is incomposite, homogeneous, unchangeable and indivisible, attributes all of which Eunomius accepted. From any other source, Gregory might have recognized something of his own position being voiced.

What then is the essential difference between the two protagonists? Eunomius concludes that this definition of God as simple unity can only be safeguarded by isolating the Supreme and Absolute One from the second and third, which came after and are therefore inferior and derivative. Ἀγεννησία (unbegottenness) becomes for him the essentially divine attribute which guarantees God's simplicity and uniqueness. Gregory, on the other hand, uses the very same description of God in order to argue that a plurality or hierarchy of separated beings is impossible: one infinite cannot be greater or less than another. There may be 'three subjects', Gregory argues, but their infinity means that they are indistinguishable alongside one another. To speak of 'large' and 'small', or 'before' and 'after' introduces compositeness into the single unity of the undivided divine substance. There is existence and non-existence; there cannot

---

English translations of I & II, see Mateo-Seco and Bastero (1988) and Karfikova, Douglass and Zachhuber (2007).

110 See Ayres in Coakley (2003); and the response in Maspero (2007). Also Barnes (2001), Turcescu (2005), Cross (2006) and Ludlow (2007) for Gregory's Trinitarianism.

111 See Pottier (1994); and articles in Mateo-Seco and Bastero (1988) and Karfikova, Douglass and Zachhuber (2007).

112 Gregory Nyssen, *Refutatio Confessionis Eunomii* 33 (Jaeger et al. (1960–) = *GNO* II, 325).

113 Meredith (1975) argues that the debate reflects current arguments within the philosophical schools, and that Eunomius, so far from being an Aristotelian, was closer to the mainstream Platonic tradition than his eclectic orthodox opponents. See further Meredith in Mateo-Seco and Bastero (1988).

be degrees of Being or priorities of Being; one cannot be more or less existent than another.

The drive of Gregory's argument, then, like Basil's before him, is against the possibility of a 'hierarchy of Being'. Eunomius' very desire to separate God in absoluteness from the created order led him into a 'hierarchical' position; since he wanted to continue using scriptural language of his derivative Logos, he could not avoid producing 'a new God springing up from nothing'.[114] Eunomius was trying to establish a distinction between God and creation; Gregory already accepted this as fundamental, but his God was a Trinitarian God.

For Gregory, Father and Son express not so much different Beings as an eternal relationship within one divine Being; for without the Son, the Father has neither existence nor name.[115] Gregory had to address the charge of 'tritheism', not least because he defines the οὐσία which Father, Son and Spirit share in an apparently generic sense, and his favourite analogy is the universal human οὐσία shared by particular men, e.g. Peter, James and John.[116] Furthermore, in speaking of generation, Gregory points out that even among men and animals the production of a son does not divide or diminish the substance of a father.[117] The obvious objection to this approach would be that it does produce a separate individual, making it difficult to call monotheistic a theology based on this way of defining the common nature. In fact Gregory's definition of divine substance resolves this difficulty for him. If divine substance is in principle indivisible, incomposite and undifferentiated, if number is inapplicable to divine simplicity so that one and one and one cannot be added together to make three, if each is infinite so that they cannot exist alongside each other but only in each other, then the oneness of God is by definition ensured. If divine substance is in principle unchangeable, then the mutual relationships within the Godhead are eternal and non-hierarchical. Polytheism and Judaism are alike avoided, and the fundamental distinction between God and creation safeguarded.[118]

Meanwhile, the Trinitarian debate involved the parties in some other interesting theological issues, one being the question of theological language and its basis.[119] Eunomius wanted to claim that all descriptions of the Logos were analogical; he was Son of God metaphorically, not literally. Gregory of course accepts the analogical character of titles like 'stone', 'door', 'way', 'shepherd',

---

114 Gregory Nyssen, *Contra Eunomium* III. 164 (Jaeger et al. (1960–) = GNO II, 106).

115 *Refutatio* 6–7 (Jaeger et al. (1960–) = GNO II, 315). See the following sections of the *Refutatio* for the arguments summarized in this paragraph.

116 *Contra Eunomium* I. 202 (Jaeger et al. (1960–) = GNO I, 85); *Ad Ablabium* 117 (Jaeger et al. (1960–) = GNO III, 38). For discussion of this analogy, see Zachhuber (2000); Ayres in Coakley (2003); Turcescu (2005); Maspero (2007). Human nature as a unity at creation and in the *eschaton* is a feature of Gregory's thought which seems to go beyond a merely generic understanding.

117 *Refutatio* 59ff. (Jaeger et al. (1960–) = GNO II, 336).

118 *Catechetical Orat.* 3 (Jaeger et al. (1960–) = GNO III.4); text and ET Srawley (1903, 1917); ET in *NPNF*.

119 The topic figures most prominently in *Contra Eunomium* II (Jaeger et al. (1960–) = GNO I, 226–409). For discussion, see Young in Schoedel and Wilken (1979); also Stead in Mateo-Seco and Bastero (1988); Zachhuber (2000); Maspero (2007); commentary and articles in Karfikova, Douglass and Zachhuber (2007), etc.

etc., but tries to distinguish between these and other names which have the function of designating his nature. 'Son' and 'only-begotten God' must be taken in a more 'literal' sense. The principle on which he makes this distinction is that images used of Christ's relationship with humanity are analogical, whereas names expressing his relationship with God are essential.[120]

Yet it was Gregory who insisted on God's incomprehensibility. How then could he justify the attempt to define God or express the essential Being of the divine? Gregory admits that all names are inadequate and humanly contrived expressions, but he goes on to argue that they are not arbitrary, for they are grounded in the prior existence and activity of God. Though God has to accommodate the divine self to the limitations of human perception, God cannot be a party to deception; so the names revealed in scripture have sufficient grounding in reality to form a basis for theological construction. They have to be critically tested; for so wide is the gulf between Creator and creature, finite and Infinite, that they are misleading as well as applicable. They also have to be multiplied, for no one epithet can express or define the totality of the infinite God; and their status has to be determined in accordance with the principle mentioned earlier, the distinction between those that apply to God absolutely and those that have a relative reference. However, critically evaluated, the variety of attributes indicated by the names derived from scripture can provide a positive theological language without endangering the transcendent unity of God's nature.

There is always, nevertheless, a 'difference of unlikeness'. Eunomius' arrogant claim to define and delimit the Being of God will not do: 'the infinity of God exceeds all the significance and comprehension that names can furnish.'[121] For all the detail of his Trinitarian discussions, Gregory stands ultimately before a mystery, and this is where his dogmatic theology and his so-called 'mysticism'[122] coalesce.

2 The Pneumatomachi

Meanwhile, the issue concerning the divinity of the Holy Spirit had had to be addressed.[123] Already Basil had argued for this in his *Contra Eunomium III*, but ongoing criticism would lead to his breach with Eustathius and the composition of his *De Spiritu Sancto*.[124] Written in 375 and used only a few years later by Ambrose when he composed his *De Spiritu Sancto*, this work laid the foundations on which the two Gregories based their definitive exposition of Trinitarian theology, even though Basil himself was chary of using the *homoousion* of the Holy Spirit, a point on which Gregory Nazianzen upbraided him. There has been some debate about the reasons for Basil's reticence – maybe it was no more than a political ploy to keep together as many as possible in the face of Valens' tendency to favour non-Nicenes. After Basil's death, Gregory of

---

120 *Contra Eunomium* III. 127–41 (Jaeger et al. (1960–) = GNO II, 46ff.).

121 *Contra Eunomium* III. 110 (Jaeger et al. (1960–) = GNO II, 41).

122 See below, pp. 165–9; NB Canévet (1983) for discussion of the link between Gregory's view of 'names' and his exegesis.

123 See Haykin (1994) for an account of this controversy.

124 Text: Pruche (1968); Sieben (1993). ET in *NPNF* and Anderson (1980).

Nyssa was embroiled in debate with the Pneumatomachi; and at the Council of Constantinople in 381 there was an attempt to reconcile their delegation, which failed, but also led to a weaker statement in the Creed than Gregory Nazianzen liked.

Discussion about the Holy Spirit raised serious questions about the relationship between tradition and innovation. Basil had tried to argue largely on the basis of scripture, but the debates soon proved that scripture was insufficiently clear on the matter. Gregory Nazianzen admitted that the Spirit's divinity was only becoming clear in the life of the Church: the Old Testament revealed the Father, the New Testament revealed the Son; so there were stages of illumination depending upon the capacity of the recipients. The disciples were not yet ready for a full revelation of the Spirit's divinity (John 16.12).[125]

Basil had maintained the overriding importance of scripture, but also relied on the experience of sanctification and the worship of the Church. Perhaps his way of rooting this in the apostolic tradition was through a distinction between *kerygma* and *dogma*. The publicly proclaimed teaching of the Church, enshrined in the creed, was *kerygma*; *dogma* was the secret and mystical tradition reserved for the initiates. The exact implications of this were once the subject of some discussion: did Basil adopt the Origenist idea of advanced secret doctrines for an élite, an idea deliberately dropped by Gregory Nazianzen?[126] That he uses that kind of language cannot be denied; yet the élite was almost certainly all the baptized. What Basil referred to, and this can be documented by examining his arguments, was the theological implication of the sacraments and the Church's customs, those aspects of the Church's life taught only to catechumens.[127] In practical terms, those who submitted to baptism in this period were an élite, and the 'mysteries' of the faith were reserved by the *disciplina arcani* from public promulgation.[128] This may explain Basil's reserve in public preaching concerning the Holy Spirit, when he was prepared to acknowledge his divinity in private correspondence. It was the liturgy which provided the data on which such a doctrine was based. So the concept of *dogma* made it possible for Basil to disclaim any charges of innovation when he argued that the divine nature of the Holy Spirit was implied by the doxology, baptism, sanctification and so on. He could circumvent the traditional accusations against heretics, that they took pride in intellectualism and philosophy, were avid for originality and prestige, and failed to accept the authority of the sacred text and the tradition of the Church,[129] because what he called *dogma* was as apostolic in origin as the *kerygma*, so far as he and his contemporaries knew. Scripture and tradition remained the bulwark against newfangled doctrines, even as doctrinal clarifications were established.

---

125 Gregory Nazianzen, *Theological Orat.* 5 (*Orat.* 31), 24ff.

126 Hanson (1968).

127 Amand de Mendietta (1965a, 1965b). Also Pruche (1966).

128 Day (2001) outlines the emergence of secrecy among strategies to account for doctrinal development, as well as to protect Christians and sacraments in times of persecution, but notes that the device of *disciplina arcani* was a decreasingly useful construct: 'there can have been few secrets left for a fourth century catechumen as he commenced his instruction' (270).

129 Coman (1966).

3 Apollinarius

As Basil thought through the issues raised by Eunomius and moved towards a Nicene position, he apparently consulted Apollinarius;[130] Gregory Nazianzen's Trinitarianism also seems indebted to him.[131] It would be some time before the Cappadocians realized that there were problems with Apollinarius' Christological teaching. However, as the problems raised by Arius were largely being resolved in Trinitarian terms, the scene of debate was shifting. The transcendence of God had once made the divine relationship with the world problematical and the Logos had filled the role of mediator. Now the Logos shared the transcendence of the divine Being. Christological difficulties were bound to ensue.

Cappadocian Christology has proved somewhat elusive when attempts are made to assess it in relation to the Christological positions that came into conflict in the succeeding decades.[132] Both Gregories were happy to use the language of 'mixture'; they also resisted the notion of 'Two Sons'. But after Constantinople both found themselves in conflict with Apollinarians. Gregory of Nazianzus wrote a couple of letters to Cledonius on the subject, where we find the well-known aphorism, 'what is not assumed is not healed', directed at the notion that the enfleshed Christ did not assume a human soul. Gregory of Nyssa tackled Apollinarius' *Apodeixis* in his *Antirrheticus against Apollinarius*,[133] to which we are indebted for the fragments of Apollinarius' work. This, together with Gregory's work as a whole, reveals how deeply he would contest the notion that Christ had no human soul. The good shepherd takes the whole sheep on his shoulders.[134] In Christ human nature is re-created; transformation in Christ 'marks the beginning of the transformation in which each of us is called to participate'.[135] For Gregory the passions were like 'warts' or growths on the soul that needed removing, and imitation of Christ through an asceticism of mind as well as body would be the process whereby that painful stripping would be effected.[136]

For Further Reading

English translations

Anderson, David (trans.), 1980. *St. Basil the Great: On the Holy Spirit*, Crestwood, NY: St Vladimir's Seminary Press.

---

130 Prestige (1956).

131 Beeley (2008) suggests that Apollinarius was a more important influence on Gregory than Athanasius.

132 For which see Chapter 6; discussion of and references to contrary estimates of Gregory's Christology will be found in Meredith (1999), p. 47; Daley in Coakley (2003), pp. 67ff.

133 Edition Jaeger et al. (1960–) = GNO III.1.

134 *Antirrheticus* 16.

135 Daley in Coakley (2003), p. 71.

136 For example, *On the Soul and Resurrection* (Migne, PG 46; ET Roth 1993); for discussion see Daley in Coakley (2003).

Daley, Brian E., 2006. *Gregory of Nazianzus*, London and New York: Routledge.

Karfikova, L., Scot Douglass and Johannes Zachhuber (eds), 2007. *Gregory of Nyssa: Contra Eunomium II. An English version with Supporting Studies* (Proceedings of the 10th International Colloquium on Gregory of Nyssa, 2004), Supplements to *VigChr*, Leiden: Brill.

Meredith, Anthony, 1999. *Gregory of Nyssa*, London and New York: Routledge.

Norris, F. W., with F. Williams and L. Wickham, 1991. *Faith Gives Fullness to Reasoning: the Five Theological Orations of St. Gregory Nazianzen*, Supplement to *VigChr*, Leiden: Brill.

Vaggione, Richard P., 1987. *Eunomius. The Extant Works*, Oxford: Clarendon Press.

Studies

Barnes, Michel Rene, 2001. *The Power of God: Δύναμις in Gregory of Nyssa's Trinitarian Theology*, Washington, DC: Catholic University of America Press.

Beeley, Christopher A., 2008. *Gregory of Nazianzus on the Trinity and the Knowledge of God*, Oxford: Oxford University Press.

Coakley, Sarah (ed.), 2003. *Re-Thinking Gregory of Nyssa*, Oxford: Blackwell.

Fedwick, Paul J., (ed.), 1981. *Basil of Caesarea, Christian, Humanist, Ascetic: A Sixteen-Hundredth Anniversary Symposium*, 2 vols, Toronto: Pontifical Institute of Mediaeval Studies.

Maspero, Giulio, 2007. *Trinity and Man: Gregory of Nyssa's* Ad Ablabium, Supplements to *VigChr*, Leiden: Brill.

Meredith, A., 1995. *The Cappadocians*, London: Geoffrey Chapman.

Prestige, G. L., 1956. *St. Basil the Great and Apollinaris of Laodicea* (ed. Henry Chadwick), London: SPCK.

Turcescu, Lucian, 2005. *Gregory of Nyssa and the Concept of Divine Persons*, Oxford: Oxford University Press and the American Academy of Religion.

Vaggione, Richard P., 2000. *Eunomius of Cyzicus and the Nicene Revolution*, Oxford: Oxford University Press.

Zachhuber, J., 2000. *Human Nature in Gregory of Nyssa: Philosophical Background and Theological Significance*, Supplements to *VigChr*, Leiden: Brill.

VI Gregory the Theologian

Unlike his fellow-Cappadocians, Gregory Nazianzen left no treatises dealing with the controversial issues of the day, and his philosophical theology has been regarded as less sophisticated than theirs.[137] Yet 'the theologian' is the title by which he has been honoured down the centuries. It is perhaps on his ability to communicate, his 'popularization', his clarity and ease of expression that his reputation rests. For him, preaching and theology were integrated; his *Five Theological Orations*[138] were a brilliant summary for the city congregation of what was becoming the accepted Trinitarian orthodoxy. These statements have been seen as the height of Gregory's achievement. But such a view may be an

---

137 See Norris's Introduction in Norris, Williams and Wickham (1991).

138 Text: Mason (1899); Gallay and Jourjon (1978). ET: Williams and Wickham in Norris, Williams and Wickham (1991).

THE CAPPADOCIANS

underestimate of his work. It has been suggested that a proper estimation of his Trinitarian theology demands a look beyond the *Five Theological Orations*, which are defensive and do not reveal the full spectrum of this thought.[139]

In the theology of Gregory Nazianzen, the Trinity is absolutely central. Where Basil had been a bit chary of openly asserting the divinity of the Holy Spirit, in spite of the general drift of his argumentation, Gregory did not hesitate to take the lead.[140] Where Basil and Gregory of Nyssa tended to stress the equality or co-ordination of the three hypostases, against hierarchical tendencies,[141] Gregory maintained the 'monarchy' by insisting on the Father as source of Son and Spirit – the unity is preserved because the Son and Spirit are referred back to a single cause: it is as Trinity that God is abundantly generative.[142] Gregory's work was one of consolidation. He was conscious of finding the 'mean' between heretical extremes, and at the same time of affirming a theology of positive significance.[143]

A study of the doctrinal controversies of the fourth and fifth centuries may leave one with a sense of frustration. Were the debates really significant? Were the contenders not hair-splitting in a matter that is beyond human knowledge? Standing back from the debates, we may be tempted to wonder how so much passion could have been expended on relatively technical issues. It is when we sense the religious significance of the issues that we begin to appreciate why emotions were roused. Athanasius, as we have seen, was driven by the urgency of his sense of salvation in Christ: Arian simplification just could not contain the depths of that reality. Gregory was likewise driven by the pressures of his religious consciousness. For him, the cold technicality of logical argumentation detracted from his sense of mystery in the divine. The Arians, he felt, were too rational by half. An adequate theology had to do justice to his experience of awe and mystery in the universe, in ascetic contemplation, in the liturgy and in scripture. Gregory knew that human beings can know nothing of God, except what God has chosen to reveal in limited human terms. So he is often hesitant and plainly aware of the complexity of the problems he is discussing. He exhorts his congregations to cling to the essentials, and particularly to the sure foundation of the cross of Christ.[144]

Gregory's theology shared the apophatic, negative stress we have already observed in the argumentation of Gregory Nyssen. God is incorporeal, ingenerate, unchangeable, incorruptible and incomprehensible. We can only understand *that* God is, not *what* God is. Yet, for Gregory, this is not the end of discussion. For God has come to meet us, and our faith is not vain. The Trinity expresses both the mystery of God's nature (θεολογία), and of his loving outreach towards his creation (οἰκονομία); the latter allows some glimpse of the 'back-parts' of the

139 Beeley (2008).
140 Gregory Nazianzen, *Ep.* 58 and *Orat. 43*.
141 Zachhuber (2000); though this can be exaggerated – Coakley (2003) et al.
142 Beeley (2008); but see Norris in Norris, Williams and Wickham (1991) for previous discussion about the validity of arguing from the Father as 'cause' rather than the Godhead.
143 Plagnieux (1951).
144 *Theological Orat.* 2 and 3 (*Orat.* 28 and 29); *Orat. 45*.

former – there is no separation of the transcendent God and the God revealed in the economy.[145]

So the Trinity is the object of Gregory's devotion, and the ground of his faith and his life. Knowledge of the Trinity comes through scripture and tradition, and through the continuing revelation of the Spirit in the Church. For all his rhetorical tricks, Gregory had an outstanding ability to draw on the vast range of imagery and symbolism, the expression of faith and worship, originating in the Bible and developing in the life of the Church. Rationalist tools he converted into urgent appeals and dire warnings for his sinful and unrepentant congregations, by drawing on the prophetic writings of the Old Testament.[146] His God is not just the God of the philosophers or dogmaticians, but the God of Abraham, Isaac and Jacob, acting in the events of his own time. The distinctive message of Christianity is expressed not in logical systems, but in evocative images. His entire approach is saturated with biblical imagery and typological symbolism, centring on the cross of Christ and brought alive for the Christian of his own day:

> Yesterday, the lamb was slain and the door-posts anointed, and Egypt bewailed her first-born, and the Destroyer passed us over ... To-day, we have escaped from Egypt, and from Pharaoh, and there is none to hinder us from keeping the feast to the Lord, our God ... Yesterday, I was crucified with him; today I am glorified with him ... yesterday, I was buried with him; today, I rise with him ...[147]

The key to Gregory's theology is the notion of θέωσις (*theōsis*), his word for 'deification' through Christ and the imitation of Christ which effects it, through sacrament, through ascetic practice, through contemplation. Only the true theologian who approaches the task through the process of purification, humility and devotion is qualified to speak of the Triune God.[148]

Gregory is true to nearly every aspect of Christian thought about salvation in the East.[149] He was able to express the faith in the pictorial and rhetorical language that appealed to his contemporaries. In all this, he was able to impart a sense of the depth, the complexity, the mystery of the Christian conception of God and of his relation with the world; thus he outshone those who indulged in the niceties of technical debate, and became revered as the theologian *par excellence*.

For Further Reading

English translations

Daley, Brian E., 2006. *Gregory of Nazianzus*, London and New York: Routledge.

---

145 Norris in Norris, Williams and Wickham (1991); Beeley (2008).
146 *Orat.* 16.
147 *Orat.* 1.
148 *Orat.* 27.
149 For Gregory's soteriology, see Winslow (1979).

Norris, F. W., with F. Williams and L. Wickham, 1991. *Faith Gives Fullness to Reasoning: The Five Theological Orations of St. Gregory Nazianzen*, Supplement to *VigChr*, Leiden: Brill.

Vinson, Martha, 2003. *Gregory Nazianzen. Select Orations, FC*, Washington DC: Catholic University of America Press.

Studies

Beeley, C. A., 2008. *Gregory of Nazianzus on the Trinity and the Knowledge of God*, Oxford: Oxford University Press.

Børtnes, J. and Tomas Hägg (eds), 2006. *Gregory of Nazianzus: Images and Reflections*, Copenhagen: Museum Tusculanum.

McGuckin, J., 2001. *Gregory of Nazianzus*, Crestwood, NY: St Vladimir's Seminary Press.

Winslow, D. F., 1979. *The Dynamics of Salvation: A Study in Gregory of Nazianzus*, Cambridge, MA: Philadelphia Patristics Foundation.

VII Gregory of Nyssa and Neoplatonic Mysticism

During the twentieth century, Gregory of Nyssa emerged from the shadows and his works came to be mined for their theology and spirituality beyond the historical interests of early Christian studies; von Balthasar, Torrance and Zizioulas had successors in feminist theologians and among the radical orthodox. There is now a multiplicity of readings of Gregory Nyssen's writings.[150] However, the most interesting aspect of his thought for the scholar of Late Antiquity is the way in which biblical exegesis modifies his fundamentally Neoplatonic outlook.

Modern studies, largely initiated by Daniélou, established Gregory's philosophical ability, and seemed to rediscover the fundamental importance of his mysticism for his theological thought.[151] That Gregory was no mere eclectic compiler of ideas but a Christian Neoplatonist who expressed his mystical experience through scriptural symbols allegorically interpreted became the standard judgment. But further study has called this consensus in question – for after all, the validity of such an estimate depends on the definition of philosopher or mystic that is operative. Thus G. C. Stead has asserted that Gregory is not a philosopher in the sense that he engages with philosophical questions, only in the sense that as a theologian, he draws eclectically from philosophy in order to systematize his theological insights;[152] and Mühlenberg's study of Gregory's thought on God's infinity inspired a reassessment of the so-called mystical work, the *Life of Moses*, suggesting that theological controversies of the time had a formative influence, and that while the symbolic language of the mysteries is certainly used, this arises out of the need to deal with cognit-

---

150 For discussion, see Ludlow (2007).

151 Daniélou (1954). Cf. Balthasar (1942); Musurillo (1961); Harl (1971); Harrison (1992).

152 See the discussion in Dörrie, Altenburger and Schramm (1976), especially Stead, but also Daniélou.

ive problems, not out of any kind of 'mystical experience'[153] – indeed, Gregory never testifies to such experience, and it is easy to see how later schemata have been read back into his works. Rather, scripture is the foundation of Gregory's thought; philosophy was used to clarify and systematize it, a didactic focus on ethics lying at the heart of his so-called mystical writings, whose concern is primarily the progress of the soul towards God.[154]

Nevertheless Plotinus' influence has surely been established. Philosophy in Gregory's day was not 'rational thought without presuppositions', but a way of life.[155] Besides, the bias of ancient culture was veneration of the past. The philosophical schools of the Hellenistic world were interpreters of the wisdom of earlier great thinkers. In the schools, this tended to become bound by tradition and scholasticism, but in Plotinus, Gregory had a predecessor who was no mere commentator tied to the mainstream of the Platonic tradition. Rather, in certain key passages in the Platonic dialogues, he found the foundations of true philosophy, opinions which accorded with his own. 'It must be the opinion of anyone who studies the *Enneads* that Plotinus' major motive for philosophizing is to rationalize his own intuitions and experiences. Plotinus is a Platonist because Plato enables him to achieve this with the most success.'[156]

Much the same can be said of Gregory, though for him Plotinus himself, along with scripture and the traditions of the Church, has become a source of his expression and understanding. His dependence he never acknowledges, but Gregory must have known at first hand both the major Platonic dialogues and also some of the treatises included in the *Enneads* – his work is more than the reflection of a general cultural atmosphere. To this can be added the observation that Gregory adopts the hermeneutical approach of another Neoplatonist, Iamblichus.[157] Yet he is neither a slavish imitator, nor a collector of quotations. The thought-world of Plato and Plotinus, their imagery and the vocabulary are wedded to the imagery, vocabulary and thought-world of Christian traditions, scripture and liturgy, so as to become the expression of Gregory's understanding, while modified at crucial points by Christian tradition. So here is no shotgun wedding, superficial and artificial – rather Gregory's sense of the way things are is expressed in a subtle amalgam of scriptural and philosophical symbols. The integration of Plato's image of the cave in Republic VII with the grotto at Bethlehem is a case in point: as Daniélou points out,[158] the combination indicates that God descends into the shadows of the cave to bring illumination, rather than humanity having to find its own way of ascent. The Christian gospel transforms the essentially Platonic motif.

So in key respects Gregory breaks with traditional Platonic presuppositions. He drops, for example, the presupposition that perfection is static, an ultimate to be reached by philosophical ascent. All change from what is perfect,

---

153 Mühlenberg (1966); Heine (1975); Heine (1995); Ludlow (2000). But cf. Macleod (1970, 1971); Harrison (1992).

154 Ludlow (2000); Ramelli (2007).

155 Verghese in Dörrie, Altenberger and Schramm (1976); Gregorios and Meredith in Mateo-Seco and Bastero (1988); etc.

156 Rist (1967), p. 185.

157 Heine (1995).

158 Daniélou (1964).

it had been thought, must be for the worse; so much of the Platonist tradition, including Origen, envisaged a fall and return, the Good being the changeless perfection lost. But Gregory saw perfection in terms of constant progress. There is no limit to virtue; so perfection cannot be grasped or possessed. The race goes on for ever; the ascent is never-ending. To gain a vision of God, it is necessary to follow in God's way. There is no danger of the soul becoming satiated and therefore being distracted from the pursuit of God, for every summit reached is a revelation of greater heights above. For participation in God only produces more intense desire: this truly is the vision of God, never to be satisfied in the desire to see him.[159]

This notion of perpetual progress (ἐπέκτασις – *epektasis*) is grounded in Gregory's most fundamental theological perceptions: human mutability, the inevitable result of being created out of nothing (another non-Platonic idea), enables constant change and progress; while God's incomprehensibility, which ensures that never can the divine be wholly grasped, means that true knowledge of God is the seeing which consists in not seeing. The incomprehensibility of God is grounded in divine infinity, and this positive use of the idea of infinity is significant.[160] In the Greek philosophical tradition, infinity had for long implied indefiniteness, formlessness. It was distasteful to a culture whose idea of the good and the beautiful was based on symmetry, proportion and mathematical categories. Goodness meant limit. The Platonic forms were finite beings. But already for Plotinus the One transcended the forms in being formless and 'beyond being'.[161] The apophatic theology of Philo and Clement of Alexandria had toyed with the idea of God's infinity. Now positive affirmation of God's infinity appears in Christian writers, anxious to assert that divine goodness, power and love have no limit; and also, in Gregory's case, that eternal progress towards the divine is likewise limitless. The soul enters a 'luminous darkness',[162] in which it can know nothing of an infinite and incomprehensible God, but yet by faith senses the divine presence in a union of love. This experience is not cyclic, lost and found over and over again, but a perpetual discovery of deeper and deeper riches, a never-ending process of 'becoming'. For God remains ever inaccessible, and yet intimately near, the divine presence being grasped by faith when discursive reason fails.[163]

One concept where Platonist and biblical traditions coalesced was in the understanding of the human soul as an image of the divine. For Plotinus and Gregory the ascent begins with purification from fleshly desires, and the turning of the soul inward upon itself, to find knowledge of God in its own purity. Gregory uses Plotinus' language and imagery to describe this process. Subtle differences have been stressed:[164] Gregory insists on the goodness of creation,

159 Ferguson (1973, 1976). Cf. J. Daniélou (1954) and his Introduction to Musurillo (1961).

160 Mühlenberg (1966). But see the criticisms of Brightman (1973); Harrison (1992); Geljon (2005).

161 Rist (1967).

162 Laird (2004) offers a critique of the emphasis on darkness in studies of Nyssen, stressing the presence of light and luminosity in his writings.

163 Laird (2004); anticipated by von Balthasar (1942).

164 For example by Daniélou (1954); Bebis (1967); etc.

and increasingly on the importance of the body as a constitutive part of human nature.[165] Yet, for Plotinus also, the ultimate source of everything is the transcendent One. The beauty and harmony of the universe reveals its divinity, and leads the soul to contemplation of the intelligible. In spite of his identification of matter with evil, Plotinus was also opposed to the Gnostics, and like some Christians defined evil as non-being – a dualist doctrine was no ultimate solution. Besides this, both stress the moral content of the process of purification, and the stripping away of distracting sense perceptions. Furthermore, some studies stressed that Plotinus' mysticism is really 'theistic': the soul is not absorbed into the One so as to lose its identity.[166] The One remains transcendent, as God does for Gregory, and if Plotinus can be described as a mystic, Gregory can too.[167]

But there is a distinctively Christian colouring to Gregory's philosophy. Biblical symbols dominate and fill out Platonic imagery.[168] Exegesis of the *Inscriptions of the Psalms*,[169] *Ecclesiastes*,[170] the *Beatitudes*,[171] the *Life of Moses*[172] and the *Song of Songs*[173] forms the vehicle for describing the ladder of ascent. Furthermore, the process is essentially sacramental, being expressed in the 'death and resurrection' symbolism of baptism, and the spiritual feeding of the Eucharist. Above all, it is Christological. An individual can only progress towards God and the experience of contact with the divine because humankind as a whole has ascended in Christ. By being in Christ, humanity is resurrected and its double (body–soul) constitution is unified.

Perhaps most significant are the differences in understanding of the One, or God. Both Gregory and Plotinus have radically apophatic thinking. Nothing can be known of the Being beyond Being. Yet there is some truth in the oversimplified generalization that Plotinus' soul has to search for God, while Gregory's God has searched for his soul. Furthermore, Plotinus' soul, like the whole universe, is ultimately derived from the One by a process of spontaneous activity, the overflow of its abundant life, but Gregory's soul is created by God out of nothing, as a conscious act of will and of love. For Gregory there is a gulf fixed between the self-existent Trinity and all creatures, bridged only

---

165 See Mosshammer in Mateo-Seco and Bastero (1988). The body, and its intimate relationship with the driving force of the soul, is clearly affirmed in the *De Opificio Hominis*. The question of the emotions/passions in Gregory's thought is worth exploring: are they just to be excised (as seems to be the case in the dialogue with Macrina, *De Anima et Resurrectione*), or harnessed and transformed into *agapē*, in the way Evagrius suggested (cf. pp. 106–7 above)? See discussion in Warren Smith (2004), and Meredith reviewing Warren Smith (2004) in *JTS* NS 57, pp. 308–9.

166 For discussion of the interpretation of Plotinus, see Armstrong (1967); Rist (1967).

167 See further Canévet in Fontaine and Kannengiesser (1972); *pace* von Stritzky (1973) who argued (subsequent to the work of Mühlenberg) that the mystical interpretation is dangerous because there is always a distinction between God and man and no mystical union as such.

168 NB Canévet (1983).

169 Jaeger et al. (1960–) = *GNO* V; ET Heine (1995).

170 Jaeger et al. (1960–) = *GNO* V; ET Hall (1993).

171 Jaeger et al. (1960–) = *GNO* VII.2; ET Graef (1954).

172 Jaeger et al. (1960–) = *GNO* XII.1; ET Ferguson and Malherbe (1978).

173 Jaeger et al. (1960–) = *GNO* VI; ET McCambley (1987).

by the grace which makes humanity in its own image, and re-creates that lost image through the incarnation.[174] Gregory's dogmatic theology and his philosophy are ultimately inseparable. Both are expressions of his understanding and experience of the Christian gospel of salvation in Christ.

For Further Reading

English translations

Ferguson, E. and A. Malherbe, 1978. *The Life of Moses*, Classics of Western Spirituality, New York: Paulist Press.
Graef, Hilda, 1954. *The Lord's Prayer. The Beatitudes*, Ancient Christian Writers, New York: Newman Press.
Heine, R., 1995. *Gregory of Nyssa's Treatise on the 'Inscriptions on the Psalms'*, Oxford: Clarendon Press.
McCambley, Casimir, 1987. *St. Gregory of Nyssa: Commentary on the Song of Songs*, Brookline, MA: Hellenic College Press.
Meredith, Anthony, 1999. *Gregory of Nyssa*, London and New York: Routledge.
Musurillo, H. (ed. and trans.), 1961. *From Glory to Glory: Texts from Gregory of Nyssa's Mystical Writings*, New York: Scribner.

Studies

Balthasar, H. Urs von, 1942. *Présence et pensée: Essai sur la philosophie religieuse de Grégoire de Nysse*, Paris: Éditions Beauchesne (ET of 1988 edition, 1995, *Presence and Thought*, by Mark Sebanc, San Francisco: Ignatius Press).
Coakley, Sarah (ed.), 2003. *Re-Thinking Gregory of Nyssa*, Oxford: Blackwell.
Harrison, V., 1992. *Grace and Human Freedom according to Gregory of Nyssa*, Lewiston, NY: Edwin Mellen.
Heine, R., 1975. *Perfection in the Virtuous Life: A study of the relationship between edification and polemical theology in Gregory of Nyssa's* De Vita Moysis, Cambridge, MA: Philadelphia Patristic Foundation.
Laird, Martin, 2004. *Gregory of Nyssa and the Grasp of Faith: Union, Knowledge, and Divine Presence*, Oxford: Oxford University Press.
Ludlow, Morwenna, 2007. *Gregory of Nyssa, Ancient and [Post]Modern*, Oxford: Oxford University Press.

VIII Preachers and Teachers of the Church

The Cappadocian Fathers were cultured leaders of the Church, steeped in the traditions of developing Christian apologetic and theology, and immersed in the moral, liturgical and mystical life of the Christian community. Basil is said to have reformed the liturgy of his cathedral at Caesarea,[175] and his *De Spiritu Sancto* defends certain innovations. There can be no doubt that he made contributions in this field. It is probable that the *Liturgy of St Basil*, still employed

---

174 NB Harrison (1992).
175 Gregory Nazianzen, *Orat.* 43.

in the Orthodox Church on a number of important occasions, does go back to Basil himself, though his contribution is likely to have been that of reviser and enlarger of an older liturgy, rather than that of creator of an entirely new rite.[176]

A considerable amount of the work of these three is in the form of homilies or sermons, and here we can see them fulfilling the role of pastors, teachers and leaders.[177] Apart from his *Letters* and *Poems*, all we have from Gregory Nazianzen is the collection of forty-five *Orations*, clearly a selection of his best sermons. As noted, they follow the style and pattern of contemporary rhetorical practice, and are not exegetical homilies; however, many were delivered on a specific occasion and deal with particular urgent problems. His attempt to avoid ordination occasioned an explanation which became a classic exposition of the responsibilities of the priesthood.[178] A terrible hailstorm destroyed the crops of his father's parishioners; so Gregory delivered an urgent call for repentance in the face of God's chastisement.[179] Of the large number of panegyrics, conventionally brilliant eulogies of great individuals, many were occasioned by the relevant 'saint's day', or were delivered as funeral orations. The liturgical sermons on Christmas and Easter are fine expressions of the essential Christian gospel in the dress of rhetoric and scriptural typology. For all his faults, Gregory knew the pastoral needs of his people; he knew how to rise to the occasion; and he was clearly influenced by the liturgical pattern of the Christian year.

A number of Basil's occasional sermons[180] have survived also, some for feast-days, some concerned with Christian duties such as fasting, vices like anger, avarice, drunkenness and jealousy, virtues like humility. A few deal with the problem of evil and God's providence, one occasioned by a period of drought and famine. The devices of contemporary rhetoric were his means of expression, but evidently his pastoral and moral concerns overrode any desire simply to give pleasure to his hearers.

Gregory Nyssen has also left a variety of homilies and orations,[181] sermons for feast-days, some moral and dogmatic homilies, panegyrics on saints, and three funeral orations delivered in Constantinople, one on the emperor's daughter, and one on the emperor's wife – a clear testimony to his reputation as an orator. Indeed, his style is generally considered more affected, more studiously rhetorical, than the style of his fellow-Cappadocians.

Basil and his brother also preached exegetically. Series of sermons following through a biblical book are characteristic. Basil's commentary on the creation-story in Genesis, the *Hexaemeron*, takes the form of nine homilies, and there are

---

176 Bobrinskoy (1969) compares the liturgy with Basil's *De Spiritu Sancto* and *Letters*, showing that the amplifications made to an older version are in line with Basil's theology. For the more archaic form, see Doresse and Lanne (1960); also discussion by Capelle in the same volume.

177 Bernardi (1970).

178 *Orat.* 2.

179 *Orat.* 16.

180 Basil, *Homiliae diversae*: text in PG 31. For some homilies in more recent editions, see Courtonne (1935); Rudberg (1962); Marti (1989); ET of *Exegetic Homilies*, Way (1963).

181 Texts in Jaeger et al. (1960–) = GNO IX; ET of some in Spira and Klock (1981).

thirteen genuine homilies on the Psalms. Gregory's eight homilies on Ecclesiastes, fifteen homilies on the Song of Songs and eight homilies on the Beatitudes are among his most important 'mystical' works.[182]

Basil wrote no formal commentaries, but his exegetical methods are evident in the homilies and other writings. He rarely turns to allegory, though often draws morals from the text and frequently uses scripture to support his rigorous ascetical demands. By contrast, his brother inclined to a 'spiritual' interpretation, following Origen, for example, in his allegorical exegesis of the Song of Songs. However, Gregory felt constrained to write an *Explicatio apologetica in Hexaemeron* to correct misunderstanding of Basil's work, and also to complete it with a treatise on the creation of humanity, the *De Opificio Hominis*.[183] It is remarkable that in these works he follows Basil's example and avoids allegory. The *De Opificio Hominis* is an important statement of Gregory's anthropology, especially of creation in the image of God and its implications. Gregory is somewhat torn between the dualistic analysis of human nature current at the time and the affirmation that humanity is the crown and perfection of God's creation, but on the whole the idea that human enjoyment of the world is part of God's creative purpose is allowed to predominate.[184] The dialogue with Macrina, *On the Soul and the Resurrection*, takes further the notion of the whole created person, body and soul, being restored and transfigured.[185]

The treatise *De Vita Moysis*[186] is perhaps the best example of Gregory's exegetical methods, as well as a fine expression of his theology. It falls into two parts, the first summarizing the historical life of Moses as depicted in Exodus and Numbers, the second using this as the symbol of the soul's ascent to God through purification, withdrawal, darkness and ecstasy. Here the allegorical method might seem to become paramount; but Gregory eschews multiple meanings and looks for the ἀκολουθία (sequence) or σκοπός (intent or aim) of the text. The latter controls the allegory.[187]

Gregory's ascetical works are also important.[188] As noted, the *De Virginitate* was his earliest work, written before he became bishop of Nyssa; already asceticism is seen as the way of spiritual ascent. The complete *De Instituto Christiano* has been rediscovered and shown to be the culmination of Gregory's ascetic thought.[189] Other important treatises include the *De Perfectione* and the *Vita*

---

182 Texts in Jaeger et al. (1960–) = *GNO* V, VI, VII.2; ET in Hall (1993); Drobner and Viciano (2000); Graef (1954).

183 Migne, *PG* 44; ET in *NPNF*.

184 See Mosshammer in Mateo-Seco and Bastero (1988) for the development of Gregory's anthropological views; discussion also in Zachhuber (2000). For the anthropology of Gregory Nazianzen, see Ellverson (1981).

185 Migne, *PG* 46; ET in *NPNF*, and Roth (1993). See, for example, Limberis in Moutsoulas (2005).

186 Text in Jaeger et al. (1960–) = *GNO* VII.1; ET Ferguson and Malherbe (1978).

187 Dünzl (1990); Heine (1995).

188 Texts in Jaeger et al. (1960–) = *GNO* VIII.1; ET Callahan (1967).

189 Jaeger (1954). Jaeger's view that 'Macarius' was dependent on Gregory initiated a major scholarly debate, involving not only the critical question but also the relationship between Gregory's ascetic teaching and that of the Messalians. For discussion, see Chapter 3, pp. 117, 121.

Macrinae, a biography of his sister which offers an ideal for imitation by the would-be ascetic.[190]

Gregory was by far the most prolific writer of the three. Apart from the many works already mentioned, attention must be drawn to the *Oratio Catechetica Magna,*[191] a significant attempt to write a comprehensive account of Christian theology. It was intended for Christian teachers to assist them in catechesis of converts. The work covers the doctrine of the Trinity, the drama of redemption in Christ, reversing the Fall and tricking the devil out of his possession of humanity, and then finally the means of receiving the benefits of this redemption, the sacraments and faith of the Church.

The importance of the Cappadocians is not confined to the history of dogma. To appreciate the life of the fourth-century Church in its tensions, its spiritual richness, its vitality and its doctrinal struggles, it is to their writings that we should turn.

For Further Reading

English translation

Srawley, J. R., 1917. *The Catechetical Oration of Gregory of Nyssa*, London: SPCK.

NB See previous lists for other relevant translations and studies.

---

190 There is some discussion in Spira (1984).
191 Edition in Jaeger et al. (1960–) = *GNO* III.4; earlier edition and translation Srawley (1903, 1917).

5

The Temper of the Times:
Some Contrasting Characters of the
Late Fourth Century

I Introduction

In studying the Cappadocians, we have already observed that their significance in the life of the Church at that time went far beyond their contribution to the development of doctrine. It is very easy for students of doctrine to isolate their study from the ongoing life and history of the Church, thus distorting their understanding of the context of theological discourse. The aim of this chapter is to widen the perspective still further.

Although they are but a selection of the authors listed in a Patrology, none of the figures that appear here have much place in the typical history of doctrine. Ephrem reminds us that the Syriac tradition was deeply intertwined with the Greek East and would have an important influence on the development of Orthodox hymnography. Cyril contributed to the development of the liturgical practices of Jerusalem, and so influenced the worldwide liturgical life of the Church through returning pilgrims. Epiphanius' encyclopaedias were widely read for centuries to come, and John Chrysostom became perhaps the most influential of all the Fathers through the extensive copying and circulation of his published homilies. The popular mind and devotion of the Byzantine Church owed its formation more to these men than to great philosophical theologians; while the effect of the Origenist controversy was to deepen suspicion of theological exploration, to enhance conservatism and to encourage careful preservation of tradition.

None of the figures that appear here, then, have much place in the story of Nicaea and Chalcedon; yet they all illustrate important aspects of the life of the Church as it was experienced in this formative period. The Arian controversy deeply affected Ephrem's theology, which came to bear similarities to that of the Cappadocians as a result; but it is a theology of a very different character, expressed as it is in poetry. Cyril's career provides interesting comment on the extent to which the difficulties created by the Arian controversy really affected conservative bishops in the middle of the century. Epiphanius represents the fanatical, slogan-shouting mind which could not distinguish central from peripheral matters or think through fundamental theological issues. The over-upright ascetic Chrysostom, who could not compromise with political realities, was caught in the highly political crossfire of the Church of this period, and in his losing battle to maintain strict moral values highlights the increasing social pressures which forced the Church to forfeit its innocence. By contrast, Nemesius and Synesius largely got away with quiet, literary pursuits in local backwaters, endeavouring to preserve the classical traditions of the philosophical life and standing for ancient humanist ideals in an increasingly intolerant age. But they too point to social pressures on the Church: discussion has raged about how far Synesius was really a Christian, even though thrust onto the bishop's throne because of his social class and his local standing in the community, and similar questions might be asked of Nemesius too.

Thus the lives, thoughts and literary remains of these five characters are of fundamental importance for understanding the period with which we are concerned.

II Ephrem the Syrian

1 Ephrem's place in this collection

It may be a matter of some surprise that Ephrem the Syrian, who probably knew little or no Greek and certainly wrote in Syriac, should be included in this survey of the principal Greek Fathers whose literary activity falls between Nicaea and Chalcedon. We can identify several good reasons. First, he very rapidly attained fame in the Greek world: it is virtually certain that Ephrem died in 373 and Epiphanius already mentions him in the *Panarion*,[1] in other words, by 374–7, while Jerome, the Latin Father who lived in the East for much of his life, included him among his 'Illustrious Men', compiled in 392. Jerome tells us he was a deacon in Edessa and wrote a great deal in the Syriac language, and continues:

> I have read a work of his on the Holy Spirit, which someone had translated from Syriac into Greek, and even in translation I could recognise the acumen of a lofty intellect.

Sozomen gives an account[2] in which he notes that translations of his work were already available in Greek during Ephrem's lifetime, and that his eloquence was admired by Basil; Palladius and Theodoret also describe him, the latter calling him 'the harp of the Spirit, who daily waters the people of Syria with the streams of grace'.[3] Second, unlike his literary predecessor, Aphrahat, who lived in Persia, Ephrem represents the Christianity of the Antiochene hinterland, the Syrian borders of the Roman Empire. His own bishop, Jacob of Nisibis, was present at Nicaea, though the tradition that Ephrem accompanied him is probably a legend; in a later generation Theodoret, as bishop of Cyrus, would oversee a largely Syriac-speaking diocese and try to stamp out use of the *Diatesseron*, the Gospel Harmony on which Ephrem wrote a commentary. So even though scholarship once saw Ephrem as culturally and linguistically

---

1 51.22.7.

2 *Ecclesiastical History* III.16.

3 *Ep.* 145.

marginal to the world of the Greek Fathers,[4] in practice he is a salutary reminder of the interlinked diversity of the Empire as it Christianized. It has even been argued that in his opposition to the error, on the one hand, of the 'outsiders', the Marcionites and Manichees, and, on the other, the 'insiders', those like the Arians who might be won back, he championed the Church of the Roman Empire at its margins.[5]

Indeed, another reason for including Ephrem lies in the fact that his work was clearly affected by the spread of Arianism, and his theology in some respects bears comparison with that of the Cappadocians as he tries to meet the challenges. Besides, as we shall see, he was even more directly affected than they were by the reign of Julian the Apostate,[6] particularly by that emperor's failed campaign against the Persians. Yet it is often said that his theological method provides an intriguing contrast to that of the Greeks; for the most part he expresses his theology in poetry, a medium which favours the use of images, symbols and types, and scholars have repeatedly contrasted this with the argumentation of Greek rationalism as it expressed its faith in philosophical terms. So Ephrem is a reminder that it is often at the margins that creative alternatives emerge, eventually, in his case, to affect what became the Byzantine mainstream through his influence on the poetry of Romanos.[7]

The final reason for his inclusion is that there has been an enormous surge of interest and research in Syriac studies, so that the availability of critical texts, translations, aids and studies now means that access is easier than it once was, even for those who do not have facility in the language.[8] This access is to be encouraged, if only because attention to the Syriac sources has discredited the 'Greek Ephrem', challenging the traditional hagiography and the mass of works in Greek which have been transmitted under his name – apparently the quantity is second only to that of John Chrysostom.[9] This Greek material makes Ephrem a monk who wrote ascetic treatises; the Syriac material which is independent of this Greek tradition presents a rather different picture, as we shall see.

2 Life

So what do we know about his life? Most of his life was spent at Nisibis, the frontier town in the Roman Province of Mesopotamia. During his lifetime it was besieged three times by the Persians (338, 346 and 350), and in 363 it was ceded to Persia after Julian's disastrous campaign. His *Hymns on Nisibis* and those *Against Julian*[10] clearly relate to the events of his own lifetime. The surrender of

---

4 For discussion see Griffith (1986), pp. 27–9.

5 Griffith (2001), pp. 395–427; and (1986), pp. 22–52.

6 See Chapter 4, above, pp. 148–9; also Griffith (1987), pp. 238–66.

7 Petersen (1985), pp. 171–87.

8 For a brief history of scholarship see Griffith (1997), pp. 3–6. In the notes to this section, references will be given to what is available in English on the assumption that most readers will not have Syriac. For a considerable bibliography, see den Biesen (2002).

9 General Introduction to Matthews, Amar and McVey (1994), p. 39.

10 ET available in McVey (1989).

Nisibis was agreed with the condition that Christian inhabitants were permitted to leave, and among the refugees was Ephrem, probably now nearing sixty. Whether or not he went straight to Edessa is a matter of discussion, but he certainly spent much of the last ten years of his life in that city.[11] Palladius only knows of his association with Edessa.

It would seem from his own writings that Ephrem had Christian parents, though the later Syriac *Life* suggests his father was a pagan. He was probably born around 306. From his *Hymns on Nisibis* we learn that he served as deacon and exegetical teacher under three bishops, all of whom he reveres, Jacob, the one who attended the Nicene Council and apparently appointed Ephrem a teacher on his return, Babu and Vologeses. A physical link with Ephrem is provided by the oldest Christian building in the East, a baptistery with the inscription:

This baptistery was erected and completed in the year 671 [= AD 359–60] in the time of Vologeses through the zeal of the priest Akepsimas. May this inscription be a memorial to them.[12]

Nisibis had a Rabbinic school, and Ephrem's school may have been conceived as the Christian counterpart, though whether there were any contacts it is impossible to determine;[13] it is clear, however, that Syriac exegesis is acquainted with Jewish traditions in targums and midrash.[14]

In Edessa, already an important centre with its own legends about the apostolic origins of Christianity there, Ephrem again served the bishop and taught many disciples, either founding the famous school there, as later tradition affirms, or perhaps just taking his place in an already existing school.[15] The Syriac *Life* says that he found nine heresies there; and his own writings show his horror at the fact that there the Marcionites were called Christians, and the orthodox were known as 'Palutians' after Palut, an early bishop of Edessa.[16] Many of his writings appear to date from this Edessene period, though it is not easy to be sure how much he composed earlier in Nisibis.[17] As early as Palladius we find the story of how he intervened during an acute famine, pleading with those hoarding grain to release it. The response was that no one could be trusted to do it fairly, but when Ephrem offered himself they recognized he was a man of God and let him get on with organizing relief. This appears to have been from early summer 372 through to the barley harvest in May of the following year, which was plentiful.[18] That would be the year of Ephrem's death.

---

11 Assumed by Brock et al. (see, for example, McVey 1989, Introduction, and Brock 1990, Introduction) – but see discussion and notes in Matthews, Amar and McVey (1994), Introduction, p. 33.
12 Quoted by Brock (1990), Introduction, p. 11.
13 Murray (2006), p. 18.
14 Discussed by Brock in many of his publications; see also Van Rompay (1996), pp. 612–41.
15 Griffith (1986), p. 25.
16 Matthews, Amar and McVey (1994), Introduction, p. 35.
17 Russell (2006), pp. 71–4, advises caution since we really know nothing!
18 Brock (1990), Introduction, p. 15.

Confirmed by some of the earliest notices in Greek, the Syriac tradition knows Ephrem mainly as a teacher. The verse homily on Ephrem by Jacob of Serugh (d.521),[19] as well as indicating that he founded women's choirs and instructed them in the singing of his hymns, says,

> He was the teacher of truth who both acted and taught, as it is written;
> For his disciples he depicted a model for them to imitate.
> . . . He did not just teach through the toil of speech,
> but he manifested in his own person the activity of perfect sainthood.[20]

He ends his poem by comparing Ephrem to a sheepdog guarding the sheep of God's household, building a sheepfold out of his poems and hymns for their safety and scattering the heresies that roam around outside.[21] Theodoret speaks of Ephrem taking over for his own orthodox poems the music of songs written by the son of the heretic Bardaisan, so giving his hearers both great delight and a healing medicine.[22] Jerome mentions that his writings were read in some churches after the scripture lections. So Ephrem 'seems to have lived his life as an unmarried disciple of Christ wholly engaged in helping and advising his bishops by preaching, teaching, writing, and fighting against heresies'.[23] The tradition that made Ephrem a monk is almost certainly a misunderstanding going back to Palladius and developed in the work of his successors. There was an old Syrian tradition of the 'Sons of the Covenant' living a celibate life in the midst of the community, and it would seem that Ephrem belonged to this,[24] rather than to the relatively new ascetic movement of fourth century, which called people away from civilization into the desert either as solitaries or to live in a monastic community.

3 Writings

Inevitably it is mainly as a writer that we can now know Ephrem. His work has been passed down in the original Syriac and in multiple translations: Greek, Armenian, Latin, Arabic, Coptic, Ethiopic, Slavonic, Georgian and Syro-Palestinian.[25] Sorting out what is genuine is no easy task. It seems that nearly all of the translated works can be traced back to the spurious Greek material, apart from the Armenian corpus, which will probably be of immense value when fully edited and accessible, since much of it no longer survives in Syriac. However, there is a good deal of uncertainty about the authenticity of much that has survived even in Syriac and Armenian. The core of the Syriac material, what is generally recognized as genuine, is the basis for most recent studies of Ephrem,

---

19 See Amar (1995).
20 ET by Brock (1990), Introduction, p. 22. Cf. Amar (1995), pp. 29 and 159 for an alternative rendering.
21 Brock (1990), Introduction, p. 24–5.
22 Theodoret, *HE* IV.26.
23 Matthews, Amar and McVey (1994), Introduction, p. 24.
24 Brock (1990), Introduction, pp. 25–33; and cf. Brock (1985), pp. 107–17.
25 Matthews, Amar and McVey (1994), Introduction, p. 39.

and the burgeoning interest is partly to be explained by the fact that critical texts are now available, principally through the editorial work of Dom Edmund Beck: published between 1955 and 1979, a considerable corpus is available in the *CSCO*, with German translation. English versions are expanding.[26]

Ephrem's hymns constitute a significant proportion of his work – 400 survive and others are known to have been lost. The hymns (*madrashe*) have been passed down in sixth-century manuscripts in cycles whose titles often refer only to a small group in the collection; thus the cycle of fifty-two hymns on virginity[27] begins with three hymns on that subject, followed by four on oil, while 42–50 meditate on Jonah, another incorporated cycle addresses biblical interpretation, and other individual hymns scattered around among other short cycles tackle a variety of different subjects; and of those on Nisibis only the first half are on that city. The arrangement seems to go back at least to the late fifth century, but it is likely that only in the case of the smaller collections, such as the *Hymns on Paradise*, does it go back to Ephrem himself.[28] This complicates the attribution of the hymns to the different periods of his life, since editorial activity in transmission may have put together work not originally associated at all. He also wrote verse homilies (*memre*), and it is in this category that a great deal has been attributed to him which is unlikely to be authentic.

A number of prose works, including biblical commentaries and anti-heretical treatises, also survive. Of special interest is the *Commentary on the Diatesseron*, of which the Syriac original was discovered in 1957.[29] There also survives his *Commentary on Genesis and Exodus*, and some fragments in Armenian of commentaries on Acts and the Pauline Epistles, possibly also the prophets.[30] His approach to biblical exegesis has been compared with the Antiochenes';[31] but there is no historical evidence of dependence.[32] He applies the principles of attending to the words of the text, of accepting the point of the parable without being distracted by all aspects of the comparison, of not taking things out of context (as Satan did when tempting Christ), and of using the Bible to interpret the Bible, taking account of the totality of scripture:[33] Ephrem has been described as having 'the freedom of a bird to move at will over the vast range of scripture, and select whatever text pleases him in the execution of his task'.[34] Consistently he appeals to the richness of scripture, likening it to a fountain, and suggesting that no one should imagine that they have received the full meaning; for scripture has many facets like a diamond, and each reader receives treasures, perceiving deeper meanings suited for their need.[35]

---

26 See list in references.

27 ET in McVey (1989).

28 Brock (1990), Introduction, p. 35.

29 See further McCarthy (1993).

30 Murray (2006) places the material on the prophets among the *Dubia*.

31 Van Rompay (1996); see also the discussion of the Commentaries in Griffith (1997).

32 Yousif (1990).

33 For example, *Commentary on the Diatesseron* IV.8; VI.1; XII.15; XIII.19; XV.14, XVIII.15.

34 McCarthy (1993), Introduction, p. 17.

35 For example, *Commentary on the Diatesseron* I.18, 19; VII.22; XXII.3.

The thirsty one rejoices because he can drink, but is not upset because he is unable to render the source dry. The well can conquer your thirst, but your thirst cannot conquer the fountain. If your thirst is satiated, without the fountain running short, whenever you are thirsty, you can drink again.[36]

Furthermore, Ephrem's hymns display the kind of binocular vision which allows him to see 'current history in the light of biblical characters and events'[37] and every human life as lived according to the 'types' provided by scripture.

4 Thinking through types and symbols

Discussion of Ephrem's approach to theological thinking has largely concentrated on the Hymns. Robert Murray's book, *Symbols of Church and Kingdom*, published in the 1970s, set Ephrem's thought in the context of early Syriac traditions and initiated discussion of his symbolism. Some ten years later Sebastian Brock developed this perspective further in *The Luminous Eye: The Spiritual World Vision of St Ephrem*. Since then there have been a number of attempts to refine the accounts of his poetic and synthetic methodology, and challenge easy oppositions between Greek and Semitic thinking.[38] The following discussion will explore Ephrem's discourse and its theological grounding, and then briefly consider some of the similarities and differences between his approach and that of the Cappadocians.

The very act of choosing to compose poetry shifts the kind of discourse a writer uses. Metaphor and imagery, double entendre, paradox and other devices become natural as the poet seeks to point beyond the limitations of human language. That Ephrem's theology is largely expressed in poetic medium is significant in itself. Key themes arise from the fluid development of images, symbols and 'types', usually drawn from scripture, to which vivid allusion is constantly made but in re-minted and arresting form, as material from different texts is melded together. Brock[39] listed some of the recurring images:

- the use of fire to represent the divinity;
- putting clothing on and off, as a way of speaking about revelation, various moments in salvation-history and the incarnation;
- conception and birth-giving, developed, for example, so that Mary's womb is associated with the womb of the Jordan and baptism, and with the womb of Sheol and the resurrection;
- the eye, light and mirror – used to explore human receptivity to revelation, and its limitations;
- medical imagery, as well as imagery from agriculture, archery, sailing, commerce and travel.

---

36 *Commentary on the Diatesseron* I.19.
37 Griffith (1987).
38 Surveyed in den Biesen (2006). Important contributions include: Bou Mansour (1988); a string of journal articles by Phil Botha; Possekel (1999).
39 Brock (1985).

Brock also explored in some depth Ephrem's use of themes, such as the robe of glory, the medicine of life and the bridal chamber, drawing together examples of how these are woven and re-woven into dynamic expressions of salvation-history, liturgy and eschatology.

It is perhaps the *Hymns on Paradise* which give most immediate access to the ways in which types and symbols are interwoven to provide such a conspectus on salvation-history. Fundamentally Ephrem believes that God intended Adam eventually to receive the fruit of both trees in Paradise, the Tree of Knowledge and the Tree of Life, but once he disobeyed with respect to one, God prevented the same thing happening with the other, essentially out of compassion – 'lest this life-giving gift ... become misery, and thus bring worse evil upon them than what they had already obtained from the tree of knowledge'; for death would eventually cast off 'the bonds of their pains'.[40] It has been said that the *Commentary on Genesis* 'is a close literal reading of the text', which 'rarely engages in the typological or symbolic that so characterises his hymns';[41] yet it supplies perspectives which illuminate the hymns, and the hymns enable us to recognize that this reading of the Paradise story sees it as not about a 'literal' place but rather as 'representing both the primordial and the eschatological state'.[42] For recapitulation in Christ would enable humanity to receive the gift from the Tree of Life.

So Adam becomes a universal 'type', and the Hymns delight in drawing this out, notably Hymns XII, XIII and XIV: the Refrain of the first is 'Praise to your grace that has compassion on sinners', and of the second, 'Through your grace make me worthy of that Garden of Happiness'. In XII, Adam's sin is illuminated by the failings of Uzziah and Abraham; in XIII the king of Babylon, then David, are each said to resemble Adam, and further examples appear – Samson, Jonah, Joseph; in XIV we should learn from Jeremiah, Daniel, Noah, Moses and Jacob. The point of all these 'types' is to show up our own sin:

> The Good One in His love
>   wished to discipline us for doing wrong,
> and so we had to leave Paradise
>   with its bridal chamber of glory ...

But the earlier Hymns hold out a vision of that Paradise for which the singer yearns, and which is God's promise in Christ:

> The tongue cannot relate
>   the description of innermost Paradise ...
> For the colors of Paradise are full of joy,
>   its scents most wonderful,
> its beauties most desirable,
>   and its delicacies glorious. (*Hymn* IV)

---

40 *Comm. on Genesis* 35 (ET in Matthews, Amar and McVey (1994).
41 Matthews, Amar and McVey (1994), p. 60.
42 Brock (1990), Introduction, p. 49.

There is no mirror adequate to reflect its beauty, or paints to portray it, says Ephrem, not even the outer reaches, which surpass 'all other treasures in the world entire'.

Cycles of Ephrem's hymns explore the depths of meaning and associations in particular symbols, such as oil, or the pearl; linguistic, scriptural, natural and sacramental are woven together. The use of oil to anoint the sick is associated with the healing received from the Anointed One, whose very name comes from this symbol. It is associated with forgiveness through the story of the sinner anointing Jesus' feet, and Mary anointing his head to show up Judas' theft.[43] Oil in lamps gives light – so associations with the Light of the World and the sun could be explored, celebrating the banishment of darkness, not to mention the links with the seven-branched candlestick! And oil runs on water, so the singer can turn to Christ's walking on the water and rescuing Simon to enlighten the world. An oil lamp found the lost coin, and the virgins awaiting the Bridegroom needed oil for their lamps. Oil smears the edge of a sword, and the Anointed polishes the mind. With many more examples Ephrem shows how oil becomes the 'key of the hidden treasure-house of symbols'.[44] But he has nowhere near finished – for the next hymn takes up the association of oil with kingship, and then explores pre-figurations of Christ in scripture through the occurrence of olive branches; and the last of the set can still find new themes, such as baptism, to which many further associations are easily attracted. The pearl might seem at first sight a less promising symbol, but it had figured in earlier tradition,[45] and because Ephrem accepted the idea that pearls came into being when lightning struck the shellfish in the sea, he was able to develop all kinds of analogies with the conception of Christ. The refrain of one of the five hymns is a reminder that Jesus himself likened the kingdom of God to a pearl, and Ephrem, after working through the parallels in the mysterious conception of pearl and Christ, even writes:

In your beauty is depicted the beauty of the Son
who clothed himself in suffering: nails went through him.
Through you the awl passed, you too did they pierce,
as they did his hands. But because He suffered He reigns
– just as your beauty is increased through your suffering.[46]

One might sum up Ephrem's approach by calling it a sacramental understanding of both nature and scripture. The words articulate a Word that is hidden. Concrete realities are themselves, yet point beyond themselves: if a bird gathers its wings and denies the extended symbol of the cross, he suggests, then the air denies the bird – it will not carry the bird unless its wings confess the Cross.[47] It is no surprise that eucharistic imagery is also well explored in key hymns,[48] and constantly and creatively woven into others.

---

43 *Virginity* 4 (ET in McVey 1989).
44 *Virginity* 5 (ET in McVey 1989).
45 cf. *Hymn of the Pearl* in the *Acts of Judas Thomas*.
46 *On Faith* 82 (Syriac and ET in Brock and Kiraz 2006).
47 *On Faith* 18.6, quoted by Brock (1985), p. 43.
48 *On Faith* 10 and 14 (Syriac and ET in Brock and Kiraz 2006, pp. 200–1).

5 Language and theology

Undergirding all this is a particular conception of the nature of language.[49] For Ephrem, human language and conception is inevitably limited. There is a great chasm between the Creator and created beings. Not to recognize this is to get involved in inappropriate 'prying' into God's nature:

Whoever is capable of investigating
  becomes the container of what he investigates;
a knowledge which is capable of containing the Omniscient
  is greater than him,
for it has proved capable of measuring the whole of him.
A person who investigates the Father and the Son
  is thus greater than them!
Far be it, then, and something anathema,
  that the Father and the Son should be investigated,
while dust and ashes exalts itself![50]

In Ephrem there is a constant dialectic between this apophaticism and a loving response to all that God has revealed, between silence and speech, humility and boldness,[51] the point being that God has reached out across the chasm.

Brock identifies three modes of divine self revelation in Ephrem's work. It happens through (i) types and symbols, which are present in both nature and scripture; through (ii) the names or metaphors, which God allows to be used of the divine self in scripture; and above all (iii) in the incarnation. For our exploration of Ephrem's discourse it is particularly significant that the first two suggest a kind of incarnation in language, somewhat parallel to the incarnation in flesh, for this justifies Ephrem's poetic theology. It is only because of God's condescension and accommodation to the human level that we can speak of God at all. Ephrem offers as an analogy an amusing picture of someone trying to teach a parrot to talk and hiding behind a mirror so that the parrot imagines it is talking to one of its own kind; that is the kind of thing God did, bending down from on high and acquiring our own habits from us. God clothed the divine self in metaphors: scripture speaks of God's ears to teach us that God listens to us, of God's eyes to show that God sees us. God clothed the divine self in our language so that we might be clothed in God's mode of life.[52]

But even so our discourse has to be oblique and multivalent, because we can never capture the reality in our limited language. Ephrem objects to those who think they can immediately grasp exactly what scripture is talking about:

If there only existed a single sense for the words of scripture, then the first commentator who came along would discover it, and other hearers would

---

49 '. . . the challenge of the Arians is met . . . by opposing the very idiom in which they raise their questions. For Ephraem it almost seems that the *madrāšâ* . . . is the only genre of human speech that is suitable for the issue of God-talk.' Griffith (1986), p. 45.
50 *On Faith* 9.16; quoted by Brock (1985), p. 13.
51 Explored in depth by den Biesen (2006); cf. also Bou Mansour (1988).
52 *On Faith* 31, quoted by Brock (1985), pp. 43–5.

experience neither the labour of searching nor the joy of finding . . . Each individual understands according to his capacity and interprets as it is granted him.[53]

Who is capable of comprehending the extent of what is to be discovered in a single utterance of Yours? For we leave behind in it far more than we take of it, like thirsty people drinking from a fountain.[54]

One of the ways in which limited human language becomes infinite is through the use of paradox and polarity – the inexpressible truth lying somewhere in the tension between the opposites. In a powerful hymn about approaching God,[55] Ephrem oscillates between the silence appropriate to his weak nature and the love that stirs him to sing in God's presence:

Your teaching is new wine: it uplifts everyone who becomes drunk with it and thereby forgets his frailty, and fearlessly he dares to speak, overcoming timidity and silence.

But reason is vehement in questioning this possibility – only silence is appropriate, because talk of what cannot be known and understood is bound to be nonsense. The dialogue between the two poles is sustained through nineteen stanzas, the climax being an appeal to Gospel narratives: John cries that he is not worthy, says reason, while love remembers the sinful woman who kissed the feet of Jesus and anointed them.

Such paradox and polarity is particularly focused on the incarnation: the antinomies immortal/mortal, great/small, height/lowness, etc. are well exploited to cultivate a sense of amazement at something that cannot be articulated. Ephrem can express this the more powerfully because of his strong affirmation of the human body and the reality of Christ's enfleshment against the Marcionites and Manichaeans. The polarity of Adam and Christ, Eve and Mary is exploited over and over again to bring out salvation-history:

Eve in her virginity put on leaves of shame,
but your mother, Lord, in her virginity
has put on a robe of glory
that encompasses all people,
while to Him who covers all
she gives a body as a tiny garment.[56]

Layers of meaning are suggested by the clothing image and the key polarity. More than any contemporary Greek patristic literature Ephrem meditates on the significance of Mary, even putting some of the *Hymns on the Nativity*[57] into her mouth.

---

53 *Commentary on the Diatesseron* 7.22, quoted from Brock (1985), p. 34–5.
54 *Commentary on the Diatesseron* 1.18, quoted from Brock (1985), p. 35.
55 *Church* 9, ET in den Biesen (2006), pp. 335–40.
56 *Nativity* 17.4, quoted from Brock (1985), p. 69.
57 ET of these hymns in McVey (1989).

6 The confluence of traditions in Ephrem's distinctive voice

However, one of his younger Greek contemporaries, Gregory of Nyssa, certainly did develop typological thinking about Mary – as 'her purity and integrity open a place within her where God can enter, where Christ can be formed', so 'the virginal soul, like Mary, receives the entrance of God and brings forth Christ, though spiritually, not physically'.[58] In other ways too, some parallels with the Cappadocians can be drawn.[59] We have already seen how, in response to Eunomius, Gregory of Nyssa resisted the idea that God could be defined, how his theology depicts the great gulf or chasm between the infinite, incomprehensible Creator and all creatures, how he insisted that all names are inadequate – yet not arbitrary since God accommodated the divine self to our level. His discussion of the difference between names that are intrinsic to God and names that are analogical bears comparison with Ephrem's own approach.[60] Again we have seen already that Gregory of Nazianzen's theology also insists on apophaticism: we can know that God is, not what God is. Yet that is not the end of the discussion, since the Trinity expresses both the mystery of God's nature and of the loving outreach of the divine towards creation. Gregory's approach is saturated with biblical imagery and typological symbolism, as well as the rhetoric of paradox and polarity. His true theologian is one who recognizes the limits of his capacity. The contrast with Greek philosophical thought should not be drawn too sharply.

Nevertheless Ephrem has a distinctive voice, one formed by the confluence of Mesopotamian, Jewish and Greek traditions. Already much has been said about his links with the Graeco-Roman Christian world. Some of Ephrem's literary patterns were ultimately derived from ancient Mesopotamia, via their previous reception in Christian Syriac literature, both 'orthodox' and 'heretical'; notable among these are his imaginative dialogues employing personification, an example being the dialogue between Satan and Death in *Hymns on Nisibis* 52.[61] His debt to Jewish traditions has also been hinted at, and can be seen in many footnotes to his works – they are all the more intriguing given the depth of his anti-Jewishness, a matter that has been much discussed among scholars, Shepardson[62] suggesting that to a considerable extent Jews figure as foils and warnings in the context of inner-Christian debate. Even so Ephrem stands in the same tradition as other patristic authors who not only assert that Christianity supersedes Judaism, but appeal to the Old Testament prophets and the fact of the crucifixion to prove that the Jews rejected God's messengers, even Christ, the Son of God. Many scholars assume that Syriac Christianity competed in a strongly Jewish environment; so the tension between Ephrem's anti-Jewishness and evident use of Jewish traditions perhaps reflects that. Be that as it may, it is

58 Harrison (1996).

59 Brock (1985), pp. 119–23; Russell (1994), discussed in den Biesen (2006), pp. 293–307.

60 Cf. Brock (1985), p. 121.

61 Brock (1985), p. 7; the confluence of different literary traditions was explored further in Brock's lecture to the Fifteenth International Conference on Patristic Studies in Oxford, 2007, entitled 'Dramatic Poems on Biblical Topics in Syriac'.

62 Shepardson (2001), pp. 502–7.

his intriguingly distinct voicing of emerging Christian orthodoxy that justifies Ephrem's place in this volume.

For Further Reading

English translations

Brock, Sebastian, 1990. *Saint Ephrem: Hymns on Paradise*, Crestwood, NY: St Vladimir's Seminary Press.
McVey, Kathleen, 1989. *Ephrem the Syrian: Hymns, Classics of Western Spirituality*, New York: Paulist Press.

Studies

Brock, Sebastian, 1985. *The Luminous Eye: The Spiritual World Vision of St Ephrem*, Rome: CIIS; republished Cistercian Publications 1992.
den Biesen, Kees, 2006. *Simple and Bold: Ephrem's Art of Symbolic Thought*, Piskataway, NJ: Gorgias Press.
Griffith, Sidney H., 1997. *'Faith Adoring the Mystery': Reading the Bible with St. Ephraem the Syrian*, Milwaukee: Marquette University Press.
Murray, Robert, 2006. *Symbols of Church and Kingdom*, 1975; rev. edn, London: T. & T. Clark.

II Cyril of Jerusalem

The catechetical lectures attributed to Cyril of Jerusalem are rightly well-known and readily accessible to students.[63] Interest once largely centred upon the information they provide for the study of fourth-century liturgical developments;[64] but Cyril is also important for his contribution to the evident enhancement of Jerusalem's importance as a Christian holy place and pilgrimage centre,[65] and for the light his career throws on Church politics in this period.

The facts of Cyril's career provide an interesting contrast to the impression created by the lectures. Although they were delivered in the mid-fourth century, when the historians made it appear that the world was in a turmoil over the issues raised by Arianism, the catechumens were given little explicit guidance on the issues; they were warned about warring bishops and advised to keep to a middle path, while being instructed in the traditional faith grounded in scripture.[66] There is no reference to the *homoousion*, but then in the 350s the

---

63 Selections, with useful introduction, in Yarnold (2000); Cross (1951) contains the *Procatechesis* and the *Mystagogical Catecheses* (that is numbers 19–23), text and translation with introduction; see also Telfer (1955). Full text in *PG* 33, though the critical edition by Reischl and Rupp (1848, 1860, reissued 1967), is to be preferred. Critical text of the *Mystagogical Catecheses*, Piédagnel (1966). Complete ET in *NPNF* and *FC* (McCauley and Stephenson (1969, 1970).

64 See Riley (1974); Baldovin (1989); Bradshaw (2002).

65 Doval (2001); Drijvers (2004). Cf. Hunt (1982); Walker (1990). Stemberger (2000).

66 *Cat. Orat.* xv.7; Yarnold (2000), p. 59; Doval (2001), p. 24.

homoousion seems to have been judiciously avoided even by Athanasius.[67] The meagre information we have about Cyril's life, however, shows that no bishop in this period could escape the vicissitudes of church politics. For one reason or another, he was exiled and restored three times.

The chief authorities on which any reconstruction must be based are the historians, Socrates, Sozomen, Rufinus and Theodoret, with some comments by Epiphanius and Jerome. Their evidence is not entirely compatible,[68] especially over the question of Cyril's doctrinal position. Jerome[69] gives an account of how Cyril obtained the episcopate, turning the whole incident into a nasty piece of Arian politics; he had personal reasons for being malicious, however, and it is possible to view the matter as Cyril simply conforming to proper church order.[70] Rufinus[71] indicates that Cyril varied in his allegiance. If he was ordained by the 'Arian', Acacius, he soon fell out with him; later he was associated with the homoiousians. Eventually Cyril was involved in the Council of Constantinople in 381. The Council's letter to the Pope speaks of him with respect, mentioning his many struggles against the Arians;[72] but others hint that he renounced his former opinions in order to join the orthodox ranks.[73] Whatever Cyril's position, all this indicates clearly the subsequent tendency, when giving an account of this period, to blacken or whitewash a leading figure simply by putting a label on him. At the time, which party represented 'orthodoxy' was not by any means obvious – opposition to Nicaea in the mid-fourth century did not 'counter-indicate Arianism',[74] and before 380, the emperors largely favoured positions other than the Nicene. In all probability Cyril found himself caught in the cross-currents of contemporary politics without being doctrinally committed to any particular party.[75] In fact, most investigators have concluded that his catechetical lectures reveal total dedication to the traditional faith – a fact which has been used to prove his essential orthodoxy.[76] It seems likely that it was not so much doctrinal issues, but matters of personal rivalry and church order which determined his position at various stages in his career[77] – indeed, it has been suggested that we should distinguish between Cyril as bishop-theologian and as bishop-politician.

---

67 Gregg (1985); Doval (2001).

68 For example, even the names of those who replaced Cyril during his exiles are incompatible.

69 Jerome, *Chronicle* for 348, in *GCS* Eusebius VII, *Die Chronik des Hieronymus* (no. 47 of whole series), 1956, 237.2–14.

70 Doval (2001); Drijvers (2004).

71 Rufinus, *HE* i.23.

72 Theodoret, *HE* v.9, quotes the Council's letter.

73 Socrates, *HE* vii.7, followed by Sozomen, *HE* v.3.

74 Gregg (1985); Gregg argues that what Cyril says resists the interests of early Arians, especially his refusal to allow *prokopē*, that is, any suggestion that the Son of God holds divine status through advancement or adoption.

75 van Nuffelen (2007) concludes that 'Nicenes' were suspicious of Cyril's opportunism, and refused to recognize him as the authentic bishop of Jerusalem despite the fact that his election was apparently uncontested if the sources are trustworthy.

76 For discussion of Cyril's Arianism, see Berten (1968); Stephenson (1972); Gregg (1985); Yarnold (2000); and Drijvers (2004), especially Appendix I.

77 Lebon (1924); Drijvers (2004), especially Appendix I.

It was certainly not over doctrine that his dispute with Acacius originated. Acacius, bishop of Caesarea, was Cyril's canonical superior who had consecrated him in 350; by the orthodox historians Acacius is presented as a leading Arian, and his subsequent opposition to Cyril is attributed to this cause. But the issue over which he and Cyril quarrelled was a matter of church property. The church at Jerusalem had been the recipient of many rich gifts and dedications, especially from the imperial household; it was also the haven of pilgrims and ascetics. In the mid-50s, famine caused much distress, especially among the 'saints'. Cyril sold church treasures, according to Sozomen in order to feed the hungry.[78] Scandal ensued when someone noticed an actress wearing a robe he had himself dedicated to the church. For two years, Cyril resisted Acacius' summons to account for his actions, but was eventually deposed in his absence in 357. Two years later his case came up at Seleucia in an atmosphere hostile to Acacius; but Cyril's reinstatement was short-lived. Constantius, for one reason or another,[79] came round to Acacius' view and sent Cyril into exile. Underlying the bitterness was undoubtedly the threat posed for Caesarea by the rising influence of the see of Jerusalem as it developed into the prime Christian holy place and became a centre of pilgrimage.[80] This certainly became an issue towards the end of the century, and in 451, at Chalcedon, Jerusalem became a patriarchate. Meanwhile, Cyril had ensured that his nephew, Gelasius, succeeded to the see of Caesarea, and had devoted much energy to the promotion of Jerusalem.

Subsequently, like many others, Cyril found his position subject to imperial whims. He was able to return under Julian the Apostate, but when Valens reverted to Constantius' policy in 367, Cyril found himself banished for the remaining eleven years of that emperor's reign. His banishment under these circumstances turned him into an anti-Arian hero, especially since he now associated himself with the neo-Nicenes, and after Valens' death joined in the movement which culminated in the council of 381. Six years later he died.

Hardly a hint of these troublesome times appears in the *Catechetical Orations*. True, it is highly probable that they were delivered during one of Cyril's first Lents as a bishop and most of the events just described were still in the future. Yet the controversy over Athanasius and his reinstatement in 346 meant that the Eastern Church could hardly forget the storms induced by Arius. It was in an unsettled atmosphere that Cyril addressed the candidates for baptism. He does so with cool authority, indicating no party position in the current debates. His hearers are warned about heretics, but those actually named are the Gnostics and Manichees,[81] not the Arians. They are warned against false teachings, and some of these include identifiable doctrines of contemporaries,

---

78 Sozomen, *HE* iv.25.

79 According to Epiphanius (*Haer.* 73.37), Cyril had taken the step of consecrating a new bishop of Caesarea during Acacius' discomfiture. This no doubt exacerbated Acacius' hostility. Constantius soon came to favour Acacius and his party, and then, according to Theodoret (*HE* ii.23), Acacius informed the emperor that one of the things sold by Cyril was a 'holy robe' dedicated by Constantine himself. It is never easy to sort out truth and slander in the controversies of this period.

80 Sozomen, *HE* iv.25.

81 Cyril, *Cat. Orat.* vi.12ff.; elsewhere others are sometimes mentioned, e.g. the Marcionites and Sabellius in xvi.4.

such as Marcellus,[82] or indeed unnamed early Arians;[83] but when Cyril reaches the stage in his exposition of the faith which obliges him to speak of the Son's generation from the Father, he advises his flock to profess ignorance on matters too high even for angels. The ordinary Christian is told to ignore party strife, and probably that is exactly what Cyril himself tried to do. The chanting mobs of Alexandria were perhaps not as typical of church life in this period as we might have supposed.

Cyril produces a straightforward statement of Christian belief, largely immune from the controversies of the time. New and old covenant must not be divided. God the Creator is One, but also Trinity; the Trinity is not three gods, not three different grades of divinity, nor coalesced into a Sabellian One. This is clearly stated in a lecture on the Holy Spirit[84] which anticipates the position still to be hammered out in the Macedonian controversy; likewise Cyril anticipates the approach of Leo's *Tome* in his simple summary of the incarnate state: 'Christ was twofold . . . As man, he ate . . ., as God, he made five loaves feed five thousand men. As man he truly died, and as God . . . he raised to life his body.'[85] These anticipations are not due to any brilliance or profundity in his theology. Cyril states the traditional faith, and fundamental to his presentation is reference to scripture.

Simplified and uncontroversial as we find his position, might it therefore be possible perhaps to discern in these lectures a 'popular' Christianity, uninvolved in the professional sophistications of the clerics? Unfortunately this is a claim difficult to make. The lectures presume the need to equip the convert with intellectual weapons to confront sceptics, pagans, Jews and heretics,[86] and define what it means to be Christian by differentiation from others, especially other versions of Christianity, named or not. Furthermore, any person who sought baptism in this period was virtually a 'semi-professional', often on the point of taking monastic vows. If one seeks to unearth the probably only half-formed belief of the nominally Christian populace rather than that of an élite, it is hardly to be found here. Cyril had a dedicated audience.

Yet one thing we do find recommended here is a more practical and less rarefied Christian lifestyle than that in the ascetic treatises of the period. Cyril follows St Paul in his advice on chastity and marriage, even allowing a second marriage.[87] Bodily needs are not to be despised. True, self-indulgence and luxury are to be avoided, but meat is not taboo, nor are riches accursed. To suggest such things belongs to the heretics. God is the source of all and to be worshipped as such; his gifts are to be put to good use.[88] On the clause 'Maker of heaven and earth', Cyril waxes eloquent on the marvels of creation, evoking a sense of wonder and worship worthy of Job and the Psalms, both of which he

---

82 *Cat. Orat.* xv. 27.

83 *Cat. Orat.* xi.13. See further Gregg (1985).

84 *Cat. Orat.* xvi.

85 *Cat. Orat.* iv.9 (after Telfer's translation).

86 Drijvers notes that in Cyril's *Catecheses* 'we catch glimpses of a world of social diversity and of religious pluralism in Late Roman Palestine', Drijvers (2004), p. 125.

87 *Cat. Orat.* iv.22–29.

88 *Cat. Orat.* viii.6–8.

here quotes.[89] The extreme otherworldliness so often attributed to this period of monastic upsurge was certainly tempered by the continued use of the biblical traditions once employed to uphold the goodness of creation against the Gnostics.

The lectures that we have consist of a *Procatechesis*, welcoming the candidates to preparation for baptism during Lent, and indicating their responsibilities; five lectures on the faith arranged by topic, leading up to the recitation of the creed which candidates then had to commit to memory; and thirteen expounding the credal formulae. The Jerusalem creed itself is not quoted, but can be reconstructed on the basis of the lectures.[90] How exactly the eighteen pre-baptismal lectures fitted into the Lent period has been the subject of some discussion – the Lent period seems to have been undergoing some development at this time.[91] In the days after Easter there followed further gatherings for the exposition of the sacraments to which the neophytes had just been admitted, and the final words of the final pre-Easter lecture anticipate these further lectures to come. Most manuscripts then contain five *Mystagogical Catecheses* which fulfil this role.

However, there has been considerable controversy over the date and authorship of the *Mystagogical Catecheses*. Strong grounds were adduced for attributing them to Cyril's successor as bishop of Jerusalem, namely John,[92] whom we shall meet again as a key figure in the Origenist controversy. There are four basic arguments favouring this view.

First, there is the manuscript evidence. Some manuscripts do not contain the *Mystagogical Catecheses* at all, which suggests they may not have originally been associated with the pre-Easter set. In one manuscript, they are actually ascribed to John, and in three others, Cyril and John are mentioned as authors of the whole collection. On the other hand, five manuscripts treat the *Mystagogical Catecheses* as continuous with the rest, and the whole is attributed to Cyril.[93] F. L. Cross[94] explained this by suggesting that Cyril used the same text year after year, and his successor John inherited it. Although it is possible that such a theory could be right in general terms, it falls to the ground with respect to the specific text of the pre-baptismal set of lectures which were clearly taken down by stenographers as delivered during one particular Lent[95] – indeed, it is poss-

---

89 *Cat. Orat.* ix.

90 The close parallels between this reconstructed Jerusalem creed and the creed of Constantinople (381) gave rise to the theory that Cyril had produced his creed at the Council and it was generally accepted by the assembled bishops. This theory was rejected by Kelly (1950), pp. 311ff.; but see Drijvers (2004), p. 46, with notes 69 and 70.

91 Doval (2001); Drijvers (2004). For liturgical developments in general, see Bradshaw (2002).

92 The full case is assembled in the important article by Swaans (1942); Doval (2001) argues in detail the case against.

93 Piédagnel (1970); see also his discussion of the authorship question in the introduction to the SC edition of the *Mystagogical Catecheses*.

94 Cross (1951), p. xxxix.

95 For one thing, Cyril gets worried in the last few lectures about running out of time. Did this happen year after year? In *Orat.* 14 he refers to 'yesterday's sermon'. Some details of this kind can be used to pinpoint the date of the lectures: see Telfer (1955), pp. 37ff.

ible to date them fairly definitely to 351,[96] while there are reasons for dating the Mystagogical Catecheses to about 383 or later, and stylistically they seem more like lecture notes.

Second, there is the literary evidence. There are references to the pre-baptismal set in fifth-century literature, whereas the Mystagogical Catecheses are not mentioned until the second half of the sixth century. Even after that people like Photius fail to allude to the Mystagogical Catecheses, even though specifically referring to Cyril's Catechetical Lectures.

Third, there is the internal evidence. The description of the lectures to come, which appears in the final lecture before Easter, does not exactly fit what we actually find in the post-Easter set. Furthermore, there are some inconsistencies between the two groups of lectures: the baptismal symbolism of Romans 6 forms the subject of the Second Mystagogical Catechesis, thus being treated as esoteric teaching for the initiated, but in the Procatechesis Cyril clearly expects the candidates to be already familiar with it. In addition to this, the character of the two sets is somewhat different: the style of the Mystagogical Catecheses is terser, on the whole, and lacks the direct address and circumstantial details of the earlier set.

Finally, there are the liturgical arguments. The practices described in the Mystagogical Catecheses seem to belong to the late fourth century, rather than the date presumed by the Lent lectures.

Such arguments appeared to carry so much cumulative weight that most investigators were accepting John's authorship, or expressing the view that certainty was impossible. However, a couple of articles and a monograph have defended the ascription of these lectures to Cyril, while assigning them to a much later date than the pre-baptismal set. Beukers[97] argued that the final catechesis must belong to a year between 383 and 386, when Cyril would still have been bishop, though his evidence need not necessarily point to that conclusion; and Yarnold put a strong case for Cyrilline authorship, suggesting that the character of the Mystagogical Catecheses and the doubt about their authorship is explained if we suppose that they were the outline notes on the basis of which Cyril was accustomed to lecture, expanding as he went along.

> Because of the disciplina arcani these notes would not be intended for publication, and would probably bear no author's name ... The ascription to John may have been a conjecture based on the fact that the MS was found in Jerusalem after Cyril's death. The dual ascription to Cyril and John would have a similar explanation. The MS may have been the work of Cyril, come into John's possession, and been used by him in his own preaching.[98]

Yarnold's arguments against John's authorship, and for the continuity of style, theology and spirituality, appear very strong, assuming as he does that the Mystagogical Catecheses bear the marks of a period thirty or so years later than

96 Doval (1997); Drijvers (2004).
97 Beukers (1961).
98 Yarnold (1978), pp. 144f. In earlier articles (1972, 1973, 1975), Yarnold demonstrated the probability of Ambrose's dependence on the Mystagogical Catecheses, which increases the likelihood of Cyril's authorship.

the pre-Lent set; and the subsequent detailed treatment of all the arguments by Doval[99] has at least established that there is really no reason why they should not be ascribed to Cyril.

The dating of the *Mystagogical Catecheses* is crucial to the historian of liturgy as they are one of the richest and earliest sources he possesses. One problem which has arisen is how to relate the evidence they provide to that found in the *Peregrinatio Etheriae*,[100] the account in Latin of a lady's pilgrimage to the Holy Places, in which the practices of the Jerusalem church are described in some detail. Both texts seem to belong to the 380s, and yet at certain crucial points they do not appear to be compatible. Probably the difficulties have been exaggerated. The 'tourist' does not always get every item of information absolutely accurate, after all,[101] and in any case many think the *Peregrinatio* should be dated twenty or more years later. Besides, liturgical developments were clearly proceeding apace in Jerusalem in this particular half-century. Specialists have in fact attributed several significant innovations to none other than Cyril himself; that Cyril had a much higher view of the Holy Places than Eusebius has been cogently argued.[102] In the *Catechetical Lectures*, there is no trace of the elaborate Holy Week celebrations characteristic of Jerusalem at the end of the century and described with enthusiasm in the *Peregrinatio Etheriae*. Yet already interest in the local sites is apparent in the lectures, and Cyril and his hearers were assembled in the beautiful new buildings provided by Constantine for Christian worship in the holy city. Already Jerusalem was the goal of pilgrimages and an attraction to the devout. The conditions for the development of a commemorative cycle already existed, and by the end of Cyril's episcopacy, the pattern had been established. The same sort of situation is apparent in the matter of the daily round of Offices; a complete cycle is described by Egeria, though observances of this kind are not mentioned to the catechumens about forty years earlier. It seems very likely that Cyril was responsible both for introducing monastic observances to the 'secular' church at Jerusalem and for the pattern of Holy Week celebration.[103] The practices of the Jerusalem church were clearly recommended to churches elsewhere by returning pilgrims, and thus Cyril had a remarkable influence on the worldwide Church.

But did Cyril also make innovations in the eucharistic celebration? The peculiar features of the rite described in the *Mystagogical Catecheses* when compared with other evidence of the period, are clear.[104] We have here the first evidence for the consecration and conversion of the elements by invocation of the Holy

---

99 Doval (2001).

100 *Peregrinatio Etheriae*: text, CCL 175 (1967), 37–90; ET, G. E. Gingras, 1970. *Egeria: Diary of a Pilgrimage*, ACW 38, New York: Newman Press. On the problems of relating this text to the evidence of the *Catechetical Lectures* see Yarnold (1978, 2000), Stephenson (1954a), Doval (2001), Drijvers (2004).

101 Yarnold (1978).

102 Walker (1990).

103 Cyril's importance as an innovator is particularly stressed by Dix (1945), p. 329, pp. 348–51.

104 For discussion, and especially comparison with the Liturgy of St James, see Dix (1945), pp. 187ff. Liturgical questions are also discussed by Swaans (1942); Kretschmar (1956); Yarnold (2000); Doval (2001); Drijvers (2004); and Day (2007).

Spirit (the *Epiclesis*), the first evidence for the use of liturgical vestments, for the carrying of lights, and for other significant details like the symbolic hand-washing and the use of the Lord's Prayer after the eucharistic prayer.[105] Such features appear elsewhere towards the end of the century, presumably spread by returning pilgrims, and are most likely to have been gradually introduced at Jerusalem as her rites were suitably elaborated for use in her lavishly constructed basilica, a process which must have taken place in the main during Cyril's episcopate. In the course of this, there may have been an increase in what was regarded as subject to the *disciplina arcani*, a possibility which would account for some of the inconsistencies between the main body of the *Catechetical Lectures* and the five *Mystagogical Catecheses*.[106]

Whatever their date and whatever Cyril's liturgical contributions, the *Mystagogical Catecheses* are not just descriptions of ritual acts. The comments on their meaning are integrated into a fascinating theological whole. The author presents the sacraments as a means by which the believer is transformed into Christ. Baptism is understood as a dying and rising with Christ: 'Christ was really crucified, really buried and truly rose ... in order that partaking in the imitation of his sufferings, in truth we might gain salvation.' Chrism means that we have become 'Christs', anointed with the Holy Spirit. By partaking of the eucharistic food, which becomes the body and blood of Christ by the invocation of the Holy Spirit, the Christian is made of the same body and the same blood with him; 'thus we become "Christ-bearers", because his body and blood are diffused through our members'. This is how we become 'sharers in the divine nature' (2 Peter 1.4).[107] The idea of salvation is one of what we might call 'Christification' conveyed in and through the mystery-sacraments.

Apart from the *Catechetical Lectures*, very little survives from Cyril's pen or pulpit. One item of interest is a letter to the Emperor Constantius.[108] The authenticity of this letter has been questioned on the grounds that the word *homoousios* occurs in the final blessing: there is MS evidence, however, that the final phrases were a later addition to the text, and in other respects the letter fits Cyril's style and the situation of 351 so well that its basic trustworthiness is to be accepted. The letter's purpose is to describe the appearance of a cross of light in the sky above Golgotha, witnessed by the whole population of the city.[109] Cyril regards this as proof that Constantius' piety towards God ensures imperial victory. He makes no reference to Constantine's decisive vision of the cross, though there are clear parallels suggesting that both phenomena may have been *parhelia*. Cyril does refer, however, to the discovery of the wood of the cross itself during Constantine's reign. Cyril particularly promoted the cult of the cross, along with the holy sites and their relics. It is not improbable that he grew up in Jerusalem when Constantine was revitalizing the city; as already noted, the special

---

105 Dix (1945), p. 350.

106 *Pace* Day (2001), see above, p. 160.

107 Dix greatly underplays the evidence for 'partaking' in Cyril's lectures. It is true that in *Myst. Cat.* 5 sacrifice predominates, but that is not so in *Myst. Cat.* 4. See further Camelot (1970).

108 Critical text: Bihain (1973), pp. 264–96. ET in Telfer (1955).

109 The story also appears in Sozomen, *HE* iv.5. Sozomen associates it with Cyril's consecration, but the letter gives no support to this dating.

position of Jerusalem is not ignored in his lectures. A legend about Cyril[110] arises from this special position. It was during the episcopacy of Cyril, in 362–3, under the Emperor Julian, that the Jews were permitted to rebuild the Temple; a prophecy of their failure was attributed to Cyril, which was then immediately fulfilled by the earthquake. The point of the story seems to be that in Jerusalem the high priest of the New Covenant inherits the prophetic powers attributed to the old high priest in John 11.51. Hearsay seems to be the only basis on which the story rests, since the supposed prophecy is almost exactly a quotation from the lectures[111] and in that context has no bearing on the Temple incident. However, the lectures were delivered a decade or so earlier, and those disposed to look for prophecy are rarely deterred by inappropriate contexts. The very existence of the story, like so much of our information about Cyril, is indicative of the atmosphere of the period. Despite the fact that Cyril apparently never mentions it,[112] the threat to Cyril of the rebuilding of the Temple must have been considerable: the Holy Sepulchre had replaced the Temple, and the Temple site was left a ruin to prove the supersession of Judaism by Christianity.[113]

The only other extant work is a sermon *On the Paralytic*.[114] By contrast with the teaching of the *Catecheses*, this sermon is firmly within the Alexandrian tradition of mystical allegory, a fact which might arouse doubts about its authorship. On the other hand, there is nothing improbable about it. There were close links between Egyptian and Palestinian Christianity, and Origen himself had eventually settled in Palestinian Caesarea. Without wanting to suggest that Cyril was an 'Origenist', Stephenson[115] has convincingly shown that certain passages in the *Catechetical Orations* are entirely compatible with the evidence of the sermon, and that Cyril embraced the view that scripture could be given a 'contemplative exegesis ($\dot{\epsilon}\xi\acute{\eta}\gamma\eta\sigma\iota\varsigma$ $\theta\epsilon\omega\rho\eta\tau\iota\kappa\acute{\eta}$) leading to a higher knowledge ($\gamma\nu\tilde{\omega}\sigma\iota\varsigma$), as well as the more literal sense normally expounded in the lectures. Indeed, the Sermon can provide an important key to understanding some aspects of Cyril's thought. The secrecy surrounding the imparting of enlightenment to those seeking baptism is itself consonant with the esoteric leanings of the Alexandrian tradition.

It was Cyril's successor who was to be embroiled in controversy as a defender of Origen, and the close links between the ecclesiastics and monks of Egypt and Palestine become entirely evident in the story of that conflict. It was Epiphanius who would provoke it.

---

110 Socrates, *HE* iii.20; Rufinus, *HE* i.57.

111 *Cat. Orat.* xv.15, where prophecies from Daniel and Matthew are used to indicate what to expect before the coming of Antichrist.

112 A letter of Cyril's, purporting to report the signs and miracles that happened when the Jews were ordered to rebuild the Temple, turned up in a Syriac manuscript at Harvard and was published by Brock in 1977. It is unlikely to be original. See Drijvers (2004), chapter 5 and Appendix III, which reprints Brock's ET.

113 Drijvers (2004), p. 135.

114 Text in *PG* 33, and Reischl and Rupp (1848, 1960).

115 Stephenson (1954b, 1957).

For Further Reading

English translations

McCauley, Leo P. and Anthony A. Stephenson, 1969, 1970. *The Works of Cyril of Jerusalem*, FC 61, 64, Washington, DC: Catholic University of America Press.
Yarnold, E., SJ, 2000. *Cyril of Jerusalem*, Introduction and ET of selections, London & New York: Routledge.

Studies

Day, J., 2007. *The Baptismal Liturgy of Jerusalem: Fourth- and Fifth-Century Evidence from Palestine, Syria and Egypt*, London: Ashgate.
Doval, Alexis James, 2001. *Cyril of Jerusalem, Mystagogue: The Authorship of the Mystagogic Catecheses*, Patristic Monograph Series 17, Washington, DC: Catholic University of America Press.
Drijvers, J. W., 2004. *Cyril of Jerusalem: Bishop and City*, Supplements to *VigChr*, Leiden: Brill.

III Epiphanius of Salamis

The work of Epiphanius is best known because it has proved a quarry for material needed by the textual critic of the New Testament and the historian of the early Church. Apart from examining his role in the Origenist controversy, scholarly work has been primarily concerned to trace Epiphanius' sources and estimate the reliability of his evidence about the many important heretical movements which he describes; very little has treated Epiphanius as interesting in himself. This is not all that surprising, but there are features of his life and work which illustrate well the atmosphere within the Church in this period.

Few would claim that Epiphanius was an original thinker or an attractive personality; yet in some ways it is precisely his intolerant conservatism which is interesting. The mere fact that he appears to rely on shouting formulae rather than careful argument is a useful reminder that Trinitarian orthodoxy won the Church over not through abstruse philosophical reasoning or the careful sustained explication of works like the great Cappadocian treatises, but by constant unquestioning affirmation in the life of the Church, backed by political strength and scornful prejudice against all possible alternatives. As a scholar reputed to be master of five languages, as an upholder of the one true faith of the holy catholic Church, Epiphanius bears comparison with Eusebius, and yet the differences are marked: for where Eusebius looked for truth, Epiphanius hunted out error, believing that κακοπιστία (bad belief) is worse than ἀπιστία (lack of belief).[116]

---

116 Epiphanius, *Ancoratus* 9.

1 The *Ancoratus*

It is clear that for Epiphanius Christianity had become a set of dogmas to be upheld in every paradoxical particular with no concessions to deviant interpretations. There are some things, he thought, about which enquiry should not be made.[117] Scripture speaks the truth in everything; heresy is false because it does not receive the Holy Spirit according to the traditions of the Fathers of the holy catholic Church of God.[118] 'Search the scriptures . . . and the Spirit itself . . . will reveal to you the knowledge of the word of the Son of God, so that you may not wander from the truth and lose your own soul.'[119] For that is the penalty for unorthodox speculation. 'Heresies and their founders are the gates of Hades.'[120]

These remarks are to be found in the *Ancoratus*. Epiphanius' most important work was, of course, the *Panarion* or *Haereses*;[121] but before he turned to that major encyclopaedia of heretical sects, Epiphanius had written in 373 this carefully crafted shorter treatise, which throws considerable light on his own position, particularly with regard to contemporary problems.[122] The work is called the *Ancoratus* (Ἀγκυρατός), the well-anchored man, because in it he sets out to reply to several Christians who had written from Syedra in Pamphylia asking him about the true faith, and particularly to a certain Palladius who described with some concern the dangers confronting one tossed in the storms of heresy. It is here that we can see how Epiphanius establishes the true faith, not so much by argument as by formulaic confessions, scriptural allusions or quotations, together with heated denial of heretical suggestions. His Greek is direct and straightforward; indeed his works were very popular, partly perhaps because they were written in 'elevated *koinē*' rather than in the artificial literary style then current.[123] But he was also popular, one suspects, because in his work the familiar ecclesiastical language is simply reproduced. It is not just that he depends on current orthodox apologetic, as when he denies such classic errors as the idea that the Father has two Sons, or on current orthodox exegesis in dealing with awkward subordinationist texts such as Proverbs 8.22; nor is it simply that he appeals to the classic Trinitarian proofs, like the threefold *Sanctus* and God's plural address at creation, 'Let us make humankind in our image.' The fact is that he is so moulded by ecclesiastical style that he actually writes in credal patterns. Not only does he quote two actual creeds at the end of his work, one of which has caused considerable discussion because of its remarkable similarity to the creed adopted at Constantinople some seven

---

117 *Ancoratus* 18.

118 *Ancoratus* 63.

119 *Ancoratus* 19.

120 *Ancoratus* 9.

121 Text of *Ancoratus* and *Panarion*, ed. Holl (1915); Holl and Dummer (1980, 1985); ET Williams (1987, 1994); Amidon (1990).

122 See further Kösters (2003).

123 Holl (1915), Introduction, p. vii. Older scholars treated Epiphanius' language as degenerate; and the MS tradition has a tendency to Atticize the text; see Holl (1910).

or eight years later,[124] but the structure and content of his phraseology echoes the familiar style of the classic confessional definitions, particularly in its piling up of participial clauses: 'the holy Word himself . . . becoming man in truth and being God in truth, not changing his nature, not altering his Godhead, begotten in flesh, the enfleshed Word, the Word become flesh . . .'[125] We seem to have direct access to the current ecclesiastical jargon and formulaic ways of confession and preaching. Over and over again, as a substitute for thought or careful explanation there appears a battery of mixed scriptural and extra-scriptural catchphrases, nominatives stretching over pages: Christ is 'the only-begotten, the perfect, the uncreated, the immutable, the unchangeable, the unknowable, the unseen, become man among us . . . the one who though rich became poor for us . . . one Lord, King, Christ, Son of God, seated in heaven on the right hand of the Father . . .' and so on.[126] Scripture and tradition provide Epiphanius with his tools, but essentially his Trinitarianism can be seen to be in a direct line from Athanasius.[127]

But for Epiphanius, the truth can only be properly maintained by avoiding error. The *Ancoratus* contains a number of anti-heretical digressions, and already we find a bitter attack on Origen and his followers, revealing the particular prejudice which was to give Epiphanius his not very honourable place in the events of the time. Again, already in the *Ancoratus*, he lists eighty heresies, and it is interesting that we find here roughly the scheme of heretical sects which provides the pattern of his later work. After Moses up to the incarnation there were eleven heresies, after the incarnation, sixty more. Before the Mosaic Law there were five heresies and the four sects of the Greeks; so that counting their 'mothers' the total number of heresies is eighty. Such is the first outline of Epiphanius' scheme, with the enumeration of the sects by name.

2 The *Panarion*

It is in fact the case that the work *Against the Heresies* developed out of this preliminary sketch in the *Ancoratus*. This time Epiphanius was approached by Acacius and Paul, archimandrites of Chalcis and Beroea in Coele–Syria, with a request to clarify the eighty heresies listed in his first work. Epiphanius replied that he had been in process of doing exactly that when their letter arrived; from his comments it is possible to date the work as completed in approximately 377. His largest work is thus devoted to the description and rebuttal of false doctrines – he wanted to provide antidotes to the poisons of heresy and entitled it the 'Medicine Chest': *Panarion*.

The medical image is not, however, the one sustained throughout this vast compendium. Epiphanius was clearly fascinated by catalogues and genealogies: a list of Roman emperors, and a list of all the nations descended from

---

124 See Kelly (1950), especially pp. 318ff.; Palachkovsky (1966); Kösters (2003). It may be that the Nicene Creed originally stood in the text, and the Creed of Constantinople replaced it through the work of a later scribe or editor.

125 *Ancoratus* 19.

126 *Ancoratus* 81.

127 See Kösters (2003) and Dechow (1988) for further discussion.

Shem, Ham and Japheth appear in the *Ancoratus*, as well as the catalogue of heresies. More lists appear in the concluding section of the *Panarion*, entitled περὶ πίστεως (*On Faith*). This interest is explicitly acknowledged in the opening paragraphs of the *Panarion*, where Epiphanius makes it clear that what he is seeking to do is to map out a genealogy of heresy. He also uses the analogy of biological classification: he wants to trace the genera and species. He is making an attempt to devise a family tree, to systematize the rise and proliferation of heresy within a world context. This image is sometimes lost in the course of this enormous work, but it is noticeable that there are references to the derivation of one group of heretics from another: Basileides and Satornilus derived their teachings from Menander, who followed Simon Magus, from whom the false-named γνῶσις took its roots. The genealogical scheme most clearly affects the first volume of the first book (Epiphanius himself divided it into seven τόμοι – volumes – arranged in three βιβλία – books[128]); for Epiphanius does not restrict heresy to Christian deviation – αἵρεσις, which means 'choice' or 'option' and so something like 'faction', is essentially the breakdown of the unity of humanity, and its parentage can be traced back to the origins of history.[129]

The first volume of Epiphanius' work, therefore, indulges in a wandering and partly repetitive survey of world history, largely drawn from the Bible though with scraps of Greek history fed into the biblical outline, and punctuated by lists of names, genealogies and enumerations of generations. Now and again Epiphanius supplies reflections on the significance of it all. In the beginning there was no heresy. There was true faith: Adam was neither an idolater nor circumcised, but in a sense held the faith of the holy catholic Church of God which existed from the beginning and was later to be revealed again. Because of Adam's sin, there appeared the opposite of true faith – adultery, rebellion, idolatry. Piety and impiety, faith and unfaith co-existed, with the great biblical figures like Abel, Enoch, Methuselah and Noah representing the former which was the image of Christianity;[130] Abraham in particular is presented as the type of the Christian, prefiguring in his departure from his father's house the call of the first disciples.[131] Several times in the text Epiphanius stresses that there was as yet no heresy, no variety of opinions, nor any device other than adultery or idolatry, that is, the opposite of the true worship and faith of the holy catholic Church; and he seems at this stage to identify the origins of heresy with the scattering of humankind after the tower of Babel. Yet, somewhat inconsistently,

---

128 *Letter to Acacius and Paul* 3.

129 There has been some discussion about Epiphanius' understanding of heresy. Pétau (who edited the *Panarion* in 1622 and whose text is reproduced in *PG* 41–2) commented that Epiphanius does not use the word αἵρεσις in the usual theological sense, and Fraenkel (1963) draws attention to the 'neutrality of the terminology' he uses, describing it as striking in the work of a 'successor to Irenaeus and Tertullian who had used the words as technical terms for denouncing error'. However, the word was in fact the classical designation for different philosophical schools. Besides, if Lipsius (1865) is right, Epiphanius' source included the pre-Christian sects: Dositheans, Sadducees, Pharisees and Herodians. Epiphanius' understanding of heresy is not entirely consistent: see further Moutsoulas (1966) and Young (1982).

130 *Panarion* i.5 (*PG* 41.181–4) = 2.4–7 (*GCS* (Holl 1915), 174.21—175.13).

131 *Panarion* i.8 (*PG* 41.189) = 4.1.2 (*GCS* (Holl 1915), 179.13–15).

Epiphanius imposes on this early history his first four heresies: Barbarism, he attributes to the period between Adam and Noah, Scythian superstition, to the period between Noah and the tower of Babel; thereafter, with the development of magic and astrology, arose Hellenism, and with the circumcision of Abraham, came Judaism. The subsequent story is concerned with the fragmentation of these four great divisions into smaller sects: Hellenism produced four, the Stoics, the Platonists, the Pythagoreans and the Epicureans; Samaritanism split off from Judaism and then produced four sects of its own; and Judaism produced seven pre-Christian heresies. Thus prior to the coming of Christ, there were twenty heresies altogether, as Epiphanius has already indicated in his outline in the *Ancoratus*.

The inconsistencies in the application of the word heresy and in the assessment of Abraham's role alert us to the artificiality of the scheme. Comparison with the summaries found in the *Ancoratus*, and even more significantly the prefatory letter to Acacius and Paul, provides further confirmation.[132] Of a number of variations in the order of the heresies as they appear in the text and in each of the summary lists, the most significant is the position of Samaritanism. In the summaries it is treated as one of the five 'mothers of heresy', and in the *Ancoratus* is even carelessly placed 'before the Law'; in the text, however, the Samaritan schism is placed after the description of the sects of Hellenism.[133] Since other variations are attributable to the fact that in his text Epiphanius faithfully follows the order of his sources,[134] it is tempting to suggest in this case that the actual course of the history which he is presenting affected his order. But the real reason is that Epiphanius' framework was controlled by his exegesis of two particular biblical texts.

The text that directs his presentation in the first volume of the *Panarion* he quotes from Paul as follows: in Christ Jesus, there is neither barbarian, nor Scythian, Greek nor Jew, but new creation. This is in fact a somewhat mixed memory of Galatians 3.28; 6.15 and Colossians 3.11; but it gives him *four* great divisions of humanity from which all subsequent heresies stemmed. That he can only enumerate further splintering in Judaism and Hellenism simply reinforces the artificiality of his analysis.

The text that determines the overall scheme is eventually divulged to us in the concluding essay *On Faith*. Epiphanius quotes from the Song of Songs (Cant. 6.7): 'There are sixty queens, and eighty concubines and maidens without number; but my dove, my perfect one, is only one.' The one dove is, of course, the holy catholic Church; and the concubines are the heresies. Now we understand why somehow or other Epiphanius has to press his heresies into

---

132 The *Anakephalaiosis* follows and partially distorts the order of the prefatory letter. It is in any case irrelevant since it is unlikely to be the work of Epiphanius himself.

133 Fraenkel's valiant attempt to schematize Epiphanius' underlying ideas surely must not be allowed to obscure the inconsistency of Epiphanius' treatment. Fraenkel argues (1963, pp. 181f.) that Epiphanius regarded Samaritanism as syncretistic, and therefore places it and its sects between Hellenism and Judaism in the text; and that this means that it is only in a secondary sense one of the basic divisions of humankind, but can still be regarded as one of the 'mothers of heresy'.

134 Lipsius (1865). The same order is found in Pseudo-Tertullian and Philastrius; it is likely they all got it from Hippolytus.

the number eighty, urging his readers not to worry about the fact that different names and subsequent sectarian splits apparently upset his calculations. There must be seventy-five sects and five 'mothers of heresies' in order to reach the correct number. Then with evident delight, Epiphanius goes on to explain also the sixty queens and maidens without number, for this is an excuse to produce more of his beloved lists and generation counts. The queens are the faithful in each generation before Christ, those like Enoch, Methuselah, Lamech and Noah described in the first volume, and there were sixty generations of them, ten from Adam to Noah, ten from Noah to Abraham and then following Matthew's genealogical table, fourteen from Abraham to David, fourteen from David to the captivity, fourteen from the captivity to Christ. The total sixty-two is no problem, for scripture provides several examples where seventy serves for seventy-two. Then the maidens without number are the countless philosophers and false teachers: Epiphanius lists forty-four Greek philosophers from Thales to Epicurus, reports that there were supposed to be seventy-two philosophers in India, including the Brahmins, and mentions the Magi and the mystery-religions. It is surely apparent that without the controlling power of the Canticles text, Epiphanius could have included many more religious and philosophical sects in his catalogue of heresies: indeed his mention of the Peripatetics in the letter to Acacius and Paul suggests a certain embarrassment at describing only four heresies of Hellenism. The word αἵρεσις, from which we get our word 'heresy', was the classical designation for different philosophical sects, and Hellenism had in fact produced many more schools of philosophy. But Epiphanius had to produce the number eighty, and this is not the only expedient he adopted in order to do so. Some distinct groups are conflated; some heresies appear to have been created out of minor allusions (for example, the Melchizedekians)[135] or out of small incidents in Epiphanius' life (for example, the Antidikomarianitae, a group to whom he wrote defending the perpetual virginity of Mary). It never seems to have entered his head that *future* heresies might be expected and that would finally undermine his attempt to show the fulfilment of his guiding prophecy.

Epiphanius' work was not only directed by theoretical applications of prophecy. His choice of targets, particularly in the later parts of the work, was undoubtedly guided by his fanatical animosities. He had no power of distinguishing between major and minor distortions of truth; schism and heresy was all the same to him. Homoiousians were no nearer salvation than Manichees, Novatians no more Christian than Gnostics. All heresies, even the defunct, were capable of generating further error, and many of the sects he describes, like the Montanists, the Novatians, Marcionites and others, did in fact still exist. So Epiphanius' work was no mere historical survey. For the early centuries he relied on older sources: from Dositheus to Noetus he seems to have followed Hippolytus' *Syntagma* extremely closely (in fact, the *Panarion* has been described as a new edition of Hippolytus, brought up to date and augmented);[136] he quotes extensively from Irenaeus and from a number of lost heretical works, so preserving the Greek text of many interesting documents – hence his value for

---

135 Horton (1976), pp. 90ff.
136 Lipsius (1865), and further Nautin (1949).

modern scholars, in spite of his inaccuracy and lack of critical sense.[137] But for him this compendium was no mere academic exercise, a fact well-illustrated by the events of his life. As a young monk in Egypt he had been subject to Gnostic attempts to entrap him, and had acquired an aversion to followers of Origen which was never to leave him – indeed, it has been argued[138] that Epiphanius regarded Origen as the epitome and exemplar of all heresies, the culmination of those before and the inspiration of those who came after. In the end his fanatical zeal against the greatest of Greek theologians was to cause untold disruption and tragedy in the Church.

3 Early life

Epiphanius was born about 315. He grew up in Palestine and his native tongue was Syriac; he learned Greek at school, though unlike most of the great Christian writers of this period he seems to have been unacquainted with the classical *paideia*. Sozomen says he was educated by Egyptian monks, and certainly as a young man he spent some time in Egypt where he acquired Coptic. (Jerome, in fact, calls him πεντάγλωττος, five-tongued,[139] but his knowledge of Latin seems to have been pretty slight and the few Hebrew words he mentions in his writings are probably the only basis of the claim that he had a fifth language.) He was an enthusiastic ascetic who on his return from Egypt founded his own monastery near his birthplace, Eleutheropolis near Gaza, and was ordained as 'convent-priest'. Clearly he maintained close Palestinian contacts even after 367 when he was elected bishop of Constantia/Salamis in Cyprus. Hilarion, another Palestinian monk, seems to have been a major influence, and may have been behind his election as bishop, a position he held until his death thirty-six years later.[140]

It was during the first ten years of his episcopate that Epiphanius wrote the works already discussed, and one interesting feature of the *Panarion* is that it reveals his estimate of the current warring factions of the 360s and 370s: the seventy-second heresy he details is that of Marcellus, and the seventy-third that of the semi-Arians or Homoiousians – clearly Epiphanius' sympathies lay with the former who did at least accept the *homoousion*, and his attitude to Apollinarius remained ambivalent through the 370s. Epiphanius, then, was an extremely ardent upholder of the Nicene formula; yet he did not participate in the Council of Constantinople in 381 which re-established the Nicene faith. The probable reason is perhaps typical of him: in the 360s a series of misunderstandings produced two anti-Arian bishops of Antioch, Paulinus and Meletius, a factor contributing to confusion and division in the anti-Arian ranks.[141] Epiphanius, together with Athanasius and Rome, supported Paulinus, but Basil of

---

137 However, Epiphanius' accuracy has been defended by Benko (1967).

138 Dechow (1988) makes this concern central to the whole of Epiphanius' compendium on heresies, chapter 64 of the *Panarion*, against Origen, being unusually long; but Kösters (2003) suggested this needs to be somewhat relativized.

139 Jerome, *Adversus Rufinum* 3.6.

140 See further Dechow (1988).

141 At one stage there were four bishops of Antioch; the complex relations of Epi-

Caesarea and many others in the East favoured Meletius, who in 381 was one of the leaders of the Council.

4 Other works

In the early 390s Epiphanius composed two more treatises, this time concerned with biblical problems, though going far beyond mere exegesis. Both of them largely survive in translations, *On Weights and Measures* in Syriac and Armenian,[142] and *On the Twelve Gems* in a number of fragments, of which the most complete is the Georgian. *On Weights and Measures*[143] is a most inadequate title for what is almost a biblical encyclopaedia, though the matter he keeps reverting to in the central section of the book is the question of the correct equivalents for the units of measure and weight used in the Bible. Epiphanius begins by explaining the conventional signs in the biblical text, the obelus, asterisk and signs of punctuation; he then gives an introduction to the various Greek translations available, telling at some length the story of the seventy-two translators of the Septuagint, dating the version of Aquila and Symmachus, and even, in spite of his anti-Origenism, describing the *Hexapla*. By now he is about a quarter of his way through the book, and he begins to list weights and measures, but his digressions take up most of the space and some are quite astounding: because the *modius* = twenty-two *xestai*, he finds occasion to list the twenty-two works of creation, the twenty-two generations from Adam to Jacob, the twenty-two letters of the Hebrew alphabet and the twenty-two books of the Old Testament. On another occasion, he meditates upon the number four – there were four books in the Ark (Genesis–Numbers), four rivers out of Eden, four quarters of the world, four seasons of the year, four watches of the night and four spiritual creatures (Ezek. 1.5) with four faces, man, lion, ox and eagle, which represent the four Gospels, Matthew, Mark, Luke and John. The last quarter of the book turns from weights and measures to geographical matters, listing and commenting upon the names of biblical places. Since Epiphanius was born and brought up in Palestine, this might have been interesting; but he seems largely dependent not on personal knowledge, but on earlier encyclopaedias like Eusebius' *Onomasticon*.

The *De Gemmis*[144] is ostensibly an elaborate exegetical exercise dealing with the twelve stones of Aaron's breastplate (Exod. 28); but in reality, it was probably intended to provide a Christian counterblast to the pagan quasi-scientific and mystical interpretation of precious stones. First, drawing on current literature, he gives a description of each gem with an account of where it is found and what medicinal properties it has; then he embarks on symbolical and allegorical expositions of the association of each gem with the particular name of one of the twelve patriarchs, a technique which enables him to wander in a disorderly fashion over a good deal of exegetical and theological ground.

---

phanius with Paulinus and Vitalis (an Apollinarian) are discussed in detail by Dechow (1988).

142 Stone and Ervine (2000).
143 Ed. and ET: Dean (1935).
144 Texts of fragments with translation: Blake and de Vis (1934).

The discursive writings of this conservative Nicene were widely read in the Christian world, an indication of their popularity being the many oriental versions of his writings. His reputation for learning was such that odd works like the *Physiologus*, the principal source of mediaeval bestiaries, came to be attributed to him. However, apart from the treatises mentioned, little else remains that is authentic. There are a few genuine letters scattered about in various collections, but most of the homilies and exegetical fragments attributed to him are regarded as spurious. Fragments exist of works against images to which the Iconoclasts appealed in the later controversies; the authenticity of these fragments has been defended by Holl,[145] who claims that they represent three separate works on the topic. That Epiphanius did have strong views on this subject is clear from an incident he describes in a letter to John, Cyril's successor in Jerusalem, which has survived in Jerome's Latin translation:[146] journeying in Palestine, he went into a village church to pray and there found an embroidered curtain bearing an image either of Christ or of one of the saints. He tore it asunder and advised the custodians to use it as a winding sheet for some poor person.

5 The Origenist controversy

This incident occurred during a fateful trip to Palestine in 394 when the Origenist controversy flared up. At Epiphanius' instigation the monasteries of Rufinus and Jerome had been challenged to reject Origen; the former refused, the latter complied, and the friendship between the two Westerners never recovered. Then in 393, Epiphanius had arrived in Jerusalem for a major festival, where he was invited by John to preach and attacked Origen very publicly. Equally publicly, John sent his archdeacon to tell him to stop discussing these matters, and then later in the day preached against simple-minded Anthropomorphites. Epiphanius agreed, suggesting both mistaken theologies should be condemned. But the seeds of conflict were sown, and soon Rufinus and John were ranged against Jerome and Epiphanius, who fuelled the dissension by ordaining a priest for Jerome's monastery at Bethlehem, thus trespassing on John's jurisdiction. The letter to John sought to patch things up, but its attack on Origen only inflamed the situation.[147]

The animosities had long been germinating.[148] From very early in his career Epiphanius clearly regarded the teaching of Origen as the cause of Arianism and many other errors. In the *Ancoratus* and the *Panarion*, long before the outbreak of controversy, he detailed his charges against the Origenist heresy: Origen said that the only-begotten Son cannot *see* the Father, nor the Spirit the Son, nor can the angels see the Spirit, nor human beings the angels; the Son is not of the *ousia* of the Father – he is altogether other (in other words, created), but called *Son* by grace. Origen spoke of the pre-existence of souls as angels, of their incarna-

---

145 Holl (1928).

146 Jerome, *Ep.* 51 = his translation of Epiphanius' Letter to John.

147 This summary is largely based on Jerome's partisan account; see further Kelly (1975) and Clark (1992).

148 See further Dechow (1988).

tion in flesh as punishment for sin; he said Adam lost the image of God and the 'coats of skin' God made for Adam and Eve (Gen. 3) were their bodies. Origen denied the resurrection of the dead. Origen allegorized Paradise and treated all scripture as riddles and parables, claiming it was hard for human beings to understand. Charges covering more or less the same ground occur nearly twenty years later in the letter to John, but the emphasis has changed a bit, focusing now on the issues of the 390s – the loss of God's image, the salvation of the devil and the 'deprecation of reproduction' implicit in the 'original bodiless condition of humans'.[149] Epiphanius now warns against Palladius, and the teaching of his teacher, Evagrius, would seem to be in the firing line.

The story of the controversy has often been told and can be found in detail elsewhere.[150] The famous quarrel between Rufinus and Jerome, the heads of rival Latin monasteries in the Holy Land, soon reached a peak of literary blast and counterblast. Jerome had been an admirer of Origen, but he was not the only actor in the drama who changed sides. In 399, the bishop of Alexandria, Theophilus, to whom John had once appealed for support, also became a turncoat and started persecution of the Origenist monks in Egypt.[151] Personality, networks of personal connections and expediency seem to have played a larger role in this controversy than conviction, though Epiphanius was characteristically consistent in his position throughout. As a result of persecution in Egypt, four of these monks, the so-called Tall Brothers, associates of Evagrius, fled to Palestine, and then travelled on to Constantinople seeking support and spreading the controversy. Their arrival in Constantinople gave Theophilus a chance to lay schemes for the downfall of John Chrysostom, and Epiphanius, now in his eighties but still burning with anti-Origenist zeal, obeyed the summons to a council in Constantinople. However, he then realized he was being used as a tool by Theophilus and hurried home, only to die at sea on the way. By now it was 403, and the controversy he had initiated had gone its way for ten years. Its tragic outcome was soon to be realized.

For Further Reading

English translations

Amidon, Philip R., 1990. *The Panarion of St. Epiphanius. Selected Passages*, New York and Oxford: Oxford University Press.
Williams, Frank, 1987, 1994. *The Panarion of Epiphanius of Salamis*, 2 vols, Leiden: Brill.

Studies

Clark, E., 1992. *The Origenist Controversy*, Princeton: Princeton University Press.
Dechow, Jon F., 1988. *Dogma and mysticism in early Christianity: Epiphanius of Salamis and the legacy of Origen*, Leuven: Peeters.

---

149 See further the discussion in Clark (1992), pp. 86–104.
150 On the Origenist controversy, see standard Church histories, along with Kelly (1975) and Clark (1992).
151 On Theophilus, see Russell (2007).

IV John Chrysostom

1 The Origenist controversy

The bitterest fruit of the Origenist controversy was the tragic end of John Chrysostom. It is ironical that one so little influenced by the great theologian of the third century was the most important victim of the campaign. Indeed, it seems clear that political factors and other personal motives were ultimately far more important. However, the occasion was provided by the current theological battle.

The most important source for understanding the events associated with Chrysostom's fall is the *Dialogue* written in his defence by Palladius.[152] The value of this is that it clearly comes from someone intimately involved in the events. Maybe it is partisan and very hostile to all considered the enemies of John; yet at the same time the criticisms which it answers give some indication of the hostility which Chrysostom aroused and the reasons why. Socrates' evidence is less direct but more impartial.[153] It is instructive, by the way, to see the high proportion of their histories that both Socrates and Sozomen devoted to these events – a clear indication of the importance attached to them at the time.

It is impossible here to record all the detail with which we are presented in the accounts. The essential movements were as follows. The Tall Brothers, accused of Origenism and hounded through Palestine by Theophilus, arrived in Constantinople and appealed to Chrysostom. Chrysostom did not receive them to communion, but out of charity and respect for their ascetic holiness, he allowed them hospitality while he communicated with Alexandria about their persecution. Theophilus refused to negotiate and demanded their expulsion. Meanwhile they appealed to the emperor, who was induced to summon Theophilus to answer charges against his conduct in the affair. Thus, Theophilus came to the capital.

Theophilus realized that somehow the tables had to be turned. He rejected conciliatory gestures from Chrysostom, and set about an attack on him rather than his own defence. Clearly he was able to play upon a large element of resent-

---

152 It is generally accepted that Palladius of Helenopolis, the author of the *Lausiac History* (see above, pp. 78–83), was also the author of the *Dialogue*, though the ascription is not absolutely certain. The title of the only complete manuscript describes it as 'An Historical Dialogue of Palladius, Bishop of Helenopolis, with Theodore, Deacon of Rome, concerning the Life and Conversation of the Blessed John Chrysostom, Bishop of Constantinople'. This identifies Palladius with the main character in the *Dialogue* itself, the anonymous bishop who tells the story. In fact, this identification is impossible; not only do the facts of the bishop's life fail to correspond with what is known of Palladius' movements, but also he refers to Palladius in the third person. The most likely explanation of the title is that the bishop is a fictional character and the title preserves a tradition of the *Dialogue*'s authorship. Stylistic comparisons with the *Lausiac History* on the whole confirm this attribution. Its value as a source for Chrysostom's life is not in any case dependent upon the authorship question. Text ed. Coleman-Norton (1928), Malingrey and Leclerq (1988); translation by Moore (1921).

153 Other evidence, notably from the unpublished *Life of Martyrius* and Photius' summary of the Acts of the Synod of the Oak, has been exploited by Ommerslaeghe (1977). See also Ommerslaeghe (1979).

ment against the archbishop. He collected a group of bishops at the Oak near Chalcedon, formed a Synod and summoned Chrysostom to answer charges. Chrysostom demanded a fair hearing before a less hostile council, but since Theophilus had by now the support of the court, his deposition was guaranteed (403). Most accounts stress the extreme wickedness of Theophilus as an agent of the devil, arriving with massive bribes and sheer insolence to carry out a well-laid plot. For all the tendency to blacken the opposition, it is hard to dismiss such charges totally, and one should not underestimate the political complexities that allowed Theophilus to operate against Chrysostom.[154]

Chrysostom was rapidly recalled when some disaster caused the empress to fear divine displeasure. Theophilus made a precipitate departure. But Eudoxia's favour was short-lived. Modelling himself on John the Baptist, Chrysostom could not resist criticism of the empress when her statue was erected and dedicated with much pomp a few months later.[155] The resultant imperial hostility was soon played upon by the agents of Theophilus, and amidst massacre, riot and arson, John and his followers were driven from the city at Easter (404). Chrysostom spent several years in exile in Armenia, but his continuing influence through correspondence riled the court, and he died in 407 while being conveyed to a more remote locality.

What were the real charges against Chrysostom,[156] and did they have any basis? His two chief accusers were two deacons that he expelled, according to his defenders, for murder and fornication. Most of the charges seem comparatively trivial, though they add up to severe treatment of his clergy, misuse of church property, an unfortunately sarcastic, almost libellous, tongue towards those who expected respect and refusal to practise the traditions of hospitality. We can deduce that Chrysostom's ascetic ideals made him a somewhat arrogant and self-righteous critic of clerical lapses, and induced him to withdraw from the luxurious entertainments expected of him; that his concern for the poor and his personal habits could easily be misrepresented by the suspicious; and that his rigorous standards caused considerable unpopularity. Chrysostom was apparently not blessed with tact or diplomacy. This impression is confirmed by Palladius' treatment of critical rumours: he defends Chrysostom for eating alone and failing to provide hospitality, denies his tyrannical deposition of sixteen Asian bishops, and tries to put his arrogant self-assertion into a better light. Chrysostom seems to have alienated enough people, including the city monks,[157] to make Theophilus' task not too difficult.

One suspects, however, that underlying all the machinations was Theophilus' suspicion of the rising power of the upstart see of Constantinople. That ecclesiastical power struggle had already begun when Alexandria contested the consecration of Gregory Nazianzen in 381; it was to continue in the Christological battle between Cyril and Nestorius; but here we have the classic case of a dispute exploited simply for the sake of weakening the church in the cap-

---

154 For a full discussion of the politics, see Holum (1982), Liebeschuetz (1990); and Kelly (1995).

155 For Chrysostom's relations with Eudoxia, see Holum (1982) and Liebeschuetz (1990).

156 Kelly (1995) lists the charges in an appendix.

157 NB discussion in Liebeschuetz (1990), chapter 20.

ital. Theophilus had opposed Chrysostom's election; now he took his revenge, and his power to do so was almost certainly enhanced, not only by Chrysostom's own personality, but also by current uncertainties about canon law. In the course of the events and afterwards, the validity of appeal to the canons of previous councils was contested, often on the grounds that the councils in question had been of an Arian character; and besides this, the status of the see of Constantinople was probably uncertain – a primacy of honour was accorded in 381, but not it seems jurisdiction. Theophilus seems to have proceeded as if the bishop of Constantinople had no metropolitan status but was himself under the jurisdiction of Heracleia whose bishop presided at the Synod of the Oak;[158] and he also made use of the resentment of the Asian bishops deposed by Chrysostom a few years earlier (401). His intervention was easily turned into charges of power-seeking and tyranny, though, whether or not Chrysostom had any canonical jurisdiction in Asia, the fact that appeal had been made to him probably justified his actions, which also apparently had the backing of the imperial court.[159]

Indeed, ultimate responsibility lay with the court and its inconsistent attitudes to Chrysostom's episcopacy. Theophilus would have been powerless if Chrysostom had not offended those in high places. Despite his attempts not to take sides, his career provides illuminating comment on the vacillating politics of the turn of the century.[160] He was implicated in the struggles between Aurelian and Gainas after the fall of Eutropius, and made enemies among those with real power behind the throne. He exacerbated the crisis over the Goths by refusing to allow Gainas and his troops to have an Arian place of worship in the city, yet later he was the only one Gainas would negotiate with. Eudoxia's initial support for Chrysostom's active campaigns for charity and against Arians is well attested; yet his fearless denunciations were deliberately reminiscent of biblical models – he apparently likened Eudoxia both to Jezebel and Herodias. Arcadius was too weak to accept criticism, or to resist the competing influence of other powerful ecclesiastical figures. So Chrysostom became a martyr, and was indeed honoured as such by Arcadius' son, Theodosius II, when he brought back his relics to the capital with much pomp and celebration.

2 Chrysostom and Christian morals

The whole unfortunate episode is also a reminder that the conduct of church leaders was as much an issue at this time as their theological beliefs. Here the accusations centred on behaviour, treatment of people and use of church property. The appeal from Asia had been concerned with charges against clerics of

---

158 This point was convincingly argued by D. L. Powell in an unpublished paper entitled 'John Chrysostom and the Synod of the Oak' read at the Oxford Patristic Conference, September 1975; I am grateful to him for supplying a copy. Paul, bishop of Heracleia, was apparently the Synod's official president; see Kelly (1995), p. 218.

159 Liebeschuetz (1990), chapter 20.

160 Liebeschuetz (1990), Cameron and Long (1993); older views that there were pro- and anti-Goth parties in Constantinople are no longer accepted. Cf. pp. 235–7 below on Synesius' presence and account of the events surrounding the Gothic influence.

giving and receiving bribes to obtain ecclesiastical office. The standards expected of churchmen presented a real problem in a period in which the Church acquired great treasures, and ecclesiastical office had become an attractive public career with power, influence, riches and patronage.[161] The Church was caught in a dilemma. Once her members had been the 'elect', a small minority of the saved with very high standards of conduct, and a tradition of opposition to the status quo. Now the Church was part of the establishment, dedicated to upholding the prosperity of the empire under God. Socrates bears witness to the fact that the old rigorist sect of the Novatians had not only survived but was attractive to his generation, and the monastic movement is powerful testimony to the fact that many saw a serious lowering of standards as the Church accommodated itself to a new role in the secular world. The preaching career of Chrysostom provides further comment on the situation. His life was a campaign for the purity of Christian life in the world as well as in the ascetic's cell and at every level of the Church hierarchy. Sadly but understandably, he reaped his reward, and his acts recoiled upon him.

As a young man, Chrysostom had embraced the monastic life.[162] He had been educated to take his place in the world; though he himself never refers to this openly, he is said to have been the most eloquent pupil of the famous sophist, Libanius, and according to Sozomen[163] was destined to be his successor if he had not been stolen by the Christians. The legacy of this is seen in his powerful use of rhetoric, employing all the standard metaphors of the textbooks,[164] and perhaps especially in his capacity to ape the theatre, which he also consistently condemned – he had a strongly ambivalent locus in relation to 'Greek' (pagan) culture, and his works suggest implicit criticism of Libanius.[165] At the age of eighteen he became dissatisfied with worldly ideals, was baptized, probably studied with Diodore, later to be bishop of Tarsus, and in his early twenties became a lector in the orthodox group in Antioch led by Meletius; these formative years were prior to the Council of Constantinople in 381, a time when Arianism was in the ascendant and the orthodox in Antioch were split. He seems to have experimented with an ascetic home-life in response to the wishes of his widowed mother, but later, possibly after her death, retired to the mountains and caves. There he permanently damaged his health with excessive mortifications of the flesh. He retreated in 378, and his earliest works[166] are

---

161 Cf. Cyril of Jerusalem and the accusations about a robe dedicated to the church, p. 187 above.

162 Brändle (2004) is a useful introductory outline of Chrysostom's biography; but see Kelly (1995) for more detail.

163 Sozomen, HE viii.2; the veracity of Sozomen's report has been contested, but see the arguments of Hunter (1988, 1989) to the effect that Chrysostom was implicitly attacking Libanius in his early works, A Comparison between a King and a Monk and Against the Opponents of the Monastic Life. Hunter defends the authenticity of the former, given, among other things, the quotations of Libanius and the similarities with the latter.

164 Ameringer (1921).

165 Hunter (1988); Leyerle (2001).

166 These include the works on monasticism and virginity listed in notes 171 and 173 below; the apologetic works – see Schatkin and Harkins (1985) and Schatkin et al. (1990); and the two treatises on the Subintroductae – see Dumortier (1955); Leyerle (2001).

dated between this return from the desert and his priesting in 386; twelve years later he was 'kidnapped' and consecrated bishop of the capital city. Already as a priest in Antioch, his fame as a pulpit orator was worldwide: as the author of many books, he appears in Jerome's *De viris illustribus* which dates from 392, six years before Chrysostom was translated to Constantinople. His homilies derive from the twelve years preaching in Antioch, and five and a half years in Constantinople.

Retreat from the caves did not mean retreat from his ideals, though his relationship with ascetics was distinctly ambivalent. A link between Chrysostom's apologetics and his ascetic works has been discerned: he was concerned for the moral life of Christians especially as perceived by pagan critics – he wanted to counter both Libanius and Julian, whose stay in Antioch was a mere twenty years or so before.[167] He particularly challenged the idealistic lifestyle of those who lived in a 'spiritual marriage' in the city, and expected monks to stay in the mountains.[168] His relations with monks and ascetics in Constantinople seem to have been particularly fraught[169] – their independence of his episcopal authority was doubtless a key factor. Yet monks lived the life of angels and provided patterns of Christian perfection.

There have been some who have suggested that Chrysostom softened his standards when he became involved in pastoral work, and certainly there is a difference in atmosphere between his negative descriptions of marriage in the early work *De virginitate* and his more positive preaching to his largely married congregations. But the change was not so much a relaxing of standards as a deeper realization of the demands of Christian perfection. Like so many of his contemporaries, Chrysostom began by understanding Christian perfection in terms of the philosophic ideals of detachment and otherworldliness; but then, like Basil, he realized that to be like God meant love and generosity towards other human beings.[170] Yet in enlarging his views, Chrysostom did not alter his fundamental position. To love meant to be involved; but it also meant detachment from the selfish passions associated with sex, with the possession of riches and with worldly success. Christian perfection was to be the aim of all believers, whether or not they withdrew from the battle and distraction of city life.

As early as his treatises on monasticism,[171] written while still young and enthusiastic about the ascetic ideal, Chrysostom refused to admit a double standard: there was no difference between the monk and the man of the world apart from

---

167 Wilken (1983); Hunter (1988).

168 Leyerle (2001).

169 Liebeschuetz (1990); Cameron and Long (1993).

170 Meyer (1933); cf. Leroux (1961, 1975); also Murphy (1972).

171 These include (1) the letters to Theodore, probably but not certainly of Mopsuestia, on his relapsing from the monastic life (see Carter 1962); text – Dumortier (1966); ET in *NPNF*; (2) an appeal to opponents of monasticism, *Adversus oppugnatores vitae monasticae*; ET Hunter (1988); and (3) a couple of works on remorse, *De Compunctione*; ET Christo (1998): texts in *PG* 47. The rhetorical exercise comparing the king and the monk, on the model of Plato's contrast between the tyrant and the philosopher in *Republic* ix, is often regarded as spurious (Aldama 1965, n. 327, and Carter 1970, p. 20); but cf. Hunter (1988) and note 163 above.

the fact that one took a wife and the other did not.[172] In his works on virginity,[173] it is clear that idealization of chastity did not mean total disparagement of marriage – that was to despise God's good creation and was the way of the heretic; it was because marriage was good that virginity was the greater attainment.[174] He always admitted that in some ways life was really easier for the monk: he battled in a less demanding arena than those who stayed in the world; he suffered less from distractions, from temptations and the demands made by others; he more readily found peace and philosophy.[175] In the *De Sacerdote*,[176] a revealing dialogue indicating his high estimate of the responsibilities of the priesthood and certainly his best-known work, Chrysostom confesses to having deceived his friend Basil and deliberately evaded the challenges and temptations of ordination (though whether the incident is historical is a matter of dispute).[177] He retreated to find solitude, to find purity and holiness. This work on the priesthood, probably composed soon after his ordination, contrasts the active and contemplative lives, and Chrysostom shows no doubt about which he now felt was superior, at least for those great enough to cope with the demands. Throughout his subsequent life, his constant problem was living and preaching his puritanical ideals as the standard for all Christians in the world. Simplicity, purity, holiness, an independence of worldly goods and concerns, concern rather for the poor and the kingdom of heaven – such are the recurring themes of Chrysostom's exhortations, and the examples to which he appeals are the monks and ascetics. If he expected such behaviour from lay people, still more did he expect it of the clergy. His demanding standards are particularly evident in his tirade against the practice of consecrated virgins housekeeping for ascetic or celibate priests:[178] the mere possibility of scandal, let alone the reality of it was enough to cause him disquiet. We can well believe that he was intolerant of clerical lapses as well as being a scathing critic of extravagance and worldliness. Chrysostom is an example of the monk-bishop who interiorized the desert while serving the city.[179]

The flavour of Chrysostom's moral teaching can readily be sampled by reading the short treatise *On Vainglory and the Education of Children*. In the eighteenth and nineteenth centuries, this little work was rejected as spurious

---

172 *Adversus oppugnatores vitae monasticae*, PG 47.372.

173 Besides the *De virginitate* (text: Musurillo and Grillet 1966; ET Shore 1983), Chrysostom wrote some small works on widowhood, against second marriages, etc. Texts: Grillet and Ettlinger (1968).

174 *De virginitate* viii–x.

175 *Adversus oppugnatores vitae monasticae*, PG 47.373–4.

176 Text: Malingrey (1980); ET in *NPNF* series I, vol. IX, and Neville (1964).

177 The friend Basil whom Chrysostom deceived was identified by Socrates (*HE* vi.3) as Basil of Caesarea; but this can hardly be correct. Basil appears nowhere else in Chrysostom's works, not even his correspondence, which is rather surprising in view of the intimacy indicated in the dialogue. Perhaps Basil was a literary fiction, or at least a fictitious name; Sterk (2004) suggests Chrysostom was inspired in this work by Gregory Nazianzen, *Orat.* 2, and Basil *was* Gregory's friend.

178 In two pastoral letters, *Adversus eos qui apud see habent virgines subintroductas*, text: Dumortier (1955). See Clark (1977); Leyerle (2001).

179 Sterk (2004), chapter 6.

(it does not appear in Migne's *Patrologia*); but it was rehabilitated by the work of S. Haidacher, and is now generally regarded as a genuine and illuminating document.[180] The integrity of the work has been questioned, but in fact the conjunction of these two topics is very significant.[181] Chrysostom begins by deploring the fact that κενοδοξία (vainglory) has even invaded the Church, and after a sophistical proof that men deceive themselves by seeking honour from others, he turns to the question of inculcating true values into the young. Interestingly enough, he repudiates any attempt to advise parents to educate their offspring for monasticism;[182] rather he wishes to establish high moral standards within the conditions of the world. His demands are rigorous – no theatre or amusements, biblical stories instead of fables, no young women;[183] yet at the same time, he admits the need for lightheartedness, for an appreciation of beauty and for genuine relationships resting on respect even for a younger brother, or indeed servants. Gold and silver may be condemned as unnecessary for life; but Chrysostom's ideals are far from wholly negative.

In fact, for all the reports of his harshness and excessive zeal for temperance, in spite of repeated condemnations of pomp and extravagance, of luxurious eating and drinking, of games and the theatre, of ornate dress and make-up, Chrysostom does show appreciation of the good things of life. It was not riches in themselves that Chrysostom blamed, but rapacity and arrogance. Wine and wealth should not be despised; they are God's good gifts. 'Wine was given by God, not that we might be drunk, but that we might be sober, that we might enjoy ourselves, not that we might suffer pain.'[184] 'God made you a rich man, why make yourself poor? God made you rich so that you could help those in need'; though Chrysostom adds that an important motive for doing so is 'that you may have release from your sins through generosity to others'.[185] Even a wife is a blessing; for she can 'gently soothe her husband when he comes home harassed from business'.[186] To despise good things was to fall into the heresy of the Manichees.

---

180 On *Vainglory and the Education of Children:* Haidacher's introduction and German translation (1907) was followed by critical editions of the text by F. Schulte (1914) and B. K. Exarchos (1954). The most recent and reliable work is the edition by Malingrey (1972). English translation in Laistner (1951).

181 The abrupt change in topic and some stylistic differences have been stressed, but do not seem sufficiently serious to suggest that this is a composite work.

182 Though earlier he had advocated sending boys to monasteries for moral education: *Adversus oppugnatores vitae monasticae, PG* 47.319–86. For a detailed study of Chrysostom's views on education, see Danassis (1971). For the pedagogical dimensions of Chrysostom's work, see Maxwell (2006).

183 For a discussion of the rhetorical role of the theatre and games as metaphors for the abyss, corruption and death, see Retzleff (2003), pp. 195f.

184 *De statuis* i.4, *PG* 49.22.

185 *De statuis* ii.8, *PG* 49.43. For Chrysostom on wealth and poverty see Roth (1999).

186 *Hom. in Jn.* lxi.3, *PG* 59.340. See Roth and Anderson (1997) for translated texts on marriage and family life.

3 The goodness of God

Indeed, the goodness and bounty of God, his mercy and φιλανθρωπία (love for humankind) is a constant theme of Chrysostom's preaching. He was adored by the populace because he chastised the Pharisaical with his wit and condemned the prosperous and insensitive, while offering the poor and the sinner the mercy of a kind and loving Father. The tension between his rigorous standards and his open acceptance of the penitent was already noted by Socrates. Throughout his account of John's life, Socrates had emphasized the excessive harshness with which he tried to root out evil in the Church, and at the end he commented:

> Indeed it is most inexplicable to me, how with a zeal so ardent for the practice of self-control and blamelessness of life, he should in his sermons appear to teach a loose view of temperance. For . . . he did not scruple to say, 'Approach although you may have repented a thousand times'. For this doctrine, many even of his friends censored him.[187]

Yet it was this which more than anything else fired Chrysostom in his exhortations. His most frequent theme is an appeal to ἐλεημοσύνη (eleēmosynē), a word which has roughly the same double sense as the English 'charity'.[188] In most cases, his appeal is a practical call to almsgiving. In a society of extreme poverty and excessive riches, Chrysostom constantly urged his hearers to practise generosity, to relieve suffering, to recognize Christ among the poor. 'The rich man is not the man who owns a lot, but the man who gives a lot.'[189] Riches, like fresh air, sun and water, should be held in common.[190] But this was no socialist programme,[191] nor was it simply a call to good works to earn treasure in heaven rather than on earth. For ἐλεημοσύνη meant more than charitable donations. On one occasion he pictured ἐλεημοσύνη as a dove interceding on our behalf at the judgment, taking us under her wings and saving us from punishment. She it was who saved humankind, for if God had not had mercy on us (ἠλέησεν ἡμᾶς – eleēsen hēmas), all would have been lost. She reconciled us while we were still enemies; she brought about myriads of good things; she persuaded the Son of God to become a slave and empty himself. 'Let us, beloved, strive after her through whom we are saved', Chrysostom continues. 'Let us love her, let us value her more than money . . .' God prizes her more than sacrifice. Nothing is more characteristic of a Christian than ἐλεημοσύνη. But it does not stem from us first; for God had already shown his mercy towards us.[192]

This mythical personification is a characteristic trick of sophistry, but for Chrysostom's age it was an effective way of making his appeal. More important

---

187 Socrates, HE vi.21.

188 Brändle (1977); Plassmann (1961); Vandenberghe (1961), chapter VII. For more general treatments of almsgiving, see Quère-Jaulmes (1966); Constantelos (1968); Young (1977); Leyerle (1994). For translated texts see Roth (1999).

189 De statuis ii.5, PG 49.40.

190 De statuis ii.7, PG 49.43.

191 Though see Greeley (1982).

192 Hom. in Heb. xxxii.3, PG 63.223.

than the style is the nature of the appeal. Philanthropic works are grounded in God's own 'philanthropy'; for φιλανθρωπία means literally 'love of humanity'. The classic studies of Chrysostom invariably enquire how far his thought was Pelagian; but surely that is an inappropriate question. The paradox of divine grace and human freedom would not become a controversial issue until four years after his death. Chrysostom was well aware that in the achievement of salvation neither God's grace nor human effort was sufficient without the other. Thus he often coupled both emphases: in willing lies everything, with grace from above;[193] virtue comes neither wholly from God nor simply from ourselves; the grace of the Spirit leads us.[194] Augustine as well as Pelagius found passages in Chrysostom to support his case.[195] Chrysostom undoubtedly urged his hearers to make considerable moral effort; yet few were more conscious of the fact that it was God's love which was the motive of all Christian action. He certainly preaches a doctrine of merit at times, but he also glories in the salvation gratuitously given by God, and is not wholly insensitive to Paul's doctrine of justification by grace through faith.[196] On Romans 1.17, for example, Chrysostom points out that it is 'not your own righteousness, but that of God. . . . For you do not achieve it by toilings and labour, but you can receive it as a gift from above, contributing one thing only, namely "believing".'[197] Further, it is because of God's love displayed in the incarnation that there are constant opportunities for repentance, at least until the final judgment. Repentance can always heal human failings, and true repentance involves not only recognition and confession of sins with humility, prayers and tears, but also much ἐλεημοσύνη, renunciation of anger, evil and all kinds of sin, conversion of others from their wanderings and bearing all things with gentleness.[198] The answer to Socrates' perplexities is that Chrysostom preached no cheap forgiveness, but a gracious though demanding God who calls on people to respond with true Christian holiness.

Chrysostom, preacher, pastor and pedagogue, was well aware that people generally respond to concrete pictures rather than abstract conceptions. God is graphically presented as Father, Judge or King; his anger appears in disaster, his love when people turn in repentance. A mixture of fear, respect and somewhat subservient love is the attitude with which God should be approached; yet the marvellous thing about being in Christ is that it gives people παρρησία (freedom of speech) before God.[199] This freedom, this possibility of standing before God with the self-confidence almost of a trusted confidant, is a frequent theme in Chrysostom. Thus, in many ways the God of Chrysostom is highly anthropomorphic; and the language used of the incarnate Son is understandably even more personal – he is our brother and companion, our leader and advocate, our guide and priest. Salvation is expressed in parables of personal relationships. Indeed, if we try to analyse in logical or literal terms the ways

---

193 *Hom. in Heb.* xiii.5, PG 63.110.
194 *Hom. in Heb.* xxxiv.2, PG 63.234.
195 See Baur (1907), pp. 6f.; Thonnard (1967).
196 *Pace* von Campenhausen (1963), p. 144. Cf. Coman (1968); Gorday (1983).
197 *Hom. in Rom.* ii.6, PG 60.409.
198 *Hom. in Heb.* ix.4, PG 63.80f.
199 Cf. van Unnik (1963).

in which Chrysostom preaches salvation, we are bound to find a fundamental inconsistency between two approaches: on the one hand, he stresses the activity of God's love in dealing with evil and overcoming the devil, on the other hand, he emphasizes the grace of our High Priest winning round an offended Father by his sacrifice. Chrysostom does not seek to integrate these graphic pictures into any theological system: both are pictorial ways of presenting the significance of the cross. Only when it comes to helping his congregations sort out the issues raised by contemporary battles with heresy, does he use the more technical formulae concerning God's nature, and even here, he avoids the abstruse to a remarkable extent. His first sermon against the followers of Eunomius is a typical example.[200] After a topical reference to the absence of Bishop Flavian, he turns to the lovely hymn to love in 1 Corinthians 13. Love is the essential characteristic of the Christian life, and it surpasses knowledge. Scripture shows this in many places and further insists that God is greater than human comprehension can conceive. 'I know God is everywhere, and wholly present everywhere, but how, I know not, I know he is without beginning, derivation or end, but how, I know not.' God's judgments are inscrutable and his ways indiscernible. We can only know in part. Scriptural allusion and quotation abounds, and far from proceeding with abstract argument, Chrysostom creates a sense of wonder and of worship, honouring a God beyond our deepest imaginings. The mystical flights and metaphysical arguments of Gregory of Nyssa seem to lie behind much of what Chrysostom says, but he turns it into a simple but profound faith for his mixed congregation of city dwellers. The blasphemous arrogance of the heretics contrasts with his call to humility and the repeated exhortations to prayer found in the subsequent homilies of this series.

4 Chrysostom's Christology

As in theology, so in Christology[201] Chrysostom's approach is fundamentally practical. Having accepted the Nicene *homoousion*, he is obliged to comment on scriptural texts which seem to imply a quite different understanding of Jesus Christ. He resorts to distinguishing between his titles, functions and attributes κατ' ἀνθρωπότητα (at the human level) and those κατα θεότητα (at the divine level), a position often characterized as fundamentally Antiochene,[202] though

---

200 There are a number of sermons against the Anomoeans, whose grouping in the manuscripts is confused; for details, see studies by Malingrey (1970, 1973) and introductions to editions and translations: Malingrey (1970, 1994) and Harkins (1984) – it is suggested that 1–10 in the Montfaucon numbering were preached in Antioch in 386–7, and 11–12 in Constantinople. Malingrey (1970) provides a critical edition of the first group of five.

201 Lawrenz (1996) offers a basic study of Chrysostom's Christology.

202 Lawrenz (1996), p. 28 notes that Grillmeier claimed that Chrysostom was more Alexandrian than Antiochene in his Christology. One must recall that Athanasius distinguished those things done *qua* man and *qua* God when faced by the same exegetical exigencies; and Lawrenz documents the fact that like Athanasius, Chrysostom tends to speak of the human nature of Christ as his *sarx*. Maybe the conventional labels are not always helpful in analysis.

not yet the subject of controversy. That Chrysostom should adopt Antiochene procedures is not at all surprising in view of the fact that his theological teacher was Diodore, who may be regarded as the father of the Antiochene School.[203] Yet for Chrysostom the procedure is not just a theoretical convenience. It has highly practical effects. For it allows him a thoroughly realistic exegesis of Jesus the man, the pioneer, undergoing suffering, overcoming temptation and leading his brethren to glory; but there are times when it leads him into paradox. How can Christ sit as Judge and stand as suppliant-priest at the same time? Chrysostom first remarks on his eternal intercession for us, and later in the same sermon insists that his priesthood is not eternal but only a function of the incarnation; he only needed to make one sacrifice and then for the future he can take his throne. His priesthood refers to his humanity (ἀνθρωπότης), though when speaking of his humanity it is humanity θεότητα ἔχουσα (having godhead) that is referred to, and the persons should not be divided.[204] Chrysostom is already, though perhaps rather naïvely, wrestling at a practical and exegetical level with the theological difficulties which became central in the ensuing controversies. He is also struggling with the terminology: on Philippians 2.5–11, he comments:

> Remaining what he was, he took that which he was not . . . Let us not confuse or divide the natures. There is one God, one Christ, the Son of God; when I say one, I mean ἕνωσις (union), not σύγχυσις (confusion); one nature did not change into the other, but was united with it.[205]

Chrysostom refused to hazard an answer to the question, How?[206] It was an ineffable, indefinable union.[207] One thing he was clear about was that the incarnation involved συγκατάβασις (descent, condescension), the divine nature being revealed by accommodation to the human level.

5 Sacramental doctrine

In dogmatics, Chrysostom popularized rather than contributed; in liturgy, however, composition and innovation have been attributed to him by tradition. It is difficult to ascertain his precise contributions and the liturgy which bears his name certainly comes from a much later date. Nevertheless, his comprehensive works provide many details illuminating the worship and liturgy of his time and his teaching on baptism and Eucharist provides important evidence for late fourth-century practice and theology.[208]

In this connection, Harkins' English translation of his *Baptismal Instructions* is of particular importance.[209] Here we have brought together for the first time

---

203 See below, Chapter 6, Section II.
204 *Hom. in Heb.* xiii.3, PG 63.106.
205 *Hom. in Phil.* vii.2, 3, PG 62.231f.
206 *Hom. in Jn.* xxvi.I, PG 59.154.
207 *Hom. in Jn.* xi.2, PG 59.89.
208 For a comprehensive introduction to the study of liturgy, see Bradshaw (2002).
209 Harkins (1963); see also Riley (1974).

in easily accessible form catechetical homilies from various partly overlapping collections. The collection of Chrysostom's works produced by Montfaucon (and reprinted in Migne) contains only two homilies delivered to candidates for baptism, but others were found and published by Papadopoulos-Kerameus in Russia in 1909, and more still, discovered at the Stavronikita monastery on Mount Athos, were published in the Sources Chrétiennes series by Wenger in 1957.[210]

A striking feature of these homilies is the vivid sense that the baptized are transferring from one side to the other in a real conflict between God and the devil. They are now soldiers of Christ, and faith is a contract made with God through the Spirit. The newly enlisted must expect ambush and attack from the enemy; he must be alert and thoroughly renounce his old ways. He is warned against worldliness and the specific manifestations of it which constantly appalled Chrysostom – luxury and gluttony, expensive adornment and make-up, the theatre and circus, oaths and superstitions. The moral demands of the Christian life figure far more than the need for correct dogmatic affirmations. These homilies provide excellent examples of Chrysostom's primary concerns, and of his preaching techniques, his superb mastery of scriptural phraseology, of typology and of image and parable.

But more to our purpose here, the discourses now available provide liturgical evidence on a par with the *Mystagogical Catecheses* of Cyril of Jerusalem,[211] and more reliably dated; for it is pretty clear that they come from Chrysostom's Antiochene period and almost certainly from the years 388–90. Quite apart from containing fairly detailed evidence concerning the actual rites practised at the time, these homilies confirm the stark realism which had already been noticed elsewhere as a feature of Chrysostom's attitude towards the sacraments. Baptism is not a simple washing away of sin, but a melting down and remoulding;[212] thus Chrysostom emphasizes that the genuine re-creation involved (the cross, the death and resurrection) is more than symbolic. The eucharistic elements are not just consecrated bread and wine symbolizing the body and blood of Christ; for 'the devil flees at the sight of one returning from the Master's table with mouth and tongue stained with his precious blood.'[213] That the eucharistic bread and wine actually constitute the body and blood of Christ slain on the altar, a fearful and holy sacrifice, Chrysostom often emphasized. On one occasion,[214] he set himself to elucidate the paradox that there is one Christ who died once for all, and yet countless and repeated celebrations of the Eucharist; the mere fact that this posed a problem is indicative of Chrysostom's usual assumption that in the elements Christ is actually present and what is offered is a real sacrifice. However, once faced with the explicit problem of the relationship between the cross and the Eucharist, Chrysostom affirms the fact that what is offered is the

---

210 Wenger (1957).

211 Riley (1974) provides a study of the evidence for baptismal rites in the work of both these and other authors.

212 *Instruction* IX.21–2: Montfaucon-Migne 1 = Papadopoulos-Kerameus 1 (Harkins 1963, p. 138).

213 *Instruction* III.12: Stavronikita 3 = Papadopoulos-Kerameus 4 (Harkins, 1963, p. 60).

214 *Hom. in Heb.* xvii.3, PG 63.131.

same, not a different sacrifice, and not even a repetition of the original sacrifice; indeed, he has to resort to the explanation that 'we celebrate a memorial of a sacrifice', and even though the word *anamnēsis* has a stronger force than its English equivalent and carries with it the notion of realistic representation, nevertheless one cannot help feeling that this explanation is tamer than his very forceful language elsewhere. Chrysostom's language comes alive when one feels the pulse of devotion and the energy of his Christian lifestyle; exact theological definitions pale before his vivid pictures and lively exhortations.

6 Chrysostom's sermons and their hearers

More than anywhere else in patristic literature, in reading the homilies of Chrysostom one feels in touch with the semi-Christian populace,[215] so thoroughly human and alive, responsive to striking image and parable, appreciative of clever speaking and yet titillated by the unsophisticated amusements of early Byzantine city life. It can be shown that people from all walks of life, including women and slaves, were present in Chrysostom's congregation. They come over as a fickle crowd, lost without leadership, easily led astray, capable of riot and arson, but also of respect and hero-worship. Historians of social and cultural conditions in this period turn primarily to Chrysostom, who provides some of the richest source material. His sermons are full of delightful touches and revealing asides: beware of pickpockets while you are engrossed in the sermon! They also reflect the pluralist society of a city like Antioch, with Jews, pagans and various different Christian groups competing for attention.[216]

A number of occasional sermons have survived which are specifically linked with incidents in Chrysostom's career. His first sermon after ordination and sermons preached before and after his first brief exile are of personal interest. Others are linked with public incidents, like the two sermons delivered in Constantinople on the occasion of Eutropius' fall from power. But the best-known group, and the ones which better than any others give a graphic picture of the Antiochene populace and Chrysostom's relationship with it, are the twenty-one discourses *De statuis*.[217] It was these which established the young priest's reputation. The story is told not only by the Church historians but also by Libanius: in 387, at the news of extra taxes, the citizens of Antioch ran riot, and among other damage, smashed the imperial statues. When they came to their senses, they rushed to the church in fear of reprisals for such an insult to the imperial family. Bishop Flavian set out on an exhausting mission of appeal to the emperor, and while they awaited news, Chrysostom comforted and harangued

---

215 Extensive researches into the composition of Chrysostom's audience have been undertaken by Allen and Mayer: for example, Allen (1997) and Mayer (1997); other references listed in Mayer and Allen (2000). See also Hartney (2004) and Maxwell (2006).

216 For the Antioch years, see Wilken (1983); Maxwell (2006). Studies on Antioch are many: Festugière (1959); Liebeschuetz (1972); Wallace-Hadrill (1982).

217 Texts and translations: Migne, *PG* 49; *NPNF* vol. 9. See Paverd (1991) for a detailed reconstruction of events and the order of the Homilies, which were delivered during Lent; also the addition of some homilies to the collection.

the people from the pulpit day after day, urging them to repent, to amend their ways and to trust in God. He castigates them for their discontent at the penalties exacted by the royal commissioners. Finally he gives a moving account of Flavian's successful audience with the emperor. Chrysostom rose to the occasion and dealt with the issues of the moment; in such sermons one appreciates most his qualities as preacher and pastor.

Chrysostom's extant works are largely sermons, sermons for specific occasions, sermons for liturgical feasts, panegyrical sermons on saints and martyrs, sermons on themes – against the theatre, or for charity; but the majority of those surviving are exegetical sets of homilies covering Genesis and the Psalms, some of Isaiah, Matthew and John, Acts and all the Pauline epistles (which for Chrysostom included Hebrews). It is not exactly clear how these running commentaries in homily form were produced and published. The comparative lack of topical reference led Baur[218] to the view that, unlike other sermons which were taken down by stenographers as they were delivered, the exegetical homilies were composed and published by Chrysostom himself as a sort of literary commentary in homiletic form. Yet this conclusion is not satisfactory for material where there are extemporaneous asides or topical reference; nor does it fit passages which suggest a loss of structure as the preacher develops his discourse on the spot.[219] In the case of the Genesis homilies, we seem to have two editions of the first eight, and the double text is usually explained by attributing one to stenographers and the other to the issue of a more official and literary version; a certain roughness in the text, and asides referring to immediate distractions like the sacristan lighting the lamps, are features characteristic of one version more than the other. Perhaps this case provides some clue to the relationship between Chrysostom's preaching on a biblical book, and the written form in which the exegetical homilies mostly survive.

The individual homilies tend to fall into exegetical and exhortatory sections, the latter stressing Chrysostom's favourite moral themes and certainly having a basis in his regular preaching rather than in literary activity. Indeed, for the modern reader, the most disturbing aspect of Chrysostom's sermons is their chaotic form – the concluding exhortation is often long and usually bears little relation to the exegesis. Sometimes he ranges over several topics in long irrelevant digressions. His themes are repeated over and over again: in his ninety homilies on Matthew, for example, it is reckoned that he spoke on almsgiving forty times, poverty thirteen times, avarice more than thirty times and wealth wrongly acquired or used, about twenty times.[220] It seems that he received criticism for such things in his own time, since he insists that he preaches daily on almsgiving and love of one's neighbour because the congregation shows little sign of having learned the lesson,[221] and justifies his habit of ranging over many topics in one sermon by saying that, like a doctor, he does not imagine the same

---

218 Baur (1929/1959), long regarded as the standard biography, but now superseded.

219 Goodall (1979), pp. 72ff., examines two sample passages to make this kind of point, arguing that Chrysostom never revised these passages for publication, but they remain as taken down by stenographers.

220 Baur (1929/59), p. 217.

221 *Hom. in Matt.* lxxxviii.3, *PG*, 58.779.

medicine is suitable for all his patients.[222] With such comments, we can hardly regard these exegetical collections as purely literary creations divorced from Chrysostom's regular preaching task.

For the study of the biblical text and of exegetical methods in use at this date in Antioch and also Constantinople, these homilies have no rival.[223] Like others in the Antiochene tradition of exegesis,[224] Chrysostom repudiates allegorical flights of fancy and treats the text as straightforwardly as possible. His main aim is to indicate and elucidate the meaning of the text for his congregation, noting where the stops should come, explaining difficult words or phrases, bringing out the sense by reference to the context or other usages elsewhere. He does not shrink from accepting that much of the Old Testament refers to mundane and even immoral matters and is to be taken as history, not symbol, as literal (though interim) commandments, not spiritual directives in veiled form; indeed he regards it as a universal law of scripture that it supplies the interpretation if an allegory is intended, so as to prevent the uncontrolled passion of those bent on allegorizing from penetrating everywhere without system or principle. Yet he recognized the presence of metaphor and symbol, and saw scripture as the supreme act of God's condescension, a text in which to observe the divine pedagogy.[225] To see prophecies of the New Testament in the Old was not to allegorize but to recognize the voice of God: the Psalms could prove the divinity of Christ, because messianic references are embedded in the text, veiled until the fulfilment was revealed.

Chrysostom's perspective is that of a fourth-century churchman regarding the scriptural text as divine oracles, miraculously delivered to humankind in spite of their barbarity, in spite of the poverty of the writer's intellect – after all, Paul was a mere tent-maker![226] All the more remarkable, then, is Chrysostom's sensitive appreciation of the Pauline epistles as 'occasional' writings reflecting Paul's efforts to deal with pastoral problems; it is noticeable that he tries to understand the particular difficulties, to interpret the mind of the writer, to show what Paul's aim and intention was in the given situation, and emphasizes Paul's adaptability to different situations.[227] Appeal to Paul's purpose even provides the criterion for deciding between conflicting interpretations: that which is in harmony with the apostle's thought takes precedence over mere attention to words. In summaries, Chrysostom seeks to trace the thread of Paul's argument. Of course, the problems of his own time intrude: wherever Christological texts appear, the dangerous heresies which threaten Chrysostom's congregation easily become the subject of his exegesis; but Paul is made to teach a post-Nicene theology because he wrote the words of the Spirit, which have a

---

222 *Hom in Jn.* xxiii. 1, *PG*, 59.137f.

223 Translations of Chrysostom's exegetical homilies on the New Testament are to be found in *The Library of the Fathers*, Oxford 1840ff.; texts in *PG* 57, 59, 60, 61, 62, 63, or F. Field, *Ioannis Chrysostomi interpretatio omnium epistularum Paulinarum*, Oxford 1845–62.

224 On Chrysostom's exegesis, see Chase (1887); Garrett (1992); Mitchell (2000); Amirav (2003); on Antiochene exegesis, see Young (1989, 1997a, 1997b).

225 Garrett (1992).

226 *Hom. in Heb.* i.2, *PG* 63.15f.

227 Mitchell (2000).

cutting edge like a sharp two-edged sword.[228] In his day, Chrysostom could hardly have approached dogmatic matters in any other way. When it comes to texts on the Christian life and the call to Christian discipleship, then he is able to speak with deep passion and with quite remarkable insight into the challenge of the Gospel sayings and the depth of Paul's faith in God's saving mercy.

Chrysostom studies are complicated by considerable critical problems, due in large part to his exceptional reputation as orator, saint and martyr. In the first place a multitude of spurious writings has been attributed to him and copied in manuscript collections of his works; then his name accompanies enormous numbers of fragments in catenae and florilegia. The task of distinguishing the authentic is by no means complete. The abundant manuscript tradition is itself an *embarras de richesses* (Baur counted nearly 2,000 MSS, and more recent researches suggest that the total number will prove to be in the region of 3,000 to 4,000); besides, there are many ancient translations of his works which also frequently pose problems of authenticity. The result is that a complete critical text of his works is not yet available.[229]

In the course of this survey, many of the more important authentic works of Chrysostom have been mentioned, though for a comprehensive list, the *Clavis Patrum Graecorum* should be consulted. Some can be dated exactly, others are difficult to place; even the criteria on which the homilies have been assigned to certain periods of his life have been challenged.[230] Many of the literary treatises seem to be early, certainly those on monasticism, virginity and the priesthood; the homilies span the years of his priesthood and episcopate – those on Acts, Colossians, Thessalonians and Hebrews have usually been said to belong to Constantinople. After his exile Chrysostom's literary activity changed again,

---

228 *Hom. in Phil.* vi. 1, *PG* 62.218.

229 The difficulties in producing a critical text, even for a very limited amount of text, can be sampled by reading Goodall (1979). There has been a continuing upsurge in Chrysostom studies, much concentrated on cataloguing manuscripts, determining the authentic, producing critical texts and generally sorting out the critical problems. See especially: (i) Aubineau and Carter (1968, 1970). This major catalogue covers manuscripts in the British Isles, Western Europe and America. (ii) Aldama (1965) is a catalogue of all those parts of the Chrysostom corpus (*PG* 47–64) which were then regarded as spurious; this is now superseded by Geerard's *Clavis Patrum Graecorum*. (iii) The Patriarchal Institute for Patristic Studies in Thessaloniki co-ordinated work on Chrysostom, compiling a comprehensive Chrysostom Bibliography, establishing a Chrysostom library and collecting microfilms of Chrysostom manuscripts. (iv) The most comprehensive access to texts and English translations remains Migne, *PG* 47–64, and *NPNF* series I. 9–14, though modern editions and translations have been steadily increasing: Dumortier (1955, 1966, 1981); Wenger (1957); Goggin (1957, 1960); Malingrey (1961, 1964, 1968, 1970, 1972, 1980, 1994); Halton (1963); Harkins (1963, 1979, 1984); Musurillo and Grillet (1966); Grillet and Ettlinger (1968); Piédagnel (1982); Dumortier and Lifooghe (1983); Shore (1983); Schatkin and Harkins (1985); Hill (1986, 1990, 1992, 1998); Hunter (1988); Sorlin and Neyrand (1988); Brottier (1989); Hagedorn (1990); Piédagnel and Doutreleau (1990); Schatkin et al. (1990); Brändle et al. (1995); Roth and Anderson (1997); Christo (1998); Roth (1999); Mayer and Allen (2000).

230 Mayer (2005) sets out the varied conclusions reached over something like 400 years of scholarship, examines the criteria used and their validity, and suggests how an improved methodology might be established.

and it is largely through correspondence that he had continuing influence. About 236 letters are extant, showing a concern for over one hundred different persons. Through his correspondence, Chrysostom supported missionary endeavours, and attempted to present his own case to Pope Innocent. His correspondence is therefore far from devoid of interest.

He wrote most intimately to the rich deaconess, Olympias,[231] who had been associated with him in generous charitable works in Constantinople, and whose conduct in the affair of the 'Tall Brothers' Palladius had to defend along with Chrysostom's own. In these letters, Chrysostom is, of course, affected by the rhetorical conventions in which he had been so well trained. Yet at the same time a personal flavour pervades them, and the austere ascetic reveals his human sensibility. He is not averse to giving dramatic descriptions of his own physical sufferings; implicitly he confesses his lack of ἀπάθεια (passionlessness). Yet the impressive thing is that the focus is away from his personal hardships, grim though they were, to concern for Olympias. Her 'loss of heart' (ἀθυμία) he regards as a deeply serious matter. Suffering can become a 'great treasure' if faced in the right way. His words have all the more force because the experience of rejection, illness and physical hardship is his as well. The thought of the letters is particularly remarkable for its subtle blend of Stoic and Christian motifs. Like the Stoic, Chrysostom sees physical suffering as merely external, and encourages Olympias to be like a rock in the tempest or an impregnable citadel. However, biblical figures, particularly Job and Paul, are his examples, and the chief encouragement is the abuse and rejection suffered by Christ himself. The attitude recommended goes beyond Stoic ἀπάθεια to glorifying and praising God in the midst of tribulation, remembering his φιλανθρωπία, his love and care for humankind.

Most biographies of Chrysostom have difficulty in avoiding a hagiographical appearance, and the more one reads his works, the more admiration one feels for the quality of his preaching. If his style and methods of sermon construction fail to appeal to our taste, they were nevertheless the most effective method of communication in his time; it is no wonder that his great collections of exegetical sermons were carefully preserved and regularly read in the Greek-speaking Church. His brilliant use of sophistical conventions with flexibility and originality is hardly matched elsewhere – he has been described as a pure Atticist;[232] nor is his remarkable grasp of the Christian message as it spoke to his own day. He tried to recall a corrupt and officially Christian society to the standards preached in the gospels, his most frequent theme revolving around the social questions of wealth and property. He unavoidably speaks the language of the past and his works read as topical for an age long gone, but his vivid imagery, together with his love and understanding of the Bible and of erring human hearts, gives his work an abiding quality and relevance. Christianity is not simply a set of disputed doctrines, but a way of life, and Chrysostom never lets this be forgotten.

---

231 Text: Malingrey (1968). A study of the theme of suffering, though not confined to these letters, is Nowak (1972).

232 Goodall (1979), quoting Wilamowitz-Moellendorf; for Chrysostom's style and language, see further Ameringer (1921); Fabricius (1962).

For Further Reading

English translations

Christo, G. G., 1998. *St. John Chrysostom. On Repentance and Almsgiving*, FC 96, Washington, DC: Catholic University of America Press.

Goggin, Sister T. A., 1957, 1960. *Saint John Chrysostom. Commentary on Saint John the Apostle and Evangelist*, FC 33 and 41, New York: Fathers of the Church.

Halton, Thomas, 1963. *In Praise of St. Paul by John Chrysostom*, Washington, DC: Catholic University of America Press.

Harkins, P. W., 1963. *John Chrysostom. Baptismal Instructions*, ET, ACW 31, Westminster, MD: Newman Press.

——, 1979. *Saint John Chrysostom. Discourses against Judaizing Christians*, FC 68, Washington, DC: Catholic University of America Press.

——, 1984. *Saint John Chrysostom. On the Incomprehensible Nature of God*, FC 72, Washington, DC: Catholic University of America Press.

Hill, R. C., 1986, 1990, 1992. *St John Chrysostom. Homilies on Genesis 1–17, 18–45, 46–67*, FC 74, 82, 87, Washington, DC: Catholic University of America Press.

——, 1998. *St. John Chrysostom. Commentary on the Psalms*, vol. 1, Brookline, MA: Holy Cross Orthodox Press.

Hunter, David G., 1988. *A Comparison between a King and a Monk / Against the Opponents of the Monastic Life. Two treatises by John Chrysostom*, Lewiston, NY: Edwin Mellen.

Laistner, M. C. W., 1951. ET of *On Vainglory and the education of children* in *Christianity and Pagan Culture*, Ithaca, NY: Cornell University Press.

Mayer, Wendy and Pauline Allen, 2000. *John Chrysostom*, London and New York: Routledge.

Mayer, Wendy and Bronwen Neil, 2006. *John Chrysostom. The Cult of the Saints: select homilies and letters*, Crestwood, NY: St Vladimir's Seminary Press.

Moore, Herbert, 1921. *The Dialogue of Palladius concerning the life of Chrysostom*, London: SPCK.

Neville, G., 1964. *St. John Chrysostom. Six books on Priesthood*, London: SPCK; revised T. A. Moxon, Crestwood, NY: St Vladimir's Seminary Press.

Roth, Catharine P., 1999. *St. John Chrysostom. On Wealth and Poverty*, Crestwood, NY: St Vladimir's Seminary Press.

—— and David Anderson, 1997. *St. John Chrysostom. On Marriage and Family Life*, Crestwood, NY: St Vladimir's Seminary Press.

Schatkin, Margaret A. and P. W. Harkins, 1985. *St. John Chrysostom. Apologist*, including ET of the *Discourse on the Blessed Babylas and against the Greeks*, and the *Demonstration against the pagans that Christ is God*, FC 73, Washington, DC: Catholic University of America Press.

Shore, Sally Rieger, 1983. *John Chrysostom. On Virginity. Against Remarraige*, Lewiston, NY: Edwin Mellen.

Studies

Brändle, Rudolf, 2004. *John Chrysostom, Bishop, Reformer, Martyr*, ET Strathfield, NSW: St. Paul's.

Kelly, J. N. D., 1995. *Goldenmouth: The Story of John Chrysostom, Ascetic, Preacher, Bishop*, London: Duckworth.

Leyerle, Blake, 2001. *Theatrical Shows and Ascetic Lives: John Chrysostom's Attack on Spiritual Marriage*, Berkeley/Los Angeles/London: University of California Press.

Liebeschuetz, J. H. W. G., 1990. *Barbarians and Bishops in the Reign of Arcadius*, Oxford: Oxford University Press.

Maxwell, Jaclyn L., 2006. *Christianization and Communication in Late Antiquity*, Cambridge: Cambridge University Press.

Mitchell, Margaret M., 2000. *The Heavenly Trumpet: John Chrysostom and the Art of Pauline Interpretation*, Hermeneutische Untersuchungen zur Theologie 40, Tübingen: Mohr Siebeck.

Sterk, Andrea, 2004. *Renouncing the World Yet Leading the Church*, Cambridge, MA: Harvard University Press.

Wilken, Robert L., 1983. *John Chrysostom and the Jews: Rhetoric and Reality in the Late Fourth Century*, Berkeley: University of California Press.

V Nemesius of Emesa

Nemesius too was concerned about ethics and God's providence, but he was an altogether different character from Chrysostom. We have absolutely no information about Nemesius apart from what we can glean from his book *On Human Nature*,[233] but the character of this work is enough to indicate how different was his approach and personality.

1 The identity of Nemesius

On Human Nature is the impersonal work of a scholar exploring the great questions of the fundamental constitution, purpose, faculties and potential of humanity, an exploration carried out by means of the then conventional scholarly methods and probably drawing all its material from standard textbooks of the time. In fact, a common estimate of Nemesius' achievement is that his work is a totally unoriginal compendium of the received scientific knowledge of antiquity – though for Nemesius himself, of course, such an estimate would not be uncomplimentary, since he belonged to a period in which the ancients were to be respected and innovation was despised. In view of this, the overall perspective given to the discussion by his own understanding and purpose is in itself a remarkable indication of thoughtful handling of the knowledge received from his sources, however conventional his methods. Occasional inconsistencies betray his dependence on others, but surprisingly few on the whole. His discussion is often a salutary reminder of the complexity of the questions, and he never concludes an argument by dogmatizing. He has difficulty in integrating the polarities of his thought, at times, but even the greatest thinkers are not entirely consistent.

The character of the work has meant that the question of Nemesius' sources has been the primary matter discussed by scholars. For he has been regarded as of interest not for his own thought – for everything was plagiarized – but rather for preserving the thought of more distinguished contributors to Hellenistic

---

233 Text in Migne *PG* 40; Morani (1987); ET Telfer (1955).

science. It is clear that Nemesius drew a great deal on Galen, whose views he often explicitly discusses, though not always simply agreeing with him. More speculative is the ultimate attribution of many of his ideas to Posidonius, who is never mentioned. On the basis of Jaeger's studies, there was wide acceptance that Posidonius' ideas played an important part in Nemesius' work;[234] but that was in the period when classicists all accepted that Posidonius, the Stoic who in the first century BC adopted many Platonic ideas, was an original contributor to the development of Hellenistic philosophy in general and Middle Platonism in particular. Subsequently, the very limited extent of our knowledge of Posidonius has become more widely recognized,[235] and this must in itself reopen the question of Nemesius' sources. In fact, his immediate sources are probably largely untraceable; for when Nemesius puts forward the views of older authorities like Plato and Aristotle, he usually seems to be quoting handbooks or commentaries rather than working from personal acquaintance with the texts.[236] The views which have been attributed to Posidonius were probably part of the received wisdom of school philosophy in Nemesius' time, and certainly some were commonplace in the more recent thinking of a Neoplatonist like Iamblichus – the unity and sympathy of all parts of the universe, for example. If it is true that only in Nemesius do we find the integration of the two ideas that the universe has a graduated ascending order of being, and that humanity provides the link between the physical and spiritual worlds,[237] it is hazardous to assume that this connection originated centuries earlier in the work of Posidonius and Nemesius alone has preserved it. His use of Galen and, in some sections, his dependence on Origen's (largely lost) *Commentary on Genesis*, is more assured, though here again the conclusions are reached to a pretty fair extent by skilled deduction rather than concrete evidence.[238]

There are other teasing questions posed by this work. Who exactly was the obscure scholar who wrote it? At what date was it produced? It is first quoted in the seventh century and was used extensively by John of Damascus in the eighth, but otherwise there is no information apart from the manuscripts themselves. Several manuscripts, together with the seventh-century citations, attribute the work to Nemesius of Emesa, but others treat all or part of it as the work of Gregory of Nyssa, and John Damascene gives no indication of the author. The most natural assumption is that the otherwise unknown name, Nemesius of Emesa, does represent the author. But who was he? And when did he live? Presumably 'of Emesa' means that he was bishop of that Syrian city. Gregory of Nazianzus knew a Nemesius who was provincial governor of Cappadocia between 383 and 389.[239] He was not a Christian, but then most of this treatise is not explicitly Christian, and since Gregory urges his acquaintance to make

---

234 Jaeger (1914). English readers may observe the effect of Jaeger's work on Telfer's introduction and notes to his translation (1955).

235 Chiefly on the basis of the careful critical work of L. Edelstein in identifying the fragments of Posidonius. See Edelstein and Kidd (1972). For further discussion, see Dillon (1977), pp. 106ff.

236 Though Streck (2005) seems to think that he knew Aristotle's *Nicomachaen Ethics*.

237 As suggested by Reinhardt (1953).

238 See the important articles by Skard (1936, 1937, 1938, 1939, 1942).

239 Gregory Nazianzen, *Epp.* 198–201 and *Poem.* II.ii.7.

a serious study of Christianity, conversion is not out of the question. An ex-provincial governor could well have become a bishop soon after his baptism.[240] It is impossible to confirm such a speculation, but the date at least seems to fit the evidence of the treatise itself. The views of Apollinarius and Eunomius are discussed as if they are contemporaries, and the work reveals a rather circumspect approach to Origen. The name of Origen is mentioned only three times; on the first occasion his views are criticized and on the third a rather derogatory story about him, no doubt in popular circulation at the time, is used as an illustration. On the second occasion a very brief statement of Origen's account of memory is offered among other accounts and without comment (Jaeger saw reason to attribute this to the Neoplatonist philosopher of the same name rather than to the Christian Origen). In other words, when Origen's name is mentioned, it is never as an appeal to a respected authority; and yet there are many passages which are probably indebted to Origen's *Commentary on Genesis*, and Nemesius' thought seems to follow a mildly Origenist line on a number of occasions.[241] We may conclude that it had become foolhardy to reveal strongly Origenist sympathies, but formal condemnation had not yet taken place. Thus a date round about 395–400 seems most likely.

Can we glean any more about the author from his work? The large amount of anatomical and physiological information in the treatise strongly suggests that the author had studied medicine and knew the works of Galen and probably some other medical texts first-hand. This does not necessarily mean he was a professional physician. Caesarius, Gregory Nazianzen's brother, is the usual parallel cited: he studied medical science as part of a gentleman's liberal education, and on the basis of his knowledge gave medical advice in the imperial household; yet Gregory explicitly tells us that he was not a professional practitioner and never took the Hippocratic oath.[242] If Nemesius is correctly identified as Gregory's correspondent, then he was a trained lawyer rather than a physician.

So all we can say with any confidence is that Nemesius was the sort of person who could have written a work like this. So what is the treatise like? What was its purpose? What are its contents?

2 The work's purpose

Nemesius begins with an overall summary of his subject. He proposes the subject of human nature, and there is a general consensus that a human person is composed of soul and body. The trouble is that there are widely differing views about the nature of the soul and its relationship with the body, and it is therefore these matters which are to occupy his attention in the first place. In the course of the first summary chapter, Nemesius refers to the following authorities: Plotinus, Apollinarius, Aristotle, Plato, Moses and Paul. The discussion moves from a review of other people's philosophical conclusions to a presen-

---

240 This identification was proposed by Tillemont. For discussion, see Telfer (1955), p. 209.

241 See the first of Skard's articles listed.

242 Gregory Nazianzen, *Orat.* vii.10.

tation of the 'dual nature' of human persons – their links both with irrational animals and spiritual beings, their potential for good or evil – and concludes with ethical exhortation. Thus the introductory chapter reveals something of Nemesius' method and his purpose, and provides an overall perspective of understanding of his subject. Ultimately his concern is with moral questions, and his address is to the cultured and educated in general. His method is that of contemporary philosophical treatises, listing authorities, acknowledging different conclusions, arguing for the most reasonable position; but his purpose is to lead beyond the standard pagan discussions to a Christian viewpoint. So this treatise has often been described as a work of apologetic, but it is not by any means a conventional apologetic work; for it is far from dominated by specifically Christian themes. Rather it is a contribution to a philosophical discussion which was going on among Christian and pagan intellectuals alike, and Nemesius is still free to explore the possibility of various answers about the origin and nature of the soul, the extent of human free will, the proper ethical ideal and so on. What he succeeds in doing is to produce a rational account of humanity which integrates certain Christian standpoints into the prevailing scientific knowledge of antiquity, producing a coherent and attractive philosophical position which would have its own apologetic force.

Nemesius' second long section confirms these conclusions about the nature and purpose of his work. Here he turns to discussion of the soul, and again begins with a review of various philosophical approaches. Democritus, Epicurus and the Stoics are said to affirm that the soul is corporeal; but various different views of its material essence have been proposed. As these proposals are listed and the discussion proceeds to other possibilities, the following names are added to the list of those whose views are considered: Critias, Hippon, Heraclitus, Pythagoras, Dicaearchus, the Manichees, Ammonius the master of Plotinus, Numenius the Pythagorean, Xenocrates, Cleanthes, Chrysippus, the characters in Plato's Phaedo, Galen, Aristotle, Eunomius, and Apollinarius – several of these are discussed more than once. Anyone who recognizes these names will immediately notice that there is no sense in which a chronological history of philosophy is being offered. Rather the arrangement is topical: different kinds of views on the soul are reviewed, and the sources span nearly 1,000 years from the pre-Socratic philosophers to contemporary Christian thinkers. (Is it chance that they all happen to be heretics?) All are treated to the same courteous discussion, but the conclusion is eventually reached that 'the soul is not body, nor harmony, nor temperament, nor any other quality', but rather it is 'incorporeal being', which survives separation from the body. In a final few sentences Nemesius adds that while the proofs of Plato and others are difficult and obscure, except for the trained philosopher, for the Christian, the teaching of holy scripture is quite sufficient anyway; but for those who do not accept the scriptures, there are good reasons for adopting his conclusion. In other words, he seeks to reach a reasonable consensus with his pagan contemporaries on the nature of humanity.[243]

Clearly it is impossible to review the whole of this lengthy treatise in such detail. The contents of the third chapter on the union of soul and body will

---

243 See discussion in Young (1983).

be discussed later in another connection, and readers may be left to study for themselves[244] the bulk of this text with its fascinating details concerning how the ancients thought the human body works, its composition out of the classic four elements, its digestive and respiratory systems, its senses, how sense-perception is related to knowledge and thought, what the different parts of the brain do, and so on. Suffice it here to comment upon a few particular emphases which permeate this work.

3 A human being is a unity

The most striking thing about Nemesius' presentation of human nature is the fact that his overall picture is far from dualistic. A person can be analysed into a being composed of soul and body, and clearly soul and body are separable, as in death; and yet a live person is a psychosomatic whole in which body and soul are intimately united. 'A living creature is composed of soul and body; the body is not a living creature by itself, nor is the soul, but soul and body together.'[245] The soul is the driving force (ἐνέργεια) of muscular move-ment: 'Whatever movement takes place by the operation of nerves and muscles involves the intervention of soul, and is accomplished by an act of will.'[246] Soul also provides the ἐνέργεια in respiration: panting and sobbing accompany moments of great grief, and soul keeps respiration going during sleep, since it is essential for human life. So the physical and the 'psychic' are intimately woven together: τὸ ψυχικὸν συνεπλάκη τῷ φυσικῷ.[247]

Quite how this intimate union is achieved Nemesius is less able to under-stand, since it is not paralleled by other cases of mixing or union in the physical world. The soul has its own independent existence (in fact Nemesius is close to embracing an Origenist view of the soul's pre-existence[248]) and it is incorporeal. Being incorporeal it cannot suffer change by its association with the body, and yet it has established its presence in every part of the body. It preserves its own identity of being and yet modifies whatever it indwells without itself being transformed. Soul is not located in body and yet it is bound by habit to the body.[249] The intimate weaving together of τὰ ψυχικά and τὰ φυσικά is attributed to the providence of the Creator.[250] The Christian doctrine of the resurrection of the body becomes a natural corollary of the anthropological position adopted by Nemesius, though Nemesius makes little use of it,[251] and has somewhat of a tendency to oscillate between this insistence on the unity of body and soul, and an acceptance of the soul's independence.

---

244 Telfer (1955) provides an easily accessible translation and commentary.

245 PG 40.733; Telfer (1955), p. 393. For the translations, I am largely though not wholly quoting Telfer's version.

246 PG 40.708; Telfer (1955), p. 372.

247 PG 40.709; Telfer (1955), pp. 375f.

248 PG 40.573–6; Telfer (1955), pp. 282–5.

249 PG 40.596–7, 600; Telfer (1955), pp. 295–9.

250 PG 40.708; Telfer (1955), p. 373.

251 Only in the passage in the introductory chapter: PG 40.521–4; Telfer (1955), pp. 244, 246. See discussion below pp. 229–30.

However, his basic picture of a person's unitary being is intimately related to his views on ethics and providence. In the early part of his work, as we have seen, Nemesius treats humanity as the link between the physical and spiritual realms; humanity thus finds itself on the border between rational and irrational, and capable of following carnal pleasures or the direction of reason.[252] Now if Nemesius had imagined a great dichotomy between these two worlds, he would have been led into a strongly dualist view of a human person as a spiritual being trapped in flesh and seeking purification of the soul by escape from it, a view more or less presupposed by some then current ascetic enthusiasm. Nemesius, however, rejoices in human nature as crown and lord of the animal creation, for whose sake all else was created,[253] and he recognizes that there is a 'this-worldly' morality. A living creature cannot avoid 'passion' (which is in any case a highly ambiguous term);[254] a person needs to distinguish between good and bad passions,[255] rather than attempting to eliminate them altogether. Deeds of virtue are themselves performed κατὰ πάθος (with emotion). So the ethical aim must be to find the Aristotelian 'mean' with regard to the passions.[256] A person of worth can face grief with proper moderation of passion (μετριο-παθής), not overwhelmed by emotion but battling for mastery over it.[257]

Yet Nemesius also presents a higher ideal: in the face of grievous circumstances, 'the contemplative will be entirely unmoved (ἀπαθής), seeing that one has severed oneself from present things and cleaves to God',[258] God being depicted as above all mutability.[259] Has he betrayed his basic position? At first sight we do seem to have an inconsistency, and Nemesius himself fails to draw the threads very closely together. He makes the ancient distinction between the contemplative and the active life,[260] and he recognizes that there are two kinds of 'good' for humanity: one kind applies to the soul and body together, or to put it another way, to the soul as it makes use of the body, and the virtues are a good example of this; the other concerns the proper functions of the soul alone without involving the body, godliness (εὐσέβεια) or philosophic contemplation (ἡ τῶν ὄντων θεωρία) being the classic expression of this alternative.[261] These two ethical standards run parallel with the oscillation between his profound recognition of the soul's union with the body in humanity as we know it, and his insistence that the soul is an independent entity. Yet there are hints that he had a more coherent picture underlying his various comments, and that his 'purer' ideal did not imply a dualist position. He adopts the view that the soul has both rational and irrational faculties; so the passions are movements of the irrational soul.[262] And even the spiritual realm cannot be regarded as

---

252 PG 40.512; Telfer (1955), p. 236.
253 PG 40.525ff., 532ff.; Telfer (1955), pp. 248ff., 254ff.
254 PG 40.673; Telfer (1955), p. 348.
255 PG 40.676f.; Telfer (1955), p. 351.
256 PG 40.729; Telfer (1955), p. 390.
257 PG 40.688; Telfer (1955), p. 359.
258 PG 40.688; Telfer (1955), p. 359; cf. PG 40.776f.; Telfer (1955), p. 419.
259 PG 40.805; Telfer (1955), p. 443.
260 PG 40.685; Telfer (1955), p. 358.
261 PG 40.513; Telfer (1955), p. 236.
262 PG 40.676; Telfer (1955), p. 379.

beyond emotion, since there are pleasures of the soul just as there are pleasures of the body.[263] The contemplative life may be purer than the active life, but contemplation is itself a form of activity, though it takes place in stillness. (Similarly, God is unmoved, and yet is also the Mover.)[264] Nemesius, not with total clarity but certainly with courage, seems to be feeling his way towards the idea of sublimation of the passions rather than their suppression or denial. He refuses to oversimplify the questions of 'passion' and 'pleasure', any more than the nature and faculties of soul. In doing this he was following in the wake of important discussions deriving from Plato and Aristotle which the tendencies of Neoplatonic teaching and the ascetic movement in Christianity were in danger of submerging.

This interpretation of Nemesius' position makes sense of his discussion of freewill. Because humankind is physically composed of the various elements which make up the material universe, it is mutable; because humanity is endowed with reason and can deliberate about courses of action, it has free will. It is by exercising the power of choice and using reason that humanity can tame and direct the passions, and even, through contemplation of God, remain immutable (ἄτρεπτος).[265] Human badness is not inherent in the physical nature, but is simply the result of habits, wrong choices.[266] The noblest purpose of human beings is fulfilled when they make the right choices, and above all when they choose the purest pleasure of the soul – the activity of contemplation. The Platonic intellectual ideal is thus married to a Christian view of creation, and no blame can be attached to the Creator for the human plight. The glory of humanity is that it is a μικρός κόσμος – a mini-universe – in which the physical and spiritual are bound together according to the purposes of the Creator.[267] Thus humanity epitomizes the unity of all creation. There is no radical dichotomy between the physical and the spiritual, the corporeal and the incorporeal, for in humanity they are wedded together, forming part of an ordered hierarchy of created being, a chain in which humanity provides the crucial link. 'We may see herein', says Nemesius,

> the best proof that the whole universe is the creation of one God,[268] ... God created both an intelligible and a phenomenal order, and required some one creature to link these two together in such wise that the entire universe should form one agreeable unity, unbroken by internal incoherences. For this reason, then, humankind was made a living creature such as should combine together the intelligible and phenomenal natures.[269]

Thus in Nemesius' work, because of his interest in the unity of creation, we find the integration of the two traditional themes: humanity as the link between

263 PG 40.677–80; Telfer (1955), pp. 352ff.

264 PG 40.685; Telfer (1955), p. 357.

265 PG 40.776f.; Telfer (1955), pp. 418f.

266 PG 40.779f.; Telfer (1955), pp. 420f.

267 PG 40.533; Telfer (1955), p. 254. Cf. PG 40.713–17, and Telfer's comments, pp. 379–82.

268 PG 40.508; Telfer (1955), p. 229.

269 PG 40.512f.; Telfer (1955), pp. 235f.

physical and spiritual, and the creation as consisting of ascending orders of being. That this comes from a source is probable, though apparently it is unique to Nemesius among extant philosophical writings.[270]

4 Ethical and theological implications

Towards the end of his work, Nemesius drifts away from the central theme, human nature. His consideration of ethics naturally leads him on to a discussion of free will, fate and providence. A doctrine of fate removes all ethical incentive; yet human freedom is circumscribed by circumstances; and God's providence over all his unified creation is the only doctrine which satisfies Nemesius' analysis both morally and scientifically. Just as his unitary view of human nature is never completely undermined by his contemplative ideal, so his occasional admissions that God transcends the mutability of the creation do not detract from his insistence that God's providence oversees the smallest details. For God the Creator cannot be profaned by intimate knowledge of and loving care for his own creatures.[271] The brilliant design and utter goodness of creation is the basis for his understanding of humanity, its nature and its purpose. It was not unnatural for him to turn to the new theme of providence, for that provides the overall context for all his earlier discussions. It is a pity that his discussion tails off with every sign of incompleteness. Perhaps Nemesius died before completing his task.

Ethics and providence were classic talking points in ancient philosophy. So was the nature of the soul and the composition of the physical universe. What is it then that gives Nemesius' work a specifically Christian colouring?

Of course, Nemesius adopts views on creation, providence, free will and so on, which are consonant with Christian views, but interestingly enough, he often fails to press elements that are specifically Christian: for example, he assumes *creatio ex nihilo*, for he mentions it twice in passing, but this particular contentious subject is not specifically debated. Nemesius seeks a consensus with pagan philosophy rather than looking for conflict or being defensive about controversial points. For the most part it is incidental hints which point to the Christian motivation of Nemesius' overall discussion – the casual introduction of references to Hebrew ideas (probably picked up from his source, Origen), or to the scriptures, to Moses or Paul, or the occasional quotation of a text. Only three passages have a strong Christian colouring, and one of these is probably the least happy section of Nemesius' work. He is trying to indicate the characteristic and distinguishing marks of human beings as distinct from other creatures, and he begins by stating that there are two choice prerogatives which humanity shares with no other creature: first, through repentance they can gain forgiveness, and, second, their mortal body can be immortalized[272] – in other words, he turns to the credal affirmations of the forgiveness of sins and the resurrection of the body to provide his distinguishing characteristics,

---

270 Reinhardt (1953).
271 *PG* 40.805; Telfer (1955), p. 443.
272 *PG* 40.521ff.; Telfer (1955), pp. 244ff.

though he explores neither very deeply. Alongside this he adopts the pagan clichés that laughter is a peculiarity of the human animal and that human ability to learn and practise arts and sciences is also a distinguishing mark of the human species. This is one of the less well-integrated sections of Nemesius' work and the Christian motifs seem to be dragged in and rather baldly stated. However, the point of the remarks is to distinguish human nature both from irrational animals and from spiritual, angelic beings, with both of whom there is a kinship; so within Nemesius' overall account of the human position, it has a certain relevance and importance.

A little earlier in his introductory summary, Nemesius gave an account of the Fall, and here an important and characteristically Christian theme apparently fitted neatly into his argument. Humanity, the link between two worlds, was created neither mortal nor immortal: human destiny depended upon the exercise of this choice, whether one should give oneself up to bodily passions or put the good of the soul first. Adam was to be kept in ignorance of his potential until he achieved perfection; so he was forbidden to eat of the Tree of Knowledge. He disobeyed and so became the slave of his bodily needs, losing his chance of a higher life.[273] Such is Nemesius' account: however, for the bulk of his work, Nemesius writes as if the Fall had never happened, as if human potentialities were the same. So it is hardly surprising that he has been accused (slightly anachronistically) of Pelagianism. As for most of the Eastern Fathers, the theme of human free will and moral potential was so important to him that he failed to grasp the seriousness of the Fall in the intense way that Augustine perceived it.[274]

Did he then take no account of redemption in Christ? Again it is there in hints and no doubt if pressed, Nemesius would have stated that Christ reversed the Fall and therefore humanity had regained its original potentialities. But these characteristic Christian themes are not central to Nemesius' study, and the one passage[275] where he deals with the incarnation is the most unexpected feature of his work. For where many Christians were solving their Christological problem by appeal to the soul–body analogy, Nemesius virtually reverses the argument and illustrates his soul–body problem by appeal to the analogy of the Incarnate Word.

As we have noticed, Nemesius is at a loss to find a suitable analogy for elucidating the mysterious union of soul and body in human nature. Physical analogies imply either mixture, and therefore the transformation of the two entities into a third, or juxtaposition, which is not a real union. Neither will satisfy Nemesius in the case of the union of soul and body. The soul cannot be changed by association with the body or it would cease to be soul. The union must be without confusion (καὶ ἥνωται τοίνυν καὶ ἀσυγχύτως ἥνωται τῷ σώματι ἡ ψυχή). There is genuine union, since there is a community of feel-

---

273 *PG* 40.513ff.; Telfer (1955), pp. 238ff.

274 Streck (2005) discusses free will in Nemesius and Gregory of Nyssa, showing that both had the kind of optimistic anthropology that explains why anti-Pelagianism had little purchase in the East. Human free will could be aligned with God's will; with God's help it is possible to counteract the Fall.

275 For the following discussion, see Chapter III, 'On the Union of Soul and Body', *passim* (*PG* 40.592–609; Telfer (1955), pp. 293–304).

ing (συμπάθεια) throughout the whole living creature – it is one thing. As an incorporeal entity, the soul has located itself in every part of the body, as if giving up its independent existence, and yet without doing so. It makes important changes to the body without being in any way changed itself (τρέπουσα, but not τρεπομένη). It is not confined by the body – it is in a sense part of the universal mind – so it is not related to the body by location (ἐν τόπῳ) but by 'a habitual relation of presence there' (ἐν σχέσει) (and here Nemesius introduces a very surprising analogy) 'even as God is said to be in us'. The soul is bound to the body by habit, or by inclination (τῇ πρός τι ῥοπῇ) or by disposition (τῇ διαθέσει). Soul cannot be 'located' and when we say it is 'there', we mean its activity is there. To parallel this kind of relation with God's presence is perhaps not surprising, especially given that some posited a transcendent soul of which the souls of human beings were part; what is surprising is that Nemesius can give no more definite account of the soul–body union in which he so strongly believes.

Now many of the terms Nemesius has used in this discussion are remarkably close to the kind of language which was to become so prominent in the ensuing Christological debates. Indeed, quite quickly, Nemesius picks up the Christological theme, drawing attention to the parallel. The union of the divine Word with his humanity can be described in the same sort of way: 'For he continued thus in union without confusion and without being circumscribed' (ἐνωθεὶς ἔμεινεν ἀσύγχυτος καὶ ἀπερίληπτος). Having introduced the parallel, however, Nemesius tries to draw out a distinction, namely that the soul does somehow seem to suffer with the body, whereas the Word does not share in human infirmities, while sharing with humanity his own Godhead; indeed he thinks that the language he has been using applies more precisely to the incarnation than it does to the soul–body union. Yet it is difficult for him to specify exactly where the distinction lies in view of his earlier insistence that the soul suffers no change by association with the body; and furthermore, he goes on to quote a passage from Porphyry, which Porphyry intended to elucidate the soul–body union, but Nemesius uses it specifically in order to indicate that the Christian doctrine of the union of God and human being is not absurd or incredible. Whether Nemesius likes it or not, his analogies undoubtedly reduce the uniqueness of the incarnation. Because the soul is incorporeal, its union with the body must be without confusion or impairment of the superior, spiritual being; the union takes place because the soul can pervade the body throughout, without being invaded or changed itself. Neither the incarnation, nor the presence of God in humanity can he describe in fundamentally different terms.

In the succeeding chapter, it will be important to recall this brief contribution of Nemesius to the Christological discussion. Quite clearly he holds an 'Antiochene' view of the union of the immutable God–Word with the whole (body + soul) human being; yet this cannot involve for Nemesius a dualist doctrine of 'Two Sons'. Nemesius is at a loss to give an adequate account of the soul–body union, yet the union of soul and body is so close as to produce one living creature, humanity; even if he, or indeed other Antiochenes were at a loss to give a satisfactory account of the union of Word and humanity in Christ, this did not necessarily mean that they envisaged anything other than a real union in one individual. This was not a union by mere divine grace (εὐδοκία) but by nature (φύσις), as Nemesius indicates in a strong aside directed against 'the opinion of certain men of note'. Nemesius may have been alluding here to extreme views expressed by Theodore of Mopsuestia – indeed, in this section, Nemesius gives the impression of being briefly sidetracked by a contemporary controversy; for he fails to draw any distinctly Christian conclusions about human nature from his excursion into Christological discussion.

Nemesius had his problems. Some of his conclusions, pieced together from his various sources, are held together in uncomfortable tension. But at least he tried to wrestle with the complexity of the questions in a relatively broad context and with a relatively broad outlook. He refused to dogmatize; he did not condemn but argued. It was because of people like Nemesius that dogmatic Christianity did not submerge the intellectual heritage of the Graeco-Roman world. Nemesius brought all his pagan philosophy into the Church and moulded together an understanding of human nature which stands out against the ascetic currents of the period for its humanity and its optimism.

For Further Reading

English translation

Telfer, W., 1955. *Cyril of Jerusalem and Nemesius of Emesa*, Library of Christian Classics, vol. IV, London: SCM Press.

Study

Young, Frances, 1983. 'Adam, the soul and immortality: a study of the interaction of "science" and the Bible in some anthropological treatises of the Fourth Century', *VigChr* 37, pp. 110–40.

VI Synesius of Cyrene

From the amount of space devoted to Synesius of Cyrene in the typical Church history, it might appear that he was a figure of considerable unimportance. As a representative of the particular period in which he lived, however, his significance is greater.[276] Synesius catches the interest of classicists, Byzantinists and historians of late antiquity, and the reason for this becomes apparent as soon as one begins to study his career.

Synesius was a well-educated, prominent, upper-class member of his local community who ended up as a bishop.[277] This would not be so surprising if it were not for his apparent lack of Christian convictions and the 'pagan' stance of his writings. In an earlier period of scholarship, many enthusiastic books were written on this cultured Hellene, and much ink expended on the question when

---

276 von Campenhausen (1963) recognized this, and included Synesius in his studies of the Fathers of the Greek Church; for his importance for understanding the politics of Constantinople during the reign of Arcadius and the episcopacy of John Chrysostom, see Liebeschuetz (1990) and Cameron and Long (1993).

277 For Synesius in his local context, see Roques (1987).

he was converted.[278] Yet there is no trace in his very personal works of any crisis or change in his faith; he did not go through the spiritual turmoils of his contemporary, Augustine of Hippo. Some have suggested he slipped quietly into the Church, hardly committing himself until episcopal honours were thrust upon him; and even then, there is no obvious break in his thinking or his circle. He complains of a change in his way of life, and among his correspondence there are epistles of an ecclesiastical character; but Christianity certainly did not appear to him to represent a fundamental change in his values or beliefs. Bregman[279] has argued that he essentially remained a Neoplatonist, but others have concluded that he was a Christian all along[280] – archaeology has turned up a house in Cyrene, which belonged to a Christian with the same name as his father.[281]

What we know of Synesius comes largely from his extant works. These include a number of small treatises, some hymns and a collection of letters.[282] Difficulties with dating his birth, death and most of the events of his life lie in lack of specific evidence. None of his letters can be dated later than 413, and he does not appear to have heard of the ghastly lynching by Christian fanatics of his heroine Hypatia, which took place in 415.[283] So the end of his life can be established with some probability, and clearly he did not survive long as a bishop, since it was apparently about 411 when Theophilus consecrated him. How old he was at either of these dates is a matter of considerable dispute; his birth has been dated as early as 360 and as late as 375.[284]

It was thought that the firmest date in his career was his visit to Constantinople, which lasted three years from 399 to 402; but this dating has been successfully challenged, and put two years earlier.[285] He was chosen by his fellow-citizens of the Pentapolis to represent them before the emperor. This area of Libya was in financial ruin, and Synesius eventually obtained some remission of taxes. It

---

278 For example, Volkmann (1869); Crawford (1901); Grützmacher (1913).

279 Bregman (1982).

280 Liebeschuetz (1990); Cameron and Long (1993); cf. discussion in Schmitt (2001).

281 See Cameron and Long (1993), p. 16, discussing a suggestion offered by Liebeschuetz (1985); see also their reinterpretation of Synesius' letters suggesting he was baptized on return from Constantinople in honour of a vow, p. 33.

282 Text of Synesius' works in *PG* 66. Critical editions and translations include: (1) treatises: Terzaghi (1944); Lamoureux and Aujoulat (2008); ET: Fitzgerald (1930); (2) hymns: Terzaghi (1939); Lacombrade (1978); ET: Fitzgerald (1930). Edition of the letters in Hercher (1873) (*PG* 66 has a slightly different numbering); also Garzya and Roques (2000a, 2000b). ET: Fitzgerald (1926), following Hercher's numbering.

283 Socrates, *HE* vii.15.

284 Synesius refers to himself as old in a couple of letters (116 and 123); but in *Ep.* 72, he is younger than his suffragans, and in *Hymn* 8 (probably though not certainly written after 405), he refers to his youth. When he wrote his *Encomium on Baldness*, he was certainly bald; but that must have been well before his consecration and suggests that he lost his hair prematurely. The question cannot be finally settled, though Roques (1989) argues for 371; he also dates his consecration as bishop as 1 January 412, offering a precision which the evidence hardly allows. See Barnes (1986b).

285 Crawford (1901) put it two years earlier, but the later date, established by Seeck (1894), was generally accepted; see Lacombrade (1951a). However, see now Barnes (1986a); Liebeschuetz (1986, 1990); Cameron and Long (1993).

is significant that his fellow-citizens turned to him to act as their ambassador in this way, since it throws light on his election as bishop of Ptolemais – it was as *patronus* rather than as spiritual father that he helped his flock, in particular defending the people against the cruel prefect, Andronicus, whose excommunication by Synesius is said to be the first recorded.[286] One of the things he dreaded about becoming a bishop was being overwhelmed by the enormous burden of arbitration in local disputes and of correspondence on behalf of individuals seeking the righting of wrongs or personal advancement. He had already done much of this kind, but without detriment to his philosophy.[287] Most of his life was clearly spent as the local landowner and leading citizen. His pursuits were 'gentlemanly', a devotion to literature (his works are almost a mosaic of allusions to classical authors, especially Plato, Plutarch and Homer)[288] and to the chase (he was a connoisseur of arms, dogs and horses).[289] He was an intensely patriotic Hellene; the solution to the military and economic problems of the Empire and his own province lay for him in a citizen-army fully committed to the defence of its property, rather than professional parasites, with no personal motivation to anything but plundering the produce of the area. His commitment to this view was put to the test several times in his life, when barbarian tribes were ranging over the countryside and Synesius found himself taking a personal lead in organizing local defence.[290] His ideal was philosophy, or quiet retirement from public life to cultivate contemplation and the arts; but true to the classical Greek spirit of loyalty to the city, he responded repeatedly to calls on his sense of duty.[291] His consecration as a bishop was simply the culmination of a lifetime of public service.

Apart from this, we know that Synesius went to Alexandria for his higher education and studied with the remarkable daughter of Theon, Hypatia; that he visited Athens and was definitely of the view that Alexandria had outstripped the more ancient centre of learning;[292] and that he married sometime after his return from Constantinople, a marriage solemnized by the patriarch,

---

286 For this incident, see *Ep.* 57 (which is a public address erroneously placed among the letters), and *Epp.* 72, 79 and 89.

287 *Epp.* 105 and 57.

288 A glance at the footnotes of Terzaghi (1939, 1944) is instructive in this regard. Many details will also be found in the notes to Fitzgerald (1926, 1930). Crawford (1901) tabulates a large collection of parallels in Appendix D.

289 According to *Ep.* 154 (no. 153 in *PG*), Synesius wrote a book on the chase, *Cynegetica*. In *Ep.* 105, he regrets having to give up a fondness for dogs and horses which he has had since childhood. In *Ep.* 40, he sends a horse to a friend with an account of its qualities. His needs in the way of horses, arrows and other military equipment are mentioned in *Epp.* 132 and 133 (131 and 132 in *PG*). Hunting analogies are frequent in his works.

290 *Ep.* 107. *De regno* 14 recommends a citizen-army. Other references to Synesius' leading military operations will be found in *Epp.* 89, 104, 108, 113, 132, 133, etc.

291 Fitzgerald's Introduction (1930) perhaps over-romanticizes Synesius' attachment to classical ideals of patriotism, but there is certainly an element of truth in his descriptions. In an age of diminishing social responsibility, Synesius was a bit of an anachronism. For a different slant on all this, see Bayless (1977).

292 *Ep.* 136 (135 in *PG*).

Theophilus, who later consecrated him as bishop.[293] His close connections with Alexandria are further shown by his correspondence.

The correspondence of Synesius seems to range in date from about 395 to the end of his life. The order in the standard editions is certainly not chronological, and in many cases it is doubtful whether the chronological order can be reconstructed. From these letters, many of them lively and personal pieces even though written in accordance with the rhetorical conventions of the day and with an eye on publication, we can glean not only personal information but also vivid impressions of the life and society of the times. Synesius had about forty correspondents, to some of whom only one or two letters survive. Most frequently appear letters to Euoptius, his brother, to Herculian and Olympias, two fellow-students in Alexandria, and to Pylaemenes and Troilus, a well-known rhetorician, both of whom he met in Constantinople.[294] In these he reveals considerable narrative powers, humour and intimacy. One of the most discussed, Epistle 4,[295] is a superb account of a disastrous sea-voyage along the coast from Alexandria to Cyrene. Everything goes wrong, and when the vessel is caught in a storm further from land than it might have been, the crowning touch comes when at dusk the captain and half the crew abandon the tiller and ropes to prostrate themselves and read their sacred rolls: they are Jews and the Sabbath has begun! The letter is written with somewhat donnish humour, savouring the slight exaggeration of an escapade after it is over, with plenty of literary quotes and allusions. It is full of current popular superstitions,[296] quite apart from the vivid picture of the cosmopolitan seafaring community of Alexandria.

Scattered among such gems of private correspondence are several letters to Theophilus referring difficult ecclesiastical matters for his judgment, as well as a number which reveal Synesius' state of mind as he considered his possible consecration. But perhaps most interesting are the seven letters to Hypatia. According to Socrates,[297] Hypatia was the most outstanding philosopher of her time, who pursued the Platonism of Plotinus and attracted pupils from afar; the daughter of an eminent mathematician, she incurred no hint of slander, even though she was constantly in masculine society. Synesius' letters indicate the degree of philosophic friendship and devotion she elicited from her pupils, and even in the sad days of his episcopacy, when everything seemed against him and his three sons had died, it was to the pagan, Hypatia, that he turned for comfort.[298] Earlier in his life, he appeals to her judgment before publishing some of his works.[299]

Synesius' treatises show a wide range of literary skills and a variety of interests. Dating from the time of his visit to Constantinople, the *De regno* purports to be the speech addressed to Arcadius on behalf of his fellow-citizens, while

---

293 *Ep.* 105: his wife was a possible obstacle to his consecration, and Synesius refused to part from a perfectly legal and proper marital position simply for ecclesiastical advancement.

294 Socrates, *HE* vii.12, 37; see further Roques (1989); Cameron and Long (1993).

295 The exact date of the letter is disputed. See Roques (1977).

296 Pack (1949).

297 Socrates, *HE* vii.15.

298 *Epp.* 10, 16, 81.

299 *Ep.* 154 (153 in *PG*).

the *De providentia* is an allegorical retelling of the myth of Osiris and Typhos which provides allusive comment on the current political and moral situation at the court in Constantinople.[300] After his return to Pentapolis,[301] he composed (i) a humorous sophistic speech *Encomium on Baldness*, a deliberate counter-weight to the treatise of Dio Chrysostom in praise of hair, (ii) a more serious work on *Dreams*, which with the *Hymns* might give us most of our insight into his philosophical and theological position, and (iii) the *Dion*, a fascinating comment on his way of life and the relationship between philosophical and sophistic ideals. A couple of Orations on the political situation in the Pentapolis,[302] and some fragments of homilies, complete the list of his extant works, apart from the interesting description of the 'astrolabe' which he sent to Paeonius with the instrument itself. Like many others in Late Antiquity, he saw himself as a Hellene, combining commitment to philosophy and rhetoric with pursuits practical, political and literary as well as mystical:[303] Synesius even constructed a machine to hurl long-distance missiles at the enemy.[304]

From the above survey, it should be apparent that Synesius' life and works are likely to provide contrasts and insights in relation to several themes raised in earlier chapters. (i) Like Eusebius, he addressed the emperor: how do their approaches compare? (ii) Like Gregory Nazianzen, he felt tension between rhetoric and philosophy, but achieved a balance: how did he reach his position of relaxed and active humanism? (iii) He hovers between Christianity and Hellenism apparently discerning no essential opposition between the two: why did he not feel the same conflicts as the Cappadocians? Each of these themes is worth pursuing further.

(i) The traditions of panegyric had an effect upon Eusebius' attitude to Constantine which seems like blind adulation, even if understandable in the circumstances. By contrast, Synesius' speech is openly critical of the situation of Arcadius' court, so much so that scholars believe it could not be the actual words he spoke in the presence of the emperor, a view challenged by Lacombrade, but later reinstated – it is now regarded as an address shared privately with Aurelian and others with similar political sympathies.[305] Synesius' speech, no less than Eusebius', draws on long-standing traditions and conventions: but he uses them to present a picture of the ideal king, with implied criticism of Arcadius' present style and policies. His indebtedness to Dio Chrysostom's *Orations on*

---

300 See Cameron and Long (1993) for detailed discussion of these works. Note that there is a dispute about the identity of Typhus (cf. Liebeschuetz (1990)), which materially affects the reconstruction of historical events in Constantinople, for which Synesius is a major witness.

301 Lacombrade (1951a) dates the *Encomium on Baldness* before the trip to Constantinople; this masterly biography presents a plausible reconstruction of Synesius' life and the sequence of his works, but much of the dating must still be regarded as tentative. Lacombrade (1961) revises the date of the hymns.

302 The *Constitutio* and *Catastasis*.

303 Bregman (1982).

304 *Ep.* 133 (132 in *PG*).

305 Lacombrade (1951b); Barnes (1986a); Liebeschuetz (1990); Cameron and Long (1993).

Kingship[306] is very considerable, but it is not slavish. What he does is to enter debates at court about policy matters, in particular voicing doubts about the power and influence of Goths in high places;[307] but he does this in the guise of exhorting the young emperor to emulate the philosopher-king who first rules over his own passions (chapters 6 and 22), the shepherd-king (chapters 5–6) whose concern for and leadership of his flock is personal, open and direct, the father-king, whose presence is the image of God on earth whose calling is to imitate the divine, especially in his goodness and providential care for his people (chapters 4–5). Synesius concludes from this ideal that Arcadius should abandon his isolated and protected luxury, open himself to suppliants, ban the foreigners and lead a citizen-army in defence of the state – a somewhat unrealistic and anachronistic plea in the conditions of the early Byzantine world. Yet clearly Synesius, so far from being a subservient flatterer like Eusebius, is at least in private, an outspoken critic. The difference is partly attributable to Synesius' very real veneration for the classical ideals of Homer and Plato. He was a literary rather than a political figure.

(ii) This desire to reinvigorate contemporary society with the ideals of the past also explains the fact that he allows no division between philosophy and rhetoric.[308] According to *Epistle* 154, Synesius wrote the *Dion* in the face of personal charges that he was faithless to philosophy because he professed grace and harmony of style and enjoyed literature. Synesius retorts with an attack on contemporary philosophers who refused to take any pleasure in beauty and harmony of speech or life. 'I know I am a man, and neither a god that I should be adamant in the face of every pleasure, nor a brute that I should take delight in the pleasures of the body.' What passionate attachment is more free from passion, he asks, than a life spent in literature? Included in his attacks are certain 'foreign philosophers' who are particularly extreme in their asceticism, take no part in public life and become unsociable in their haste to release themselves from nature. In spite of opinions to the contrary,[309] it seems impossible not to identify this as a criticism of the excesses of Christian monks. Synesius in this treatise stands for the Hellenic 'mean' in contrast with all current extremism. In Charles Kingsley's historical novel *Hypatia* (1853), Synesius is aptly described as 'the only Christian from whom he had ever heard a hearty laugh'.

If he professes philosophy but refuses to subscribe to fashionable extremist ideals, much the same is true of the sophistic way of life. The lawyer and rhetorician, growing fat and prosperous on the rewards of his services, or composing elegant speeches with no content, were equally to be criticized. In his letters, Synesius begs his friends to withdraw from ambitious careers and devote themselves to philosophy. This does not mean a lack of patriotism or a total withdrawal from public service: for philosophy should be the crown of rhetoric, and no other science will be able to govern affairs as well

---

306 Dio Chrysostom, *Orat.* I—IV and LXII.

307 Bregman (1982) follows the 'standard' view of the dating and politics; for challenges to this, consequent on the redating of Synesius' time in Constantinople, and a re-reading of the evidence, see Barnes (1986a); Liebeschuetz (1990); Cameron and Long (1993).

308 Bregman (1982).

309 Fitzgerald (1930) I, p. 227.

as this philosophy. Synesius regrets that in his day circumstances afforded no room for the philosopher to control the state. As noted already, he idealizes the philosopher-king.[310] Dio Chrysostom provides his model, because even as a philosopher he retained his sophistry, his linguistic elegance and his political influence with Trajan.

Synesius, the self-styled philosopher, both enjoyed sophistic exercises (the *Encomium on Baldness* is a classic of this type), and involved himself in public life. He anachronistically believed that the philosopher had a contribution to make to society. Even though he bitterly regrets his loss of leisure when faced with the episcopacy, he liked to think of himself as a philosopher-priest.[311]

(iii) Synesius' theology is particularly fascinating. Apart from the *Hymns* and the treatise on *Dreams*, there is little direct discussion of theological or even philosophical matters, but his unguarded allusions give us some important clues. Even his *Encomium on Baldness* has theological comments: baldness is related to the divine, a shrine to the God through whom we have wisdom; whereas hair has lack of reason, brute tendencies and all that is opposed to God – it is an excrescence of imperfect matter.[312] In the political works, we find the old monotheistic idealism of the Empire, with a general belief in God's providential favour when human beings behave themselves. This general theism has precious little to differentiate it from that of Christianity, though there is no hint of specific Christian beliefs and much use of pagan myths, at least in their literary forms. The *Dion* reveals that Synesius shared with pagan and Christian philosophers the ideal of freedom from passion and contemplation of the divine. In his treatise on *Dreams*, he displays a fascination with the possibility of divination and prediction, theoretically based on the Neoplatonic doctrine of the sympathy of the whole universe which is one organism. He argues for the importance of dreams as a way of ascent to God for the soul, provided the imaginative faculty is tempered by philosophical discrimination. But the *Hymns* indicate how little difference he saw between his lifelong Neoplatonic mysticism and the kind of Christianity he espoused. Whether he uses Christian or pagan imagery, pagan or Christian devotional language, or a mixture of the two, his piety is much the same. There is no abrupt transition in style or content or atmosphere. Whether addressing God as 'Master of the thunderbolt, higher than the gods' as in pagan hymns to Zeus, or as 'Source of the Son, Form of the Father', or 'God, the glorious Son of the eternal God', the same basic spirituality is present.[313] Bregman[314] argued that in Synesius' case there was never a conversion from paganism to Christianity: rather in alliance with Christians who shared loyalty to the Hellenic traditions of the Empire, he was happy to replace pagan symbols and cultic practices with those of the Church, all alike being inadequate to the true divine. Others, as noted above, suppose he was never anything other than a Christian whose literary expression simply conformed to classical precedent.[315]

---

310 *De regno*; cf. *Epp.* 101, 103; *Ad Paeonium de dono astrolabii*.

311 *Epp.* 57, 62.

312 *Calvitii Encomium* 20.

313 *Hymns* 3, 5 and 6 provide the examples.

314 Bregman (1982). Cf. Marrou (1936).

315 Liebeschuetz (1990), p. 141.

If put to the test, Synesius might have been condemned for 'that eclectic farrago of his which he calls philosophic Christianity'.[316] There does not seem to have been any clear break, or even an evolution, in his thinking, since the *Hymns* all seem to date from approximately the same time, whether using philosophic or Christian phraseology.[317] Synesius never seems to have acquired the usual Christian temper of 'exclusiveness'. Most of the Fathers, for all that they embraced classical education, felt the need to carry on the tradition that Christianity was different, distinctive and incapable of syncretistic compromise; in theory, if not in practice, paganism must be confronted, not taken into partnership. As a bishop, Synesius conformed to the ecclesiastical habit of objecting to deviations from orthodoxy and proper moral standards, and he had a healthy respect for his office as a priest of God.[318] But this was continuous with his patriotism: even in the early philosophical work *De providentia*, he says of the 'Arian' Goths that they bring innovations into 'our religion', clearly identifying himself with official orthodoxy. The Roman Empire had always been a 'divine institution' which owed its success and stability to the gods or God, and to that extent deviation and antisocial conduct were alike politically intolerable. Theologically, Synesius himself required the possibility of honest dissent, but divisiveness he could not countenance.

Before he took up his ecclesiastical duties, Synesius made it clear exactly where he stood:

> For my own part, I can never persuade myself that the soul is of more recent origin than the body. Never would I admit that the world and the parts which make it up must perish. The resurrection, which is an object of common belief, is nothing for me but a sacred and mysterious allegory . . . The philosophic mind, albeit the discerner of truth, admits the employment of falsehood, . . . the false may be beneficial to the populace, and the truth injurious to those not strong enough to gaze steadfastly on the radiance of real being . . . I can take over the holy office on condition that I may prosecute philosophy at home, and spread legends abroad . . .[319]

For Synesius, the real distinction was not between Christianity and paganism, but between philosophy and popular myths. His conversion to philosophy was arguably the most significant turning point in his life.[320] Maybe, to state whether one thinks Synesius was really a Christian or not, says more about one's own understanding of Christianity than about Synesius himself or even the times in which he lived.

---

316 Charles Kingsley, 1853. *Hypatia*, London: J. W. Parker & Son, p. 116.

317 The dating of Synesius' *Hymns* has been seen as the clue to his so called conversion. However, Lacombrade (1961) has argued that they all date from approximately the same period. In 1951a, chapter 14, he dated them to 405–9, and detected a shift towards more explicitly Christian language, suggesting that it was the language of a sympathizer rather than a theologian. In 1961, he dates them even earlier, pp. 402–4.

318 *Ep.* 5 and *Catastasis*.

319 *Ep.* 105.

320 Bregman (1974, 1982).

For Further Reading

English translations

Fitzgerald, A., 1926. *Letters of Synesius*, Oxford and New York: Oxford University Press.

Fitzgerald, A., 1930. *Essays and Hymns of Synesius*, 2 vols, ET, Oxford and New York: Oxford University Press.

Studies

Cameron, Alan and Jacqueline Long with Lee Sherry, 1993. *Barbarians and Politics at the Court of Arcadius*, Berkeley: University of California Press.

Bregman, Jay, 1982. *Synesius of Cyrene: Philosopher-Bishop*, Berkeley/Los Angeles/London: University of California Press.

Liebeschuetz, J. H. W. G., 1990. *Barbarians and Bishops in the reign of Arcadius*, Oxford: Oxford University Press.

6

The Literature of Christological Controversy

I. Introduction: Eustathius

The problems of Christology were a direct result of the Arian controversy and the adoption of Nicene theology as orthodoxy. Different ways of meeting 'Arian' positions produced different Christological approaches which eventually came into conflict. The tensions between two types of Christology left a continuing mark on subsequent Church history, for there survive in the Middle East to this day non-Chalcedonian churches (both 'Monophysite' and 'Nestorian', though the labels are not really appropriate), while in the West, Chalcedon has proved less a solution than the classic definition of a problem which constantly demands further elucidation.

The Nicene formula changed the whole theological landscape. God's transcendent Being, immutable and impassible, eternal and underivative, was an assumption which went unquestioned by all parties. Prior to Arius most theologians presupposed a hierarchy of Being whereby this transcendent, unoriginate God was linked on the ladder of existence with creation through the mediating Logos: in Platonic terms, the One–Many or Indefinite Dyad provided the link between the Many and the ultimate One.[1] As a result of the 'Arian' controversy, the hierarchy was destroyed and a radical distinction was established between the Creator and everything which derived its being from the divine creative activity; or, to put it another way, the question was pressed on which side of the fundamental divide between the self-existent and the contingently existent was the Logos to be found. One way or another, the Platonic hierarchical scheme had to be abandoned. New questions changed the ground of debate.

Arius insisted that the Being of the Logos was derivative and contingent and therefore mutable. He supported his contention by appeal to scriptural texts which attributed weakness or fallibility to Jesus Christ, that is, the Logos. The basic presupposition with which he worked was that the Logos was the subject of all the human experiences of Jesus.

How were the opponents of Arius to account for those texts which ascribe weakness and fallibility, and indeed passion and death, to the incarnate Logos? The Nicene formula insisted that the Being of the Logos was not derivative, but in every respect of the same transcendent nature as the self-existent God. The supporters of such a claim were inevitably confronted with extreme difficulties

---

1 See above, pp. 17–18.

in dealing with the mediatorial activity of the Logos in creation and incarnation. The Logos could no longer belong to both sides of the divide and provide the link between Creator and creature. Being immutable and impassible, how could he become involved in the world of 'becoming' and change and destruction. The Christological problem was bound to become the next major issue.[2]

We have already explored the answer given by Athanasius. The Logos himself did not experience weakness, suffering and death in his essential Being; it was the flesh he took which was subject to these human limitations. It might look as though Athanasius was 'dividing the Christ',[3] but in fact the Logos remained the subject of the incarnation, adopting human constraints and experiences as his own: 'he imitated our condition'.[4] There is a sense in which the heresy of Apollinarius can be seen as the logical extreme of Athanasius' position; and the fully developed Alexandrian Christology found in the works of Cyril is its mature outcome. In this Christological tradition, the Logos is seen as existing in two states, a pre-existent eternal transcendent state and a voluntarily accepted incarnate state in which he allows himself fleshly experience, even though in his essential nature he is incapable of development, addition or change. The Logos remains the essential subject; the flesh is 'impersonal humanity' and the reality of the human nature of Jesus Christ is in constant danger of being merely an outer skin – the result being, as Hanson put it, a 'space-suit Christology'.[5]

Another approach to the problem emerged during the fourth century, and produced a theological tradition associated with Antioch and its hinterland. This may have had roots in earlier Antiochene trends, in the Christology of Paul of Samosata, for example; but there are some grounds for the view that it only developed as a response to the Christological problems posed by 'Arianism'. The alternative way of answering Arius was to accept that the transcendent Logos could not in reality be the subject of the incarnate experiences and to attribute weakness, fallibility and passion to 'the Man' he assumed. The difference between these two kinds of thought, Alexandrian and Antiochene, has classically been expressed in the formulae *Word–Flesh Christology* and *Word–Man Christology*, but these terms are increasingly subject to criticism; the two sides tended to use overlapping terminology rather than a consistently distinct set of terms. It is perhaps better, therefore, to see the difference as variant answers to the question, 'Who was the subject of the incarnate experiences of Jesus Christ?'[6] For the Alexandrians the subject remained the Word, who though transcendent accommodated himself to the conditions of human nature. For the Antiochenes, the corollary of Nicaea was that the Word could not possibly be regarded as the immediate subject of the incarnate experiences without a blasphemous denigration of his essential divinity; naturally this produced a dualistic Christology in which the unity of the Christ as the Word incarnate was hard to maintain. Neither Christological tradition was without its difficulties,

---

2 For a collection of significant texts in English, see Norris (1980).

3 Indeed Theodoret would be able to include Athanasius in florilegia concerned with the 'two natures'. See below, p. 334.

4 See above, p. 63.

5 Hanson (1988), p. 448.

6 For a clear and forceful presentation of this distinction, see Sullivan (1956). His approach is now widely adopted.

and through the twentieth century scholarly discussion has tended to reflect shifting theological preferences.[7]

The fact that these patterns of approach to the Christological problem emerged explicitly out of the new theological demands of the post-Nicene situation is suggested by the case of Eustathius of Antioch. Various vague accounts of Eustathius' deposition leave the historian guessing to some extent, but the consistent witness of the sources is that he was violently opposed to 'Arianism', and unable to compromise in the period after Nicaea.[8] Many fragments of his writings have survived because over a century later Theodoret of Cyrus was able to appeal to Eustathius as a hero of the anti-Arian struggle accepted by both sides in the later Christological debate. Eustathius was at loggerheads with Eusebius of Caesarea, and suffered the same fate as that other uncompromising anti-Arian, Athanasius. It is hardly surprising that his vehement defence of Nicaea was widely interpreted as Sabellian, and Antioch lost its bishop, as Alexandria did some years later, in the reaction against the Nicene position.

Traditionally, then, Eustathius' error was regarded as Trinitarian rather then Christological. In the last century, however, the idea has gained currency that Eustathius stands in a continuous Syrian tradition providing the link between later Antiochenes, like Theodore of Mopsuestia, and the earlier heretic Paul of Samosata.[9] His Trinitarian ideas, it is said, tend in a Sabellian direction, the Logos being treated as divine 'energy' rather than as a 'person', and his Christology is exaggeratedly dualistic to the point of Adoptionism. Careful editing and examination of the fragments, however, has suggested that this judgment is only partially true.[10] Eustathius' Trinitarian views seem perfectly in line with those of his orthodox contemporaries (Athanasius, for example). Certainly some of his Christological formulae foreshadow those of the later Antiochenes, but dualistic statements predominate among the fragments because a high proportion were preserved in 'Dyophysite' collections (florilegia). Besides they are drawn largely from his anti-Arian writings, and elsewhere he often affirms the unity of the Saviour. It was the Arian controversy which turned Eustathius into an 'Antiochene'.

'Why do they think it important to show that Christ assumed a body without a soul?' he asks.[11] This was a perceptive question for so early a stage in the discussion. Like Didymus later,[12] he saw that the presence of a human soul in the Christ would avoid the difficulties of attributing creaturely weakness and

---

7 From Bethune-Baker (1908) through Sellers (1940) and Anastos (1962) there was a tendency to defend the discredited Antiochene tradition for taking seriously the genuine humanity of Christ. Wickham (1983) and McGuckin (1994) represent the reaction, claiming that only Cyril really understood the incarnation. McLeod (1999, 2005, 2009) and Pásztori-Kupán (2006) provide more recent defence of the Antiochene approach; while Fairbairn (2003) prefers the Cyrilline view.

8 See further, Sellers (1928).

9 Loofs (1914) and (1924). Sellers (1928) develops this line of approach. See also Sellers (1940).

10 Spanneut (1948) and (1954); see now the new edition of Eustathius' complete surviving works, including the fragments, in CCG, Declerck (2002).

11 Fr. 15, ed. Spanneut.

12 See above, pp. 99–100.

fallibility to the divine Logos. The Logos, he insisted, remained impassible and omnipresent, but the Man he assumed, the temple he built for himself, was born, was crucified, was raised and glorified. Athanasius in a sense 'divided the natures' to counter Arius, but Eustathius came much closer to treating the Man rather than the Logos as Christ's personal subject, so avoiding the potentially docetic tendencies of Athanasius' approach. 'Not in appearance and supposition but in very reality God was clothed with a whole man, assuming him perfectly'.[13] To insist on the integrity of Christ's humanity was one way of meeting the Arian challenge.

Eustathius' only complete surviving work is a homily on the Witch of Endor, which is directed, among other things, against Origen's allegorical exegesis, thus anticipating another position characteristic of the Antiochenes.[14] The argument Eustathius advances is rather more complex than a straightforward attack on allegorical method;[15] however, attacks on allegory are characteristic of Diodore, Theodore, Chrysostom and Theodoret – the principal characters identified as 'Antiochene'. That there is a connection between their exegetical and Christological positions is likely – in both cases they were concerned with the 'concrete realities' (πράγματα) and the narrative sequence (ἀκολουθία), insisting that allegory as practised by Origen destroyed the overarching story of God's purposes from Beginning to End enshrined in the Rule of Faith.[16]

Athanasius and Eustathius, then, were the classic defenders of Nicaea; bishop of Antioch and bishop of Alexandria, they shared the distinction of being deposed for their resolute opposition to Arianism. Almost incidentally, they mapped out two different Christological approaches as part of their response to the Arian challenge, each of which was to develop into a distinctive Christological tradition in the succeeding period. In the persons of Cyril and Nestorius, the two traditions came into open and damaging conflict. The extreme forms of each Christology were condemned, possibly through exaggerated misinterpretations by the opposing side. Meanwhile in the generation after Nicaea, the two ways of approach were represented by Apollinarius of Laodicea and Diodore of Tarsus.

For Further Reading

English translations

Froehlich, K., 1984. *Biblical Interpretation in the Early Church*, Sources of Early Christian Thought, Philadelphia: Fortress Press.

Greer, Rowan A. and Margaret M. Mitchell, 2007. *The 'Belly-Myther' of Endor. Interpretations of 1 Kingdoms 28 in the Early Church*, Atlanta, GA: SBL.

Norris, Richard A., Jr, 1980. *The Christological Controversy*, Sources of Early Christian Thought, Philadelphia: Fortress Press.

---

13 Fr. 41, ed. Spanneut.

14 Young (1997b); cf. Schäublin (1974) and standard works on patristic exegesis.

15 See Greer and Mitchell (2007), and previous discussion in Young (1989) and (1997a).

16 Young (1997b); for a negative view of this connection, see O'Keefe (2000).

Price, Richard and Michael Gaddis, 2005. *The Acts of the Council of Chalcedon: vols. I–III*, Liverpool: Liverpool University Press.
Stevenson, K., 1966. *Creeds, Councils and Controversies*, London and New York: SPCK.

Studies

Grillmeier, A., 1965/75. *Christ in Christian Tradition*, ET, London and Oxford: Mowbrays.
Sellers, R. V., 1928. *Eustathius of Antioch*, Cambridge and New York: Cambridge University Press.
——, 1940. *Two Ancient Christologies*, London: SPCK.
——, 1953. *The Council of Chalcedon*, London: SPCK.
Young, Frances M., 1997a. *Biblical Exegesis and the Formation of Christian Culture*, Cambridge: Cambridge University Press.
——, 1997b. 'The Fourth Century Reaction against Allegory', *SP* 30, pp. 120–5.

II Apollinarius and Diodore

1 Apollinarius and the Alexandrian tradition

It can be misleading to identify the two types of Christology with geographical locations. In a later period, Syriac Christianity was divided between 'Nestorian' and 'Monophysite' groups, and Antioch had its 'Monophysite' bishops just as did Alexandria. Even in the Nestorian controversy when Antioch and the Oriental bishops seem solidly identified with the 'two natures' Christology, Cyril had his supporters in the city and among Syriac-speaking monks and bishops, an example being Rabbula. In fact, Syria was the scene of the first round in the conflict, for the Laodicea with which Apollinarius is connected was a Syrian seaport not far from Antioch. Antioch was where Jerome heard Apollinarius lecture in 373; and it was in Antioch that Apollinarius took the step of consecrating Vitalis, so initiating the Apollinarian schism.

However, Apollinarius is naturally associated with Alexandria, for his father originated from there, settling in Laodicea as a teacher; and all our sources testify to Apollinarius' friendship with Athanasius. This seems to have been initiated in 346 when Athanasius was returning to Alexandria from one of his periods of exile; the bishop of Laodicea, having refused to receive him to communion himself, excommunicated Apollinarius for doing so. From then on Apollinarius seems to have headed a separated group of loyal Nicenes in Laodicea, and was eventually consecrated their bishop. His friendship with Athanasius was lasting – there was an extensive correspondence between the two, and Athanasius seems to have consulted Apollinarius on theological points, apparently even submitting to him the draft of his *Epistle to Epictetus* for comment.[17] As far as Athanasius was concerned Apollinarius was a staunch supporter of Nicene orthodoxy, and for most of his life that remained Apollinarius' reputation.

---

17 Raven (1923), p. 105, quoting fragments 159–61 from Lietzmann (1904), pp. 253f. (cited henceforth as L 253f., etc.).

It is also natural to associate Apollinarius with Alexandria because of the close links between his theological stance and what became the typical Alexandrian Christology. After his views had been condemned a number of Apollinarian treatises were circulated under the names of others, that of Athanasius being one of the most important. Cyril of Alexandria unwittingly took some of his Christological slogans from such works, thinking that they came from his authoritative predecessor. A notable example is the confession of faith addressed to the Emperor Jovian.[18] One of Apollinarius' followers, Polemon, quoted this letter as from his master, so confirming the impression given by its style and contents that its superscription is fraudulent. This confession follows a somewhat credal pattern (its title suggests that it was an exposition of the Nicene Creed), affirming that the same one is pre-existent and incarnate, and describing the Son of God as the one begotten before all ages, and at the end of the ages born according to the flesh from Mary for our salvation. This double γέννησις (one Greek word serves for begetting and giving birth), and the unity of subject in the Nicene Creed, were both to become typical of Cyril's standpoint. So were statements like 'the same one is Son of God κατὰ πνεῦμα (according to the Spirit) and Son of Man κατὰ σάρκα (according to the flesh)', or 'one Son has not two natures but one'. Most notorious, however, is the catchphrase μία φύσις τοῦ Θεοῦ Λόγου σεσαρκωμένη (one enfleshed nature of the God–Word), which was to become a slogan for Cyril's party. So perhaps it is hardly surprising that the Antiochenes mistook Cyril's position to be Apollinarian, though presumably they too were unaware of the provenance of Cyril's sources. Later it will be worth considering in what ways Cyril's Christology differed from that of Apollinarius. Both of them claimed to be upholding the teaching of Athanasius.[19]

Reconstructing what Apollinarius actually taught is a very complicated process, even though study has been facilitated by Lietzmann's careful edition of the fragments. As already noted, the Apollinarians secured the survival of a number of works under false names. Inevitably there is some doubt as to which may be confidently attributed to Apollinarius himself; two pseudo-Athanasian pieces, the *Quod unus sit Christus* and the *De Incarnatione Dei Verbi*, Lietzmann attributed to Apollinarius' followers. Besides this, there are a considerable number of fragments, mostly preserved in anti-Apollinarian works such as Gregory Nyssen's systematic refutation of Apollinarius' *Apodeixis*. Sometimes it is hard to decide whether a purported fragment is a quotation or a comment on the character of his teaching, especially when contradictory statements are found elsewhere. Apart from this we are dependent upon reports, and given the possibility that both his friends and his enemies may have misrepresented his teaching, it is no wonder there are a number of unsettled issues of interpretation. It can be stated without too much fear of contradiction that Apollinarius thought of the incarnation as the Logos taking the place of the human mind in Jesus Christ, but the corollaries of this theory, precisely how and why it was worked out, whether this was the central feature of his theology – all these matters raise more difficulties.

---

18 Apollinarius, *Letter to Jovian* (L 250ff.).
19 Apollinarius, *Letter to the Bishops of Diocaesarea* 1 (L 255).

2 Problems of interpretation

The first problem concerns the situation out of which Apollinarius' teaching arose. In spite of his well-known opposition to Arianism, there is a basic Christological similarity in that both assumed that the Logos replaced the human soul in the Christ. Did Apollinarius get his ideas from his opponents? The little treatise *Kata meros pistis* (*The faith in detail*) is largely concerned with Trinitarian questions, but there are several paragraphs which discuss the incarnation. Here Apollinarius is not only opposed to those who attach human things to the deity as if they belonged to God, things like progress, sufferings, attaining to glory and so on (clearly the Arians are in view here), but he also criticizes those who divide human things from the Godhead, emphasizing in his treatment the uniting of Godhead with flesh.[20] He states that 'if anyone calls him Son of God as being filled with deity, not as being begotten from divinity, he denies the Logos . . . and destroys knowledge of God'.[21] He outlines a view of the σάρκωσις (enfleshment) of the Logos which involves God living on earth while remaining the same, filling everything and at the same time 'being mixed (συνκεκράμενος) with flesh'.[22] Whoever he is criticizing does not agree with this idea of God being made flesh but instead attaches a man to God.[23] He can hardly now be referring to Arius. What he has in mind has appeared to be the so-called Antiochene Christology, for again in the *De Unione* he warns against denying the Godhead by speaking of the 'whole man'.[24] When we notice that in his *First Letter to Dionysius*[25] he expresses concern about contemporary followers of Paul of Samosata, and that he certainly wrote a treatise against Diodore, the suspicion grows that one factor in his thinking was profound opposition to the kind of Christological ideas found in Eustathius and actively propagated in his own generation by Diodore.

This view certainly makes better sense than the extraordinary idea that he poached his main idea from the Arian opposition. What is much more likely is that he and the Arians shared presuppositions which were very widespread, and Apollinarius made them explicit under quite different pressures. However, it may be that the influence of his opposition to the Antiochenes has been exaggerated. There are reasons for thinking that the two sides did not come into direct conflict until after Apollinarius' condemnation, and we have yet to discuss at what point Diodore's Christological views had developed and become notorious. Might some other situation have stimulated Apollinarius' thinking?

In an interesting study by Mühlenberg, Apollinarius' thought was set against a quite different background.[26] Beginning from the *Apodeixis*, he argues that Apollinarius' prime concern was to contrast Christ, the θεὸς ἔνσαρκος (God enfleshed) with the ἄνθρωπος ἔνθεος (man inspired) or divine man through

---

20 *KMP* 3 (L 168).
21 *KMP* 6 (L 169).
22 *KMP* 11 (L 171).
23 *KMP* 30 (L 178).
24 *De unione* 4 (L 186).
25 *Letter to Dionysius* (L 256ff.).
26 Mühlenberg (1969); but see the review articles by Kannengiesser (1971) and Hübner (1972).

whom, in the philosophical tradition, knowledge of God was mediated. From this philosophical tradition Apollinarius accepted that God was νοῦς (Mind), and that salvation was knowledge of God; from the Christian tradition he accepted that knowledge of God came through the incarnation. Thus he developed further the 'revelation' aspect of Athanasius' soteriology. His emphasis on the fact that the divine mind was enfleshed arose from his sense that what Christianity had to offer was truth – direct and genuine knowledge of God. Inevitably he reacted to Christologies of the Antiochene type as a betrayal of Christianity to Jews and pagans. For him Jesus was to be absolutely identified with God. To compromise that identification by introducing a human mind was to undermine the distinct truth which Christianity claimed. When worked out in detail with its attendant criticisms of other expositions of Apollinarius' whole standpoint, this interpretation of Apollinarius' theology has not proved entirely convincing, but there are enough hints in the fragments to suggest that this motive may have played some part in Apollinarius' thinking. Another suggestion, however, seems to have more bite,[27] namely that Apollinarius was reacting against Marcellus. It seems that all the ideas he is criticizing in the *Kata meros pistis* were attributed to Marcellus of Ancyra, who was accused of following Paul of Samosata as the Antiochenes would be later on, and also that the Christological assumptions of Apollinarius are anticipated in Eusebius' critique of Marcellus. Of all the theories about what initially stimulated Apollinarius to make his views explicit, this seems the best.

In general terms, the Arian controversy and reactions to it, provided the main context within which Apollinarius' basic ideas arose.[28] In many ways, his views were a natural development from the principles and assumptions of Athanasius' theology. Athanasius had argued that only God could save, and this is a frequent refrain of Apollinarius'.[29] Athanasius had argued that only one who was truly Son of God could reveal God to humanity, and Apollinarius shared that viewpoint: 'The very man who speaks to us the things of the Father is God the Creator of the ages'.[30] Athanasius had insisted that redemption depended on the Logos being ἄτρεπτος (immutable); likewise Apollinarius argues that it is only because the Logos is ἄτρεπτος and ἀπαθής (impassible) that the fallibility and passibility of humanity is overcome and salvation achieved. Athanasius never seems to have faced the question whether Christ had a human soul or mind; in Apollinarius' time, however, this question was gradually coming into the open, the Christological implications of Arius' views being increasingly recognized. Apollinarius assumed that every mind was an αὐτοκράτωρ, a self-moving, self-governing will, and he came to the conclusion that two such entities could not exist in one person.[31] Apollinarius also assumed that the human mind was τρέπτος (*treptos*), changeable, fallible and liable to sin, and he found a mixture of the ἄτρεπτος and the τρέπτος impossible to conceive. They would be bound to conflict with one another.[32]

---

27 Spoerl (1994).
28 Spoerl (1993).
29 For example *De fide et inc.* 4 (L 195).
30 Fr. 38 (L 213).
31 Fr. 150 (L 247).
32 Fr. 151 (L 248).

Given these assumptions, it is hardly surprising that he interpreted Athanasius' teaching as implying a denial of a human mind or soul in the Christ. Salvation depended upon the incarnation of the unchangeable power of divinity. 'The human race is not saved by the assumption of a mind and a whole man, but by the taking of flesh ... An ἄτρεπτος νοῦς (immutable Mind) was needed which would not fail through weakness of understanding.'[33] Interestingly enough the evidence suggests that Apollinarius not merely accepted but approved of both the *Tomus ad Antiochenos* and Athanasius' later Christological writings, a fact which both confirms the view that these writings were directed not against Apollinarius but others, and enhances the possibility that Athanasius himself did not interpret the Christological language of these documents as affirmations of the presence of a human mind or soul in the Christ.[34] Even Apollinarius could say that the Saviour did not have a σῶμα ἄψυχον (a body without soul) or ἀναίσθητον (without sense) or ἀνόητον (without mind), in the same breath asserting that he did not assume a human mind;[35] for he thought of the Logos as providing the body's intelligence and vitality.

The second problem of interpretation concerns Apollinarius' anthropology. Rufinus suggested that Apollinarius began by teaching that Christ 'assumed only a body and not a soul at all', but that in the course of controversy he shifted his ground and 'said that he did possess a soul, but only on its animating and not its rational side, and that to supply the place of a rational soul there was the Word of God'.[36] It will be recalled from the section on Nemesius that contemporary Platonism commonly recognized a distinction between the rational and irrational parts of the soul; Nemesius, however, mentions Plotinus and Apollinarius as protagonists of the view that the soul and the mind are two different things, man being composed of three elements, body, soul and mind. Others like Theodoret[37] set out to disprove the 'trichotomist' view of human nature as a way of confuting Apollinarius. The evidence is therefore quite strong that Apollinarius' anthropology did not follow the more usual dualism of soul and flesh.

To complicate things further the fragments contradict one another. Some imply a dichotomist soul–flesh or spirit–flesh position, others the more controversial trichotomist analysis. The fact of the matter seems to be that a specific anthropological theory is not central to Apollinarius' thought. He basically thinks of a person as a νοῦς ἔνσαρκος (a mind enfleshed) or as a composite of πνεῦμα and σάρξ (spirit and flesh)[38] deriving his various different sets of terminology from the language of St Paul. Paul himself, while most often seeming dualistic almost to the point of Gnosticism, can also speak in what appear to be trichotomist terms. Apollinarius adopts the apostle's language. A human person is a νοῦς ἔνσαρκος, the Logos is also νοῦς ἔνσαρκος. That is what it meant for him to be in the likeness of humanity. 'Because of this he was man; for man is a νοῦς ἐν σαρκί (mind in flesh) according to Paul.' 'Paul calls the last (Adam)

33 Fr. 76 (L 222).
34 See above, p. 67.
35 *Letter to the Bishops of Diocaesarea* 2 (L 256).
36 Rufinus, *HE* ii.20; cf. Socrates, *HE* ii.46.
37 *Eranistes*, the opening discussion of Book II.
38 For example, Fr. 69 (L 220); *Tomus Synodalis* (L 263).

life-giving Spirit.' 'The Christ having God as spirit, that is, mind, together with soul and body, is reasonably called the "man from heaven".' 'If man is composed of three and the Lord is man, the Lord is of three, spirit, soul and body, but he is "heavenly man and living Spirit".'[39] Precise anthropological terms were not Apollinarius' prime concern; his main interest was to contrast his view of the θεὸς ἔνσαρκος (God enfleshed) with the more generally acceptable idea of an ἄνθρωπος ἔνθεος (man inspired). Even Jews and pagans could stomach the latter, but it was inadequate because it would imply a human mind enlightened by wisdom (as is the case with other human beings), and so the arrival of Christ would not be ἐπιδημία θεοῦ (God's stay on earth) but the birth of a man.[40]

So we turn to a third problem. Paul speaks of a 'heavenly man' and Apollinarius, as we have just seen, adopts his terminology. His ancient critics represent him as having taught that the Logos' flesh pre-existed from the beginning, and much effort was expended in confuting this view. However, modern studies of Apollinarius, notably those of Raven and Prestige,[41] have asserted that at this point Apollinarius has been misrepresented; this was a view held by some of his more extreme followers, but not by Apollinarius himself. Gregory of Nyssa misinterpreted what he wrote.

Now it is true that Apollinarius took the virgin birth very seriously and frequently spoke of the Son of God receiving flesh from Mary. He also specifically denies the heavenly origin of the flesh.[42] Yet he did apparently make a good deal of the 'man from heaven' in the *Apodeixis*, contrasting him with the man from earth, and he seems to speak of the man Christ pre-existing as life-giving Spirit.[43] There are hints that he may have thought of God having always been in some sense 'enfleshed': thus he is reported to have said 'God having been ἔνσαρκος before the ages, afterwards was born through a woman.'[44] One thing he insists on is that the Trinity is three, not four, by implication attributing to his opponents the view that the Trinity was expanded into four by the assumption of the glorified Man. Perhaps then his view of God's changelessness led him to posit the eternal union of Logos and flesh. A passage from the *First Letter to Dionysius*, however, suggests that the only thing Apollinarius really cared about was the union, and he was not disposed to examine too closely its corollaries:

we are not afraid of the false charges of those who divide the Lord into two *prosōpa* (persons), if they blaspheme us, pretending that in maintaining the evangelical and apostolic unity we say the flesh comes from heaven, since we read the holy scriptures describing the one from heaven as Son of Man. [He alludes to John 3.13.] Nor when we say the Son of God was born of a woman can we be blamed for saying that the Word is from earth and not from heaven. We say both, the whole is from heaven through the Godhead

---

39 Quotations from Frs. 72, 29, 25, 89 (L 221, 211, 210, 227); and see especially Frs. 69ff. (L 220ff.).

40 Fr. 51 (L 216); and Fr. 70 (L 220).

41 Raven (1923) and Prestige (1940).

42 *De fide et inc.* 3 (L 194).

43 Fr. 32 (L 211).

44 Fr. 50 (L 216).

and the whole is from woman through the flesh; we do not know division of the one *prosōpon*, nor do we separate the earthly from the heavenly, nor the heavenly from the earthly.[45]

3 The union of Christ

Whatever the problems or implications, the union is Apollinarius' chief concern, and what gives this overriding importance in his eyes is its soteriological implications. It is not just that Apollinarius has adopted Athanasius' perception that salvation depends upon God remaining ἄτρεπτος (immutable) so as to free humanity from sin and mortality; he has reflected upon the problem of mediation. A mediator stands in the middle. The pre-Arian view saw the Logos as standing in the middle by being a link in the chain of Being; but for Apollinarius he is mediator in the sense of being the mean between God and humanity. The mean between a horse and a donkey is a mule, between white and black is grey, between winter and summer is spring. The mean between God and humanity is Christ. He is neither wholly human nor wholly God, but a mixture of God and humanity. He is God by the enfleshed spirit and human by the flesh assumed by God.[46] Thus he is mediator as the one who unites humanity and God, and it is this new creation, the divine mixture, God and flesh perfected in one nature,[47] that brings θεοποίησις (divinization) and salvation to humanity. Apollinarius is far from being chary of explaining the union in terms of μῖξις (mixture) or σύγκρασις (combination); for him the union is an organic or biological union exactly analogous to the composition of a human person out of flesh and spirit.[48] The virgin birth is important precisely because it produces a biological freak; there is no male sperm charged with vivifying power – instead there is the descent of the Spirit. So the 'one nature' did not mean for Apollinarius that the Logos took on a new condition of existence (as it would for Cyril), but it meant that Christ is a unique kind of being combining God and humanity. That is why 'eternal enfleshment' is an idea not wholly foreign to the tendencies of his thought. Nor is it strange to find the idea of the flesh being *homoousios* (of one substance) with God: 'Flesh did not become an addition to the Godhead by grace, but it is συνουσιωμένη (united in *ousia*) with the Godhead and σύμφυτος (innate, natural) to it.' 'His flesh gives us life because it is συνουσιωμένη with the Godhead.'[49] (This union of *ousia* was what offended Diodore more than anything else; his treatise against Apollinarius is called *Contra Synousiastes*.) This concept of union may also help to explain Apollinarius' anthropological confusion. For in this unique individual, the Logos is not just the Mind, he is also the life-giving principle – the πνεῦμα ζωοποιοῦν. So whether Apollinarius uses dichotomist or trichotomist language depends upon whether he is thinking of the moral issues at stake (and therefore treating the Logos as

---

45 *First Letter to Dionysius* 7 (L 259).
46 Frs. 113 (L 234) and 19 (L 209).
47 Frs. 113 (L 234) and 19 (L 209).
48 Fr. 11 (L 207); *De unione* 5 (L 187); *De fide et inc.* 7 (L 199). See Riedmatten (1948) and (1956, 1957).
49 Fr. 36 (L 212); Fr. 116 (L 235).

νοῦς – Mind), or whether he is concentrating his attention on the imparting of divine life and immortality to humanity. Far from clearly distinguishing spirit, mind and soul, his only interest really was to establish the organic unity of this unique mediator. The 'compound unity' which he posited meant that Apollinarius did in a sense recognize the two natures (as Theodoret could show in his florilegia) and that for him, unlike the later Eutychians, the flesh was not transformed into divinity,[50] but was united with divinity to form a unique *tertium quid*.

We have noticed several points where Apollinarius' views seem to be derived from scripture; yet Raven and Mühlenberg have each regarded his Christology as the culmination of the Hellenic tradition of Christian theology. Broad generalizations of this kind should be treated with caution. If Raven thought the 'Monophysite' type of theology was Hellenic, and regarded the Antiochene 'two natures' Christology as representing the more realistic biblical tradition native to Syria, Wigram[51] reversed the assessment, regarding the 'Dyophysite' position as belonging to Greek intellectualism and attributing Monophysitism to the simple Syrian ascetic. Yet there is no doubt that Apollinarius' teaching was highly sophisticated, and Apollinarius himself was a highly cultured intellectual who had received a thoroughly Greek education. We should never forget that he and his father remained schoolteachers though becoming clerics, and that the few details of his life that we have are connected with his love of the classics. The first incident that we know anything about was when the two Apollinarii, father and son, were excluded from communion and sent to do penance for attending the recital of a hymn in honour of Dionysus. The incident arose because of their friendship with Epiphanius the Sophist, whose lectures they both attended. Some thirty years later (AD 360), when the Emperor Julian forbade Christians to teach pagan literature in schools, the two Apollinarii published a rewritten Bible for school use in the form of Homeric epics, Euripidean tragedies, comedies like those of Menander, Pindaric lyrics and Platonic dialogues. All this has been lost; some have argued that Apollinarius was the author of an extant paraphrase of the Psalms in hexameters, but its authenticity has been seriously undermined by more recent critical examination.[52]

One way or another Apollinarius proved a notable defender of the faith, against Julian, against Arius. He also wrote thirty books against Porphyry and many commentaries on scripture. He was a powerful and respected academic. It was not only Athanasius who had consulted him; Basil as a young man wrote to enquire about the meaning of *homoousios* – a correspondence whose authenticity was doubted in the light of Basil's later embarrassed denials, but was successfully defended by Prestige and de Riedmatten.[53] Although most attention has inevitably been given to Apollinarius' Christology, his Trinitarian views, as expressed in the *Kata meros pistis* and the Basil correspondence, are not without interest. Apollinarius succeeds in upholding the *homoousion*, the Trinity as a whole being the one holy God to whom worship is due, while at

---

50 Fr. 121 (L 237).
51 Wigram (1923).
52 Text: Ludwich (1912). See Golega (1960).
53 Prestige (1956); Riedmatten (1956, 1957).

the same time preserving some of the traditional subordinationism as a defence against Sabellianism. The Son is God because he has 'the Father's Deity naturally' (τὴν πατρικὴν θεότητα φυσικῶς);[54] 'we say the Trinity is one God, not as knowing one by a combination of three but thus – what the Father is as source and origin (ἀρχικῶς τε καὶ γεννητικῶς), this the Son is as image and offspring (εἰκὼν καὶ γέννημα) of the Father.' He is not the Father's brother.[55] This is not far from the position reached by the Cappadocians.

How was it then that this respected leader of the faithful Nicenes in Laodicea came to be condemned for heresy? This is the historical puzzle raised by the career of Apollinarius. He is supposed to have taught his dangerous doctrines for thirty years without meeting any opposition. He was eventually excluded by the Council of Constantinople (381), though in somewhat ambiguous terms. Prior to that, in the late 370s he had been condemned by the Roman pope and by a local synod at Antioch. As already noted, the idea that earlier in the 360s his condemnation was implied by the *Tomus ad Antiochenos*, or that Athanasius criticized him in the *Epistle to Epictetus*, seems very unlikely. In the 370s Jerome attended his lectures in Antioch – he was still respected by the wider Church. About the same time, however, Epiphanius found dangerous views being expressed in Antioch, at this stage associating them with Vitalis. A few years later he wrote very strongly against Apollinarius in the *Adversus haereses*. Most people, however, were still much more worried by the Arian ascendency and the tragic split among the anti-Arians in Antioch, where the Eustathian party had the support of Rome while the Melitians were favoured by the majority of Eastern bishops. (Jerome, when in Antioch, was most perplexed as to which party he ought to communicate with.) Basil expressed concern about Apollinarius' activities about this time, but he was less worried by his doctrinal position than by his formation of yet another schismatical group in the Syrian capital. Even after his condemnation Apollinarius was accorded great respect by his critics for his life and his scholarship, and clearly he enjoyed the support of many Nicenes almost until the Nicene cause emerged triumphant. Apart from Epiphanius' criticisms, it was not until after 381 that energetic refutations of his doctrine were produced by the two Gregories of Cappadocia, Gregory Nazianzen in his letters to Cledonius, and Gregory Nyssen in his *Antirrheticus*, a point-by-point refutation of Apollinarius' *Apodeixis*.[56]

---

54 *KMP* 27 (L 176).

55 *KMP* 18–19 (L 173).

56 Daley (2002), pp. 469f., argues that both Gregories object to what they perceive to be a fundamentally different soteriology in Apollinarius' description of Christ from their own. Apollinarius understood the significant feature of Christ's saving power depending upon his *difference from* fallen human nature. The Gregories 'understood the mystery of salvation as the incipient transformation of all humanity through the communication, by God the Word, of divine virtue and life to a complete and normal human being united personally to himself'.

4 Diodore of Tarsus

Another critic of Apollinarius, Diodore of Tarsus, was more local and more directly involved to the extent that he eventually provided some of the grist for Apollinarius' mill. They must have been contemporaries, Apollinarius probably being somewhat the older man; for Diodore became bishop of Tarsus just as Apollinarius was being rejected, and Apollinarius seems then to have been well into his sixties. Though sharply divided in their Christology, in other ways they had a number of similarities. Both seem to have been well educated in the classics, for Diodore apparently studied at Athens as a young man. Like Apollinarius, he used his learning to confute paganism – both apparently wrote lengthy tomes against Porphyry, and Diodore is said to have written on many other philosophical topics, astronomy, providence, first principles, the elements and so on. Both were involved in the struggle against Julian; for if Apollinarius tried to foil him with his massive literary productions, the sources attribute heroic acts to Diodore when Julian settled on Antioch and began his programme of re-establishing pagan rites. Julian himself confessed that he found Diodore a great thorn in his side:

> Diodore, a charlatan priest of the Nazarene . . . is clearly a sharp-witted sophist of that rustic creed . . . For he sailed to Athens to the detriment of the public welfare, rashly taking to philosophy and literature, and arming his tongue with rhetorical devices against the heavenly gods.

Julian went on to suggest that Diodore's pitifully wasted condition was a sign not of his philosophic habits (referring to his asceticism), but of the punishment of the gods.[57] It is difficult to reconcile such reports with Jerome's somewhat disparaging remarks suggesting that Diodore was an inferior imitator of Eusebius of Emesa and 'unacquainted with literature'.[58]

So Diodore, like Apollinarius, seems to have been advanced in secular learning and to have confronted paganism. Both also confronted heresy, Arianism and Sabellianism being enemies they had in common – indeed, Diodore's Trinitarian teaching seems to have had a remarkable similarity to that of Apollinarius with its tendency towards subordinationism.[59] Both also made a distinctive contribution to the musical life of the Christian community; for Apollinarius' sacred songs became popular for festivals and were even sung by men at their work and women at the loom, while Diodore introduced the practice of antiphonal psalm-singing, dividing the choir into two groups.[60] Both were steeped in the scriptures and both produced biblical commentaries characterized by economy of explanation and lack of speculative allegory.[61]

---

57 Julian, *Ep.* 55 (fragments from a letter to Photinus preserved by Facundus), in *Works* III, LCL 1923.

58 Jerome, *Vir.* 119.

59 Abramowski (1931).

60 Sozomen, *HE* vi.25 for Apollinarius; Theodoret, *HE* ii.19 for Diodore.

61 Jerome, *Vir. ill.* 104, on Apollinarius' exegetical work. Exegetical fragments can be found in Staab (1933/84), and in Mühlenberg (1975). On Diodore's exegesis, see Schweizer (1941); Schäublin (1974); Young (1997a); O'Keefe (2000); Hill (2005).

It was Diodore, however, who acquired the greater reputation in this particular area. Most of Diodore's life was spent in a monastery near Antioch, and there he exercised a profound influence on two outstanding figures of the next generation, John Chrysostom and Theodore of Mopsuestia. The most important thing Diodore seems to have done was to lay the foundations of biblical exegesis, which enabled the latter to develop his great work of scriptural commentary, becoming known as 'The Interpreter', and the former to earn his great name for exegetical preaching.

Some fragments of Diodore's commentaries have been preserved in the Catenae, but the work of collecting, editing and publishing them has not yet been effectively carried out. There is continuing debate about the authenticity of the available material, and considerable confusion between extracts attributed to Diodore and extracts attributed to Theodore. The general lines of Diodore's approach seem fairly clear, however; he insisted primarily on the 'historical' dimension of the text,[62] and rejected excessive allegorizing. His main concern was elucidation of the actual words and sentences of scripture, providing etymologies, trying to discern the 'scriptural' sense of words by comparing texts, looking at the context and sequences of thought, paraphrasing to bring out the meaning. His detractors found his work prosaic and unexciting. However, he did not abandon the traditional view that the Old Testament had a prophetic sense, that an action or event might be a 'type' pointing beyond itself to fulfilment in Christ. What he repudiated was the elaborate and artificial interpretation of every verbal detail according to imaginative allegorical symbols. What he emphasized was the importance of taking the factual reference of the text seriously. Altogether Diodore does not seem to have gone far beyond the commonsense practice of many exegetes in this period, and parallels to his methods and comments can be traced in many contemporaries not associated with the Antiochene tradition, people like Eusebius of Caesarea, Eusebius of Emesa, Epiphanius, Basil, occasionally even Gregory of Nyssa though he stood nearer to the Origenist approach. Diodore's successors, especially Theodore, were to develop some of his ideas to extremes; but Diodore himself seems to have concentrated primarily on refining the techniques of explication without calling in question too many traditional assumptions about the Christological reference of the whole of scripture. This general assessment is upheld by the identification of his *Commentary on the Psalms*,[63] an important addition to the evidence concerning the famed scripture teacher who taught key Antiochene exegetes. Here we can read his own comments on allegory and how to proceed in interpreting a text.

5 Diodore's Christology

If the fragmentary character of Apollinarius' work makes reconstruction of his Christological teaching difficult, how much more is this so in the case of

---

62 For the difference between Antiochene and modern understandings of 'history', see Young (1997a, 1997b); O'Keefe (2000); etc.

63 Text: Olivier (1980); ET Hill (2005); cf. Froehlich (1984) and discussion in Young (1997a) and O'Keefe (2000).

Diodore! Of his huge output very little remains, and concerning the reliability of the surviving dogmatic fragments serious doubts have been raised because mostly they come from hostile sources. Fragments in Latin and a few in Greek can be found in the literature of later Christological controversy, but nearly all that has survived has been preserved by hostile Syrian 'Monophysite' writers in their native Syriac. All this material appears to derive ultimately from collections of quotations (florilegia) drawn up by the opponents of the Antiochene theology at the time of the Nestorian controversy. Later 'Monophysites' used Cyril's now lost work, *Contra Diodorum et Theodorum*, and Cyril seems not to have consulted the original works of his opponents himself, but to have based his work on previously prepared florilegia. These, it has been suggested, originally came from Apollinarians who had tampered with the material to blacken Diodore's name.[64] The basis of that final claim seems little more than speculation, and most recent discussions have assumed the authenticity of the fragments if only because the terminology used has not been adapted to conform with the later formulae of the Antiochene school – in other words, Diodore's Christology as portrayed in the fragments is distinctive and therefore not likely to have been falsified.[65] Yet doubts remain; obviously selection will have lifted his more controversial remarks out of context, and a complete picture of the basic shape and motives of his theological position is unlikely to be obtainable. Furthermore, the majority of the extracts are drawn from his work *Against the Synousiasts*, so that they are likely to reflect strong reaction against Apollinarius and not necessarily give a balanced view of Diodore's own theology. Access to the extant fragments is less straightforward than is the case for Apollinarius, but they have been collected and published in periodical articles, the Syriac being supplied with French or German translation.[66]

The difficulties posed by lack of evidence used to be resolved by the assumption that Diodore was an important representative of the Antiochene school; his doctrine, like his exegesis, was associated with that of his pupil Theodore, though regarded as probably less extreme since his other famous pupil, John Chrysostom, was clearly nearer to the orthodox mainstream. So no one questioned the fact that he was instrumental in developing the Word–Man or 'two natures' Christology which Antiochene theologians so determinedly defended in the ensuing Christological controversies. A fragment of Cyril complains that having abandoned the Macedonian heresy, Diodore consorted with the orthodox until he fell into another sickness, saying and writing that the one born of the holy virgin from the seed of David was a different Son from the Word of the Father.[67] This summary of his position was taken as typical, and while the question how far he was a 'Nestorian before Nestorius' was repeatedly debated, the generally Antiochene bent of his Christological thinking went unchallenged. It was assumed that he must have been the most important of those described by Apollinarius as followers of Paul of Samosata, who divided the Christ and

---

64 Richard (1946/77).

65 Grillmeier (1965), p. 270 (2nd ed., 1975, p. 360), n. 34; a considerable discussion of the question of authenticity will be found in Sullivan (1956).

66 Brière (1946) publishes the fragments from British Museum Codex 12156. Abramowski (1949) includes also Greek, Latin and Syriac fragments from elsewhere.

67 Schwartz, *ACO* I.i.6, 151f., quoted in Abramowski (1949), p. 62.

taught 'two Sons'. Grillmeier's suggestion[68] that he actually started out from a Word–Flesh type of Christology was therefore an innovation which stimulated some strong replies.[69]

Diodore's terminology, argued Grillmeier, is predominantly of the Word–Flesh type. Like Athanasius, he not merely attributes Jesus' increase in age and wisdom to the flesh, not the Logos, but even understands this increase not as human progress but as the gradual imparting of wisdom to the flesh by the Godhead. Never does the human soul of Jesus play a positive role in his Christological formulations, nor is it the central point in his debate with Apollinarius, where he is chiefly concerned with the theological dangers of Apollinarius' fusion of Word and flesh into one unique entity. Only gradually did his thinking shift from the Word–Flesh pattern which, Grillmeier suggests, he got from Eusebius of Emesa, a key link in the history of Christology. Even when Apollinarianism drove him to modify his thinking, the soul never became a 'theological factor', a positive element in his Christological thinking.

It must be admitted that Diodore does speak of the Logos taking flesh rather than 'a man'. Even Cyril accuses Diodore of trying to get away with his Nestorianism by deceptively speaking of 'soulless flesh'.[70] Theodore's formula 'the Man assumed' is never found in the fragments of Diodore, and it is proper that we should be warned against assuming that Diodore was the source of all his pupil's ideas. Yet the fragments we have do assert a Christological dualism which Grillmeier, according to his critics, has only succeeded in obscuring. Over-concentration on the Word–Flesh/Word–Man formulae can result in imposing a preconceived framework on the material and so distort the interpreter's perception. The terminology should not be regarded as decisive: representatives of both sides in the Christological controversies continued to use 'flesh' and 'man' interchangeably, asserting that this was scriptural usage. Nor is the use or absence of a 'human soul' in a Christology an infallible guide to the basic Christological principles in operation: Didymus of Alexandria, for example, affirmed the soul but did not develop an Antiochene dualism.[71] Soul or no soul, what makes Diodore's Christology Antiochene is his refusal to make the Logos the direct subject of the incarnate experiences. 'The one who is the seed of David', 'the one born of Mary', he it is who suffers and dies and is raised, not the Logos.[72] The Logos did not submit to two γεννήσεις (meaning 'begetting' and 'birth'), one before the ages from God and one from the virgin; rather he built himself a temple in Mary's womb. He was not *mixed* with flesh; for the one who was begotten from the Father before all ages did not receive change or suffering. He was not changed into flesh, he was not crucified, he did not eat or drink or grow tired, but remained incorporeal and undefiled, never departing from his Father's likeness.[73] According to Diodore, 'the likeness of

---

68 Grillmeier (1965, ET of German original 1951), with revisions in 2nd edn (1975).

69 Sullivan (1956); Greer (1966).

70 Cyril of Alexandria, Frs., in Pusey (1872a) III, p. 494. Abramowski (1949) does not give the full quotation.

71 See above, pp. 99–100.

72 For example Frs. 15, 17, 19 (Brière and Abramowski, henceforth cited as B. and Ab.).

73 These statements are found in Frs. 22, 28, 19, 20 (B. and Ab.); 35 (Ab. only).

the Father' must be distinguished from 'the likeness of a servant'. Paul speaks not of the God–Word becoming a child from Mary, but of the Man born of Mary being sent for our salvation. The one born of Mary, being really a man, could not have existed before the heaven and the earth; if he did, he was not man. If he was from Abraham, how could he be before Abraham? If he was son of David, how could he be before the ages?[74] Given statements of this kind, it is not surprising that a Monophysite excerpter could parallel Diodore's remarks with those of Leo the blasphemer (meaning the Pope whose *Tome* was canonized at Chalcedon).[75] Diodore did teach a 'two natures' Christology with a strongly dualistic basis. Only καταχρηστικῶς (inexactly) could the son of David be iden-tified with the Son of God.[76] Naturally enough, Diodore's opponents accused him of preaching 'two Sons'; and his reply avoided the point. He asserted that he did not say two sons of David, for he did not say that the God–Word became Son of David; nor did he say two Sons of God, for he did not say two came from God's *ousia*, but that the God–Word dwelt in the seed of David.[77] Diodore failed to see that what worried his critics was precisely that refusal to identify the Son of God with the son of David, which suggested two different sons in a loose collocation.

So, on the basis of the surviving fragments, Grillmeier's critics undoubt-edly appear to have the stronger case, especially when it is recognized that one important fragment in which Diodore appears to assert the unity of Christ is in fact an attempt to summarize Apollinarian teaching. If at first sight it looked as though Diodore accepted the body–soul analogy as a Christological paradigm and affirmed a unity of subject, the same one being from God and in the man-ger, on the cross and in heaven, such an interpretation cannot be maintained in the light of another fragment where Diodore subjects the body–soul analogy to searching criticism and asserts clearly that 'they confess that the same one is of God before the ages and of David in the last times . . . they confess that the same one is impassible and passible . . .'. In both passages[78] Diodore is stating the Apollinarian position in order to highlight their error. He could not see how any identification could be made between the divine and human subjects.

There is nothing quite like paucity of evidence for producing new theories and lively debates, and when that evidence is clearly slanted and is drawn almost entirely from one work related to one controversy, the potential for pro-ducing reconstructions with quite different emphases is greatly enhanced. Of course, Grillmeier admitted that Diodore develops a Christology of 'distinc-tion' or 'division', but he put his emphasis on the fact that this is built onto a Word–Flesh framework. What his critics do not seem to have fully grasped is the fact that Grillmeier's main point concerns the background and develop-ment of Diodore's ideas rather than their eventual shape. What he is arguing is that Diodore did not start out with a ready-made Word–Man framework

---

74 These statements are drawn from Frs. 14, 12, 4 (B. and Ab.); cf. 44 (Ab. only).

75 Frs. 46–9 (Ab. only).

76 Fr. 27 (B. and Ab.).

77 Fr. 42 (Ab. only); cf. Fr. 30 (B. and Ab.).

78 The two fragments concerned are 2 and 26 (B. and Ab.); for discussion, see Richard (1945). See esp. Greer (1966). Both these passages are misinterpreted by Abramowski (1931).

inherited from some long-standing Antiochene tradition. He repudiated Paul of Samosata; direct influence from Eustathius is unlikely in view of the fact that Diodore belonged not to the Eustathian but the Melitian party, nor regarded the soul as an important issue. So Grillmeier makes much of the link with Eusebius of Emesa that Jerome mentions, and on this basis posits a development from *Logos–Sarx* roots. If Grillmeier is right, it reduces the likelihood that Apollinarius developed his views in conscious opposition to Diodore, and there are certainly indications that they did not come into direct doctrinal conflict with one another until the 380s, that is, after Apollinarius had been condemned; thus, while their positions may have hardened because of their reaction to one another, this reaction did not create their differing Christologies.

Why then did Diodore develop a Christological duality? Grillmeier suggests that the debate with Julian was instrumental. Julian credits Diodore with having invented the divinity of Christ, and elsewhere accuses some who distinguish Jesus Christ from the Logos of evading the issue. 'Was Diodore driven to work out two subjects for Christological sayings by the attacks of the pagan emperor?' asks Grillmeier. Certainly the starting-point of Diodore's theology seems to be the need to preserve 'the Godness of God' in the person of the Logos. To identify a man with God was nothing other than blasphemous, and certainly laid the Christians open to ridicule from philosophers. The God–Word simply could not accept change or suffering, since he was incorporeal, infinite and in every way shared the divinity of the Father; Diodore complains of the injury done to the Word by putting him in composition with the body.[79] But could it not be that Diodore inherited this concern for the unalterable divinity of the Logos from the debate with the 'Arians', which was by no means over at the time when his theology must have been developing? His process of reasoning could well have followed the same pattern as that of Eustathius, even though he did not adopt the notion of the human soul as a way of explicitly working out the problems. By implication if not terminology, he made the man descended from David and born of Mary the subject of those incarnate experiences which he could not attribute to the Logos. He had taken a parallel if not identical step, and the Arian controversy is sufficient to account for it.

We can find further confirmation of this. Undoubtedly in many respects Diodore anticipated the 'two natures' Christology of Theodore and the later Antiochenes, and this includes treating the union between divine and human in Christ as one not of nature but of grace. There was one Son of God by nature, affirmed Diodore, and the Man from Mary, though by nature from David, was from God by grace; he shared the one Sonship, one glory, one immortality and one worship, by grace. Like his successors Diodore had to defend himself from the charge that he regarded the one from David's seed as no different from the prophets; the prophets, he explained, enjoyed only particular grace in moderate quantities, whereas he had it permanently and was entirely filled with the glory and wisdom of the God–Word.[80] However, even at this point, where Diodore so clearly anticipates the later Antiochenes, his thinking can be seen to be

---

79 Frs. 19, 20 (B. and Ab.); 31 (Ab. only).

80 These statements are drawn from Frs. 30 (B. and Ab., and cf. also 27); 31, 34 (Ab. only); and 38 (Ab. only). For discussion, see Fairbairn (2003).

related to earlier opponents of Arius. Like Athanasius, he attributes weakness, mutability and so on to the flesh, and to the God–Word things like miracles, exceptional powers, superhuman knowledge; and among the achievements of the Godhead he appears to have reckoned the conquest of temptation.[81] In other words, where the later Antiochenes insisted on the moral victory of the Man, Diodore seems to have followed the older view that only one who was immutable by nature could have remained immutable in the face of temptation. Similarly he treats the progress of the Saviour as the gradual revelation of the Logos, rather than the advancement of human maturity.[82] His thought still moves along the lines of the anti-Arian arguments developed by Athanasius, and thus what offended Diodore about Apollinarian teaching was not its denial of a human soul or mind in the Christ, but its blending of flesh and Word into one entity so compromising the utter divinity of the Logos. Indeed, there is a sense in which each of these antagonists was developing different aspects of Athanasius' answer to Arius.

There is a good deal to be said, therefore, for accepting Grillmeier's argument that Diodore did not start out with a ready-made Word–Man Christology. Yet the surviving fragments, most of which come from his work against Apollinarius, do suggest that, whatever the roots of his theology, it had developed along the lines which in many ways foreshadow the ideas, if not the terminology, of the later Antiochenes, and over and over again in his debate with Apollinarius arguments later used in Christological conflicts were anticipated.

Diodore and Apollinarius had a good deal in common, even in the doctrinal area. They shared opposition to Arianism, had similar Trinitarian views, appealed to scripture and acted in loyal devotion to Nicene orthodoxy. They even used Christological language which to a considerable extent overlapped.[83] But each was associated with a different anti-Arian group in Antioch, and each approached the Christological question in a totally different way. So it happened that at the time when Apollinarius was losing the support of the catholic Church, Diodore rose to prominence; elected bishop of Tarsus in 378, he was present at the Council of Constantinople three years later and, together with Gregory of Nyssa and one or two others, he was officially designated an exponent of orthodoxy. Both Diodore and Apollinarius lived until the early 390s; but if Diodore, unlike Apollinarius, died in the peace of the Church, his teaching became highly controversial within half a century and was eventually condemned. So by a curious irony, the two opponents came to share the same fate, and though both had lived as defenders of the faith, most of their writings are lost in obscurity.

For Further Reading

English translations

Hill, R. C., 2005. *Diodore of Tarsus. Commentary on Psalms 1–51*, Atlanta, GA: SBL.

---

81 Frs. 46–9 (Ab. only).
82 Fr. 36 (Ab. only).
83 Abramowski (1931) comments on the parallels, though she probably overestimates them by her misinterpretation of Frs. 2 and 26.

Studies

Prestige, G. L., 1956. *St Basil the Great and Apollinarius of Laodicea*, London: SPCK.

Raven, C. E., 1923. *Apollinarianism*, Cambridge and New York: Cambridge University Press.

Greer, R. A., 1966. 'The Antiochene Christology of Diodore of Tarsus', *JTS* NS 17, pp. 327–41.

Grillmeier, A., 1965/75. *Christ in Christian Tradition*, ET, London and Oxford: Mowbrays.

Spoerl, K. M., 1993. 'Apollinarius and the Response to Early Arian Christology', *SP* xxvi, pp. 421–7.

——, 1994. 'Apollinarian Christology and the anti-Marcellan tradition', *JTS* (NS) 45, pp. 545–68.

Young, Frances M., 1997a. *Biblical Exegesis and the Formation of Christian Culture*, Cambridge: Cambridge University Press.

——, 1997b. 'The Fourth Century Reaction against Allegory', *SP* 30, pp. 120–5.

III Theodore of Mopsuestia

Now is the time for me to say, 'Sing unto the Lord a new song, for he has done marvellous things.' Indeed a new song is required for new things, as we are dealing with the New Testament which God established for the human race through the Economy of our Lord Jesus Christ, when he abolished all old things and showed new things in their place. Everyone who is in Christ is a new creature; old things are passed away and all things are become new ... He gave us this new covenant which is fit for those who are renewed; and because of this covenant we receive the knowledge of these mysteries so that we should put off the old man and put on the new man which is renewed after the image of him who created him, where there is neither Jew nor Greek, bond nor free, but Christ is all and in all. This will take place in reality in the next world ... Because it was necessary that the faith in the truth of the future gifts should remain in us, ... these awe-inspiring mysteries were confided to us in order that through them as through symbols we might gradually approach our future hope ...[84]

These were the words with which Theodore greeted prospective Christians in his catechetical lectures. In true Pauline fashion, and indeed in Pauline language, he confronted them with the *newness* of the gospel and the exhortation to conform their lives to the promise of incorruptibility in Christ. What a striking appreciation of the eschatological dimension of New Testament thought, an appreciation which considerably modifies, if it does not quite remove, the then current Platonic emphasis on escape from the world below to the world of spiritual realities in heaven! While at times retaining the language of earthly and heavenly, of time and eternity, Theodore also points to successive stages in the creative purposes of God, of a new creation anticipated in Christ and awaiting its final consummation.

---

84 Theodore, *Catechetical Homilies* i (Mingana, 1932), text pp. 118f., ET pp. 19f.

Those doctrines recognized as characteristic of Theodore are closely related to this perception. His sense of the overarching story of God's purposes from Beginning to End reinforced his emphasis on the *pragmata* (concrete realities) of scripture; the writings of the Old Testament addressed themselves to their own situation, while the New Testament proclaims a new saving act of God and points forward to the consummation of God's purposes in the future. Allegorical method was to be eschewed, if only because it destroyed this perspective and undermined the newness of the gospel by finding Christ everywhere in the Old Testament. Also clearly linked with his eschatological perspective is Theodore's so-called doctrine of the two ages; he criticized the current tendency to see a human being as primarily a spiritual being trapped in flesh by the Fall, and explored the Pauline contrast between man-in-Adam and man-in-Christ, creation and new creation, two καταστάσεις (states). Such thinking is again the basis of his characteristic emphasis on the genuine and complete humanity of Christ – indeed, Christ is 'image' of God as the one who fulfils what Adam was meant to be.[85] The 'Man assumed' has a crucial place in the shape of Theodore's Christology, because for Theodore salvation depends upon a Christ who is the first fruits of this new creation.

Given these characteristic doctrines, it is hardly surprising that some modern studies display a tendency to adulate Theodore as a much misunderstood forerunner of modern theology and exegesis.[86] But this estimate will not altogether do. Theodore was still a child of his own time; current debates and current presuppositions inevitably coloured his thinking. The features congenial to modern thought are easily exaggerated, and factors which seem of supreme importance to him are glossed over or disregarded. Yet Theodore's rehabilitation was due, and the narrowly defined debate as to whether he was a heretic or not is in danger of missing the more interesting aspects of his contribution.[87] Like Origen he was a man of outstanding influence and importance, with a particularly interesting place in the history of theology; like Origen he was condemned in the sixth century by an edict of Justinian I, having been a contentious figure since his own day. The supreme allegorist and allegorism's prime critic were both victims of Byzantine politics, and both alike deserved reassessment. That reassessment has been facilitated by modern scholarship, by its collection and critical examination of alleged fragments, by its rediscovery, translation and interpretation of lost works.

What then do we know of this remarkable figure? The only fact about Theodore's life of any interest to Socrates and Sozomen was his early association with John Chrysostom.[88] They were fellow students under Libanius, and together gave up secular pursuits for an ascetic life, concentrating on biblical studies under Diodore. When Theodore, attracted by marriage and a legal career, abandoned the monastery, Chrysostom wrote two eloquent letters which succeeded

---

85 See further McLeod (1999, 2002, 2005, 2009).

86 For example, Patterson (1926).

87 For the debate since the mid-nineteenth century about whether Theodore was Nestorian before Nestorius, see the useful summaries in Kalantzis (2004); Clayton (2007 – that is chapter 2 on the Antiochene tradition inherited by Theodoret); and McLeod (2009).

88 Socrates, *HE* vi.3; Sozomen, *HE* viii.2.

in persuading him against his intentions.[89] It is evident that Theodore, though still under twenty, had won Chrysostom's admiration and respect for the intensity of his commitment to study and for the joy with which he practised ascetic self-discipline. Further details of his life are shrouded in mist, but it seems likely that he stayed on as Diodore's pupil until Diodore left to become bishop of Tarsus in 378. Probably about 383 he was ordained priest in Antioch, and he was consecrated bishop of Mopsuestia in 392. There he is reputed to have been an active evangelist who turned many from the errors of idolatry and paganism, as well as establishing the truth against Arian and other heretics. His defenders later spoke of him expounding scripture 'in all the churches of the East',[90] but this probably refers to the widespread influence of his scriptural commentaries rather than extensive travels. Theodore died in 428.

So on the whole Theodore's life was uneventful. When he died he was held in great respect, especially in those regions under the influence of the Patriarchate of Antioch. But within three years the Nestorian controversy had broken out. Theodore's name was associated with that of Nestorius, and so were Theodore's doctrines. The Antiochenes steadfastly refused to countenance his condemnation even when they compromised over the case of Nestorius, but for the 'Monophysites' his work was always to be suspect, once Cyril had identified him and Diodore as the true originators of Nestorianism. His eventual condemnation meant the disappearance of most of his works, apart from quotation and misquotation in controversial writings and histories. Yet for a century they had enjoyed wide dissemination among the 'Dyophysites', particularly in Syria. Prior to Chalcedon – indeed, in the early stages of the Christological battle – Syriac translations of the revered works of Theodore 'the Interpreter' had been produced, and it is to Syriac sources that we now look for a considerable amount of our information about Theodore and his work. Four treatises have been known in Syriac versions in modern times: his *Disputation with the Macedonians* (published 1913),[91] his *De Incarnatione* (lost before publication – one of the less generally known tragedies of World War One), his *Catechetical Homilies* (published 1932)[92] and his *Commentary on John* (published 1940).[93] Syriac catalogues of the thirteenth and fourteenth centuries give us an idea of the quantity of works once available.

Theodore's output seems to have been largely commentaries on scripture and dogmatic works. The Syriac catalogues suggest that he commented on almost all the books of the Bible, but prior to the publication of the Syriac version of the *Commentary on John*, only two exegetical works survived in their entirety, the complete Greek text of his *Commentary on the Minor Prophets*[94] and a Latin version of the *Commentary on the Ten Minor Epistles of St Paul*,[95] which escaped destruction by being attributed to Ambrose. Now more is known to be extant, if

89 Chrysostom to Theodore, PG 47.277–316; the second letter is personal, the first more like a treatise and not entirely applicable to Theodore's situation. See Carter (1962).
90 John of Antioch, quoted by Facundus, *Defence of the Three Chapters* ii.2.
91 Nau (1913).
92 Mingana (1932, 1933); also Tonneau (1949).
93 Vosté (1940).
94 Text in Migne, PG 66; ET Hill (2003).
95 Swete (1880–2); Latin version with Greek fragments.

only in fragments; some awaits publication.[96] From the Catenae quite extensive Greek fragments of his *Commentaries on Genesis, on the Psalms* and *on the Gospel of John* have been gleaned[97] – indeed, the Greek fragments of the last are thought by some to be a preferable guide to Theodore's work than the more complete Syriac.[98]

The most important of his dogmatic works were those against Apollinarius and Eunomius,[99] and above all his *De Incarnatione*. Of these we now have only a collection of fragments from various sources: the *Acta Conciliorum* quoting the documents on the basis of which Theodore was condemned; the *Defence of the Three Chapters* written in Latin by Facundus, and the treatise of Leontius of Byzantium *Against the Nestorians and the Eutychians*. The authenticity and accuracy of these fragments has been seriously questioned, particularly by Richard and Devreesse,[100] who brought charges of deliberate falsification against the compilers of hostile florilegia (collections of extracts). Discrepancies between the Greek fragments and various Syriac discoveries seemed to provide evidence of tampering with the tradition at some point. A spirited defence of the integrity of the Greek fragments by F. A. Sullivan[101] reopened the question; he argued that absolute confidence in the word for word accuracy of the Syriac translator was misplaced, and serious modification or interpolation of the Greek text was unproven. Not all have been convinced, however;[102] there is at least substantial evidence that the compiler did not shrink from deliberate suppression of the context, so putting Theodore's views in the blackest possible light.[103] The question of context is what makes the Syriac evidence so indispensable. The Syriac version of the *Catechetical Homilies* provides us with our only complete dogmatic work in which suspicious statements can be seen in a total context and therefore in better perspective. However, the continuing critical problems mean that the student of Theodore is hampered by lack of a convenient and reliable collection of extant texts; Migne is hopelessly out of date and in need of critical revision, and the more recently discovered material in the Catenae and in Syriac are scattered about in learned articles and oriental collections. So for initial studies of Theodore the English translation of selections which appeared in 2009 is all the more important.[104]

As we have noticed, the churches of the East honoured Theodore as 'the Interpreter'; and there are indeed good reasons for seeing interpretation of scripture

---

96 For example, the Syriac of some of his *Commentary on the Psalms* is extant – van Rompay (1982); the *Commentary on Ecclesiastes* was discovered early in the twentieth century, but has never been published.

97 Devreesse (1939, 1948). Some material is available in Migne, *PG* 66, but it needs critical examination and supplementation; cf. Staab (1933/84). Further relevant articles can be traced in the Patrologies and McLeod (2009).

98 Kalantzis (2004), who translates the Greek material collected by Devreesse (1948).

99 For fragments of the *Contra Eunomium*, see Abramowski (1958) and Vaggione (1980).

100 Richard (1943/77); Richard (1946/77); Devreesse (1948).

101 Sullivan (1956).

102 McKenzie (1958); cf. Sullivan (1959).

103 McKenzie (1953).

104 McLeod (2009).

as his main interest, as well as the basis of much of his characteristic theology. How then did Theodore interpret? What methods did he use? What presuppositions can we discern underlying his work?

1 Interpretation of scripture

Theodore's commentaries are brief and largely confined to the basics of scriptural exegesis.[105] Where appropriate he discusses problems of translation and text, within the limitations of available techniques and his lack of Hebrew. He discusses the meanings of words and phrases, especially those distinctive and characteristic of biblical usage. He notes where metaphorical expressions are used, for he knows that it is nonsense to take some phrases literally. Frequently he makes use of summaries and paraphrases to bring out the gist of the argument in the text before him, and he regularly writes historical and circumstantial introductions to fill in and explain the background. The result, it must be admitted, is often dull, but it conforms to the basic philological principles of ancient rhetorical schools.[106] Where recent work commends his historico-critical sense, earlier scholars commented upon the dry, pedestrian character of his commentaries compared with the imaginative insights of allegorical and mystical exegesis.[107]

It is reported that Theodore wrote a book *On Allegory and History* and the universal comment of ancient witnesses was that Theodore avoided allegory and concentrated on 'historical' interpretation[108] – indeed, he was accused of interpreting the Old Testament like the Jews. The Church in general found his attitude problematical not simply because of the deeply engrained influence of allegory against which the Antiochene standpoint was a healthy reaction, but because of the long tradition of Christological interpretation of the Old Testament which went right back to the New Testament itself. Theodore's early work was the most startling. He himself almost admits that he overplayed his hand in the *Commentary on the Psalms*.[109] For most commentators the fact that verses from Psalms 22 and 69 appear on the lips of Jesus in the Gospel accounts of the passion was enough to establish their prophetic character; and an extension of the principle meant that large areas of the Psalter were traditionally interpreted as direct prophecy of the Messiah. For Theodore, however, the only direct prophecy to be found was Psalm 16.10, 'Thou wilt not abandon my soul to Hades, Nor let thy holy one see corruption.'[110] Occasionally by prophetic inspiration the psalmist spoke in the person of the Messiah, Psalms 2 and 8

---

105 The work of Bultmann (published posthumously 1984) is a comprehensive study.

106 See further Young (1989, 1997a, 1997b).

107 For example, Pirot (1913).

108 McLeod (2009) translates a fragment of *On Allegory and History*; for the suggestion that the concentration on history in Diodore and Theodore may have been heightened by opposition to Julian, see p. 20.

109 In a fragment quoted by Facundus, *Defence* iii.6.

110 The hyperbole shows that its reference goes beyond the immediate situation and its full meaning is to be found in Christ. See comment in Wiles (1970).

being examples;[111] but most of the traditional messianic psalms were to be given quite different interpretations. How was Theodore led to conclusions so extreme for his age?

Some of the basic principles along which Theodore worked were exemplary. Texts were not to be lifted out of context. Arbitrary shifts of subject were not plausible. So to take individual verses from the psalms as messianic prophecies when the rest of the psalm did not fit had to be disallowed. That immediately excluded a number of the traditional Christological texts; in the Septuagint version, the subject of Psalm 22 mentions his 'transgressions', and therefore he cannot be identified with Christ. Another principle was that passages in the Old Testament belonged to one specific historical context, usually contemporary with the prophet or writer; thus David sang, 'My God, my God, why hast thou forsaken me?' as a lament over Absalom. Certainly Christ took over David's lament on the cross, but its primary meaning was to be referred to the original event in David's life. Unfortunately in the case of the Psalter, Theodore was unable to rid himself of the tradition that David was the author of the entire collection; and that being the case the good directions he followed led him into some strange alleys. Solomon is clearly the subject of Psalm 72; so it must have been composed prophetically by David in Solomon's person. If this explanation worked in this case, there was no reason why it should not work in the case of other historical difficulties. Certain psalms undoubtedly referred to the disasters under the Maccabees and not to events which occurred in David's lifetime; so David was again prophesying. Each psalm Theodore attributed in its entirety to a particular situation, unearthing the most plausible context. Rarely was this the events of the life and death of the Christ.

If Theodore's principles produced some aberrations in the case of the Psalms, they proved more reasonable when he turned to the Minor Prophets. Here he insisted that each prophet was preaching a message for the people of his own day. He sketched the situation, the doom overhanging the people in pre-exilic times, the judgment that came upon them, the hopes of restoration held out to them; he set the later prophets correctly in the context of the Return and its problems. The circumstances of the prophets were Theodore's preoccupation, for therein lay the key to understanding their message. If the prophetic words appeared to point to Christ, it was because they were shadows, glimmerings of the providential care of God for his people which reached its fullness in Christ. Zechariah cannot have had a vision of the Son of God; for God was not known as Father and Son until the New Testament.

It is this last argument which reveals Theodore's basic reasoning and accounts for the oddities in his exegesis. Theodore had not rejected the current idea that prophecy was inspired prediction. He accepted that the prophets and supremely David, predicted events which occurred centuries later in the history of Israel. So why could he not accept that the prophets of the Old Testament predicted Christ? Fundamentally it was because such a notion flattened out the difference between the Old and New Testaments; it undermined the Christian claim to new revelation in Christ. Before the time of Christ, nothing was clear; what indica-

---

111 McLeod (2009) translates the commentary on Psalm 8, noting that Theodore takes four psalms only as Messianic.

tions there were, were merely shadows, vague pre-figurations. It was the need to preserve the distinctiveness of the New Testament which stimulated Theodore's radical criticism of the traditional Christological understanding of the Old Testament, thus producing results scandalous in contemporaries' eyes – he even asserted that the Song of Songs was Solomon's love poem and had nothing to do with the marriage of Christ and the Church. Yet he did recognize that the same God was God of both Testaments, and that both Testaments pointed in the same direction. So he admitted some of the classic 'types', though only if he could recognize a genuine correspondence (μίμησις), an Old Testament situation closely paralleling a New Testament situation.[112] Thus the sprinkling of blood which marked the end of Israelite slavery in Egypt was a prophetic image of deliverance from sin and death through the blood of Christ; and the historical Jonah prefigured the historical Jesus, the extraordinary events of his life signifying by μίμησις Christ's rejection, resurrection and conversion of the Gentiles. Such pre-figurations Theodore could acknowledge as long as neither the factuality of the original events was undermined, nor the newness of the New Testament compromised. This was the kind of thing meant by Paul in the 'allegory' of Sarah and Hagar (Gal. 4);[113] it was abusing the apostle's words, Theodore insisted, to take ἀλληγορούμενα as justifying the fables and fantasies of allegorical interpretation. There are two different covenants (or Testaments) though they have a certain rapport which is discerned in the 'types'.

If the New Testament was to be seen as radically different, was the commentator to approach its interpretation along quite different lines? Certainly there is a difference apparent in Theodore's New Testament commentaries, but there are also similarities. There is the same concentration on 'concrete realities': Theodore takes the chronology of John's Gospel very seriously indeed, and goes to considerable trouble to indicate the circumstances of Paul's epistles. The method of commentary remains similar, concentrating on the background situation, problems in the text, explication of obscurities, and elucidation of the argument or the sequence of the narrative. The key difference is that for Theodore the New Testament, unlike the Old Testament, contains the truth and the whole truth in the matter of Christian doctrine. In other words, Paul and the author of John's Gospel actually taught the theology of Theodore and his orthodox contemporaries. So dogmatic concerns play a very important part in his efforts to interpret – in fact, he stated it as a principle that commentators should concentrate on problem texts, particularly those twisted by the heretics.[114]

The effect of this presupposition is considerable. In his concern to establish the truth as far as the controversial issues of the day were concerned, Theodore fails to present the subtle unity and irony of the Johannine portrait of Christ. He labours to distinguish things said of the Logos from those said of the 'Man assumed' – though Kalantzis notes that this is not the terminology he uses in the Greek fragments, where his comments are largely directed against Arianism and Apollinarianism, the two heretical positions perceived as most dangerous in Theodore's day. This dogmatic focus, together with the fact that his gener-

---

112 Theodore discusses this point in the Introduction to his commentary on Jonah, PG 66.317–28.

113 Swete (1880–2), I, pp. 73ff.; ET in Froehlich (1984) and McLeod (2009).

114 *Comm. in Jn.*, Vosté (1940), pp. 4f. (Latin p. 2).

ally over-literal bent blinds him to the symbolic overtones of this, the 'spiritual gospel', renders this commentary less successful than that on the minor Pauline epistles. With Paul Theodore shows a greater affinity and depth of appreciation (indeed there are passages in the *Commentary on John* which can only be described as Pauline exegesis of the Johannine text, the high-priestly prayer of John 17 being a particularly striking example).[115] As already observed, his religious perception focused like Paul's upon the newness of the gospel, the end of the old order, the creation of a new humanity in Christ, the gift of the Holy Spirit, foretaste of the age to come in the grace received through baptism and Eucharist. Yet the dogmatic interest is not absent from his commentaries on the Pauline epistles; a major purpose of New Testament interpretation is the establishment of orthodox doctrine and the confusion of the heretics.[116] It is this standpoint which sharply distinguishes Theodore's approach from that of modern critical scholarship. For all his sense of history, Theodore had no awareness of doctrinal development. Anachronistic interpretation of the Old Testament in terms of Christ he discerned and criticized; but it was inconceivable to him that the New Testament writers did not share his basic theological assumptions.

Yet the interrelationship between theology and exegesis is never entirely straightforward. For all that has just been said, one important element in Theodore's thought seems to lie in his readiness to disregard certain presuppositions of contemporary Platonism – the basic context in which Christian theology was operating at this time; and this readiness seems to have been induced, partially at least, by his reading of the Bible. The extent to which he abandons metaphysical terms in favour of biblical images is probably rather exaggerated by Rowan Greer,[117] but we have already observed this happening in the case of his eschatology, and this is not the only area of his theology affected. Theodore's anthropology is significantly different from that of, say, Gregory of Nyssa, not to mention Apollinarius, and as R. A. Norris has shown,[118] the difference lies not in his supposed Aristotelianism, but in the degree to which Platonic assumptions are modified, or at any rate balanced, by certain biblical insights, by his overriding concern with morality and by the understanding of salvation consequent upon his perception that human rationality consists in mutability and freedom of choice. For Theodore's primary interest centred on the will, rather than the intellect, on the soul's involvement in practical moral action within the created order, rather than its contemplative transcendence of the flesh and the material world. Humanity was created to perform a certain function in the universe, as the keystone of the whole; so Adam's fall had cosmic consequences.[119] The new age depended on the re-creation of humanity, rather than its translation to a co-existent spiritual realm. The resurrection of humanity meant the restoration of the cosmos and established a bond of harmony for the whole creation.[120]

115 *Comm. in Jn.*, Vosté (1940), p. 314 (Latin p. 224).
116 On the above points, see further Wiles (1960, 1967); and the excellent summary article, Wiles (1970). Also Greer (1961).
117 Greer (1961), chapter 1.
118 Norris (1963).
119 For further development of this point, see McLeod (1999, 2005, 2009).
120 Swete (1880–2), I, pp. 128–31.

There remain many tensions and inconsistencies in Theodore's thought, for many of the current Platonic commonplaces he took for granted alongside his fresh understanding.[121] Thus the two states are characterized in rather Platonic terms as mortal and immortal, mutable and immutable, passible and impassible. Furthermore, Theodore oscillates between regarding the present mutable state of humanity as providential and necessary for the exercise of the will, and accepting the tradition of Christian Platonism that mortality is the tragic result of a fall from perfection. Yet this moral interest remained predominant, and needless to say, markedly affected Theodore's Christology.

2 Christology

Apart from scriptural exegesis, Christology was clearly the matter of most concern to Theodore. He not only wrote specific treatises against what he regarded as misguided Christological theories, but he composed a massive work on the subject of the incarnation. We are told[122] that the De Incarnatione contained fifteen books and showed by the clearest reasoning and the testimony of scripture that just as the Lord Jesus possessed deity in its fullness, so he possessed humanity in its fullness. It also discussed what full humanity means, arguing that a person consists of two substances, soul and body, and that the spirit and the senses are inborn faculties of the soul rather than different substances. The fourteenth book, we are told, dealt with the divine nature; and the fifteenth clinched the whole dissertation with citations from the Fathers. It is unfortunate that all the access we have to this work is through fragments, most of them quoted to show that Theodore's views were heretical.

The general characteristics of Theodore's Christology have been frequently described. His emphasis was upon the two distinct natures of Christ. In the face of Neo-Arianism, Theodore asserted that the Son was true God of true God, consubstantial with the Father. In the face of Apollinarianism, Theodore asserted that the 'Man assumed' was a complete man, perfect in everything which belongs to human nature and composed of a mortal body and a rational soul. The extent to which this dual stress arose out of the controversial background is debated. What has caught people's interest in modern times has been Theodore's highly realistic emphasis on the genuine human experience of Jesus, and many, like Norris, would argue that this is no mere response to Apollinarius but a deeply ingrained aspect of his total thought. Similarly it can be argued that his emphasis on the transcendence of the Logos is no mere safeguard in the face of contemporary conflicts, but an essential element in his religious consciousness. If God is to be God, God's divine nature cannot be compromised. Theodore regards as utterly foolish those who imagine that there is a natural kinship between God and humankind.[123] There is a great chasm between the eternal and the contingent.[124] That God transcended time and space, passion, limitation and change was no mere theological axiom, but a central element

---

121 Norris (1963).
122 Gennadius, Vir. 12.
123 A fragment from DI ii, in Swete (1880–2), II, pp. 291ff.
124 Hom. cat. iv, Mingana (1932) = WS v, p. 152, ET p. 45.

in Theodore's understanding of God's otherness. Yet this very transcendence implied immanence, for the uncircumscribed must be everywhere. Schooled by Nicaea, Theodore was bound to attribute the same universality to the divine Logos. The Logos could not move from place to place,[125] nor 'become' flesh, except κατὰ τὸ δοκεῖν[126] – he meant 'metaphorically' rather than 'docetically' because he continued: 'In appearance, not in the sense that he did not take real flesh, but in the sense that he did not *become* flesh.' For Theodore truer expressions are to be found in the phrases 'he tabernacled among us' or 'he assumed flesh' – 'flesh' being a term which he explicitly takes to mean human nature in its entirety.[127] So the incarnation could not imply any change in the essential Godhead any more than it could undermine the autonomy of the humanity.

It is hardly surprising that the standard criticism of Theodore's Christology has been that in his concern to avoid compromising either the divinity or the humanity of the Christ, he failed to give an adequate account of the unity. He was himself offended by language of 'two Sons',[128] but he nevertheless insisted in effect on two subjects.[129] The following comments may help to put this dualism into better perspective.

(i) Within the basic framework of Theodore's thought, both God and humanity were each required to perform their own appropriate action in order that salvation could be achieved: on the one hand, an act of God's creative grace was required to refashion humanity and to bring the new state or age into being; on the other hand, since the human will was the seat of sin, humanity had to achieve perfection by exercising that will in obedience to God. God could not play that part, any more than humanity could play God's part. The two have to co-operate, each contributing its own proper action. In spite of certain tales of Theodore's association with Pelagians, really his thought does not belong to either side in that contemporary Western dispute.[130]

(ii) Current anthropology operated with a dualism of body and soul in which the mode of unity remained a puzzle, though its actuality could not be denied. If Nemesius could speak of the soul dwelling in the body by habit, inclination or disposition and take it that this was a sufficient account of the basic unity of a human person,[131] it is not surprising that Theodore should regard terminology not dissimilar as adequate for expressing the unity of Christ. The God–Word united the 'Man assumed' to himself by habit of will (κατὰ σχέσιν τῆς γνώμης)[132] or by favour (κατ' εὐδοκίαν), and though there remained two distinct natures, there was nevertheless one subject (πρόσωπον – *prosōpon*) to which all the actions of the Saviour could be referred, one Son because of the union (ἕνωσις).

(iii) Theodore meant a great deal more by this union κατ' εὐδοκίαν than might

---

125 *Hom. cat.* v, Mingana (1932) = WS v, p. 161, ET p. 52.
126 *DI* ix.1, Swete (1880–2), II, p. 300.
127 *DI* ix.1, Swete (1880–2), II, p. 300; see also *Comm. in Jn.* 1.14, Vosté (1940), pp. 33f. (Latin p. 23).
128 *Hom. cat.* viii, Mingana (1932) = WS v, p. 207, ET p. 90.
129 Sullivan (1956), especially pp. 219ff.
130 Norris (1963).
131 See above, pp. 230–2.
132 *DI* vii, Swete (1880–2), II, p. 310.

appear at first sight. Since God is everywhere, unlimited and uncircumscribed, it is a specific act of favour (εὐδοκία) for God to be specially or particularly present. Thus God is present in a special way in the apostles and in the elect, as a particular act of grace. But when God chose to dwell in the 'Man assumed', he did so ὡς ἐν υἱῷ (as in a Son), uniting the whole of the 'assumed' to himself. [133] This 'unified relationship that Christ's humanity possesses with God the Word' he spoke of as an 'indwelling of good pleasure in one *prosōpon*';[134] it was a unique case of God's particular presence, produced by a deliberate act of divine Will, unique because God operated completely in him[135] 'as in a Son'.

(iv) The unity of *prosōpon* meant more than a unity of appearance;[136] for when Theodore speaks of a unity of subject in his scriptural exegesis he uses the word *prosōpon*. Furthermore, it has been shown[137] that Theodore placed great weight on the notion of 'participation', in both his Christology and his soteriology. His theology has its roots in the sacrament of baptism; baptism and the gift of the Spirit effected a sharing in the divine immutability, an anticipation of the life of the age to come. The Saviour was one in whom that participation was uniquely realized in all its fullness. On the one hand, this enabled the participation of others in divine grace by adoption into Christ; on the other, in the case of Christ such a unity of *prosōpon* was effected that he shared the honour, the worship, the lordship of the God-Logos.

(v) Although Theodore occasionally uses unguarded expressions which suggest that a perfect man was adopted by the divine Logos as his special dwelling-place, this is not really the drift of his meaning. For Theodore, Jesus was no 'mere man'; at no point was the Logos separated from the man he assumed. Their perfect union was never destroyed, otherwise a 'mere man' he would indeed have been. If Theodore stresses the duality, it is because for him the unity is obvious. In analysis of scriptural texts, he often notes that the unity is assumed, while carefully balanced phrases ensure that the truth about the two natures is not obscured. In speaking of the 'economy of his humanity', or of the divine condescension, Theodore constantly affirms the basic unity of the dual saving action, and asserts the priority of the divine initiative.[138]

3 A rounded view of Christianity

In the context of controversy, the temptation to exaggerate particular points against the opposition is easy. For this reason, the positive outline of Christianity according to Theodore which we now possess in his *Catechetical Lectures* is likely to present a truer picture of Theodore's theology than pointed quota-

---

133 *DI* vii, Swete (1880–2), II, pp. 294ff.

134 McLeod (2009), p. 34.

135 Dewart (1975); Fairbairn (2003), pp. 46–50, suggests both that this was a 'unique case of grace' and that it remained different essentially in degree only – Christ was a 'uniquely graced man'.

136 On Theodore's understanding of *prosōpon* (as distinct from *hypostasis*), see McLeod (2009), chapter 6.

137 Abramowski (1961).

138 *Hom. cat.* viii *passim* and often elsewhere.

FROM NICAEA TO CHALCEDON

tions from works like that against Apollinarius, if only because it will be a more rounded one. The *Catechetical Lectures* consist of ten homilies on the creed,[139] and a further six homilies explaining the Lord's Prayer and the liturgies of baptism and Eucharist. Though tending to seem repetitive, a feature further exaggerated by the peculiarities of Syriac idiom, this set of discourses contains a remarkable conspectus of the heart of what Theodore believed. A sense of wonder and mystery, of awe and thanksgiving pervades much of what he has to say. We have already met his opening proclamation of new creation in Christ, of the kingdom to come in which Christians begin already to participate through the mysteries of the sacraments. To share in these mysteries, Christians must keep the faith handed down to them. So Theodore begins his exposition of the credal profession to be made at baptism. From time to time, he gives the conventional warnings against Jews and polytheists, against heretics and schismatics, but he concentrates upon a positive outline of what the Fathers meant, illustrating the clauses of the creed with passages from scripture carefully expounded. Patiently the precise distinctions of Christian theology are elucidated. If in the homilies concerned with Christology Theodore labours the distinction between the natures, this is set in the overall context of an exposition of Christian teaching on the doctrine of God, of salvation, of the Christian life and sacraments.[140] It is thus no mere controversial theory but an integral part of the whole presentation, and balanced by the wider perspective of the one central act of the divine initiative taken on humanity's behalf. Thus the dogmatic sections are framed in the proclamation of Theodore's faith, which is moulded at the deepest level by his response to Paul's eschatological perspectives, the present gift of the Spirit and the future hope anticipated in the sacraments.

Entry to the future kingdom depends upon adoption as sons of God. Adoption is an important theme in Theodore's thinking about salvation. For Theodore, the Logos was genuinely Son of God; the 'Man assumed' was united with that sonship, and the 'Man assumed' paved the way for all human beings. When he raised the body he assumed, he raised us and made us sit with him in heaven so that we might be glorified in him.[141] Theodore's theological presuppositions meant that he could not countenance θεοποίησις (divinization), but he rejoiced in υἱοποίησις (filiation). In the homilies on the sacraments, Theodore was able to work this theme out in highly dramatic terms. Needless to say, the details of the liturgy to which he refers are of immense value to liturgiologists, but it is his interpretation of the liturgical acts which is so forceful. Both baptism and Eucharist perform sacramentally the events that took place in connection with Christ our Lord, in the belief that what happened to him will happen to us. Passion and resurrection are re-enacted so that the believer can participate in the action. The elements represent Christ lying stretched out on the altar as a sacrifice, but by the invocation of the Holy Spirit, these elements are transformed so as to become immortal, invisible, incorruptible, impassible and immutable, just as the body of Christ was made immortal by the resurrection. When we partake of the body and blood, we expect to be changed into an immortal and incor-

---

139 For discussion of Theodore's Creed and the Creed of Nicaea, see Gerber (2000).

140 McLeod (2002).

141 Fragment from Theodore's *On Priesthood*, in Mingana (1934) = WS vii, pp. 95f. Cf. *Comm. in Jn.*, Vosté (1940), p. 315 (Latin p. 225).

ruptible nature. Through the sacrament we will be united to Christ our Lord whose body we believe ourselves to be. He was the first to receive this change; and 'we believe that through these symbols, as through unspeakable signs, we possess sometime beforehand the realities themselves.'[142] As the newborn baby is weak, so the newly baptized possesses only potentially the faculties of his immortal nature, but that possession is the ground of his future hope. Newborn babes need suitable food, and the sacramental food of the Eucharist is nourishment suitable to our present state, though really a symbol which will cease in the age to come.

Theodore frequently speaks of the sacraments as 'mysteries', but what he seems to mean by this is 'signs' or 'symbols'; for he was not really interested in mystical theology, but rather in practical Christian action. As newborn babes, Christians cannot expect to be perfect, but they should endeavour to live in a manner worthy of their heavenly citizenship. Human weakness should not deter the believer from the sacrament, for 'if we do good works . . . and truly repent . . . undoubtedly we will obtain the gift of remission of sins in our reception of the holy sacrament.'[143] The Lord's Prayer indicates that we can have confidence in forgiveness if we forgive others. Theodore's exposition of the Lord's Prayer in fact highlights his interest in action rather than contemplation: 'Thy will be done on earth as it is in heaven' means that we must strive to imitate the life we will live in heaven, for heaven contains nothing contrary to God. True prayer, says Theodore in his introduction, does not consist in words, but in good works, love and zeal for duty.[144] It would be interesting if some of his writings on the ascetic life had survived and we could see more clearly how he applied his understanding of Christian salvation to its practical outworking in life. The only bit of information we have is that in his work *On Perfection*,

> he taught, admonished and warned the solitaries to be assiduous in solitude and confirmed his words by testimonies from the books of the prophets, from the gospels and from the Pauline epistles. Anyone who reads with care this book on the perfection of solitaries will easily learn the things said by the Interpreter about solitude and how much he rebukes and reproves the solitaries who are distracted by worldly works outside it.[145]

Such expressions might suggest contemplative leanings in Theodore's asceticism, and likewise he tells his catechumens to avoid 'the commerce of this world'. Yet we can be pretty sure that when it came to working out the practical implications, scripture provided Theodore with the supreme guide for shaping a Christian lifestyle and making the ethical decisions so central to his understanding of human rationality. Obedience to God's law was fundamental, though set in the context of the gracious activity of a God who creates and re-creates.

---

142 *Hom. cat.* xvi, Mingana (1933) = WS vi, p. 256, ET p. 115; cf. *Hom. cat.* xii–xvi, *passim*.

143 *Hom. cat.* xvi, Mingana (1933) = WS vi, p. 259, ET p. 118.

144 *Hom. cat.* xi, Mingana (1933) = WS vi, p. 126, ET p. 3.

145 Quoted in Mingana (1934) = WS vii, pp. 109f.

Thus Theodore and Chrysostom, the two pupils of Diodore, shared a common outlook, and their mutual regard was lifelong, for Theodore was one of those to whom Chrysostom wrote from exile. It is a strange twist of fate that Chrysostom, having suffered in his lifetime, rapidly became one of the most honoured saints of the Church, whereas Theodore was posthumously anathematized even though honoured and respected all his days. Little did Theodoret foresee his fate when he made the divine Theodore's death the culmination of his *Ecclesiastical History*.

For Further Reading

English translations

Hill, R. C., 2003. *Commentary on the Twelve Prophets*, FC, Washington, DC: Catholic University of America Press.

——, 2006. *Theodore of Mopsuestia. Commentary on Psalms 1–81*, SBL, Leiden: Brill.

Kalantzis, George, 2004. *Theodore of Mopsuestia. Commentary on the Gospel of John*, Strathfield, NSW: St Paul's Publications.

McLeod, Frederick G., 2009. *Theodore of Mopsuestia*, Abingdon and New York: Routledge.

Mingana, A., 1932, 1933. *Theodore, Catechetical Homilies*, Syriac text and ET, Commentary of Theodore of Mopsuestia on the Nicene Creed (= Hom. cat. i–x) and Commentary . . . on the Lord's Prayer and the Sacraments of Baptism and the Eucharist (= Hom. cat. xi–xvi), Woodbrooke Studies v and vi, Cambridge: Heffer.

Studies

Dewart, Joanne, 1971. *The Theology of Grace of Theodore of Mopsuestia*, Washington, DC: Catholic University of America Press.

Fairbairn, Donald, 2003. *Grace and Christology in the Early Church*, Oxford: Oxford University Press.

Greer, Rowan, 1961. *Theodore of Mopsuestia: Exegete and Theologian*, London: Faith Press.

Norris, R. A., 1963. *Manhood and Christ*, Oxford and New York: Clarendon Press.

Patterson, L., 1926. *Theodore of Mopsuestia and Modern Thought*, London: SPCK.

Sullivan, F. A., 1956. *The Christology of Theodore of Mopsuestia*, Rome: Analecta Gregoriana.

Wiles, M. F., 1960. *The Spiritual Gospel*, Cambridge: Cambridge University Press.

——, 1967. *The Divine Apostle*, Cambridge: Cambridge University Press.

——, 1970. 'Theodore of Mopsuestia as Representative of the Antiochene School', in *The Cambridge History of the Bible* I, Cambridge and New York: Cambridge University Press, pp. 489–510.

IV Polemical Correspondence and a Pamphlet War

The very year that Theodore died, Nestorius was consecrated bishop of Constantinople. Within a few months disturbances were beginning to surface. The story of the Nestorian controversy has been often told; the course of its history, of synod and counter-synod, of compromise and breakdown, can easily be read elsewhere.[146] Suffice it here to highlight the character of the controversy and the issues at stake by surveying the correspondence between Cyril and Nestorius, and the literary history of the notorious Twelve Anathemas.

The documents which concern us are to be found in the Conciliar Acts. For although most literature from the hands of those branded as heretics met destruction, from the time of the Council of Ephesus on, collections were made of documents relating to the controversial issues discussed at the oecumenical councils, and these were preserved together with the Conciliar minutes; so the *Acta Conciliorum Oecumenicorum*[147] become an important literary source from this date onwards. For the Council of Ephesus (431), there are a number of different collections, some in Greek, some in Latin, with partly but not entirely overlapping material. The most important is the *Collectio Vaticana*, in which most of the material now to be discussed is to be found.[148] Here, then, we can read the correspondence of the principal actors in this doctrino-political battle, and in the process notice not only the explicit issues but hints of the 'hidden agenda' in the conflict.

1 The letters

Cyril began the correspondence by writing to Nestorius. His opening address has the conventional form of polite patriarchal diplomacy: 'To Nestorius most reverent and pious fellow-servant, greetings in the Lord'; and personal reference throughout is to 'your Piety' rather than 'you'. This respectful formality is maintained throughout the correspondence, even as it becomes more barbed.

Cyril proceeds to explain the occasion for writing. He has had reports from Constantinople that Nestorius is getting upset. On enquiry he discovered that the cause of Nestorius' annoyance was a letter that he, Cyril, had written to the holy monks, a copy of which had found its way to the capital. Here then are hints of the activities of the spies and counter-spies employed by the patriarchs to keep a watch on each other's activities. The letter which caused Nestorius' distress is also to be found in the *Acta Conciliorum*. That Cyril had written it suggests that he may well have been preparing to use tactics against Nestorius

---

146 Apart from the standard Church histories and introductions, see Sellers (1953); Grillmeier (1965/75); McGuckin (1994).

147 Schwartz (1927–) = *ACO*; French translation (of Acts of Ephesus and Chalcedon) Festugière (1982, 1983); ET (of Acts of Chalcedon) Price and Gaddis (2005).

148 The *Collectio Vaticana* (*ACO* I.i.1–6) contains all except Cyril's *Apology against the Orientals*, which is to be found in the *Collectio Atheniensis* (*ACO* I.i.7). For the documents discussed here, see Bindley and Green (1955) for ET and notes; Wickham (1983) for text and ET; and McGuckin (1994) for ET of Cyril's second and third letters to Nestorius; McGuckin (1994) and Russell (2000) for ET of Cyril's *Explanation of the Twelve Chapters*; Pásztori-Kupán (2006) for ET of Theodoret's *Refutation of the Twelve Anathemas*.

similar to those employed by his uncle Theophilus against Chrysostom. The monks had long been the shock troops used by the Alexandrian patriarchs to further their political aims; the alliance had been forged by Athanasius and was consolidated by his successors. Now Cyril had made sure of the monks' support by circulating a pastoral letter which raised a number of controversial Christological points in a manner designed to arouse the emotions of the faithful while not seeming unreasonable or contentious himself. The Nicene Creed, he had written, established the divinity of Christ and so the virgin must be *Theotokos* – Mother of God. The title *Theotokos* is implied, if not always used, by scripture, the Fathers, the great Athanasius and Nicaea. It was the Word of God himself who became flesh; and that Logos of God who was made flesh, suffered, died and rose, we name the one Lord Jesus Christ. He was no 'mere man like us'. He was God even if he became flesh. You cannot sever the one Lord Jesus Christ into two, separating what was from the Holy Virgin from what was from God. The Logos emptied himself, fulfilling the economy of his humanity, and when he became man he was born of woman. Emmanuel is no mere 'God-bearing man', nor a mere instrument of the divine. If Christ is not truly Son nor God by nature, but a mere human being like us, a mere instrument of the divinity, how can our salvation be from God? The target was clearly Nestorius' Christology. That Nestorius was upset is hardly surprising.

In his letter to Nestorius, however, Cyril expresses surprise that Nestorius had not considered his own position. After all, uproar had arisen prior to Cyril's letter to the monks. Was it not Nestorius' own statements which had started it all? Cyril had been labouring to straighten out distorted propositions found in certain papers and sermons. Some had nearly reached the point of holding back from confessing that Christ was God and proposing instead that he was an instrument or tool of the divinity, a 'God-bearing man' and such like. How could anyone keep silent when the faith was being injured and such ideas being bandied about? Cyril suggested that if he did not respond, he would have to answer for his silence before Christ's judgment seat. Besides Celestine, bishop of Rome, together with his local bishops, had expressed concern, and wanted to know whether these papers really originated from Nestorius or not. Clearly when they wrote from Rome they were deeply offended. (In fact, though Cyril does not mention it here, he had himself alerted Celestine to the dangers of Nestorius' preaching, and Cyril was now writing to Nestorius at Celestine's instigation. The letters of Celestine provide clear evidence of the Rome–Alexandria axis carefully fostered by Cyril.) So, continued Cyril, there was upset and uproar all over the place. Nestorius had better explain himself, and stop the worldwide scandal. If there was to be peace, he had better call the Holy Virgin *Theotokos*, because everyone else was prepared to suffer for their faith in Christ.

For all Cyril's diplomatic address, this was clearly a declaration of war. Nestorius tried to play it cool. He only answered the letter because of the strong pressure exerted by Cyril's representative, upon whose praiseworthy qualities he chiefly dwelt, suggesting almost incidentally that Cyril's letter, to speak plainly, was not written in brotherly love, yet he would bear it patiently.

So Cyril had not got very far. The affair rumbled on, and a few months later Cyril wrote again. This was the famous *Second Letter to Nestorius* which was adopted as a standard of orthodoxy alongside Leo's *Tome* at the Council of Chalcedon. It deals much more explicitly with the specific Christological issues.

Cyril's opening paragraph is further evidence of behind-the-scenes activity. Cyril states that he has been informed that 'certain persons are gossiping to your Piety to the detriment of my character'. No doubt they expected 'to delight your ears', as he puts it, suggesting that the overt hostility between the two sees was ripe for exploitation by fugitives from justice, the ambitious, or the plain malicious – this kind of thing had already happened in the Origenist controversy after all. Cyril insists that Nestorius' informants were all condemned criminals whose appeal to Constantinople was quite unjustified. But however difficult it was becoming to keep the correspondence polite, Cyril continues to address Nestorius as a 'brother in Christ', and appeals to him as a pastor and teacher with responsibility to the Church.

When a lot of people have been offended, he suggests, it is necessary to remove the offence and establish healthy doctrine. As in the letter to the monks, Cyril takes as his standard of orthodoxy the creed of Nicaea. The proper way of proceeding is to hold the Nicene Creed in high esteem and allow it to determine the shape of one's doctrine. He then states what he thinks the Nicene Fathers meant. They said that it was the only-begotten Son himself who was incarnate, lived as man, suffered, rose and ascended; without actually stating it in so many words, he was trying to insist that the Logos was the subject of the incarnate experiences. This, he continued, is the line all must follow, while recognizing what is meant by being incarnate:

For we do not say that the Nature of the Word was *changed* and became flesh, nor that he was *transformed* into a complete human being (I do mean one of soul and body); but this rather, that the Word became man, having in his own hypostasis united to himself flesh, animated with a rational soul, in an ineffable and inconceivable manner.

Cyril thus acknowledges the propriety of the Antiochene concern to preserve God's immutability and repudiates the suggestion that his own Christology involves the Logos in change. He also affirms the full humanity of Christ, excluding Apollinarianism by his formula 'flesh animated by a rational soul'. However, it is quite plain that he cannot say how the incarnation is to be conceived. Several times in the letter he refers to its 'ineffable and inconceivable' character. The one point he keeps reiterating is that, whatever the difficulties, it must be affirmed that it was the Logos who was incarnate, and there is only one Lord and Christ and Son. He admits that two Natures are involved, but their union, he says, is hypostatic, because the Logos united humanity to himself 'in his own *hypostasis*'.

In expounding this position further Cyril deals with a number of difficulties which had already arisen in the debate. He asserts that it is possible to say that the Logos had his γέννησις (generation) from the Father, and also that he had a γέννησις κατὰ σάρκα (birth according to the flesh) from a woman. This he had asserted in his letter to the monks, and the following words suggest that he had laid himself open to misinterpretation. (It was after all an Apollinarian idea.)[149]

---

149 See above, p. 246.

He denies that this means either that the Divine Nature began its existence in the Holy Virgin, or that the eternal Logos lacked something or had need of a second beginning of existence. He is simply said to have been born according to the flesh on the occasion when he united humanity to himself hypostatically for our sakes and our salvation, he explains.

But Cyril refuses to go on the defensive. This was no ordinary man who was born of the Holy Virgin; it was the Word himself who made his own the birth of his own flesh. The Word himself suffered and died – not that he suffered in his own proper nature, for the Divine is impassible because it is incorporeal. But when his own body suffered, he is said to have suffered for us himself, for the impassible was in the suffering body. In other words, Cyril is trying to say that the incorporeal had accepted a corporeal, and therefore passible, state.

So, continues Cyril, we acknowledge one Christ and Lord, not worshipping a man alongside the Word and allowing division to creep in. If we reject this hypostatic union, we end up saying 'two Sons'. A unity of *prosōpon* just does not meet the case. 'For the scripture has not declared that the Word united to himself a man's person, but that he became flesh.' Accordingly there is no objection to calling the Holy Virgin *Theotokos*.

Cyril had made a serious attempt in this letter to expound his position, and had given attention to some of the problems involved. He concluded by saying that he had written 'out of the love which I have in Christ', and beseeching Nestorius 'thus to think and teach with us that the peace of the churches may be preserved and the bond of unanimity and love between the priests of God remain unbroken'. We should trust his motives sufficiently to realize that Cyril did fear deeply for the truth of the incarnation, and here at any rate he avoided extremist statements in the interest of achieving peace. Possibly he relished the prospect of forcing the bishop of Constantinople to knuckle under Alexandrian ascendency, but for the moment he avoided dictating and demanding.

Nestorius, however, was not the type to give way to anyone, least of all his greatest ecclesiastical rival. He was a determined and intolerant character with little tact, if Socrates' assessment is to be believed;[150] and at the moment he had the advantage that he was in favour with the court. So this time Nestorius replied to Cyril with some force, giving not an inch, but replying directly to Cyril's points. He begins by explicitly ignoring the insults at the start of Cyril's letter and coming straight to the theological points. He quotes Cyril's remarks about Nicaea and points out that the holy Fathers did not say that the consubstantial Godhead was passible or that the one co-eternal with the Father was γεννητής (begotten/born). In the phrase 'the one Lord Jesus Christ, his only-begotten Son', the Fathers carefully laid alongside each other the names belonging to each nature so that the one Lord is not divided, while at the same time the natures are not in danger of confusion because of the singleness of sonship. Paul taught the same thing in Philippians 2.5f. (a passage discussed by Cyril in the letter to the monks, and one that constantly reappears in the debate): since he was about to speak of passion, in order to avoid the implication that the divine Logos was παθητός (subject to suffering), he used the name 'Christ', so indicating the single *prosōpon* of passible and impassible nature; for Christ can

___
150 Socrates, *HE* vii.29; see below, pp. 291–3.

be called ἀπαθής (impassible) and παθητός (susceptible to suffering) without any danger – for he is ἀπαθής in his Godhead and παθητός in his body.

Nestorius indicates that he could make many other observations on this, but in the interests of brevity he will proceed to Cyril's next point. He claims that the division of the natures is perfectly orthodox and the Fathers never spoke of a second γέννησις (birth) from woman. Cyril's pernickety account he finds inconsistent: he began by stressing that the Logos was ἀπαθής (impassible) and unable to accept a second γέννησις (birth) and then somehow he introduced the idea that he was παθητός (susceptible to suffering) and newly created.

Scripture, claims Nestorius, attributes the economy, the birth (γέννησις) and the suffering (πάθος), not to the Godhead but to the humanity. Therefore the Holy Virgin is *Christotokos*, not *Theotokos*. He proceeds to quote long scriptural proofs. The body was the temple of the Godhead; the Godhead made it its own by an exact and divine συνάφεια (one of the words used for union or conjunction). This is the view that fits with the gospel tradition. To attribute birth and suffering and death to the Logos is to fall into pagan thinking and follow the heresies of Apollinarius and Arius.

Nestorius sympathizes with Cyril's desire to avoid conflict, quoting Paul's condemnation of the contentious, and he signs off with expressions of brotherliness and respect.

Reasoned debate, however, was becoming impossible. Cyril's *Third Letter to Nestorius* was not a personal reply to Nestorius' arguments, some of which were acute, but a demand for submission from a synod of Egyptian bishops. The 'anti-Nestorius' campaign had acquired more and more momentum. When Cyril informed Celestine that he had had no success in getting Nestorius to recant, the pope held a synod in Rome (August 430), and in the *Acta Conciliorum* there appear several letters from Celestine announcing the verdict of this synod to interested parties in the East, to the clergy and people of Constantinople, Cyril, John of Antioch and of course Nestorius himself. The verdict was an ultimatum: if Nestorius did not recant and confess the same faith as Rome and Alexandria within ten days of receiving the letter, he would be excommunicated. Cyril's synod in November confirmed the Roman synod and despatched the third letter, but the ultimatum was forestalled by an imperial summons to a General Council the following year. More water was to flow under the bridge before that council, however, and by the time it was held, the controversy was no longer merely a question of Nestorius' orthodoxy. The Eastern Church had been split into two hostile camps. The third letter was instrumental in thus deepening the conflict.

The tone of Cyril's third letter to Nestorius is no longer charitable and persuasive. The letter is a categorical demand for submission. The faith is being wronged; the law of affection must be abjured. Silence can be maintained no longer. The Egyptian synod is acting in harmony with the synod at Rome in counselling Nestorius to desist from his mischievous and perverse doctrines or he will be excommunicated. The disturbance of the churches and the scandalizing of the laity can no longer be tolerated. Nestorius has already been warned by Celestine's own letter.

The letter continues by saying that it is not sufficient for Nestorius simply to affirm the Nicene faith because the whole problem centres on the fact that he has interpreted it wrongly. What he has to do is to anathematize his own foul doctrines and promise to teach what is taught by all bishops, teachers and leaders of the churches throughout West and East. This is contained in the letters Nestorius has already received from Celestine and Cyril himself, but, to be sure there is no misunderstanding, the teaching is again stated in this letter.

There is no need to rehearse in detail the contents of the ensuing exposition, since much the same series of positive arguments and formulae are advanced as in the second letter. One addition, however, is sufficiently important to be mentioned, namely Cyril's appeal to the Eucharist: we do not receive 'common flesh' or 'the flesh of a man sanctified', he says, but the flesh of the Word himself, which is life-giving only because it is the flesh of the Word who as God is himself Life. Apart from this new line of argument, the major difference between the two letters is the greater extent to which there appears explicit rejection of many typically Antiochene christological formulae. 'Indwelling' is not a strong enough account of the union; the Logos did not 'inhabit' the body, dwelling in it by grace in the same way as he indwells the saints. There is one Christ and Son and Lord, not a man conjoined with God in a unity of dignity and authority. Conjunction (συνάφεια) is not enough to describe the union since it suggests mere juxtaposition rather than a union of nature or hypostatic union. It is false exegesis to divide up scriptural texts between the natures as Nestorius does; human sayings and divine were spoken by one person. It is equally false to ascribe his titles and saving actions to the two different natures; and Cyril proceeds to discuss certain titles and texts which had become notorious in the course of the controversy. This more negative approach is crowned by Cyril's final demand that Nestorius anathematize twelve statements which are appended to the letter.

2 The Twelve Anathemas[151]

Of all Cyril's acts, the drawing up of the Twelve Anathemas was the most divisive; for they themselves became the focus of controversy and aroused the deep suspicions of all the Antiochene party. They are bald hostile statements asserted without the necessary niceties and safeguards which Cyril had taken the trouble to include in his more discursive explanations. To the Antiochenes they were not merely provocative but blasphemous and doctrinally dangerous. As the controversy developed it became more important to them to ensure the withdrawal of the Twelve Anathemas than to defend Nestorius. Antiochene tracts attacked them; Cyril defended them in a series of apologies and counterattacks. The pamphlet war was born.

The Antiochene party took the offensive. When Nestorius informed John, the bishop of Antioch, of the contents of Cyril's latest letter, almost immediately two critical treatises were produced, one by Andrew of Samosata representing the 'Orientals', and the other by Theodoret of Cyrus, the greatest of the Antiochene scholars. These survive through their extensive quotation in Cyril's replies, his *Apology against the Orientals* and his *Apology against Theodoret*, Cyril

---

151 Discussion of the anathemas will be found in, for example, Wickham (1983); McGuckin (1994); Clayton (2007); et al.

produced a further *Explanation of the Anathemas* during the course of the Council of Ephesus, realizing the extent to which they were one of the biggest contributory factors in the breakdown of communications between the two parties. Somehow they had to be justified to the outside world, and especially the imperial court. The Antiochenes were convinced that they were Apollinarian, and were not afraid of broadcasting this view. Theodoret was not alone in hardly being able to believe that they were the work of Cyril, or of any real pastor in the Church, because of their Apollinarian and blasphemous character. Someone even produced a series of counter-anathemas, which were attributed to Nestorius and survive in a Latin translation; but since they do not appear to be authentic and were not part of the immediate debate, they will be ignored in the discussion here.

The first anathema was directed against those denying that Emmanuel was truly God and refusing the title *Theotokos* to the Holy Virgin; in explanation of this demand it is asserted that the Word which originated from God (ὁ ἐκ Θεοῦ Λόγος) was born in a fleshly manner when he became flesh.

The Orientals fastened first on the explanatory clause and asked how anyone could agree that he was born 'in a fleshly manner', which would imply a denial of the virgin birth. Was his birth 'fleshly' or 'God-befitting' (θεοπρεπής)? But the Antiochene criticisms centred on the main problem: how can the divine admit change? His 'becoming flesh' cannot be any more literal than his becoming sin or a curse; it means his dwelling (σκήνωσις) in flesh. Theodoret concentrates on this point. Change cannot be attributed to the deity; God 'took' flesh according to Philippians 2.7. Theodoret is prepared to accept the title *Theotokos*, but only with careful explanations: what she bore was the temple (ναός) of the divine in which all the fullness of the divine dwelt bodily.

How then did Cyril meet the attack? To the Orientals he began by asserting that John 1.14 is a statement of the mystery of the incarnation; and Nicaea said that the Word which originated from God was incarnate and made man. Of course this union must have happened without change or mixture (ἀτρέπτος and ἀσυγχύτως), for the Logos is unchangeable (ἀναλλοίωτος) by nature. Second, he suggested that if they insisted on his birth being θεοπρεπής (God-befitting), there was no reason why they should not call the virgin *Theotokos*; does an ordinary man have a God-befitting birth? Furthermore it was ridiculous to suggest that he became flesh in the same way as he became sin or a curse; since he was sinless, the corollary of that argument is that he was not really incarnate at all. He was truly made flesh and made man without change or confusion; the manner of the Economy is ineffable. Cyril appends patristic citations to support his case.

Much the same kind of reply he gives to Theodoret: we do not speak of mixture or change when we say that the Logos became flesh, but of his indescribable and ineffable union with a holy body having a rational soul. The language of 'indwelling a temple' is not sufficient to describe this union, because that language can also be used of God's presence in the saints, and he quotes 1 Corinthians 3.16–17.

In his *Explanation* Cyril reiterates his main point that according to the Nicene Creed, the Logos submits himself to the incarnate experiences, as well as being consubstantial with the Father. The Logos remained God, and was incarnate without change; the manner of the incarnation is simply beyond our conception or speech.

The second anathema is directed against those who deny that the Word which originated from God the Father was united hypostatically with the flesh. Now the notion of hypostatic union was precisely the problem for the Antiochenes. They wished to affirm a unity, but to call it 'hypostatic' had all the wrong connotations for them, implying Apollinarianism, implying a mixture and confusion of natures, implying a 'natural union', that is, one brought about by something inherent in the nature of things and so by necessity, rather than one voluntarily undertaken by the gracious will of God. For Cyril it was the only way of speaking of a 'real' union. There seems to have been a genuine difference in use of terminology.[152] To suggest, as some have,[153] that Theodoret should have realized what Cyril meant, since *hypostasis* had been given a specific meaning in the Trinitarian formula, 'One *ousia* and three *hypostaseis*', is not quite fair. It was used there to distinguish a single individuality, and to affirm a single individuality in Jesus Christ could well imply a mixture or confusion if the phrase were approached from the Christological standpoint of the Antiochenes. The explanation produced by Cyril probably did not reassure Theodoret. Besides, it seems likely that the formula καθ' ὑπόστασιν (hypostatically) was invented by Cyril and introduced an entirely novel terminology into the Christological debate.[154] It is noticeable that years later, when Nestorius wrote *The Bazaar of Heraclides*, he was still perplexed by the term.[155]

Discussion of this anathema does not appear at all in Cyril's *Apology to the Orientals*. Theodoret, however, insists that the Antiochenes, persuaded by the scriptures, do agree that there was a real union; but they reject the description hypostatic as being foreign to the scriptures and to the Fathers who interpreted them. If by describing the union as hypostatic a mixture of flesh and divinity is intended, then they oppose the term with zeal and condemn it as blasphemy. Mixture implies confusion; confusion undermines the peculiar character of each nature. By the text 'Destroy this temple and in three days I will raise it again', the Lord indicated the two natures – the destroyed temple and the raising God. Ἕνωσις (union) is quite enough; it safeguards the distinction of natures and the one Christ.

Cyril retorts by stating what he means by καθ' ὑπόστασιν: it is the very nature and *hypostasis* of the Logos which was united to human nature, by some means other than confusion, as he has often stated before. Theodoret, he suggests, is really saying the same thing. In his *Explanation* Cyril again insists that it is the Logos which was incarnate – granted, without change in his own nature – and it is not legitimate to divide the one Christ into Man on his own (ἰδικῶς) and

---

152 McGuckin (1994), pp. 138ff., provides a lengthy account of the terminology and the different senses in which it was taken by the two sides; summary accounts are provided by Russell (2000) and Pásztori-Kupán (2006) in their Introductions. See also Clayton (2007).

153 For example Sellers (1940), p. 10. Pásztori-Kupán (2006) indicates that the use of *hypostasis* in Christology was an innovation.

154 Richard (1945/77). See also the comments in Chadwick (1951).

155 See below, pp. 294 and 295.

God on his own (ἰδικῶς) or we think in terms of two Sons and undermine the whole idea of incarnation.

The third anathema is directed against those who divide the natures after the union, and describe the union as an association (συνάφεια) in dignity, authority or power, rather than a conjunction (σύνοδος) by natural union (φύσει, that is, by nature).

The issue here is much the same as in the previous anathema, but it introduces terminology which remained contentious; the non-Chalcedonians rejected the Definition because it spoke of '*in* two natures' rather than '*out of* two natures', that is, because it implied the continuing presence of two separate natures after the union. Here the Orientals pointed out that Cyril himself had spoken of two natures in his letter to the monks; had he now forgotten himself in confusing the two natures into one hypostasis and calling it a 'natural union'? Who could accept a physical union which excludes the action of grace? This must be an Apollinarian idea. In reply Cyril restates his familiar ground: the same Son and Lord before the incarnation and after the incarnation – no division into two Sons. He quotes passages from Nestorius and proceeds to confute them. Nestorius consistently divides the natures, uniting them merely in a common worship, authority and a union of dignity alone. He quotes and defends his own statements concerning the two natures, insisting that the natures are not divisible after the union. He explains that by φύσει he means κατ' ἀλήθειαν, a real or true union – not a confusion; and he repudiates the teaching of Apollinarius.

Theodoret regarded the subtle distinction between συνάφεια and σύνοδος as unintelligible, and also drew attention to the necessity implied in a natural union. 'Naturally' we drink, sleep, breathe – that is, they are natural necessities, not acts of will. If the union was natural it was inevitable; it was not a voluntary act of God's love towards humanity. A union by intention and will is surely superior to a natural union. If of a human being Paul can speak of an 'outer man' and an 'inner man', what is wrong with speaking of two natures after the union? To Theodoret, Cyril spells out his meaning. What he denies is the view that two independent natures were joined σχετικῶς (by habit), or simply in dignity, authority or by having the common title 'Son'. The anathema opposes such empty language and affirms a 'natural union', that is, one not by habit, but in truth, and one that is indivisible. To think it means confusion or necessity is to misunderstand. The Logos could not be compelled to become man and suffer unwillingly, since in his own nature he is not susceptible to suffering and necessity. You cannot simply identify 'by nature' and 'by necessity'. All that the natural union means is a real union.

Cyril's *Explanation* of this anathema simply reiterates his basic objections to a dualistic Christology.

The fourth anathema pursues the point by condemning those who differentiate scripture texts, assigning them to each appropriate nature. This was of course an important exegetical procedure among the Antiochenes, but what Cyril momentarily disregards was that it had been an important element in the great Athanasius' polemic against Arius. In the Formulary of Reunion, Cyril was obliged to climb down. In his *Explanation* Cyril justified the anathema by appeal to Philippians 2.6–11. Everything, divine and human, is ascribed here to the same subject. So all scripture texts should be applied to the one *prosōpon* (subject), since we believe Jesus Christ to be the one Son, that is the Word of God incarnate. The danger of ascribing texts to two subjects (*prosōpa*) is that it easily suggests two Sons. While giving nodding recognition to a distinction between 'divine' and 'human', he insists that the latter are to be referred to the incarnate state of the Logos, and is silent about his rejection of an important tradition.

In reply to the Antiochenes, however, he had been forced to admit the propriety of distinctions. Theodoret had suggested that Cyril might as well be Arius or Eunomius, and explicitly raised the question of the texts referring to the hunger, thirst, tiredness, sleep, ignorance, fear and loneliness of Jesus, texts which had long figured in orthodox polemic against Arianism. If they are applied to the God–Word, how, he asks, can Wisdom be ignorant? Both he and the Orientals accuse Cyril yet again of 'mixture' and 'confusion'. Cyril repudiates that accusation, and insists that even though some things are said of Jesus Christ 'humanly' and others 'divinely', all apply to the one person of the incarnate Logos.

The fifth anathema was directed against those who say that Christ is a God-bearing man (θεόφορος ἄνθρωπος) not the Word made flesh, and *the seventh* was against those who say that Jesus was a man energized by the Word. Here the typically Antiochene vocabulary is singled out for condemnation, as it is also in *the eighth anathema*, which rules out any suggestion of an independent man assumed by the Logos and so co-worshipped and co-glorified. Also to be anathematized is the suggestion that Christ was empowered to do his mighty acts by the Spirit, as if the Spirit were foreign to himself and not his own (*anathema 9*), and the statement that a man born of woman was made high priest and apostle (*anathema 10*). The underlying accusation is one of Adoptionism. How then do the Antiochenes defend such terms?

The Orientals firmly repudiate the idea that their formulae imply that Christ was energized simply like a man, like a prophet or an apostle or a righteous individual. They assert the scriptural basis for language like 'energizing' and doing signs by the power of the Spirit, and explain that his uniqueness consists in the fact that he was energized 'as a Son'. By co-worship is meant the single worship we offer to the one Son. As for *the tenth anathema*, they insist that God cannot be the subject of many texts in the Epistle to the Hebrews: how can God offer prayers and supplications with many tears, how can God learn obedience through suffering? In fact, they made a plausible case on the basis of realistic scriptural exegesis, though they did not meet Cyril's real difficulties: how is this 'Man Assumed' different from a saint or a prophet? How can this be described as an incarnation of the Logos?

Theodoret covers several of the same points. We do offer one worship to the one Christ who is both God and Man; but we must insist that the Word did not change into flesh, nor did the Man change into God. Scripture speaks of Christ's anointing with the Holy Spirit (and he produces a battery of texts); and it must be the humanity, not the Godhead, that was anointed. Is Cyril going to anathematize the prophets, the apostles and even Gabriel? The Epistle to the Hebrews makes quite plain the weakness of the assumed nature. The unchangeable nature did not change into flesh and learn obedience by experience. The

Logos is not a creature; rather the one who is of David's seed was made high priest and victim and offered himself to God as a sacrifice. Compared with the Orientals, however, Theodoret insists rather more on the unity of person while defending the characteristic Antiochene expressions: when the Son of David made his sacrifice, he did it 'having the Logos united to himself and inseparably conjoined.' There is no suggestion that θεόφορος ἄνθρωπος (God-bearing Man) implies that he had just some particular divine grace; rather it means he was wholly united with the Godhead of the Son.

Was Cyril satisfied with these explanations? Hardly. In his later *Explanation* he feels no difficulty in making the same charges against the Antiochene position as he had done all along. The discussion has made no difference. Whatever Theodoret or the Orientals said, a God-bearing man still meant to him an ordinary saint; *we* are temples of the Holy Spirit, he replied. It is just not the same thing to say 'the Word became man' and 'God dwelt in a man'. Paul said, 'In him the whole fullness of the Godhead was pleased to dwell *bodily* – σωματικῶς, not σχετικῶς – by habit. The saints are energized by the Spirit; Jesus was different, for the energy and the Spirit were his own. Unless the same one is God and Man, the claim to offer a single worship is false. As for the Epistle to the Hebrews, the contentious texts refer, of course, to the incarnate state, but the subject of all the experiences and activities is nevertheless the Logos, not a second subject – the 'Man Assumed'. Furthermore, any idea that the Man progresses to union with the Logos must be repudiated.

The remaining three anathemas condemn those who do not subscribe to certain Alexandrian Christological statements. *The sixth anathema* produced little discussion: it anathematized anyone who said that the Logos was the God or Lord of Christ, and did not agree that the same one is God and Man, the Word having become flesh. Theodoret hardly disputes Cyril's words; we do agree, he says, that 'the form of a servant' is God because of the union. Did he miss the point? Cyril's discussions confirm the suspicion that what he really had in mind was the affirmation that the Logos was the immediate subject of the incarnate experiences, though he never clearly states this in so many words. If they had realized what was at stake, the Antiochenes would certainly have qualified this statement, but as it stands it was perfectly consistent with Theodoret's Christological position.[156]

The eleventh anathema raises the question of the Eucharist. Anyone suggesting that the flesh is not the Logos' very own flesh, and therefore life-giving, is anathematized. Needless to say the Antiochenes promptly accuse Cyril of Apollinarianism. Cyril has failed to say that the flesh was ours. We have to be very careful about speaking of the Logos' own flesh or we introduce confusion of the natures. Theodoret points out that Cyril keeps talking about the flesh like Apollinarius, and neither mentions that it was 'intelligent', nor agrees that what was assumed was perfect humanity. The flesh is life-giving because it is united with the Logos, and there is no escaping the two natures implied by such a statement. Cyril is obliged to defend himself from these charges. He explains

---

156 Clayton (2007) argues that Theodoret could admit a *communicatio nominum* but not a *communicatio idiomatum*. He also argues that Theodoret's Christological position at this stage remains essentially that of Theodore of Mopsuestia.

that his language was merely intended to exclude the Nestorian suggestion that the flesh belonged to a separate human person. Of course 'flesh' means 'man in his completeness'; of course he took flesh from the virgin; of course the union is without confusion and the Logos remains unchanged.

The final anathema was the most provocative of all: Let anyone be anathema who does not confess that the Logos which originated from God 'suffered in the flesh, and was crucified in the flesh, and tasted death in the flesh.' Without qualification, suffering and death were predicated of the Logos. In the epistles Cyril had been more guarded. Was he just careless in framing the anathema? But anathemas were to be taken seriously. So did he wish to force the issue? If he did, he succeeded, but he also laid himself open to severe criticism. It was blasphemous to suggest that God was passible. If the Son was παθητός (susceptible to suffering) while being ὁμοούσιος τῷ Πατρί (of one substance with the Father), then the Father was passible. The logical outcome of Cyril's statement was either Patripassianism or Arianism. Is it any wonder that the Antiochenes were sufficiently scandalized to condemn Cyril and his anathemas at the rival session of the Council of Ephesus? This final anathema confirmed all their suspicions of the basic intent of the rest.

In his attack Theodoret declared that the ἀπαθής (impassible) is above παθῆ; only the παθητός can suffer. The 'form of a servant' suffered, the 'form of God' being with it, assenting to its suffering for the salvation of human beings and making the suffering its own through the union. When forced to explain, Cyril too spoke of the Logos making the sufferings of the flesh his own, while remaining ἀπαθής (impassible) in his own nature. At this crucial point it seems as though the two sides were really not far apart in wrestling with the paradox; and yet it was here that each gave the deepest offence to the other. For the essential difference remains: the Antiochenes could not make the Logos directly the subject of incarnation, passion and death, whereas that was precisely what Cyril was trying to do. Both sides were haunted by the contests with Arians, Eunomians and Apollinarians.

With passions aroused, the bishops proceeded to Ephesus.[157] Is it any wonder that communications broke down? Both saw the issues in terms of another serious heresy-hunt, each accusing the other. The fact that a Formulary of Reunion was reached two years later is really more remarkable than their reciprocal excommunication in 431. A few years later Cyril and Theodoret were engaged in a new exchange, Theodoret defending Diodore and Theodore from their Alexandrian critic. (Unfortunately these treatises exist only in fragmentary form, but they had an important place in the discussion which led to the eventual condemnation of the great Antiochene teachers, the 'Fathers of Nestorianism'.) The two sides remained suspicious of one another. There has been a tendency to argue that there was no real difference between the two contenders,[158] that their theologies were in reality very close and if only they could have talked out the issues calmly and sorted out their terminology in the peace and quiet of a seminar room, all discrepancies could have been ironed out; politics

---

157 For a full account of the proceedings at Ephesus, see McGuckin (1994), though he reads the sources to put Cyril's actions into the most favourable light possible.

158 For example, Sellers (1940, 1953); Prestige (1940); also Anastos (1962).

got mixed up with theology and the condemnation of Nestorius was all a horrible mistake. But the actors thought they were fighting for truth, and surely we should pay both Cyril and his opponents the compliment of attending to their views on the subject of their quarrel. Nestorius cared only, in the end, that truth should prevail,[159] and so did Cyril. Of course, no serious human dispute is carried on in isolation from political, social or personal factors, but that does not mean that these exhaust everything there is to say about the issues. Of course, many arguments proceed because of emotion, prejudice and failure to listen to the other side, and these factors are particularly strong when people feel their faith under attack. But surely there were real issues: How could God be the subject of incarnate experiences? How could Christ be genuinely human if identified with God incarnate? The Antiochenes gave serious attention to the difficulties, and aroused the suspicions of the faithful by refusing to allow a direct identification; Cyril insisted on that direct identification and waved aside the difficulties, thinking that the reiteration of certain provisos met the problem sufficiently well. Controversy meant the exaggeration of each position, and many of the side-issues and mutual misunderstandings tended to obscure the point at which the real difference lay. But a real difference there was.

It is time to put this controversy into perspective. How much did it dominate the lives and literature of the three main figures we have found involved? Cyril and Theodoret had long episcopates and were by no means monopolized by this issue. But first let us turn to Nestorius whose life was inevitably coloured by his tragic role in the confrontation between two Christological traditions.

For Further Reading

English translations

Bindley, T. H. and F. W. Green, 1955. *The Oecumenical Documents of the Faith*, London: Methuen.
Pásztori-Kupán, István, 2006. *Theodoret of Cyrus*, London and New York: Routledge.
Russell, N., 2000. *Cyril of Alexandria*, London and New York: Routledge.
Wickham, L. R., 1983. *Cyril of Alexandria: Select Letters*, ed. and ET, Oxford: Clarendon Press.

Studies

Clayton, Paul B. Jr, 2007. *The Christology of Theodoret of Cyrus: Antiochene Christology from the Council of Ephesus (431) to the Council of Chalcedon (451)*, Oxford: Oxford University Press.
McGuckin, J. A., 1994. *Cyril of Alexandria: The Christological Controversy: Its History, Theology and Texts*, Leiden: Brill / republished St Vladimir's Seminary Press.

---

159 See below, p. 288.

V Nestorius

It is my earnest desire that even by anathematizing me they may escape from blaspheming God [and that those who so escape may confess God, holy, almighty and immortal, and not change the image of the incorruptible God for the image of corruptible man, and mingle heathenism with Christianity ... but that Christ may be confessed to be in truth and in nature God and Man, being by nature immortal and impassible as God, and mortal and passible by nature as Man – not God in both natures, nor again Man in both natures. The goal of my earnest wish is that God may be blessed on earth as in heaven]; but as for Nestorius, let him be anathema; only let men speak of God as I pray for them that they may speak. For I am with those who are for God, and not with those who are against God, who with an outward show of religion reproach God and cause him to cease from being God.[160]

It could be said that a great Christian wrote those words. There have been many who were prepared to die as martyrs for what they believed to be the truth, but Nestorius was prepared to live cursed and consigned to oblivion, as long as God was not dishonoured. The saving of God's honour, the exclusion of blasphemy and pagan mythology from the language of religious devotion, was what had motivated him all along; and we now know that he not only lived to see his theology vindicated, but even rejoiced to see it even though it meant no reprieve or recognition for him and his followers. As long as truth prevailed, he was prepared to suffer, to efface himself, rather than arouse renewed conflict, prejudice and misunderstanding. In tribulation he showed a greater generosity of spirit than many who have received the name saint rather than heretic.

Was Nestorius orthodox? Was Nestorius a 'Nestorian'? These questions have been repeatedly debated in the twentieth century, and there is a real sense in which the terms of the debate make the discussion fruitless and uninteresting. Each investigator tends to presuppose a different standard of 'orthodoxy'; do we measure by Chalcedon or by subsequent Christological developments? If by Chalcedon, then Nestorius himself affirms that he could have accepted its main tenets; for he welcomed Leo's *Tome* to Flavian as a summary of his own theology.[161] Then, what is meant by Nestorianism? If we mean the traditional thumbnail sketch of this heresy – teaching two Sons, dividing the Christ or treating him as a mere man, reintroducing Adoptionism and the false views of Paul of Samosata – then it is quite clear that Nestorius repeatedly repudiated the views attributed to him. If we mean the theology of the 'Nestorian Church', the Church of the East 'established' in Persia and throughout the Orient for many centuries though out of communion with the West, then in the light of Chalcedon it is by no means clear that that church was heretical – though it may once have harboured extremist 'Dyophysites' who found their home

---

160 Nau (1910), p. 323; Driver and Hodgson (1925), p. 370. According to Abramowski (1963) the section in brackets bears the marks of the interpolator; however the same attitude is found in the surrounding sentences, so the main point is not affected by that literary-critical hypothesis.

161 Nau (1910), p. 298; Driver and Hodgson (1925), p. 340.

over the border. There are those for whom the definition of orthodoxy and heresy remains ecclesiastically vital, but for those interested in the workings of theological argument, it seems much more important to try and understand Nestorius against the background of his own time, the situation in the Church and the theological questions at issue. In that situation, did Nestorius have an interesting contribution to make?

1 The sources

The upsurge of interest in Nestorius in the twentieth century was caused by the fact that just as Loofs was publishing a collected edition of his surviving frag-ments,[162] news was gradually percolating through that there existed a Syriac manuscript of his lost apology, the *Book of Heraclides*. South of Armenia and west of the Caspian Sea is a mountainous area that falls within Iran (Persia). Here, in the late nineteenth century, some American missionaries heard of a manuscript in the possession of the Nestorian patriarch which contained this lost work of Nestorius. Eventually copies reached Europe and the work of publication and translation slowly began.[163] Meanwhile, though the *Book of Heraclides* was still unpublished, Bethune-Baker was able to use it together with Loofs's fragments to produce his vindication of Nestorius in 1908,[164] quoting long sections in Eng-lish translation. Careful literary analysis of the *Book of Heraclides* had to wait for another half century,[165] but reconsideration of Nestorius' position was initiated. *The Book of Heraclides* provided a wider perspective against which the fragments could be more fairly judged. A fair assessment, however, depends upon giving due consideration to chronology and literary-critical problems; for Nestorius' stance in his later apology may not necessarily be simply equated with his posi-tion during the crisis – memory is affected by hindsight, after all – and the *Book of Heraclides* has to be used with care, for it seems to have been interpolated and may well be composite. What sources do we have, then, what is their chrono-logy, and what is their character?

Nestorius is said to have composed many treatises on various questions; but virtually nothing survived Theodosius' decree that all his works should be burned. Like John Chrysostom, Nestorius became bishop of Constantinople on the strength of his reputation for preaching; so at one time there were doubtless numerous sermons in circulation, but most of what has survived did so because its contents were regarded as damaging to Nestorius' position. Extracts from his sermons were quoted against him at the Council and in Cyril's controversial writings. Some complete sermons were included in the *Conciliar Acts*, though these are in Latin translation, as is the material preserved by Marius Mercator, an African writer resident in Constantinople at the time of the controversy; but Greek fragments of the notorious sermons on *Theotokos* confirm parts of the text. Some fragments have established the Nestorian authorship of a sermon attrib-uted to John Chrysostom, thus giving us at least one complete Greek homily

---

162 Loofs (1905).
163 Syriac text: Bedjan (1910); ET: Driver and Hodgson (1925).
164 Bethune-Baker (1908).
165 Abramowski (1963).

which is undisputed. Various others have been attributed to Nestorius by certain modern scholars, but general agreement about their authenticity has so far not been reached.[166] In addition to these homiletic materials, we have a number of letters dating from the controversy, not just those to Cyril already examined, but also Latin versions of his letters to Celestine in Rome, and various other relevant letters, to the emperor, to John of Antioch, and to certain other contacts. Of course, all this material derives from hostile sources and may therefore give a distorted picture; brief quotations lack a context, and the selection of passages was no doubt determined by the desire to incriminate Nestorius. But the more complete examples of letters and sermons probably convey a reasonably accurate impression of Nestorius' stance during the controversy.[167]

After Ephesus Nestorius asked permission to return to his monastery near Antioch, and for a short period he was allowed to do that. Imperial decrees of 435, however, not only ensured the destruction of his books but banished him to Oasis in Upper Egypt; perhaps after the Formulary of Reunion his proximity had become an embarrassment to John of Antioch, who had essentially sacrificed Nestorius for the sake of the peace of the churches. During the years of retreat and exile Nestorius turned to literary activity. Probably during the period in his monastery he composed an apology called *Tragedy* which gave his side of the case; and at some point he wrote a dialogue refuting Cyril called *Theopaschites*. Fragments of each of these are to be found in Loofs's collection. But by far the most significant of his extant works is the rediscovered *Book of Heraclides*, sometimes called *The Bazaar*.

It was the Syriac title which suggested the translation 'Bazaar', but the word was probably a rendering of the Greek πραγματεῖα (*pragmateia*); the translation should therefore be the less enigmatic 'treatise'. But why Heraclides? It seems as though the author was attempting to prevent immediate destruction of the book by adopting a pseudonym, but there is no attempt in the body of the book to conceal the identity of its author. Anyone who looked further than the title page was not going to be deceived. It is apparently a work of apology and explanation composed by Nestorius himself. The book is not quite complete and the contents are not homogeneous. The first part is in dialogue form, Nestorius discussing various different Christological proposals with one Sophronius, rejecting docetism and 'mixture', and eventually proposing a Christology that both preserves the two natures intact and affirms a unity of *prosōpon*. But the dialogue form is eventually abandoned and Nestorius in his own person gives an account of the events which doomed him, quoting letters and documents at length, discussing the theological and terminological points at issue, arguing with Cyril, accusing him of a serious miscarriage of justice, claiming that proper enquiry would have shown that he was orthodox and innocent of the charges brought against him, and that the great Fathers, Gregory, Ambrose and Athanasius taught his doctrine. Nestorius was out to prove that Cyril was deeply hostile and the whole affair turned on personal animosity; really he and Cyril were not far apart, and where they differed, Cyril was confused or

---

166 The additional material published by Nau appended to his translation of the *Liber Heraclidis* is generally accepted. For other suggestions, consult the Patrologies.

167 The material described in this paragraph will be found collected together in Loofs (1905).

wrong. The first major literary analysis suggested that the treatise as it stands is a compilation of two different works, and the opening dialogue is not in fact the authentic work of Nestorius;[168] this view has not met with universal acceptance[169] – though the literary case is quite strong, stronger than the theological differences observed.[170]

The work is frustrating to read, as Anastos points out:

> It must be admitted that his style is often turgid and confusing. The repetitiousness of his great theological treatise, the *Bazaar of Heraclides*, is frustrating, wearisome and painful. It would have been vastly more effective if some expert rhetorician had pruned it of tautology, eliminated contradictions, added the necessary logical definitions which Nestorius unhappily eschewed, and reduced its length by a half or three quarters. Still, even in a morass of verbiage, the *Bazaar* is a document that merits careful consideration.[171]

From the historian's point of view this is undoubtedly true, but we have yet to consider whether Anastos is right in thinking that in spite of its defects we find here 'the subtlest and most penetrating study of the mystery of the incarnation in the whole of patristic literature'. Its diffuse and chaotic form makes it a highly difficult work to comprehend and assess, and the fact that it is a constructive work of theology going deeper than the general Antiochene treatment of the subject is by no means immediately obvious.

2 Nestorius' position in the controversy

A number of interesting problems are posed by these literary remains of Nestorius. In the first place there is the question of consistency: does Nestorius give a fair account of the controversy in his apology, or did he as bishop of Constantinople act with greater provocation than he was later prepared to admit? Did he modify his position and refine it with qualifications in the years of reflection? Then there is the question of significance: were Nestorius' reflections really the product of subtle metaphysical analysis or was he simply confused and inconsistent? Finally there is the question of personality: what was Nestorius really like? How do we reconcile the self-effacing monk in exile with the headstrong bishop in Constantinople? Did character contribute to his tragedy as it did in the somewhat parallel case of Chrysostom? Clearly these questions need to be reviewed not only in the light of Nestorius' own statements, but also set against the impression he made on his contemporaries, one of whom was the Church historian Socrates.

Socrates[172] explains Nestorius' downfall as the result of his own contentious spirit. Immediately after his consecration he said in public: 'Give me, my prince,

---

168 Abramowski (1963).
169 For example, Scipioni (1975). See also Chesnut (1978).
170 Turner (1975).
171 Anastos (1962), p. 123.
172 Socrates, *HE* vii.29, 31–2.

the earth purged of heretics, and I will give you heaven as a recompense. Assist me in destroying heretics, and I will assist you in vanquishing the Persians.' He then set in motion a vicious persecution of heretics in the capital and in Asia Minor, earning the nickname 'Firebrand' after an Arian chapel had gone up in smoke. Socrates' estimate was that his own expulsion was no more than he deserved: as the proverb says, 'Drunkards never want wine, nor the contentious strife.'

As far as Socrates was concerned, the doctrinal charges brought against Nestorius had no substance:

> Having myself perused the writings of Nestorius, I have found him an unlearned man and shall candidly express the conviction of my mind concerning him . . . I cannot concede that he was either a follower of Paul of Samosata or of Photinus, or that he denied the divinity of Christ; but he seemed scared at the term *Theotokos* as though it were some terrible 'bugbear'. The fact is, the causeless alarm he manifested on this subject just exposed his extreme ignorance; for being a man of natural fluency as a speaker, he was considered well-educated, but in reality he was disgracefully illiterate.

This judgment Socrates bases upon the fact that he had not bothered to check up biblical and patristic authorities for using the title *Theotokos* of Mary; if he had, he would have found it in the works of Origen as well as others, Socrates states. However, 'puffed up with his ease of expression, he did not give his attention to the ancients, but thought himself the greatest of all'.

That Nestorius tended to act in haste and that he was over-sure of his own position can hardly be doubted. The high-handed way he addressed the bishop of Rome in the extant letters, his total want of tact in paying attention to some Western adherents of Pelagius who had been condemned at Rome some years before, all this suggests that he set himself up as the sole judge of heresy and was not disposed to accept advice or meddling from his fellow-patriarchs. He was determined and impetuous in dispute and liable to make strong statements open to misunderstanding; he himself admits that he had made some remark about not calling God an infant two or three months old.[173] Simple believers reacted to such comments as they did to his refusal to call Mary *Theotokos*, and it was of course that 'bugbear' around which the whole controversy revolved.

There are different accounts of how the question of using that title for Mary set off the conflict. Socrates states that Nestorius took a strong line against *Theotokos* in support of a presbyter, Anastasius, one of those who had come from Antioch in his entourage. Nestorius' strongly worded sermons against *Theotokos* are consistent with this account. Nestorius himself, however, claims[174] that he did not start the trouble but was drawn into it by an appeal from mutually hostile groups in Constantinople. The Apollinarian controversy lay behind the whole business: some gave the name 'Mother of God' to Mary, others 'Mother of Man', and each attached heretical labels to the other, Manichaeans or Apollinarians on

---

173 Nau (1910), pp. 120f. / Driver and Hodgson (1925), pp. 136f. Socrates reports a similar remark as having given scandal.

174 Nau (1910), pp. 91f. / Driver and Hodgson (1925), pp. 99f. Cf. Loofs (1905), pp. 185 and 203, for parallel accounts in a letter to John and a fragment of the *Tragedy*.

the one side, Photinians or followers of Paul of Samosata on the other. Nestorius questioned each group and found that the first did not deny the humanity and the others did not deny the divinity; so he went for compromise – both titles were acceptable with certain reservations, but it would be better to avoid difficulties by using *Christotokos*. The groups went away happy and reconciled, he claims. Only the interference of outsiders like Cyril prolonged the question. Hints in his first sermon suggest that a debate had recently taken place in Nestorius' presence concerning the question whether Mary should be called *Theotokos* or *Anthropotokos*;[175] so his story finds some confirmation in sources from the time of the dispute. However, it does not seem altogether consistent with the fact that his sermons appear to exclude the title *Theotokos* entirely. Besides, that is what everyone apparently took him to mean at the time. So Nestorius must have been a determined critic of the term, whatever he said later. Yet there are several hints that even during the controversy he was prepared to allow it, if it were accompanied with proper safeguards: to the Pope he admitted that the term might be tolerated,[176] and to Cyril he confessed that he had nothing against it – 'only do not make the virgin a goddess'.[177] What worried Nestorius was not so much the term itself as the theological implications of careless usage; it too easily carried with it so many unacceptable corollaries. Only with great care and subtlety could one speak of God being born, God suffering, God dying. The unguarded language of faith could lead into all kinds of heretical snares. With characteristic resolution Nestorius waded into the attack.

Years later, writing the *Bazaar*, Nestorius was still sure he was right. He insists that he has not changed.[178] He rejoices that God has raised up others to defend the truth.[179] Maybe his apparent self-effacement for the sake of truth is consistent with his earlier brusque activity on truth's behalf. In both cases he was trying to ensure that God was not blasphemed but given his due honour; and when he wrote the *Bazaar*, he still thought he was fighting Arians and Apollinarians in the unguarded statements of Cyril. However, at the time of the conflict it would appear that he was inexperienced, over-zealous, tactless, insensitive to popular feeling and politically inept. To some extent he may have brought his condemnation at Ephesus upon his own head.[180] Socrates seems to have put his finger on aspects of Nestorius' incompetence.

But how consistent and intelligent is his doctrine? Socrates apparently dismissed it as all froth and no substance. Are we to accept his judgment?

3 His own doctrinal position

The persistent criticism brought against the Antiochene theology has been that, dominated by the need to distinguish the two natures, it failed to give any

175 Loofs (1905), pp. 251f.
176 Loofs (1905), p. 167.
177 Loofs (1905), p. 353.
178 Nau (1910), p. 88 / Driver and Hodgson (1925), p. 95; Nau (1910), p. 330 / Driver and Hodgson (1925), p. 378.
179 Nau (1910), p. 327 / Driver and Hodgson (1925), pp. 374f.
180 See the account given in McGuckin (1994).

account of the unity of the Christ. Most twentieth-century studies were at pains to show how much Nestorius was concerned with Christ's unity of person,[181] and some have gone so far as to suggest[182] that Nestorius' 'prosopic union' was a serious attempt to give a metaphysically sound basis to the often-repeated Antiochene claim that they accepted one Son and one worship, without abandoning any of the hard-won principles of Antiochene theology in the process. Nestorius, it is said, worked with three basic metaphysical terms, *ousia* (substance), *physis* (nature) and *prosōpon* (person). A thing's *ousia* is what it is in itself; its *physis* is its totality of qualities, what gives it its distinctive characteristics; its *prosōpon* is its concrete manifestation, its external presentation. Divine *ousia* and human *ousia* being 'alien to one another' or mutually exclusive, could not be identified or united, so the union did not take place at that level. A union of *physis* could not mean anything but confusion – either an Apollinarian mixture producing a *tertium quid* or the complete absorption of one nature by the other.[183] So the only possible level at which the union could take place was that of *prosōpon*. The concrete manifestation is the one Son, our Lord Jesus Christ, who cannot be divided or separated into two; but underlying the common *prosōpon* are two natures and two *ousiai*, the divine and the human. What of the term *hypostasis*? Nestorius usually seems to have identified this with *ousia*;[184] in the Trinitarian context he preferred to speak of three *prosōpa* rather than three *hypostaseis*, and in Christology he speaks of each nature having its own *hypostasis*. But he recognizes that the term is ambiguous, even stating that Cyril's phrase 'hypostatic union' could be acceptable if it meant not a union of *ousia* or *physis* but a union of *prosōpon*[185] (after all *hypostasis* and *prosōpon* were interchangeable in the Trinitarian formula).

The 'prosopic union' thus becomes Nestorius' attempt to provide a metaphysical account of Christ's unity of person which did not involve the difficulties of a 'natural' or 'substantial' union, and Nestorius meant it to convey a 'real union'. The one Christ has 'two grounds of being', he is 'in two natures', as Chalcedon was later to affirm. God the Word and the Man in whom he came to be are not numerically two.[186] Christ is indivisible in his being Christ, but he is twofold in his being God and his being Man.[187] In other words the unity and the duality belong to different metaphysical levels.

---

181 Bethune-Baker (1908); Amann (1931); etc. Survey in Turner (1975).

182 Anastos (1962). Cf. Hodgson (1918/25).

183 For example Nau (1910), pp. 263f. / Driver and Hodgson (1925), pp. 298f. Various other sections revolve around the question of definition, for example Nau (1910), pp. 127–63 / Driver and Hodgson (1925), pp. 143–85. The alternatives are discussed at length in the dialogue (especially Nau (1910), pp. 18f. / Driver and Hodgson (1925), pp. 20f.), which Hodgson and Anastos took to be authentic Nestorius. There seems little reason to doubt that it represents with slightly more clarity what Nestorius himself attempts to say elsewhere.

184 Driver and Hodgson (1925), p. 156 n. 2; cf. Vine (1948), pp. 113ff. Abramowski (1963), pp. 213ff., notes that the word is not used in Christological contexts until well into the controversy. This confirms Richard's view that Cyril introduced it, and it was by no means a natural term for the Antiochenes. See above, p. 282.

185 Nau (1910), pp. 138f. / Driver and Hodgson (1925), pp. 156f.

186 Loofs (1905), p. 224.

187 Loofs (1905), p. 280.

The claim that Nestorius had begun to work out such a sophisticated account of the union even at the time of the controversy deserves some attention. It seems clear that whereas the Antiochenes in general tended to distinguish two classes of scriptural titles and sayings, those referring to the God–Logos and those referring to the Man, Nestorius chose to use three categories. Certain terms like Logos are specific references to his divine nature, and certain others specifically indicate his human nature; but the majority of titles refer neither to one nature alone nor the other, but to the common *prosōpon*, the Lord Jesus Christ. Hence his recommendation of *Christotokos* as a solution to the difficulties of using either *Theotokos* or *Anthropotokos* exclusively. God in his own essential nature was not born. The Trinity did not enter the virgin's womb. But Christ who was both God and Man, was born. Christ was not mere man, nor was he identical with God. To speak of the Logos becoming twofold in his nature, as Cyril did, was impossible for Nestorius. The Logos could not be the *prosōpon* of union; the two natures were not two states of the Logos' being, but the two 'grounds of being' of the one Christ. Of course, this implies a typically Antiochene 'symmetry', equal emphasis on the Godhead and the humanity; and the typically Antiochene safeguards for each nature are rigidly maintained. But whereas Theodore had tended to envisage each nature in very concrete terms, each being almost a separate person acting independently, Nestorius was anxious to present an account of one concrete individual with two distinguishable metaphysical bases.

However, if this was what Nestorius had in mind, he was certainly not very adept at making the point clearly. He inherited the Antiochene terminology and he was not altogether able to discard their very concrete ways of thinking. Thus he found it impossible to reserve the term *prosōpon* for the union; he could not avoid talk of a human *prosōpon* and a divine *prosōpon*. Thus each nature had its own *prosōpon* and the two natures remain personalized to the extent that his opponents were not altogether unfair in accusing him of teaching a 'double Christ', two persons acting independently. Nestorius himself speaks of them as 'self-sustaining',[188] and it is doubtful if he would have accepted the idea that the two natures were distinguishable merely in thought. Thus he was not sufficiently strict in his terminology to avoid misunderstanding. This is also true of his alleged distinction between *ousia* and *physis*. He often seems to identify the two and be very unclear about their specific application.[189] We may well ask whether he was not really rather confused by this metaphysical terminology, especially when we recall his difficulties with *hypostasis*. Socrates did not after all find his logical capabilities very impressive.[190]

So what did Nestorius' 'prosopic union' mean? Was it one *prosōpon* with two underlying 'grounds of being'? Or was it two *prosōpa* uniting into a third? – in which case he faced the same difficulties about mixture as his opponents. Or was the word *prosōpon* used in two different senses, as Anastos suggests? Nestorius may have become dimly aware of these puzzles, for in the *Bazaar*

---

188 Nau (1910), p. 265 / Driver and Hodgson (1925), p. 300.

189 Turner (1975).

190 Nor does McGuckin (1994), who provides an account of Nestorius' unclarity and the way the two sides misheard each other because of different understandings of the terminology.

we find a way of speaking not in evidence elsewhere, either in Nestorius' fragments or the other Antiochenes. Nestorius introduces the idea of an exchange
of *prosōpa*, or a mutual reciprocity of *prosōpa*. He speaks of the divinity making
use of the *prosōpon* of the humanity, and the humanity of that of the divinity.[191]
In other words, the two *prosōpa* do not constitute a third by combination, but
rather it is at the level of the *prosōpon* that two complete beings can interpen-
etrate without damage to the essential nature of either. On the basis of this idea
it can be argued that Nestorius came to admit a *communicatio idiomatum*, though
he remained well aware of the way in which this tradition could be misused by
the unwary. (*Communicatio idiomatum* describes the doctrine that because of the
union of natures in Christ, properties which are properly divine may be predicated of the human nature and properties properly human may be predicated
of the divine.)

Nestorius does seem to be searching for a substantial basis for the union of
two natures in Christ. The fact that this was his aim is most clearly indicated by
his willingness to draw parallels between Christological and Trinitarian concepts:[192] 'As in the Trinity there is one *ousia* of three *prosōpa*, but three *prosōpa* of
one *ousia*, here there is one *prosōpon* of two *ousiai* and two *ousiai* of one *prosōpon*';
'Confess then the Assumer and the Assumed, each being one and in another,
one not two, after the same manner as the manner of the Trinity.' Nestorius was
attempting to provide a way of conceiving a real unity. But how successful he
was is another question. One is tempted to think he was the victim of his own
lack of definition, though part of the problem was that he did not have suitable metaphysical tools; but besides that, his thought was still overshadowed
by the legacy of the Arian and Apollinarian controversies. The sharp division
between the divine and the human, the Creator and the created, was an axi-
omatic principle to be defended at all costs, and this in itself made his task
well-nigh impossible. Chalcedon itself made no attempt to resolve the problem,
content simply to affirm two in one and one in two without separation or mixture. It was precisely that confession that Nestorius was trying to establish.

So Nestorius was wrestling with the problems of the Antiochene theology he
had inherited. In reaction to Arianism and Apollinarianism, it had produced
an over-concrete picture of the man Jesus struggling against temptation, while
the Logos remained transcendent and unconfined to the human temple he had
fashioned for himself. Nestorius strove to put back into the centre the one Lord
Jesus Christ, while refusing to compromise the 'Godness of God' or the 'human-
ness of the human'. In this endeavour he seems to have been fairly consistent,
and we should probably take his word for it that he did not change or seriously
modify his Christological position over the years. He carried the can for all the
faults and difficulties of the Antiochene position while actually seeking ways

---

191 For example Nau (1910), pp. 140f. / Driver and Hodgson (1925), p. 159, and often,
especially Nau (1910), p. 183 / Driver and Hodgson (1925), p. 207 and Nau (1910), pp. 212f.
/ Driver and Hodgson (1925), pp. 240f.: the humanity making use of the *prosōpon* of the
divinity and the divinity of the *prosōpon* of the humanity. For an interesting discussion
of this, see Chesnut (1978).

192 Grillmeier (1965), pp. 439ff. (2nd ed., 1975, pp. 508ff.), quoting Nau (1910), p. 219
/ Driver and Hodgson (1925), pp. 247; 448 (2nd ed., p. 516), quoting Nau (1910), p. 183 /
Driver and Hodgson (1925), p. 207 (altered).

to resolve them. That he was thoroughly misrepresented by his enemies cannot be doubted, though he may have asked for it by making manifestly provocative statements. When Theodoret was finally forced to anathematize Nestorius together with anyone who did not say the holy Mary was *Theotokos* and divided the one only-begotten Son, he must have known that he was associating Nestorius' name with a thoroughly misleading caricature of his actual teaching. It is hardly surprising that he conscientiously refused to desert Nestorius and his friends throughout twenty years of attack. With his own rather different approach, he was attempting to perform the same task as Nestorius – namely find a way of maintaining the traditional Antiochene insights while rediscovering the one Saviour, the one Lord Jesus Christ.

Nestorius was the victim. He has become the symbol of one type of Christological position taken to extremes. And for that he suffered. He could legitimately complain that his condemnation had been unfair: Cyril had plotted his downfall; Cyril chaired the synod; Cyril was his accuser and his judge; Cyril represented Pope and Emperor. 'Cyril was everything!'[193] Nestorius had no chance of a hearing. From his point of view the proceedings at Ephesus were indefensible.[194] Then his friends deserted him, and he went into exile in Egypt. There he was captured by invading barbarians, and on his escape surrendered himself to the Roman governor 'lest all future generations should be told the tragic story that it was better to be captured by barbarians than to take refuge with the Roman empire'.[195] The governor, however, kept him on the move, transferring him from place to place, while he lived in constant pain from injuries. But Nestorius was a monk, schooled to patience and endurance. There is no better testimony to the depth of his commitment than his refusal to appeal to Leo even though it was evident that Leo's *Tome* was a vindication of what he had himself stood for. He did not want the truth to suffer by association with his blackened name.[196] Did he live to hear of Chalcedon? In a recently published collection of Nestorian texts, it is stated that he lived twenty-two years after Ephesus,[197] which implies that he did; but the *Liber Heraclidis* provides no unambiguous evidence, though it certainly indicates that he saw the death of Theodosius and looked forward to a new council with assurance that truth would prevail. But 'as for me,' he concludes,

I regard the sufferings of my life and all that has befallen me in this world as the suffering of a single day; and I have not changed all these years. Now my death approaches and every day I pray to God to dismiss me – me whose eyes have seen the salvation of God. Rejoice with me, Desert, thou my friend, my nurse, my home; and thou exile, my mother, who after my death will keep my body until the resurrection by the grace of God. Amen.

---

193 Nau (1910), p. 117 / Driver and Hodgson (1925), p. 132.

194 McGuckin (1994), however, puts a rather different light on the proceedings, suggesting that Cyril acted within the canons and Nestorius behaved in a way that lost him support.

195 Loofs (1905), p. 199.

196 Nau (1910), p. 330 / Driver and Hodgson (1925), p. 378.

197 Abramowski and Goodman (1972), vol. II, p. 24.

For Further Reading

English translations

Driver, G. R. and L. Hodgson, 1925. *Nestorius. The Bazaar of Heraclides*, ET, Oxford and New York: Clarendon Press.

Studies

Anastos, Milton V., 1962. 'Nestorius was Orthodox', *Dumbarton Oaks Papers* 16, pp. 119–40.
Bethune-Baker, J. F., 1908. *Nestorius and his Teaching*, Cambridge: Cambridge University Press.
Chesnut, Roberta C., 1978. 'The Two Prosopa in Nestorius' *Bazaar of Heraclides*', *JTS* NS 29, pp. 392–409.
Hodgson, L., 1918. 'The Metaphysic of Nestorius', *JTS* 19, pp. 46–55 (republished as Appendix IV in Driver and Hodgson 1925).
Loofs, F., 1914. *Nestorius and His Place in the History of Christian Doctrine*, Cambridge and New York: Cambridge University Press.
McGuckin, J. A., 1994/2004. *Cyril of Alexandria: The Christological Controversy: Its History, Theology and Texts*, Leiden: Brill / republished Crestwood, NY: St Vladimir's Seminary Press.
Turner, H. E. W., 1975. 'Nestorius Reconsidered', *SP* 13, pp. 306–21.

VI Cyril of Alexandria

1 Cyril's reputation

Cyril has provoked extreme reactions in both ancient and modern times. He has always been for some the great Doctor of the Incarnation: his letters were given canonical status at Chalcedon and proved a foundation on which later thinkers would build. Chalcedonians and Non-Chalcedonians agreed that Cyril was to be regarded as the prime authority on this question. Some modern studies have hailed Cyril as the one great fifth-century thinker to perceive the essentials for an incarnational theology and to seek ways of upholding them in a philosophical atmosphere which made his task formidable. True he was a bit hasty, but an extract from a letter penned by him in the early phases of the controversy throws light on an aspect of his character of which few are aware:

> I love peace; there is nothing that I detest more than quarrels and disputes. I love everybody, and if I could heal one of the brethren by losing all my possessions and goods, I am willing to do so joyfully; because it is concord that I value most . . . But there is question of the faith and of a scandal which concerns all the churches of the Roman Empire . . . The sacred doctrine is entrusted to us . . . How can we remedy these evils? . . . I am ready to endure with tranquillity all blame, all humiliations, all injuries provided that the faith is not endangered. I am filled with love for Nestorius, nobody loves him more than I do . . . If, in accordance with Christ's commandment, we must

love our very enemies themselves, is it not natural that we should be united in special affection to those who are our friends and brethren in the priesthood? But when the faith is attacked, we must not hesitate to sacrifice our life itself. And if we fear to preach the truth because that causes us some inconvenience, how, in our gatherings, can we chant the combats and triumphs of our holy martyrs?[198]

To some then, Cyril was a saint, primarily concerned with the defence of Christian truth. To others, Cyril has appeared as an unscrupulous political operator, a true successor to his uncle Theophilus who contrived the downfall of John Chrysostom, a nasty piece of work out to achieve maximum power for the Alexandrian see by whatever possible means.[199] And modern emphasis on the part played by politics and personality receives some support from contemporaries. Isidore of Pelusium was a good friend of Cyril's, so much so that he could afford to offer him a rebuke for his conduct at Ephesus, implying that animosity had blinkered his judgment: 'Sympathy does not see distinctly; but antipathy does not see at all. If then you would be clear of both sorts of poor-sightedness, do not indulge in violent negations, but submit any charges made against you to a just judgment.'[200] His following remarks are revealing:

Many of those who were assembled at Ephesus speak satirically of you as a man bent on pursuing his private animosities, not as one who seeks in correct belief the things of Jesus Christ. 'He is sister's son to Theophilus,' they say, 'and in disposition takes after him. Just as the uncle openly expended his fury against the inspired and beloved John, so also the nephew seeks to set himself up in his turn, although there is considerable difference between the things at stake.'

Socrates[201] certainly disliked Cyril and most of the information he gives about him is designed to bring discredit on his early years as bishop – indeed, relatively speaking, his behaviour in the Nestorian controversy appears restrained, for in Socrates' eyes, the chief blame for that affair rested on Nestorius' tactlessness and ignorance. Clearly Cyril made enemies easily, and it is hardly surprising that in a letter quoted as Theodoret's[202] among the Acts of Chalcedon, we find expressed heartfelt relief at Cyril's death and the suggestion that a large, heavy stone be placed on his tomb lest he provoke the dead so much that they send him back!

So Cyril's character, as well as his theology, has been subject to critique; yet one may justifiably ask whether he was any different from, say, Athanasius,

---

198 Extract from Kerrigan (1952), p. 7, quoting Schwartz, *ACO* I.i.1, 108f. Kerrigan here follows very closely the material and judgments of du Manoir (1944). Latterly Wickham (1983); McGuckin (1994); and Weinandy and Keating (2003) have defended Cyril against criticisms ancient and modern.

199 See, for example, von Campenhausen (1963), chapter 12; the discussion in Chadwick (1951); and the assessments in many of the major histories of the early Church.

200 As quoted in Stevenson (1966), p. 300 (translation slightly altered).

201 Socrates, *HE* vii.13ff.

202 Theodoret, *Ep.* 180.

in his forthright defence of what he saw as the essential truth about the Word Incarnate.[203] The extreme reactions on both sides are surely exaggerated; yet Cyril must have been a strong character with the ability to attract and repel. If we are to judge him as a scheming politician with little interest in anything but success, we have systematically to distrust his own protestations. Doubtless his was a strong-principled personality who found compromise difficult; like many other figures of history, he identified his standpoint with Truth, and was prepared to stop at little to ensure its triumph. This would make it hard for him to listen to others with sympathy, and he can be convicted of misunderstanding and unfairness from his own writings. Yet we have to acknowledge that he did eventually come to terms with the Orientals in the Formulary of Reunion.

What then do we know of his life and work prior to the great controversy? Do the first fifteen or so years of his episcopate throw any light on his motivations?

2 Earlier years

The first recorded fact about Cyril's life is that he accompanied his uncle, Theophilus, to the Synod of the Oak which deposed John Chrysostom;[204] and that prejudice lasted – after the rest of the Church had restored the name of John to the diptychs (i.e. the roll of those whose names should be included in the prayers of the liturgy), Cyril at first refused to follow suit – he was not one to see any reason for going back on a decision once made.[205] Nor can Theophilus' political tactics have escaped his notice; there is surely a certain parallel between John's deposition and that of Nestorius thirty years later.

Cyril probably owed his education and advancement to his uncle, though nothing directly is known of his early years. It is possible he spent time with monks,[206] likely that he pursued the usual grammatical and rhetorical curriculum, plausible that he studied some philosophy despite the usual estimate that he was no philosopher. From his writings we may deduce that he was less enamoured of Hellenic learning than, say, the Cappadocians, but he does seem to have profited from the standard *cursus*.[207] His work *Against Julian* betrays some independent knowledge of the classics,[208] and it has been shown[209] that his mind was 'educated to think in a particular way', the evidence being his

---

203 McGuckin (1994) addresses the charges against Cyril, pointing to the climate of the age and the attitudes of others, including Nestorius; cf. also McGuckin in Weinandy and Keating (2003).

204 On Theophilus, see Russell (2007).

205 His agreement to restore John's name two years later may have been the result of a compromise deal with Constantinople; Burns et al. (1991).

206 Wickham (1983).

207 The fact that he speaks of it as 'vain and pointless', and suggests that it 'requires much effort for no reward' (*Against Julian* 5, Migne, *PG* 773D, ET Russell (2000), p. 203), would not of itself establish this, given he quotes Plato to support his view, and even Basil purported to reject it when a bishop!

208 See further below, p. 320.

209 See the important study by Siddals (1987); cf. Boulnois (1994).

deployment of terms which derive from the logic of Aristotle and Porphyry to demolish Eunomian and Arian arguments, and to ground his own Christological position. His style suggests a somewhat studied antiquarianism, though coupled with some fresh linguistic forms, and a combination of austere argument with widespread use of image and metaphor.[210] How widely read he was in Christian literature is contested, but many discern echoes of at least the Cappadocians in addition to the Alexandrian tradition.

When his uncle died in 412, Cyril was not elected his successor unopposed, but he soon asserted himself in the city of Alexandria. His first act was the suppression of the Novatianist sect and the seizure of their ecclesiastical property.[211] He rapidly came into conflict with the prefect, Orestes, and Socrates suggests that his major fault was meddling in secular affairs.[212] The real problem is to assess the degree of Cyril's responsibility for the dreadful events Socrates proceeds to relate. Alexandria was in any case a cosmopolitan city given to tumult and riot, with inter-racial feuds of an endemic nature.[213] The 'third race' – the Christian populace – stood flanked by pagans and Jews, still strong in influence and numbers. Did Cyril stir up trouble? Or did a series of coincidences trigger the conflicts, as so often happens when a closely packed urban population is divided by race or religion? It is a matter of judgment.

The first outbreak of violence came when a great devotee of Cyril – the leader of applause when Cyril was preaching – was caught eavesdropping on an occasion when the prefect was issuing regulations for theatricals on the Jewish Sabbath. Orestes was already annoyed at Cyril's meddling in the city administration and, according to Socrates,[214] arrested his supposed spy, and there and then publicly tortured him. Cyril complained to the Jewish leaders, who promptly plotted against the Christians. At night they raised an outcry that a certain church was on fire, and then slaughtered all the Christians who turned out to save it. Cyril promptly led a great army of Christians to the synagogues and drove all Jews out of the city, permitting the crowd to loot their property.

Alexandria was no stranger to anti-Semitic riots:[215] it had all happened before, even as long ago as the reign of Claudius, before Christian influence was appreciable. As then, reports and appeals went to the emperor. Orestes was particularly annoyed at the damage done to the city, no doubt economic damage in particular, by the loss of so large a section of the population. However, popular feeling could no longer stand the power conflict between civil and ecclesiastical authorities and in response to demand, Cyril made peaceful overtures to Orestes, only to have them rejected.

Subsequent events did nothing to help. About 500 monks came to the city from the Nitrian desert to defend their Patriarch, and caught Orestes out in his chariot.[216] It is clear that the monks saw Orestes as a representative of paganism,

---

210 Wickham (1983); Russell (2000), p. 205 n. 11.

211 Wessel (2001) suggests that this was the reason for Socrates' hostility to Cyril; see Wessel (2004) for a study of Cyril's early years.

212 Socrates, *HE* vii.15.

213 For the city of Alexandria in late antiquity, see Haas (1997).

214 Socrates, *HE* vii.13.

215 Bell (1941); cf. Bell (1924).

216 Socrates, *HE* vii.14.

in spite of his protestations that he had been baptized by the bishop of Constantinople. They started abusing him and one threw a stone which struck Orestes on the head. The city population now rushed to the rescue and the monk who had injured the prefect was tortured so severely that he died. Cyril again sent a report to the emperor and, much to everyone's disgust, treated the victim as a martyr for the cause of Christ.

Worse was to follow. The most distinguished pagan of the time was a woman, Hypatia, a Neoplatonist philosopher who could hold her own in any academic circle.[217] Orestes was clearly impressed by her and they were frequently in each other's company. The Christian mob decided it was she who was influencing Orestes against Cyril – the pagan connection again! They waylaid her, took her into a church, there lynched her and then burnt her mangled remains at a place called Cinaron. As Socrates states, 'Surely nothing can be further from the spirit of Christianity than to tolerate massacres, fights and such doings.' The reputation of the Alexandrian Church was tarnished. But while this event was particularly horrible because of the personal nature of the atrocity, Alexandria was no stranger to anti-pagan riots. The suppression of paganism had been the subject of imperial edicts, but the authorities had often acted weakly or not at all, and it was fanatical monks who set fire to temples; twenty-five years earlier, Alexandria had witnessed the destruction of the Mithraeum and the Serapeum under the direction of Cyril's uncle, Theophilus.

It is hard to decide how far Cyril was responsible for the events described; but clearly he gave more than tacit support to any who acted for Christianity against its two powerful religious rivals, sometimes to the point of serious misjudgment. These events occurred in the first four years of his episcopate, and given the absence of evidence for further trouble, Cyril's involvement has been put down to inexperience.[218] Nevertheless, it is interesting to see that his literary activity reflects the continuing struggle with non-Christians. His work *Against Julian*,[219] possibly begun in these years, would be praised by Theodoret, and its publication proves that the Nestorian controversy did not monopolize Cyril's interests even as late as the 430s. Paganism was still a prime issue. And the Jewish question has been described as 'the backdrop to Cyril's exegesis' in an important study by Robert Wilken:[220] Cyril needed to prove that the Old Testament belonged, not to the Jews, but to the Christians, and this issue has a predominant place, particularly in the Old Testament commentaries which seem to have been his earliest literary output.

From the very beginning, then, Cyril stood for the Christian cause, and was unbending in his determination. He had one aim in view, namely the establishment of Christian truth. If the triumph of truth was at stake, Cyril was not one to attempt passive resistance rather than positive, if violent, action. And he had the traditions of his see to encourage him – the unflinching boldness of Athanasius, the determination of Theophilus and the long-standing alliance between the archbishop and the monks, the shock-troops of orthodoxy. Precedent was

217 Socrates, *HE* vii.15.
218 Wickham (1983) – an 'untried leader attempting, and initially failing, to master popular forces'; quoted with approval by McGuckin (1994), pp. 14–15.
219 See further below, p. 320.
220 Wilken (1971).

of particular importance to Cyril – he it was who developed the 'patristic argument' in theology, the appeal to statements of the Fathers alongside scripture as a means of ascertaining the proper tradition of interpretation. So, like his predecessors, Cyril was not afraid to take an uncompromising stand against all opposition, against heresy, paganism and the Jews, and with principle and precedent behind him, he was sure he was in the right. Just occasionally he seems to have been persuaded that his unbending attitudes had carried him a bit too far and, if he did not retract, at least he allowed things to drop. Silence about the anathemas permitted his reconciliation with John of Antioch, and it was not the first time that discretion had rescued his reputation: for Socrates reports that he allowed the memory of his pseudo-martyr to be gradually obliterated by silence. In the end it was not Cyril who so overstepped the mark that Alexandrian ascendency was shattered and its theological legacy compromised, but his less worthy successor, Dioscorus. The Second Council of Ephesus, the 'Robber-Synod' of 449, was not entirely out of line with the First – Cyril had set something of a precedent for playing on popular passions and encouraging the shouting of oversimplified theological formulae. Yet starting the council without John and the Orientals may not have been quite so high-handed as often depicted,[221] and the emperor surely bears some responsibility for the impasse that was the immediate result.

Cyril's early years, then, afford us some insight into the kind of man he was when the controversy with Nestorius broke out; and the works he wrote prior to the controversy also provide significant pointers for understanding the position he took up. The dating of Cyril's early works (that is, those written before 428 and the start of the Christological conflict) is conjectural;[222] the bulk of his output was exegesis of scripture, though at some point he also turned to anti-Arian polemics. Such was the training-ground in which his theological skills were refined, and in both areas he was steeped in Alexandrian traditions.[223] His anti-Arian writings, though largely a restatement of the ideas and arguments of Athanasius, nevertheless clarified the doctrine of the Trinity in significant ways;[224] his exegesis, avowedly a digest of the work of predecessors (though who they were he does not say),[225] takes up the spiritualizing heritage that descended from Philo, through Clement and Origen, to Didymus, but with distinctive emphases relating to his holistic view of salvation in Christ. To understand the Nestorian controversy it is important to recognize that in his Christology likewise, Cyril espoused an essential conservatism, and that his characteristic stance was a straightforward appeal to tradition, which he sought to clarify. Originality, then generally regarded as dangerous innovation, was remote from Cyril's ambitions. It is this background which enables us

---

221 McGuckin (1994).

222 Liébaert (1951); but see the article by Jouassard (1945). Liébaert did not accept Jouassard's argument. For Jouassard's reply, see his article in *Revue Bénédictine* (1977).

223 Wessel (2004) suggests that Cyril was skilful in identifying his cause against Nestorius with that of Athanasius against Arius; his rhetoric made the Christ of Nestorius look like the Logos of Arius.

224 See Boulnois (1994); cf. Boulnois and Daley in Weinandy and Keating (2003).

225 Kerrigan (1952), pp. 246ff.; cf. Wilken (1971); McKinion (2000); Wilken and Young in Weinandy and Keating (2003).

to appreciate the sheer dynamic of his campaign. As far as his party was concerned, Cyril was not re-laying the foundations or even building on them; he was simply doing a bit of repointing to the brickwork. Yet Cyril was not simply a literary parrot like the later Byzantine scholastics.[226] His profound dependence on the past was married to a brilliant judgment of contemporary needs and an ability appropriately to recycle the traditional inheritance.

3 Old Testament exegesis

Cyril would probably have been remembered as a biblical commentator, if it had not been for the Christological controversy[227] – the majority of his writings may be regarded as exegetical in some sense, though they are not all by any means formal commentaries. Cyril seems to have been drawn to the dialogue form, which is first evidenced in a series of dialogues between himself and a certain Palladius, *On Worship in Spirit and Truth*.[228] The opening question is this: how is the statement in Matthew's Gospel that not a jot or tittle of the Law will pass away to be reconciled with that in the Gospel of John that the Father will not be worshipped in Jerusalem but in spirit and in truth?[229] So, though sometimes treated as if it were a commentary on passages from the Pentateuch, this is really an exploration of the proper Christian attitude to the Law.

Cyril's approach is fundamentally conventional: righteousness comes not through the Law but through Christ. Moses is unable to free humanity from the tyranny of the devil; for Moses' Master is Christ. New Testament references provide Cyril with the starting-point for showing that the Mosaic covenant is a type and shadow, that Christian righteousness must exceed that of the scribes and Pharisees. The prophetic condemnation of Jewish sacrifices points forward to the pure sacrifice to be offered under the new covenant (an age-old Christian apologetic argument here refurbished). The Law was written δι' ἡμᾶς (for us), and its prescriptions operate at two levels, at the literal, practical level for the historical Israelites, but also as an image and type for the spiritual law of the Church. All manner of legal prescriptions (for example those in Exodus 22 concerning restitution for theft) can be turned into meaningful spiritual commands, especially injunctions to goodness and loving one another. The Law is holy, especially if its double significance is properly appreciated. Indeed, the whole Law is summed up in loving God and one's neighbour (a claim based on Matthew 22.40, Paul in Romans 13 and 1 John 4.20); this provides the model for understanding the continuing relevance of the Decalogue to Christians.

Besides this, however, Cyril has perceived that the true meaning of the Law is to be expounded in terms of the drama of Fall and redemption.[230] The pattern of exile and spiritual famine, followed by repentance and return to a better life, is traced in various biblical narratives: Abraham's migration and the exodus

226 The difference in method is explained by Liébaert (1951), p. 38.
227 McGuckin (1994); Russell (2000).
228 Cyril, *De adoratione in Spiritu et veritate*: text, PG 68.
229 Wilken (1971) provides an account of how Palladius sets out the problem and Cyril's opening reply.
230 See further Young in Weinandy and Keating (2003).

are taken as paradigms of God's grace bringing conversion. This, then, is no conventional commentary on selected Pentateuchal passages; what we have here is a thematic treatment aimed at presenting what might be called a 'biblical theology', worked out in relation to the five books of the Law. The aim is to expose the human predicament and its solution in Christ, showing how the Christian use of the Jewish scriptures is an integral part of the whole theological construction.

Nearly everything here can be found in pre-Cyrilline writings. Cyril does not introduce new types or new ideas. But somehow the impact of this work is a magnificent justification of a whole method of approach which can seem arbitrary; instead of being dissipated in verse by verse allegory, it is concentrated in an impressive coherence, remarkable for its total grasp of the distinctive Christian claim. Allegory naturally plays a considerable part, but it is integrated into an overall typological setting by which the two Testaments are shown to cohere with one another through a systematic theological presentation into which each link fits. For Cyril's time, for the contemporary battle with the Jews, it must have provided powerful ammunition of a kind far more worthwhile than the stones and looting of the street battles.

Cyril's other effort on the Pentateuch, possibly composed concurrently since each work refers to the other, is of a quite different character – indeed, the approach in the *Glaphyra* is much closer to a commentary.[231] But once again Cyril makes no overall attempt to go through it verse by verse; in some sections he quotes the text for detailed exegesis, but this is by no means always the case: for example, the Genesis narrative of Adam is never quoted – the story is treated entirely in the light of its ἀνακεφαλαίωσις (recapitulation) in Christ and what biblical quotations there are come almost exclusively from the New Testament. So, keeping to the Pentateuchal order but not tied to every detail of its text, Cyril presents a selection of narratives or themes from which he can obtain maximum Christian capital. Thus, like most great theologians, he operates a 'canon within the canon' concentrating on prize passages which have stimulated his particular theological emphases, or can provide a vehicle for their expression. Interestingly enough, the creation story is given no attention at all. Cosmogony preoccupied Basil and many others, but Cyril shows no interest in the subject outside his apologetic treatise against Julian. In his Old Testament exegesis he is preoccupied with the Christian claim to have the true key to its meaning.[232] Thus in his introduction he states that everything in Moses' writings signifies the mystery of Christ in riddles, and his tendency throughout is to choose narratives or themes with ancient typological meanings so as to bring out the spiritual sense of the Old Testament. This being the case it is perhaps not surprising to find that one book each suffices for Leviticus, Numbers and Deuteronomy, whereas Exodus takes three and Genesis predominates with seven.

Cyril's works on the Pentateuch have a particular interest since their very selectivity is indicative of the primary theological concerns with which he was exercised at the time of writing. While there can be little doubt that Wilken is

---

231 Cyril, *Glaphyra in Pentateuchum*: text, PG 69.
232 This observation is made by Wilken (1971); see especially chapter 4.

right in seeing conflict with the Jews as the setting against which these works were produced, they also provide considerable insight into Cyril's basic understanding of humanity, sin, redemption, Christ and the essentials of Christian practice. As Wilken has also noted, the superiority of Christ to Moses and the Adam–Christ typology stand out as soteriological themes of great importance for Cyril's Christology.[233] Christ's uniqueness lay in his role as the one who restored the lost image of God to humanity – the old 'recapitulation' theme is Cyril's link with the past and his presupposition for the future. It was because Nestorius threatened his basic Christian perceptions that Cyril's opposition was aroused.

Cyril's work on the prophets takes a more conventional commentary form and provides a clearer overall picture of his exegetical methods. Extant in their entirety are his commentaries on the Minor Prophets and on Isaiah, though many further fragments are traceable in the Catenae (authenticity is as usual a problem with this material, and the collections in Migne need to be examined with care). It is particularly interesting that his *Commentary on the Minor Prophets*[234] exists in full and can therefore be compared in detail with that of Theodore of Mopsuestia, the radical Antiochene. Needless to say, unlike Theodore, Cyril gives plenty of attention to prophetic and spiritual meanings, often teased out of the text by elaborate allegorical devices. More unexpected are the extensive explanations of historical background, and the attention he pays to the literal reference of the text. His introductory outlines, together with his interest in the prophet's intention, 'are features which bear comparison with the work of the Antiochenes, though often differing in detail'.[235] The reality of the text's historical dimension and of its original message to the Israelites is fully admitted, even though it is by no means given the primacy accorded to it by Theodore. Kerrigan has argued that Cyril's exegesis is eclectic, and that Jerome in particular exercised a considerable influence on him, drawing him away from exclusive dependence on the Alexandrian tradition.[236] Certainly the excesses of Origenism have been abandoned, partially no doubt because the Origenist controversy had tempered current exegetical practice. But there may be other factors operating too: the prophets' denunciations provided fuel for Cyril's attacks on the Jews, the exile was an important indication of God's judgment upon them, and for Cyril their rejection of the prophets, who had after all heralded the coming transformation of Judaism through the Christ, was symptomatic of their continuing religious blindness. The two levels of meaning were equally important to Cyril where the prophetic books were concerned – for both pointed to the superiority of Christianity.

The two levels of meaning were also essential because they had a metaphysical basis of fundamental theological importance, and it is here that Cyril reveals his real kinship with the Alexandrian tradition. Cyril's conception of reality dis-

---

233 Wilken (1971); cf. his articles, Wilken (1966) and in Weinandy and Keating (2003).

234 Text: Pusey (1868); ET Hill (2007, 2008).

235 Kerrigan (1952) tabulates comparable passages; cf. Hill (2007), Introduction.

236 Russell (2000) provides some translations of the *Commentary on Isaiah*, with an introductory note on the possible debt to Jerome. Text of the Isaiah Commentary in Migne, *PG* 70. On this work, see also Wilken in Weinandy and Keating (2003).

tinguished in Platonic manner between τὰ αἰσθητά (realities perceived by the senses) and τὰ νοητά (realities perceived by the mind) – the latter he regarded as the true realities (τὰ ἀληθινά), the spiritual realm (τὰ πνευματικά) discovered only through contemplation (θεωρία). These two realities co-existed in parallel, the former representing the latter in parables, signs and symbols (his words for this include: τύποι, παραδείγματα, σκιαί, αἰνίγματα and εἰκόνες).[237] Thus the sensible and intelligible worlds are distinct yet intimately related. God is transcendent (Cyril will have nothing to do with Anthropomorphites),[238] but the harmony of the created order is a symbol or sign of God's wisdom,[239] and humanity was intended to incarnate the image of God in the sensible world. There is a real sense in which Cyril's Christology is grounded in this metaphysical theory, the Word Incarnate fulfilling the role that Adam failed to play, and guaranteeing the cohesion of the two distinct realms of reality. For Cyril the text of scripture likewise belonged to both worlds; the literal meaning referred to the objects of the sensible world, the spiritual sense to spiritual realities.

Closely parallel to his treatment of the Old Testament is Cyril's approach to the parables, as evidenced in his *Commentary on Luke*.[240] The parables are images of things not seen, of realities belonging to the intelligible and spiritual world. They illustrate theological truths or point to aspects of Christian conduct. The obvious outer sense of the parable requires no explanation; but the object of the exposition is to explore its inward, secret, unseen meaning. At times, perhaps more particularly in his earlier works, Cyril denigrates the literal meaning of scripture, and often he stresses that it is something to be surpassed; but his regard for the literal meaning, elsewhere expressed, parallels a refusal to admit to docetism. The sensible world is not an illusion, but rather the vehicle of truth. This is the core of Cyril's spirituality, and it coheres with his sacramental understanding of the divine life communicated through the elements of the Eucharist. This is why it is misleading to attach party labels to his exegesis, suggesting that he combines features of the Antiochene approach with the Alexandrian tradition – rather he incorporates into the Alexandrian tradition a positive affirmation of the physical and material realities of history and human existence.

Cyril's biblical interests were not confined to the Old Testament, but his New Testament exegesis seems to date from a somewhat later period. The two works which survive pretty extensively are commentaries on the Gospels of Luke and John, though sizeable fragments of other commentaries are also extant. Pusey's three-volume edition of the *Commentary on John* adds the most important of these fragments, though as usual material drawn from the Catenae needs to be treated with caution. The *Commentary on John* must have been composed before the Nestorian controversy, since its Christological discussions never explicitly

---

237 Cyril's exegetical terminology is studied in detail by Kerrigan (1952), pp. 35ff., 112ff., and is related to his metaphysical assumptions, pp. 42ff., 126ff.

238 See further Wickham (1983), who distinguishes those Cyril addresses directly in certain writings with the Anthropomorphites of the Origenist controversy in the time of his uncle, Theophilus.

239 du Manoir (1944), chapter 2.

240 Kerrigan (1952), pp. 198, 394ff.

take up the characteristic issues of the controversy, whereas the *Commentary on Luke* does.

4 Doctrinal debate and a 'more dogmatic exegesis'

Meanwhile, however, dogmatic issues had begun to exercise Cyril. The *Thesaurus de sancta Trinitate*[241] seems to have preceded the *Commentary on John*, and some features of that commentary are more readily understood if we consider the anti-Arian writings first.[242] Jouassard argued that it was in the mid-420s that these questions began to claim Cyril's attention, since his paschal letters show no anxiety about heresy prior to the encyclical of 424;[243] but Boulnois[244] detects the beginnings of defence against Arian errors in earlier festal letters, and suggests that, while a resurgence of Arianism is possible, Cyril may have had in mind, at least in composing the *Dialogues on the Trinity*, pagan intellectuals who had heard about these internal Christian debates.

Liébaert[245] showed that the *Thesaurus* was almost entirely based on Athanasius' work *Contra Arianos* (Book III in particular) and a lost work *Contra Eunomium*, which was probably the work of Didymus. Yet for all its dependence on past material, it is a striking example of Cyril's ability to systematize and re-present the well-worn arguments. As Boulnois points out,[246] he always begins with clear statements about the mystery of the Trinity, which surpasses human understanding – a point clarified in response to Eunomius; yet we can gather a kind of reflected knowledge through subtle imagery, assembling in our minds a vision which is like a riddle, and so acquire a solidity of faith. Cyril's images, then, are illustrations that obliquely convey difficult concepts in symbolic form.[247]

The *Thesaurus* consists of thirty-five chapters, each of which presents a thesis (*logos*), which is then defended on the basis of a series of listed arguments or a compilation of scriptural testimonies. The sixth *logos*, for example, is 'that the Father begat the Son of himself without division or outflow'. This is followed by a number of Eunomian objections, each answered by a series of counter-arguments. The thirty-second *logos* is 'that the Son is God by nature, and if this, not something made or created'; and this is established on the basis of some 170 scriptural testimonies and arguments. Athanasius' work is never copied word for word – even his quotations from the writings of Arius are paraphrased. Athanasius' ideas are used but they are reordered and given totally new expression so as to present a more rigorous form of argument. Cyril has really sorted the subject out and provided a treatise which highlights the essential elements in the debate, clarifies the points one by one, and affords much more

---

241 Cyril, *Thesaurus de sancta Trinitate*: text, PG 75.
242 For a useful overview, see Russell (2000), pp. 21–30.
243 Jouassard (1977); on the *Festal Letters*, see further p. 313 below.
244 Boulnois in Weinandy and Keating (2003).
245 Liébaert (1951), especially chapters 1 and 2.
246 Boulnois (1994) and in Weinandy and Keating (2003), referring to the Prefaces to both the *Thesaurus* and the *Commentary on John*.
247 Boulnois (1994); McKinion (2000).

ready access to patristic theological method than the diffuse polemics of earlier writers. This matter of form is important for the John commentary; for here he indulges in dogmatic excursuses similarly ordered, with points marshalled into neat lists – theological mini-treatises of a form similar to that adopted for the whole of the *Thesaurus*.

There has been some debate about the sources of the *Thesaurus*, many scholars affirming that Cyril had access to the works of Epiphanius and the Cappadocians. Liébaert maintained that his information was exclusively Alexandrian, and that there is no direct link with, for example, the works against Eunomius written by Basil or Gregory of Nyssa. If sustained, this would be an important conclusion, for it suggests that Cyril's theological awareness was very much bound by the Alexandrian situation and inheritance, and that he had little contact with the directions that theology and exegesis were taking in Antioch and elsewhere – unlike the Antiochenes, he showed little concern about post-Arian developments like Apollinarianism, prior to the outbreak of Christological controversy.[248] Arianism remained for him the great dogmatic issue, and the Nicene faith was the answer to it. This could be another significant pointer to Cyril's position at the outbreak of the Christological battle.

So closely associated with the *Thesaurus* are the seven *Dialogues on the Trinity*[249] that we can hardly overlook them at this point. Having set out the anti-Arian argumentation in a methodical form, Cyril proceeded to give the case a more literary presentation. This is a more personal work, not so rigorous, freer in style; but as Liébaert noted,[250] it follows the same outline scheme of subjects and is closely parallel to the first work. Cyril dedicated the work to the same Nemesinos as the *Thesaurus* and explains in the prologue that he proposes to treat the issue by presenting a debate between himself and Hermias, the dramatis personae being identified in the text by the use of A and B respectively; question and answer will facilitate the organization and effectiveness of the attack when a matter of such subtlety is at issue. So in the dialogues, B fulfils the role of reporting heretical theses, and A replies in arguments analogous to the *Thesaurus*. We have already noticed Cyril's liking for this particular form of literature. That he regarded these dialogues on the Trinity as a particularly effective work is shown by the fact that later he wrote an additional dialogue with Hermias on the questions raised by the Nestorian controversy. It has generally been assumed that to do this he rewrote the material used in his *De recta fide*, following the text so closely that Pusey found it convenient to print the two works on facing pages;[251] but the priority of the *De recta fide* has since been questioned.[252]

The seven dialogues, then, treat the central issues in the debate with Arius: that the Son is co-eternal and consubstantial with the Father; that the Son is

---

248 Liébaert (1951), pp. 154ff., followed by Grillmeier (1965), p. 330; this point of view may be a little exaggerated in view of the contents of *Paschal Letter* viii, but it is plausible to suggest that Cyril merely adopts current formulae and has no real appreciation of the post-Arian developments in Antioch.
249 Text: de Durand (1976, 1977, 1978).
250 Liébaert (1951), chapter 3.
251 Text: Pusey (1877).
252 de Durand (1964); see Introduction.

begotten of him κατὰ φύσιν (by nature); that he is true God, just like the Father; that the Son is not a κτίσμα or ποίημα (something created or made); that all things proper to the Godhead, including its glory, belong φυσικῶς (naturally) to the Son, just as they do to the Father. Then, before adding a final dialogue on the divinity of the Holy Spirit, Cyril spends the sixth dialogue discussing how human attributes are properly ascribed to the Son, insisting that they do not belong to the nature of the Logos inasmuch as he is conceived to be and is God, but rather are attributed to him τῇ μετὰ σαρκὸς οἰκονομίᾳ (by the economy with flesh). This dialogue is particularly interesting for several reasons. (i) It alerts us to the fact that sanctification is at the heart of Cyril's soteriology – the Logos did not need to be sanctified, but the sanctification of his humanity by the coming of the Spirit meant the sanctification of human nature in him. This was basically Cyril's understanding of θεοποίησις (deification). (ii) The emphasis on the Logos' κένωσις (literally 'emptying') or ταπείνωσις (humiliation) is already to be found as a constituent motif in Cyril's thinking; he limited himself to the human condition and that is why human attributes are applicable to him. (iii) At this point, Cyril is prepared to speak of the Logos raising 'his own temple' (using John 2.9) – a form of speech which, coming from the Antiochenes, he was later to attack mercilessly. This is not the only case of inconsistency perpetrated by Cyril in the heat of the battle; he had also used the phrase 'assuming the woman-born man or shrine like a robe' in the Thesaurus, and later vehemently attacked such expressions.[253]

Generally speaking, then, we find here in the Dialogues the same situation as in the Thesaurus. Cyril has taken over the language and theology of Athanasius, but clarified and re-presented it. He focuses on worship as the basis of his position: the baptismal formula justifies Trinitarian belief, and prayer must be Trinitarian – through the Son and in the Spirit we have access to the Father.[254] Cyril tends to be more concerned with human sinfulness than Athanasius;[255] he tends to speak of 'humanity' rather than 'flesh'; he also gives a little more stress to the 'psychological' weaknesses of human nature, like fear and dread. Yet at this stage, he does not seem to have noticed that positive affirmation of a human soul in the Christ could resolve some of the difficulties in confuting the Arians.[256] In the Alexandrian tradition, that affirmation was to be found only in the works of the notorious Origenist, Didymus, and Cyril inherited his uncle's anti-Origenism. Nor was he yet alive to the necessity of refuting Apollinarius.

The Commentary on John[257] sums up all that we have so far learned of Cyril, demonstrates the close link between Cyril's theology and his exegesis,[258] and highlights the basic theological stance from which his campaign against Nestorius was launched. The twelve books of the Commentary exist in their entirety apart from Books VII and VIII; for these, Pusey pieces together extensive fragments from the Catenae and some Syriac sources, but doubts have been

---

253 Prestige (1940), p. 156 develops this point.

254 Boulnois in Weinandy and Keating (2003).

255 Burghardt (1957) develops a number of points of difference between Cyril and his great predecessor.

256 Liébaert (1951), pp. 117, 172ff., 179; followed by Grillmeier (1965/75).

257 Text: Pusey (1872a); ET Pusey (1874, 1885); selections in Russell (2000).

258 Boulnois in Weinandy and Keating (2003).

expressed about the reliability of this material. The form of the work is a verse by verse commentary, and Cyril's interest in the two levels of interpretation remains an important element in his exegesis. He is not too concerned about historical discrepancies between John and the other Gospels, even though he assumes that the literal sense is accurate and has some natural explanation. Far more interesting to him, however, are possible symbolic explanations. His interest in the spiritual sense of the Gospel enables him to plumb the depths of Johannine symbolism in the signs and discourse material, particularly where it points to one of his favourite themes, the superiority of Christianity to Judaism, and the transference of the gospel from the Jews to the Gentiles.[259] It also stimulates allegorical interpretations of a less convincing kind.

But Cyril, in this commentary, is avowedly looking for a δογματικώτερα ἐξήγησις (a more dogmatic exegesis). For him, the evangelist foresaw the heresies that would later appear and forestalled them; so his main interest is in propounding orthodox rather than heretical interpretation, and this gives this commentary its chief characteristics. Indeed, so prominent is this that thesis-type chapter headings have been supplied for much of the commentary, outlining the main purport of the dogmatic argument in each section. This dogmatic purpose leads to a concentration on controversial texts with Christological implications, though Christology and the anti-Arian argument are not the only interest: Book I.9 provides a lengthy refutation of the idea of the pre-existence of souls, in the same argumentative format as is found in other dogmatic excursuses. Inevitably in a work of commentary, the text of the Johannine Gospel suggests the themes pursued, and since the Gospel is primarily concerned with the person of Christ, it is not surprising that this theme predominates. This was after all Cyril's main concern at this stage – at least in so far as the Arian debate posed the problem.

The approach of Athanasius is still Cyril's model. To counter the Arian argument, Cyril points out that certain things were said by Jesus as a man, or even as a Jew, and insists that from such texts no ultimate conclusions about the nature of the Logos can be deduced. Really he is the transcendent Logos, *homoousios* with the Father. But the features of his earthly life are the outcome of his voluntary ταπείνωσις (humiliation) of which Philippians 2.5–11 is the classic expression. He remained what he was, and yet became man, subjecting himself to human limitations.[260] Like Athanasius, Cyril himself distinguished between divine and human attributes in the context of the anti-Arian argument, but it is noticeable that already he is insisting on the subjection of the Logos to human conditions in the incarnation, and occasionally criticizing the tendency to divide the Christ, though he does not yet explicitly attack characteristic Antiochene terminology.[261] As in the case of Athanasius, his statements occasionally have a near-docetic ring: 'he trembles and feigns (πλάττεται) confusion', 'to suffer the appearance (σχῆμα) of confusion', 'he seems to submit to death'.[262]

---

259 See Wiles (1960) for further development of this and the following points, especially pp. 32ff.

260 The opening of Book II.5 contains this particular explanation. Cyril is discussing the story of the Samaritan woman.

261 Liébaert (1951).

262 *On John* 11.33; 13.21; 6.38 (Pusey II, p. 280; II, p. 363; I, p. 487).

Cyril does not merely speak of Jesus acting ὡς θεός (as God) or ὡς ἄνθρωπος (as man) in parallel; but he uses the phrase ὡς ἄνθρωπος σχηματίζεται (he is in the form of a man), which 'could easily suggest that the whole human life of Jesus was a pretence'.[263] Yet Cyril's underlying thought is that the humanity is genuine enough as the external manifestation of the one Christ, the aspect of Christ which belongs to the world of the sensible.[264] The gospel for him is all about the self-limitation of the Logos to the conditions of the created order. But for some interpreters the human factor in Cyril's Christ is indispensable and complete, precisely because it is necessary for the salvation of humanity, and it is in the pre-controversy exegetical works that it is possible to discern this.[265]

It is clear that for Cyril, biblical exegesis was his major theological activity. Though distracted into pamphleteering and controversy soon after composing the *Commentary on John*, his interpretative work did not cease. Exegetical treatises fill seven out of ten volumes of Migne's edition of Cyril's work; yet sizeable portions of his biblical work have disappeared. Indeed, the other major surviving work, the *Commentary on Luke*, we mostly have not in the original but in a Syriac translation.

The *Commentary on Luke* in fact shows Cyril in a new light, for it is not really a formal commentary at all, but a series of homilies. Three complete homilies are actually extant in Greek; but a Syriac version of a great deal more was discovered in the last century and published by Payne Smith.[266] Further fragments have since appeared, and a new edition of the whole text has started to appear in the *CSCO* series.[267] It is often said that the Syriac version comprises 156 homilies, but some sections are so brief that they must clearly be extracts rather than complete texts. Nevertheless it has proved a significant find.

Cyril's interests in these homilies are primarily practical. He focuses on the gospel themes and places a great deal of emphasis upon ethical teaching, exhortation and above all, imitation of Christ through obedience and humility. Christ is the 'type' to be imitated, the example to be followed, through baptism, through temptation in the wilderness, through suffering and death. The Christian is to be united with Christ in living a life like his. The kingdom of God is a spiritual kingdom, found when one forsakes all for love of Christ; and as we have seen, the parables, like the Old Testament, point beyond themselves to spiritual realities, to divine grace and human obedience.[268] The needs of the congregation, then, are uppermost in his mind. Occasionally, however, those needs include warnings about dangerous interpretations. Thus the Nestorian controversy clearly lies behind his comments on Christ's baptism. True the Logos of God did not need to be baptized, but that is no reason for separating off the 'seed of David'; the baptism of Christ is justified as part of the 'economy', his acceptance of the human condition for the salvation of human beings.

---

263 Wiles (1960), p. 138.

264 Du Manoir (1944), pp. 155ff.

265 See, for example, Meunier (1997); for Cyril's soteriology, see Koen (1991) and Keating (2004).

266 Text: Payne Smith (1858); ET (1859). Greek homilies in *PG* 77.

267 Text: Chabot (1912); Tonneau (1953, 1954).

268 For the importance of grace in Cyril's thought, and how it differs from the Antiochene understanding, see Fairbairn (2003).

5 The Nestorian controversy

Even though biblical exegesis largely occupied Cyril, there is no doubt that for a few important years the Christological controversy came to dominate his literary activity as well as his politics. The first indication of his alarm at Nestorius' teaching is to be found in his seventeenth *Paschal Letter*, the one for 429. Cyril's letters announcing the date of Easter[269] cover the years 414–442 (twenty-nine in all), and provide some indication of the Patriarch's interests at various points in his career. They are predominantly of a practical character, exhorting the congregations to fasting and prayer, to celebration of the festival, to love and almsgiving; but they also reveal Cyril's polemical zeal against Jews and pagans, and particularly those Christians who tried to have it both ways, combining their Christian profession with participation in the festivities of other religions. These themes, together with exposition of the spiritual significance of the Old Testament as a shadow and type of the New, keep recurring over the years. The letter for 424, however, introduces discussion of the Trinity and the ἀγέννητος (ingenerate) nature of the Son; and the letter for 429, though not mentioning Nestorius by name or even using the term *Theotokos*, launches into a discussion of the incarnation, insisting that the child born of Mary is indissolubly Son of God and therefore Mary should be called 'Mother of God'. Cyril had already used a Paschal Letter to discuss the incarnation some years before (the eighth Letter, for 420); but here the object of his attack is obvious.

The second indication of Cyril's dawning concern is the *Letter to the Monks*. Cyril's efforts in the controversy were at first largely concentrated in correspondence – letters to the Roman Pope Celestine, to Nestorius himself, and to many other influential figures; some of the more important have already been discussed.[270] It has been suggested that the letters speak more directly to the reader than his longer treatises;[271] the selection edited and translated by Wickham only underlines the potential value of a collected, critical edition of Cyril's correspondence. Various new discoveries are scattered about in a variety of publications;[272] the collection in Migne includes a number of spurious epistles, while for the most significant letters it has been superseded by the work of Schwartz on the *Acta Conciliorum*.

Cyril also turned quite smartly to polemical treatises.[273] Five volumes *Adversus Nestorii blasphemias* were circulated in 430.[274] Here Cyril subjects to searching criticism the sermons of Nestorius which had become so notorious, quoting and pulling apart various sections, some of them particularly damning out of context. In the same year he submitted three papers to the imperial court *De*

---

269 Text: Burns et al. (1991, 1993, 1998).

270 See above, pp. 275–80.

271 Wickham (1983), p. xii.

272 For details, see *Clavis Patrum Graecorum* on Cyril, and the Introduction to McEnerney (1987). The collection translated includes letters preserved in Latin, Syriac and Coptic, and provides the bibliographical reference for the critical text of each letter.

273 The text of the most important of these is found in Pusey (1875, 1877). The most recent and best text for the majority of them is to be found in Schwartz, *ACO*. See also de Durand (1964).

274 ET of selected passages in Russell (2000).

recta fide, one addressed to the Emperor Theodosius, another to Arcadia and Marina, his younger sisters, and the other to his wife Eudocia and his elder sister, Pulcheria. These were widely circulated as propaganda documents, although at the time they were not successful in turning imperial favour from Nestorius. Rabbula, bishop of Edessa, switching his support to Cyril, made a translation of the first in order to promulgate Cyril's theology in the Syriac speaking areas of the Eastern Empire. As previously noted, the same work was probably readapted by Cyril himself as an eighth *Dialogue with Hermias*, known as the *Dialogus de incarnatione Unigeniti*.

Cyril's pamphleteering, however, could not remain purely offensive. He soon had to defend his own position. We have already surveyed his three treatises written in defence of the Anathemas; he also wrote an *Apology to the Emperor* on his return from Ephesus, justifying his somewhat dubious carryings-on at the council.

After the Formulary of Reunion had been negotiated, the flood of Christological treatises came to an end; but Cyril's interest did not entirely subside. He later summarized his Christological position in two works which received wide distribution and were highly valued especially by the churches of the East: though in Greek surviving only in fragments, his *Scholia de incarnatione unigeniti* exists in Latin, Syriac and Armenian translations, an indication of its widespread appeal; and the *Quod unus sit Christus* is regarded as the mature culmination of all Cyril's Christological work.[275] As so often before, he here chose the dialogue form to give his views definitive literary expression.

The only other major work in this area was his treatise *Contra Diodorum et Theodotum*,[276] which gave offence to Theodoret and nearly ruptured the delicate union which had been achieved. Quotations from Cyril's treatise are our chief source for the Christological fragments of Diodore and Theodore; for Cyril's work provided the material on the basis of which they were eventually condemned, and it was used and quoted by such important later controversialists as Severus of Antioch. Cyril does not seem to have read the works of the great Antiochene theologians for himself, but apparently based his work on hostile florilegia, collections of quotations from their works supplied by extreme anti-dualists, possibly Apollinarians;[277] for there is evidence that he was confused about the correct authorship of some of the statements he attacked.

Such were Cyril's Christological writings; what then do they reveal of his Christological thinking? A perusal of these works gives an overriding sense of repetitiveness. Certain phrases and arguments keep on recurring: the appeal to the title 'Emmanuel' – God with us; to the Nicene Creed; to Paul's account of the incarnation in Philippians 2. Mary must be called *Theotokos*, since she gave birth to 'God made man and enfleshed' (θεὸν ἐνανθρωπήσαντα καὶ σαρκώθεντα). There is one Son, one Lord Jesus Christ, both before and after the 'enfleshment' (σάρκωσις). There is not one Son who is the Logos of God the Father and another who is from the holy virgin. The Logos who is before the ages (προαιώνιος) *is said* to be born from her *according to the flesh*. The flesh is *his own* (ἴδια), just

---

275 ET McGuckin (1995).
276 Fragments in Pusey (1872a), vol. III.
277 Richard (1946/77).

as each one of us has his own body. Cyril insists on an 'exact union' (ἕνωσις ἀκριβής). These phrases come from the *First Letter to Succensus*,[278] where Cyril is answering queries about his theology from his correspondent, the bishop of Diocaesarea, but they could be paralleled from almost anywhere else in his Christological work. Anticipating the usual criticisms, he goes on to say in this letter that this doctrine does not imply σύγχυσις (confusion) or σύγκρασις (mixture) of the Word, nor transformation of the body into the nature of the Godhead; what he intends to say is that 'inconceivably and in a way that is inexpressible, he united to himself a body ensouled with a rational soul' (σῶμα ἐψυχωμένον ψυχῇ νοερᾷ). He bore the likeness of a servant, while remaining what he was. This letter provides an excellent summary in brief of Cyril's recurring themes.

6 Cyril, Athanasius and Apollinarius

Yet for all the repetitiveness, it seems certain that Cyril's Christology did not remain static over the years, but he responded to the demands of the controversy, introducing new elements into his Christology to oppose the exaggerated dualism of Nestorius. Liébaert[279] took the line that it is necessary to study the pre-Nestorian writings to get an exact idea of Cyril's basic Christological position. We have already observed the fact that fundamentally Cyril's early Christology was theologically conservative, even unadventurous; he was mostly interested in clarifying the anti-Arian tenets of his great master, Athanasius. This in fact gave him a number of abiding principles which stood him in good stead against Nestorius. Cyril would have opposed a dualist Christology anyway, as the *Commentary on John* shows, as well as the much earlier *8th Paschal Letter*.[280] Here he had insisted that the Son of God was one and the same before and after his σάρκωσις (enfleshment); and on the authority of Athanasius, spoke of a σύνοδος (conjunction) of two things, Godhead and manhood. 'The God-Logos dwelt in his own temple, the body assumed from woman, having a rational soul', he stated, using language he later rejected to emphasize the Christological union. Cyril's early Christology, then, gave him the launch pad from which he fired his attack on Nestorius. In an important article, Liébaert[281] demonstrated that his first two attacks on Nestorius, the *17th Paschal Letter* and the *Letter to the Monks*, are entirely based on his previous, essentially Athanasian position, apart from a few fresh themes which are specific reactions to points raised by Nestorius himself in the sermons and papers to which Cyril had access. Interestingly enough, these new ideas include his appeal to the body–soul analogy as a model for understanding unity in Christ. Nevertheless, as the controversy progressed, some phrases which he had once been happy to use himself became suspect, and new elements and new vocabulary undoubt-

---

278 Text of the *Letters to Succensus*: Schwartz, *ACO* I.i.6, pp. 151–62; text and ET in Wickham (1983).

279 Liébaert (1951), p. 78.

280 Chadwick (1951), pp. 145–64, attributes Cyril's opposition to dualism in his early writings to an already existing tradition in Alexandria.

281 Liébaert (1970).

edly entered his anti-Nestorian writings. Where did Cyril get these new slogans from? He was the last person to develop a new theological direction, and his whole stance was based on his conservatism – his conservation of the tradition. One of his most important activities was the assembly of patristic quotations to support his understanding of the tradition.

Indeed it is that very conservatism which is the key to Cyril's innovations. The new and specifically anti-dualist formulae which he adopted and made his own, came from what he believed to be important patristic sources. About the time of the controversy someone must have brought to his notice a work of Athanasius which spoke of the 'one enfleshed nature of the Logos'; a work of Gregory Thaumaturgus entitled *Kata meros pistis*, which affirmed a single worship and condemned dual worships, one divine and one human; a couple of works of Pope Julius, including a treatise *De Unione*, which affirmed not two beings, the Word and a man, or two *hypostases*, but one *hypostasis* of the incarnate Word; and a letter apparently connected with Dionysius, bishop of Corinth.[282] These were among the range of authoritative authors to which Cyril appealed. The precise, detailed correspondence between Cyril's works and these documents is set out clearly in an important article by P. Galtier;[283] particularly striking is the dependence of the Anathemas on these works. So Cyril thought he was appealing to the authority of respected figures of the past; but every one of these treatises came from Apollinarian circles.[284] Thus Cyril inherited his insistence on 'the one nature and/or hypostasis of the Logos enfleshed' from Apollinarian works asserting the composite unity of Christ's person.[285]

Given this documentary evidence of Cyril's unsuspecting dependence on Apollinarius, the question how far his theology is of an Apollinarian tendency becomes the more fascinating. It has been commonly accepted that Cyril's position belongs to the Word–Flesh tradition of Alexandria, and that he never really makes the soul of Christ a 'theological factor' in his Christology. Some have suggested that Cyril is incapable of doing real justice to the humanity of Christ, and his rejection of Apollinarianism is merely superficial. Nevertheless, alerted to the condemnation of Apollinarius, he did consistently explain σὰρξ (flesh) as meaning a human being with a soul and a mind, and some have argued that the complete humanity of Christ is an indispensable element in his soteriological thought.[286]

---

282 The first edition of *From Nicaea to Chalcedon* included the following sentence at this point, 'These were the authoritative authors to which Cyril appealed and the authoritative documents on the basis of which he composed his anti-Nestorian writings'. McGuckin (1994), p. 85 n. 141, quotes and challenges this statement with some justification. It is true that Cyril's patristic argument rested on a far wider range of testimonies. Nevertheless it does appear that certain phrases drawn from these writings entered his terminology around 430, and significantly compounded the misunderstanding of his position by Theodoret and other Antiochenes, who, with some justification, took the Anathemas as fundamentally Apollinarian.

283 Galtier (1956).

284 The texts will be found in Lietzmann (1904).

285 Such phrases appear first in the *Five Tomes Against Nestorius* of the year 430; see above, p. 313.

286 For example, Meunier (1997); essays in Weinandy and Keating (2003).

Grillmeier,[287] drawing heavily on the *Second Letter to Succensus* where Cyril answered charges of Apollinarianism, argued strongly that Cyril, though using Apollinarian formulae, nevertheless gave these phrases an essentially non-Apollinarian interpretation. Others stressed the incompatibility of Cyril's various assertions, suggesting that he never reached a satisfactory synthesis of views which arose out of his reactions to the controversial situation. A helpful insight into Cyril's position was offered by R. A. Norris;[288] he suggested that the problems of assessment and interpretation arose from the fact that the discussion was too much confined to the Word–Flesh, Word–Man models, neither of which adequately accounts for what Cyril was trying to confess. The fifth-century debate was conducted in terms of the conjunction of two natures, the union of Godhead and humanity in the Christ, and these were the parameters within which Cyril had to operate; but Cyril basically approached the problem from a quite different perspective. His primary mode of Christological thinking was in terms of a 'narrative' concerning the Logos, who though being in the form of God, took upon himself the form of a servant. Philippians 2 and the Nicene Creed he repeatedly appealed to, because he wanted to affirm that it was the pre-existent Logos who was incarnate. He was feeling after a theology of 'predication' which made the Logos the subject of both divine and human attributes, rather than a 'physical theory' of 'natures in union'. The problem, which he clumsily resolved by using undetected Apollinarian formulae, was to express his own approach in the current terminology. 'One nature' formulae were bound to prove more conducive to his purposes. But, as was inevitable, his use of these formulae has been constantly misunderstood, even though he consistently explained them, at any rate whenever explanation seemed necessary, not in terms of 'mixture', but in terms of the Logos' self-limitation to the conditions of human existence. Cyril was himself quite clear that this self-limitation included his submission to psychological as well as physical restraints; and on those grounds vociferously reiterated his rejection of Apollinarianism. Thus the clue to Cyril's thinking lies in his view of *kenōsis*, a theme already prominent in the pre-Nestorian writings, and his constant refrain thereafter. The Word 'abased himself by submitting . . . to the limitations of the human condition', says Cyril in the *Quod unus sit Christus*.[289] The Word 'made man and enfleshed' is Cyril's most frequent form of words, and supplied the meaning of his most notorious slogan: μία φύσις τοῦ θεοῦ Λόγου σεσαρκωμένη (or interchangeably, σεσαρκωμένου) – one nature of the God–Logos enfleshed (enfleshed agreeing with 'nature' or 'Logos'). The Logos did not cease to be himself in entering upon human existence; but on the other hand his human existence is entirely genuine. What Cyril could not admit was a potentially independent human being assumed by the Logos – ἄνθρωπος θεόφορος. The Logos had to be the only subject, his (impersonal) humanity having no independent existence, but merely being the way of stating the conditions of existence to which the Logos subjected himself. The Logos is for Cyril the only *hypostasis*, and that was what he intended to convey by his formula 'hypostatic union'. That is also what he

---

287 Grillmeier (1965), pp. 400ff. (2nd ed., 1975, pp. 473ff.).
288 Norris (1975).
289 De Durand (1964), p. 396.

meant by 'one nature', not the result of a compounding of two independent natures, though his use of the phrase 'out of two natures' came near to suggesting that it did.

This basic picture explains the apparent docetism sometimes detected in the Cyrilline position, as well as other frequently discussed difficulties, like the paradoxical phrase ἀπαθῶς ἔπαθεν (he suffered without suffering)[290] and his appeal to the soul–body analogy.[291] The Logos could not undergo temptation or progress in his own nature; yet as human he was tempted and learned by experience, while already having the perfection and knowledge proper to divinity.[292] Docetism? Not so for Cyril; both conditions were real. Cyril admitted that in his own nature the Logos was impassible and immortal, but whatever the difficulties he was determined to maintain the ancient tradition that the Son of God himself suffered and died on the cross. The soul–body analogy was some help here, since many then regarded the soul as by nature impassible on the grounds that it was incorporeal, though subject to passions by its association with the body. Cyril insisted that in the same way the Logos suffered through his own flesh, while remaining in his essential nature impassible. Basically, however, Cyril regarded the whole matter as beyond human explanation and yet still true; paradox is the best way of stating such truths. Analogies and images also prove to be the only way of expressing things beyond human comprehension, and Cyril knew perfectly well that the inseparable union of body and soul in a human being was no more than an analogy for what happened in the incarnation, like the many other analogies employed: light and eye, word and voice, thought and mind, scent and flowers.[293] Furthermore, he insisted that the flesh assumed by the Logos was an entire man complete with a soul and mind, thus excluding a literalist application of the analogy.

> He makes his own all that belongs, as to his own body, so to the soul, for he had to be shown to be like us through every circumstance both physical and mental, and we consist of rational soul and body; and as there are times when in the incarnation he permitted his own flesh to experience its proper affections, so again he permitted the soul to experience its proper affections, and he observed the scale of the κένωσις in every respect.[294]

So what happened to Cyril's Christology was that he adopted 'monophysite' formulae to counter the 'dyophysite' position he thought he faced; and became more and more insistent that his description of the Logos' humanity included the human soul and mind as well as the flesh. Apollinarianism is in the background of both moves; its error was repudiated, its contribution undetected. Cyril had an important contribution to make, however – a basic appeal to

---

290 On divine suffering in Cyril and Nestorius, see Hallmann (1997).

291 Further discussion of the problems of Cyril's Christology will be found in Chadwick (1951), section III; Young (1971), pp. 103–14; while McGuckin (1994) defends Cyril against his detractors.

292 This kind of statement is particularly common in Cyril's exegesis of the Epistle to the Hebrews, of which extensive fragments survive; see Young (1969).

293 McKinion (2000).

294 Cyril, De recta fide ad Augustas 11.55.

Christian tradition that it was the Son of God himself who was incarnate, suffered, died and was raised. That basic popular appeal was the secret of what success he had. Translation into 'physical' terms, the language of *physis* and *hypostasis*, required the adoption of formulae which became slogans open to misinterpretation.[295] Safeguards were not always carefully propounded, and this was especially so in the case of the Anathemas; but the slogans are not the real indicators of Cyril's thinking. Cyril spoke for the many faithful who received the Eucharist as the flesh of the incarnate Logos and trusted that in this way they were assured resurrection by participating in the new humanity sanctified by the presence of the Logos himself.[296] The union of the spiritual and material worlds in the incarnation was at the heart of Cyril's metaphysical assumptions. He was wedded to the Alexandrian tradition of θεοποίησις, of deification realized by the saving initiative of God himself. So for him there was no point in winning the battle against Arius at the price of divorcing the Logos from humankind. The opposition to Nestorius was the natural corollary of Cyril's Athanasian heritage. It is really no wonder that Cyril's characteristic argument was an appeal to tradition, to scripture and the Fathers, whereas Nestorius appealed rather to a priori theological assumptions. Cyril was prepared to sacrifice everything to his championship of what he saw as the saving realities and the truth passed down by tradition; in this he expressed the fundamental instincts of the Christian tradition.

For all that, Cyril probably deserved the rebuke of his mentor, Isidore, even if he did proceed according to the canons at Ephesus.[297] Yet he himself came to recognize the mistake of alienating the entire section of the Church under the influence of the Antiochene Patriarchate, as is clear from his positive and conciliatory reaction to the negotiations which produced the Formulary of Reunion, a peace treaty which he then had some difficulty in justifying to his more extreme followers. For the moment, however, Cyril was prepared to let the battle subside, and he tried to cultivate easier diplomatic relations with the see of Antioch, politely sending to Bishop John his work *Against Julian*,[298] a fact which indicates that it must have been completed at some point between 433 (the year of reunion) and 441 (the date of John's death). John's close friend and supporter, Theodoret of Cyrus, actually wrote congratulating Cyril on his excellent effort on behalf of the truth of Christianity.[299] There has been a suggestion that Cyril wrote the work deliberately to supersede that of Theodore of Mopsuestia, whose heretical views he objected to; but its reception by the Antiochenes suggests that no trace of such a motive was apparent to them.

---

295 McGuckin (1994) provides useful discussion of the different ways in which Cyril and his opponents understood the language of *ousia, physis, hypostasis, prosōpon*, etc. Cf. Russell (2000), p. 40.

296 Chadwick (1951); Gebremedhin (1977); Welch (1994).

297 As argued by McGuckin (1994) in detail, and followed by Russell (2000).

298 Cyril, *Against Julian*: text – Burguière and Evieux (1985); ET of selections in Russell (2000).

299 Theodoret, *Ep.* 83.

7 *Against Julian*

The Emperor Julian the Apostate had written a blistering attack *Against the Galileans*, all the more damaging because he knew the sect from inside, was familiar with its apologetics and could quote its scriptures. Cyril dedicated his reply to the Christian Emperor Theodosius, and justified his work, written eighty to ninety years after Julian's, on the grounds that many believers had been shaken by Julian's arguments. Paganism was still very much alive in Alexandria and Julian's work gave encouragement to it. In the first book, Cyril, quoting extensively from a wide range of the classics, seeks to show that the scriptures are more ancient and more full of truth than the authorities of Greek literature and philosophy. The work against Julian has been regarded as the major evidence for Cyril's classical learning; elsewhere he appears as a thoroughly ecclesiastical figure, and without this work of apology, his education in the traditional *paideia* appeared open to question,[300] especially in view of his lack of a polished rhetorical style. Then R. M. Grant[301] showed that Cyril's knowledge of pagan literature does come from independent researches, undertaken for the purpose of refuting Julian, but often by following up references in Eusebius' *Praeparatio Evangelica* and the works of other Christian predecessors.

From the second book on, Cyril quotes passages from Julian's work and sets about refuting them, rather as Origen had done in his reply to Celsus. On the basis of these quotations, some of them being quite extensive, a reconstruction of the first book of Julian's treatise has been possible,[302] though it is to some extent tentative since Cyril states that he rearranged Julian's material in order to avoid repetitions and bring similar subjects together. Furthermore Cyril was careful to omit invectives against Christ and other matter which might contaminate the minds of Christians. Ten books of Cyril's work are extant, and they cover only the first book of Julian's three-volume attack. Fragments of later books have been found in Greek and Syriac.

The arguments on both sides, pagan and Christian,[303] are not fundamentally different from the earlier exchanges between Celsus and Origen. Julian regards Plato as better than Moses, and attacks the Genesis accounts of creation and the Fall. This he can do to some effect since he knew the scriptures first-hand. Moses did not teach *creatio ex nihilo*, for the 'deep', the 'darkness' and the 'waters' were apparently there already; and there is no account of the God of the Jews creating anything incorporeal – he just reordered pre-existent matter. The serpent was actually the benefactor of humanity because the ability to distinguish good and evil constitutes human wisdom. The story is detrimental to God who appears jealous of his own rights and powers; and in any case it is all just as much myth as the myths of the Greeks – what about the talking serpent? Julian objects to the favouritism of a God who is only concerned with a small tribe recently settled in Palestine, and attacks the scriptural accounts of his anger

---

300 Though see above, p. 320 for Cyril's education.

301 Grant (1964).

302 Julian, *Against the Galilaeans:* text and translation of this reconstruction are conveniently available in the Loeb Classical Library, Julian, *Works* III, 1923.

303 These are surveyed by Malley (1979).

and resentment as anthropomorphic. The philosophers taught a God who is the Creator and universal Father of all, and bade human beings imitate the gods who are free from all passion and emotion. The Christians are not faithful to the teachings of the apostles; for Paul, Matthew, Luke and Mark did not call Jesus God – that was only introduced by John. The claim to fulfilment of prophecy is based on fabrications, and not even good ones at that – for Matthew and Luke disagree about the genealogy of Jesus. Julian also reiterates the ancient claim to Hellenic superiority in culture, learning, war and politics; in any case, if scripture is sufficient, why do Christians dabble in the learning of the Hellenes?

Cyril's reply has all the faults of partisanship. He attacks the myths of the Greeks without seeing the force of the pagan criticism of the scriptures. He defends the scriptures by appealing to the spiritual meanings discovered by allegory, and by proving thus that the Old Testament, contrary to Julian's argument, does in fact contain the doctrines of the Church, Trinity and all. The Jews misunderstood their own writings. But apart from the first book, Cyril's reply is entirely piecemeal, concentrating on individual points and not attempting any synthesis or integrated response to the overall case Julian had mustered. Once again he shows himself wedded to the traditions of the past, this time the age-old apologetic arguments of the Fathers, while capable of adapting them to the immediate need before him. So, for all its faults, his treatise was welcomed and admired as a necessary contribution to the continuing battle against paganism; and it did something to paper over the cracks that still existed between the Patriarchates of Antioch and Alexandria.

It was the attack on Diodore and Theodore which revealed Cyril's continuing suspicions and once again exposed the nerves of such as Theodoret. No wonder his death was greeted with relief. Sadly Cyril, though hasty and intransigent, proved more tractable than his successor. Theodoret's position deteriorated rather than improved. It is time to examine the life and works of Cyril's most distinguished opponent.

For Further Reading

English translations

Hill, R. C., 2007, 2008. *St. Cyril of Alexandria. Commentary on the 12 Prophets*, 2 vols, FC, Washington, DC: Catholic University of America Press.

McEnerney, J. I., 1987. *St Cyril of Alexandria: Letters 1–50*, FC, Washington, DC: Catholic University of America Press.

——, 1987. *St Cyril of Alexandria: Letters 51–110*, FC, Washington, DC: Catholic University of America Press.

McGuckin, J. A., 1995. *St. Cyril of Alexandria: On the Unity of Christ*, Crestwood, NY: St Vladimir's Seminary Press.

Russell, N., 2000. *Cyril of Alexandria*, London and New York: Routledge.

Wickham, L. R., 1983. *Cyril of Alexandria: Select Letters*, ed. and ET, Oxford: Clarendon Press.

Studies

McGuckin, J. A., 1994. *Cyril of Alexandria: The Christological Controversy: Its History, Theology and Texts*, Leiden: Brill / republished Crestwood, NY: St Vladimir's Seminary Press.

McKinion, S. A., 2000. *Words, Imagery, and the Mystery of Christ: A Reconstruction of Cyril of Alexandria's Christology*, Leiden: Brill.

Norris, R. A., 1975. 'Christological Models in Cyril of Alexandria', *SP* 13, pp. 255–68.

Siddals, Ruth M., 1987. 'Logic and Christology in Cyril of Alexandria', *JTS* NS 38, pp. 341–6.

Weinandy, Thomas G. and Daniel A. Keating, 2003. *The Theology of St Cyril of Alexandria: A Critical Appreciation*, London / New York: T. & T. Clark.

Welch, L. J., 1994. *Christology and Eucharist in the Early Thought of Cyril of Alexandria*, San Francisco: International Scholars Press.

Wessel, Susan, 2004. *Cyril of Alexandria and the Nestorian Controversy: The Making of a Saint and a Heretic*, Oxford: Oxford University Press.

Wilken, Robert L., 1971. *Judaism and the Early Christian Mind: A Study of Cyril of Alexandria's Exegesis and Theology*, New Haven: Yale University Press.

VII Theodoret of Cyrus

We have already met Theodoret several times in this book. That he should appear in three different places is indicative of his wide-ranging interests and his major contribution to the life of the Church in the fifth century. He has already appeared as a consciously 'orthodox' ecclesiastical historian, as a cultured apologist and as a rather pious hagiographer. He was also a fine theologian and exegete of the Antiochene school, who found himself deeply involved in the controversies which led up to Chalcedon, his attack on Cyril's Anathemas has already been described and his defence of Diodore and Theodore has been mentioned. It is time to pull the threads together and get a clearer picture of Theodoret's life, personality and wide-ranging literary accomplishments.

1 Life

Theodoret turns out to be a highly attractive individual. We know him and his life quite intimately because of a wealth of his correspondence has been preserved. Like Paul, when under attack he was reluctantly drawn into surveying his life and his achievements, 'boasting' in self-justification, and thus passing on some fascinating information about his activities.[304] But these were the outbursts, not of a proud self-assertive man, but of a highly sensitive and conscientious servant of the Church who was unable to accept that all he had done was to be written off by people he seriously regarded as dangerous heretics.[305]

---

304 For example, *Theodoret, Epp.* 81, 113, 116, 119 in *SC* II and III (see n. 325 below); also in *PG* 83 and *NPNF*.

305 *Epp.* 121, 122, 125.

The mood passed. He returned to his monastery, found renewed calm and tranquillity, and then responded to dawning hopes of truth's vindication with a forgiving and thankful spirit.[306]

But this is to begin at the end. The date of Theodoret's birth, like that of most figures of antiquity, is very uncertain – probably 393 is all we can say. The circumstances of his birth, however, he reveals himself in his writings – they were after all rather exceptional. He was the child of a prosperous Antiochene couple who had been childless for many years. Encouraged by the fact that his rather flashy socialite mother had been cured of a serious eye complaint and converted to a sober life by Peter the Galatian (an ascetic living in an unoccupied tomb in the locality and described in Theodoret's *Historia Religiosa* 9, from which we get this information), Theodoret's parents sought further help from the famous local holy men in her barrenness. For years their hopes were fed but not fulfilled, until Macedonius the Barley-Eater (Theodoret's *Historia Religiosa* 13 is now the source) promised that a son would be born to her, provided that like Hannah she devoted him from birth to the service of God. So it is that in Epistle 81 Theodoret can describe himself as consecrated to God before his conception, and given an appropriate education.

What then was that education? The actual information Theodoret gives suggests that his education was exclusively religious. He paid weekly visits to Peter, was instructed by Macedonius and other ascetics, and at an early age became a lector. He speaks of Diodore of Tarsus and Theodore of Mopsuestia as his teachers, though certainly the former and probably the latter he can only have known through books. Undoubtedly it was their theological tradition in which Theodoret was brought up.

But Theodoret was the child of prosperous parents in a city which had long been a centre of secular learning and culture. There Libanius the pagan sophist had taught Chrysostom and Theodore. It would be surprising if Theodoret had not followed the classical *paideia* – and for all his silence, it is quite plain that he did. His correspondents included the sophists Aerius and Isokasius, with whom he was quite capable of exchanging pleasant nothings of a traditional rhetorical kind, complimenting them on the Attic purity of their language. In his letters he quotes from Homer, Sophocles, Euripides, Aristophanes, Demosthenes and Thucydides, he uses the ancient proverbs of Pittacus and Cleobulus, μηδὲν ἀγάν (nothing to excess) and μέτρον ἄριστον (due measure is best).[307] There can be no doubt that he shared the common literary culture of the sophisticated urban upper classes, and that this was one reason for the fine quality of his apologetic work.[308] Yet he was also deeply imbued with the native Syrian culture; he spoke the vernacular and shared the simple piety of the Syrian peasants and ascetics. Indeed, Canivet has suggested that his first language was Syriac, and the very purity of his Greek proves that it was to him an acquired literary language.[309] He was a bridge between cultural extremes in the society of the late Roman

---

306 *Epp.* 133–5, 138–41.

307 *Ep.* XLIII (*SC* I; the Roman numerals indicate those Epistles belonging to the shorter collection discovered by Sakkelion and published by him in 1885).

308 See above, pp. 37–9.

309 Canivet (1958), p. 25, n.3.

Empire, and this no doubt was the result of the 'dual education' ensured by the peculiar circumstances of his birth.

In his early twenties Theodoret inherited his parents' wealth, but it is hardly surprising, given his background, that he immediately gave it all up and distributed it to the poor. After his condemnation he was to write that he had nothing, no house, no land, no money, no tomb;[310] true to his principles he had not used his episcopate to enrich himself.

So Theodoret became a monk, apparently leaving Antioch to enter a monastery near Apamea – for when later deprived of his see, he begs permission to return there, explaining that it is seventy-five miles from Antioch and twenty miles from his episcopal city.[311] There he lived for about seven years, and then only left because he had been elected bishop of Cyrus, a small city deep in the Syriac-speaking countryside, not all that far from the Euphrates. His bishopric he always regarded as a charge entrusted to him by God, frequently saying in his letters that he preferred the withdrawal and peace of an ascetic's life. He made nothing for himself out of his position and contributed much in terms of energy, influence and finance to the local community for which he was responsible. With ecclesiastical revenues he put up public buildings, built two bridges and ensured a water supply by constructing an aqueduct. Thus he provided employment and improved the facilities of the little backwater[312] over which he had been given charge. He clearly realized how desperate the social and economic position was. Peasant-farmers were being forced off the land by their inability to produce enough to meet their taxes and still have a livelihood. So we find a considerable number of letters in the collections which were written to officials or people with influence in the capital trying to get a reduction in dues and to encourage better administration.[313] Though still a young man when elected, Theodoret must rapidly have shown the powers of leadership and devotion to the community which lasted and developed in his thirty-odd years as a bishop, and when he was under attack he could take pride in the fact that there had been no cause of complaint against him, no whisper of bribery or corruption, and neither he nor his clergy had ever been involved in any kind of lawsuit with anyone. It is a sad comment on the state of the Church in this period that such a clean sheet was noteworthy.

The other achievement of which Theodoret boasted was his complete eradication of heresy in the 800 parishes of his diocese. He claims to have delivered 1000 souls from Marcion and whole villages from Arius and Eunomius. He had many battles with heretics, pagans and Jews.[314] Yet his letters have no tone of rancour or hard intolerance. Here we see a man who was sure he knew what was right and true, sincerely carrying out what he believed to be his duty in

---

310 *Ep.* 113; cf. 81.

311 *Ep.* 119.

312 Theodoret himself (*Ep.* 138) speaks of the wretched and solitary little town he improved with these works. However, Cyrus was the chief city of Cyrrhestica, a province of Euphratensis, and the bishopric had 800 parishes in an area of 40 × 40 miles; doubtless it felt small and remote compared with Antioch.

313 See especially *Epp.* 42–7, but there are a number of others scattered about in the collections.

314 *Ep.* 113, to Pope Leo.

love for the souls lost in error and falsehood. All the more devastating to such a man was the judgment of a Church council against him. Even then he was sure he was right, and subsequent events did vindicate him.

Something of Theodoret's involvement in the wider Church struggle we have already observed. He must have been in his late thirties when he was drawn into battle against Cyril and in response to the request of John of Antioch wrote his *Refutation of the Twelve Anathemas*. He was present at Ephesus, stood out against Cyril's determination to open the council before John and the other Orientals arrived, and then led the delegation from the Antiochene splinter group when the two sides were summoned to the capital. His uncompromising campaign against Cyril and the Anathemas may have contributed to the Antiochene loss of favour at court.[315] Theodoret knew his own mind.

Theodoret did indeed know his own mind. John of Antioch had some difficulty in persuading him to accept the Formulary of Reunion two years later. He doggedly refused to condemn Nestorius; as far as he was concerned Nestorius' views were not what the opposition suggested and were perfectly orthodox. Theodoret maintained a close friendship with Nestorius' fellow-exile, Count Irenaeus. One of the earliest letters we possess Theodoret wrote to Irenaeus, wondering why he had not come to visit him.[316] He had been told Irenaeus was coming soon, and the letter describes how he kept dreaming of his arrival, expecting and hoping, and how he could not understand his disappointment. This must have been written before Irenaeus' sentence of exile was confirmed in 434. Later Irenaeus became bishop of Tyre, and we find more letters passing between him and Theodoret.[317] Theodoret's support for Irenaeus, who as bishop soon became the target of the opposition, and his long-standing refusal to condemn Nestorius, meant that when controversy broke out again in the late 440s, he was inevitably tarred with the same doctrinal brush.

However, for ten years or so the conflict remained quiescent. Though Theodoret reacted strongly against Cyril's attack on Diodore and Theodore, the peace was not seriously disrupted again until after Cyril's death. By then Antioch had a new patriarch, John's nephew, Domnus, who leaned very heavily upon Theodoret, the veteran theologian of the Antiochene party. Cyril's death was greeted with relief,[318] and the new patriarch of Alexandria received from Theodoret a remarkably friendly and welcoming letter, praising his moderation and asking for his prayers.[319] The writer can hardly have known what Dioscorus was really like. They were soon to be the chief antagonists in a renewed doctrinal struggle. Theodoret's next letter to Dioscorus[320] was a statement of his theological position, drawn up in reply to a written complaint addressed by Dioscorus to Domnus about the tenor of Theodoret's preaching. Theodoret appeals to the myriads of listeners who can testify to the orthodoxy of his preaching in Antioch during six years under Theodotus, thirteen years under

---

315 Sellers (1953), pp. 14f. Some vehement denunciations of Cyril immediately after the council have been preserved in the *Acta*.

316 *Ep.* XIV.

317 *Epp.* 3, 12, 16; ET of 16 in Pásztori-Kupán (2006).

318 *Ep.* 180, though its attribution to Theodoret has been questioned.

319 *Ep.* 60.

320 *Ep.* 83.

John, who himself joined in standing ovations during Theodoret's sermons, and a further seven years under Domnus. This letter, with its defensive outline of Theodoret's Christological position, became very important in later discussions of Theodoret's orthodoxy, and is found among letters preserved with the *Acta Conciliorum*.

It appears then that Theodoret had been a regular preacher in Antioch; as we have seen, it is likely that his *Ten Discourses on Providence* were given on one of his preaching tours to the metropolitan centre. Under Domnus his visits there seem to have been prolonged. The removal of Theodoret was clearly to be an important step in the campaign to weaken Antioch, especially since his theological reputation, or notoriety, had been further enhanced, by the publication of the *Eranistes*, of which more later. Sure enough in 448 an imperial decree confined Theodoret to his own see on the pretext that he had been summoning too many synods and disturbing the ecclesiastical peace. A number of letters express Theodoret's dismay and annoyance at the arbitrariness of this ban.[321] He had no objection to returning to his pastorate. He liked peace and his duty was to his people. He had never left except after repeated, pressing invitations. But if heretics of all kinds were allowed freedom of movement, why should he be excluded from all major cities? He had done nothing blameworthy. He had simply tried to uphold the faith. He was the victim of calumny. He proceeded to justify his life and his doctrine. Could not Anatolius or Nomus (both of whom held high office in the state) bring some influence to bear on his behalf? In his own personal difficulties, Theodoret addressed letters to those contacts at court which he had already approached on behalf of others.

But the emperor, Theodosius, allowed Dioscorus to make all the running. The Second Council of Ephesus met in 449. Christened the 'Robber Synod' by Pope Leo, it not only condemned all the 'Nestorians', including Theodoret (who was not permitted to attend and was therefore unable to defend himself), but it even gave full approval to all the acts of the earlier Council of Ephesus under Cyril, including the acceptance of the notorious Twelve Anathemas. At this Theodoret's letters reached a new pitch of urgency and dismay. He wrote an appeal to Leo, bishop of Rome – Epistle 113, from which we get so much information about Theodoret's career. He wrote again to Anatolius,[322] seeking imperial permission to go to the West to plead his case, or else to retire to his monastery. He sorted out some last-minute affairs in his diocese, but he could not take his position lying down – as he explained to the bishop of Emesa, Uranius,[323] virtue includes courage and opposition to injustice; silence or resignation is inappropriate. Yet monastic life soon calmed him, and the death of Theodosius brought renewed hope. Almost the last new letter we possess is a request to Anatolius that he should press for a new council to set everything straight. And that, as we know, is exactly what happened – Chalcedon. Theodoret attended the Council of Chalcedon, and his orthodoxy was vindicated. All that was required of him was to condemn Nestorius, which he finally agreed to do.

---

321 *Epp.* 79–82.
322 *Ep.* 119.
323 *Ep.* 122.

Thereafter Theodoret's life is lost to view. It used to be assumed that he died only a few years later, but he may have lived until 466.[324]

Theodoret's *Epistles*[325] have survived in two collections which hardly overlap, giving a total of 232 letters; some others have been preserved elsewhere, for example in the *Acta*. The correspondence is clearly of enormous interest from a biographical point of view, but there are other reasons why it is significant. As examples of the early Byzantine letter form, his epistles cannot be bettered.[326] There are patronage letters and letters of consolation; these follow rhetorical conventions, but that does not mean they are artificial – we too have conventional letter-writing styles, and Theodoret's letters have an attractive personal touch. There are many letters of Easter greeting, expressing the joy of the festival. There are invitations to feasts and dedications: To the Archōn Theodotus, the bishop writes (I paraphrase),

> Children are scared of Bony [μορμώ – the current bugbear used by nurses to keep their charges in order], students are scared of their tutors and teachers, men are scared of judges and officials, and lack of experience doubles their terror. So come and join in our festival so that everyone can see you are human.[327]

Through these letters the life of the fifth century becomes vivid. So does the life of a bishop, consulted on matters of faith and order by his colleagues, exercising pastoral care of individuals, especially those in distress or bereavement. It is clear that, however out of the way Cyrus seemed, Theodoret did not live in isolation from the wider world: he wrote to two bishops in Persian Armenia where the church was suffering persecution from the state, offering sympathy, encouragement and guidance on the question of readmitting to communion those who had succumbed under pressure.[328] And he wrote many letters on behalf of African refugees, particularly a Christian senator and a bishop who had lost everything when the Vandals swept into Carthage and Libya.[329] There are also, as we have noted, a number of letters of particular interest from the doctrinal point of view, and it is to Theodoret's doctrinal work that we will now turn our attention.

2 His theological position

Was Theodoret a Nestorian? This question has been repeatedly discussed during his lifetime and since. He was vindicated at Chalcedon, but his anti-Cyrilline writings were condemned along with his master, Theodore of Mopsuestia, in the later Three Chapters controversy in 553. Many modern scholars have discussed the question, and there is some measure of agreement that Theodoret

---

324 Honigmann (1953).
325 Text: Azéma (1955, 1964, 1965); ET *NPNF*.
326 Wagner (1948).
327 *Ep.* XXXVI.
328 *Epp.* 77–8.
329 *Epp.* XXIII, 29–35, 52, 53.

began as a Nestorian but changed his position in the course of time, some dating the change at Chalcedon, others considerably earlier.[330] It seems doubtful, however, whether the question is worth pursuing along these lines – after all, Nestorius himself has been vindicated in the eyes of many scholars by the discovery of the *Bazaar of Heraclides*. The interesting question is whether Theodoret's basic Christological position did change or advance during the course of the controversy; and to answer that question it may be more important to observe his basic theological concerns than to focus attention merely on his formulae.

But first, the evidence: what doctrinal works do we possess from the hand of Theodoret? There are a number of letters, as we have noticed already, all dating from the period between Ephesus (431) and Chalcedon (451); most of those of doctrinal interest belong to the latter part of that period when renewed controversy necessitated self-justification and the building of alliances. Also from this later period comes the *Eranistes*, a work of great importance which will be described in more detail later. From the time of the Council of Ephesus, we have the fragmentary remains preserved in the *Acta*: Theodoret's *Refutation of the Anathemas* (embedded in Cyril's defence),[331] some sermons, some letters, some conciliar statements which seem to have been drafted by Theodoret's pen. Various other fragments and descriptions of works that he composed have come down to us; more important, however, are several works which survived among the works of other writers but have now been restored to Theodoret through the researches of modern scholarship. In the nineteenth century A. Ehrhard[332] showed that *On the Holy and Vivifying Trinity* and *On the Incarnation of the Lord*, works ascribed to Cyril, in fact present the doctrinal views of Theodoret, and some fragments, quotations cited under Theodoret's name, prove that these treatises did indeed originate not from Cyril but from his opponent. Theodoret himself refers to both these works in his letters,[333] and they evidently share the standpoint of Theodoret's *Refutation of the Anathemas*. Another work with a similar history is the *Expositio rectae fidei*,[334] preserved among the writings of Justin Martyr, though clearly belonging to a much later period. Quite independently, two scholars[335] recognized it as the work of Theodoret, and there can be little doubt that this restoration is correct. In spite of the fact that one researcher, R. V. Sellers, assigned it to the same period as the *Eranistes*, the arguments for dating it early are much more compelling[336] – indeed, it seems

330 The range of views was summarized by Mandac (1971). Clayton (2007) argues that his views never changed, and remained essentially those of Theodore of Mopsuestia and other Antiochenes, with the limitations of a two-subject model and no real *communicatio idiomatum*; Pásztori-Kupán (2006) insists that Theodoret's position should not be judged in terms of later Christological standards.

331 See above, pp. 280ff.

332 See Lebon (1930). The text of these works will be found in Ehrhard (1888) and PG 75 (that is, attributed to Cyril). ET of selections in Pásztori-Kupán (2006). See also discussion in Clayton (2007), chapter 4.

333 *Ep.* 133 and Schwartz, *ACO* 1.4, 85.

334 Text in Otto (1880).

335 Lebon (1930); Sellers (1945).

336 Richard (1935/77); Brok (1951).

likely that it pre-dates the outbreak of the Christological controversies. If this is the case, then we have an excellent chance of plotting the shifts and continuities in Theodoret's thinking.[337]

Between Ephesus and Chalcedon, a shift in emphasis might appear to have occurred. We have already reviewed Theodoret's debate with Cyril over the Anathemas. It is interesting to contrast Theodoret's attitude there with that found in his Epistle 83 to Dioscorus. Here many of his affirmations are distinctly reminiscent of Cyril's:

> One Saviour Jesus Christ, only-begotten Son of God, begotten of the Father before all ages, incarnated and made man . . . born of the Virgin Mary according to the flesh, who therefore is called 'Theotokos' . . . He exists eternally as God, and is born of the Virgin Mary as Man . . . Only one Son exists, the God-Word made man.

Theodoret is concerned to defend himself from misrepresentation, asserting that he does not preach 'two Sons', supporting his statements from scripture, and from the Fathers, Alexander and Athanasius, Basil and Gregory, even acknowledging a debt to the writings of Theophilus and Cyril. He still insists that there must be no confusion between the flesh and the divine: 'We teach clearly the distinction of two natures, proclaiming the immutability of the divine nature.' But he is prepared to call the flesh of the Saviour divine inasmuch as it has become the flesh of the God–Word, as long as the idea that it is transformed into the divine is rejected as impious. Theodoret claims here that he had a friendly correspondence with Cyril (nothing of which has survived) and admired his work against Julian the Apostate. He begs Dioscorus to turn away from those who speak falsely, to consider the peace of the Church, to make every effort to cure those who dare to alter true doctrines or else drive them out. He insists that if anyone says the virgin is not *Theotokos*, or that our Saviour Jesus Christ is only man, or divides the only-begotten and first-born of all creatures into two Sons, he should be cast from the Christian hope with the acclamation of all Christian people. This, he says, is what he really believes; it is no sail-trimming. This is Theodoret in very different mood from when faced with Cyril's Anathemas; he is conciliatory and it certainly seems as if he had recognized that the basic stance of the Alexandrians was an attempt to preserve an essential aspect of the tradition which, provided certain safeguards were included, he was not averse to adopting himself. He confesses the one Saviour both as existing eternally as God and as born of Mary. Is this the result of a significant shift in his thinking?

One of the most influential studies of the subtle modifications which took place in Theodoret's Christological formulae is that of M. Richard.[338] His main point is that Theodoret's later works use abstract expressions for the humanity of Christ (ἡ ἀνθρωπίνη φύσις (human nature), τὸ ἀναληφθέν (the assumed), ἡ ἀνθρωπότης (humanity), etc.), whereas his early works do not hesitate to speak of 'the man', or 'the perfect man' (ὁ τέλειος ἄνθρωπος), treating him as a con-

---

337 For a much fuller discussion of each of Theodoret's works in chronological order with the aim of tracking changes in his Christology, see Clayton (2007).
338 Richard (1936/77).

crete individual. Following this hint, a corresponding shift in his soteriological language has been discovered:[339] in the *De Incarnatione* he is prepared to use graphic language of the man assumed being justified 'by his own toils' and prevailing over the devil 'by human φιλοσοφία (philosophy), not by the power of divinity'; whereas later he gives little positive role to the human soul and emphasizes the saving activity of the Logos who used the assumed humanity as an instrument. Again, in the *Refutation of the Anathemas*, the humanity, as priest and victim, offered the sacrifice to the divinity; later, in his exegesis of Hebrews, this dichotomy between the natures is played down, the subject of the sacrificial action being the incarnate God–Word. Many have been convinced that this represents a remarkable change in Theodoret's position. Few theologians involved in controversy have had the humility to listen to the other side and concede that the opposition has a point; Theodoret apparently had the grace to do so. Cyril had convinced him that there were dangers in treating the humanity as a concrete individual alongside the God–Word, that such expressions could lead to unacceptable division and imply a 'two Sons' doctrine.

But has Theodoret's essential theological stance been modified? A number of reasons have been advanced for thinking that the contrast, though present, seems to have been over-pressed. Concrete language for the humanity of Christ was common to all traditions in the previous century, and Cyril himself seems to have made a similar shift in his linguistic habits.[340] As for Theodoret's own position, his basically 'symmetrical' Christology remains the same:[341] he still balances divine and human expressions, giving both equal weight and failing to recognize the 'metaphysical dependence of the human on the divine'; and besides, in his later works, he still finds it difficult to attribute suffering to the Logos, so failing to make full allowance for the *communicatio idiomatum*. Thus his theology remains fundamentally dualistic. On the other hand,[342] he had always been concerned with the unity of Christ. Even in the works written prior to the controversy, this concern can be detected. In speaking of the union, he uses precisely the same vocabulary as he uses for the unity of the Trinity (ἑνόω, συνάπτω, μετέχω, κοινωνέω and related nouns). He speaks of the Son or Christ existing as God and as Man. The majority of references to the human nature are already of the abstract, impersonal kind. Furthermore there are many sentences where the Logos is both the initiator and the subject of the saving action, the Logos even being the one who justifies the human nature 'by its own toils'. In these early works, his primary emphasis was directed against Arian and Apollinarian misinterpretations of the incarnation, and it was his conviction that the anathemas were Apollinarian which gave rise to his strong language in the *Refutation*. In this kind of controversial situation, he was bound to uphold hard-won truths about the distinction of natures; yet even here we noticed that Theodoret did not bother to contradict the Sixth Anathema because he accepted the point that there is one Lord Jesus Christ who is both God and Man.[343]

---

339 Parvis (1975); he explores this question on pp. 293–307.
340 Gesché (1962), pp. 67ff.; and de Durand (1964), Introduction.
341 McNamara (1955). See further Clayton (2007).
342 Mandac (1971).
343 See above, p. 285.

So from somewhat contrasting angles it looks as though the essential features of Theodoret's Christology were not fundamentally modified, and if we concentrate on the inner motivation of his Christology, namely his soteriology,[344] this becomes even more apparent. Theodoret's ideal for a human person was the ἀπάθεια (passionlessness) and ἀτρεπτότης (changelessness) of the perfect monk who had overcome sin and fallibility. This was the ideal depicted in his *Historia religiosa*. In the *Eranistes*, however, he argues that God alone is truly ἀπαθής and ἄτρεπτος. Is he consistent here?[345] It is his Christology which redeems his consistency. Christ being the true mediator, the God-Man, united the two natures and so clothed human nature with ἀπάθεια, with the character of God himself. For Theodoret salvation did not mean the transformation of humanity into God (θεοποίησις), nor the realization of a natural kinship between the human and the divine, but rather the union of human nature with God by participation, neither God nor humanity sacrificing their integrity, but humanity becoming the image of God by being made like him. Such a soteriology Theodoret maintained throughout his life, and it remained fundamental to the structure and character of his Christology.

We may observe Theodoret's position further by examining two doctrinal works from very different dates.

3 The *Expositio recta fidei*[346]

The *Expositio* is a neat little treatise expounding the essentials of the Christian faith. Theodoret seems to regard it as the culmination of a series of works: having refuted the Jews and Greeks, he will now expound the healthy doctrine of faith. The work is catechetical or apologetic in flavour rather than controversial. The first half is concerned with the doctrine of the Trinity: one God, known in Father, Son and Holy Spirit. He explains with beautiful clarity the difference between *ousia* and *hypostasis*; and how the epithets ἀγέννητος, γεννήτος and ἐκπόρευτος (unbegotten, begotten and proceeding) describe not a difference in *ousia* but in τρόποι ὑπάρξεως (manners of existing). This is one of the briefest and most lucid statements of Trinitarian orthodoxy to be found in patristic literature. Theodoret goes on to speak of the great divide between Creator and created, and offers proofs that all three divine Persons belong to the superior category (thus refuting Arianism); they are united in a single activity and energy, both in the operation of grace and in creation. The human mind, he continues, is incapable of grasping the divine (thus excluding the views of Eunomius), we know in part and through a glass darkly. Through θεωρία (contemplation) humanity may attach itself to God, and analogies give us some glimpse of what God is like, but God is ἀκατάληπτος (incomprehensible) and

---

344 For Theodoret's soteriology and its relationship to his Christology, see Koch (1974).

345 See Fairbairn (2007), who provides a review of scholarly evaluations of Theodoret's Christology (pp. 105f.), and proposes that Theodoret mostly sees the Logos as the personal subject of Christ, apart from when he is referring to the death of Christ, where his view of divine impassibility leads him to view the subject in this context to be the human Jesus.

346 The text is to be found in Otto (1880).

ἄρρητος (ineffable), both in himself and in his οἰκονομία (his providential plan and outreach).

Theodoret now turns to expounding this οἰκονομία – by which he means the incarnation. Seeing the mess humanity was in as a result of Adam's fault, the Logos 'without leaving the heavens, came down to us' – in other words, his descent was not a physical act, but a voluntary act of the divine energy. He made a 'temple' for himself – a perfect man – and by a perfect union clothing himself with it, fulfilled the saving action on our behalf. As man he lived blamelessly, and through death paid what was owed; as God he raised up the destroyed and completely overcame death. There was one Son who as man was destroyed, and as God rose; but with respect to this one Son, it is necessary to divide the natures, assigning divine attributes or activities to the divine nature, and human to the human nature. As to the manner of the union, Theodoret is not afraid to confess ignorance – in fact, he is prepared to boast about it, for he believes in things which are simply not expressible. No one should expect complete clarification. But he is prepared to discuss certain analogies and he proceeds to explore the union of body and soul in the human being – another example of two natures in one person. There are certain qualifications to be made – the soul, for example, is involved in the passions of the body; indeed, it often suffers before the body does – but we cannot think that of the divinity of Christ. This analogy being only partially applicable, he explores another: the embodiment of light in the sun. After dealing with various difficulties and questions, Theodoret eventually confronts those who object to the division into two natures, accusing them of introducing confusion, mixture and change; they agree that he remained God while becoming flesh, so their refusal to accept two natures just produces nonsense. The idea that the body was divinized after the union, Theodoret also demolishes. The basic distinction between the natures must hold. Yet in the end all arguments and questions lead to ἀπορία (perplexity). When I reach that point, says Theodoret, I cry out with wonder at the Christian mystery, that our faith is beyond mental grasp, beyond words, beyond understanding. The only suitable response in the end is praise.

Was this treatise written early, before the Nestorian controversy broke out? It seems very likely that it was. The emphasis is not exclusively Christological; the controversial passages are explicable in the light of the Arian and Apollinarian controversies; and although there are interesting parallels with arguments that appear later, the work lacks discussion of some of the most contentious issues of the later controversy. Furthermore, later on Theodoret seems less inclined than here to fall back on agnosticism to avoid explaining the union – perhaps because he had learned that Cyril could also play that game. But if this is an early work then it is extremely significant; for here the bare bones of Theodoret's position are expressed, to some extent in terms which are elsewhere submerged, and this shows that whatever happened to Theodoret's formulae in the course of controversy, his position was not basically altered. The features to which I refer are (i) the basic distinction between Creator and created; (ii) the insistence that the Logos remains what he is in spite of the incarnation; and (iii) the assumption that the Logos is the subject of the act of incarnation, even though incarnate experiences are attributed to the humanity.

Theodoret does share Theodore's concern that it should be human nature in its completeness which should be saved, and accepts his view that only a genuine reversal of human moral failure will accomplish this.[347] But the emphasis of Theodoret's work is much more pointedly and consistently directed towards the preservation of God's 'Godness'. This appears in what has been said about the *Expositio*, and it is reinforced not only by the emphasis of his arguments in the *Refutation of the Anathemas*, but also by the very titles he gives to the three dialogues that make up the *Eranistes*: ἄτρεπτος (unchangeable), ἀσύγχυτος (unconfused), ἀπαθής (impassible). Theodoret was determined to keep a hold on the hard-won ground taken from the Arians and Apollinarians. The Logos belonged to uncreated Being, humanity belonged to the created order. There is no mean between these. The uncreated *ousia* cannot be mixed, changed or affected by anything external to itself. Only by an act of divine favour or will can God approach his creatures. The Alexandrian talk of the Word *becoming* flesh, of the flesh being *divinized*, of the *one nature* after the union, to Theodoret compromised all his basic theological instincts, and that remained true throughout his life and explains his dogged resistance first to Cyril, then to Eutyches. He seems to have recognized towards the end that he had misjudged Cyril's meaning; but then he thought that the Alexandrians seriously misjudged him and his Antiochene associates. Theodoret's basic position did not, it seems, undergo any serious modification.

4 The *Eranistes*[348]

Like the *Expositio*, this work beautifully illustrates the clarity and conciseness of Theodoret's style. It is a refreshing change from so much patristic literature. It also illustrates, as did the apologetic work described earlier (*The Cure of Pagan Maladies*), the brilliant way in which Theodoret could take over conventional forms and material from other sources, and yet produce a work which is no mere slavish copying, but a genuinely original creation within the constraints of the tradition.

The *Eranistes* consists of three dialogues between 'Collector' and 'Orthodoxus'. The characters are named to indicate their roles – for, as he explains in his prologue, Theodoret sees Orthodoxus' opponent as a 'collector' picking up various ideas from heretical sources and producing doctrine that is neither traditional nor coherent. The dialogue form enabled his argument to proceed through question and answer, propositions, elucidations, antitheses and other dialectical procedures, but the format, he explains, he modified by putting the name of the character speaking at the head of each statement made, rather than adopting a kind of narrative of the discourse with the names embedded in the text. (In other words, unlike Plato's dialogues, Theodoret's appear in the form in which a modern play is set out.) Each dialogue culminates in the production of a florilegium of patristic citations supporting the position for which Orthodoxus has argued – a device which on each occasion finally forces Eranistes to

---

347 For the theological roles of human nature in Antiochene methodologies and Theodoret's relation to these, see Schor (2007).

348 For text and ET, see Ettlinger (1975, 2003).

accept that Orthodoxus is right, especially as Orthodoxus has rounded off each collection with quotations from Apollinarius, in order to show that Eranistes' Monophysite position is even more extreme than that of that notorious heretic. As a consequence these florilegia have preserved some important fragments from the writings of Apollinarius, as well as others like Eustathius of Antioch.

Use of florilegia as a method of theological argument seems to have developed during the Christological controversies. Lists of patristic quotations had been used extensively by Cyril, and Theodoret retaliated in kind. Both sides felt the need to appeal to the authority of scripture and the tradition of the Fathers, particularly as set out at Nicaea, thus to produce quotations from such generally revered teachers as Athanasius, the Cappadocians and John Chrysostom was an excellent method of procedure. At the very beginning of the First Dialogue, Eranistes and Orthodoxus agree that the question at issue is how to follow in the footsteps of the apostles, prophets and holy men – they are not indulging in a speculative exercise. The florilegia fit this intention exactly. It is likely that in the *Eranistes* Theodoret drew on earlier florilegia and there are a number of collections, for example in Leo's *Tome* and in the Chalcedonian *Acta*, which are related to those found here. However, Theodoret's originality has once again been recognized, in this case by Ettlinger,[349] who argues that his primary source was his own earlier work, the lost *Pentalogus* written against Cyril in 432. The passages from Leo's *Tome* were added later by a post-Chalcedonian copyist; and the Chalcedonian florilegium was dependent on Theodoret. In other respects Theodoret left his mark – he appealed to the works of ante-Nicene Fathers providing the link right back to the apostles, he deliberately avoided appealing to his own great authorities, Diodore and Theodore, on the grounds that they carried no weight with the opposition, and he chose instead to quote from Theophilus and Cyril of Alexandria – not to mention Apollinarius. Heretics were usually cited to prove their heresy – only here do we find heretical citations used to support the case being presented. Theodoret never stuck merely to convention!

The fourth part of the *Eranistes* often appears in manuscripts independently under the Latin title *Demonstratio per syllogismos*; but it is quite clear that it originally belonged with the dialogues and provided a concise restatement of the principal arguments covered.

In the first of the dialogues, Orthodoxus seems to make all the running. He gets Eranistes to agree that unchangeability is a divine characteristic which belongs to the whole Trinity, and then demands to know how John's Gospel can say 'The Word became flesh', attaching change to the unchangeable nature. Eranistes confesses ignorance as to how ('only he knows'), but he is prepared to assert the truth of the gospel willy-nilly. 'I do not know what this change into flesh is,' he says, 'but I have read "The Word became flesh".' Orthodoxus accepts that one should not enquire into hidden things, but asserts that one should not display ignorance of what is perfectly plain, either. The change into flesh cannot be literally true, no matter how much Eranistes protests that 'taking flesh' or 'dwelling in flesh' is different from 'becoming flesh'. Ortho-

---

349 For the critical details in this paragraph, I am indebted to Ettlinger (1975), Introduction.

doxus gets him to agree that God's unchangeability is scriptural, that scripture uses certain phrases symbolically, and so gradually leads him on to admitting the possibility that this text has to be interpreted in the light of others, like Hebrews 10.5, Philippians 2.6f. and the second half of the same verse, John 1.14; that is, he 'became flesh' by 'taking flesh' and 'dwelling among us' as in a temple. Eranistes enquires how the ancient teachers of the Church understood this text, and so a preliminary florilegium is introduced into the dialogue, dealing simply with the exegesis of John 1.14. The main florilegium on the incarnation shortly follows, and the dialogue ends with Eranistes forced to accept that the God–Word is ἄτρεπτος (changeless), that he was not changed into flesh but took flesh. Certainly in this dialogue the characterization of Eranistes is weak compared with that of his opponent. Apart from a few spirited replies he appears as a rather dogged, unthinking fundamentalist taking refuge in the limits of human understanding, appealing to scripture texts in a rather literal-minded way, or reiterating that he became flesh without change, whatever that may mean. Orthodoxus on the other hand agrees on the necessity of sticking to scripture and tradition, but clearly believes that their meaning requires elucidation.

In the second dialogue, Eranistes is a more active participant. He is presented as offering for consideration and defending a number of the Christological formulae which were to remain sacrosanct to the Monophysite party. The subject is now ἀσύγχυτος (unconfused), which means that the dialogue ranges over the whole question of whether two distinct natures are to be confessed. In the opening discussion, the debaters agree on the dismissal of Apollinarius' views and the completeness of Christ's human nature; but then Eranistes enquires whether it is right to call Jesus God or Man. Orthodoxus makes a very traditional statement about the Logos being incarnate, from which Eranistes deduces that he is to be called God, and adds that since they have agreed he was made man without change – indeed, remaining what he was – one must call him what he was, namely God. Orthodoxus replies that it is necessary to speak both of the assumer and the assumed; as scripture sometimes refers to man as soul and sometimes as body or flesh, so Christ must be confessed in two natures, as God and Man. But God, says Eranistes, fits him better, because God is the name of his nature, and Man is merely the name of the οἰκονομία ('economy' – incarnation). Orthodoxus protests that the οἰκονομία was real, and therefore the name Man is equally appropriate. Eranistes eventually accepts the idea of two natures, but says there were two only before the union; after the union there was just one. At that, Orthodoxus is easily able to demonstrate the inappropriateness of speaking of both natures pre-existing: the humanity did not exist before the union, only the Logos. Two natures after the union, yes; but not two natures before. Eranistes retorts 'out of two natures not two natures', and pressed to explain, speaks of the union as ineffable and incomprehensible. Orthodoxus agrees but insists that each nature must remain pure and unmixed after the union, each having its own properties. Eranistes agrees to be persuaded by scripture, but sticks to his slogan: one nature after the union. He counteracts Orthodoxus' appeal to various texts by attributing them all to the incarnate Logos. All texts, he states, refer to the one enfleshed nature of the Logos. At that Orthodoxus refers back to their previous discussion: how can you talk of enfleshed God without attributing change to the Godhead or confusing the natures? Eranistes replies that two natures implies two Sons, and for a while takes over the initiative in the discussion. He gets Orthodoxus to admit that divine and human attributes are alike to be attributed to the one Christ. Orthodoxus, however, adds that both mixture and division have to be avoided, for to attribute confusion or mixture to the Godhead is blasphemous. He returns to the attack: how can Eranistes meet the challenge of Arius or Apollinarius? The ensuing discussion produces considerable agreement on the kind of Christology needed to counter various heresies, but Eranistes is not yet satisfied that two natures does not imply two sons. Orthodoxus produces various arguments, showing, for example, that union without confusion is possible in the physical world, and that the humanity of Jesus was not swallowed up in his divinity. Eranistes eventually tries to clinch his case by adducing the eucharistic parallel, with which Orthodoxus both agrees and differs – for the bodily form, he points out, remains the same. When Eranistes protests that he sticks by the teachings of the Church whatever arguments Orthodoxus may produce, the second florilegium is introduced, this time to establish that the flesh remains after the ascension, and that two natures without confusion are to be recognized in our Lord Jesus Christ.

Considering that Orthodoxus represents the author's view, one feels that in this dialogue Eranistes has been given quite a good chance to present his position. Theodoret had listened to the slogans and arguments of the opposition and was able to compose a fairly realistic and sympathetic picture of a typical Monophysite debater. He no longer misrepresents his opponent as an Apollinarian. He recognizes that there is a good deal of common ground, and he has the skill to use the dialogue form effectively to present both sides of the case, even though the total impact is of course a vindication of his own orthodox position. That position does not appear to be fundamentally different from that outlined in the *Expositio Rectae Fidei*. Theodoret may have been betrayed into more extreme statements by Cyril's provocative tactics over Nestorius, but his basic Christological understanding was not transformed during the course of the controversy.

The third dialogue gives much the same impression. This dialogue tackles the heart of the problem – the Passion. In essence many of the arguments are not dissimilar from those that have gone before, but the debate is nearer the bone. Once again Eranistes is allowed to take the initiative in the discussion, and he is not often merely a foil for Orthodoxus' arguments. He has an important case to contribute and he does not let it go by default.

Orthodoxus states that they have agreed that the God–Word is ἄτρεπτος, that he was incarnate without change, that he took perfect humanity; scripture and the teachers of the Church agree that after the union he remained what he was – unmixed, impassible, unchangeable, uncircumscribed and so on. So the question of the passion remains. Eranistes opens: 'Who suffered?' 'Our Lord Jesus Christ', says Orthodoxus. 'So a man provided our salvation? Define what you believe Christ is.' When Orthodoxus offers the definition, 'The Son of the living God made man', Eranistes states, 'God underwent suffering'. Orthodoxus, of course, cannot accept such a bald statement undermining the impassible with passion. As the discussion proceeds each side produces qualifications. Eranistes states that of course his divine nature is impassible, but he suffered in the flesh – that was why he became incarnate. Orthodoxus speaks of the body suffering, but this is no 'mere man', since it is the body of the God–Word and they were joined in an indivisible union. Both of them struggle with the paradox of the immortal dying and the impassible suffering, one dissolving it by attributing suffering and death to the body, the other asserting it on the basis of scripture. One accuses the other of blasphemy for suggesting that the ἀπαθής nature can be subject to πάθος; the other counters with the charge that anything else implies division of the one Lord Jesus Christ. They have an interesting discussion about what God can or cannot do, Orthodoxus suggesting that suffering is as alien to his nature as sin; the good cannot do evil, truth cannot be false, so all things are not possible to God. They discuss salvation, Orthodoxus emphasizing that sin is the greater problem, Eranistes tending to emphasize death; so for Eranistes the saving action of God is of primary importance, but Orthodoxus eventually brings convincing arguments from scripture that the suffering, death and resurrection were of the body, and that is why his resurrection can also be ours. He presses this point later by drawing attention to the fact that it is his flesh which is given for the life of the world; and that at the Last Supper he said 'This is my Body given for you.' Scripture never connects suffering with God himself, he asserts, even though he accepts the many texts adduced by Eranistes to prove that the Lord Jesus Christ suffered. Orthodoxus ought perhaps to have admitted that he was outmanoeuvred on this when Eranistes produced the text 'They crucified the Lord of glory'; but typically he gets round it by accepting that, on the basis of the *communicatio idiomatum*, the name of either nature can be applied to the one Christ. Basically the discussion revolves around the fact that Orthodoxus is prepared to say of the one Christ that as God he is immortal, impassible, unchangeable, etc., and as man he is mortal, passible, etc., whereas Eranistes wishes to make a stronger statement designating the Logos as the subject of the incarnate experiences: by nature he is impassible, etc., but by being incarnate he took on a state in which he could in some real sense experience suffering and death. When Eranistes comes up with Cyril's slogan ἀπαθῶς ἔπαθεν (he suffered without suffering), Orthodoxus laughs him to scorn; and yet sometimes they really do not seem all that far apart. Both agree that the Nicene Creed states that the one *homoousios* with the Father was also the one who suffered and was crucified, each being prepared to admit that it is not straightforwardly true and certain qualifications have to be made.

Once more the concluding florilegium gives Orthodoxus an apparent victory over Eranistes, but the discussion has not been unfairly presented. If the other side had been able to read Theodoret's work with an open mind, there is little doubt that accommodation could have been reached. In a sense it was reached at Chalcedon, if only the 'Monophysites' had not objected to the omission from the Definition of certain favourite slogans, the weakness of which Theodoret had here effectively demonstrated. They did after all disown Eutyches, just as the Antiochenes had come to disown Nestorius. Perhaps the purpose of the *Eranistes* was to try and convince the less extreme Alexandrians that they should abandon Eutyches and recognize how much common ground they had with the moderate Antiochenes.

In any case, it seems clear that Theodoret still stood by the basic theological principles outlined in his earlier work – the distinction between Creator and created is maintained, together with its implication, namely the recognition of two natures in Christ; but so is the acknowledgment that the Logos is the subject of the act of incarnation, even though incarnate experiences are properly attributed to the assumed nature and not to the Logos in his essential Being. What has changed is not so much his thought as his attitude and his emphases, to some extent also his terminology – the Christological formulae which he had come to adopt through twenty years of debate.

5 Biblical exegesis

Theodoret belonged to the Antiochene tradition in his doctrine. He also belonged to the Antiochene tradition in his exegesis. Apart from everything else, Theodoret wrote an enormous number of biblical studies, some treatises in the form of question and answer concerning problem passages, others more straightforward commentaries. Between them, these works cover the Pentateuch with Joshua, Judges and Ruth; the books of Kings and Chronicles; the Psalms, the Song of Songs, Daniel, Ezekiel, Isaiah and Jeremiah; and the fourteen Epistles of St Paul.[350] The *Quaestiones*, covering the Old Testament books from Genesis to Chronicles, were written late in his life, after Chalcedon, the commentaries on the prophets and the apostle all seem to have been compiled during the period 433–8. These are not extended works of scholarship, nor are they homilies, but they have a devotional dimension and traces of oral delivery, features which suggest that like the *Discourses on Providence* they may well have been originally produced as lectures in Antioch.[351] All of this exegetical work survives (only his writings against Cyril were proscribed), and it provides us with our most extensive access to the Antiochene methods and exegetical achievement.[352]

Indeed, that was once regarded as their only importance. Theodoret was thought to have reproduced Theodore to such an extent that his commentaries could supply gaps in what was known of Theodore's work.[353] If his commentaries had no other value, at least he had helped to preserve the Interpreter's work from oblivion. All the more interesting therefore has been the work of Godfrey Ashby and Paul Parvis, who have clearly established Theodoret's independence.[354] Even though he loyally leapt to the defence of Theodore when his master was attacked by Cyril, Theodoret did himself pass critical judgments on the exegetical work of his predecessors, among whom Theodore can

---

350 The text of Theodoret's biblical works will be found in *PG* 80–2. For more recent editions of the *Questions on the Octateuch* (text and ET), see Petruccione and Hill (2007), and of the *Commentary on Isaiah*, see Möhle (1932) and Guinot (1980, 1982, 1984). For ET of the Commentaries on the Psalms, the Song of Songs and the epistles of Paul, see Hill (2000, 2001, 2001a, 2001b).

351 See above, p. 38. On the date and form of Theodoret's commentaries I follow Parvis (1975).

352 On Theodoret's exegesis, see Ashby (1972); Parvis (1975); Guinot (1995).

353 Swete (1880–2) assumes that gaps in Theodore's work can be filled by referring to Theodoret.

354 Ashby (1972); Parvis (1975). I am indebted to these studies for the following paragraphs.

be clearly identified. Comparisons between their commentaries where they overlap reveals the very considerable extent to which Theodoret departed from Theodore, while also highlighting Theodore's all-pervasive influence.

In the mechanics of exegesis (the dividing up of sentences, the definition of words, background explanations, tracing the connections of thought, elucidating the historical circumstances, and so on), Theodoret follows very closely the methods of Theodore. There are, however, few verbal parallels, and it certainly appears that, even though he was saturated in Theodore's work, Theodoret did not in fact refer to his commentaries when composing his own. Theodoret often approaches a particular passage rather differently, asking quite different questions. There are a number of occasions where he definitely disagrees with Theodore: Theodoret makes a great deal of the fact that Paul visited Colossae and knew the Colossians when he wrote his epistle; Theodore had asserted the opposite. The debate between them over this rumbles on through Theodoret's commentary. In other words, this was no slavish copying, and the suggestion that Theodoret duplicates Theodore[355] does not prove true on examination.

If the commentaries of Theodore and Theodoret have a similarity in method, they are marked by a difference in flavour. Lying behind this is not merely the difference in style (Theodore tends to write repetitive and cumbersome Greek, Theodoret's language is clear and concise). There is also a fundamental shift in perspective. For Theodore, as we have seen, there was a radical distinction between the old order and the new, a strong eschatological outlook which favoured discontinuity between the two Testaments. This perspective, so characteristic of Theodore, led him to deny the Christological character of many Old Testament texts, to refuse to see any indications of the Trinitarian nature of God in the Old Testament writings, and to reduce to a bare minimum direct prophecies of the New Age: a few types were permitted with rigidly defined safeguards and rules, a few predictions were acknowledged where hyperbolic expressions made certain statements inappropriate to the old order. The abandonment of this radical Two Ages dichotomy enabled Theodoret to develop a more explicitly Christian view of the Old Testament. As he tells us in the *Preface to the Psalms*,

I have consulted various commentaries, of which some fell into allegory, whilst others adapted the prophecies themselves to the history of the past, so that their interpretation applied more to Jews than to Christians. I have felt it my duty to avoid equally the two extremes. All that is relevant to ancient history ought to be recognized. But predictions concerning Christ our Saviour, the Church of the Gentiles, the expansion of the gospel, the preaching of the apostles, ought not to be diverted from their proper sense and applied to other things as if they had been fulfilled by the Jews.

It must be Theodore he has in mind.

Theodoret, without sacrificing the historical content of the original works, is prepared to see the Christian dispensation foreshadowed and predicted in the Old Testament. So, unlike Theodore, Theodoret can relate Old and New

---

355 Greer (1973), p. 296.

Testament texts, using them to interpret each other. Much more than Theodore, Theodoret perceives a unity in the whole of scripture. The Old Testament does contain reference to the Trinity, and indeed points to the two natures of Christ. For Theodoret allows also a great deal of θεωρία – spiritual meanings. A text need no longer have one σκοπός (subject, intent): it can have both a historical reference and a predictive role, pointing to the messianic fulfilment. This makes an enormous difference to the *Commentary on the Psalms*: the LXX title εἰς τὸ τέλος (to the End/fulfilment) provided Theodoret with a clue, embedded in the scriptural text, to the messianic reference of any Psalm to which it is attached. (It actually represents the obscure Hebrew word translated by the RSV as 'To the Choirmaster'.) Some psalms belonged to the context of David's life, some referred to the great saving events of Israel's history, but many psalms were allowed a specifically Christological reference, and many more were regarded as having a double, or even triple level of meaning. Similarly the prophets, while belonging to their own time and speaking to their contemporaries, nevertheless made predictions, and these were more often than not predictions of Christ. Theodoret emphatically rejects views which clearly came from Theodore, like the idea that Micah 4.1–3 refers to the return from Babylon to Jerusalem, insisting that its fulfilment is seen in the gathering of the Gentiles to the Church. Whereas Theodore had suggested that the Song of Songs was just Solomon's love poem, Theodoret indignantly repudiates 'those who slander the Song of Songs and believe the book is not spiritual'. It does describe a marriage, but it is the marriage of Christ and the Church – and Theodoret is clearly dependent upon Origen for much of his exegesis. It is particularly interesting that Theodoret could adopt such an independent line in what was almost certainly his first commentary.[356] Consciously rejecting allegory and asserting the principles of historical interpretation like other Antiochenes, Theodoret is yet able to give full weight to the Church's traditions of spiritual exegesis. Not that every Old Testament verse can produce *theōria* – but certain basic biblical themes are to be interpreted in relation to their Christian fulfilment. Threefold invocations, mention of the Spirit, insistence on God's uniqueness – such texts show that the God of the Old Testament was the triune God of the Christians. Humanity, the creation of God but lost in sinfulness, finds its redemption and fulfilment in Christ. Christian salvation is prefigured in the great saving events of the Old Testament. Many images have their fulfilment in Christian baptism and Eucharist. Theodoret reverts to the traditional types and messianic prophecies, many of which were enshrined in the liturgy, while still grasping the priority of historical interpretation.

When it comes to the New Testament, the contrast is perhaps less marked. There is less scope for θεωρία and Theodoret's comments are largely confined to explanatory notes. But there is still a contrast. Theodore's eschatological hope is reduced and the emphasis is placed on the present, the moral life of the believer or the sacramental life of the Church. Theodoret's more guarded Christological language and his tendency to make the Word the initiator of the saving actions gives a different slant to his exegesis of key Pauline texts. Theodoret is briefer

---

356 Is Theodoret's acceptance of types and images to be associated with a knowledge of Syriac traditions? Cf. Chapter 5, Section I on Ephrem.

and less heavily theological than Theodore, indeed, 'paradoxically Theodoret is probably closer to Theodore in content and to John (Chrysostom) in spirit'.[357] Practical issues submerge vague eschatological tensions. Like Chrysostom, Theodoret identified himself with the 'mainstream' Church which had to find a practical mode of life and faith in the fifth-century world. It is ironic that one so solidly orthodox in intention should have had such a stormy career.

6 Other works

One of the last things Theodoret did was to compile an encyclopaedia of heresies: the *Compendium Haereticorum Fabularum* or *Epitome of Heretical Myths*.[358] Theodoret had to prove himself in yet another field of ecclesiastical literature. The strange thing is that he does not seem to have used the work of Epiphanius – he mentions those he has consulted, including Justin, Irenaeus, Clement, Origen, Eusebius, Diodore and various others, but not Epiphanius. In contrast to Epiphanius, Theodoret attempted a logical rather than genealogical arrangement. His first book covers those who make another Creator and hold a docetic view of Christ: this covers all the Gnostic movements from Simon Magus to Mani. The second book deals with the opposite type – those who acknowledge one God but treat Christ as a mere man: among these Theodoret includes Ebion, Theodotus, Paul of Samosata, Sabellius and Marcellus. Book III takes in various other heresies which fall between the two extremes – the Montanists, Novatians, Quartodecimans and others who in many ways were very close to the orthodox. New heresies, by which is meant the post-Nicene crop of deviations, fill the fourth book: Arius, Eunomius, Apollinarius and others are accompanied by the Donatists and Meletians. In this book there appears a section on Eutyches, and more surprisingly, one on Nestorius. Probably the idea that this was an interpolation has to be rejected; Theodoret was writing after Chalcedon and might have feared reprisals if Nestorius had been conspicuous by his absence. The fifth book is almost a Theodoretan *De principiis*, giving an account of orthodox teaching, beginning at the ἀρχή (*archē*) – the first principle – and passing through the doctrine of God, creation, angels, demons, men, providence, the Saviour's οἰκονομία, Christological questions, baptism, judgment, the End and various ethical matters.

In his self-justificatory letters, Theodoret gives three slightly different lists of his earlier writings,[359] specifying that they were written some twenty years, others eighteen, fifteen or twelve years previously. His purpose was to show that he had always been orthodox, but these references are useful because many of the works can be identified with surviving treatises and so some approximation can be made of the date of each writing.[360] A little conflation of the lists indicates the range of his literary achievement: he had written against

---

357 Parvis (1975), p. 204.

358 Selections are translated in Pásztori-Kupán (2006).

359 *Epp.* 82, 113, 116.

360 There has been considerable discussion as to how rigidly these indications of date can be interpreted, and what precisely they indicate in terms of the relative dating of Theodoret's works; see Richard (1935/77); Canivet (1958); and articles in Patrologies and

heretics – Arius, Eunomius, Apollinarius, Marcion and others; against Jews and Gentiles and the Persian Magi; on providence, theology and the incarnation; a mystical book and the lives of saints; commentaries on the prophets and the apostle Paul. We know that he also wrote an *Ecclesiastical History* and at a later date his encyclopaedia of heresies and the *Quaestiones* on the Old Testament historical books – not to mention his letters and various controversial tracts. It is an impressive range, and it would not be surprising if he had produced a whole lot of imitative materials.

This was once the standard estimate of Theodoret's achievement – a mere imitator and epitomizer, drawing upon the previous work of historians, apologists and exegetes. The interesting thing about recent work is that over and over again a closer look at Theodoret's work has shown that he did make an original contribution to each of the tasks he undertook, that he did not merely copy slavishly but undertook independent researches, adapted the material to his own ends, modified what he had inherited and gave everything a shape and a clarity which increased its appeal to his readership.

Of course, Theodoret had no ambition to be original. All he wanted to do was to preserve the tradition of the scriptures and the Fathers who interpreted them. But he seems to have realized that mere repetition was no way to fulfil that function, that there was a proper place for enquiry, for restatement, for reformulation, as new problems and circumstances arose. Each generation in promulgating the orthodox teaching of the Church faced the task of assimilating the tradition and giving it application in its own situation. Theodoret was loyal to his friends, but he retreated from the extremes of Antiochene theology and exegesis in the interest of preserving the integrity and unity of the Christian tradition. His rather belligerent orthodoxy in the *Ecclesiastical History*, his unhappy role in the doctrinal controversies, should not be allowed to obscure his fundamentally Christian personality; ascetic and pastor, he typified fifth-century tendencies, acted as a bridge between different cultural levels and between pagan and Christian society, and proved to be a literary churchman of remarkably wide-ranging interests and abilities.

For Further Reading

English translations

Ettlinger, G. H., 2003. *Theodoret: Eranistes, FC*, Washington, DC: Catholic University of America Press.

Hill, R. C., 2000, 2001. *Theodoret of Cyrus. Commentary on the Psalms*, 2 vols: Psalms 1–82, Psalms 73–150, FC, Washington, DC: Catholic University of America Press.

——, 2001a. *Theodoret of Cyrus. Commentary on the Song of Songs*, Brisbane: Centre for Early Christian Studies.

——, 2001b. *Theodoret of Cyrus. Commentary on the Letters of St Paul*, 2 vols, Brooklyne, NY: Holy Cross Orthodox Press.

Encyclopedias, for example, Bardy's article on Theodoret in the *Dictionnaire de Théologie Catholique*, and Chesnut (1981).

Pásztori-Kupán, István, 2006. *Theodoret of Cyrus*, London and New York: Routledge.
Petruccione, John F. and R. C. Hill, 2007. *Theodoret of Cyrus. The Questions on the Octateuch*, Greek text and ET, Washington, DC: Catholic University of America Press.

Studies

Ashby, G. W., 1972. *Theodoret of Cyrrhus as Exegete of the Old Testament*, Grahamstown: Rhodes University.
Brok, M. F. A., 1951. 'The Date of Theodoret's *Expositio Rectae Fidei'*, *JTS* NS 2, pp. 178–83.
Clayton, Paul B. Jr, 2007. *The Christology of Theodoret of Cyrus: Antiochene Christology from the Council of Ephesus (431) to the Council of Chalcedon (451)*, Oxford: Oxford University Press.
Greer, Rowan A., 1973. *The Captain of Our Salvation*, Tübingen: Mohr Siebeck.

Bibliography

The lists below provide full references for works cited in the footnotes, first primary sources (editions and translations) and then secondary material (studies by modern scholars). The material is subdivided to provide bibliographical guides to the individual authors or classes of material treated in the volume, and these are arranged alphabetically, as are the lists in each sub-section. Whatever does not fit into such categories, or is referred to in more than one section or chapter, is to be found in the opening Miscellaneous or General Section; in the case of the Studies section this is subdivided so as to group works on Christology together. This arrangement may occasionally make it less easy to check a particular reference, but should enable direct access to an introductory list of key material on a particular subject or figure. There is no attempt to provide comprehensive up-to-date bibliographies (as in the first edition), since there are now many other bibliographical aids available, such as *Bibliographia Patristica (Internationale Patristische Bibliographie)* (Berlin: Walter de Gruyter, 1959–), *Clavis Patrum Graecorum* (Turnhout: Brepols, 1974–) or the Internet.

Editions and Translations

Miscellaneous

Bindley, T. H. and F. W. Green, 1955. *The Oecumenical Documents of the Faith*, London: Methuen.

Festugière, A.-J., 1982. *Ephèse et Chalcédoine: Actes des Conciles*, Paris: Beauchesne.

——, 1983. *Actes du concile de Chalcédoine: Sessions III–VI*, Geneva: Patrick Cramer Éditeur.

Froehlich, K., 1984. *Biblical Interpretation in the Early Church*, Sources of Early Christian Thought, Philadelphia: Fortress Press.

Musurillo, H. A., 1972. *Acts of the Christian Martyrs*, Oxford Early Christian Texts, Oxford: Oxford University Press.

Norris, Richard A., Jr, 1980. *The Christological Controversy*, Sources of Early Christian Thought, Philadelphia: Fortress Press.

Price, Richard and Michael Gaddis, 2005. *The Acts of the Council of Chalcedon: vols I–III*, Liverpool: Liverpool University Press.

Russell, N., 2007. *Theophilus of Alexandria*, London: Routledge.

Schwartz, E., 1927–. *Acta Conciliorum Oecumenicorum*, Berlin/Leipzig: de Gruyter.

Staab, K., 1933/84. *Pauluskommentare aus der griechischen Kirche*, Münster: Aschendorf.

Stevenson, K., 1966. *Creeds, Councils and Controversies*, London and New York: SPCK.
Vaggione, Richard P., 1987. *Eunomius: The Extant Works*, Oxford: Clarendon Press.

Apollinarius of Laodicea

Migne, *PG* 33.
Lietzmann, H., 1904. *Apollinaris und seine Schüle*, Tübingen: Mohr.
Ludwich, A., 1912. *Apollinaris: Metaphrasis in Psalmos*, Leipzig: Teubner.
Mühlenberg, E., 1975. *Psalmenkommentare aus der Katenenüberlieferung*, vol. I, Apollinarius and Didymus, Berlin: de Gruyter.

Apophthegmata Patrum

Migne, *PG* 65.
Draguet, R., 1968. *Les cinq recensions de l'Ascéticon syriaque d'abba Isaie*, CSCO 294 (Scriptores Syriaci 123), Louvain: Sécretariat du CSCO.
——, 1970. *Abbé Isaïe: Recueil ascétique*, Introduction et traduction française par les moines des Solesmes, Begrolles: Abbaye de Bellefontaine.
Guy, J.-C. (ed.), 1968. *Les apophtegmes des pères du désert (série alphabétique)*, Étoilles (Essonne): Les Dominos.
—— (ed.), 1993. *Les Apophtegmes de Pères: collection systematique, books 1–9*, SC 387, Paris: Éditions de Cerf.
Nau F., 1907–9, 1912–13. *Codex Coislinianus*, published in instalments in the *Revue de l'Orient Chrétien* 12–14 and 17–18.
Regnault, L., 1981. *Les sentences des Pères du désert: collection alphabétique*, Sarthe: Éditions de Solesmes.
——, 1985. *Les Sentences des Pères du désert: Série des anonymes*, Solesmes: Éditions de Solesmes.
——, 1992. *Les chemins de Dieu au désert: collection systematique des Apophtegmes de Pères*, Solesmes: Éditions de Solesmes.
—— (introd.), J. Dion and G. Oury, and the monks of Solesmes (trans.), 1966, 1970, 1976. *Les sentences des pères du désert* I (Pélage et Jean), II & III (Coislin. 126 and Greek, Syriac, Coptic, etc.), Sarthe: Éditions de Solesmes.
Waddell, Helen, 1936. *The Desert Fathers*, London and New York: Burns, Oates & Washbourne.
Ward, Benedicta, 1975a. *The Sayings of the Desert Fathers*, London: Mowbrays.
——, 1975b. *The Wisdom of the Desert Fathers*, Oxford: SLG Press.

Athanasius

Migne, *PG* 25–28. ET in *NPNF* II.4.
Anatolios, K., 2004. *Athanasius*, London: Routledge.
Bartelink, G. J. M., 1994. *Vie d'Antoine. Athanase d'Alexandrie*, Introduction, texte critique, traduction, notes, SC 400, Paris: Les Éditions du Cerf.
Brennecke, H. C., U. Heil, A. von Stockhausen and A. Wintjes, 2007. *Athanasius Werke, 3.1, Dokumente zur Geschichte des arianischen Streites, 3 Lieferung*, Berlin and New York: de Gruyter.
Bright, W., 1884. *Orationes Contra Arianos I–III*, Oxford: Clarendon Press.

Camelot, P. T., 1977. *Athanase d'Alexandrie, Contre les Paiens,* texte grec, introduction et notes, *SC* 18, Paris: Les Éditions du Cerf.

Cureton, W., 1848. *The Festal Letters of Athanasius* (Syriac text), Society for the Publication of Oriental Texts, London: Madden & Co.

Draguet, René, 1980. *La Vie primitive de Saint Antoine conservée en syriaque, CSCO* 417–18, Louvain: Sécretariat du CSCO.

Gregg, Robert C., 1980. *Athanasius: Life of Antony and Letter to Marcellinus,* ET and introduction, New York: Paulist Press.

Heil, Uta, 1999. *Athanasius von Alexandrien de Sententia Dionysii,* Einleitung, Übersetzung und Kommentar, Berlin and New York: de Gruyter.

Kannengiesser, C., 1973/2000. *S. Athanase. Sur l'incarnation du Verbe,* Introduction, texte critique, traduction, notes, *SC* 199, Paris: Les Éditions du Cerf.

Lebon, J. S., 1947. *S. Athanase. Lettres à Serapion, SC* 15, Paris: Les Éditions du Cerf.

Lefort, L.-Th., 1955. *S. Athanase. Lettres festales et pastorals en copte,* with French translation, Louvain: L. Durbecq.

Martin, A., with M. Albert, 1985. *Histoire 'acephale' et Index syriaque des Lettres festales d'Athanase d'Alexandrie, SC* 317, Paris: Les Éditions du Cerf.

Meijering, E. P., 1984. *Athanasius. Contra Gentes,* introduction, translation and commentary, Leiden: Brill.

——, with J. C. M. van Winden, 1989. *Athanasius. De Incarnatione Verbi,* Einleitung, Übersetzung, Kommentar, Amsterdam: Gieben.

Meyer, Robert T., 1950. *Athanasius. Life of Antony,* ET, Westminster, MD: Newman Press.

Opitz, H. G., 1934. *Urkunden zur Geschichte des arianischen Streites, Athanasius Werke,* vol. III.l, Berlin: de Gruyter.

——, 1935a. *Die Apologien, Athanasius Werke,* vol. II.l, Berlin: de Gruyter.

Shapland, C. R. B., 1951. *The Letters of St. Athanasius concerning the Holy Spirit,* London: Epworth.

Szymusiak, Jan M., 1958/87. *Athanase d'Alexandrie. Deux Apologies à l'empereur Constance et pour sa fuite,* introduction, texte critique et notes, *SC* 56, Paris: Les Éditions du Cerf.

Tetz, M., 1996, 1998, 2000. *Athanasius Werke, Band I. Die dogmatischen Schriften,* 3 vols, Berlin: de Gruyter.

Thomson, Robert W., 1971. *Athanasius. Contra Gentes–De Incarnatione,* text and ET, Oxford: Clarendon Press.

Basil of Caesarea

Migne, *PG* 29–32. ET in *NPNF* II.8.

Amand de Mendietta, D. and Stig Y. Rudberg, 1997. *Basilius von Caesarea. Homilien zur Hexaemeron, GCS,* Berlin: Akademie Verlag.

Anderson, David (trans.), 1980. *St Basil the Great: On the Holy Spirit,* Crestwood, NY: St Vladimir's Seminary Press.

Boulenger, F. (ed.), 1935. *Saint Basile: Aux Jeunes Gens,* Budé, Paris: Les Belles Lettres.

Clarke, W. K. L., 1925. *The Ascetic Works of St Basil,* London: SPCK.

Courtonne, Y. (ed.), 1935. *Homélies sur la richesse,* Paris: Firmin-Didot.

——, 1957, 1961, 1966. *Saint Basile: Lettres,* 3 vols, Budé, Paris: Les Belles Lettres.

Deferrari, R. (ed. with ET), 1926, 1928, 1930, 1934. *Basil, The Letters,* 4 vols, LCL, London: Heinemann / Cambridge, MA: Harvard University Press.

Giet, S., 1968. *Basile de Césarée. Homélies sur l'Hexaémeron, SC* 26, Paris: Les Éditions du Cerf.

Hauschild, Wolf-Dieter, 1973, 1990, 1992. *Briefe: Basilius von Caesarea,* 3 vols, Stuttgart: Anton Hiersemann.

Marti, Heinrich, 1989. *De ieiunio I, II: Zwei Predigten über des Fasten nach Basileios von Kaisareia und Rufin von Aquileia. Ausgabe mit Einleitung, Übersetzung und Anmerkungen,* Leiden: Brill.

Pruche, B., 1968. *Basile de Césarée. Traité du Saint-Esprit, SC* 17, Paris: Les Éditions du Cerf.

Risch, F. X., 1992. Pseudo-Basilius, *Adversus Eunomium IV–V. Einleitung, Übersetzung and Kommentar,* Leiden: Brill.

Rudberg, S. Y., 1962. *L'Homélie de Basile de Césarée sur le mot 'Observe-toi toi-même',* Stockholm: Almqvist & Wicksell.

Sesboüé, B., G.-M. de Durand and L. Doutreleau, 1982, 1983. *Basile de Césarée. Contre Eunome I & II, SC* 299 & 305, Paris: Les Éditions du Cerf.

Sieben, Herman Josef, 1993. *De Spiritu Sancto,* Freiburg im Breisgau: Herder.

Silvas, Anna M., 2005. *The Asketicon of St. Basil the Great,* Oxford: Oxford University Press.

Smets, Alexis and M. van Esbroek, 1970. *Basile de Césarée. Sur l'origine de l'homme: Homélies X et XI de l'Hexaémeron, SC* 160, Paris: Les Éditions du Cerf.

Wagner, M. M., 1950. *Saint Basil. Ascetical Works, FC,* Washington, DC: Catholic University of America Press.

Way, Sister Agnes Clare, 1951, 1955. *Saint Basil. Letters,* 2 vols, FC, Washington, DC: Catholic University of America Press.

——, 1963. *Saint Basil. Exegetic Homilies, FC,* Washington, DC: Catholic University of America Press.

Wilson, N. G., 1975. *Saint Basil on the Value of Greek Literature,* London: Duckworth.

Cyril of Alexandria

Migne, *PG* 68–77.

Burguière, P. and P. Evieux, 1985. *Cyrille d'Alexandrie: Contre Julien,* vol. 1, SC 322, Paris: Les Éditions du Cerf.

Burns, W. H. et al., 1991, 1993, 1998. *Lettres festales* (I–VI), (VII–XI), (XII–XVII), SC 372, 392 & 434, Paris: Les Éditions du Cerf.

Chabot, J. B., 1912. *S. Cyrilli Alexandrini commentarii in Lucam I, CSCO,* reprinted with Latin trans. by R. M. Tonneau, 1953, 1954. 2 vols, Paris: E Typographeo Reipublicae.

Durand, G. M. de, 1964. *Cyrille d'Alexandrie. Deux dialogues christologiques, SC* 97, Paris: Les Éditions du Cerf.

——, 1976, 1977, 1978. *Cyrille d'Alexandrie. Dialogues sur la Trinité, SC* 231, 237 & 246, Paris: Les Éditions du Cerf.

Hill, R. C., 2007, 2008. *St. Cyril of Alexandria. Commentary on the 12 Prophets,* 2 vols, FC, Washington, DC: Catholic University of America Press.

McEnerney, J. I., 1987. *St Cyril of Alexandria: Letters 1–50, FC,* Washington, DC: Catholic University of America Press.

——, 1987. *St Cyril of Alexandria: Letters 51–110, FC,* Washington, DC: Catholic University of America Press.

McGuckin, J. A., 1994. *Cyril of Alexandria: The Christological Controversy: Its History,*

Theology and Texts, Leiden: Brill / republished Crestwood, NY: St Vladimir's Seminary Press.

——, 1995. *St. Cyril of Alexandria: On the Unity of Christ*, Crestwood, NY: St Vladimir's Seminary Press.

Payne Smith, R., 1858. *S. Cyrilli Alexandriae archiepiscopi Commentarii in Lucae evangelium quae supersunt syriace e manuscriptis apud Museum Britannicum*, Oxford: Clarendon Press.

——, 1859. *A Commentary upon the Gospel according to St Luke by St Cyril, Patriarch of Alexandria*, 2 vols, Oxford: Oxford University Press (reprinted in one vol. New York: Studion, 1983).

Pusey, P. E., 1868. *S. Cyrilli Archiepiscopi Alexandrini in XII Prophetas*, 2 vols, Oxford: Clarendon Press.

——, 1872a. *S. Cyrilli Archiep. Alex. in S. Ioannis Evangelium*, 3 vols, Oxford: Clarendon Press.

——, 1872b. *The Three Epistles of St Cyril*, LFC, Oxford: James Parker.

——, 1874. *Commentary on the Gospel according to St John by S. Cyril Archbishop of Alexandria*, vol. 1, LFC, Oxford: James Parker.

——, 1875. *S. Cyrilli Alexandrini epistolae tres oecumenicae, Libri V contra Nestorium, XII Capitum Explanatio, XII Capitum Defensio utraque, Scholia de Incarnatione Unigeniti*, Oxford: James Parker.

——, 1877. *S. Cyrilli Alexandrini De Recta Fide ad Imperatorem, De Incarnatione Unigeniti Dialogus, De Recta Fide ad Principissas, De Recta Fide ad Augustas, Quod unus sit Christus Dialogus, Apologeticus ad Imperatorem*, Oxford: James Parker.

——, 1881. *S. Cyril Archbishop of Alexandria: Five Tomes against Nestorius, Scholia on the Incarnation, Christ is One, and Fragments against Diodore of Tarsus, Theodore of Mopsuestia, and the Synousiasts*, LFC, Oxford: James Parker.

——, 1885. *Commentary on the Gospel according to St John by S. Cyril Archbishop of Alexandria*, vol. 2, ET by T. Randell, LFC, London: James Parker.

Russell, N., 2000. *Cyril of Alexandria*, London and New York: Routledge.

Wickham, L. R., 1983. *Cyril of Alexandria: Select Letters*, ed. and ET, Oxford: Clarendon.

Cyril of Jerusalem

Migne, *PG* 33. ET in *NPNF* II.7.

Bihain, E., 1973. 'L'épitre de Cyrille de Jérusalem à Constantine sur la vision de la croix (BHG3 413)', *Byzantion* 43, pp. 264–96.

Cross F. L., 1951. *St Cyril of Jerusalem's Lectures on the Christian Sacraments* (Texts for Students), London: SPCK.

McCauley, Leo P. and Anthony A. Stephenson, 1969, 1970. *The Works of Cyril of Jerusalem*, FC 61, 64, Washington, DC: Catholic University of America Press.

Piédagnel, A., 1966. *Cyrille de Jérusalem: Catéchèses mystagogiques*, trans. P. Paris, SC 126, Paris: Les Éditions du Cerf.

Reischl, W. K. and J. Rupp, 1848, 1860. *S. Cyrilli: Opera quae supersunt omnia*, 2 vols, Munich: Sumptibus Librariae Lentnerianae; reissued Hildesheim: Georg Olms, 1967.

Telfer, W., 1955. *Cyril of Jerusalem and Nemesius of Emesa*, introduction and translation of selections (Library of Christian Classics IV), London and Philadelphia: SCM Press.

Yarnold, E., SJ, 2000. *Cyril of Jerusalem*, Introduction and ET of selections, London and New York: Routledge.

Didymus the Blind

Migne, *PG* 39.

Binder, G., L. Liesenborghs, J. Kramer, B, Krebber and M. Gronewald (eds), 1969–83. *Didymos der Blinden. Kommentar zum Ecclesiastes*, 6 vols, Pap. Texte und Abhandlung 9, 13, 16, 22, 24–6, Bonn: Rudolf Habelt Verlag.

Doutreleau, Louis (ed.), 1962. *Didyme l'Aveugle. Sur Zacharie*, 3 vols, SC 83–5, Paris: Les Éditions du Cerf.

—— (ed.), 1992. *Didyme l'Aveugle: Traité du Saint-Ésprit*, SC 386, Paris: Les Éditions du Cerf.

——, A. Gesché and M. Gronewald (eds), 1968–70. *Didymos der Blinden. Psalmenkommentar*, 5 vols, Pap. Texte und Abhandlungen 4, 6–8, 12, Bonn: Rudolf Habelt Verlag.

Hadegorn, Ursula and Dieter Hadegorn, 1994–2000. *Die älteren grieschichen Katenen zum Buch Hiob*, Vol. 1, Patristische Texte und Studien 40, 48, 53. Berlin: de Gruyter.

Henrichs, A., U. and D. Hadegorn and L. Koenen (eds), 1968–85, *Didymos der Blinden. Kommentar zu Hiob*, 4 vols, Pap. Texte und Abhandlungen 1–3, 33.1, Bonn: Rudolf Habelt Verlag.

Hill, R. C. (trans.), 2006. *Didymus. Commentary on Zechariah*, FC, Washington, DC: Catholic University of America Press.

Hönscheid, J, (ed.), 1975. *De Trinitate I von Didymus der Blinde*, Hrsg. und übersetzt, Meisenheim: Verlag Anton Hain.

Mühlenberg, Ekkehard, 1975–8. *Psalmenkommentare aus der Katenenüberlieferung*, 3 vols, Berlin: de Gruyter.

Nautin, P. and L. Doutreleau, 1976, 1978. *Didyme l'Aveugle. Sur la Genèse*, SC 233 & 244, Paris: Les Éditions du Cerf.

Petit, François, 1986. *Catenae Graecae in Genesim et in Exodum. Vol 2: Collectio Coisliniana in Genesim*, CCG, 15. Turnhout: Brepols.

Petit, François, 1992–1995. *La chaîn sur Genèse: édition integral*. 3 vols, Traditio Exegetica Graeca 1–3. Leuven: Peeters.

Risch, F. X., 1999. Pseudo-Basilius, *Adversus Eunomium IV–V. Einleitung, Übersetzung und Kommentar*, Leiden: Brill.

Seiler, I (ed.), 1975. *De Trinitate II.1–7 von Didymus der Blinde*, Hrsg. und übersetzt, Meisenheim: Verlag Anton Hain.

Diodore of Tarsus

Migne, *PG* 33.

Abramowski, R., 1949. 'Der Theologische Nachlass des Diodor von Tarsus', *ZNW* 42, 1949, pp. 19–69.

Brière, M., 1946. 'Fragments syriaques de Diodore de Tarse réédités et traduits pour la première fois', *Revue de l'Orient Chrétien* 10, pp. 231–83.

Hill, Robert C., 2005. *Diodore of Tarsus. Commentary on Psalms 1–51*, Atlanta, GA: SBL.

Olivier, Jean-Marie, 1980. *Diodori Tarsensis commentarii in Psalmos I–L*, CCG, Turnhout: Brepols.

Ephrem Syrus

Brock, Sebastian, 1990. *Saint Ephrem: Hymns on Paradise*, Crestwood, NY: St Vladimir's Seminary Press.
—— and George A. Kiraz, 2006. *Ephrem the Syrian: Select Poems*, Text and ET: Provo, UT: Brigham Young University Press.
Matthews, Edward G. and Joseph P. Amar, ed. Kathleen McVey, 1994. *St Ephrem the Syrian: Selected Prose Works*, FC 91, Washington, DC: Catholic University of America Press.
McCarthy, Carmel, 1993. *Saint Ephrem's Commentary on Tatian's Diatesseron, Journal of Semitic Studies*, Supplement 2, Oxford: Oxford University Press.
McVey, Kathleen, 1989. *Ephrem the Syrian: Hymns, Classics of Western Spirituality*, New York: Paulist Press.

Epiphanius of Salamis

Migne, *PG* 41–3.
Amidon, Philip R., 1990. *The Panarion of St. Epiphanius. Selected Passages*, New York/ Oxford: Oxford University Press.
Blake, R. P. and H. de Vis, 1934. *Epiphanius, De Gemmis*, eds and trs (Studies and Documents 2), London: Christophers.
Dean, J. E., 1935. *Epiphanius' Treatise on Weights and Measures*, ed. and ET, Chicago, IL: University of Chicago Press.
Holl, K., 1915. *Ancoratus. Panarion 1–33, GCS*, Leipzig: Hinrichs.
——, rev. ed. J. Dummer, 1980. *Panarion 34–64, GCS*, Berlin: Akademie Verlag.
——, rev. ed. J. Dummer, 1985. *Panarion 65–80, De Fide, GCS*, Berlin: Akademie Verlag.
Stone, Michael E. and Roberta Ervine, 2000. *The Armenian Texts of Epiphanius of Salamis, De Mensuris et ponderibus*, Leuven: Peeters.
Williams, Frank, 1987/94. *The Panarion of Epiphanius of Salamis*, 2 vols, Leiden: Brill.

Eusebius of Caesarea

Migne, *PG* 19–24. ET in *NPNF* II.1.
Amacker, R. and E. Junod, 2002. *Apologie pour Origène/Pamphile et Eusèbe de Césarée*, SC 464, Paris: Les Éditions du Cerf.
Bardy, G. (ed.), 1952–60. *Eusèbe de Césarée. Histoire Ecclésiastique*, SC 31, 41, 55 & 73, Paris: Les Éditions du Cerf.
Cameron, A. and Stuart G. Hall, 1999. *Eusebius. The Life of Constantine* (introd., trans. and commentary), Oxford: Clarendon Press.
Conybeare, F. C., 1921. *Philostratus, the Life of Apollonius of Tyana, the Epistles of Apollonius, and the Treatise of Eusebius*, 2 vols, LCL, London: Heinemann.
Drake, H. A., 1976. *In Praise of Constantine: a Historical Study and New Translation of Eusebius' Tricennial Orations*, Berkeley: University of California Press.
Ferrar, W. J., 1920. *The Proof of the Gospel (Demonstratio Evangelica)*, 2 vols, London: SPCK.
Forrat, M., with E. des Places (eds), 1986. *Eusèbe de Césarée. Contre Hiéroclès, SC 333*, Paris: Les Éditions du Cerf.

Freeman-Grenville, G. S. P., Joan E. Taylor and R. L. Chapman III, 2003. *The Onomasticon by Eusebius of Caesarea—Palestine in the Fourth Century*, Jerusalem: Carta.

Gifford, E. H., 1903. *Eusebii Pamphili Evangelicae Praeparationis Libri XV*, Oxford: Oxford University Press.

Gressmann, H. (ed.), 1904. *Die Theophanie: die griechischen Bruchstücke und Übersetzung der syrischen Überlieferung. Eusebius Werke III*, GCS (2nd edn A. Laminski, 1992), Berlin: Akademie Verlag.

Helm, R. (ed.), 1913. *Die Chronik des Hieronymus. Eusebius Werke VII*, GCS (3rd edn U. Treu, 1984), Leipzig: Hinrichs.

Heikel, I. (ed.), 1913. *Die Demonstratio evangelica. Eusebius Werke VII*, GCS, Leipzig: Hinrichs.

Karst, J., 1911. *Die Chronik des Eusebius aus dem armenischen übersetzt. Eusebius Werke V*, GCS, Leipzig: Hinrichs.

Klostermann, E., 1904. *Das Onomastikon der biblischen Ortsnamen, Eusebius Werke III*, GCS, Leipzig: J. C. Hinrichs.

——, (ed.), 1906. *Gegen Marcell, über die kirchliche Theologie, die Fragmente Marcells. Eusebius Werke IV*, GCS (3rd edn G. C. Hansen, 1991), Berlin: Akademie Verlag.

Lawlor, H. J. and J. E. L. Oulton, 1927. *Eusebius, Bishop of Caesarea, The Ecclesiastical History and the Martyrs of Palestine*, ET and notes, 2 vols, London: SPCK.

Lee, S., 1843. *Eusebius. On the Theophaneia*, Cambridge: Cambridge University Press.

Mras, K. (ed.), 1982–3. *Die Praeparatio evangelica. Eusebius Werke VIII*, GCS (2nd edn E. des Places), Berlin: Akademie Verlag.

Notley, R. S. and Z. Safrai, 2005. *Eusebius*, Onomasticon. *The Place-Names of Divine Scripture. A Triglott edition with Notes and Commentary*, Leiden: Brill.

Places, E. des, et al. (eds), 1974–91. *Eusèbe de Césarée, la Préparation Évangélique*, SC 206, 228, 262, 266, 215,369, 292, 307 & 338, Paris: Les Éditions du Cerf.

Schwartz, E. (ed.), 1903–9. *Die Kirchengeschichte. Eusebius Werke II*, GCS, 3 vols, Leipzig: Hinrichs.

Stevenson, J., 1957. *A New Eusebius*, London: SPCK.

Williamson, G. A., 1965/89. *Eusebius. The History of the Church from Christ to Constantine*, rev. edn A. Louth, Harmondsworth and Baltimore: Penguin Books.

Winkelmann, F. (ed.), 1975. *Über das Leben des Kaisers Konstantin. Eusebius Werke I*, GCS (2nd edn 1991), Berlin: Akademie Verlag.

Ziegler, J. (ed.), 1975. *Der Jesajakommentar. Eusebius Werke IX*, GCS, Berlin: Akademie Verlag.

Eustathius of Antioch

Migne, *PG* 18.

Declerck, J. H., 2002. *Eustathii Antiocheni, Opera quae supersunt omnia*, CC Series Graeca 51, Turnhout: Brepols.

Greer, Rowan A. and Margaret M. Mitchell, 2007. *The 'Belly-Myther' of Endor. Interpretations of 1 Kings 28 in the Early Church*, Atlanta, GA: SBL.

Spanneut, M., 1948. *Recherches sur les écrits d'Eustathe d'Antioche avec une édition nouvelle des fragments dogmatiques et exégétiques*, Lille: Facultés catholiques.

Evagrius Ponticus

Migne, *PG* 40.

Casiday, A. M., 2006. *Evagrius Ponticus*, The Early Christian Fathers, London and New York: Routledge.

Driscoll, Jeremy, OSB, 2003. *Evagrius Ponticus: Ad Monachos*, Translation and Commentary, Ancient Christian Writers 59, New York: Newman Press.

Géhin, Paul, 1987. *Évagre le pontique: Scholies aux Proverbes*, SC 340, Paris: Les Éditions du Cerf.

—— (ed.), 1993. *Évagre le pontique: Scholies à l'Ecclésiaste*, SC 397, Paris: Les Éditions du Cerf.

Guillaumont, A., 1958. *Les six centuries des 'Kephalaia Gnostica' d'Évagre le Pontique*, *Patrologia Orientalis* 28.1, Paris: CNRS.

—— and C. Guillaumont, 1971, 1972. *Évagre le pontique: Traité pratique ou le moine* I & II, SC 170 & 171, Paris: Les Éditions du Cerf.

—— and C. Guillaumont, 1989. *Évagre le pontique: Le Gnostique*, SC 356, Paris: Les Éditions du Cerf.

Harmless, William and Raymond R. Fitzgerald, 2001. '"The Sapphire Light of the Mind": The *Skemmata* of Evagrius Ponticus', *Theological Studies* 62, pp. 498–529.

Hausherr, I., 1959, 1960. 'Le *Traité de l'Oraison* d'Évagre le Pontique: Introduction, authenticité, traduction française et commentaire', *Revue d'Ascétique et de Mystique* 137, pp. 3–26; 138, pp. 121–46; 139, pp. 241–65; 140, pp. 361–85; 141, pp. 3–35; 142, pp. 137–87.

Muyldermans, J., 1931. 'Evagriana', *Le Muséon* 44, pp. 37–68.

Sinkewicz, Robert E., 2003. *Evagrius of Pontus. The Greek Ascetic Corpus*, Oxford Early Christian Studies, Oxford: Oxford University Press.

Gregory of Nazianzus

Migne, *PG* 37–8. ET in *NPNF* II.7.

Bernardi, J., 1978. *Saint Grégoire de Nazianze. Discours 1–3*, SC 247, Paris: Les Éditions du Cerf.

——, 1983. *Saint Grégoire de Nazianze. Discours 4–5, Contre Julien*, SC 309, Paris: Les Éditions du Cerf.

——, 1992. *Saint Grégoire de Nazianze. Discours 42–3*, SC 384, Paris: Les Éditions du Cerf.

Calvet-Sebasti, M., 1995. *Saint Grégoire de Nazianze. Discours 6–12*, SC 405, Paris: Les Éditions du Cerf.

Daley, Brian E., 2006. *Gregory of Nazianzus*, London and New York: Routledge.

Gallay, P., 1964, 1967. *Saint Grégoire de Nazianze. Lettres*, 2 vols, Budé, Paris: Les Belles Lettres.

——, 1969. *Gregor von Nazianzus. Briefe*, GCS, Leipzig and Berlin: Akademie-Verlag.

—— and M. Jourjon, 1974. *Saint Grégoire de Nazianze. Lettres théologiques*, SC 208, Paris: les Éditions du Cerf.

—— and M. Jourjon, 1978. *Saint Grégoire de Nazianze. Discours théologiques (27–31)*, SC 250, Paris: les Éditions du Cerf.

Gilbert, Peter, 2001. *On God and Man: The Theological Poetry of St. Gregory of Nazianzus*, Crestwood, NY: St Vladimir's Seminary Press.

Jungck, Christoph (ed.), 1974. *Gregor von Nazianz. De Vita Sua*, Heidelberg: Carl Winter Universitätsverlag.

Mason, A. J. (ed.), 1899. *The Five Theological Orations of Gregory of Nazianzus*, Cambridge Patristic Texts 1, Cambridge: Cambridge University Press.

McCauley, Leo P. et al., 1953. *Funeral Orations of St. Gregory Nazianzen and St. Ambrose*, FC 22, New York: Fathers of the Church.

McGuckin, J. A., 1986/9. *St Gregory Nazianzen: Selected Poems*, Oxford: SLG Press.

Meehan, D., 1987. *St Gregory of Nazianzus. Three Poems*, FC 75, Washington, DC: Catholic University of America Press.

Meier, Benno, 1989. *Gregor von Nazianz. Über die Bischöfe* (Carmen 2, 1, 12), Paderborn: Schöningh.

Moreschini, C., 1985. *Discours 32–37*, SC 318, Paris: Les Éditions du Cerf.

——, 1990. *Discours 38–41*, SC 358, Paris: Les Éditions du Cerf.

—— (ed.) and D. A. Sykes (ET and Commentary), 1997. *Gregory of Nazianzus: Poemata Arcana*, Oxford: Clarendon Press.

Mossay, J. and Guy Lafontaine, 1980. *Discours 20–23*, SC 270, Paris: Les Éditions du Cerf.

—— and Guy Lafontaine, 1981. *Discours 24–26*, SC 284, Paris: Les Éditions du Cerf.

Norris, F. W., with F. Williams and L. Wickham, 1991. *Faith Gives Fullness to Reasoning: The Five Theological Orations of St. Gregory Nazianzen*, Supplement to *VigChr* 13, Leiden: Brill.

Palle, Roberto, 1985. *Gregor von Nazianz: Carmina de virtute 1a/1b*, Graz: Institut für ökumenische Theologie und Patrologie de Universität Graz.

Simelidis, Christos, 2006. 'Selected Poems of Gregory of Nazianzus', critical edn with introduction and commentary, Oxford University DPhil thesis.

Tuilier, A. and G. Bady (ed.), with T. Bernardi (trans. and notes), 2004. *Saint Grégoire de Nazianze. Œuvres poétiques: I. Poèmes personnels*, Paris: Les Belles Lettres.

Vinson, Martha, 2003. *Gregory Nazianzen. Select Orations*, FC, Washington, DC: Catholic University of America Press.

Werhahn, H. M., 1953. *Gregorii Nazianzeni: 'Synkrisis Bion'*, Wiesbaden: Harrassowitz.

White, C., 1996. *Gregory of Nazianzus: Autobiographical Poems*, Cambridge Medieval Classics, Cambridge: Cambridge University Press.

Gregory of Nyssa

Migne, *PG* 44–6. ET in *NPNF* II.5.

Callahan, V. Woods, 1967. *Gregory of Nyssa. Ascetical Works*, FC 58, Washington, DC: Catholic University of America Press.

Drobner, H. R. and A. Viciano (eds), 2000. *Gregory of Nyssa. Homilies on the Beatitudes*, Leiden: Brill.

Ferguson, E. and A. Malherbe, 1978. *The Life of Moses*, Classics of Western Spirituality, New York: Paulist Press.

Graef, Hilda, 1954. *The Lord's Prayer. The Beatitudes*, Ancient Christian Writers 18, New York: Newman Press.

Hall, S. G. (ed.), 1993. *Gregory of Nyssa. Homilies on Ecclesiastes*, Proceedings of the Seventh International Colloquium on Gregory of Nyssa, 1990, Berlin and New York: de Gruyter.

Heine, R., 1995. *Gregory of Nyssa's Treatise on the 'Inscriptions on the Psalms'*, Oxford: Oxford University Press.

Jaeger, W. et al., 1960–. *Gregorii Nysseni Opera*, Leiden: Brill

——, Vols I and II: *Contra Eunomii Libri;*

——, Vol. III (in five parts): *Opera Dogmatica Minora;*

——, Vol. V: *In Inscriptiones Psalmorum. In Sextum Psalmum. In Ecclesiastes Homiliae;*

——, Vol. VI: *In Canticum Canticorum;*

——, Vol. VII (in two parts): *De Vita Moysis. De Oratione Dominica. De Beatitudinibus;*

——, Vol. VIII (in two parts): *Epistolae;*

——, Vols IX and X (in two parts): *Sermones.*

Karfikova, L., Scot Douglass and Johannes Zachhuber (eds), 2007. *Gregory of Nyssa: Contra Eunomium II. An English version with Supporting Studies*, Proceedings of the Tenth International Colloquium on Gregory of Nyssa, 2004, Supplements to *VigChr* 82, Leiden: Brill.

Mateo-Seco, L. F. and J. L. Bastero (eds), 1988. *El 'Contra Eunomium I' en la produccion literaria de Gregorio de Nisa*, Pamplona: Editiones Universidad de Navarra.

McCambley, Casimir, 1987. *St. Gregory of Nyssa: Commentary on the Song of Songs*, Brookline, MA: Hellenic College Press.

Meredith, Anthony, 1999. *Gregory of Nyssa*, London and New York: Routledge.

Musurillo, H. (ed. and trans.), 1961. *From Glory to Glory: Texts from Gregory of Nyssa's Mystical Writings*, New York: Scribner.

Peroli, E., 1997. 'Gregory of Nyssa and the Neoplatonic Doctrine of the Soul', *VigChr* 51(2), pp. 117–39.

Roth, Catherine, 1993. *On the Soul and the Resurrection*, Crestwood, NY: St Vladimir's Seminary Press.

Silvas, Anna M., 2007. *Gregory of Nyssa: The Letters. Introduction, Translation and Commentary*, Leiden: Brill.

——, 2008. *Macrina the Younger, philosopher of God*, Turnhout: Brepols.

Spira, Andreas and Christoph Klock (eds), 1981. *The Easter Sermons of Gregory of Nyssa*, Translation and Commentary, Proceedings of the Fourth International Colloquium on Gregory of Nyssa, 1978, Cambridge, MA: Philadelphia Patristic Foundation.

Srawley, J. R., 1903. *The Catechetical Oration of Gregory of Nyssa*, Cambridge: Cambridge University Press.

——, 1917. *The Catechetical Oration of Gregory of Nyssa*, London: SPCK.

John Chrysostom

Migne, *PG* 47–64. ET in *NPNF* I.9–14.

Aubineau, M. and R. E. Carter, 1968, 1970. *Codices Chrysostomici Graeci I, II and III*, Paris: Éditions de CNRS.

Brändle, Rudolf and Verena Jegher-Bucher, 1995. *Johannes Chrysostomos. Acht Reden gegen Juden*, Stuttgart: Anton Hiersemann.

Brottier, Laurence, 1989. *Jean Chrysostome, neuf sermons sur la Genèse*, Lille: A.N.R.T. Université de Lille III.

Christo, G. G., 1998. *St. John Chrysostom. On Repentance and Almsgiving, FC* 96, Washington, DC: Catholic University of America Press.

Dumortier, J., 1955. *Saint Jean Chrysostome. Les cohabitations suspects; Comment observer la virginité*, Budé, Paris: Les Belles Lettres.

——, 1966. *Jean Chrysostome. À Theodore, SC* 117, Paris: Les Éditions du Cerf.

——, 1981. *Jean Chrysostome. Homélies sur Ozias*, SC 277, Paris: Les Éditions du Cerf.

—— and Arthur Lifooghe, 1983. *Jean Chrysostome. Commentaire sur Isaïe*, SC 304, Paris: Les Éditions du Cerf.

Exarchos, B. K., 1954. *Johannes Chrysostomos über Hoffart und Kindererziehung*, Munich: Hüber.

Goggin, Sister T. A., 1957, 1960. *Saint John Chrysostom. Commentary on Saint John the Apostle and Evangelist*, FC 33 and 41, NY: Fathers of the Church.

Grillet, Bernard and G. H. Ettlinger, 1968. *Jean Chrysostome. À une jeune veuve*, SC 138, Paris: Les Éditions du Cerf.

Hagedorn, Ursula and Dieter, 1990. *Johannes Chrysostomos. Kommentar zu Hiob*, Berlin: de Gruyter.

Haidacher, S., 1907. *Des hl. Johannes Chrysostomos über Hoffart und Kindererziehung*, Freiburg: Herder.

Halton, Thomas, 1963. *In Praise of St. Paul by John Chrysostom*, Washington, DC: Catholic University of America Press.

Harkins, P. W., 1963. *John Chrysostom. Baptismal Instructions*, ET, Ancient Christian Writers 31, Westminster, MD: Newman Press.

——, 1979. *Saint John Chrysostom. Discourses against Judaizing Christians*, FC 68, Washington, DC: Catholic University of America Press.

——, 1984. *Saint John Chrysostom. On the Incomprehensible Nature of God*, FC 72, Washington, DC: Catholic University of America Press.

Hill, R. C., 1986, 1990, 1992. *St John Chrysostom. Homilies on Genesis 1–17, 18–45, 46–67*, FC 74, 82 & 87, Washington, DC: Catholic University of America Press.

——, 1998. *St. John Chrysostom. Commentary on the Psalms*, vol. 1, Brookline, MA: Holy Cross Orthodox Press.

Hunter, David G., 1988. *A Comparison between a King and a Monk / Against the Opponents of the Monastic Life. Two treatises by John Chrysostom*, Lewiston: Edwin Mellen.

Laistner, M. C. W., 1951. ET of *On Vainglory and the education of children* in *Christianity and Pagan Culture*, Ithaca, NY: Cornell University Press.

Malingrey, A. M., 1961. *Jean Chrysostome. Sur la providence de Dieu*, SC 79, Paris: Les Éditions du Cerf.

——, 1964. *Jean Chrysostome. Lettre d'exil à Olympias et tous les fidèles*, SC 103, Paris: Les Éditions du Cerf.

——, 1968. *Jean Chrysostome. Lettres à Olympias*, SC 13, Paris: Les Éditions du Cerf.

——, 1970. *Jean Chrysostome. Sur l'incomprehensibilité de Dieu*, SC 28; 2nd ed., Paris: Les Éditions du Cerf.

——, 1972. *Jean Chrysostome. Sur la vaine gloire et l'éducation des enfants*, SC 188, Paris: Les Éditions du Cerf.

——, 1980. *Jean Chrysostome. Sur la sacerdoce: dialogue et homélie*, SC 272, Paris: Les Éditions du Cerf.

——, 1994. *Jean Chrysostome. Sur l'égalité du Père et du Fils: contre les anoméens homélies vii–xii*, SC 396, Paris: Les Éditions du Cerf.

Mayer, W. and P. Allen, 2000. *John Chrysostom*, London and New York: Routledge.

Mayer, W. and N. Bronwen, 2006. *John Chrysostom. The Cult of the Saints: Select Homilies and Letters*, Crestwood, NY: St Vladimir's Seminary Press.

Musurillo, H. and B. Grillet (eds), 1966. *Jean Chrysostome, La Virginité*, SC 125, Paris: Les Éditions du Cerf.

Neville, G., 1964. *St. John Chrysostom. Six books on Priesthood*, London: SPCK; revised T. A. Moxon, Crestwood, NY: St Vladimir's Seminary Press.

Piédagnel, A., 1982. *Jean Chrysostome. Panégyriques de S. Paul*, SC 300, Paris: Les Éditions du Cerf.

—— and Louis Doutreleau, 1990. *Trois catéchèses baptimales*, SC 366, Paris: Les Éditions du Cerf.

Roth, Catharine P., 1999. *St. John Chrysostom. On Wealth and Poverty*, Crestwood, NY: St Vladimir's Seminary Press.

—— and David Anderson, 1997. *St. John Chrysostom. On Marriage and Family Life*, Crestwood, NY: St Vladimir's Seminary Press.

Schatkin, Margaret A. and P. W. Harkins, 1985. *St. John Chrysostom. Apologist*, including ET of the *Discourse on the Blessed Babylas and against the Greeks*, and the *Demonstration against the pagans that Christ is God*, FC 73, Washington, DC: Catholic University of America Press.

Schatkin, Margaret A. et al., 1990. *Jean Chrysostome. Discours sur Babylas, Homélie sur Babylas*, SC 362, Paris: Les Éditions du Cerf.

Schulte, F., 1914. *Johannes Chrysostomos, De inanani Gloria et de educandis liberis*, Progr. 627 Collegium Augustinianum Gaesdonck, Münster: Schöningh.

Shore, Sally Rieger, 1983. *John Chrysostom. On Virginity. Against Remarraige*, Lewiston, NY: Edwin Mellen.

Sorlin, Henri and Louis Neyrand, 1988. *Jean Chrysostome. Commentaire sur Job*, SC 346 & 348, Paris: Les Éditions du Cerf.

Wenger, A. (ed.), 1957. *Jean Chrysostome. Huit catéchèses baptismales inédites*, SC 50, Paris: Les Éditions du Cerf.

'Macarius'

Migne, *PG* 34.

Berthold, H. (ed.), 1973. *Makarios/Symeon: Reden und Briefe. Die Sammlung I des Vaticanus Graecus 694 (B)*, 2 vols, GCS, Berlin: Akademie Verlag.

Desprez, Vincent (ed.), 1980. *Pseudo-Macaire. Homélies propres à la collection III*, SC 275, Paris: Les Éditions du Cerf.

Dörries, Hermann, Erich Klostermann and Matthias Kroeger (eds), 1964. *Die 50 Geistlichen Homilien des Makarios*, PTS 4, Berlin: de Gruyter.

Klostermann, E. and H. Berthold (eds), 1961. *Neue Homilien des Makarios/Symeon aus Typus III*, TU 72, Berlin: Akademie-Verlag.

Maloney, G. A., SJ (trans.), 1992. *Pseudo-Macarius. The Fifty Spiritual Homilies and the Great Letter*, Classics of Western Spirituality Series, New York: Paulist Press.

Mason, A. J. (trans.), 1921. *Fifty Spiritual Homilies of St. Macarius the Egyptian*, London: SPCK.

Staats, R. (ed.), 1984. *Makarios-Symeon: Epistola Magna. Eine messalianische Mönchsregel und ihre Umschrift in Gregors von Nyssa 'De Instituto Christiano'*, Göttingen: Vandenhoeck and Ruprecht.

Marcellus of Ancyra

Vinzent, M., 1997. *Markell von Ankyra: Die Fragmente und der Brief an Julius von Rom*, Supplement to *VigChr* 39, Leiden: Brill.

Nemesius of Emesa

Migne, *PG* 40.
Edelstein, L. and I. G. Kidd (eds), 1972. *Posidonius*, Vol. I: The Fragments, Cambridge: Cambridge University Press.
Morani, M., 1987. *Nemesius. De Natura Hominis*, Leipzig: Teubner.
Telfer, W., 1955. *Cyril of Jerusalem and Nemesius of Emesa* (Library of Christian Classics, vol. IV), London: SCM Press.

Nestorius

Abramowski, L. and A. E. Goodman, 1972. *A Nestorian Collection of Christological Texts*, Cambridge and New York: Cambridge University Press.
Bedjan, P., 1910. *Le Livre d'Héraclide de Damas*, Syriac text, Paris: Letouzey et Ané.
Driver, G. R. and L. Hodgson, 1925. *Nestorius, The Bazaar of Heraclides*, ET, Oxford and New York: Clarendon Press.
Loofs, F., 1905. *Nestoriana*, Halle: Max Niemeyer.
Nau, F., 1910. *Le Livre d'Héraclide de Damas*, French, trans. with Introduction and notes, Paris: Letouzey et Ané.

Palladius, *Lausiac History* and *Historia monachorum*

Migne, *PG* 34 and 47.
Berghoff, W. (ed.), 1967. *Palladius. De gentibus Indiae et Bragmanibus*, Meisenheim am Glan: Verlag Anton Hain.
Butler, Cuthbert, 1904. *The Lausiac History of Palladius: A critical Discussion, together with notes on Early Monachism* in Texts and Studies 6, Cambridge: Cambridge University Press.
Coleman-Norton, P. R. (ed.), 1928. *Dialogus de vita S. Joannis Chrysostomi*, Cambridge: Cambridge University Press.
Derrett, J. D. (ed.), 1960. *The History of Palladius on the Races of India and the Brahmans* (Classica et Mediaevalia), Copenhagen: Gyldendal.
Festugière, A.-J., 1961/71. *Historia Monachorum in Aegypto*, édition critique du text grec, Brussels: Société des Bolandistes.
——, 1965. *Enquête sur les moines d'Egypte, Les Moines d'Orient*, vol. IV.1 (French trans. of *Historia Monachorum*), Paris: Les Éditions du Cerf.
Halkin, F., 1932. *S. Pachomii Vitae graecae* (Subsidia hagiographica 19), Bruxelles: Société des Bollandistes.
Malingrey, A. M. and Philippe Leclerq, 1988. *Palladius. Dialogue sur la vie de Jean Chrysostome*, SC 341, 342, Paris: Les Éditions du Cerf.
Meyer, R. T., 1965. *Palladius: The Lausiac History*, Ancient Christian Writers 34, New York: Newman Press.
Moore, Herbert, 1921. *The Dialogue of Palladius concerning the life of Chrysostom*, London: SPCK.
Nau, F., 1908. *Histoire de S. Pachome*, Patrologia Orientalis 4, pp. 425–503.
Preuschen, Erwin, 1897. *Palladius und Rufinus: ein Beitrag zur Quellenkunde des ältesten Mönchtums, Texte und Untersuchungen*. Giessen: J. Rickersche Buchhandlung.
Russell, Norman, 1981. *The Lives of the Desert Fathers: The 'Historia monachorum in Aegypto'*, CS 34, Kalamazoo, MI: Cistercian Publications.

Philostorgius

Migne, *PG* 65.
Bidez, J., 1972/81. *Kirchengeschichte mit dem Leben des Lucian von Antiochen und den Fragmenten eines arianischen Historiographen*, GCS, 2nd/3rd edn F. Winkelmann, Berlin: Akademie-Verlag.

Socrates Scholasticus

Migne, *PG* 67. ET in *NPNF* II.2.
Hansen, G. C., 1995. *Sokrates. Kirchengeschichte*, GCS, Berlin: Akademie-Verlag.
——, P. Périchon and P. Maraval, 2004, 2005, 2006, 2007. *Socrate de Constantinople. Histoire ecclésiastique*, SC 477, 493, 505 & 506, Paris: Les Éditions du Cerf.

Sozomen

Migne, *PG* 67. ET in *NPNF* II.2.
Bidez, J. and G. C. Hansen, 1960. *Sozomenus Kirchengeschichte*, GCS, 2nd ed., Berlin: Akademie Verlag.
Bidez, J., B. Grillet, Guy Sabbah and A.-J. Festugière, 1983, 1996. *Sozomène. Histoire ecclésiastique*, SC 306 & 418, Paris: Les Éditions du Cerf.

Synesius of Cyrene

Migne, *PG* 66.
Garzya, A. and D. Roques, 2000a. *Synésios de Cyrène II. Lettres I–LXIII*, Budé, Paris: Les Belles Lettres.
Garzya, A. and D. Roques, 2000b. *Synésios de Cyrène III. Lettres LXIV–CLVI*, Budé, Paris: Les Belles Lettres.
Fitzgerald, A., 1926. *Letters of Synesius*, Oxford and New York: Oxford University Press.
——, 1930. *Essays and Hymns of Synesius*, 2 vols, ET, Oxford and New York: Oxford University Press.
Lacombrade, C., 1951b. *Le Discours sur la Royauté de Synésios de Cyrène à l'empereur Arcadios*, Paris: Les Belles Lettres.
——, 1978. *Synésios de Cyrène I. Hymnes*, Synésios de Cyrène I, Budé, Paris: Les Belles Lettres.
Lamoureux, J. and N. Aujoulat, 2008. *Synésios de Cyrène IV. Opuscula*, Budé, Paris: Les Belles Lettres.
Hercher, R. (ed.), 1873. *Epistolographi Graeci* (includes Synesius' letters, pp. 638–739), Paris: Didot.
Terzaghi, N. (ed.), 1939. *Synesius Cyrenensis Hymni*, Rome: Typis Regiae Officinae Polygraphicae.
—— (ed.), 1944. *Synesius Cyrenensis Opuscula*, 2 vols, Rome: Typis Regiae Officinae Polygraphicae.

Theodore of Mopsuestia

Migne, *PG* 66.

Abramowski, L., 1958. 'Ein unbekanntes Zitat aus "Contra Eunomium" des Theodor von Mopsuestia', *Le Muséon* 71, pp. 97–104.

Devreesse, R., 1939. *Le Commentaire de Théodore de Mopsueste sur les Psaumes* (Studi e Testi 93), Rome: Vaticana.

——, 1948. *Essai sur Théodore de Mopsueste* (Studi e Testi 141), Rome: Vaticana; appendix includes the Greek text of the *Commentary on John*.

Hill, R. C., 2003. *Commentary on the Twelve Prophets*, FC 108, Washington, DC: Catholic University of America Press.

——, 2006. *Theodore of Mopsuestia. Commentary on Psalms 1–81*, SBL, Leiden: Brill.

Kalantzis, George, 2004. *Theodore of Mopsuestia. Commentary on the Gospel of John*, Strathfield, NSW: St Paul's Publications.

McLeod, Frederick G., 2009. *Theodore of Mopsuestia*, Abingdon and New York: Routledge.

Mingana, A., 1932. *Theodore, Catechetical Homilies*, Syriac text and ET, Commentary of Theodore of Mopsuestia on the Nicene Creed (= *Hom. cat.* i–x], Woodbrooke Studies v; Cambridge: Heffer.

——, 1933. *Theodore, Catechetical Homilies*, Syriac text and ET, Commentary . . . on the Lord's Prayer and the Sacraments of Baptism and the Eucharist (= *Hom. cat.* xi–xvi), Woodbrooke Studies vi; Cambridge: Heffer.

——, 1934. *Early Christian Mystics*, Woodbrooke Studies vii; Cambridge: Heffer.

Nau, F., 1913. *Théodore, Controverse avec les Macédoniens*, Patrologia Orientalis 9, Paris: Firmin–Didot, pp. 637–67.

Rompay, Lucas van, 1982. *Fragments syriaques du Commentarie des Psaumes (Pss. 118 et 138–148)*, Louvain: Peeters.

Sprenger, H. N., 1977. *Theodori Mopsuesteni, Commentarius in XII Prophetas*, Wiesbaden: Harrassowitz.

Swete, H. B., 1880–2. *Theodori Episcopi Mopsuesteni in epistolas B. Pauli commentarii*, 2 vols, Cambridge: Cambridge University Press.

Tonneau, R., 1949. *Les Homélies Catéchétiques de Théodore de Mopsueste*, with French trans., Studi e Testi 145, Rome: Vaticana.

Vaggione, R. P., 1980. 'Some neglected Fragments of Theodore of Mopsuestia's Contra Eunomium', *JTS* (NS) 31, pp. 403–70.

Vosté, J.-M., 1940. *Theodori Mopsuesteni Commentarius in Evangelium Iohannis Apostoli*, CSCO, Louvain: Officina Orientali.

Theodoret of Cyrus

Migne, *PG* 80–84. ET in *NPNF* II.3.

Azéma, Y., 1954. *Théodoret de Cyr. Discours sur la providence*, Budé, Paris: Les Belles Lettres.

——, 1955, 1964, 1965. *Théodoret, Correspondence*, 3 vols, SC 40, 98, 111 & 429, Paris: Les Éditions du Cerf.

Canivet, P. (ed.), 1958/2000. *Théodoret de Cyr, Thérapeutique des Maladies Helléniques*, 2 vols, SC 57, Paris: Les Éditions du Cerf.

—— and A. Leroy-Molinghen (eds), 1977, 1979. *Théodoret de Cyr, Histoire des Moines de Syrie*, 2 vols, SC 234 & 257, Paris: Les Éditions du Cerf.

Doran, Robert, 1992. *The Lives of Simeon Stylites*, trans. with introd., Kalamazoo, MI: Cistercian Publications.

Ehrhard, A., 1888. *Die Cyrill von Alexandrien zugeschriebene Schrift περὶ τῆς τοῦ κυρίου ἐνανθρωπήσεως; ein Werk Theodorets von Cyrus*, Würtzburg 1988–9, Tübingen: H. Laupp, Jr.

Ettlinger, G. H., 1975. *Theodoret: Eranistes*, Oxford: Oxford University Press.

——, 2003. *Theodoret: Eranistes, FC* 106, Washington, DC: Catholic University of America Press.

Guinot, J.-N., 1980, 1982, 1984. *Théodoret de Cyr. Commentaire sur Isaïe*, 3 vols SC 276, 295 & 315, Paris: Les Éditions du Cerf.

Halton, Thomas, 1988. *Theodoret. On Divine Providence*, New York, NY: Newman Press.

Hill, R. C., 2000, 2001. *Theodoret of Cyrus. Commentary on the Psalms*, 2 vols, Psalms 1–82, Psalms 73–150, FC 101 & 102, Washington, DC: Catholic University of America Press.

——, 2001a. *Theodoret of Cyrus. Commentary on the Song of Songs*, Brisbane: Centre for Early Christian Studies.

——, 2001b. *Theodoret of Cyrus. Commentary on the Letters of St Paul*, 2 vols, Brookline: Holy Cross Orthodox Press.

Möhle, A., 1932. *Theodoret von Kyros. Kommentar zu Jesaia*, Berlin: Weidmannsche Buchhandlung.

Otto, J. T. C., 1880. *Corpus Apologetarum Christianorum saeculi secundi*, vol. 4, Jena: Gust. Fischer.

Parmentier, L., 1954/98. *Theodoret. Kirchengeschichte, GCS* 2nd/3rd edn rev. F. Scheidweiler, Berlin: Akademie-Verlag.

——, G. C. Hansen, J. Bouffartique, A. Martin and P. Canivet, 2006, 2009. *Theodoret de Cyr. Histoire ecclésiastique, SC* 501, 530, Paris: Les Éditions du Cerf.

Pásztori-Kupán, István, 2006. *Theodoret of Cyrus*, London and New York: Routledge.

Petruccione, John F. and Robert C. Hill, 2007. *Theodoret of Cyrus. The Questions on the Octateuch*, Greek text and ET, Washington, DC: Catholic University of America Press.

Price, R. M., 1985. *Theodoret of Cyrrhus. A History of the Monks of Syria*, trans., Kalamazoo, MI: Cistercian Publications.

Studies

General: (a) miscellaneous

Altaner, B., 1960. *Patrology*, ET New York: Herder & Herder.

Amand de Mendietta, D., 1945. *Fatalisme et liberté dans l'antiquité grèque*, Louvain: Bibliothèque de l'Université de Louvain.

Armstrong, A. H. (ed.), 1967. *Cambridge History of Later Greek and Early Medieval Philosophy*, Cambridge: Cambridge University Press.

Bell, H. I., 1924. *Jews and Christians in Egypt*, London: British Museum.

——, 1941. 'Anti-semitism in Alexandria', *JRS* 31, pp. 1–18.

Bradshaw, Paul, 2002. *The Search for the Origins of Christian Worship*, 2nd edn, London: SPCK.

Brock, S. P., 1973. 'Early Syrian Asceticism', *Numen* 20, pp. 1–19.

Brown, Peter, 1971a. 'The Rise and Function of the Holy Man in Late Antiquity', *JRS* 61, pp. 80–101.

——, 1971b. *The World of Late Antiquity*, London and New York: Thames & Hudson.

——, 1988. *The Body and Society: Men, Women and Sexual Renunciation in Early Christianity*, London/Boston: Faber & Faber.

Cameron, Alan and Jacqueline Long, with Lee Sherry, 1993. *Barbarians and Politics at the Court of Arcadius*, Berkeley: University of California Press.

Campenhausen, H. von, 1963. *The Fathers of the Greek Church*, ET London: A. & C. Black.

Chadwick, H., 2003. *The Church in Ancient Society: From Galilee to Gregory the Great*, Oxford: Oxford University Press.

Chesnut, Glenn F., 1977. *The First Christian Histories: Eusebius, Socrates, Sozomen, Theodoret and Evagrius*, Paris: Beauchesne.

Christensen, M. J. and J. A. Wittung (eds), 2007. *Partakers of Divine Nature: The History and Development of Deification in the Christian Traditions*. Madison and Teaneck, NJ: Fairleigh Dickinson University Press / Grand Rapids, MI: Baker Academic.

Clark, Elizabeth A., 1992. *The Origenist Controversy: The Cultural Construction of an Early Christian Debate*, Princeton, NJ: Princeton University Press.

Constantelos, B., 1968. *Byzantine Philosophy and Social Welfare*, New Brunswick, NJ: Rutgers University Press.

Crislip, Andrew T., 2005. *From Monastery to Hospital: Christian Monasticism and the Transformation of Health Care in Late Antiquity*, Ann Arbor: University of Michigan Press.

Day, J., 2001. 'Adherence to the *Disciplina Arcani* in the Fourth Century', *SP* 35, pp. 266–70.

Dillon, J., 1977. *The Middle Platonists*, London: Duckworth.

Dix, G., 1945. *The Shape of the Liturgy*, London: Dacre Press.

Downey, G., 1965. 'The Perspective of the Early Church Historians', *Greek, Roman and Byzantine Studies* 6, pp. 57–70.

Edwards, M. J. and S. Swain (eds), 1997. *Portraits: Biographical Representation in the Greek and Latin Literature of the Roman Empire*, Oxford: Clarendon Press.

Elm, Susanna, 1994. *'Virgins of God': The Making of Asceticism in Late Antiquity*, Oxford: Clarendon Press.

Festugière, A. J., 1959. *Antioche paienne et chrétienne*, Paris: Éditions de Boccard.

——, 1961–5. *Les Moines d'Orient*, 4 vols, Paris: Les Éditions du Cerf.

Finn, Richard, 2006. *Almsgiving in the Later Roman Empire: Christian Promotion and Practice (313–450)*, Oxford: Oxford University Press.

Frank, Georgia, 2000. *The Memory of the Eyes: Pilgrims to the Living Saints in Christian Late Antiquity*, Berkeley: University of California Press.

Frend, W. H. C., 1965. *The Early Church*, London: SCM Press.

Greer, Rowan A., 1973. *The Captain of our Salvation*, Tübingen: Mohr Siebeck.

Haas, Christopher, 1997. *Alexandria in Late Antiquity: Topography and Social Conflict*, Baltimore and London: Johns Hopkins University Press.

Harnack, A. von, 1931. *Lehrbuch der Dogmengeschichte*, 5th edn, reprint of 4th (1909), Tübingen: Mohr.

Haykin, Michael A. G., 1994. *The Spirit of God: The Exegesis of 1 & 2 Corinthians in the Pneumatomachian Controversy of the Fourth Century*, Leiden: Brill.

Holum, Kenneth G., 1982. *Theodosian Empresses: Women and Imperial Dominion in Late Antiquity*, Berkeley: University of California Press.

Horton, Jr, F. L., 1976. *The Melchizedek Tradition*, Cambridge: Cambridge University Press.

Hunt, E. D., 1982. *Holy Land Pilgrimage in the Later Roman Empire*, Oxford: Clarendon Press.

Kelly, J. N. D., 1950. *Early Christian Creeds*, London: Longman.

——, 1958. *Early Christian Doctrines*, London: A. & C. Black.

——, 1975. *Jerome*, London: Duckworth.

Liebeschuetz, J. H. W. G., 1972. *Antioch: City and Imperial Administration in the Later Roman Empire*, Oxford: Oxford University Press.

——, 1990. *Barbarians and Bishops in the reign of Arcadius*, Oxford: Oxford University Press.

Louth, Andrew, 1981. *The Origins of the Christian Mystical Tradition: From Plato to Denys*, Oxford: Clarendon Press.

Luchman, Harriet A. and Linda Kulzer (eds), 1999. *Purity of Heart in Early Ascetic and Monastic Literature*, Collegeville, MN: Liturgical Press.

Malone, E. E., 1950. *The Monk and the Martyr: the monk as successor of the martyr*, Washington, DC: Catholic University of America Press.

McLeod, Frederick, 1999. *The Image of God in the Antiochene Tradition*, Washington, DC: Catholic University of America Press.

Mitchell, Margaret and Frances Young, 2006. *The Cambridge History of Christianity: Origins to Constantine*, Cambridge: Cambridge University Press.

Murray, Robert, 1975. 'The Features of the Earliest Christian Asceticism', in Peter Brooks (ed.), *Christian Spirituality: Essays in Honour of Gordon Rupp*, London: SCM Press, pp. 63–77.

O'Keefe, John J., 2000. '"A Letter that Killeth": Toward a Reassessment of Antiochene Exegesis, or Diodore, Theodore, and Theodoret on the Psalms', *JECS* 8, pp. 83–104.

Prestige, G. L., 1936. *God in Patristic Thought*, London: SPCK.

——, 1940. *Fathers and Heretics*, London and New York: SPCK.

Quasten, J., 1960. *Patrology III*, Westminster, MD: Newman Press.

Riedmatten, H. de, 1956, 1957. 'La correspondence entre Basile de Césarée et Apollinaire de Laodicée', *JTS* (NS) 7, pp. 199–210; 8, pp. 53–70.

Riley, Hugh M., 1974. *Christian Initiation: a comparative study of the interpretation of the baptismal liturgy in the mystagogical writings of Cyril of Jerusalem, John Chrysostom, Theodore of Mopsuestia and Ambrose of Milan*, Washington, DC: Catholic University of America Press.

Rist, J. M., 1967. *Plotinus: The Road to Reality*, Cambridge: Cambridge University Press.

Rousseau, Philip, 1978. *Ascetics, Authority and the Church in the age of Jerome and Cassian*, Oxford: Oxford University Press.

Russell, Norman, 2004. *The Doctrine of Deification in the Greek Patristic Tradition*, Oxford: Oxford University Press.

Schäferdiek, K. (ed.), 1997. *Bibliographia Patristica: Internationale Patristische Bibliographie*. Berlin and New York: de Gruyter.

Schäublin, Christoph, 1974. *Untersuchungen zu Methode und Herkunft der Antiochenischen Exegese*, Köln: Hanstein.

Setton, K. M., 1941. *The Christian Attitude to the Emperor in the Fourth Century*, New York: Columbia University Press.

Steenberg, M. C., 2009. *Of God and Man: Theology as Anthropology from Irenaeus to Athanasius*, London: T. & T. Clark International.

Stemberger, Gunter, 2000. *Jews and Christians in the Holy Land: Palestine in the Fourth Century*, Edinburgh: T. & T. Clark.

Sterk, Andrea, 2004. *Renouncing the World Yet Leading the Church: The Monk-Bishop in Late Antiquity*, Cambridge, MA: Harvard University Press.

Vööbus, A., 1958, 1960. *A History of Asceticism in the Syrian Orient*, 2 vols, Louvain: Secretariat du CSCO.

Walker, P. W. L., 1990. *Holy City, Holy Places? Christian Attitudes to Jerusalem and the Holy Land in the Fourth Century*, Oxford: Oxford University Press.

Wallace-Hadrill, D. S., 1982. *Christian Antioch: A Study of Early Christian Thought in the East*, Cambridge: Cambridge University Press.

Wiles, M. F., 1960. *The Spiritual Gospel*, Cambridge: Cambridge University Press.

Wilken, Robert L., 1992. *The Land Called Holy: Palestine in Christian History and Thought*, New Haven, CT and London: Yale University Press.

Young, Frances M., 1977. 'Christian Attitudes to Finance in the First Four Centuries', *Epworth Review* 4, pp. 78–86.

——, 1989. 'The Rhetorical Schools and their Influence on Patristic Exegesis' in Rowan Williams (ed.), *The Making of Orthodoxy: Essays in honour of Henry Chadwick*, Cambridge: Cambridge University Press, pp. 182–199.

——, 1997a. *Biblical Exegesis and the Formation of Christian Culture*, Cambridge: Cambridge University Press.

——, 1997b. 'The Fourth Century Reaction against Allegory', *SP* 30, pp. 120–5.

General: (b) Christology

Daley, B. E., 2002. '"Heavenly Man" and "Eternal Christ": Apollinarius and Gregory of Nyssa on the Personal Identity of the Savior', *JECS* 10, pp. 469–88.

Fairbairn, Donald, 2003. *Grace and Christology in the Early Church*, Oxford: Oxford University Press.

Galtier, P., 1956. 'Saint Cyrille et Apollinaire', *Gregorianum* 37, pp. 584–609.

Grillmeier, A., 1965/75. *Christ in Christian Tradition*, ET, London and Oxford: Mowbrays.

Loofs, F., 1924. *Paulus von Samosata*, Leipzig: Hinrichs.

Lyman, R. J., 1993. *Christology and Cosmology: Models of Divine Activity in Origen, Eusebius and Athanasius*. Oxford: Oxford University Press.

Richard, M., 1945/77. 'L'Introduction du mot 'hypostase' dans la théologie de l'incarnation', *Mélanges de Science Religieuse* 2, pp. 5–32, 243–70; republished in M. Richard, 1977. *Opera Minora* II, Turnhout: Brepols.

——, 1946/77. 'Les traités de Cyrille d'Alexandrie contre Diodore et Théodore et les fragments dogmatiques de Diodore de Tarse', *Mélanges F. Grat I*, pp. 99–116; republished in M. Richard, 1977. *Opera Minora* II, Turnhout: Brepols.

Robertson, J. M., 2007. *Christ as Mediator: A Study of the Theologies of Eusebius of Caesarea, Marcellus of Ancyra, and Athanasius of Alexandria*, Oxford Theological Monographs, Oxford: Oxford University Press.

Sellers, R. V., 1940. *Two Ancient Christologies*, London: SPCK.

——, 1953. *The Council of Chalcedon*, London: SPCK.

Spoerl, K. M., 1993. 'Apollinarius and the Response to Early Arian Christology', *SP* 26, pp. 421–7.

——, 1994. 'Apollinarian Christology and the anti-Marcellan tradition', *JTS* (NS) 45, pp. 545–68.

Vine, A. R., 1948. *An Approach to Christology*, London: Independent Press.
Wigram, W. A., 1923. *The Separation of the Monophysites*, London: Faith Press.
Wiles, M. F., 1965. 'The Nature of the Early Debate about Christ's Human Soul', *JEH* 16, pp. 139–51.
Young, Frances M., 1969. 'Christological Ideas in the Greek Commentaries on the Epistle to the Hebrews', *JTS* (NS) 20, pp. 150–63.
——, 1971. 'A Reconsideration of Alexandrian Christology', *JEH* 22, pp. 103–14.

Apollinarius of Laodicea

Golega, Joseph, 1960. *Der Homerische Psalter: Studia über die dem Apollinarios von Laodikeia zugeschriebene Psalmenparaphrase*, Ettal: Buch-Kunstverlag Ettal.
Hübner, R., 1972. 'Gotteserkenntnis durch die Inkarnation Gottes. Zu einer neue Interpretation der Christologie des Apollinaris von Laodicea,' *Kleronomia* 4, pp. 131–61.
Kannengiesser, C., 1971. 'Une nouvelle interprétation de la christologie d'Apollinaire', *RSR* 59, pp. 27–36.
Mühlenberg, E., 1969. *Apollinaris von Laodicea*, Göttingen: Vandenhoeck & Ruprecht.
Raven, C. E., 1923. *Apollinarianism*, Cambridge and New York: Cambridge University Press.
Riedmatten, H. de, 1948. 'Some Neglected Aspects of Apollinarist Christology', *Dominican Studies* I, pp. 239–60.

Apophthegmata Patrum and Monasticism in general

Bousset, W., 1923. *Apophthegmata: Studien zur Geschichte des ältesten Mönchtums*, Tübingen: Mohr.
Burton-Christie, 1993. *The Word in the Desert: Scripture and the Quest for Holiness in Early Christian Monasticism*, New York and Oxford: Oxford University Press.
Chitty, Derwas, 1966.*The Desert a City*, Oxford: Oxford University Press.
——, 1971. 'Abba Isaiah', *JTS* (NS) 22, pp. 47–72.
——, 1974. 'The Books of the Old Men', *Eastern Churches Review* 6, pp. 15–21.
Goehring, James E., 1999. *Ascetics, Society and the Desert: Studies in Egyptian Monasticism*, Harrisburg, PA: Trinity Press International.
Gould, Graham, 1993a. *The Desert Fathers on Monastic Community*, Oxford: Clarendon Press.
Gould, Graham, 1993b. 'Recent Work on Monastic Origins: A Consideration of the Questions Raised by Samuel Rubenson's *The Letters of St Antony*', *SP* 25, pp. 405–16.
Guy, J.-C., 1955. 'Remarques sur le texte des Apophthegmata Patrum', *RSR* 43, pp. 252–8.
——, 1962. *Recherches sur la tradition grèque des Apophthegmata Patrum*. Subsidia Hagiographica 36, Brussels: Société des Bollandistes.
——, 1974. 'Educational innovation in the Desert Fathers', *Eastern Churches Review* 6, pp. 44–51.
Harmless, William, SJ, 2004. *Desert Christians: An Introduction to the Literature of Early Monasticism*, New York: Oxford University Press.

Regnault, L., 1987. *Les Pères du désert à travers leurs Apophtegmes*, Sarthe: Solesmes.

———, 1990. *La vie quotidienne des Pères du désert en Égypte au iv siècle*, Mesril-sur-l'Estrée: Éditions Hachette.

Rousseau, Philip, 1999. *Pachomius: The Making of a Community in Fourth-Century Egypt*, updated (original publication 1985), Berkeley, Los Angeles and London: University of California Press.

Rubenson, S., 1990. *The Letters of St. Antony: Origenist Theology, Monastic Tradition and the Making of a Saint*, Bibliotheca Historico-Ecclesiastica Lundensis 24, Lund: Lund University Press.

Arius, Arianism and the shaping of Nicene orthodoxy

Ayres, L., 2004a. *Nicaea and its Legacy: An Approach to Fourth-Century Trinitarian Theology*, Oxford: Oxford University Press.

Bardy, G., 1927. 'La Thalie d'Arius', *Revue de Philologie* 53 (3rd series I), pp. 211–33 (reproduced in Bardy 1936, pp. 246–74).

———, 1936. *Recherches sur Lucien d'Antioche*, Paris: Beauchesne.

Barnard, L. W., 1970. 'The Antecedents of Arius', *VigChr* 24, pp. 172–88.

———, 1972. 'What was Arius' Philosophy?' *Theologische Zeitschrift* 28, pp. 110–17.

Barnes, M. R. and D. H. Williams (eds) 1993. *Arianism After Arius: Essays on the Development of the Fourth Century Trinitarian Conflicts*, Edinburgh: T. & T. Clark.

Barnes, T., 2009. 'The Exile and Recalls of Arius' *JTS* (NS) 60, pp. 109–29.

Baynes, N. H., 1948. 'Sozomen, *Ecclesiastica Historia* 1.15', *JTS* 49, pp. 165–9.

Böhm, T., 1992. 'Die *Thalia* des Arius: Ein Beitrag zur Frühchristlichen Hymnologie', *VigChr* 46(4), pp. 334–55.

Boularand, E., 1972. *L'Hérésie d'Arius et la 'Foi' de Nicée*, Paris: Éditions Letouzey et Ané.

Edwards, M. J., 1995. 'The Arian Heresy and the *Oration to the Saints*', *VigChr* 49(4), pp. 379–87.

Gregg, Robert and Dennis Groh, 1977. 'The Centrality of Soteriology in Early Arianism', *Anglican Theological Review* 59, pp. 260–78.

———, 1981. *Early Arianism: a View of Salvation*, Philadelphia: Fortress Press.

Hanson, R. P. C., 1985. 'The transformation of images in the Trinitarian Theology of the Fourth Century' in *Studies in Christian Antiquity*, Edinburgh: T. & T. Clark.

———, 1988. *The Search for the Christian Understanding of God*, Edinburgh: T. & T. Clark.

Leroux, J. M., 1966. 'Acace évêque de Césarée de Palestine (341–365)'. *SP* 8, pp. 82–5.

Pollard, T. E., 1958. 'The Origins of Arianism', *JTS* (NS) 9, pp. 103–11.

Stead, G. C., 1964. 'The Platonism of Arius', *JTS* (NS) 15, pp. 14–31.

———, 1978. 'The *Thalia* of Arius and the Testimony of Athanasius', *JTS* (NS) 29, pp. 20–52.

Telfer, W., 1936. 'Arius Takes Refuge at Nicomedia', *JTS* 37, pp. 60–3.

———, 1946. 'When did the Arian Controversy begin?' *JTS* 47, pp. 129–42.

———, 1949. 'Sozomen 1.15. A reply', *JTS* 50, pp. 187–91.

Vaggione, R. P. C., 2000. *Eunomius of Cyzicus and the Nicene Revolution*, Oxford: Oxford University Press.

Vinzent, M., 1993. *Asterius von Kappadokien: Die Theologische Fragmente*, Leiden: Brill.

Wiles, Maurice, 1962. 'In Defence of Arius', *JTS* (NS) 13, pp. 339–47.
——, 1996. *Archetypal Heresy: Arianism through the Centuries*, Oxford: Clarendon Press.
Williams, R. D., 1983. 'The Logic of Arianism', *JTS* (NS) 34, pp. 56–81.
——, 1986. 'Arius and the Melitian Schism', *JTS* (NS) 37, pp. 35–52.
——, 1987. *Arius: Heresy and Tradition*, London: Darton, Longman & Todd.

Athanasius

Anatolios, K., 1998. *Athanasius: The Coherence of his Thought*, Routledge Early Christian Monographs, London: Routledge.
Armstrong, C. B., 1921. 'The Synod of Alexandria and the schism of Antioch in AD 362', *JTS* 22, pp. 206–21, 347–55.
Ayres, L., 2004b. 'Athanasius' Initial Defense of the term *homoousios*; re-reading the De Decretis', *JECS* 12, pp. 337–59.
Barnard, L. W., 1974. 'The date of Athanasius' *Vita Antonii*', *VigChr* 28, pp. 169–75.
——, 1975. 'Athanasius and the Meletian Schism in Egypt', *Journal of Egyptian Archaeology* 59, pp. 183–9.
Barnes, Timothy D., 1986. 'Angel of Light or Mystic Initiate: The Problem of the *Life of Antony*', *JTS* (NS) 37, pp. 353–68.
——, 1993. *Athanasius and Constantius: Theology and Politics in the Constantinian Empire*, Cambridge, MA and London: Harvard University Press.
Blennan, B. R., 1976. 'Dating Athanasius' *Vita Antonii*', *VigChr* 30, pp. 52–4.
Bouyer, L., 1943. *L'Incarnation et l'Église-Corps du Christ dans la théologie de S. Athanase*, Paris: Les Éditions du Cerf.
Brakke, David, 1994. 'The Greek and Syriac Versions of the Life of Antony', *Le Muséon* 107, pp. 29–53.
——, 1995. *Athanasius and the Politics of Asceticism*, New York: Oxford University Press; published in paperback as *Athanasius and Asceticism*, Baltimore and London: Johns Hopkins University Press, 1998.
Campbell, T. C., 1974. 'The Doctrine of the Holy Spirit in the Theology of Athanasius', *SJT* 27, pp. 408–40.
Cross, F. L., 1945. *The Study of St Athanasius*, Oxford: Clarendon Press.
Dörries, Hermann, 1966. 'Die *Vita Antonii* als Geschichtsquelle', in Dörries, *Wort und Stunde* I, Göttingen: Vandenhoeck und Ruprecht, pp. 145–224.
Ernest, James D., 2004. *The Bible in Athanasius of Alexandria*, Leiden: Brill.
Frazier, F., 1998. 'L'Antoine d'Athanase à Propos des Chapitres 83–88 de *La Vita*', *VigChr* 54(3), pp. 227–56.
Frend, W. H. C., 1976. 'Athanasius as an Egyptian Church Leader in the Fourth Century', in Frend, *Religion Popular and Unpopular in the Early Christian Centuries*, London: Variorum, pp. 20–37.
Galtier, P., 1955. 'S. Athanase et l'âme humaine du Christ', *Gregorianum* 36, pp. 552–89.
Gywnn, D. M., 2007. *The Eusebians: The Polemic of Athanasius of Alexandria and the Construction of the 'Arian Controversy'*, Oxford Theological Monographs, Oxford: Oxford University Press.
Haarlem, A. van, 1961. *Incarnatie en verlossing bii Athanasius*, Wageningen: Veenman.
Kannengiesser, C., 1964a. 'Le témoignage des Lettres Festales de S. Athanase sur

la date de l'apologie *Contre les païens, Sur l'incarnation du Verbe'*, *RSR* 52, pp. 91–100; Reproduced in Kannengiesser, *Arius and Athanasius*, Aldershot: Variorum, 1991.

——, 1964b, 1965. 'Le texte court du *De Incarnatione* Athanasien', *RSR* 52, pp. 589–96; 53, pp. 77–111.

——, 1966. 'Les différentes recensions du traité *De Incarnatione Verbi* de S. Athanase', *SP* 7, pp. 221–9.

——, 1970a. 'Ou et quand Arius composa-t-il la Thalie?', in P. Granfield and J. A. Jungmann (eds), *Kyriakon: Festschrift Johannes Quasten*, Vol. 1, Münster: Aschendorff, pp. 346–51.

——, 1970b. 'La date de l'Apologie d'Athanase "Contre les Paiens" et "Sur l'incarnation du Verbe"', *RSR* 58, pp. 383–428; reproduced in Kannengiesser, *Arius and Athanasius*, Aldershot: Variorum, 1991.

——, 1972. 'λόγος et νοῦς chez Athanase d'Alexandrie', *SP* 11, pp. 199–202.

——, 1973. 'Athanasius of Alexandria and the Foundation of Traditional Christology', *Theological Studies* 34, pp. 103–13; reproduced in Kannengiesser, *Arius and Athanasius*, Aldershot: Variorum, 1991.

—— (ed.), 1974. *Politique et Théologie chez Athanase d'Alexandrie*, Paris: Beauchesne.

——, 1975. 'Le mystère pascal du Christ selon Athanase d'Alexandrie', *RSR* 63, pp. 407–42. Reproduced in Kannengiesser, *Arius and Athanasius*, Aldershot: Variorum, 1991.

——, 1982. 'Athanasius of Alexandria, Three orations against the Arians: a reappraisal', *SP* 18, pp. 981–95. Reproduced in Kannengiesser, *Arius and Athanasius*, Aldershot: Variorum, 1991.

Lorenz, R., 1989. 'Die griechische *Vita Antonii* des Athanasius und ihre syrische Fassung: Bemerküngen zu einer These von R. Draguet', *Zeitschrift für Kirchengeshchichte* 100, pp. 77–84.

Louth, Andrew, 1985. 'Athanasius' understanding of the humanity of Christ', *SP* 16, pp. 309–18.

——, 1988. 'St Athanasius and the Greek *Life of Antony*', *JTS* (NS) 39, pp. 504–9.

Martin, Annik, 1996. *Athanase d'Alexandrie et l'Église d'Égypte au IVe siècle (328–373)*, Rome: École Française de Rom.

Meijering, E. P., 1968. *Orthodoxy and Platonism in Athanasius*, Leiden: Brill.

——, 1996. 'Zur Echtheit der Dritten Rede des Athanasius *Gegen die Arianer* (*Contra Arianos* III)', *VigChr* 50(4), pp. 364–86.

Meyer, J. R., 1998. 'Athanasius' Use of Paul in His Doctrine of Salvation', *VigChr* 52(2), pp. 146–71.

Nordberg, H., 1961a. 'A reconsideration of the date of Athanasius' *Contra Gentes* and *De Incarnatione*', *SP* 3, pp. 262–6.

——, 1961b. *Athanasius' Tractates Contra Gentes and De Incarnatione: An attempt at Redating*, Helsinki: Societas Scientarum Fennica.

Opitz, H. G., 1935b. *Untersuchungen zur Überlieferung der Schriften des Athanasius*, Berlin: de Gruyter.

Pettersen, Alvyn, 1980. *Athanasius and the Human Body*, Bristol: Bristol Press.

——, 1982. 'A reconsideration of the date of the *Contra Gentes-De Incarnatione* of Athanasius of Alexandria', *SP* 18, pp. 1030–40.

——, 1995. *Athanasius*, London: Geoffrey Chapman.

Prestige, G. L., 1933. 'ΑΓΕΝ[Ν]ΗΤΟΣ and cognate words in Athanasius', *JTS* 34, pp. 258–65.

Richard, M., 1947. 'S. Athanase et la psychologie du Christ, selon les Ariens',

Mélanges de Science Religieuse 4, pp. 5–54; republished in Richard, 1977. *Opera Minora* II, Turnhout: Brepols.

Roldanus, J., 1968. *Le Christ et l'homme dans la théologie d'Athanase d'Alexandrie*, Leiden: Brill.

Rondeau, M. J., 1968. 'Une nouvelle preuve de l'influence littéraire d'Eusèbe de Césarée sur Athanase: l'interprétation des psaumes', *RSR* 56, pp. 385–434.

Ryan, G. J. and R. P. Casey, 1945/6. *The De Incarnatione of Athanasius* (Studies and Documents 14), (Part I, The Long Recension, by G. J. Ryan, Part II, The Short Recension, by R. P. Casey), London: Christophers.

Slusser, M., 1986. 'Athanasius, *Contra Gentes* and *De incarnatione*: Place and Date of Composition', *JTS* 31, pp. 114–17.

Stead, G. C., 1976. 'Rhetorical Method in Athanasius', *VigChr* 30, pp. 121–37.

——, 1992. 'Athanasius' in A. di Berardino, *Encyclopedia of the Early Church*, Cambridge: James Clarke, pp. 93–5.

Tetz, M., 1973. 'Markellianer und Athanasios von Alexandrien: Die markellinnische Expositio fidei ad Athanasium des Diakonos Eugenios von Ankyra', *ZNW* 64, pp. 75–121.

——, 1975. 'Über Nikäische Orthodoxie. Der sog. Tomus ad Antiochenos des Athanasios von Alexandrien', *ZNW* 66, pp. 194–222.

——, 1983. 'Athanasius und die *Vita Antonii*: literarische und theologische Relationen, *ZNW* 73, pp. 1–30.

Vinzent, M., 1996. *Pseudo-Athanasius, Contra Arianos IV: eine Schrift gegen Asterius von Kappadokien, Eusebius von Cäsarea, Markell von Ankyra und Photin von Sirmium*, Leiden: Brill.

Weinandy, T. G., 2007. *Athanasius: A Theological Introduction*, Aldershot: Ashgate.

Winden, J. C. M. van, 1975. 'On the Date of Athanasius' Apologetical Treatises', *VigChr* 29, pp. 291–5.

Basil of Caesarea

Amand de Mendietta, D., 1949. *L'Ascèse monastique de S. Basile*, Denée: Éditions de Maredsous.

——, 1965a. 'The Pair Κήρυγμα and Δόγμα in the Theological Thought of St Basil of Caesarea', *JTS* (NS) 16, pp. 129–45.

——, 1965b. *The Unwritten and Secret Apostolic Traditions in the Theological Thought of St Basil of Caesarea*, SJT Occasional Papers no. 13, Edinburgh: Oliver & Boyd.

——, 1976. 'The Official Attitude of Basil of Caesarea as a Christian Bishop towards Greek Philosophy and Science', in D. Baker (ed.), *The Orthodox Churches and the West*, Studies in Church History 13, Oxford: Blackwell, pp. 25–49.

Bobrinskoy, B., 1969. 'Liturgie et ecclésiologie trinitaire de S. Basile', *Verbum Caro* 89, pp. 1–32.

Coman, J., 1966. 'La démonstration dans le traité *Sur le Saint Esprit* de Saint Basile le Grand. Préliminaires', *SP* 9, pp. 172–209.

Courtonne, Y., 1934. *S. Basile et l'Hellénisme*, Paris: Firmin Didot.

Doresse, J. and E. Lanne, 1960. *Un témoin archaïque de la liturgie copte de S. Basile*, Louvain: Publications Universitaires.

Fedwick, Paul J., 1979. *The Church and the Charisma of Leadership in Basil of Caesarea*, Toronto: Pontifical Institute of Mediaeval Studies.

—— (ed.), 1981. *Basil of Caesarea, Christian, Humanist, Ascetic: A Sixteen-Hundredth*

Anniversary Symposium, 2 vols, Toronto: Pontifical Institute of Mediaeval Studies.

——, 1993–2004. *Bibliotheca Basiliana Universalis*: I—V, *CCG*, Turnout: Brepols.

Gribomont, J., 1953. *Histoire du texte des Ascétiques de S. Basile*, Louvain: Muséon.

——, 1957. 'Les Règles Morales de S. Basile et le Nouveau Testament', *SP* 2, pp. 416–26.

——, 1963. 'L'Origénisme de S. Basile', in *L'Homme devant Dieu. Mélanges H. Lubac*, Vol. 1, Paris: Aubier, pp. 281–94; reprinted in *Saint Basile: Évangile et église. Mélanges*, 2 vols, Bégrolles-en-Mauges: Abbaye de Bellefontaine, 1984.

——, 1975. 'Les lemmes de citation de S. Basile indice de niveau littéraire', *Augustinianum* 14, pp. 513–26.

Hanson, R. P. C., 1968. 'Basil's doctrine of tradition in relation to the Holy Spirit', *VigChr* 22, pp. 241–55.

Hayes, W. M., 1972. *The Greek Mss Tradition of (Ps.-) Basil's Adversus Eunomium*, Leiden: Brill.

Hildebrand, Stephan M., 2007. *The Trinitarian Theology of Basil of Caesarea: a Synthesis of Greek Thought and Biblical Truth*, Washington, DC: Catholic University of America Press.

Lèbe, L., 1965. 'S. Basile et ses Règles morales', *Revue Benédictine* 75, pp. 193–200.

Lim, R., 1990. 'The Politics of Interpretation in Basil of Caesarea's *Hexaemeron*', *VigChr* 44, pp. 351–70.

Loofs, F., 1878. *Eustathius von Sebaste und die Chronologie der Basiliusbriefe*, Halle: Niemeyer.

Moffatt, A., 1972. 'The Occasion of Basil's Address to Young Men', *Antichthon* 6, pp. 74–86.

Murphy, F. X., 1976. 'Moral and Ascetical Doctrine in St Basil', *SP* 14, pp. 320–6.

Orphanos, M., 1975. *Creation and Salvation according to Basil of Caesarea*, Athens: Gregorios Parisianos.

Prestige, G. L., 1956. *St. Basil the Great and Apollinaris of Laodicea* (ed. Henry Chadwick), London: SPCK.

Pruche, B., 1966. 'Δόγμα et Κήρυγμα dans le traité *Sur le Saint-Esprit* de Saint Basile de Césarée en Cappadoce', *SP* 9, pp. 257–62.

Rousseau, Philip, 1994. *Basil of Caesarea*, Berkeley/Los Angeles/London: University of California Press.

Rudberg, S. Y., 1953. *Études sur la tradition manuscrite de S. Basile*, Uppsala: AB Lundequistska Bokhandeln.

Cappadocians in general

Balas, D., 1976. 'The Unity of Human Nature in Basil's and Gregory of Nyssa's Polemics against Eunomius', *SP* 14, pp. 275–81.

Bernardi, J., 1970. *La Prédication des Pères Cappadociens*, Paris: Presses Universitaires de France.

Gregg, Robert C., 1975. *Consolation Philosophy: Greek and Christian 'Paideia' in Basil and the Two Gregories*, Philadelphia: Philadelphia Patristic Foundation.

Holman, Susan R., 2001. *The Hungry are Dying: Beggars and Bishops in Roman Cappadocia*, Oxford: Oxford University Press.

Junod, E., 1972. 'Remarques sur la composition de la *Philocalia* d'Origène par Basile de Césarée et Grégoire de Nazianze', *Revue d'histoire et de philosophie religieuse* 52, pp. 149–56.

Meredith, A., 1995. *The Cappadocians*, London: Geoffrey Chapman.

Mitchell, Stephen, 1993. *Anatolia: Land, Men and Gods in Asia Minor*, 2 vols, Oxford: Oxford University Press.

Rousseau, P., 2005. 'The Pious Household and the Virgin Chorus: Reflections on Gregory of Nyssa's *Life of Macrina'*, *JECS* 13, pp. 165–86.

Smith, J. Warren, 2004. 'A Just and Reasonable Grief: the Death and Function of a Holy Woman in Gregory of Nyssa's *Life of Macrina'*, *JECS* 12, pp. 57–84.

Van Dam, Raymond, 2002. *Kingdom of Snow: Roman Rule and Greek Culture in Cappadocia*, Philadelphia: University of Pennsylvania Press.

——, 2003a. *Families and Friends in Late Roman Cappadocia*, Philadelphia: University of Pennsylvania Press.

——, 2003b. *Becoming Christian: The Conversion of Roman Cappadocia*, Philadelphia: University of Pennsylvania Press.

Cyril of Alexandria

Boulnois, M.-O., 1994. *Le paradoxe trinitaire chez Cyrille d'Alexandrie*, Paris: Institut des Études Augustiniennes.

Burghardt, W. J., 1957. *The Image of God in Man according to Cyril of Alexandria*, Washington, DC: Catholic University of America Press.

Chadwick, H., 1951. 'Eucharist and Christology in the Nestorian Controversy', *JTS* (NS) 2, pp. 145–64.

Gebremedhin, E., 1977. *Life-Giving Blessing: An Inquiry into the Eucharistic Doctrine of Cyril of Alexandria*, Uppsala: Borgströms.

Grant, R. M., 1964. 'Greek Literature in the Treatise *De Trinitate* and Cyril *Contra Iulianum'*, *JTS* (NS) 15, pp. 265–79.

Hallmann, Joseph M., 1997. 'The Seed of Fire: Divine Suffering in the Christology of Cyril of Alexandria and Nestorius of Constantinople', *JECS* 5, pp. 369–91.

Jouassard, G., 1945. 'L'activité littéraire de S. Cyrille d'Alexandrie jusqu'à 428', *Mélanges E. Podechard*, Lyons: Facultés Catholiques, pp. 159–75.

——, 1977. 'La date des écrits antiariens de S. Cyrille d'Alexandrie', *Revue Bénédictine* 87, pp. 172–8.

Keating, D. A., 2004. *The Appropriation of Divine Life in Cyril of Alexandria*, Oxford: Oxford University Press.

Kerrigan, A., 1952. *St Cyril of Alexandria: Interpreter of the Old Testament*, Analecta Biblica 21, Rome: Pontificio Istituto Biblico.

Koen, L., 1991. *The Saving Passion: Incarnational and Soteriological Thought in Cyril of Alexandria's Commentary on the Gospel according to St. John*, Uppsala: Graphic Systems.

Liébaert, J., 1951. *La Doctrine Christologique de S. Cyrille d'Alexandrie avant la querelle Nestorienne*, Lille: Facultés Catholiques.

——, 1970. 'L'évolution de la christologie de S. Cyrille d' Alexandrie à partir de la controverse nestorienne. La lettre paschale XVII et la lettre aux Moines (428–9)', *Mélanges de Science Religieuse* 27, pp. 27–48.

Malley, William J., 1979. *Hellenism and Christianity: The Conflict between Hellenic and Christian Wisdom in the* Contra Galilaeos *of Julian the Apostate and the* Contra Julianum *of St. Cyril of Alexandria*, Analecta Gregoriana 210, Rome: Università Gregoriana.

Manoir, H. du, 1944. *Dogme et Spiritualité chez S. Cyrille d'Alexandrie*, Paris: J. Vrin.

McGuckin, J. A., 1994/2004. *Cyril of Alexandria: The Christological Controversy: Its History, Theology and Texts*, Leiden: Brill / republished Crestwood, NY: St Vladimir's Seminary Press.

McKinion, S. A., 2000. *Words, Imagery, and the Mystery of Christ: A Reconstruction of Cyril of Alexandria's Christology*, Leiden: Brill.

Meunier, B., 1997. *Le Christ de Cyrille d'Alexandrie: L'humanité, le salut et la question monophysite*, Paris: Beauchesne.

Norris, R. A., 1975. 'Christological Models in Cyril of Alexandria', *SP* 13, pp. 255–68.

Siddals, Ruth M., 1987. 'Logic and Christology in Cyril of Alexandria', *JTS* (NS) 38, pp. 341–6.

Weinandy, Thomas G. and Daniel A. Keating, 2003. *The Theology of St Cyril of Alexandria: A Critical Appreciation*, London and New York: T. & T. Clark.

Welch, L. J., 1994. *Christology and Eucharist in the Early Thought of Cyril of Alexandria*, San Francisco: International Scholars Press.

Wessel, Susan, 2001. 'Socrates' Narrative of Cyril of Alexandria's Episcopal Election', *JTS* (NS) 52, pp. 98–104.

——, 2004. *Cyril of Alexandria and the Nestorian Controversy: The Making of a Saint and of a Heretic*, Oxford: Oxford University Press.

Wilken, Robert L., 1966. 'Exegesis and the History of Theology: Reflections on the Adam-Christ Typology in Cyril of Alexandria', *Church History* 35, pp. 139–56.

——, 1971. *Judaism and the Early Christian Mind: A Study of Cyril of Alexandria's Exegesis and Theology*, New Haven, CT: Yale University Press.

Cyril of Jerusalem

Baldovin, John F., 1989. *Liturgy in Ancient Jerusalem*, Nottingham: Grove Books.

Berten, I., 1968. 'Cyrille de Jérusalem, Eusèbe d'Emèse et la théologie semi-arienne', *Revue des Sciences Philosophiques et Théologiques* 52, pp. 38–75.

Beukers, C., 1961. '"For our Emperors, Soldiers and Allies": An attempt at dating the 23rd Catechesis by Cyrillus of Jerusalem', *VigChr* 15, pp. 177–84.

Camelot, P. T., 1970. 'Note sur la théologie baptismale des Catéchèses attribuées à S. Cyrille de Jérusalem', in P. Granfield and J. A. Jungmann (eds), *Kyriakon: Festschrift Johannes Quasten*, Vol. 2, Münster: Aschendorff, pp. 724–9.

Day, J., 2007. *The Baptismal Liturgy of Jerusalem: Fourth- and Fifth-Century Evidence from Palestine, Syria and Egypt*, London: Ashgate.

Doval, Alexis James, 1997. 'The Date of Cyril of Jerusalem's *Catecheses*', *JTS* 48, pp. 129–32.

——, 2001. *Cyril of Jerusalem, Mystagogue: The Authorship of the Mystagogic Catecheses*, Patristic Monograph Series 17, Washington, DC: Catholic University of America Press.

Drijvers, J. W., 2004. *Cyril of Jerusalem: Bishop and City*, Supplements to *VigChr*, Leiden: Brill.

Gregg, Robert C., 1985. 'Cyril of Jerusalem and the Arians', in Gregg (ed.), *Arianism: Historical and Theological Reassessments*, Cambridge, MA: Philadelphia Patristic Foundation, pp. 85–109.

Kretschmar, G., 1956. 'Die frühe Geschichte der Jerusalemer Liturgie', *Jahrbuch für Liturgik und Hymnologie*, pp. 22–46.

Lebon, J., 1924. 'La position de S. Cyrille de Jérusalem dans les luttes provoquées par l'Arianisme', *Revue d'Histoire Écclésiastique* 20, pp. 181–210, 357–86.

Piédagnel, A., 1970. 'Les Catéchèses Mystagogiques de S. Cyrille de Jérusalem. Inventaire de la tradition manuscrite grecque', *SP* 10, pp. 141–5.

Stephenson, A. A., 1954a. 'The Lenten Catechetical Syllabus in Fourth-century Jerusalem', *Theological Studies* 15, pp. 103–14.

——, 1954b. 'St. Cyril of Jerusalem and the Alexandrian heritage', *Theological Studies* 15, pp. 573–93.

——, 1957. 'St Cyril of Jerusalem and the Alexandrian Christian Gnosis', *SP* 1, pp. 142–56.

——, 1972. 'St Cyril of Jerusalem's Trinitarian Theology', *SP* 11, pp. 234–41.

Swaans, W. J., 1942. 'A propos des "Catéchèses Mystagogiques" attribués à S. Cyrille de Jérusalem', *Le Muséon* 55, pp. 1–43.

van Nuffelen, P., 2007. 'The Career of Cyril of Jerusalem (c.348–87): A Reassessment', *JTS* (NS) 58, pp. 134–46.

Yarnold, E. J., 1972. 'Baptism and Pagan Mysteries in the Fourth Century', *Heythrop Journal* 13, pp. 247–67.

——, 1973. '"Ideo et Romae fideles dicuntur qui baptizati sunt": a note on *De Sacramentis* 1.1', *JTS* (NS) 24, pp. 202–7.

——, 1975. 'Did St Ambrose know the Mystagogical Catecheses of St Cyril of Jerusalem?', *SP* 12, pp. 184–9.

——, 1978. 'The Authorship of the *Mystagogic Catecheses* attributed to Cyril of Jerusalem', *Heythrop Journal* 19, pp. 143–61.

Didymus the Blind

Bardy, G., 1910. *Didyme l'Aveugle*, Paris: Beauchesne.

——, 1937. 'Aux origènes de l'école d'Alexandrie', *RSR* 27, 65–90.

——, 1942. 'Pour l'histoire de l'école d'Alexandrie', *Vivre et Penser* (the wartime *Revue Biblique*) 2, pp. 80–109.

Béranger, L., 1963. 'Sur deux énigmes du *De Trinitate* de Didyme l'Aveugle', *RSR* 51, pp. 255–67.

Bienart, W. A., 1972. '*Allegoria' und 'Anagoge' bei Didymos dem Blinden von Alexandria*, Patristische Texte und Abhandlungen 13, Berlin: de Gruyter.

Bouteneff, P. C., 2001. 'Placing the Christology of Didymus the Blind', *SP* 37, pp. 389–95.

de Regnon, T., 1892–8. *Études de théologie positive sur la Sainte Trinité*, 4 vols, Paris: Victor Retaux.

Doutreleau, L., 1957. 'Le *De Trinitate* est-il l'oeuvre de Didyme l'Aveugle?', *RSR* 45, pp. 514–57.

——, 1961. 'Ce quel' on trouvera dans l'*In Zachariam* de Didyme l'Aveugle', *SP* 3, pp. 183–95.

—— and J. Aucagne, 1955. 'Que savons-nous aujourd'hui des papyrus de Toura?', *RSR* 43, pp. 161–93.

—— and L. Koenen, 1967. 'Nouvel inventaire des Papyrus de Toura', *RSR* 55, pp. 547–64.

Gauche, W. J., 1934. *Didymus the Blind, an Educator of the Fourth Century*, Washington, DC: Catholic University of America Press.

Gesché, A., 1959, 'L'âme humaine de Jesus dans la Christologie du IVe Siècle. Le témoignage du commentaire sur les Psaumes découvert à Toura', *Revue d'Histoire*

Ecclésiastique 54, pp. 385–425.
——, 1962. *La christologie du 'Commentaire sur les Psaumes' découvert à Toura*, Gembloux: J. Duculot.
Hayes, W. M., 1982. 'Didymus the Blind *is* the author of *Adversus Eunomium* IV–V', *SP* 17, pp. 1108–14.
Holl, K., 1928. *Gesammelte Aufsätze zur Kirchegeschichte II*, Tübingen: Mohr, pp. 298–309.
Hübner, R., 1989. *Die Schrift des Apollinarius von Laodicea Gegen Photin (Pseudo-Athanasius, Contra Sabellianos und Basilius von Caesarea)*, PTS 30, Berlin: de Gruyter.
Layton, Richard A., 2000. '*Propatheia*: Origen and Didymus on the Origin of the Passions', *VigChr* 54(3), pp. 262–82.
——, 2004. *Didymus the Blind and His Circle in Late-Antique Alexandria*, Urbana and Chicago, IL: University of Illinois Press.
Lebon, J., 1937. 'Le Pseudo-Basile (*Adv. Eunom.* IV–V) est bien Didyme d'Alexandrie', *Le Muséon* 50, pp. 61–83.
Pruche, B., 1970. 'Didyme l'Aveugle est-il bien l'auteur des livres *Contre Eunome* IV et V attribués à Saint Basile de Césarée?', *SP* 10, pp. 151–5.
Tigcheler, J. H., 1977. 'Didyme l'Aveugle et l'exégèse allégorique. Étude sémantique de quelques termes exégétiques importants de son Commentaire zur Zacharie', Nijmegen: Dekker and van de Vegt.

Diodore of Tarsus

Abramowski, R., 1931. 'Untersuchungen zu Diodor von Tarsus', *ZNW* 30, pp. 234–62.
Greer, R. A., 1966. 'The Antiochene Christology of Diodore of Tarsus', *JTS* (NS) 17, pp. 327–41.
Schweizer, E., 1941. 'Diodor von Tarsus als Exeget', *ZNW* 40, pp. 33–75.

Ephrem Syrus

Amar, Joseph P., 1995. 'A Metrical Homily on Holy Mar Ephrem by Mar Jacob of Sarug', *Patrologia Orientalis* 47, pp. 1–76.
Bou Mansour, P. Tanios, 1988. *La pensée symbolique de saint Ephrem le Syrien*, Kaslik, Lebanon: Bibliothèque de l'Université Saint-Esprit.
Brock, Sebastian, 1985. *The Luminous Eye: The Spiritual World Vision of St Ephrem*, Rome: CIIS; republished Cistercian Publications 1992.
den Biesen, Kees, 2002. *Bibliography of Ephrem the Syrian*, Giove in Umbria: self-published.
——, 2006. *Simple and Bold: Ephrem's Art of Symbolic Thought*, Piskataway, NJ: Gorgias Press.
Griffith, Sidney H., 1986. 'Ephraem, the Deacon of Edessa, and the Church of the Empire', in Thomas Halton and Joseph P. Williman (eds), *Diakonia: Studies in Honor of Robert T. Meyer*, Washington, DC: Catholic University of America Press, pp. 22–52.
——, 1987. 'Ephraem the Syrian's Hymns "Agaist Julian": Meditations on History and Imperial Power', *VigChr* 41, pp. 238–66.

——, 1997. 'Faith Adoring the Mystery': Reading the Bible with St. Ephraem the Syrian, Milwaukee, WI: Marquette University Press.

——, 2001. 'The Thorn among the Tares: Mani and Manichaeism in the Works of St. Ephraem the Syrian', SP 35, pp. 395–427.

Harrison, Verna, 1996. 'Gender, Generation, and Virginity in Cappadocean Theology', JTS (NS) 47, pp. 38–68.

Murray, Robert, 2006. Symbols of Church and Kingdom, rev. edn (originally published 1975), London: T. & T. Clark.

Petersen, William L., 1985. 'The Dependence of Romanos the Melodist upon the Syriac Ephrem; its importance for the Origin of the Kontakion', VigChr 39, pp. 171–87.

Possekel, Ute, 1999. Evidence of Greek Philosophical Concepts in the Writings of Ephrem the Syrian, CSCO supplement 102, Louvain: Peeters.

Russell, P. S., 1994. St. Ephraem the Syrian and St. Gregory the Theologian Confront the Arians, Kottayam.

——, 2006. 'Avoiding the Lure of Edessa: A Plea for Caution in Dating the Works of Ephraem the Syrian', SP 41, pp. 71–4.

Shepardson, Christine, 2001. 'Anti-Jewish Rhetoric and Intra-Christian Conflict in the Sermons of Ephrem Syrus', SP 35, pp. 502–7.

Van Rompay, Lucas, 1996. 'The Christian Syriac Tradition of Interpretation', in Magne Saebo (ed.), Hebrew Bible/Old Testament: The History of Its Interpretation, Vol. I, Göttingen: Vandenhoeck & Ruprecht, pp. 612–41.

Yousif, P., 1990. 'Exegetical principles of St. Ephraem of Nisibis', SP 18, pp. 296–302.

Epiphanius of Salamis

Benko, S., 1967. 'The Libertine Sect of the Phibionites according to Epiphanius', VigChr 21, pp. 103–19.

Dechow, Jon F., 1988. Dogma and Mysticism in early Christianity: Epiphanius of Salamis and the legacy of Origen, Leuven: Peeters.

Fraenkel, P, 1963. 'Histoire sainte et hérésie chez S. Epiphane de Salamine', Revue de Théologie et Philosophie 12, pp. 175–91.

Holl, Karl, 1910. Die handschriftliche Überlieferung des Epiphanius, TU 36.2, Leipzig: Hinrichs.

——, 1928. 'Die Schriften des Epiphanius gegen die Bilderverehrung', in Gesammelte Aufsätze zur Kirchengeschichte II, Tübingen: Mohr Siebeck, pp. 351–87.

Kösters, Oliver, 2003. Die Trinitätslehre des Epiphanius von Salamis, ein Kommentar zum 'Ancoratus', Göttingen: Vandenhoeck & Ruprecht.

Lipsius, R. A., 1865. Zur Quellenkritik des Epiphanius, Vienna: Wilhelm Braumüller.

Moutsoulas, E., 1966. 'Der Begriff "Häresie" bei Epiphanius von Salamis', SP 7, pp. 362–71.

Nautin, P., 1949. Hippolytus, Contre les hérésies, Paris: Les Éditions du Cerf.

Palachkovsky, V., 1966. 'Une interpolation dans l'Ancoratus de S. Epiphane', SP 7, pp. 265–73.

Young, F. M., 1982. 'Did Epiphanius know what he meant by heresy?' SP 18, pp. 199–205.

Eusebius of Caesarea

Attridge, H. W. and G. Hata (eds), 1992. *Eusebius, Christianity and Judaism*, Leiden: Brill.

Barnes, T. D., 1981. *Constantine and Eusebius*, Cambridge, MA: Harvard University Press.

Baynes, N. H., 1929. 'Constantine the Great and the Christian Church', *Proc. of British Academy* XV, pp. 341–442.

——, 1933/55. 'Eusebius and the Christian Empire', originally published in *Mélanges Bidez*; reprinted in *Byzantine Studies and Other Essays*, London: Athlone Press, pp. 168–72.

——, H. J. Lawlor and G. W. Richardson, 1924-5. 'The Chronology of Eusebius', *Classical Quarterly* 19, pp. 95–100.

Burgess, R. W., (1997). 'The Dates and Editions of Eusebius' *Chronici Canones* and *Historia Ecclesiastica*', *JTS* (NS) 48, pp. 471–504.

Cangh, J. M. van, 1971, 1972. 'Nouveaux Fragments Hexaplaires. Commentaire sur Isaie d'Eusèbe de Césarée', *Revue Biblique* 78, pp. 384–90; 79, p. 76.

Carriker, Andrew James, 2003. *The Library of Eusebius of Caesarea*, Leiden: Brill.

Delcogliano, Mark, 2006. 'Eusebian Theologies of the Son as the Image of God before 341', *JECS* 14, pp. 459–84.

Frede, Michael, 1999. 'Eusebius' Apologetic Writings' in Mark Edwards, Martin Goodman and Simon Price (eds), *Apologetics in the Roman Empire. Pagans, Jews and Christians*, Oxford: Oxford University Press, pp. 223–50.

Grafton, Anthony and Megan Williams, 2006. *Christianity and the Transformation of the Book: Origen, Eusebius, and the Library of Caesarea*, Cambridge, MA: Harvard University Press.

Grant, R. M., 1972. 'Eusebius and his Church History', in J. Reumann (ed.), *Understanding the Sacred Text: Studies in Honor of M. S. Enslin*, Valley Forge, PA: Judson Press, pp. 233–47.

——, 1975. 'The Case against Eusebius, or Did the Father of Church History Write History?' *SP* 12, pp. 413–21.

——, 1980. *Eusebius as Church Historian*, Oxford and New York: Clarendon Press.

Hollerich, Michael J., 1999, *Eusebius of Caesarea's Commentary on Isaiah: Christian Exegesis in the Age of Constantine*, Oxford: Clarendon Press.

Jones, A. H. M., 1954. 'Notes on the genuineness of the Constantinian documents in Eusebius' *Life of Constantine*', *JEH* 5, pp. 196–200.

Kofsky, Aryeh, 2000. *Eusebius of Caesarea Against Paganism*, Leiden: Brill.

Lawlor, H. J., 1912. *Eusebiana: Essays on the Ecclesiastical History of Eusebius, Bishop of Caesarea*, Oxford: Oxford University Press.

Lienhard, J. T., 1999. *Contra Marcellum: Marcellus of Ancyra and Fourth Century Theology*, Washington, DC: Catholic University of America Press.

Louth, Andrew, 1990. 'The Date of Eusebius' *Historia Ecclesiastica*', *JTS* (NS) 41, pp. 111–23.

Luibheid, C., 1978. *Eusebius of Caesarea and the Arian Crisis*, Dublin: Irish Academic Press.

Lyman, Rebecca, 1993. *Christology and Cosmology: Models of Divine Activity in Origen, Eusebius and Athanasius*, Oxford: Clarendon Press.

Markus, R. A., 1975. 'Church History and the Early Church Historians' in D. A. Baker (ed.), *The Materials, Sources and Methods of Ecclesiastical History*, Studies in Church History 11, Oxford: Blackwell, pp. 1–17.

Möhle, A., 1934. 'Der Jesaiakommentar des Eusebios von Kaisareia fest vollständig wieder aufgefunden', *ZNW* 33, pp. 87–9.

Momigliano, A., 1963. 'Pagan and Christian Historiography', in Momigliano (ed.), *The Conflict between Paganism and Christianity in the Fourth Century*, Oxford and New York: Clarendon Press, pp. 79–99.

Mosshammer, A. A., 1979. *The* Chronicle *of Eusebius and Greek Chronographical Tradition*, Cranbury, NJ and London: Associated University Presses.

Nautin, P., 1961. *Lettres et écrivains chrétiens des IIe et IIIe siècles*, Paris: Les Éditions du Cerf.

Places, E. des, 1975. 'Numenius et Eusèbe de Césarée', *SP* 12, pp. 19–28.

Ricken, F., 1967. 'Die Logoslehre des Eusebios von Caesarea und der Mittelplatonismus', *Theologie und Philosophie* 42, pp. 341–58.

Sirinelli, J., 1961. *Les vues historiques d'Eusèbe de Césarée durant la période prénicéenne*, Dakar: Université de Dakar.

Stead, G. C., 1973. 'Eusebius and the Council of Nicaea', *JTS* (NS) 24, pp. 85–100.

Storch, R. H., 1971. 'The Eusebian Constantine', *Church History* 40, pp. 145–55.

Tabbernee, W., 1997. 'Eusebius' "Theology of Persecution": as seen in the various editions of his *Church History*', *JECS* 5, pp. 319–34.

Wallace-Hadrill, D. S., 1955. 'The Eusebian Chronicle: The Extent and Date of Composition of its Early Editions', *JTS* (NS) 6, pp. 248–53.

——, 1960. *Eusebius of Caesarea*, London: Mowbray.

Weber, A., 1965. *APXH. Ein Beitrag zur Christologie des Eusebius von Caesarea*, Rome: Pontifica Universita Gregoriana.

Eustathius of Antioch

Sellers, R. V., 1928. *Eustathius of Antioch*, Cambridge: Cambridge University Press.

Spanneut, M., 1954. 'La position théologique d'Eustathe d'Antioche', *JTS* (NS) 5, pp. 220–4.

Evagrius Ponticus

Guillaumont, A., 1962. *Les 'Kephalaia Gnostica' d'Évagre le Pontique et l'histoire de l'origénisme chez les Grecs et chez les Syriens*, Patristica Sorbonensia 5, Paris: Éditions du Seuil.

Konstantinovsky, Julia, 2009. *Evagrius Ponticus: The Making of a Gnostic*, Farnham: Ashgate.

Stewart, Columba, 2001. 'Imageless Prayer and the Theological Vision of Evagrius Ponticus', *JECS* 9, pp. 173–204.

Young, R. D., 2001. 'Evagrius the Iconographer: Monastic Pedagogy in the *Gnostikos*', *JECS* 9, pp. 53–71.

Gregory of Nazianzus

Beeley, Christopher A., 2008. *Gregory of Nazianzus on the Trinity and the Knowledge of God*, Oxford: Oxford University Press.

Bernardi, J., 1995. *Saint Grégoire de Nazianze: Le Théologien et son temps (330–390)*, Paris: Les Éditions du Cerf.

Børtnes, J. and Tomas Hägg (eds), 2006. *Gregory of Nazianzus: Images and Reflections*, Copenhagen: Museum Tusculanum.

Coman, J., 1976. 'Hellénisme et Christianisme dans le 25ᵉ discourse de saint Grégoire de Nazianze', *SP* 14, pp. 290–301.

Cross, R., 2006. 'Divine Monarchy in Gregory of Nazianzus', *JECS* 14, pp. 105–16.

Demoen, K., 1996. *Pagan and Biblical Exempla in Gregory Nazianzen: A Study in Rhetoric and Hermeneutics*, Corpus Christianorum, Turnhout: Brepols.

Ellverson, Anna-Stina, 1981. *The Dual Nature of Man: A Study in the Theological Anthropology of Gregory of Nazianzus*, Uppsala: Acta Universitatis Upsaliensis.

Fleury, E., 1930. *Hellénisme et Christianisme: S. Grégoire de Nazianze et son temps*, Paris: Gabriel Beauchesne.

McGuckin, J., 2001. *Gregory of Nazianzus*, Crestwood, NY: St Vladimir's Seminary Press.

Plagnieux, J., 1951. *Saint Grégoire de Nazianze théologien*, Études de science religieuse 7, Paris: Éditions Franciscaines.

Ruether, Rosemary, 1969. *Gregory Nazianzen, Rhetor and Philosopher*, Oxford: Clarendon Press.

Spidlik, T., 1971. *Grégoire de Nazianze: Introduction à l'étude de sa doctrine spirituelle*, Rome: Ponitificum Institutum Studiorum Orientalium.

Sykes, D. A., 1970. 'The *Poemata Arcana* of St Gregory Nazianzen', *JTS* (NS) 21, pp. 32–42.

Winslow, Donald F., 1979. *The Dynamics of Salvation: A Study in Gregory of Nazianzus*, Cambridge, MA: Philadelphia Patristics Foundation.

Gregory of Nyssa

Balthasar, H. Urs von, 1942. *Présence et pensée: Essai sur la philosophie religieuse de Grégoire de Nysse*, Paris: Éditions Beauchesne (ET of 1988 edition, 1995, *Presence and Thought*, by Mark Sebanc, San Francisco: Ignatius Press).

Barnes, Michel René, 2001. *The Power of God: Δύναμις in Gregory of Nyssa's Trinitarian Theology*, Washington, DC: Catholic University of America Press.

Bebis, G., 1967. 'Gregory of Nyssa's *De Vita Moysis*: a philosophical and theological analysis', *Greek Orthodox Theological Review* 12, pp. 369–93.

Brightman, R. S., 1973. 'Apophatic Theology and Divine Infinity in St Gregory of Nyssa', *Greek Orthodox Theological Review* 18, pp. 404–23.

Canévet, Mariette, 1983. *Grégoire de Nysse et l'herméneutique biblique: Étude des rapports entre le langage et la connaisance de Dieu*, Paris: Études Augustiniennes.

Cherniss, H. F., 1930. *The Platonism of Gregory of Nyssa*, New York: Burt Franklin.

Coakley, Sarah (ed.), 2003. *Re-Thinking Gregory of Nyssa*, Oxford: Blackwell.

Cross, R., 2006. 'Divine Monarchy in Gregrory of Nazianzus', *JECS* 14(1), pp. 105–16.

Daniélou, J., 1954. *Platonisme et théologie mystique*, Paris: Aubier.

——, 1964. 'Le symbole de la caverne chez Grégoire de Nysse', in A. Stuiber and A. Hermann (eds), *Mullus: Festschrift für Theodor Klauser*, Münster: Aschendorf, pp. 43–51.

——, 1965. 'Grégoire de Nysse à travers les lettres de saint Basile et de saint Grégoire de Nazianze', *VigChr* 19, pp. 31–41.

——, 1966a. 'La chronologie des oeuvres de Grégoire de Nysse', *SP* 7, pp. 159–69.

——, 1966b. 'Le traité "Sur les enfants morts prematurement" de Grégoire de Nysse',

VigChr 20, pp. 159–82.

——, 1967. 'Grégoire de Nysse et le néoplatonisme de l'Ecole d'Athènes', *Revue des Études Grecques* 80, pp. 395–401.

Dörrie, H., M. Altenburger and A. Schramm, 1976. *Gregor von Nyssa und die Philosophie*, Zweites internationales Kolloquium über Gregor von Nyssa, Freckenhorst bei Münster 1972, Leiden: Brill.

Dünzl, F., 1990. 'Gregor von Nyssa *Homilien zum Canticum* auf dem Hintergrund seiner *Vita Moysis*', *VigChr* 44, pp. 371–81.

Ferguson, E., 1973. 'God's Infinity and Man's Immutability Perpetual Progress according to Gregory of Nyssa', *Greek Orthodox Theological Review* 18, pp. 59–78.

——, 1976. 'Progress in perfection: Gregory of Nyssa's *Vita Moysis*', *SP* 14, pp. 307–14.

Fontaine, J. and C. Kannengiesser (eds), 1972. *Epektasis: Mélanges patristiques offerts au Cardinal J. Daniélou*, Paris: Beauchesne.

Geljon, A.-K., 2005. 'Divine Infinity in Gregory of Nyssa and Philo of Alexandria', *VigChr* 59, pp. 152–77.

Harl, M. (ed.), 1971. *Écriture et culture philosophique dans la pensée de Grégoire de Nysse*, Actes du colloque de Chevetogne, Leiden: Brill.

Harrison, V., 1992. *Grace and Human Freedom according to Gregory of Nyssa*, Lewiston, NY: Edwin Mellen.

Heine, R., 1975. *Perfection in the Virtuous Life: A study of the relationship between edification and polemical theology in Gregory of Nyssa's* De Vita Moysis, Cambridge, MA: Philadelphia Patristic Foundation.

Jaeger, W., 1966. *Gregor von Nyssa's Lehre vom Heiligen Geist* (ed. H. Dörries), Leiden: Brill.

Laird, Martin, 2004. *Gregory of Nyssa and the Grasp of Faith: Union, Knowledge, and Divine Presence*, Oxford: Oxford University Press.

Ludlow, Morwenna, 2000. *Universal Salvation: Eschatology in the Thought of Gregory of Nyssa and Karl Rahner*, Oxford: Oxford University Press.

——, 2007. *Gregory of Nyssa, Ancient and [Post]modern*, Oxford: Oxford University Press.

Mann, F., 1977. 'Gregor, Rhetor et Pastor: Interpretation des Proömiums der Schrift Gregors von Nyssa, *De Infantibus praemature abreptis*', *VigChr* 31, pp. 126–47.

Maspero, Giulio, 2007. *Trinity and Man: Gregory of Nyssa's Ad Ablabium*, Supplements to *VigChr*, Leiden: Brill.

May, G., 1966. 'Gregor von Nyssa in der Kirchenpolitik seiner Zeit', *Jahrbuch der österreichischen Byzantinistischen Gesellschaft* 15, pp. 105–32.

Macleod, C. W., 1970. 'ΑΝΑΛΥΣΙΣ: A Study in Ancient Mysticism', *JTS* (NS) 21, pp. 43–55.

——, 1971. 'Allegory and Mysticism in Origen and Gregory of Nyssa', *JTS* (NS) 22, pp. 362–79.

Meredith, A., 1975. 'Orthodoxy, Heresy and Philosophy in the Later Half of the Fourth Century', *Heythrop Journal* 16, pp. 5–21.

——, 1976. 'Traditional Apologetic in the *Contra Eunomium* of Gregory of Nyssa', *SP* 14, pp. 315–19.

Moutsoulas, E. D. (ed.), 2005. *Jesus Christ in St. Gregory of Nyssa's Theology*, Athens: Eptalophos.

Mühlenberg, E., 1966. *Die Unendlichkeit Gottes bei Gregor von Nyssa*, Göttingen: Vandenhoeck & Ruprecht.

Pottier, B., 1994. *Dieu et le Christ selon Grégoire de Nysse*, Namur: Culture et Vérité.

Ramelli, I. L. E., 2007. 'Christian Soteriology and Christian Platonism: Origen, Gregory of Nyssa, and the Biblical and Philosophical Basis of the Doctrine of Apokatasis', *VigChr* 61, pp. 313–56.

Schoedel, W. R. and R. L. Wilken (eds), 1979. *Early Christian Literature and the Classical Intellectual Tradition*, in honorem Robert M. Grant, Paris: Beauchesne.

Smith, Warren J., 2004. *Passion and Paradise: Human and Divine Emotion in the Thought of Gregory of Nyssa*, New York: Crossroad.

Spira, Andreas (ed.), 1984. *The Biographical Works of Gregory of Nyssa*, Proceedings of the Fifth International Colloquium on Gregory of Nyssa, 1982, Cambridge, MA: Philadelphia Patristic Foundation.

Stritzky, M. von, 1973. *Zum Problem der Erkenntnis bei Gregor von Nyssa*, Münster: Aschendorf.

Turcescu, Lucian, 2005. *Gregory of Nyssa and the Concept of Divine Persons*, Oxford: Oxford University Press and the American Academy of Religion.

Zachhuber, J., 2000. *Human Nature in Gregory of Nyssa: Philosophical Background and Theological Significance*, Supplements to *VigChr*, Leiden: Brill.

John Chrysostom

Aldama, J. A., 1965. *Repertorium pseudo-Chrysostomicum*, Paris: CNRS.

Allen, Pauline, 1997. 'John Chrysostom's Homilies on I & II Thessalonians: The Preacher and his Audience', *SP* 31, pp. 3–21.

Ameringer, T. E., 1921. *The Stylistic Influence of the Second Sophistic on the Panegyrical Sermons of St John Chrysostom*, Washington, DC: Catholic University of America Press.

Amirav, Hagit, 2003. *Rhetoric and Tradition: John Chrysostom on Noah and the Flood*, Leuven: Peeters.

Baur, C., 1907. *S. Jean Chrysostome et ses oeuvres dans l'histoire littéraire*, Paris: Fontemoing.

——, 1929/59. *St Chrysostom and His Time* (German original 1929), ET by M. Gonzaga, Westminster, MD and London: Sands.

Brändle, R., 1977. 'Jean Chrysostome: l'importance de Matt. 25:31–46 pour son éthique', *VigChr* 31, pp. 47–52.

——, 2004. *John Chrysostom, Bishop, Reformer, Martyr*, ET Strathfield, NSW: St. Paul's.

Carter, R. E., 1962. 'Chrysostom's *Ad Theodorum Lapsum* and the early chronology of Theodore of Mopsuestia', *VigChr* 16, pp. 87–101.

——, 1970. 'The Future of Chrysostom Studies', *SP* 10, p. 20.

Chase, F. H., 1887. *Chrysostom: A Study in the History of Biblical Interpretation*, Cambridge: Deighton, Bell.

Clark, E. A., 1977. 'John Chrysostom and the *Subintroductae*', *Church History* 46, pp. 171–85.

Coman, J., 1968. 'Le rapport de la justification et de la charité dans les homélies de S. Jean Chrysostome à l'Epitre aux Romains', *Studia Evangelica* 5 (TU 103), pp. 248–71.

Danassis, A. K., 1971. *Johannes Chrysostomos: Pädagogisch-psychologische Ideen in seinem Werk*, Bonn: Bouvier Verlag.

Fabricius, C., 1962. *Zu den Jugendschriften des Johannes Chrysostomos: Untersuchungen zum Klassizismus des vierten Jahrhunderts*, Lund: Gleerup.

Garrett, Duane A., 1992. *An Analysis of the Hermeneutics of John Chrysostom's Commentary on Isaiah 1–8 with an English Translation*, Lewiston, NY: Edwin Mellen.

Goodall, Blake, 1979. *The Homilies of John Chrysostom on the Letters of Paul to Titus and Philemon: prolegomena to an edition*, Berkeley: University of California Press.

Gorday, Peter, 1983. *Principles of Patristic Exegesis: Romans 9–11 in Origen, John Chrysostom, and Augustine*, New York and Toronto: Edwin Mellen.

Greeley, D., 1982. 'St. John Chrysostom. Prophet of Social Justice', *SP* 17, pp. 1163–8.

Hartney, Aideen M., 2004. *John Chrysostom and the Transformation of the City*, London: Duckworth.

Hunter, David G., 1989. 'Libanius and John Chrysostom: New Thoughts on an Old Problem', *SP* 22, pp. 129–35.

Kelly, J. N. D., 1995. *Goldenmouth: The Story of John Chrysostom, Ascetic, Preacher, Bishop*, London: Duckworth.

Lawrenz III, Melvin E., 1996. *Christology of John Chrysostom*, Lewiston, NY: Edwin Mellen.

Leroux, J. M., 1961. 'Monachisme et communauté chrétienne d'après saint Jean Chrysostome', in *Théologie de la vie monastique*, Études sur la tradition patristique, Paris: Aubier, pp. 143–90.

——, 1975. 'Saint Jean Chrysostome et le monachisme', in C. Kannengiesser (ed.), *Jean Chrysostome et Augustin*, Paris: Beauchesne, pp. 125–44.

Leyerle, Blake, 1994. 'John Chrysostom on almsgiving and the use of money', *Harvard Theological Review* 87, pp. 29–47.

——, 2001. *Theatrical Shows and Ascetic Lives: John Chrysostom's Attack on Spiritual Marriage*, Berkeley, Los Angeles and London: University of California Press.

Malingrey, A. M., 1970. 'La tradition manuscrite des homélies de Jean Chrysostome *De Incomprehensibilité*', *SP* 10, pp. 22–8.

——, 1973. 'L'édition critique de Jean Chrysostome. Actualité de son oeuvre. Volumes parus. Projets', in P. C. Christou, *Symposion: Studies on Saint John Chrysostom*, Thessaloniki: Patriarchikon Hidryma Paterikon Meleton, pp. 77–90.

Maxwell, Jaclyn L., 2006. *Christianization and Communication in Late Antiquity*, Cambridge: Cambridge University Press.

Mayer, Wendy, 1997. 'John Chrysostom and his Audiences: distinguishing different congregations at Antioch and Constantinople', *SP* 31, pp. 70–5.

——, 2005. *Homilies of St. John Chrysostom: Provenance—reshaping the foundations*, Roma: Pontificio Istituto Orientale.

Meyer, L., 1933. *S. Jean Chrysostome: Maître de perfection chrétienne*, Paris: Beauchesne.

Mitchell, Margaret M., 2000. *The Heavenly Trumpet: John Chrysostom and the Art of Pauline Interpretation*, Hermeneutische Untersuchungen zur Theologie 40, Tübingen: Mohr Siebeck.

Murphy, F. X., 1972. 'The Moral Doctrine of St John Chrysostom', *SP* 11, pp. 52–7.

Nowak, E., 1972. *Le chrétien devant la souffrance: Étude sur la pensée de Jean Chrysostome*, Paris: Beauchesne.

Ommerslaeghe, F. van, 1977. 'Que vaut le témoignage de Pallade sur la procès de S. Jean Chrysostom?', *Analecta Bollandiana* 95, pp. 389–414.

——, 1979. 'Jean Chrysostome en conflit avec l'impératrice Eudoxie', *Analecta Bollandiana* 97, pp. 131–59.

Paverd, Frans van de, 1991. *St. John Chrysostom. Homilies on the Statues. An Introduction*, Roma: Pont. Institutum Studiorum Orientalium.

Plassmann, O., 1961. *Das Almosen bei Johannes Chrysostomus*, Münster: Aschendorf.
Quère-Jaulmes, F., 1966. 'L'aumone chez Grégoire de Nysse et Grégoire de Nazianze', *SP* 8, pp. 449–55.
Retzleff, A., 2003. 'John Chrysostom's Sex Aquarium: Acquatic Metaphors for Theatre in *Homily 7 On Matthew*', *JECS* 11, pp. 195–207.
Thonnard, F.-J., 1967. 'S. Jean Chrysostome et S. Augustine dans la controverse pélagienne', *Revue des Études Byzantines* 25, pp. 189–218.
Vandenberghe, Bruno H., 1961. S, *Jean Chrysostome et la parole de Dieu*, Paris: Les Éditions du Cerf.
Wilken, Robert L., 1983. *John Chrysostom and the Jews: Rhetoric and Reality in the Late Fourth Century*, Berkeley: University of California Press.

'Macarius'

Dörries, H., 1941. *Symeon von Mesopotamien: Die Überlieferung der Messalianischen 'Makarios'-Schriften*, TU 55, Leipzig: Hinrichs.
——, 1978. *Die Theologie des Makarios-Symeon*, Göttingen: Vanderhoeck & Ruprecht.
Golitzin, A., 2002. 'A Testimony to Christianity as Transfiguration: The Macarian Homilies and Orthodox Spirituality' in S. T. Kimbrough, Jr (ed.), *Orthodox and Wesleyan Spirituality*, Crestwood, NY: St Vladimir's Seminary Press, pp. 129–56.
Jaeger, W., 1954. *Two Rediscovered Works of Ancient Christian Literature: Gregory of Nyssa and Macarius*, Leiden: Brill.
Plested, Marcus, 2004. *The Macarian Legacy: The place of Macarius-Symeon in the eastern Christian tradition*, Oxford Theological Monographs, Oxford: Oxford University Press.
Staats, R., 1968. *Gregor von Nyssa und die Messalianer*, PTS 8, Berlin: de Gruyter.
Stewart, Columba, 1991. *'Working the Earth of the Heart': The Messalian Controversy in History, Texts, and Language to AD 431*, Oxford: Clarendon Press.
Villecourt, L., 1920. 'La date et l'origine des "Homélies spirituelles" attribuées à Macaire', in *Comptes rendus de l'Académie des Inscriptions et Belles-Lettres*, Paris, pp. 250–8.
Young, Frances M., 1987. 'Allegory and Atonement', *Australian Biblical Review* 35, pp. 107–14.
——, 2002. 'Inner Struggle: Some Parallels between John Wesley and the Greek Fathers,' in S. T. Kimbrough, Jr (ed.), *Orthodox and Wesleyan Spirituality*, Crestwood, NY: St Vladimir's Seminary Press, pp. 157–72.

Marcellus of Ancyra

Lienhard, J. T., 1982. 'Marcellus of Ancyra in Modern Research', *ThS* 43, pp. 486–503.
——, 1993. 'Did Athanasius Reject Marcellus?', in M. R. Barnes and D. H. Williams (eds), *Arianism After Arius: Essays on the Development of the Fourth Century Trinitarian Conflicts*, Edinburgh: T. & T. Clark, pp. 65–80.
——, 1999. Contra Marcellum: *Marcellus of Ancyra and Fourth-Century Theology*. Washington, DC: Catholic University of America Press.
Loofs, Friedrich, 1902. 'Die Trinitätslehre Marcell's von Ancyra und ihr Verhältnis zur älteren Tradition', in Loofs, *Patristica: ausgewählte Aufsätze zur Alten Kirche*, ed.

H. C. Brennecke and J. Ulrich, Berlin: de Gruyter, 1999, pp. 123–42.

Parvis, S., 2006. *Marcellus of Ancyra and the Lost Years of the Arian Controversy, 325–345*, Oxford Early Christian Studies, Oxford: Oxford University Press.

——, 2008. "'Tὰ τίνων ἄρα ῥήματα θεολογεῖ?'": The Exegetical Relationship between Athanasius' *Orationes contra Arianos I–III* and Marcellus of Ancyra's *Contra Asterium'*, in L. DiTommaso and L. Turcescu (eds), *The Reception and Interpretation of the Bible in Late Antiquity: Proceedings of the Montréal Colloquium in Honour of Charles Kannengiesser, 11–13 October 2006*, Leiden and Boston: Brill, pp. 337–67.

Vinzent, M., 1996. *Pseudo-Athanasius Contra Arianos IV: Eine Schrift gegen Asterius von Kappadokien, Eusebius von Cäsarea, Markell von Ankyra und Photin von Sirmium*, Supplement to *VigChr* 36, Leiden: Brill.

Nemesius of Emesa

Jaeger, W. W., 1914. *Nemesios von Emesa: Quellenforschungen zum Neuplatonismus und seinen anfängen bei Posidonios*, Berlin: Weidman.

Reinhardt, K., 1953. 'Poseidonios von Apamea', in A. F. Pauly, G. Wissowa and W. Kroll (eds), *Real-Encyclopädie der klassischen Altertumswissenschaft* 22, Stuttgart: Metzler, col. 773.

Skard, E., 1936, 1937, 1938, 1939, 1942. 'Nemesiosstudien', *Symbolae Osloenses* 15, pp. 23–43; 17, pp. 9–25; 18, pp. 31–41; 19, pp. 46–56; 22, pp. 40–8.

Streck, Martin, 2005. *Das Schönste Gut: der menschliche Wille nach Nemesius von Emesa und Gregor von Nyssa*, Göttingen: Vanderhoeck & Ruprecht.

Young, Frances, 1983. 'Adam, the soul and immortality: a study of the interaction of "science" and the Bible in some anthropological treatises of the Fourth Century', *VigChr* 37, pp. 110–40.

Nestorius

Abramowski, L., 1963. *Untersuchungen zum Liber Heraclidis des Nestorius*, CSCO 242 (Subsidia 22), Louvain: Secretariat du CSCO.

Amann, E., 1931. 'Nestorius', in *Dictionnaire de Théologie Catholique* XI, pp. 76–157.

Anastos, Milton V., 1962. 'Nestorius was Orthodox', *Dumbarton Oaks Papers* 16, pp. 119–40.

Bethune-Baker, J. F., 1908. *Nestorius and his Teaching*, Cambridge: Cambridge University Press.

Chesnut, Roberta C., 1978. 'The Two Prosopa in Nestorius' *Bazaar of Heraclides*', *JTS* (NS) 29, pp. 392–409.

Hodgson, L., 1918. 'The Metaphysic of Nestorius', *JTS* 19, pp. 46–55 (republished as Appendix IV in G. R. Driver and L. Hodgson, *Nestorius. The Bazaar of Heraclides*, ET, Oxford and New York: Clarendon Press, 1925).

Loofs, F., 1914. *Nestorius and His Place in the History of Christian Doctrine*, Cambridge and New York: Cambridge University Press.

Scipioni, L. I., 1975. *Nestorio e il concilio di Epheso*, Studia Patristica Mediolanensia, Milan: Pubblicazioni della Università Cattolica del Sacro Cuore.

Turner, H. E. W., 1975. 'Nestorius Reconsidered', *SP* 13, pp. 306–21.

Palladius, *Lausiac History* and *Historia monachorum*

Bammel, C. P., 1996. 'Problems of the *Historia Monachorum*', *JTS* (NS) 47, pp. 92–104.

Bousset, W., 1917. 'Komposition und Charakter del Historia Lausiaca', in *Nachrichten von der königlichen Gesellschaft der Wissenschaften zu Göttingen, Phil.–hist. Klasse*, pp. 173–217.

——, 1922. 'Zur Komposition del Historia Lausiaca', *ZNW* 21, pp. 81–98.

Buck, D. F., 1976. 'The Structure of the *Lausiac History*', *Byzantion* 46, pp. 292–307.

Chitty, D. J., 1955. 'Dom Cuthbert Butler and the Lausiac History', *JTS* (NS) 6, 239–58.

Coleman-Norton, P. R., 1926. 'The Authorship of the *Epistola de Indicis gentibus et de Bragmanibus*', *Classical Philology* 21, pp. 154–60.

Draguet, R., 1944. 'Le chapitre de l'*Histoire Lausiaque* sur les Tabénnesiotes', *Le Muséon* 57, pp. 53–146.

——, 1945. 'Le chapitre de l'*Histoire Lausiaque* sur les Tabénnesiotes', *Le Muséon* 58, pp. 15–96.

——, 1946. 'L'Histoire Lausiaque, une oeuvre écrite dans l'esprit d'Evagre', *Revue d'Histoire Ecclésiastique* 41, pp. 321–64.

——, 1947a. 'L'Histoire Lausiaque, une oeuvre écrite dans l'esprit d'Evagre', *Revue d'Histoire Ecclésiastique* 42, pp. 5–49.

——, 1947b. 'Une nouvelle source Copte de Pallade: le chapitre viii (Amoun)', *Le Muséon* 60, pp. 227–55.

——, 1949. 'Un nouveau témoin du texte G de l'Histoire Lausiaque (MS. *Athènes 281)*', *Analecta Bollandiana* 67, pp. 300–8.

——, 1950. 'Butler et sa Lausiac History face à un ms. de l'édition I Wake 67', *Le Muséon* 63, pp. 203–30.

——, 1955. 'Butleriana: Une mauvaise cause et son malchanceux avocat', *Le Muséon* 68, pp. 239–58.

Festugière, A.-J., 1955. 'Le problème littéraire de l'*Historia Monachorum*', *Hermes* 83, pp. 257–84.

Halkin, F., 1930. 'L'Histoire Lausiaque et les vies grecques de S. Pachome', *Analecta Bollandiana* 48, pp. 257–301.

——, 1929. 'Les vies grecques de S. Pachome', *Analecta Bollandiana* 47, pp. 376–83.

Hunt, E. D., 1973. 'Palladius of Helenopolis: A Party and its Supporters in the Church of the late Fourth Century', *JTS* (NS) 24, pp. 456–80.

Meyer, R. T., 1970. 'Palladius and Early Christian Spirituality', *SP* 10, pp. 379–90.

Molinier, Nicolas, 1995. *Ascèse, contemplation et ministre: d'après l'Histoire Lausiaque de Pallade d'Hélénopolis*, SO 54, Bégrolles-en-Mauges: Abbaye de Bellefontaine.

Peeters, P., 1936. 'Une vie copte de S. Jean de Lycopolis', *Analecta Bollandiana*, 54, pp. 359–83.

Telfer, W., 1937. 'The Trustworthiness of Palladius', *JTS* 38, pp. 379–83.

Socrates Scholasticus

Chesnut, Glenn F., 1975. 'Kairos and Cosmic Sympathy in the Church Historian Socrates Scholasticus', *Church History* 44, pp. 69–75.

Urbainczyk, Theresa, 1997. *Socrates of Constantinople, Historian of Church and State*, Ann Arbor: University of Michigan Press.

Synesius of Cyrene

Crawford, W. S., 1901. *Synesius the Hellene*, London: Rivingtons.

Barnes, T. D., 1986a. 'Synesius in Constantinople', *Greek, Roman and Byzantine Studies* 27, pp. 93–112.

——, 1986b. 'When did Synesius become Bishop of Ptolemais?', *Greek, Roman and Byzantine Studies* 27, pp. 325–9.

Bayless, W. N., 1977. 'Synesius of Cyrene: A Study of the Roles of the Bishop in Temporal Affairs', *Byzantine Studies: Études Byzantines* 4, pp. 147–56.

Bregman, Jay, 1974. 'Synesius of Cyrene: Early Life and Conversion to Philosophy', *California Studies in Classical Antiquity* 7, pp. 55–88.

——, 1982. *Synesius of Cyrene: Philosopher-Bishop*, Berkeley/Los Angeles/London: University of California Press.

Grützmacher, G., 1913. *Synesius von Kyrene*, Leipzig: Dechert.

Lacombrade, C., 1951a. *Synésios de Cyrène: Héllène et chrétien*, Paris: Les Belles Lettres.

——, 1961. 'Perspectives nouvelles sur les hymnes de Synésios', *Revue des Études Grecques* 74, pp. 439–49.

Liebeschuetz, J. H. W. G., 1985. 'Synesius and Municipal Politics of Cyrenaica in the Fifth Century', *Byzantion* 55, pp. 146–64.

——, 1986. 'Why did Synesius become Bishop of Ptolemais?', *Byzantion* 56, pp. 180–95.

Marrou, H. I., 1936. 'Synesius of Cyrene and Alexandrian Neoplatonism', in A. Momigliano (ed.), *The Conflict between Paganism and Christianity in the Fourth Century*, Oxford: Oxford University Press, pp. 128–50.

Pack, R., 1949. 'Folklore and Superstitions in the Writings of Synesius', *Classical Weekly* 43, pp. 51–6.

Roques, D., 1977. 'Le Lettre 4 de Synésios de Cyrène', *Revue des Études Grecques* 90, pp. 263–95.

——, 1987. *Synésios de Cyrène et la Cyrenaique du Bas-Empire*, Paris: Éditions du CNRS.

——, 1989. *Études sur la correspondence de Synésios de Cyrène*, Bruxelles: Latomus.

Schmitt, T., 2001. *Die Bekehrung des Synesios von Kyrene: Politik und Philosophie, Hof und Provinz als Handlungsräume eines Aristokraten bis zu seiner Wahl zum Metropoliten von Ptolemais*, München: K. G. Saur.

Seeck, O., 1894. 'Studien zu Synesios', *Philologus* 52, pp. 442–83.

Volkmann, R., 1869. *Synesius von Cyrene*, Berlin: Ebeling & Plahn.

Theodore of Mopsuestia

Abramowski, Luise, 1961. 'Zur Theologie Theodors von Mopsuestia', *Zeitschrift für Kirchengeschichte* 72, pp. 263–93.

Bultmann, R., 1984. *Die Exegese des Theodor von Mopsuestia*, ed. H. Field and K. Schelke, Stuttgart: W. Kohlhammer.

Carter, R. E., 1962. 'Chrysostom's *Ad Theodorum lapsum* and the Early Chronology of Theodore of Mopsuestia', *VigChr* 16, pp. 87–101.

Devreesse, R., 1948. *Essai sur Théodore de Mopsueste*, Studi e Testi 141, Rome: Vaticana.

Dewart, J., 1971. *The Theology of Grace of Theodore of Mopsuestia*, Washington, DC: Catholic University of America Press.

——, 1975. 'The Notion of "Person" underlying the Christology of Theodore of Mopsuestia', *SP* 12, pp. 199–207.

Gerber, S., 2000. *Theodor von Mopsuestia und das Nicanum: Studien zu den katechetischen Homilien*, Leiden: Brill.

Greer, R., 1961. *Theodore of Mopsuestia: Exegete and Theologian*, London: Faith Press.

McKenzie, J. L., 1953. 'The Commentary of Theodore of Mopsuestia on Jn. 1.46–51', *Theological Studies* 14, pp. 73–84.

——, 1958. 'Annotations on the Christology of Theodore of Mopsuestia', *Theological Studies* 19, pp. 345–73.

McLeod, F., 2002. 'The Christological ramifications of Theodore of Mopsuestia's Understanding of Baptism and the Eucharist', *JECS* 10, pp. 37–75.

——, 2005. *The Role of Christ's Humanity in Salvation: Insights from Theodore of Mopsuestia*, Washington, DC: Catholic University of America Press.

Norris, R. A., 1963. *Manhood and Christ*, Oxford and New York: Clarendon Press.

Patterson, L., 1926. *Theodore of Mopsuestia and Modern Thought*, London: SPCK.

Pirot, L., 1913. *L'Oeuvre exégétique de Théodore de Mopsueste*, Rome: Sumptibus Pontificii Instituti Biblici.

Richard, M., 1943/77. 'La tradition des fragments du traité Περὶ τῆς ἐνανθρωπήσεως de Théodore de Mopsueste', *Le Muséon* 56, pp. 55–75; republished in M. Richard, 1977. *Opera Minora* II, Turnhout: Brepols.

Sullivan, F. A., 1956. *The Christology of Theodore of Mopsuestia*, Rome: Analecta Gregoriana.

——, 1959. 'Further Notes on Theodore of Mopsuestia. A Reply to Fr. McKenzie', *Theological Studies* 20, pp. 264–79.

Unnik, W. C. van, 1963. 'παρρησία in the "Catechetical Homilies" of Theodore of Mopsuestia', in *Mélanges offerts à Mlle Christine Mohrmann*, Utrecht: Spectrum, pp. 12–22.

Wiles, M. F., 1960. *The Spiritual Gospel*, Cambridge: Cambridge University Press.

——, 1967. *The Divine Apostle*, Cambridge: Cambridge University Press.

——, 1970. 'Theodore of Mopsuestia as Representative of the Antiochene School', in *The Cambridge History of the Bible* Vol. 1, Cambridge and New York: Cambridge University Press, pp. 489–510.

Theodoret of Cyrus

Ashby, G. W., 1972. *Theodoret of Cyrrhus as Exegete of the Old Testament*, Grahamstown, South Africa: Rhodes University.

Brok, M. F. A., 1951. 'The Date of Theodoret's *Expositio Rectae Fidei*', *JTS* (NS) 2, pp. 178–83.

Canivet, P., 1957. *Histoire d'une entreprise apologétique de Ve siècle*, Paris: Bloud & Gay.

——, 1977. *Le monachisme Syrien selon Théodoret de Cyr*, Paris: Éditions Beauchesne.

Chesnut, G. F., 1981. 'The Date of Composition of Theodoret's Church History', *VigChr* 35, pp. 245–52.

Clayton, P. B., Jr, 2007. *The Christology of Theodoret of Cyrus: Antiochene Christology from the Council of Ephesus (431) to the Council of Chalcedon (451)*, Oxford: Oxford University Press.

Delahaye, H., 1923. *Les Saints Stylites*, Bruxelles: Société des Bollandistes.

Devos, P., 1979. 'La structure de l'*Histoire Philothée* de Théodoret de Cyr: Le nombre de chapitres', *Analecta Bollandiana* 97, pp. 319–36.

Fairbairn, D., 2007, 'The puzzle of Theodoret's Christology: A Modest Suggestion', *JTS* (NS) 58, pp. 100–33.

Guinot, J.-N., 1995. *L'exégèse de Théodoret de Cyr*, Paris: Beauchesne.

Honigmann, E., 1953. 'Theodoret of Cyrrhus and Basil of Seleucia: The Time of Their Death', *Patristic Studies* (Studi e Testi 173), Rome: Vaticana, pp. 174–84.

Koch, G., 1974. *Strukturen und Geschichte des Heils in der Theologie des Theodoret von Kyros*, Frankfurter Theologischen Studien 17, Frankfurt am Main: Verlag Josef Knecht.

Krueger, D., 1997. 'Typological Figuration in Theodoret of Cyrrhus's *Religious History* and the Art of Postbiblical narrative', *JECS* 5, pp. 393–419.

Lebon, J., 1930. 'Restitutions à Théodoret de Cyr', *Revue d'Histoire Ecclésiastique* 26, pp. 524–50.

Leroy-Molinghen, A., 1964. 'A propos de la Vie de Syméon Stylite', *Byzantion* 34, pp. 375–84.

Mandac, M., 1971. 'L'Union christologique dans les oeuvres de Théodoret anterieures au concile d'Ephèse', *Ephemerides Theologicae Lovanienses* 47, pp. 64–96.

McNamara, K., 1955. 'Theodoret of Cyrus and the Unity of Person in Christ', *Irish Theological Quarterly* 22, pp. 313–28.

Parvis, P. M., 1975, 'Theodoret's Commentary on the Epistles of St Paul', Oxford University, unpublished D.Phil. thesis.

Peeters, P., 1943. 'S. Symeon Stylite et ses premiers biographes', *Analecta Bollandiana* 61, pp. 29–71; republished in *Le tréfonds oriental de l'hagiographie byzantine* (Subsidia Hagiographica 26), Brussels: Société des Bollandistes, 1950, chapter V.

Richard, M., 1935/77. 'L'activité littéraire de Théodoret avant le concile d'Ephèse', *Revue des Sciences Philosophiques et Théologiques* 24, pp. 83–106; republished in Richard, *Opera Minora* II, Turnhout: Brepols, 1977.

——, 1936/77. 'Notes sur l'évolution doctrinale de Théodoret', *Revue des Sciences Philosophiques et Théologiques*, 25, pp. 459–81; republished in Richard, *Opera Minora* II, Turnhout: Brepols, 1977.

——, 1946/77. 'Théodoret, Jean d' Antioche et les moines d'Orient', *Mélanges de Science Religieuse* 3, pp. 148–61; republished in Richard, *Opera Minora* II, Turnhout: Brepols, 1977.

Schor, A. M., 2007. 'Theodoret on the 'School of Antioch': A Network Approach', *JECS* 15, pp. 517–62.

Sellers, R. V., 1945. 'Pseudo-Justin's *Expositio Rectae Fidei*, a Work of Theodoret', *JTS* 46, pp. 145–60.

Urbainczyk, T., 2002. *Theodoret of Cyrrhus: The Bishop and the Holy Man*, Ann Arbor: University of Michigan Press.

Wagner, M. M., 1948. 'A Chapter in Byzantine Epistolography', *Dumbarton Oaks Papers* 4, pp. 119–81.

Index of Subjects and Names

Diodore of Tarsus, 244–5; 251; 254–63; 265; 274; 286; 314; 321–5; 334; 341
Diogenes Laertius, 7
Dionysius of Alexandria, 6; 47; 247; 250–1
Dionysius, Bishop of Corinth, 316
Diotogenes, 14
Dioscorus, 303; 325; 326; 329
Disciplina arcani, 160; 170; 190; 192
Docetism, 17; 63–4; 99; 244; 270; 290; 307; 311; 318; 341
Dogma, 20; 35; 40; 56; 61; 69; 87; 95–6; 99–100; 150; 156; 169–70; 172; 195; 203; 214–5; 219; 222; 232; 255; 263–4; 267–8; 272; 308–9; 311
Domnus, 325–6
Dorotheus, 82
Dositheus, 199
Dyophysite, 243; 252; 263; 288

Ebion, -ite, 6; 47; 341
Economy, 58; 124; 254; 251; 261; 271; 276; 281; 310
Eden, 75; 77; 201; *see also* Paradise
Education, 19; 23; 32; 37; 47; 88–9; 93–4; 97; 135–6; 138; 145–51; 209–11; 224; 234; 239; 252; 300; 320; 323–4
Egypt, 2; 5; 33; 40; 42–4; 49–51; 64; 66; 68–70; 73–6; 78–80; 82–4; 86–7; 89; 91–2; 94–5; 102–3; 111; 114; 116; 118; 122; 127; 129–30; 133–4; 137; 141; 144; 164; 193–4; 200; 203; 267; 279; 290; 297
Ephrem, 117; 121; 122; 128; 131; 173–185; 340
Epicurus, -eans, 198–9
Epiphanius of Salamis, 42–3; 57; 60; 117; 173–4; 186–7; 193; 194–204; 253
Epiphanius the Sophist, 252
Eschatology, 5; 108; 180; 268
Etheria, 191
Eudoxia, 205–6
Eunomius, -ians, 31–3; 47; 66; 156; 286; 301; 308
Euripides, 93; 242; 323
Eusebius, Bishop of Caesarea in Cappadocia, 137–8
Eusebians, 25; 41; 59; 62

Eusebius of Caesarea (in Palestine), 1–44; 47–8; 52–3; 57; 61; 65; 66; 73; 80; 176; 191; 194; 243; 254–5; 257
Eusebius of Emesa, 254–5; 257; 259
Eusebius of Nicomedia, 41–4; 57
Eustathius, 2–3; 20; 25; 57; 137; 144; 152–4; 156; 159; 241; 243–5; 247; 259; 334
Eutropius, 206; 216
Eutyches, -ians, 252; 264; 333; 337; 341
Evagrius Ponticus, 24; 39; 74; 76; 79; 81–3; 89; 91–2; 94; 101–18; 124; 127; 168; 203
Exegesis, of Arius, 44; 46; 94; of Athanasius, 46; 53; 63–4; of Basil, 139; 147; of Cyril, of Alexandria, 280; 284; 302–13; 318; 322; of Jerusalem, 193; of Didymus, 97; 99; of Diodore, 254–6; 261; of Ephrem, 176; 178; of Epiphanius, 195; 198; 201; of Eusebius, 17; 21–3; 53; of Eustathius, 244; of Evagrius, 105; 115; of Gregory Nazianzen, 24; 141; of Gregory Nyssen, 142; 165; 168; 171; of John Chrysostom, 214; 217–8; monastic, 90; of Theodore, 268–271; of Theodoret, 330; 335; 338–42

Facundus, 254; 263–5
Fall, 10; 45; 54–5; 59; 99; 100; 110; 112; 122; 167; 172; 230; 253; 262; 268–9; 304
Fasting, 70; 74; 118; 132; 170; 313
Flavian, bishop, 117; 213; 216–7; 288
Florilegia, 40; 219; 242–3; 252; 256; 264; 314; 334

Galen, 74; 131; 223–5
Gaza, 84; 200
Gelasius, 24; 187
George the Cappadocian, 50
Gnosis, Gnostic, -ism, 48; 119; 168; 187; 189; 199–200; 249; 241
Gregory of Alexandria, 50
Gregory of Nazianzus, 49; 51; 71; 75; 94; 102–3; 107–8; 135–65; 169; 171; 184; 205; 209; 223–4; 236

223–5; 228; 234–5; 237; 241; 249;
252; 261; 268–9; 300; 307; 333
Plotinus, 47; 76; 138; 146; 150; 166–8;
224–5; 235; 249
Plutarch, 34; 246–7; 234
Poemen, 84; 87; 88–90; 128
Poems, 44; 141; 149–51; 170; 177; 184;
267
Politics, 3; 8; 18; 34; 40; 51–2; 69; 82;
137–9; 144; 185–6; 205–6; 232; 237;
240; 262; 286; 299; 313; 321
Polemon, 246
Porphyry, 5; 9–11; 32; 93; 150; 231;
252; 254; 301
Posidonius, 223
Potamiaena, 80; 128; 137; 175; 184
Property, of Church, 187; 205; 220;
234; 301
Prophecy, prophets, OT, 11–12; 22;
29; 24; 80; 193; 199; 165–6; 321
Providence, 8, 11–16; 29; 31; 34–5; 38;
94; 109; 113; 170; 222; 226–7; 229;
254; 326; 338; 341–2
Psalms, 22; 53; 90; 95–6; 98–100; 104;
132; 168–9; 171; 188; 217–8; 221;
252; 254–5; 260; 264–6; 274; 338–342
Pythagoras, -ean tradition, 10; 17–8;
58; 198; 225

Revelation, 11–2; 19; 45; 54–6; 61; 68;
71; 123; 160; 164; 167; 179; 182; 248;
250; 266
Rhetoric, sophists, 93; 136; 146; 148;
170; 184; 222; 236; 303
Rome, 13; 25; 31–2; 40–1; 59; 74–6;
82–3; 92–3; 95; 98; 107; 117; 149;
174; 177; 202–3; 245; 253; 259; 276;
279; 292
Rufinus, 2; 24; 29; 36; 42; 73; 78; 82;
91–5; 102–3; 114; 176; 202–3; 249

Sabellianism, 42–3; 58; 60; 95; 187–8;
243; 253–4; 341
Sabinus, 30
Sacraments, 109; 118; 124; 150; 154;
168; 162; 171; 189; 192; 214–6; 271–
4; 307; 340
Salvation, soteriology, see Christ,
salvation in
Samaritan, -ism, 198; 311
Sasima, 139–41; 145
Satan, demons, 10–1; 17; 36; 76; 81;
97–8; 103; 106; 109; 114; 119; 122;
133–4; 178; 184; 341
Satornilus, 197
Scete, -is, 81; 84; 87
Scholasticus, 26; 73
Septuagint, ix; 5; 201; 266; 340
Simon Magus, 197; 341
Sin, 19; 55; 59; 62–3; 67–8; 76; 77; 97;
100; 105; 107; 112; 118–9; 124–5;
180; 197; 210; 212; 215; 229; 248;
251; 267; 270; 273; 281; 306; 331; 337
Socrates (historian), 20; 24; 26–36; 39;
42–5; 79; 82; 93–4; 100; 102–3; 107;
114; 186; 193; 204; 207; 209; 211–3;
233; 235; 249; 262; 278; 291–3; 295;
299; 301–3
Socrates (philosopher), 143; 150
Society, 12; 74; 87; 89; 130; 133–4; 152;
154; 156; 211; 216; 220; 235; 237;
238; 313; 342; 346
Sophocles, 93; 323
Sotades, 44
Soteriology, see Christ, redemption in
Sozomen, 24; 26; 30–1; 33–36; 39; 42;
44–5; 48; 79; 93; 102; 138; 153; 174;
186–7; 196; 200; 204; 207
Spirit, Holy, 58; 62–3; 66; 69; 88; 92;
99; 112–3; 118–124; 126; 129; 132;
140–1; 156–61; 163–4; 174; 192; 195;
202; 212; 215; 218; 250–1; 268; 272;
284–5; 304; 310; 331; 340
Stoicism, 57; 198; 220; 223; 225
Subordinationism (Christ as
intermediary), 18–9; 23; 47; 57; 63;
195; 253–4
Symeon of Mesopotamia, 117
Symeon Stylites, 128; 131; 133–4
Symmachus, 201
Synesius of Cyrene, 174; 206; 232–240;
258
Synod of the Oak, 82; 204–6; 298; 300
Syria, -ac, 10; 33; 35; 70; 73–5; 116;
127–8; 130; 134; 137; 154; 174; 194;
245; 252

Index of Modern Authors

Select Index of Greek Words